D1733707

LIVY ON THE HANNIBALIC WAR

Livy on the
Hannibalic War

D. S. LEVENE

OXFORD
UNIVERSITY PRESS

OXFORD
UNIVERSITY PRESS

Great Clarendon Street, Oxford OX2 6DP

Oxford University Press is a department of the University of Oxford.
It furthers the University's objective of excellence in research, scholarship,
and education by publishing worldwide in

Oxford New York

Auckland Cape Town Dar es Salaam Hong Kong Karachi
Kuala Lumpur Madrid Melbourne Mexico City Nairobi
New Delhi Shanghai Taipei Toronto

With offices in

Argentina Austria Brazil Chile Czech Republic France Greece
Guatemala Hungary Italy Japan Poland Portugal Singapore
South Korea Switzerland Thailand Turkey Ukraine Vietnam

Oxford is a registered trade mark of Oxford University Press
in the UK and in certain other countries

Published in the United States
by Oxford University Press Inc., New York

© D. S. Levene 2010

British Library Cataloguing in Publication Data

Data available

Library of Congress Cataloging in Publication Data

Data available

Typeset by SPI Publisher Services, Pondicherry, India
Printed in Great Britain
on acid-free paper by
CPI Antony Rowe, Chippenham, Wiltshire

ISBN 978–0–19–815295–8

1 3 5 7 9 10 8 6 4 2

In memoriam
Leighton Reynolds

Preface

Woll't ihr nach Regeln messen,
was nicht nach euren Regeln Lauf,
der eignen Spur vergessen,
sucht davon erst die Regeln auf!

If you want to measure by rules
that which does not run according to your rules,
forgetting your own ways
first seek *its* rules!

Richard Wagner, *Die Meistersinger von Nürnberg*, Act I

Livy's Third Decade, his narrative of the Hannibalic War, is the most remarkable and brilliant piece of sustained prose narrative in the whole surviving corpus of classical literature.

That is a bold claim. It is a bold claim even if one gives full weight to the qualifications implicit in the words 'sustained', 'prose', and 'narrative' (we do not have to weigh here the claims of the *Iliad* or the *De Corona*, of Lucretius or the *Agricola*). In order to justify so bold a claim I would have to spend the next twenty pages tediously damning with faint praise such distinguished rivals as Herodotus and Thucydides, Tacitus and Apuleius, something I have no intention of doing. Instead I shall simply state that in its concentrated and single-minded coherence over ten long volumes, but even more in its challenges to the most fundamental presuppositions about the nature of the world, the work Livy created here is of unparalleled richness and depth. This too may sound a bold and indeed surprising judgement, especially to those who have long imbibed the common picture of Livy as a naïve and uncritical romantic of secondary historical value. Bold or surprising it may be: the object of this book is to explain it.

I emphasize that this is a claim—and a book—about Livy's narrative *of the Hannibalic War*. It is not a claim about Livy's entire surviving corpus. Some years ago I published a book in which I demonstrated, *inter alia*, that different parts of Livy's work have radically different characteristics.[1] Naturally it is possible despite this to make valid points about Livy's work as a whole. After all, *The Pickwick Papers* and *Bleak House* have radically different characteristics, but many excellent books have been written on Dickens which focus on

---

[1]Levene (1993).

his novels' obvious commonalities: *The Pickwick Papers* and *Bleak House* together reveal highly typical Dickensian features which are not shared by (for example) Henry James. And the individual parts of Livy's surviving work are linked more closely than Dickens's novels are, since they narrate sequentially the history of a single state, focusing on a number of aspects which do not vary much from book to book. Nevertheless, while it is certainly the case that many of the techniques and much of the conceptual apparatus revealed in the Hannibalic books are present in other parts of the work, we are not entitled to *assume* that any particular aspect of these books is replicated elsewhere. In some areas that is demonstrably false, with others it is more likely to be true, but that requires empirical verification in each case, and attempting to perform such verification, while possible in principle, would have required me to lengthen considerably what is already a considerably lengthy book. Perhaps even more importantly, my argument is that the different aspects of the Hannibalic books unite to form a single coherent and distinctive whole. That argument would not be assisted by an analysis of those themes in other books which either do not unite so coherently with one another at all, or at least do so to entirely different ends. I shall leave that comparison for other studies.

It is reasonable that readers should initially approach these claims about Livy's Third Decade with scepticism. If these books are indeed at least as remarkable as Thucydides or Tacitus, why has this not already been widely recognized? Why are they not the subject of as many books and doctoral dissertations as Thucydides and Tacitus? Why do they not appear on syllabuses in schools and universities with the same frequency as those other authors? Why indeed do they appear less often on syllabuses than certain *other books of Livy himself*?

A proper answer to these questions would require an account of the entire reception of Livy in the Western world in the last 200 years, an account which I am not qualified to write. I will simply offer here a few suggestions which might go some way towards explaining these books' relative neglect. Their themes are certainly narrow by comparison with many ancient histories (though admittedly not with Thucydides): it seems more pertinent to many people to read of the intimate travails of a Croesus, a Lucretia, or even a Tiberius, than to grind through the apparently endless sequence of battles which makes up much of the narrative of the Third Decade. Moreover, the one-sided and overtly celebratory approach to Roman victories jars badly against modern enlightened opinion: people tend to prefer the radical cynicism and pessimism of Sallust or Tacitus, or at least to find someone who can be read as damning all sides equally. The complex relationship with Polybius, which I discuss in Chapter 2, has not helped: it is not a significant encouragement to give a close reading to a lengthy history when one is aware of the existence of an earlier historian of unquestionably greater historical value who treats much the same topic, and who may even be Livy's source in part.

But perhaps the single factor that has contributed most to the books' neglect is the very feature which I believe constitutes their greatest strength. This work is unified in a way that no other surviving ancient history of comparable length can match. To understand Livy 21–30 one needs to read it as a whole, to see how themes raised are subsequently explored and completed, how stories begun are concluded. One can no more get a true impression of its qualities from reading a small portion than one could get a sense of *Moby Dick* if one had read nothing more than the first fifteen chapters and had given up before Ishmael had seen the Pequod or heard of Captain Ahab. But to read the whole of Livy 21–30 in Latin would obviously not be feasible in school or university syllabuses: it feels burdensome even to many professional classicists. If this book accomplishes nothing else, I hope that it will encourage people to explore the Third Decade beyond the safe confines of those books that are habitually read in schools and universities, and to appreciate that though it may appear an effort to work through so lengthy a text, the rewards for doing so are considerable.

I have drawn my examples from across the entire work, though with a particular concentration on Books 21 and 30, which are currently those which most commonly appear on syllabuses—for while, as I have said, I regard Livy's Third Decade as fundamentally indivisible, I felt it necessary to make some concessions to the practical reality that people for the moment will continue to read it divided and will wish to see some discussion of the parts most familiar to them. And I have inevitably had to be selective. Every page of Livy's account of the Hannibalic War is replete with complexities and subtleties that are well worth analysing, but to give a comprehensive analysis of every page would require a shelf of volumes, not merely one: I apologize to anyone who finds that their favourite passages have been bypassed.

The book contains five chapters, each covering a different aspect of Livy's writing in the Third Decade. The first examines the articulation of the narrative, the way Livy shapes individual books and the decade as a whole, the chronological arrangement of his material, and the way he maintains connections between the different parts of the world in which the Hannibalic War was fought. The second chapter considers the relationship between Livy's account of the war and other texts, both those texts which he employed as source material and the literary works more broadly to which he alludes. The third chapter looks at his handling of people, both individual characters and ethnic groups. The fourth examines his battle narratives, and in particular the question of how he explains the outcomes of battles—what factors make the difference between victory and defeat. The final chapter looks more broadly at Livy's account of historical causation and his explanation for why things in history happen—and, by extension, what he thinks his own role is as an historian.

Describing the book as I have done in the last paragraph, however, is misleading in one crucial respect. Although each chapter deals with a self-contained topic, there is a continuous thread of argument running through the entire book. Chapters 1 and 2 provide the essential justification for the methodological approach to reading Livy that I adopt in Chapters 3, 4 and 5. Meanwhile Chapters 1 and 4, and to a lesser extent Chapter 3, draw attention to a number of odd anomalies in Livy's picture of the world, and the major purpose of Chapter 5 is to bring those different features together and to provide a comprehensive explanation for them. A number of the readers of my draft manuscript told me that they found it frustrating to have to wait so long between reading of possible problems and discovering the ultimate solutions that I would offer to those problems. I understand and sympathize with the frustration, but the empiricist in me baulks at providing a conclusion to my argument ahead of assembling the data in full, especially since many of the answers I provide to these problems are radical and counterintuitive, and it is only once one has examined the full range of anomalies and difficulties that one discovers in Livy's narrative that it becomes clear that it is necessary to postulate a radical and counterintuitive solution to them rather than merely (and facilely) attributing them to some brand of authorial incompetence, as has usually been the case in the past.

I am nevertheless immensely grateful to those readers of my draft, even if I have here (and in some other respects too) not always taken their advice. In particular, Jane Chaplin, Joy Connolly, Christina Kraus, and Tony Woodman read the entire book and offered detailed and acute comments throughout: there are few if any pages of the book which have not benefited from their keen criticisms. Individual chapters were also read and commented on by Denis Feeney, Damien Nelis, Victoria Pagán, and Michael Peachin, to whom I am once again most grateful. I have taught courses based on these books of Livy in Oxford, Durham, Leeds, and New York, and in all cases the input from the students taking those courses has been invaluable and salutary. I have also delivered versions of the arguments developed in this book as papers in Oxford, Durham, Leeds, London, Lampeter, Nottingham, Edinburgh, Manchester, Mannheim, New York, Reading, and Vienna, and the comments I have received on those occasions have been important to me as the book developed. Other people I have consulted include Roger Brock, Andrew Feldherr, Dennis Glew, Malcolm Heath, Brooke Holmes, John Kahn, Andrew

Laird, Michèle Lowrie, Robert Maltby, Ellen O'Gorman, Stephen Oakley, and Michael Strevens: I greatly appreciate their time and attention, as also that of Joel Ward and Olivia Geraci, from whom I received clerical assistance in the crucial final stages of the project. Much of the book was written in the two years in which I held a Major Research Fellowship funded by the Leverhulme Trust, and it was all but completed during a further year of leave provided by New York University: I am grateful to both institutions for their generosity, without which it is unlikely that the book could have been written at all.

The book is dedicated to a great scholar, teacher, and friend, who died shortly after I commenced work on it. I am not sure that he would have agreed with all of its conclusions, but I like to think that he would have seen in it an echo of his own commitment to scholarship.

D.S.L.

Contents

Abbreviations

CAH	*The Cambridge Ancient History* (2nd edn., Cambridge: Cambridge University Press, 1971–2005).
CIL	T. Mommsen *et al.* (eds.), *Corpus Inscriptionum Latinarum* (Berlin: Georg Reimer, 1853–).
FGrH	F. Jacoby, *Die Fragmente der griechische Historiker* (Berlin: Weidmann, 1923–30; Leiden: E. J. Brill, 1940–58).
HRR	H. Peter, *Historicorum Romanorum Reliquiae*, vol. 1 (2nd edn., Leipzig: B. G. Teubner, 1914).
ILS	H. Dessau, *Inscriptiones Latinae Selectae* (Berlin: Weidmann, 1892–1906).
L&S	C. T. Lewis and C. Short, *A Latin Dictionary* (Oxford: Clarendon Press, 1879).
LSJ	H. G. Liddell, R. Scott, H. S. Jones *et al.*, *A Greek-English Lexicon* (9th edn., Oxford: Clarendon Press, 1940, with supplement of 1968).
MRR	T. R. S. Broughton with M. L. Patterson, *The Magistrates of the Roman Republic.* Vol. 1: 509 B.C.—100 B.C. (New York: American Philological Association, 1951).
OCD^3	S. Hornblower and A. Spawforth (eds.), *The Oxford Classical Dictionary* (3rd edn., Oxford: Oxford University Press, 1996).
OLD	*Oxford Latin Dictionary* (Oxford: Clarendon Press, 1968–82).
ORF	E. Malcovati (ed.), *Oratorum Romanorum Fragmenta Liberae Rei Publicae* (4th edn., Turin: I. B. Paravia, 1976–9).
POxy	B. P. Grenfell and A. S. Hunt *et al.* (eds.), *The Oxyrhynchus Papyri* (London: Egypt Exploration Society, 1898–).
RE	A. F. von Pauly *et al.*, *Paulys Real-Encyclopädie der classischen Altertumswissenschaft* (Stuttgart: J. B. Metzler, 1894–1963).
SIG	W. Dittenberger, *Sylloge Inscriptionum Graecarum* (3rd edn., Leipzig: S. Hirzel, 1915–24).
SVF	H. von Arnim, *Stoicorum Veterum Fragmenta* (4 vols., Leipzig: B. G. Teubner, 1903–24).
TLL	*Thesaurus Linguae Latinae* (Leipzig: B. G. Teubner, 1890–).
W-M	W. Weissenborn, H. J. Müller, and O. Rossbach (eds.), *Titi Livi ab urbe condita libri* (Berlin: Weidmannsche Verlagbuchhandlung, 1880–1924).

Unless otherwise stated, all quotations of Livy 21–30 are taken from the Teubner edition of T. A. Dorey (Books 21–5) and P. G. Walsh (Books 26–30).

1

Narrative Organization

When Livy came to write his account of the Hannibalic War, he had to deal with the most commonplace of problems: how to organize his narrative. Any history requires some level of selection and organization. To some extent this may be decided in advance by the form of history that the historian has chosen to write: Livy, like many historians before and since, narrated his work chronologically, year by year. There are occasional exceptions to this, some of which I shall be discussing later in the chapter, but in general he works within that basic chronological framework. In this he aligns himself with (for example) Thucydides and Polybius, both of whom narrated the bulk of their works according to calendar years, and is entirely unlike (for example) Herodotus, who often focuses on one particular geographic location for extended sections of his narrative, and regularly moves backwards or forwards in time in order to give the background or consequences of a sequence of events.[1]

So far this is all obvious. But this natural decision to create a chronological account left Livy with two further problems, one the consequence of his material, the second largely self-imposed. On the one hand he had to cope with the geographical spread of the events; on the other, with the division and organization of his books.

To begin with the former, though Livy is, as we shall see, narrating the Hannibalic War as a single story, this also represents for him the history of Rome in 218–202 BC, a time when her power already encompassed much of the Western Mediterranean, and she was just beginning to focus attention eastwards as well. The Romans were fighting in Italy, Spain, Sicily, and ultimately Africa (to name only the most important); they also had their own domestic affairs to deal with. In any one year Livy might have information about all of these which he wished to incorporate into his account, with some stories naturally crossing several years. Maintaining strict annual chronology inevitably involved fragmenting some narratives of particular areas.

---

[1] Cf. de Jong (2001).

Now, this was not a new problem, either for Livy himself or within the historical tradition. Most obviously, the so-called 'universal historians' from Ephorus onwards had sought to intertwine narratives of several different countries, sometimes within a chronological framework that narrated each year separately.[2] But the same issue potentially arose even for those working on a more limited scale. Even the historian of a single war, like Thucydides, might well find himself having to narrate events on multiple fronts. The historian of a single state might well find that he had to cover apparently unrelated events occurring simultaneously; and the more powerful the country, the more likely it was that a multiplicity of events would appear important enough to require inclusion. As a generalization one can say that the wider the geographic focus, the more awkward the historian was likely to find the limitations of a strict chronology,[3] but this did not necessarily preclude the use of the latter, even when one was seeking to cover the broadest range, as the year-by-year format of much of Diodorus Siculus' work demonstrates.

As so often in ancient historiography, a key (though polemical) discussion of the issue is found in Polybius. His explicit justification for his own choice of subject-matter was that this was the point in history where the stories of separate nations came together into one, as Rome defeated first Carthage and then the Hellenistic kingdoms, spreading her hegemony across the entire Mediterranean (1.3.3–6). At such a time merely narrating the separate wars cannot provide a true perspective on events (3.32):[4] he describes his own history by contrast as 'woven together in a series' (3.32.2 κατὰ μίτον ἐξυφασμένας),[5] which he claims makes it easier to follow. But this is not an entirely comfortable claim. At 38.5–6 he addresses potential critics of his approach who might complain about his chronological framework and the consequent fragmentation of his narrative; but his (possibly disingenuous) response is now to abandon claims of greater ease of understanding, and instead to defend himself by pointing to the variety that such a narrative offered the reader. At the very least, this suggests that even at such a late stage in his history, when the unification of the Mediterranean under Rome had already happened, the effective interconnectedness of these

---

[2] On the tension in universal historians between the desire to give a clear chronological perspective and the wish to maintain narrative continuity in a particular area see Clarke (1999b) (cf. Fornara (1983: 43–6)), though she is perhaps too ready to assume that the issues she identifies are distinctive to that particular subset of historians. For a broader perspective see Jal (1997), and compare n. 7 below.

[3] So e.g. Marincola (1999: 305–6).

[4] Compare Sacks (1981: 104–21) for a critique of Polybius' argument that Rome's conquest of the Mediterranean can only be understood if one combines a diachronic narrative with a synchronic dimension.

[5] For the significance of this phrase see Walbank (1957: 359–60).

different narratives was less obvious to readers than his earlier statements had implied. His difficulties can be seen in his actual practice. His obvious problem was that since he was narrating the process of Rome's unifying conquest and not merely its result, for much of his work, especially in its earlier parts, he was required to maintain separate narratives for the different nations he was treating (cf. 4.28.2–6, 5.31.4–5). To this end, in his first five books he delivers extended narratives covering first the background and then the whole of Olympiad 140 (220–216 BC) for each state separately. Then he pauses for his account of the Roman constitution in Book 6, and only then does he switch to annual narratives. Even after that point a good deal of his account in fact still proceeds along parallel tracks which intersect only rarely, and the sequence of interconnected events which he has led his readers to expect is often hard to discern.[6]

Livy himself had to cope with a not dissimilar issue. Already in the previous twenty books he had narrated the history of a Rome that was expanding into many areas, and where potentially a number of different stories running across several years might have to be covered simultaneously. In a sense the Hannibalic War might be thought an easier task for him, in as much as he sees the very existence of Rome as threatened, and so all Roman events in the period could comfortably be subsumed within the framework of that war alone. And indeed, he explicitly states at the start of Book 21 that his subject matter in this section of his work is 'the most memorable of all wars that have ever been fought' (21.1.1 *bellum maxime omnium memorabile, quae umquam gesta sint*): in other words he presents it as the narrative of a single war, rather than a general history of Rome at the time. But that very fact gives him an additional hurdle, again not unlike Polybius, because he creates expectations of a linear narrative that he may in practice struggle to fulfil.[7] Like Diodorus he faces the problem of maintaining narrative continuity in a particular place. But at least Diodorus could, we may

---

[6] On this issue see Walbank (1975). As Walbank also shows, however, the very fact of interweaving his narrative is used by Polybius to demonstrate the growing connections between the different Mediterranean states, as events in one area more and more frequently impinge directly on another.

[7] Compare Dionysius of Halicarnassus' criticisms of Thucydides (*Thuc.* 9, *Ep. Pomp.* 3.13–14) for his chronological arrangement by seasons which, according to Dionysius, leads to his fragmenting his narratives and makes him hard to follow (*Ep. Pomp.* 3.13 πλανώμεθα δὴ καθάπερ εἰκός, καὶ δυσκόλως τοῖς δηλουμένοις παρακολουθοῦμεν ταραττομένης τῆς διανοίας—'as one would expect, we wander, and irritatedly follow his descriptions with our minds in confusion'). Nor was Dionysius alone in finding this aspect of Thucydides problematic: note Theon, *Prog.* 80.10–24 (Spengel); though see *POxy* 853 ii.15–iii.4 for a response. Similarly Polybius 14.12 and 32.11.2–7 explains that he has conflated several chronologically distinct episodes where they might appear too trivial if told separately; and Appian, *Praef.* 12 says that while originally researching and writing the history, he was 'like a wanderer' (ὥσπερ ἀλώμενον) from place to place, but that he ultimately reworked it according to different countries, so that one could see the progress of their relationship with Rome. See Heath (1989: 85–7); also Walbank (1972: 110–14).

presume, rely on most of his readers being less bothered by the diffuseness of his history, since that is intrinsic to its subject-matter, and ancient readers were anyway more willing than moderns are to find an acceptable unity in a well-balanced amalgam of disparate elements.[8] A reader of Livy who expects a single war may find the sheer spread of events difficult to assimilate.

What this suggests is that, at least with regard to narrative arrangement, there is no clear distinction to be made between the issues faced by a 'universal' historian like Diodorus and a 'local' historian like Livy.[9] Rather there is a continuum extending between those who treat the affairs of multiple states separately, those who treat the interrelated affairs of multiple states, and those who treat the affairs of a single state in multiple areas. A more significant difference lies in the extent to which each historian appears to be leading the reader to expect a linear narra-tive. Here Livy, by advertising his subject-matter as a single war, has set the bar high enough to cause himself potential difficulties when narrating the different fronts on which events took place. How he addressed those difficulties, and indeed made creative use of them, will be a major theme of this chapter.

The second issue for Livy is more specific to his own work. Virtually all ancient historians wrote works in multiple volumes. But with the earliest historians the book divisions do not even stem from the historians them-selves, and many of the later ones do not seem to be engaging in any elaborate patterns or structures. Livy is unusual, and possibly innovative,[10] in the careful patterning that he applied to (at least) the extant books of his history (it is much more controversial how far that extended into the lost books).[11] The extant books fall very clearly into groups of five and ten 'pentads' and 'decades'. It is naturally no accident that his account of the Hannibalic War

---

[8] For this vital but often underappreciated point see the key arguments of Heath (1989), especially 48–9 and 77–87, for his specific account of the selection and arrangement of material in historians. This will be relevant to my discussion of Livy's book divisions, on which see Section 1.1 below. With regard to Diodorus, however, Heath appears to have misinterpreted his preferred arrangement of material (86). He seems to take 16.1.1–2 (recommending that the historian should wherever possible include 'actions complete from beginning to end'—πράξεις αὐτοτελεῖς ἀπ' ἀρχῆς μέχρι τοῦ τέλους) to mean avoiding 'discontinuity in the narrative' similar to that which Dionysius disliked in Thucydides (n. 7 above). However, the actual content of Diodorus' Book 16 involves frequent breaks in narrative continuity, as Diodorus intersperses his account of Philip with lengthy descriptions of unrelated but contemporaneous events in (for example) Sicily and Persia. This makes it clear that Diodorus is talking here about book division, not narrative continuity *per se*: he is recommending that historians should try to cover each story within a single volume, not that they should do so without narrative breaks (cf. also 17.1.1–2). This too will be relevant to Livy.

[9] This conclusion is reasonable on other grounds too: for a general critique of the whole concept of 'genre' as it applies to ancient historiography see Marincola (1999).

[10] See Vasaly (2002).

[11] On this issue, see e.g. Syme (1959: 29–37), Stadter (1972: 292–302), Wille (1973: 56–117), Luce (1977: 9–24).

begins exactly at the very start of Book 21 and concludes at the very end of Book 30, nor that Book 21 and Book 31 each begins with a new preface, formally setting the Hannibalic narrative off from the events preceding and succeeding it: I shall be discussing this in more detail below. Moreover, the care he takes over book division goes beyond simply blocking out five- and ten-book sets: individual books have been shaped to mark them as unities, and scholars have frequently identified patterns of repetition and balance between the separate books of a pentad or decade.[12]

But this creates for Livy his second structural problem. We may reasonably surmise that the Hannibalic War did not in fact divide perceptibly into ten (or any other number of) distinct movements. Still less may we assume that each section was exclusively marked with features that would allow it to be grouped or paralleled neatly with others. So Livy was faced with competing pressures, between on the one hand the desire to divide his narrative as far as possible into these neat and carefully organized segments, but on the other hand having to deal with features of the transmitted story that might resist such straightforward categorization.

We therefore have three separate elements around which Livy has to organize his narrative of the war. First there is book division, second chronology. The third is what we might call narrative sequencing, and this itself falls into two parts: the need to maintain the different narrative threads in a way that leaves the stories separately comprehensible, but also to interweave them in a way that makes sense to a reader anticipating a single narrative.

1.1. BOOK DIVISION

Before I begin a detailed analysis, it is desirable to set out briefly the contents of these books of Livy. Realistically, I am aware that many of my readers may not (yet) have read the decade in its entirety; moreover, given its complexity, even those who are familiar with all ten books may benefit from having a summary of the narrative to refer to.

Table 1.1 accordingly shows the events of the Hannibalic War in Livy. I should emphasize that, although it may look detailed, it already involves a great deal of simplification, omitting or conflating many brief scenes. For the reader's convenience I have sometimes divided episodes in ways which may seem a little

---

[12] This has been studied extensively for Books 1–5: see Burck (1964); Vasaly (2002). Likewise Luce (1977: 25–138) provides a detailed analysis in these terms for Books 31–45. For Books 21–30 see below.

arbitrary, since they do not all correspond to clear breaks that Livy himself marks. Nevertheless this should give some sense of how the narrative proceeds. The phrases 'End of year' and 'New year' in the table signify the places where Livy introduces formal, 'annalistic' material associated with the change of annual magistrates at Rome. I should also point out that the chronology given here is Livy's own, not one that modern historians would accept, at least without significant qualification. At a number of points Livy has probably placed events in the wrong year: the most striking example is at the very start of the war, since the siege of Saguntum was pretty certainly in 219, not 218. Sometimes Livy seems to be aware of the problem, at other times not. I shall be looking at some of these issues later in the chapter; in the meantime the reader should be wary of taking the whole of the chronology here as representing historical reality.

Table 1.1. The narrative of the Second Punic War

Book	Date	Events
21	218 BC	21.1–15 Hannibal takes command of the Carthaginian forces in Spain. He launches an attack on the Spanish town of Saguntum, allied to Rome, and captures it. 21.16–20 The Romans respond to the fall of Saguntum by sending embassies to Africa, Spain, and Gaul. 21.21–38 Hannibal prepares to invade Italy. He crosses first the Pyrenees, then Gaul, where he engages Gallic and Roman forces at the Rhône, and then the Alps. Meanwhile, the Boii Gauls in north Italy revolt against Rome. 21.39–48 Hannibal defeats the consul Publius Scipio at the battle of the River Ticinus. 21.49–56 After campaigning in Sicily, the other consul Sempronius joins his colleague in Italy. They engage Hannibal at the River Trebia, but are defeated. 21.57–59 Elections in Rome; Hannibal continues his campaign, attempting (but failing) to cross the Appennines. 21.60–61 Gnaeus Scipio campaigns in Spain. 21.62–63 End of year; conflict between the incoming consul Flaminius and the Senate.
22	217	22.1.1–7.5 New year. Hannibal traps Flaminius at Lake Trasimene, kills him and destroys his army. 22.7.6–11.9 Fabius Maximus chosen as dictator, with M. Minucius as his deputy. 22.12–18 Fabius, despite the opposition of Minucius, campaigns against Hannibal by refusing to engage him in battle while circumscribing his movements. 22.19–22 Further campaigns in Spain. 22.23–30 Minucius gets the better of Hannibal in Fabius' absence; as a result the Romans give him equal command with Fabius. Hannibal then traps Minucius, who is only rescued by Fabius' last-minute intervention. 22.31 Servilius raids Africa.
	216	22.32–40 End of year and new year. Terentius Varro is chosen as consul in a contentious election, despite Fabius' fears.

22.41.1–54.6 Hannibal traps Varro and massacres the Roman armies at Cannae, killing the other consul, Aemilius Paullus.
22.54.7–61 A state of emergency is declared at Rome. Hannibal offers to return Roman prisoners for a ransom: after a debate the Senate refuses.

23   23.1–10 Capua decides to abandon her alliance with Rome and invites Hannibal to the city.
23.11.1–14.4 The Romans receive a response from the Delphic oracle; the victory at Cannae is reported to Carthage.
24.14.5–20.10 Hannibal makes attempts on other Italian towns; he winters in Capua.
23.21–25 The Romans hold elections and seek to make up their losses, but are defeated in Gaul.
23.26–29 The Scipio brothers achieve substantial victories in Spain.
23.30 Hannibal captures more southern Italian towns; end of year.

215   23.31–32 New year; Carthage sends reinforcements to Spain and Sardinia.
23.33.1–41.12 Hannibal makes a treaty with Philip V of Macedon; the consuls Gracchus and Fabius Maximus campaign in Italy. Roman victories in Sardinia.
23.41.13–48.3 Marcellus defeats Hannibal at Nola.
23.48.4–49.14 Further Roman victories in Spain.

24   24.1–3 Hannibal takes further Italian towns.
24.4.1-7.9 The youthful Hieronymus succeeds to the throne of Syracuse and breaks the alliance with Rome, but is assassinated.
24.7.10–9.6 End of year.

214   24.9.7–11.9 New year.
24.12–20 Fighting in Italy over Beneventum, Casilinum, and Tarentum.
24.21–39 Civil conflict in Syracuse. The Carthaginian allies Hippocrates and Epicydes take control of the city and manipulate the people to take up arms against Rome. Marcellus attacks the city, but is held off by the inventions of the scientist Archimedes. The Romans forestall the defection of Henna and massacre the inhabitants.
24.40 Beginning of the First Macedonian War against Philip.
24.41–42 Carthaginians rally in Spain but the Romans regain control.
24.43.1–8 End of year.

213   24.43.9–44.10 New year.
24.45-47 Fabius Maximus (the younger) captures Arpi.
24.48-49 The Scipio brothers make a treaty with the African king Syphax, who is however defeated by the Numidian prince Masinissa.

25   25.1–2 A scratch army of Italian allies is raised but defeated; end of year.

212   25.3.1–7.9 New year. The misdeeds of tax farmers are dealt with; the survivors of Cannae send a deputation to Marcellus.
25.7.10–12.15 Tarentum defects from Rome; the Roman garrison escapes to the citadel. Meanwhile the Romans discover the 'prophecies of Marcius'.
25.13–22 The Romans campaign against Hannibal in Italy; they besiege Capua. Hannibal lures the proconsul Gracchus into a trap and kills him, and defeats the praetor Gnaeus Fulvius.
25.23–31 Marcellus captures Syracuse; Sicily returns to Roman control.
25.32–39 The Scipio brothers are defeated and killed in Spain, but the Romans rally under the emergency command of Lucius Marcius.
25.40–41 Marcellus mops up opposition in Sicily; end of year.

(continued)

Table 1.1. (Continued)

Book	Date	Events
26	211	26.1–3 New year; Cn. Fulvius is tried and convicted of negligence in losing his army.
		26.4–16 The Romans recapture Capua; Hannibal marches on Rome in an unsuccessful attempt at distraction, but then pulls back. The Capuans are punished for their defection.
		26.17.1–20.6 Claudius Nero is tricked by Hasdrubal in Spain; the Romans appoint the young Scipio ('Africanus') to take command there.
		26.20.7–21.17 Blockade of Tarentum; Marcellus is awarded an ovation for his victory in Sicily.
		26.22–23 End of year.
		26.24.1–26.4 The Romans make a treaty with the Aetolians against Philip.
	210	26.26.5–37 New year. Envoys from Syracuse and Capua appeal to the Senate; the former receive sympathetic treatment, the latter do not.
		26.38–40 Salapia defects back to Rome, Tarentum is under blockade, and the final Carthaginian troops are removed from Sicily.
		26.41–51 Scipio in Spain captures the Carthaginian stronghold of New Carthage.
27		27.1–3 Hannibal defeats a further Roman army, but fails to trap Marcellus.
		27.4–7.6 End of year.
	209	27.7.7–11.16 New year. Conflict over conscription from Roman colonies.
		27.12–16 Marcellus defeats Hannibal, Fabius recaptures Tarentum.
		27.17.1–20.8 Scipio defeats Hasdrubal in Spain, but allows him to escape.
		27.20.9–21.10 End of year.
	208	27.22.1–25.10 New year.
		27.25.11–29.8 Hannibal traps and kills Marcellus.
		27.29.9–33.5 Philip fights successfully in Greece but disgraces himself at the Nemean Games.
		27.33.6–36.9 End of year.
	207	27.36.10–38.12 New year.
		27.39–51 Hasdrubal crosses the Alps. He is met by the consuls Livius and Claudius Nero, the latter leaving Hannibal behind to cross Italy with his army in forced marches. The consuls defeat and kill Hasdrubal at the River Metaurus.
28		28.1–4 Scipio achieves further victories in Spain.
		28.5–8 Fighting in Greece between Philip, the Romans, and their respective allies.
		28.9.1–10.7 End of year.
	206	28.10.8–12.9 New year.
		28.12.10–37.10 Scipio defeats Hasdrubal son of Gisgo and finally ends Carthaginian power in Spain. He makes treaties with Masinissa and Syphax. He continues the conquest of Spanish tribes, but is faced by a munity among his own troops, which he suppresses.
		28.38.1–11 End of year.
	205	28.38.12–46.16 New year. Scipio, now consul, requests from the Senate and is given permission to launch an invasion of Africa, despite the opposition of Fabius. Meanwhile, Hannibal's brother Mago attacks Liguria.

29		29.1–5 Scipio in Sicily prepares to invade Africa, and sends a preliminary raiding party under Laelius. Meanwhile a revolt in Spain is swiftly repressed by Rome.
		29.6–9 The Romans retake Locri; Hannibal retreats before Scipio. In Locri Scipio leaves his lieutenant Pleminius in charge, who treats the inhabitants brutally.
		29.10–11 End of year.
		29.12 A peace treaty is agreed with Philip, ending the Macedonian War.
	204	29.13–22 New year. Locrian envoys appeal to the Senate, who send a commission which deposes Pleminius from his command, but clears Scipio of wrongdoing.
		29.23–27 Syphax betrays Rome to the Carthaginians. Scipio launches his invasion of Africa.
		29.28–35 Scipio in Africa is joined by Masinissa.
		29.36 Sempronius defeats Hannibal in Italy.
		29.37–38 Censorship of Livius and Claudius; end of year.
30	203	30.1–2 New year.
		30.3–15 Scipio and Masinissa defeat and capture Syphax. Masinissa secretly marries Syphax's wife Sophoniba; when rebuked by Scipio he helps her to commit suicide.
		30.16–20 The Carthaginians propose a peace treaty to Scipio, who agrees to a truce while envoys are sent to Rome. Meanwhile the Romans defeat Mago, and the Carthaginians recall Hannibal from Italy.
		30.21–25 The peace proposal from Carthage is rejected by the Roman Senate; the truce in Africa is broken.
		30.26 End of year.
	202	30.27–28 New year.
		30.29.1–38.5 Scipio and Hannibal meet at Zama. Hannibal again proposes a peace, which Scipio rejects. In the ensuing battle the Carthaginians are defeated. Scipio imposes terms on them.
	201	30.38.6–39.8 End of year and new year.
		30.40–45 The Senate accepts Scipio's settlement. He returns from Africa and celebrates his victory with a triumph.

As I have already said, Livy clearly marks Books 21–30 as a distinct unit of his work. He opens it with a prefatory statement which sets out the theme for the decade (21.1.1):[13]

---

[13] This introduction of course slyly draws on the standard historiographical trope that the topic of the particular history under discussion is the greatest of all. The claim is made most extravagantly by Thucydides' extensive demonstration that the Peloponnesian War surpassed all of its predecessors, but by Livy's day it had become a commonplace: see Marincola (1997: 34–43). Livy has a linguistic nod in particular to Sallust, *Jug.* 5.1, *bellum scripturus sum quod populus Romanus cum Iugurtha rege Numidarum gessit* ('I am about to write of the war which the Roman people waged

in parte operis mei licet mihi praefari, quod in principio summae totius professi plerique
sunt rerum scriptores, bellum maxime omnium memorabile, quae umquam gesta sint,
me scripturum, quod Hannibale duce Carthaginienses cum populo Romano gessere.

I may preface a part of my work with the words that most historians state at the
beginning of the whole thing: that I am about to write of the most memorable war of
all that have ever been fought, namely the one which the Carthaginians under their
general Hannibal waged with the Roman people.

From this beginning, the narrative of the war continues until Book 30,
concluding with Scipio's triumph over the Carthaginians (30.45). After this,
the next book, Book 31, begins with a new preface in which Livy refers to the
Punic War as having ended and looks forward to the Roman expansion into
the Eastern Mediterranean that he is about to narrate (31.1.1–6):

me quoque iuvat, velut ipse in parte laboris ac periculi fuerim, ad finem belli Punici
pervenisse . . . pacem Punicam bellum Macedonicum excepit, periculo haudquaquam
comparandum aut virtute ducis aut militum robore, claritate regum antiquorum
vetustaque fama gentis et magnitudine imperii, quo multa quondam Europae
maiorem partem Asiae obtinuerant armis, prope nobilius.

It is a pleasure for me too, as if I myself had taken part in the effort and danger, to have
reached the end of the Punic War . . . The Punic peace was succeeded by the Macedonian
War, hardly comparable in danger or the courage of the general or the strength of the
soldiers, but almost more distinguished in the fame of ancient kings and the historic
reputation of the people and the extent of the empire by which they had once conquered
by force much of Europe and most of Asia.

So Book 30 is explicitly marked as the end-point to the topic prefigured in
Book 21. What is more, Book 30 ends with a series of descriptions to reinforce
that sense of closure.[14] Ending with Scipio's triumph is itself the obvious
example, since the triumph was the ceremony that for the Romans represented
the formal closure to the war in reality.[15] The triumph opens with the words

---

with Jugurtha king of the Numidians'), although Sallust in fact had defied convention by playing
down rather than heightening the importance of his theme (see Levene 1992: 55–6).

[14] On 'closure' in the ancient world see in particular Fowler (1989) and the essays in Roberts,
et al. (1997), including Fowler's own 'Second Thoughts on Closure' (= Fowler 1997a)—though
Fowler's 'second thoughts', unlike his first, claim that the identification of closure or non-closure
is simply dependent on an individual reader's preferences (Fowler 1997a: 4–6), a position which,
as will be apparent from my argument here, I do not accept. For closure in historians see
Marincola (2005), though he examines only the ends of entire works, not internal sections.

[15] Book 45, a book with even more strongly marked closural features (cf. Levene 2006a:
105–6), likewise culminates with a series of triumphs (45.40–43), though in this case a few other
brief incidents are subsequently narrated. Sallust's *Jugurtha* famously ends with the triumph of
Marius, though, equally famously, the triumph is given a colour that undermines its closural
force (cf. Levene 1992: 53–5).

pace terra marique parta (30.45.1: 'Peace having been procured on land and sea'). This has in turn been preceded by explicit statements to the effect that the war is over: notably the announcement of victory by L. Veturius Philo at 30.40.2[16] and the chronological summary that Livy gives in 30.44.1–2.[17] More broadly, the whole narrative of the Carthaginian settlement in 30.42.11–44.13 reinforces the sense of Roman control over their enemies which itself seals the victory. The death of Syphax, reported (though also queried) in 30.45.4–5, introduces a further standard closural motif at the very end.[18]

Naturally, this is not all there is to the ending of Book 30. Livy is still writing a history of Rome, and there are already pointers to the next stage of that history. Macedonian ambassadors appear before the Senate (30.42.1–10), and are warned that Philip has broken his treaty (cf. 30.26.2–3) and that Rome will respond with force. Earlier (30.40.5–6) the Senate had decided to defer the assignment of the consular provinces until the Macedonian and Carthaginian embassies have been heard (though in the event the consuls' ambitions led to the provinces being assigned immediately (30.40.7–16)). Livy's comment is *belli finem alterius, principium alterius prospiciebant animis* (30.40.6: 'they were looking forward mentally to the end of one war and the start of the other').

Moreover, the end of Book 30 also contains numerous hints at a much wider future. Hannibal's later fight against Rome as a supporter of the Seleucid king Antiochus III is prefigured in the variant (though unhistorical) notice that he left to join him immediately, rather than several years later (30.37.13). Before Zama Scipio and Hannibal warn their troops that they are fighting for permanent control of the world (30.32.1–3), a result which Romans saw themselves as having accomplished in Livy's own day.[19] The

---

[16] *pugnatum cum Hannibale esse suprema Carthaginiensibus pugna finemque tandem lugubri bello impositum*—'there had been a fight with Hannibal, in the last battle for the Carthaginians, and an end had at last been put to the mournful war.'

[17] *annis ante quadraginta pax cum Carthaginiensibus postremo facta erat Q. Lutatio A. Manlio consulibus. bellum initum annis post tribus et viginti P. Cornelio Ti. Sempronio consulibus; finitum est septimo decimo anno Cn. Cornelio P. Aelio consulibus.* ('Peace had last been made with the Carthaginians forty years earlier in the consulships of Q. Lutatius and A. Manlius. The war began twenty-three years later in the consulships of P. Cornelius and Ti. Sempronius; it ended in the seventeenth year in the consulships of Cn. Cornelius and P. Aelius').

[18] Cf. Smith (1968: 101–2, 172–82). Note also Pelling (1997a: 228–9 = Pelling 2002: 365–6), who observes how commonly Plutarch's *Lives* end with the death of someone other than the protagonist.

[19] Obvious parallels include Virgil, *Aeneid* 1.278–9: *his ego nec metas rerum nec tempora pono: / imperium sine fine dedi*—'To them I place neither limits of space nor times: I have given them empire without end'. Livy's general sentiments here are in fact taken over from the parallel passage in Polybius (15.9.2–5; cf. 15.10.2); but he has added the pointed phrase *non in unum diem sed in perpetuum* (30.32.1: 'not for one day but forever').

ultimate destruction of Carthage is alluded to in the report that Scipio would have liked to destroy the city himself but was prevented by the consuls' *cupiditas* (30.44.3): the destruction was of course in the event accomplished in 146 BC by another Scipio, his adopted grandson. The Carthaginians similarly anticipate their own destruction. The burning of their ships is described by Livy as *conspectum repente incendium tam lugubre fuisse Poenis quam si ipsa Carthago arderet* (30.43.12: 'the flames suddenly seen were as mournful to the Carthaginians as if Carthage itself were burning').[20] Hannibal's final words to the Carthaginians (30.44.6–11) hint at this future disaster, with his warning that the loss of power will lead to their ruin. Perhaps even more importantly, Hannibal also appears to be pointing to ultimate disaster for the victors as well as the defeated (30.44.7–8):[21]

nec est cur vos otio vestro consultum ab Romanis credatis. nulla magna civitas diu quiescere potest. si foris hostem non habet, domi invenit, ut praevalida corpora ab externis causis tuta videntur suis ipsa viribus onerantur.

Nor is there any reason why you should think that the Romans were concerned for your peace. No great state can rest for long. If it does not have an enemy abroad, it finds one at home, as superlatively powerful bodies seem safe from outside influences but are burdened by their own strength.

Hannibal here moves from the idea of Rome as a threat to Carthage to the implication that the absence of Carthage will cause Rome to turn in upon herself: the well-known *metus hostilis* theory that was supposedly cited in the Roman debates over the destruction of Carthage at the time of the Third Punic War.[22] It also alludes to Livy's own diagnosis of the current state of Rome in his Preface, using a similar medical metaphor: *iam pridem praevalentis populi vires se ipsae conficiunt* (*Praef.* 4: 'a long-powerful people is destroying itself by its own strength'); it also appears to draw on Horace, *Epodes* 16.2: *suis et ipsa Roma viribus ruit* ('Rome herself too is collapsing under her own strength').[23] And the final words of the book (30.45.6–7) refer to Scipio's acquired *cognomen* Africanus: the first general to have been so dignified with the name of his conquests, but a precedent which then was taken up by those

---

[20] This interpretation is reinforced by the fact that the passage also alludes to an image in the *Iliad* (22.410–11), where the mourning at the death of Hector is just as if Troy were being destroyed by fire, famously prefiguring the end of the city that is not described within the poem itself.

[21] Burck (1962: 165–6); cf. Hoffmann (1942: 119).

[22] So Diodorus 34.33.3–6. For its historicity see Gelzer (1931), *contra* Hoffmann (1960); but either way it is clear that by the time Livy was writing the association between *metus hostilis* and the Third Punic War was generally accepted.

[23] Suggested by Reeve (1987: 320–1).

nequaquam victoria pares (30.45.7: 'by no means equal in their victory')—again a hint at future decline.[24]

One might read these gestures to a distant future as anti-closural, much as the forward glances to the Second Macedonian War certainly are: they remind us that the Second Punic War is not the end of the story, but rather one stage in Rome's simultaneous march towards external political dominion and internal moral collapse. But the effect is quite as much the opposite: they convey a sense of completeness, incorporating into the story of the Second Punic War the ultimate end of the history for both Carthage and Rome. Carthage did not meet her destruction after her defeat by Rome in 202; but Livy ends the war with a glance to the time when she did meet that destruction. The defeat of Carthage in the Second Punic War did not give Rome literal power over the whole Mediterranean, since (to name only the most important) Macedon, Egypt, and the Seleucid empire were all still extant; but Livy treats the defeat of Carthage as tantamount to Rome obtaining that power. And the collapse of Rome into civil war had apparently not yet begun at the point when she defeated Carthage, but Livy sees the seeds already there, and alludes to the collapse as something that is now at hand.[25] Livy rounds off his story with a series of episodes and allusions that not only put the war to an end in a formal sense, but widen the perspective to introduce a teleological reading of Roman and Carthaginian history, a teleology which is not of course Livy's own invention, but which through its very familiarity is accepted by the reader as a proper close to the events.[26]

Just as Book 30 uses allusions and formal devices to close the story of the war, similarly Book 21 marks the war's advent in ways that go beyond simply narrating the start of the story. The introductory narrative of the book gives the entire background to the war, going back twenty years to describe Hamilcar's resentment at the earlier Carthaginian defeat and how this influenced Hannibal as a child; Livy then narrates the progress of Carthaginian power in Spain through the commands of Hamilcar and Hasdrubal, and then the appointment of Hannibal himself. Not until 21.6.3 can the reader see the

---

[24] Livy's strictures cannot have included the acquisition of the *cognomen* 'Germanicus' by Augustus' stepson Nero Drusus, since that came as a result of his conquests in 12–9, almost certainly after Book 30 was written. However, he was right to note the increasing popularity of the honour (and also the decreasing significance of the conquests celebrated): merely within the family of the Caecilii Metelli the last century of the Republic produced a Macedonicus, a Numidicus, a Delmaticus, a Creticus, and a Baliaricus.

[25] Compare Fowler (1989: 81–2 = Fowler 2000: 245–6) on the end of the *Iliad*.

[26] One can add that the final contrast between Scipio's achievements and the lesser claims of his successors has the effect of magnifying the Second Punic War itself, and such magnification of one's own topic is a regular closural device in history (see Marincola 2005: 290–9).

narrative returning to its proper chronological place, when the story intersects with Rome. This major violation of Livy's standard chronological format (a transgression, however, less noticeable to the modern reader because of the loss of Book 20, which contained the previous Roman narrative) makes Book 21 appear to begin a distinct new story, with all the necessary explanation and background provided.

In addition, Livy repeatedly marks the book as the opening to the war by pointedly introducing motifs and people that will be significant later.[27] The most obvious example is the appearance of Scipio Africanus, rescuing his father at the Ticinus (21.46.7–8). This episode is not Livy's invention, of course, but it certainly was not universally accepted to include the story or to include it here. Coelius Antipater had attributed the rescue of the elder Scipio to a slave (21.46.10 = Coelius fr. 17P); Polybius does not mention the rescue at his account of the Ticinus in Book 3, but introduces it in Book 10 when Scipio is appointed to the command in Spain. And Livy makes the point explicit with a reference to the victory that Scipio will accomplish.[28] Similarly, in the symbolically resonant scene in Carthage where the Roman ambassador declares war (21.18.13–14), Livy gives the role to the other iconic Roman commander in the war, Q. Fabius Maximus (21.18.1–3). All other surviving accounts either fail to name the ambassador or else identify him (probably correctly) as M. Fabius Buteo.[29] The fighting around Sicily (absent from Polybius), including a reference to Hiero's role as the archetypal Roman ally (21.49–51, esp. 21.50.7–10), looks forward to the central role of Syracuse in the war after Hiero's death in Books 24 and 25. Hannibal's dream at 21.22.6–9 points to the destruction that his invasion will accomplish, but also hints at his ultimate failure, when he declines to obey his guide's instruction not to look back and in response is told to allow the fates to remain hidden.[30] The ultimate Roman victory is foreshadowed both in the warnings of Hanno (21.3

---

[27] Cf. Fuhrmann (1983: 22–5).

[28] 21.46.8 *hic erit iuvenis, penes quem perfecti huiusce belli laus est, Africanus ob egregiam victoriam de Hannibale Poenisque appellatus*—'This was to be the young man who obtained the glory of completing the war, and was called Africanus because of his outstanding victory over Hannibal and the Carthaginians'.

[29] De Sanctis (1968: 1), *MRR* (241 n.7). As Hoyos (1998: 229–30) notes, the absence of the episode from Plutarch's *Fabius* and the *elogium* in the Forum Augustum (*ILS* 56) also tells against Fabius Maximus having had this role. Silius Italicus 2.3, 2.368, 382, presumably dependent on Livy, calls the ambassador 'Fabius' without further qualification.

[30] This final point, as far as we can tell, did not appear in Livy's source, Coelius Antipater fr. 11P (cited in Cicero, *Div.* 1.49), though that is possibly the result of Cicero's reworking rather than Livy's. In Levene (1993: 45–7) I interpreted the dream as largely positive from Hannibal's point of view, but note the qualification offered by Pelling (1997b: 201–4): that aspects of it point ominously to Hannibal's eventual defeat; cf. also Cipriani (1984: 103–28).

and 21.10) and in the opening skirmish (21.29.1–4), where Livy describes the bloody Roman victory as 'simultaneously the start and an omen of the war' (21.29.4 *principium simul omenque belli*).[31]

Hence even if Livy cannot conform to Diodorus' ideal (16.1.1–2 quoted n.8 above) of completing a story within a single book (though, as we shall see, he does make some moves in that direction as well), he at any rate completes it within an explicitly marked section of his history. The decade is in this way strongly unified in the terms expected by ancient aesthetic theory.[32]

Livy's use of book structure in Books 21–30, however, might be argued to extend beyond merely using the decade to cover the war: it appears vastly more intricate. The decade looks to have a general 'arc'. It begins with the rise of Hannibal and his invasion of Italy, and the first two books contain his increasingly devastating victories. Then the Romans begin to recover across the next three books, while still sustaining a number of significant defeats. Book 25, halfway through the decade, ends on a note of balance: the major Roman success in the recapture of Syracuse is followed by the last substantial Carthaginian victory of the war, the defeat and death of the Scipio brothers in Spain. Then the Roman recovery accelerates from Book 26 onwards, with victories in Italy, Spain, and ultimately Africa itself.

Moreover, Livy marks the halfway point with a firm caesura. Book 25 is one of three books in the decade that ends at a year-end, the others being 21 and 29: the centre point and the first and last books of the decade are thus the only

---

[31] Cf. Edgeworth (1989), who suggests that Livy's description of the fall of Saguntum at the beginning of Book 21 highlights themes and motifs from later in the war, such as the aggressive role of Maharbal (21.12.1–3), whose vigour leads to success at Saguntum, but who is fatally overruled by Hannibal after Cannae (22.51.1–4). He also suggests, however, that the destruction of Saguntum has more far-reaching overtones, prefiguring the ultimate destruction of Carthage in Book 51.

[32] Note Heath (1989: 41–3) on Aristotle's advocacy of a 'closed structure' in tragedy, where there is a causal end-point beyond which the dramatist does not invite exploration; also Heath (1989: 48–9) on Aristotle's suggestion that history may similarly be unified, albeit chronologically not causally (*Poetics* 1459a17–30). Heath (1989: 89, 151) however claims that Aristotle is anomalous among ancient theorists in finding that history can be unified in its subject-matter; but this conclusion does not appear to be supported by his own detailed analysis of the theorists in question (1989: 71–89), especially once Diodorus is added to the mix (n. 8 above). Heath rightly notes that Polybius did not *prescribe* unity of subject-matter for historians in general; he seems (1989: 80–1, 151) to infer from this that Polybius did not *conceptualize* unity in historians in terms of their subject-matter. But this is a false inference, and not borne out by Polybius' text (esp. 1.3–4 and 3.1.4–11). What rather seems to be the case is that some types of historical subject-matter were conceived of as more conducive to unity than others: namely historical matter where there is a central story with a clear beginning and end-point, these moreover defined (*contra* Aristotle) in causal as much as purely chronological terms, such as the career of Philip II or the Roman conquest of the Mediterranean – or indeed the Second Punic War. And even where the history as a whole cannot be unified in those terms, Diodorus, at any rate, suggests that it is preferable for individual sections to be structured along those lines.

ones separated off by chronological markers (see Section 1.2 of this chapter for further discussion).[33] The closing sections of Book 25 put a decisive end to Marcellus' Sicilian campaign while referring to the deleterious impact of the spoils from Syracuse (25.40.1–2), which thus signals the ultimate Roman decline much as the closing sections of Book 30 do. Livy also marks the period of Books 25 and 26 as a central pivot when at 26.37, immediately prior to describing Scipio's campaigns in Spain, he has a long summary of the state of the war from both the Roman and Carthaginian perspective, concluding that it was in the balance (26.37.9 *aequante fortuna suspensa omnia utrimque erant*).[34]

This 'arc' also appears to correspond to a more complex patterning. It has long been noticed, for example, that Book 30 contains a number of detailed parallels with and allusions to Book 21. These connections partly act as a further closural device, reinforcing the general sense of completion as the war comes to its end, but also suggest the overall reversal of the combatants' positions. The best-known instance is the meeting of Hannibal and Scipio before Zama (30.30–31), where each makes a speech. Before the first major battle of the war, at the River Ticinus, there had similarly been a pair of speeches by Hannibal and Scipio's father (21.40–44).[35] The mere existence of such speeches is admittedly of less significance than might initially appear, since both pairs were found in Polybius too (3.63–64, 15.6–8), who is likely to have been Livy's source (see Chapter 2). But Livy has included a few elements that bring out parallels more expressly. For example, both pairs of speeches begin with the commanders' mutual admiration (21.39.7, 30.30.2).[36] Livy's Hannibal alludes at the start of his speech before Zama to the fact that Scipio's father was his first opponent (30.30.5); conversely Hannibal's speech before

---

[33] Cf. Burck (1962: 11–13, 16–17); Wille (1973: 50). Hasse (1996) observes that this appears to be Livy's preferred way of articulating his decades, since Books 31, 35, 39, 41 and 45 all likewise end with the end of a year.

[34] This issue is complicated by the fact that the sentiments of 26.37 are partly derived from Polybius 9.21, and it may be, as Burck (1962: 13–26) argues, that Polybius dated the deaths of the Scipios a year later, and so saw the balance and turning point in the war at the end of 211 (i.e. corresponding to the middle of Livy Book 26), not the end of 212 (the end of Livy Book 25). Livy has, in Burck's view, relatively uncritically inserted here a version of Polybius' judgement adapted by an annalistic source, despite not following the chronology on which it was based. However, as I shall argue in Chapter 2, Livy's use of Polybius is more direct and self-conscious than Burck suggests, and in any event, despite Burck's elaborate arguments to the contrary, the shift in relative fortunes between the end of 25 and this point in Book 26 is not strongly significant—certainly not significant enough to make the reference to a turning point here appear anomalous within Livy's narrative structure. For a quite different analysis of 26.37, centring on Livy's presentation of the subjective feelings of the antagonists prior to the crucial campaign in Spain, see Gärtner (1975: 28–38).

[35] Burck (1962: 50), Wille (1973: 52).

[36] The former is paralleled—though in a very different form—in Polybius 3.61.1–6; the latter has no Polybian equivalent.

Ticinus had, with some dramatic irony, anticipated the future, claiming that the Romans' true ambition was to cross to Africa (21.44.7):[37] neither are in the Polybian originals. Scipio in Book 21 had reminded his troops that they were fighting for the city of Rome itself (21.41.16–17), Hannibal in Book 30 recognizes the reversal that has placed him in the same position (30.30.8, 30.30.17).[38] There are other reminders in Book 30 of the events of Book 21. The original Carthaginian aggression is acknowledged by both Hannibal himself at the start and end of his speech (30.30.3, 30.30.30, neither of which is in Polybius) and by the Carthaginian envoy Hasdrubal Haedus at 30.42.21.[39] The original Carthaginian opponent of the war from Book 21, Hanno, is recalled by Hannibal and Hasdrubal at 30.20.4 and 30.42.15; the treaty of Lutatius that had been the original point of contention in 21.18 is (contentiously) appealed to by the Carthaginians in 30.22.4–6. Hannibal from the summit of the Alps looks out at Italy on the point of entering it (21.35.8–9); this is mirrored in his final look back at Italy on his departure from it (30.20.7–9).[40] The description of Hannibal's return to Carthage at 30.35.10-11 refers to his leaving it thirty-six years previously as a boy, the departure alluded to by Livy at the very start of 21 (21.1.4). This extends even into a minor episode: at 30.19.7–8 the consul Servilius recovers his father and a colleague who had been captured by the Boii Gauls years before (21.25.7).

So it looks as if Book 30 is being presented, at least in part, as concluding and reversing the events of Book 21. Livy's patterning, however, may be argued to go beyond this. One can draw significant parallels between the opening books of the separate pentads, as the Roman recovery reverses the original Carthaginian advance.[41] Livy at the conclusion of his 'war summary' at 26.37 says that for the Romans and Carthaginians it was 'as if then they were beginning their first war' (26.37.9 *velut illo tempore primum bellum inciperent*); his narrative patterns seem to bear this out. Hannibal takes over his father's old command in Book 21 by public acclaim; his counterpart Scipio takes over from his own father in Book 26 with similar popular support (compare esp. 21.3.1 with 26.18.8). Hannibal moves from Spain to Italy at the

---

[37] As noted by Walsh (1973: 207), Hannibal's statement is in one sense literally true, since the Senate at 21.17.6 licensed Sempronius to attack Africa, but he was in fact recalled to Italy before he was able to do so. But the future resonances of the passage can hardly be irrelevant to its effect.

[38] The former is not in Polybius, the latter is based on Polybius 15.6.4, but Livy phrases it in a far more pointed way.

[39] Hasdrubal is however partially disingenuous in denying *collective* Carthaginian responsibility for the war (30.42.13–14), an interpretation which Livy's own narrative has disproved: see 159–60 below.

[40] Cf. Jaeger (2006: 402–3).

[41] Wille (1973: 51), Luce (1977: 27–8).

centre of Book 21, Scipio from Italy to Spain at the centre of Book 26; significantly, although the former was by land and the latter by sea, Livy makes a point of mentioning that Scipio sailed past the Alps, Gaul, and the Pyrenees (26.19.11), thus retracing Hannibal's route. In Book 26 Hannibal approaches the walls of Rome for the one and only time, during his abortive march on Rome, when he rides up to the Colline Gate (26.10.3). This is repeatedly prefigured in Book 21. The Senate reacts to the siege of Saguntum 'as if the enemy were already at the gates' (21.16.2 *velut si iam ad portas hostis esset*), which is an apparent reference to the iconic phrase *Hannibal ad portas*;[42] similarly when Hannibal crossed the Alps he described them to his troops as 'the walls not only of Italy but of the city of Rome' (21.35.9 *moeniaque...non Italiae modo sed etiam urbis Romanae*). At the start of Book 21 Hannibal captured and plundered the Roman allied city of Saguntum, whose inhabitants collectively commited suicide (21.14); at the start of Book 26 the Romans capture and plunder the Carthaginian ally Capua, with a similar (though smaller-scale) suicide by the inhabitants (26.14.1–5). Some of this patterning extends to later books.[43] Hannibal's greatest and most decisive victory comes at Cannae at the end of Book 22; the Roman counterpart at the Metaurus comes at the end of Book 27.[44] Livy explicitly parallels the battles (27.49.5 *redditaque aequa Cannensi clades vel ducis vel exercitus interitu videbatur*—'and a defeat equal to Cannae, whether in the destruction of the general or of the army, seemed to have been repaid'),[45] following this with Hannibal's comment that he 'recognized the fortune of Carthage' (27.51.12 *adgnoscere se fortunam Carthaginis*). To some extent this is reflected even by the reverses of the dominant side: just as the Romans in Book 22 managed to rally under Fabius' command and defeat Hannibal, Hannibal pulls off his last major coup in trapping and killing Marcellus in Book 27. The Carthaginian victory was offset in Book 23 by the troops' decline into luxury as they

---

[42] Fuhrmann (1983: 23). For the proverbial use of this phrase see Otto (1890: 158–9), who cites Cicero, *Phil.* 1.11 and *Fin.* 4.22. Otto also notes that Livy uses it in a literal sense not only here but at 23.16.1; the latter however is ironic, since the gates in question are those of Nola, not of Rome, and the Nolans' response is not heroic resistance but to seek to defect.

[43] Note Burck (1962: 130–3).

[44] Wille (1973: 52), Luce (1977: 28). As I shall discuss further in Chapter 3 (below, 187–9), there are also significant parallels between the election prior to Cannae in Book 22 and the election prior to the Metaurus in Book 27: in both cases the consul first chosen is considered too aggressive, and a more cautious colleague is chosen as a counterweight, a policy that fails at Cannae but succeeds at the Metaurus, albeit (as I shall explain) in a very surprising fashion.

[45] Appian, *Hann.* 53 similarly saw the Metaurus as paralleling and responding to Cannae: θεὸς δέ μοι δοκεῖ τόδε Ῥωμαίοις ἀντιδοῦναι τῆς ἐπὶ Κάνναις ἀτυχίας, οὐ πόρρω τε ἐπ' ἐκείνῃ καὶ ἰσοστάσιόν πως ἐκείνῃ γενόμενον —'It seems to me that God gave this to the Romans in return for the misfortune at Cannae: it both came not long after it and was in some respects a counterbalance to it'.

wintered at Capua (23.18.10–16); Scipio's successes in Spain are similarly undermined by his own troops' mutiny, their discipline damaged by the licence of peace (28.24.6–11, although one should note that in this case the troops' indiscipline is fostered more by the absence of abundant supplies than by the presence of luxury: see further below, 350–1).

One might object that this balance and patterning is generated entirely by the historical events themselves rather than anything that Livy himself provided. However, the evidence suggests otherwise. Livy did not need to distribute the events of the decade in that way. First, he had some leeway even to adjust the years in which certain episodes happened.[46] This is clearest in the Spanish campaign, where he was faced with uncertainty within the tradition about the years to which the campaigns in Spain should be assigned (cf. 27.7.5–6). This has a major effect on his handling of Books 25–28. In particular, he could have dated the death of the Scipio brothers a year later and so placed it in Book 26 rather than Book 25. Likewise Scipio Africanus' first Spanish victories could have fallen a year later, or his final campaign a year earlier: hence either episode could have appeared in Book 27 – a book which as it currently stands has relatively little Spanish narrative despite covering more years than any other in the decade. Similar licence was available to him with Hannibal's capture of Tarentum in Book 25 (cf. 25.11.20) and the events of the First Macedonian War. Movements of events within years were even easier, since many of the narratives are presented as simultaneous and so could (theoretically) appear in any order. For example, Livy could have exchanged most of what he narrates at the end of Book 23 with the beginning of Book 24 without the slightest violation of narrative expectations.

Second, he had considerable leeway over the lengths of his books. While the Third Decade is relatively evenly balanced, containing neither the longest nor the shortest of his surviving books, nevertheless the longest book, Book 27, is nearly 40 per cent longer than the shortest, Book 29.[47] This obviously gave him considerable scope to shape his books by adjusting the places where he drew the boundary.

His third, and perhaps most far-reaching, licence is that he had vast scope to build up or skate over particular events. It is noteworthy that most modern historians of the Second Punic War tend to focus their attention much more closely on the opening years, which appear more dramatic and decisive, and treat the later period far more cursorily. This approach was anticipated in

[46] Burck (1962: 13–16), Wille (1973: 50).
[47] See Stadter (1972: 304).

antiquity, for example by Silius Italicus and Florus.[48] Livy measures the years of war more evenly. This extends beyond mere chronology. He allots the victory of the Metaurus, for example, more space relative to the length of his narrative than does any other surviving writer: he builds it into one of his greatest dramatic climaxes, matched only by his description of Cannae, to which, as I said, it is presented as a counterpart. Conversely he omits altogether episodes in the African campaign that he could have included in Book 30, moving directly from Hannibal's return to Africa to the battle of Zama itself.[49]

But there is a further, perhaps more subtle, objection that might be raised along similar lines. Granted that one can find elements of patterns and balance between particular books in the history, one might object that, given Livy's long and multifarious narrative, similar parallels could be identified between any pairs of books that one happened to choose. The claim for elaborate patternings might, it could be argued, rest more in the subjective preferences of the reader in choosing certain episodes to highlight, rather than anything intrinsic in the text.[50] For example, if one is prepared to highlight Books 21 and 26 as a pair partly because of Hannibal's march into Italy being reversed by Scipio's sailing to Spain, why would we not equally identify Books 21 and 27 as a pair, with Hannibal's march into Italy being replayed by Hasdrubal some years later—especially since Livy explicitly compares these two episodes at some length (27.39, 27.44.7–8), something he does not do with Scipio in Book 26? Why should we not see a significant link between Fabius' brutal recapture of Tarentum at 27.15.9–16.9 and Hannibal's capture of Saguntum at 21.14? Why not between the victory-then-defeat of Sempronius against Hannibal at the Trebia on the one hand (21.52–6), and the defeat-then-victory of Marcellus against Hannibal near Canusium on the other (27.12–14)? The same applies to other possible pairings. The debate on war-strategy between Scipio and Fabius in Book 28—a central thematic episode, as I shall discuss in a later chapter—has its most obvious counterpart

---

[48] In Silius' seventeen-book epic, the first ten books cover the events of Livy 21–22, with the rest of the war crammed into the remaining seven; the same balance is visible in Florus' brief summary of the war (1.22). According to modern editions of Dio, he similarly devoted five books to the war (13–17), half of them (up to the middle of Book 15) on just those first three years. Much of this is speculative (cf. Boissevain 1895: e.g. LV–LVI, 168), since few of Dio's fragments—and none from those three years—are transmitted with book numbers; but it is worth noting that Zonaras, who is abridging Dio in this part of his work, spends about as long on the three opening years as on the rest of the war (8.21–9.2 compared with 9.3–14).

[49] For episodes that Livy is omitting here, see e.g. Frontinus, *Strat.* 3.6.1, Appian, *Pun.* 24 and 29–30, and Zonaras 9.12.

[50] For a similar point in a different context cf. Sharrock (2000: esp. 15–16), likewise Laird (2000).

in the debates over strategy in Book 22 between Fabius, Minucius, Varro, and Paullus: again, a parallel drawn explicitly (28.40.10–11). The mass suicide of the Saguntines in Book 21 looks much closer to that of the people of Astapa at 28.22.5–23.5 than to the relatively small number of people who kill themselves at Capua in Book 26.

Certainly it is the case that some scholars have seen patterns to the decade other than those I have identified above. Most obviously, Hoffmann treats the decade in groups of two books, analysing as units 21/22, 23/24, 25/26, 27/28, and 29/30;[51] moreover Burck, while rejecting this analysis of the overall structure, accepts the grouping 29/30, suggesting that the invasion of Africa in these books corresponds to the Carthaginian victories of Books 21/22.[52] And one can certainly see some points to support Hoffmann. For example, the account of the internal conflicts at Croton and then Syracuse at the start of Book 24 bear more than passing similarities to the revolt of Capua at the start of Book 23; and when the Syracusan Zoippus takes refuge in Egypt at 24.26.1 he is replaying the actions of the Capuan Decius Magius at 23.10.11–13.

But the problem is that such sequential groupings have to be exclusive for the argument to work. Hoffmann's analysis collapses if Book 24 has as many links to Book 25 as it does to Book 23—and in fact it is even closer. Books 24 and 25 are the two 'Syracusan' books, narrating the story of the Syracusan revolt from its beginning under Hieronymus to Marcellus' final capture of the city. That narrative dominates those two books, and hence appears a far more significant feature than the relatively minor parallels that one can adduce between 23 and 24. There likewise does not seem to be any stronger reason to link Book 27 to Book 28 than to Book 26, since Book 28 is dominated by Scipio and Spain, neither of which has a major role in Book 27, whereas Book 26 and Book 27 together have the culmination of the story of Marcellus. The coupling of 29 and 30 supported by Burck appears superficially more attractive—except that Book 29, as I shall discuss shortly, is perhaps the most anomalous book in the decade, and once again its themes might appear to link it as much to its predecessor as to its successor, since Scipio does not invade Africa until more than halfway through the book.

Still, even if one can legitimately reject certain particular patterns, the main challenge remains unmet. Hoffmann's analysis is demonstrably flawed: but it does not follow that the parallelisms and patterns to which I alluded above are not themselves arbitrary. Perhaps there are no patterns to be discovered at all, except within the fantasies of overinterpreting scholars. Is there any reason to

---

[51] Hoffmann (1942).
[52] Burck (1962: 12), supported by Wille (1973: 49–50).

suggest that some apparent parallels (such as between Book 21 and 26) should count for more than others (such as between Book 21 and 27)?

At this point we need to acknowledge something I have already mentioned (5). While it is true that Livy had considerable leeway to shape his book divisions and his narrative of the war, that leeway was not total. Nor, even if we assume that setting up balances and parallels between particular books was one of his aims, should we assume that creating such patterns was his sole—or even necessarily primary—interest. As we shall see, he is also concerned to shape individual books in a coherent and dramatic fashion; in addition he has to accommodate the constraints of his broad chronological framework. He also has many wider historiographical concerns about the meaning of particular events—though, as we shall also see shortly, those concerns are themselves not divorced from these questions of narrative arrangement. It would be implausible—indeed ridiculous—to suggest that Livy would eschew narrating a striking episode concerning Fabius or Marcellus merely because it happened to parallel an episode in Book 21 and his chronology did not allow him to accommodate it comfortably in Book 26 rather than Book 27. Indeed, he might well actively wish such parallels to be maintained for wider historiographical ends: as I shall be discussing in Chapter 3, the repetition and alteration of models of behaviour is a central concern of Livy's across the whole decade.

But in that case, even if we assume that Livy had an interest in patterns, did he have any way of signalling them to his readers? For the best answer, we need to return to the question of subjectivity. It is certainly the case that, if we are simply assembling passages in the abstract, the critic can find quite as many parallels to draw between Book 21 and 27 as between 21 and 26. But we are not and should not be looking at the question in the abstract. The search for and recognition of parallels is governed by our expectations of where we could expect to find parallels and what sort of parallels we would expect. This is subjective in a sense, but not necessarily based on the subjectivity of an individual interpreter. Rather it depends on the aesthetic context within which the text is read, and that is influenced by the norms of interpretation for texts within different communities.[53]

This brings us to contemporary poetry. It is here, rather than in prose, that one finds the most direct model for book-patterning of the sort claimed for Livy. In particular Livy's ten-book Hannibalic War narrative finds its clearest precedent in two books that appeared in the years immediately prior to Livy's beginning his history, namely Virgil's *Eclogues* and Horace's *Satires* 1, each of

---

[53] Cf. Laird (2000: 167–8), Heath (forthcoming).

which contains ten poems. Tibullus 1, which is approximately contemporary with Livy's first books, likewise contains ten poems, as do Ovid's later *Tristia* 4 and *Epistulae ex Ponto* 1. When we add books that contain other multiples of five poems, including Horace *Odes* 2, 3, and 4 and *Epistles* 1, Ovid *Amores* 1 and *Metamorphoses* (and possibly *Amores* 2 and 3 and *Tristia* 3 and 5 as well),[54] it is apparent that structuring works by multiples of five was commonplace at this period: the structure which Livy adopted for his history immediately makes sense in those terms.[55]

So the broad structural framework that Livy adopted looks pointed. But more important for us is whether poetry books exhibit internal structural patterns. On the face of things it is far more likely that patterns can be securely identified here than they can in Livy, since authors of poetry had a freer choice of subject-matter and treatment than he did, and also often a greater range of formal devices that could be used to mark parallels (such as varying metres, or the alternation between dialogue and monologue as in the *Eclogues*, or matching numbers of lines allocated to particular poems). One may add that poetry books are typically shorter than prose—and individual poems within such books shorter still—which gives a practical reason for seeing patterns as more easily recognizable there.

There is a vast quantity of scholarship on the architecture of Augustan poetry books: I cannot do more here than skate over the surface. The immediate problem is that interpreters of Augustan poetry books are even more divergent in the architectural schemes that they hypothesize than interpreters of Livy are. Certain broad patterns have received a degree of consensus: for example, the centre of the book often appears to be significant, either as a pivot around which poems may be chiastically arranged, or where a new beginning can be signalled explicitly with a 'second proem'[56]—or indeed both. Opening and closing poems and/or central and closing poems often show thematic or formal links to one another. But, for the rest, the conviction that an elaborate and detailed structure of some sort exists has been widespread; agreement on what form that structure takes has not.[57] This does not offer a great deal of reassurance to those who seek a secure basis for identifying similar architectural structures in Livy: providing it exhibits some sort of

---

[54] The precise division and hence number of poems in these books is controversial; see McKeown (1987: 91–2).

[55] Cf. Vasaly (2002).

[56] Cf. Conte (1992).

[57] Rudd's sceptical comparison of the various contradictory architectural schemes discovered in the *Eclogues* still has a great deal of force (Rudd 1976: 119–44). Perhaps the most persuasive analysis of the structure of Horace *Satires* Book 1 (Zetzel 1980) in fact suggests that the book deliberately muddies the waters by offering multiple possible structures simultaneously.

systematic balance, one might feel that almost any structure that one might identify could find a parallel in someone's interpretation of some Augustan poet.

Still, even the broad consensus about beginnings, openings, and centres provides us with enough for at least the basic identification of a structure. As I pointed out above, Livy, though having far less scope than a poet for marking patterns by formal variation, signals a sharp break between Book 25 and Book 26, and explicitly states at 26.37 that the war is starting afresh (but now, of course, the tide is running in the direction of the Romans rather than the Carthaginians). That fact, when combined with the significance of centres to mark 'new beginnings' that the parallel with the poets suggests, provides us with at least some reason for suggesting that a Roman reader would be likely to allot particular interpretative significance to parallels between Book 21 and 26, and even perhaps to extend it into parallels between Books 22 and 27—though it is also to be expected that, in the absence of further markers, such parallels would impose themselves less insistently unless Livy explicitly highlights the comparison (as he does with Cannae and the Metaurus). Likewise we could note the striking appearance of the paired speeches of Books 21 and 30, paired not only by the identities of the speakers, but also by the fact that it is rare—indeed, in Livy's surviving work, unique—to have pairs of speeches prior to battles.[58]

Hence it seems reasonable to allot significance to those—admittedly relatively limited—parallels, and to see them as providing a broad architectural framework that would be identified and recognized by contemporary readers. But it is hard to feel secure about any other claimed structures, no matter how apparently persuasive or extensive the assemblage of parallels might seem. For example, one might note apparent points of symmetry between Books 26 and 30, framing the second pentad. There is one explicit reference: in the Sophoniba episode, Scipio rebukes Masinissa partly by contrasting Masinissa's lack of continence with his own refusal in Book 26 to be seduced by even the most beautiful of his captives (30.14.3, 30.14.5–7: compare 26.49–50). Other points could also be identified. The capture of the (appropriately named)[59] New Carthage in Book 26 mirrors the final defeat of Carthage proper. The double embassies of the Carthaginians in Book 30 (the first apparently treacherous, the second genuine) mirror the double embassies of the Syracusans and the

---

[58] Luce (1977: 27).

[59] Livy in fact generally calls the Spanish city simply *Carthago*. This has some historical justification, since that is what the Carthaginians themselves called it—the name of both the mother and daughter city being the Phoenician for 'New Town' (see Polybius 2.13.1 with Walbank 1957: 167, and cf. Lazenby 1978: 285). Nevertheless, Livy's using the same name has the additional effect of accentuating the parallel between the fates of the two cities.

Capuans which occupied such a large portion of Book 26. Scipio's triumph in Book 30 is prefigured in Marcellus' ovation for his Syracusan victory in Book 26, a victory which is specifically described as having a Carthaginian component (26.21.9 *Punicae quoque victoriae*). Following Zama Scipio assesses the site of Carthage but without ultimately besieging the city, much as Hannibal had assessed the site of Rome in Book 26.[60] But the trouble is that in the absence of clear structural signals, or of any firm evidence for a structural arrangement of that particular sort being highlighted in contemporary aesthetics, it is unclear whether this pattern would be regarded as more significant than any other parallels that could be identified between any other books. (This is not to say that it would *not* have been regarded as significant: merely that our evidence is insufficient to judge.) There is the extra problem that the very awareness that Livy is writing history—in other words to some degree representing (or purporting to represent) reality—means that the reader would know something of the constraints on his narrative (indeed, might even regard them as greater than they in fact were, since Livy does not explicitly mark all of his chronological manipulations, for example). This would militate against the recognition of too complex or elaborate a structural arrangement.

The constraints on Livy can also be seen in something with which he was certainly concerned, namely the structure of individual books. Here too some caution is needed. In the context of the Fourth and Fifth Decades Luce argued that Livy's practice was to try to create major episodes at the start, middle, and end of individual books, though he carefully made it clear that this represents Livy's general preference when his source-material permitted it rather than a universal straitjacket into which all books should be forced.[61] However, even given that qualification, Books 21–30 hardly fit Luce's model—unless one allows such a liberal definition of 'start, middle, and end' (or indeed of 'major') that almost anything would qualify short of outright triviality.

The only books in the Third Decade which have a tripartite structure of Luce's type are 21, 25, and 26. Book 21 certainly centres on three substantial episodes: Hannibal's capture of Saguntum at the start, his march into Italy in the centre, and his victories at Ticinus and Trebia at the end.[62] Book 26 has the fall of Capua and Hannibal's march on Rome at the start, the embassies of the Syracusans and the Capuans at the centre, and Scipio's capture of New

---

[60] Compare 26.10.3 *moenia situmque urbis obequitans contemplabatur* with 30.36.6 *ad contemplandum Carthaginis situm*.

[61] Luce (1977: e.g. 33–8). Luce recognizes that books in other parts of Livy were sometimes patterned according to different principles—he notes, for example, the bipartite structure of Book 5 (Luce 1977: 27)—but does not analyse Books 31–45 in those terms.

[62] Burck (1962: 57).

Carthage at the end. Book 25 has the fall of Tarentum and death of Gracchus at the start, followed by the capture of Syracuse and the deaths of the Scipios in Spain—though here the three parts are not as evenly balanced, since the siege of Syracuse and the Scipios' death both fall clearly in the second half of the book.

But the other books—including perhaps the two most powerful in the decade, 22 and 27—are structured quite differently. Book 22 has a bipartite, rather than a tripartite structure. The defeat at Trasimene at the very beginning runs straight into the dictatorship of Fabius and his conflict with Minucius. The elections for 216 then create a clear break in the exact centre of the book, followed by the campaign that culminates in Cannae and its aftermath. Book 27 has not so much a balanced as a cumulative structure: it builds from the early fighting between (in particular) Hannibal and Marcellus to the death of Marcellus, and culminates with Hasdrubal's arrival in Italy and his defeat at the Metaurus. Books 23 and 30, like Book 22, have structures which are closer to bipartite than tripartite[63] (though in the case of Book 23 the division is not as clearly marked as in the others). Book 23 balances Hannibal's taking of Capua at the start with his defeat at Nola at the end. In Book 30, as in Book 22, the elections and new magistrates (for 202) divide the book between the defeat of Syphax and the subsequent abortive truce, and the victory at Zama and its aftermath. On the other hand, Books 24 and 28 have a cumulative structure closer to Book 27. Book 28 focuses on Scipio, building from his victories in Spain to the suppression of his soldiers' mutiny to his election as consul and his debate with Fabius. Book 24 is dominated by the story of Syracuse, culminating in Marcellus' unsuccessful attack on the town followed by the massacre at Henna – though here, unlike Books 27 and 28, there are also a number of further episodes following the major climax (cf. 32–3 below).

All of this suggests that, at least in these books, a tripartite structure is not Livy's only model. Indeed, it is not even his preferred model. Lack of suitable material to create three major episodes might conceivably explain the handling of Book 23, much of which is relatively piecemeal; it hardly applies to Books 22, 27, 28, or 30. It is clear that a different, more flexible account is needed.[64]

---

[63] Cf. Burck (1962: 102–3).

[64] Vasaly (2002: 280–5) gives such an account (in summary), centring on Books 1–5, but even her analysis could not be applied to Books 21–30 without a good deal of qualification: for example, her suggestion that 'Symmetry is created through the division of most books into two or three major parts' (Vasaly 2002: 284).

First, every book of the decade—with one exception—has a large-scale dramatic and often emotionally resonant episode in its final third. The Trebia in 21, Cannae in 22, Nola in 23, the Roman assault on Syracuse and Henna in 24, the Scipios' death and the rally of Marcius in 25, the capture of New Carthage in 26, the battle at the Metaurus in 27, the Scipio–Fabius debate in 28, and Zama in 30, all conform to this pattern. In several of these cases—in particular 22, 24, 27, and 30—that climactic episode is quite clearly the most powerful in the book, and in none of the others is it obviously overshadowed by anything earlier.[65] The precise positioning of the episode varies: in 23, 25, 26, 27, and 28 it comes quite close to the end, whereas in the other books there is a substantial aftermath; but the basic pattern remains intact.

Second, despite the disparate subject-matter of each book, Livy seems to be making an effort to unify them. Here we need to think about what precisely counts as 'unity' (cf. above, nn. 8 and 32). Sometimes scholars have discussed the unity of Livian books in terms of the repetition of particular abstract topics – *libertas* in Book 2, *modestia* in Book 3, and *pietas* in Book 5, for example.[66] Even if unity around such abstractions can indeed be hypothesized for the early books,[67] there was clearly little or no scope for Livy to continue it in the Third Decade. But a degree of unity of another sort was certainly sometimes available. One ancient concept of a unified narrative in historiography, as I discussed above (nn. 8 and 32), was to maintain a core story from start to finish. This unity would not be compromised even if the story was interleaved with others, since that would simply represent the balanced variety which was held by ancient aesthetics—though rarely in modern—to be entirely compatible with and indeed often expected in a unified work.

Now, Livy is not writing the Hannibalic War as a whole within one volume. But the story could be broken into component episodes and movements, and these provide a focus for most of the individual books (for an exception, see 30 below). For example, Book 21 covers Hannibal's invasion of Italy up to the end of the first year of his campaign, culminating in the Trebia, which forces a pause while the Romans regroup. From the very start of the book Livy repeatedly places the plan to invade Italy at the centre of attention and as the focus of all Hannibal's prior actions (e.g. 21.2.2–3, 21.5.1, 21.16). Book 28 has a strong focus on Scipio: it begins with the renewal of his campaign in Spain and moves through his final victory there to his election as consul, and

---

[65] We can contrast, for example, Book 3, where the most powerful and dramatic episode of the book comes in the central section, with the story of the decemvirate.

[66] So e.g. Ogilvie (1965: 30).

[67] But one should approach such claims sceptically even there: compare Heath (1989: e.g. 5–8) on problems with the modern critical tendency to 'thematic integration', where texts are assessed according to the critic's ability to relate the subject-matter to one single theme.

culminates with his great debate with Fabius over war strategy and his obtaining the (qualified) endorsement of his plan to invade Africa. Book 26 has two major narrative components, each substantially completed within the book: the recapture of Capua and the punishment of the Capuans, and the challenge faced by the Romans in Spain after the Scipios' defeat, leading to Scipio Africanus' command in Spain and his providing a new basis for Roman victory with the capture of New Carthage. Book 23 begins with an apparent success by Hannibal in taking Capua, but that success proves disastrous for him: his troops are enervated by the luxury there, with the consequence at the end of the book that he receives his first significant defeat from Marcellus at Nola, a connection which both Marcellus and Hannibal make explicitly (23.45.1–6). Book 27 might on the face of things appear the hardest for Livy to unify in these terms, since it covers more years than any other in the decade. However, it is tied together by two stories. First there is the constant back-and-forth of victory and defeat between Marcellus and Hannibal, which begins in the very first lines of the book and concludes with Marcellus' death in its centre. Woven with that is the story of Hasdrubal's flight from Spain and his crossing into Italy to join Hannibal, something long anticipated (23.28.7–8, 23.29.7, 25.32.2, 26.41.13), but which is now repeatedly presented as imminent (27.5.11–12, 27.7.3, 27.20.1–8, 27.35.10–36.4). This then culminates with the panic at Rome and the remarkable Roman victory.

This last example shows something further: how Livy can shape a book into a unity by alluding to its climactic episode from early on. Sometimes this is transparent, as in Book 27, sometimes it is more covert. A particularly neat example is near the opening of Book 28. Here Silanus has just completed a victory over Mago, and Scipio sees a chance of consolidating Roman power in Spain (28.2.14):

conlaudato benigne Silano Scipio spem debellandi, si nihil eam ipse cunctando moratus esset, nactus, ad id quod reliquum belli erat in ultimam Hispaniam adversus Hasdrubalem pergit.

After generously praising Silanus Scipio, acquiring the hope of finishing the war, if he himself made no delay by holding up that hope, pursued the remaining part of the war against Hasdrubal in Further Spain.

The ostensible allusion here is to the campaign in Spain, which Scipio does indeed complete within a few chapters. But his intentions are described in general terms which have a wider reference as well. The term *debellandi* does not specifically allude to Spain, and the book, as I said, climaxes with Scipio's great debate with Fabius, where he puts forward his plan to end the entire Punic war by invading Africa. Moreover, the refusal to delay, expressed in the apparently pleonastic phrase *cunctando moratus esset*, looks forward to

Fabius' opposition to that plan – Fabius was of course the proverbial 'delayer', as he himself notes at the start of his speech (28.40.6: cf. below, 191). Livy begins his book with a glance forward to its conclusion.

Likewise one can see Livy employing closural devices to round off individual books. Book 27 concludes the victory of the Metaurus on a magnificent final note, as Claudius Nero returns to confront Hannibal and contemptuously throws the head of his defeated brother before his camp (27.51.11–12). In Book 22 Livy summarizes the effect of Cannae by listing the defections of individual Italian communities to the Carthaginians (22.61.10–12), even though the actual defections in many cases will be described much later in his narrative. He then ends with the symbolically resonant scene of Varro, despite his responsibility for the defeat, returning to Rome to be hailed for not despairing of the state (22.61.14–15). Book 28 concludes with Hannibal dedicating an inscription of his deeds (28.46.16): again a symbolically resonant action, for with the recent election of Scipio as consul and his planned invasion of Africa Hannibal's years of success are over, and the writing of an inscription suggests that Hannibal is providing a narrative close to his own career.[68] One can find similar examples with every book.[69]

One should not, of course, exaggerate this. It would be foolish to argue that any individual book is unified as strongly as the decade as a whole demonstrably is. Even major episodes within a single book, such as those I have outlined above, are always presented with an eye to their background and consequences in the war as a whole. But unity (though scholars sometimes seem to imply otherwise) should not be conceived as an absolute, especially in the relatively liberal terms allowed in ancient aesthetics. Books can be more or less unified; Livy, by repeatedly constructing distinct narrative movements and confining them within a single book, allows these books some sense of individual unity while still maintaining the primary arc of the Hannibalic War as a whole.

These two aspects of Livy's book construction—providing a final climactic episode to each book, and a degree of narrative unity within it—are naturally not independent of one another. The existence of a climax as a conclusion to a central narrative movement in the book is one of the main things that identifies a central narrative movement in the first place. It may well be partly for this reason that, although Livy allows a significant variety of devices to

---

[68] Cf. Burck (1971: 22), and especially Jaeger (2006: 391–3, also 396), for the way in which Livy elsewhere employs monuments for closural effect. Jaeger moreover notes that Hannibal's monumental account of his own deeds suggests parallels with Livy himself, who famously described his own work as a *monumentum* (*Praef.* 10).

[69] Cf. Aly (1936: 10).

provide balance and symmetry in his Hannibalic War books, the creation of a final climax is common to (almost) all of them: in this way books receive a distinct narrative identity.

As I have said, however, Livy's freedom is not total. Even within the books I have discussed one may reasonably feel that the material available in some books (like Book 22) allowed climaxes and unified narratives to be created more strongly and distinctly than in others (like Book 23). One book in particular shows the problem: Book 29. This is the shortest book in the decade. It is also the only book in the decade which does not work towards a dramatic climax.[70] Instead, at the place where one might expect a dramatic climax, Livy substitutes something quite different: a long digression—indeed, the longest in his entire surviving corpus—giving the past history of Masinissa (29.29.6–33.10). This digression (unlike others in Livy) has been remarkably little studied;[71] I shall have more to say about it in Chapter 3. But for now we simply should note that the motivation for its introduction here is fairly tenuous. It is prompted by Masinissa joining Scipio in Africa, but Masinissa has been playing an increasingly significant role since his original introduction at 24.49.1, and this background narrative, while thematically important, could have appeared almost anywhere.[72] Rather it seems primarily to be because while Livy, for the reasons discussed above, wishes to have a book at this point in order to maintain the overall structure of the decade, he appears short of suitable material to maintain it at a reasonable length; he also has no obvious material out of which to form a significant climax (though cf. 32 below). Instead he offers an episode which, while certainly fascinating and distinctive, is not given any especial emotional force, and is overtly digressive rather than forming a dramatically satisfactory completion of the book's narrative.

The discussion so far might make it appear that Livy's decisions over book division and narrative structure were merely aesthetic in a formal sense: that in as much as his material allowed him to do so, his aim was to divide and organize his books in order to provide an aesthetically satisfying experience, with climaxes at appropriate moments, narratives of the appropriate length, and appropriate structures of balance and symmetry both within and between

---

[70] Cf. Hoffmann (1942: 9): 'XXIX aber endigt als einziges Buch der dritten Dekade ohne bedeutsames Ereignis', though Hoffmann is looking more narrowly for significant events at the very end of books, rather than climaxes of the sort I am discussing here.

[71] Exceptions include Johner (1996: 238–41) and Chlup (2004: 101–4).

[72] Cf. Soltau (1894a: 590–1, 1897: 49), who suggests that the episode would more naturally belong with the earlier appearances of Masinissa in Book 28 or Book 29. He attributes its inclusion here to Livy inserting the episode carelessly after he had already completed the book, but overlooks its structural importance.

individual books. But it would be seriously misleading to present it simply in those terms. Those aesthetic decisions about narrative structure and book division were inextricably intertwined with issues of historical interpretation.[73] To identify a particular moment as climactic, for example, involves regarding it as important in itself and often as the culmination of the earlier narrative. Book 23 provides a clear example. It is far from obvious that Marcellus' success at Nola was as impressive a victory or as significant a mark of Carthaginian decline as Livy makes it out to be.[74] No other source treats it as such, even Plutarch, who is avowedly drawing on Livy and has an interest in magnifying Marcellus' achievements.[75] It is hard to avoid the conclusion that Livy's decision to adopt Nola as the climactic end-point of his book and his boosting its importance in the war go hand in hand. But it is impossible to say which came first: whether it was the desire to have a climax around the time of Nola that led Livy to build up its significance, or whether the identification of Nola as a key moment was what led him to select it as the climactic moment in his book. Indeed, it is not clear that the distinction even makes sense. Historiographical structuring of itself implies historical interpretation. The organization of the books and the creation of an interpretation which matches that organization are likely to have been a single simultaneous process.

The same applies elsewhere. It was naturally not hard for Livy to identify Cannae or Zama as centrally important; it was much more distinctive to treat the debate on war strategy in Book 28 as a climactic moment parallel to them. Yet to do so made perfect sense within his conception of the war, where the question of the appropriate strategy with which to confront Hannibal – and the uncomfortable implications of adopting certain strategies—is a problem that recurs endlessly within his narrative. Likewise, forming parallels between Hannibal's invasion of Italy in Book 21 and Scipio's move to Spain in Book 26 is just one part of a general process by which Scipio is shown—uncomfortably and partially—to obtain victory for the Romans by employing Hannibalic methods. (I shall discuss this issue further in Chapter 3.)

And just as Livy might boost particular moments to form a climax, so he might play down others. The death of Marcellus in Book 27 is one such moment. It is easy to see how Livy could have treated the killing of one of the three leading Roman commanders of the war as a major disaster to rival the

---

[73] Cf. Lipovsky (1981: 6–21).

[74] If indeed it even occurred: de Sanctis (1968: 244) suggests that it is a patriotic invention; cf. also Seibert (1993a: 237). But even if this is so, it is unlikely to have been Livy's invention, though he does, as I argue, boost its significance.

[75] Hoffmann (1942: 51).

great defeats of the opening books, or could have turned it into a tragic climax comparable to heroic deaths in epic poetry. In fact he does neither.[76] When he uses the sinister prodigy list at 27.23.1–4 to anticipate Marcellus' death, he explicitly denies that it will be a national disaster (27.23.4 *in capita consulum re publica incolumi exitiabilis prodigiorum eventus vertit*—'The destructive outcome of the prodigies turned against the heads of the consuls, <u>leaving the state unharmed</u>'). The death itself is narrated briefly and in passing, the focus being on the flight of the Fregellan soldiers when they see him fall.[77] The skirmish in which he falls is given no more space than its aftermath, in which Hannibal attempts unsuccessfully to use Marcellus' ring to trick the Salapians. The result is that the loss of Marcellus, while not negligible, is built into but also subordinated to the sequence leading up to the Metaurus, which forms the true climax of the book. Livy presents the episode not so much as a major setback for Rome, but rather as a disastrous personal misjudgement which indeed put the country at risk (27.27.11), but whose actual consequences were considerably less significant.

The absence of a climax to Book 29 can be seen similarly, for Livy does in fact narrate two Roman victories at the end of Book 29: Scipio and Masinissa defeat and kill Hannibal's brother Hanno at 29.34, and Sempronius Tuditanus defeats Hannibal himself in Italy at 29.36.8-9. Livy could theoretically have treated either of these episodes as a powerful climactic moment. But to do so would have meant magnifying a victory by Scipio over a minor and anonymous commander (this is Hanno's first and last appearance in the war) or else a success by the otherwise unimportant Tuditanus. This would have altered drastically the interpretation of the overall narrative, which has increasingly stressed the decisive nature of the conflict that is now imminent between two iconic figures: Scipio and Hannibal. Rather than have a grand drama that would carry the wrong implications, he has no drama at all.

But once again we can see elements of tension. Livy's structure is not infinitely flexible, nor could his interpretation of the war always be conceptualized straightforwardly in structural terms: he has numerous competing pressures. He uses the massacre at Henna as part of the climax of Book 24. That is a complex episode, with many different implications: it is an immediate Roman success, and in the longer term prefigures the ultimate victory in Sicily, but it also badly damages the Roman campaign in the medium term, as

---

[76] Cf. Mensching (1996: 263), though he sees it as the specific consequence of Livy's unsympathetic treatment of Marcellus rather than connected to his broader narrative strategy.

[77] 27.27.7 *sed postquam volneratos ambo consules, Marcellum etiam transfixum lancea prolabentem ex equo moribundum videre, tum et ipsi... effugerunt*—'But after they saw both consuls wounded, Marcellus in fact pierced by a spear and falling dying from his horse, then they too... made their escape'.

their treachery and brutality at Henna alienate other Sicilians from their cause (24.39.8–9). The story also reveals something relevant about Marcellus, who is not directly involved in the massacre but condones it after the event, believing—wrongly—that it will prevent further defections (24.39.7). All of these matter: it is typical of Livy's subtlety that he presents events with such intricate and finely nuanced ramifications, and his selection of this episode as a climax draws the reader's attention to it. But if we are looking to interpret the role of this climactic moment in the dynamics of the war, it is hard to ascribe a clear significance to it.

There thus is a distinction to be drawn between an example such as this on the one hand, and Cannae, Nola, the Metaurus, or Zama on the other. These episodes, too, have many subtleties of their own. But however complex and nuanced the detail of what Livy is doing there, the reader of those books can relate the basic fact of 'defeat' or 'victory' to the episode's key structural position, and so understand clearly the direction that Livy regards the war as taking. One cannot readily make sense of the climax of Book 24 in those terms.

In short, book structure, while a significant aspect of Livy's narrative construction, is a blunt instrument: of itself it gives little opportunity for nuanced interpretation. An author can use it to mark certain episodes as more or less 'important', but it does not always allow clarity about the degree of importance or the aspects of the episodes which are most relevant to it. That very fact, of course, is something that an author may use creatively. The difficulty of interpreting Henna as a climax in terms of the dynamics of the war may be connected with Livy's willingness to use it as one. The destabilizing effect of such a climax may reinforce the finely balanced uncertainty and complexity implicit in the episode. It may also be relevant to observe that this climax, unlike others in the decade, fails to offer a completion to the narrative movement of the book. The Sicilian campaign, which has formed the single main topic of Book 24, is ostentatiously not completed but left in the balance. This book is thus the hardest to see as 'unified' in ancient terms (though, interestingly, it might appear one of the more 'unified' to the modern reader, since it contains one of the longest unbroken narratives in the decade); but it is hard to give a clear reason why Livy should have felt appropriate to leave it disunified—or indeed whether it is deliberate or merely the result of the intractability of the material. And the climax is then followed by a significant number of disconnected episodes apparently unrelated to the primary narrative of the book (above, 27). This may to a certain extent diminish the climactic effect of the episode—but again, it is hard to ascribe a meaning to that. While the formal structure of the books implies an historical interpretation, it does so only within certain circumscribed limits.

1.2. CHRONOLOGY

Another way Livy structures his narrative is via chronology.[78] Here one must raise some general caveats before beginning the discussion. Time is not something that people naturally tend to regard as culturally determined. For the most part we feel that we experience it passively rather than conceptualizing it as an entity; and even if the issue is drawn to our attention we tend to regard our own understanding as a universal substratum of human experience. However, there is a considerable (though not uncontroversial) anthropological literature to suggest that the experience of time is something that varies substantially between different cultures;[79] directly relevant here is that various scholars have suggested that perceptions of time in Greece and Rome were in certain key ways unlike our own. When it comes to historiography, the most obvious point is the absence of a universally agreed 'absolute' dating scheme. Years were not numbered according to an accepted distance from a fixed point in the past; instead modes of time-reckoning varied from culture to culture, with various local systems in place, such as identifying years according to eponymous magistrates, or by the regnal years of kings. Reckoning an era according to a fixed starting-point was not unknown, but it was not widely employed. In this context, it was much more natural for historians to present events in terms of their relationship to other events than to try to date each event within an overall chronological framework.[80] As we shall see, Livy strongly conforms to this pattern; but there are also

---

[78] The study of Roman attitudes to time has recently received a fundamental and ground-breaking study by Feeney (2007).

[79] For a general survey of the literature see Munn (1992). Gell (1992) gives a detailed though sceptical summary of earlier studies, arguing against total relativism while accepting the substantial practical difference that different societies' apparatus of time-concepts makes to their world-view. Adam (1990: esp. 70–148) seeks to give a broad theoretical basis for this, contrasting universal perceptions derived from human biology with aspects of time experience specific to particular societies. Feeney (2007: 4) likewise suggests that 'we may resist the deep relativism . . . while still allowing plenty of room for cultural specificity'; he also offers the important caveat that we should not attribute to the Romans, any more than to any other society, a single unified and coherent concept of time (Feeney 2007: 3).

[80] E.g. Hunter (1982: 166–9, 219–24, 237–64), Möller and Luraghi (1995), Shaw (2003: 25–9, 239–53), Feeney (2007: 7–16). See also Wilcox (1987: esp. 51–118), though many of his generalizations are badly overstated, such as his claim (readily disproved by reference to Diodorus—cf. Clarke 2008: 127–39) that 'When the historians saw no interaction or relation, there was no need to synchronize events' (Wilcox 1987: 74); Asheri (1991–2) is similar but more measured, distinguishing 'didactic' synchronisms, which drew a message from the coincidence of time, from 'technical' synchronisms, which did not imply such a connection.

It should however be pointed out that, unlike some other cultures, the Greeks and Romans (contrary to what more extreme versions of this thesis sometimes claim) had the *concept* of an absolute reified time available to them (see Stern 2003: 90–102; cf. Möller and Luraghi 1995:

aspects of his presentation of chronology which allow us to draw some more detailed and perhaps surprising conclusions about his conception of historical time.

Narration by years, such as we find in Livy, is surely the single most common structuring device among historians both ancient and modern. But the texture of Livy's chronology is highly distinctive because of the prominent role he gives to formal elements of the Roman political year. Each year begins with the new consuls and other magistrates formally taking up their office on 15 (the Ides) March, and ends with the election of the new magistrates for the following year. The taking up of office is typically associated with the allocation of provinces and armies to the various magistrates, and often with other formal material as well, such as the reception of embassies or the reporting and expiation of prodigies. The end of the year will likewise often see formal material introduced: typical examples might be the celebration of games or reports of the deaths of important figures, especially priests. All this material is generally described as 'annalistic'.

So awareness of the Roman year is something that is constantly forced upon the reader by the narrative: there is no other surviving ancient historian where we can see anything comparable.[81] But that makes it especially remarkable how little Livy's years correlate with his carefully designed book-structures.[82] Year-markers are occasionally used, as I have noted (above, 15–16), to reinforce key structural points, providing firm caesuras at the ends of Books 21, 25, and 29, which suggests that the year had sufficient narrative identity for its end to possess closural force. Likewise year-breaks can sometimes be used to articulate the internal structure of a book, as in Book 22 and Book 30. But more commonly book divisions cut across years, and moreover do so in ways that suggest that chronology is overwhelmingly subordinated to the thematic issues which govern the book structure. So, for example, even the

12–13), even if this was not expressed in a universal dating system that could be used for practical historiographical purposes. Moreover Livy, unlike his Greek predecessors, had in the Roman calendar a standard and recognized 'absolute' dating system for dates *within* years, even if not for dates *of* years; cf. Feeney (2007: 209–11). This may help explain why, although he introduces few such dates, when he does so the potential for chronological violations is something that he appears to be concerned about: see below, 48–52.

[81] Tacitus, *Annals* 1–6 is likewise structured around 'annalistic' years, but these appear to be a subversive device to show the hollowness of the Republican façade when set against imperial reality: see Ginsburg (1981). Accordingly the quantity of such material is greatly attenuated by comparison with Livy.

[82] This is true of Livy's history generally: see the table in Stadter (1972: 304–6). In Tacitus, *Annals* 1–6, by contrast, book divisions regularly correlate to year-breaks (see Woodman and Martin 1996: 78); though cf. McCulloch (1984: 137–69) arguing that for Tacitus, too, shaping books generally took precedence over annalistic structure even when the latter is present.

strongest closure of all, at the end of Book 30, does not correspond to the end of a year, since most of the material for 201 related to the beginning of the Second Macedonian War is reserved for Book 31.[83] The division between Book 27 and Book 28 is similar: the material for 207 related to the defeat of Hasdrubal is completed in Book 27; Book 28 then opens with the campaigns of Scipio in the same year, whose activities will form the book's primary theme. Likewise for the year 215 Livy unites Marcellus' campaign in Italy with that of the previous year by keeping it in Book 23, while he joins the beginning of the Syracusan revolt to its later developments by placing it in Book 24. Nor do year-breaks within books usually mark strong structural divisions. In Book 25 the end of the year 213 appears less than two pages into the book; in Book 27 the annalistic material for the year-break 208/7, far from marking a structural division, itself forms part of the dramatic build-up to the arrival of Hasdrubal in Italy (below, 43, 189).

In other words, the annalistic year in Livy 21–30, while extensively—indeed obsessively—marked, is rarely treated as a primary narrative unit. It seems to serve a quite different purpose.

What is the effect of the inclusion of annalistic material? It is known that the Romans kept official records of such items that historians used for their source material (though it is controversial which historians used what records and when).[84] It has usually been held that there was a genre of history prior to Livy whose authors organized their narrative according to these formal patterns, and that Livy is formulaically replicating their material;[85] these historians are collectively known as the 'annalists'.[86] If so, the insistence on the pattern in Livy would not be as distinctive to a Roman reader as it is to us, since it would simply be part of a familiar generic format.

However, this picture is open to question. John Rich has argued persuasively that while most early Roman historians doubtless narrated their history year by year, the detailed formalization of the annalistic year that we find in Livy was not in fact a standard feature of pre-Livian Roman historiography: he suggests that it

---

[83] It should be noted, however, that the last year change in the war, 202/1, is narrated in an anti-closural fashion. The chronology of the annalistic material is deliberately confounded and the election does not take place until the new year has already begun (30.40.5–6). The change of year itself is only marked in passing (30.39.5: see below, 51–2). This too suggests that a year-end narrated in the normal way would have some closural force, at least when it is appearing near to the end of the book. Livy avoids the misleading suggestion that the end of the year will mark the end of the book, narrating the year-end in such a way as to avoid that sense of closure.

[84] For the nature of the records themselves and their use by Roman historians see esp. Frier (1979).

[85] So e.g. McDonald (1957: 155–6), Frier (1979: 270–4), Fornara (1983: 23–8), Walter (2003).

[86] This is however a problematic and question-begging term: see Verbrugghe (1989).

was essentially the creation of a single historian, probably Valerius Antias, from whom Livy has taken it over.[87] He also shows that even Livy himself (demonstrably) did not employ it in Books 1–10, and (probably) did not for much of Books 71–142 either. It is also demonstrable that Livy substantially manipulated at least some of these annalistic elements when forming his narrative: he did not simply adopt the format unquestioningly (cf. below).

If the device was not simply a standard feature of Roman historiographical tradition, it follows that for Roman readers its inclusion would not simply appear as innocent traditionalism, the more so since much of the formal apparatus of the Roman political year had fallen into abeyance in the period leading up to the time when Livy was writing. Even Augustus' ostensible restoration of Republican institutions in 27 had inevitably been only partial and superficial, given his need to restructure elements of them to preserve his own control. Livy is ostentatiously demonstrating the political workings of mid-Republican Rome to an audience, many of whom will not have experienced anything comparable at first hand.[88] And in the Hannibalic War he is showing the system at the time when it had to cope with its greatest existential crisis, when the entire state was under threat from outside. In the event, of course, the ultimate collapse of the system in the later Republic was the result of internal pressures rather than external. As we shall see, some of Livy's most interesting manipulations of his annalistic material precisely involve the representation of comparable internal pressures which, although smoothed over within the system at the time, prefigure the tensions that were to come increasingly to the fore from the time of the Gracchi onwards.

One clear example of Livy's creative use of annalistic material comes with prodigy lists. Every year during the Second Punic War has an example of these supernatural events, signs of the gods' ill-favour which are collected, reported to the Senate at Rome, and formally expiated. These usually appear at the beginning of the year, which is assumed by Livy to be the regular procedure.[89] But Livy regularly manipulates the lists in both position and length in order to reinforce his wider narrative by minimizing or enhancing their negative impact, removing it where it would seem inappropriate or introducing it at the most appropriate spot.[90] The long list for 218 is displaced to the end of the

[87] Rich (1997). He also considers, but on balance rejects, the idea that Cn. Gellius might have originated it and Antias taken it from him.
[88] Cf. Walter (2003: 143–5) for the argument that the adoption of annalistic organization by writers of the Sullan period emphasized in a time of political chaos the strength of Roman tradition. See also Zorzetti (1978: 81–127) for an interesting discussion of the broader political and ideological implications of Livy's annalistic structure.
[89] Levene (1993: 35–6).
[90] For fuller discussion of the following examples, see Levene (1993: 38–77).

year, after the election of Flaminius as consul (21.62), and is thus associated with the impiety which is shortly to lead to his defeat and death at Lake Trasimene. This defeat is likewise signalled by the equally long list for 217, which comes immediately after he takes up his consulship (22.1.8–20). Book 26, as I said above, marks a new beginning, with the tide turning towards Rome; accordingly the list for 211 is both short and displaced from the start of the book until after the elections for the following year (26.23.4–6). The list for 202 is displaced until after the victory of Zama, and moreover presented so as to bring out the Romans' success in obtaining the gods' favour rather than the loss of that favour in the first place (30.38.8–12); similarly the list for Scipio's consulship in 205 is extremely brief, deferred to the end of the year, and simply forms the trigger for Rome's successful introduction of the Magna Mater (29.10.4–8). Conversely the long list for 207, before the Metaurus, is treated in a way that matches the dramatic crisis: waves of prodigies appear and are expiated, only for more to appear in their wake, and the sequence ends with a massive expiation—the Romans are faced with potential disaster, but pull out every stop to overcome it (27.37).

The relatively circumscribed formulae of prodigy lists mean that their manipulation can only have fairly broad-brush effects. When it comes to the changing of consuls for the new year the possible variations are far greater. Usually elections come with other annalistic material at the very end of the year, and the new year is then marked by an explicit reference to the new consuls taking up office. But all too often things do not go nearly so smoothly.

A good example is the material in the middle of Book 23 dealing with the end of 216—the year of the crisis of Cannae—and the start of 215. To appreciate what Livy is doing here we should look at the section in some detail. At 23.21.1–7 we find a set of 'annalistic' material which appears to suggest the end of the year is at hand: in particular the account of the elections of *pontifices* to make up for those who had died during the year (23.21.7), which is a regular formula concluding the year (below, 48–52). However, this proves not to be the end, because Livy gives it an added significance by the fact that the three priests had all died at Cannae,[91] and accordingly the election of new priests is immediately followed by further moves to recover from those losses, with a long account of the controversial arrangements to make up the numbers of the senate (23.22–23). Only then does M. Junius Pera (who had been appointed as dictator in the wake of Cannae (22.57.9)) come to Rome to hold the elections for the new year (23.24.1–5).

[91] Cf. Rich (1997).

We would naturally expect the new year now to begin with the consuls taking up office. Instead a disaster is reported: one of the newly elected consuls, L. Postumius Albinus, has been killed in Gaul (23.24.6–13). The Romans have to discuss their response to this, and make some arrangements for a new election and for the assignments of armies in the following year (23.25). So this too appears to signal the end of the year—but once again our expectations are defeated, as the scene moves to Spain, and we are given the Spanish campaign for 216 (23.26–9), followed by reports of further Carthaginian campaigns in Italy and the beginnings of anti-Roman moves in Sicily (23.30.1–13). Then we finally reach the words *exitu anni* (23.30.13: 'at the end of the year'), with some notes of temple foundations and games that were held.

So now at last the true change of year is marked: *circumacto tertio anno Punici belli Ti. Sempronius consul idibus Martiis magistratum init* (23.30.18: 'with the third year of the Punic War completed the consul Tiberius Sempronius entered his magistracy on the Ides of March'). But this is itself an anomalous formula, because it reminds us of unfinished business: no second consul has yet been chosen. Nor is one appointed immediately: first we are given further allocations of provinces and armies for the year (23.30.18–31.6). Elections are now held, though not without problems, as Marcellus is first elected and then abdicates following a bad omen (23.31.12–14); Fabius takes his place. Then there is a (remarkably perfunctory) prodigy list (23.31.15), and finally the two consuls for 215 can begin the duties of their office in earnest, with a further assignment of troops (23.32.1–4).

It should be clear that 'formulaic' would be an extremely poor characterization of this extended sequence. On the contrary, Livy appears to be manipulating and subverting the formulae, repeatedly appearing to close the year only to reopen matters with a new crisis.[92] The new year, when it arrives, still has only one consul, and the process of acquiring another creates further crises. Three separate reports are given of troop allocations for the year, following each successive revision of senior personnel. While (of course) Livy did not invent the death of one elected consul and the vitiation of another,[93] the way he

---

[92] This may even begin before the annalistic material, since Hannibal's moving his troops into winter quarters at 23.18.10 might appear also to suggest the impending end of the year. However, these seasonal markers in Livy raise separate problems: see 52–63 below.

[93] Postumius' death while consul-designate is recorded in the *Fasti Capitolini*. However, even this could have been handled differently. Polybius 3.118.6 dates it to just a few days after Cannae, so far earlier in the sequence of the year's events (Cannae took place on August 2, according to Claudius Quadrigarius fr. 53P). Livy places his account later, although he is aware of the Polybian version, since he alludes to it by drawing directly on Polybius' language even while changing the date (cf. below, 147–62): compare 23.24.6 *nova clades nuntiata, aliam super aliam cumulante in eum annum fortuna, L. Postumium consulem designatum in Gallia ipsum atque exercitum deletos* ('a new disaster was announced—fortune was piling one after another that

structures the narrative, with the year-end repeatedly deferred and then interspersed with other material, is distinctive and undermines our assumptions and expectations about the sequence of events.

In effect the disaster that came on Rome at Cannae seems to be affecting the year itself. The series of deceptive closures is not simply the result of Livy playing games with the reader's expectations, but graphically illustrates a central political point: that the emergency that Rome is facing has undermined the normal workings of the Roman year. The destruction of upper-class priests and senators at Cannae and the defeat of Postumius are both directly linked to the military crisis. The conflict over the enlargement of the Senate and the repeatedly deferred and failed elections are the indirect consequence of the same crisis, as those deaths leave a political vacuum which urgently needs filling, but how precisely they should be filled opens out tensions and controversies of a sort all too familiar from the later history of the Republic and indeed from Livy's own day. Livy's narrative constantly draws attention to those issues.

So, for example, the attempt to reinforce senatorial numbers runs into the immediate objection from Sp. Carvilius that there are not enough appropriate candidates, and he proposes appointing Latins instead. But this is contentious: Livy reminds the reader of the proposal in 340 BC to do the same thing,[94] and a descendant of the chief opponent then, Manlius Torquatus, is at hand to oppose it with equal violence now (23.22.4–7: cf. 8.5). Fabius Maximus says that it is an inappropriate time for such a discussion, and persuades the senate to make it forgotten and as if never spoken. But the overblown language in which Fabius' point is expressed[95] gives the passage an ironic tone: the proposal manifestly was not forgotten (since Livy is recording it),

---

year. L. Postumius the consul designate had been wiped out in Gaul along with his army') with Polybius 3.118.6 καὶ γὰρ ὥσπερ ἐπιμετρούσης καὶ συνεπαγωνιζομένης τοῖς γεγονόσι τῆς τύχης, συνέβη μετ᾽ ὀλίγας ἡμέρας... τὸν εἰς τὴν Γαλατίαν στρατηγὸν ἀποσταλέντ᾽ εἰς ἐνέδραν ἐμπεσόντα παραδόξως ἄρδην ὑπὸ τῶν Κελτῶν διαφθαρῆναι μετὰ τῆς δυνάμεως ('And just as if fortune was going over the top and joining the fight against them, it happened a few days later ... that the general they had sent to Gaul had fallen unexpectedly into an ambush, and he and his army were utterly wiped out by the Celts').

[94] Livy has already earlier in the book (23.6.6–8) drawn to the readers' attention the events of 340 BC and their possible salience to the time of the Hannibalic War, in the course of recording a version of the Capuan revolt in which the Campanians made a similar demand. However, Livy there says that he doubts the historicity of the Campanians' demand, partly because it is too close to the events he had narrated in Book 8.

[95] 23.22.9 *eam unius hominis temerariam vocem silentio omnium extinguendam esse et, si quid umquam arcani sanctive ad silendum in curia fuerit, id omnium maxime tegendum, occulendum, obliviscendum, pro indicto habendum esse. ita eius rei oppressa mentio est* ('That rash voice of one man should be wiped out by the silence of everyone and, if there had ever been anything in the Senate house secret and holy enough to warrant silence, this thing most of all should be concealed, covered over, forgotten, treated as never spoken. In this way mention of this issue was suppressed').

and the issue was one that would not go away, but eventually came to a head with the Social War (see Chapter 3). Then M. Fabius Buteo is appointed as dictator to carry out the measure—an appointment which he objects to as unconstitutional on several grounds. He eventually agrees to act only in a limited way, after which he immediately resigns (23.22.11–23.8).

Livy's treatment of this whole episode, as so often, shows a subtle and fine political balance. His narrative is given a sharp edge by the fact that senatorial membership was a live and controversial issue in his day. Caesar had substantially expanded the Senate, partly with people who appeared unqualified and indeed with foreigners;[96] he was followed by the Triumvirs, who (allegedly) introduced people even further down the social scale.[97] Augustus reduced the numbers in 29 by removing about 200 of the less-qualified;[98] he carried this still further in 18, bringing the Senate's membership down to 600.[99] Livy indeed touches all these issues.[100] Carvilius' suggestion of the lack of appropriate Roman candidates is apparently disproved by the subsequent narrative, in which 170 acceptable new senators are easily found (23.23.6–7); but some are qualified by courageous soldiering rather than existing rank or fortune, which puts them closer to some of Caesar's more controversial choices.[101] The Senate's hostile response to the idea of Latin senators is excessive, and Fabius' excuse for suppressing debate is that it will provoke allies whose loyalty is already in doubt—which recognizes that Roman–Italian relations are a problem rather than resolving it. Fabius Buteo's argument that no single person should have the power of judging senatorial reputations (23.23.4) carries a pointed charge when one remembers the bitter resentment that attached to Augustus following his senatorial revisions in 29—resentment which led to his complex (but unsuccessful) manoeuvres in 18 to involve other people in

[96] So e.g. Cicero, *Fam.* 6.18.1, *Phil.* 11.12; Suetonius, *Div. Jul.* 76.3. However, Syme (1938) shows that Caesar's new senators were generally less *declassé* than these hostile reactions implied.

[97] Dio 48.34.4–5.

[98] Dio 52.42.1–3.

[99] Dio 54.13–14. According to Dio 54.14.1 he wanted to return it to its historical total of 300, but was dissuaded by the hostility of those likely to be removed. This may simply be Dio's invention, since the proposal appears highly impractical unless more substantial administrative reforms were contemplated (cf. Talbert 1984: 131–2). But if there is any truth at all to it, it reinforces the point that historical accounts of senatorial membership were not simply of antiquarian interest, but had strong contemporary relevance in the Augustan period.

[100] Cf. Petersen (1961: 442–3, 450), who similarly sees in Livy's account of Tarquin reducing the Senate in number and downgrading its influence (1.49.6–7) a specific allusion to Augustus' actions in 29. However, this depends on dating Livy's first book later than 29, which is dubious (see Luce 1965, Woodman 1988: 128–35).

[101] On the unacceptability of common soldiers rising to the Senate see Wiseman (1971: 74–7), who also considers how far Caesar's appointments infringed that taboo.

the decisions to ensure that this time he would avoid being blamed by those dismissed.

Then the elections come; but immediately problems arise here too. The consul Varro deliberately avoids presiding over them by returning to his army without informing the Senate (23.23.9). Junius Pera presides instead—and uses the opportunity to promote the candidacy of his deputy, Ti. Sempronius Gracchus (23.24.3), though Gracchus' only actions so far in the war (23.19) hardly suggest the *gloria* that Pera ascribes to him. The alert reader will notice the tacit omission: Marcellus, who has genuinely distinguished himself (23.16), and who, like Gracchus, has accompanied Pera to Rome (23.24.1), receives no mention from him, although it will soon become apparent that Marcellus would be the people's preferred—and preferable—candidate (cf. 23.30.19). The loss of Postumius leads to the need for further elections, which the Senate orders to take place as soon as possible (23.25.9). Instead nothing happens until after the beginning of the following year—and this too is contentious, since people accuse Gracchus of timing the election to coincide with Marcellus being sent from Rome to assist with the reassignment of troops (21.31.5). Gracchus denies that this was his intention, and promises to delay the election until Marcellus' return (23.31.7–9), but the structure of Livy's narrative, where several episodes have intervened since the order to hold immediate elections, suggests the disingenuousness of his denial. Finally Marcellus is chosen as consul, but with a bad omen: the patricians claim that the gods are displeased by the election of two plebeian consuls (23.31.12–13). Livy's phrasing implies that this claim is a spurious ploy,[102] but it successfully forces Marcellus' abdication.

With none of this is Livy suggesting imminent disaster for Rome: indeed, that may be why he makes the prodigy list so perfunctory, which could otherwise be taken to foreshadow just such a disaster.[103] Gracchus does not in the event prove a bad commander, Fabius is a more than worthy substitute for Marcellus (who anyway maintains his command as proconsul), Fabius Buteo's exemplary handling of his constitutional scruples is acclaimed (23.23.8), and the issue of the political rights of Italians is successfully deferred. But this is precisely the point: Livy can manipulate the annalistic material subtly, so as to indicate the undercurrents of events without labouring them crudely, and leave the reader to draw the appropriate conclusions

---

[102] 23.31.13 *volgoque patres ita fama ferebant, quod tum primum duo plebei consules facti essent, id deis cordi non esse*—'And the patricians spread the rumour widely about that the gods were displeased because that was the first time two plebeian consuls had been elected'. On the election and the significance of the omen see Linderski (1986: 2168–72), who emphasizes that the patricians' interpretation was not in fact unreasonable under augural law.

[103] Levene (1993: 51–2).

from his apparently simple statements of fact. Despite the magnitude of the crisis after Cannae, the Romans for now show themselves able to deal with these issues more or less successfully. We should be aware that this will not always be true.

Nor is the 'annalistic' sequence in Book 23 unusual in this. At least half of the changes of magistrates in the decade involve comparable manipulation and variation of formulae to bring out political tensions, and sometimes are no less lengthy and intricate, though the precise issues naturally vary from episode to episode. To give some examples briefly: Book 27 (as so often) is the most dramatic: two consuls died in a single year (208), a dictator was appointed to hold elections for 207 in an emergency situation—but one of the consuls chosen, Livius Salinator, proves resentful and hostile both to the people who elected him and to his new colleague (27.33.6–38.12): neither elections nor provincial assignments can go smoothly under those circumstances (see below, 187–91). In Book 26 Marcellus is once again chosen as consul (for 210) as second-best, after Torquatus refuses the office; but he loses his consular province when the Syracusans complain to the Senate about his behaviour at their conquest (26.26.5-32.8).[104] Book 24 sees another problematic election (215/14): Fabius forces the voting to be rerun when it appears that his niece's husband T. Otacilius will be elected despite his (apparent) unsuitability (24.7.10–9.5: the beneficiaries are Marcellus—yet again elected as second choice—and Fabius himself). In Book 28 Scipio's election as consul (206/5) is treated as the natural development from his successful Spanish campaign, but then his plan to invade Africa means that the assignment of provinces becomes a point of bitter contention (28.38-45).

Book 21 provides another interesting example. In the very first elections of the war Flaminius and Servilius are chosen as consuls for 217—apparently uncontentiously (21.57.4). But here too the expected end of the year is deferred: the narrative immediately moves away from Rome, to describe Hannibal's winter campaign in Italy (21.57.5–59.10) and Cn. Scipio's Spanish campaign (21.60–61). Only then do we return to the annalistic material, and we are instantly thrown into the long delayed prodigy-list (above, 37–8) followed by a report of Flaminius' conflict with the Senate and his refusal to take up his office at Rome in the accepted fashion.[105] It quickly becomes apparent that he owes his election to popular support, which he acquired by attacking the senators' right to own large

---

[104] This year also has the complication of M. Valerius Laevinus being chosen as consul while campaigning in Greece, something that requires further manipulations (below, 46–7).

[105] This last is unlikely to be historical, since *Inscriptiones Italiae* XIII.1 p. 149 reports that Flaminius and Servilius jointly celebrated the *feriae Latinae* at the start of their consulship, contrary to what Livy indicates in 21.63.5 and 22.1.6.

ships for transporting their goods (21.63.3–4). Livy's comment on this is typically non-committal:[106] it is not obvious that Flaminius is in the wrong. But he clearly is in the wrong in his consequent refusal to acknowledge senatorial authority, and the Senate's objection to his violation of constitutional—and especially religious—values is indicated as well founded, not least by the bad omen which he receives on taking up office (21.63.13–14). And the dangerous abandonment of protocol is illustrated by Livy by a striking change in the standard formula to open the year. Though Flaminius and Servilius must have chronologically begun their consulships on the same day, in Livy they do so in separate books, the former at the very end of Book 21, the latter at the start of Book 22.[107] The division between Roman leaders, which will repeatedly prove a problem in the war, is graphically represented.

Book 22 is more radical still. The year-change within it (217/16) is one of only two in the decade where the movement between the years is not clearly marked (22.33.9–36.9).[108] First the elections are delayed by problems over who is to preside over them: the consuls decline to do so, the dictator created to hold the elections proves to be improperly selected. An interregnum has to be proclaimed, and the elections are postponed into the new year. Then, still more seriously, the whole process of electing new magistrates and assigning provinces is undermined by Varro's candidacy, which he promotes by appealing to class conflict, entangling it with the issue of the correct strategy for the war. This entanglement was not something particular to this election: it has accelerated through the entire previous year (covering the first half of Book 22), from the election of Flaminius through the dispute between Fabius and Minucius, as popular leaders advocate aggressive policies and accuse their senatorial opponents of culpable temporizing. It is noteworthy that even the creation of an interregnum at this time is treated as more than mere formality, but is itself bound up with the class conflict, as Baebius Herennius accuses the Senate and the augurs of manipulating the process in order to keep Varro from the consulship (22.34.9–11).[109] The self-destructive political conflict has now taken over the very structure of the Roman political year.

---

[106] 21.63.4 *id satis habitum ad fructus ex agris vectandos; quaestus omnis patribus indecorus visus*—'That [size of ship] was held to be sufficient for transporting produce from estates; all trade seemed to be unsuitable for senators'.

[107] 21.63.13 *paucos post dies magistratum iniit*—'After a few days he entered on his magistracy'; 22.1.4 *Cn. Servilius consul Romae idibus Martiis magistratum iniit*—'The consul Cn. Servilius entered on his magistracy at Rome on the Ides of March'.

[108] The other is 30.39.4–8, where the elections for 201 are not held until after the start of the new year, which accordingly begins with no consuls in place at all (see below, 51–2).

[109] The historicity of the whole election process in 217/16 is disputed: see the different reconstructions of (e.g.) Jahn (1970: 119-24), Sumner (1975), Gruen (1979), Twyman (1984). One concern has been the contradiction between Baebius' accusation that the Senate was

So annalistic material in Books 21–30 is far from being simply a formulaic marker of chronological years: it is a dynamic tool for the representation of political issues. But chronology does matter as well, since the annalistic material contains many explicit chronological markers and implicit chronological assumptions—that indeed is one of the things that enables it to be manipulated. This is true throughout Livy's narrative: he repeatedly introduces markers to allow readers to orientate themselves chronologically. However, as we shall see, this chronology is less transparent than might initially appear.

Let us start with an obvious point. As Livy moves between different scenes and different theatres of war, he regularly introduces an episode with a short phrase to place it in the year or relate it chronologically to the episode before. We have already seen a couple of examples: the formulae to open the new year, and the phrase *exitu anni* as the year comes to its close. The year always begins and ends in Rome (with the partial exception of 21.63.13 quoted above). Except at 22.34–6 and 30.39.4–8 (above, 44) the start is always marked with a statement about the new consuls entering office, and one sometimes finds phrases such as *principio eius anni* as well (e.g. 26.2.1), while phrases like *exitu anni* are also employed at 24.7.10, 25.41.8, 27.7.1, 27.33.6, and 30.26.2. These beginning- and end-of-year formulae relate to what we might call 'textual', as well as chronological years:[110] they only occur at the very start and end of Livy's year-narratives, and are at least on the face of things assumed to describe events at those points of the political year (though as we shall see below, this is not always unproblematic).

A more common device is to mark simultaneity: phrases like *per eosdem dies* or *per idem tempus*, indicating that a new scene takes place around the same time as the one before. Examples are far too numerous to need citing, and indeed are not surprising given that, as I have already indicated, time was primarily conceived in antiquity in terms of the relationship between events rather than absolute dates within an overarching system. We should note that, though many of these expressions of apparent simultaneity are probably Livy's invention in order to link his different narratives, he does not, at least on the face of things, use them where the narrative context would make it clearly impossible for them to be true, such as where the same person would apparently be required to be in two places at once. Hence these formulae too

---

deliberately avoiding a dictatorship but was seeking an interregnum (22.34.9–11), and Livy's direct statement that they were seeking the opposite (22.33.11). It is perhaps revealing of scholars' assumptions about Livy that too many overlook the obvious conclusion: Baebius is lying.

[110] I draw this distinction from Kraus (1994a: 11).

appear to unite textual and chronological years: they signal that Livy is narrating events in (allegedly) their chronological place—subject to the important caveat that, as Diodorus Siculus famously observes (20.43.7), the simultaneity of events is to some extent misrepresented by the mere fact that in practice they are presented sequentially.

However, things are not always quite so straightforward. At 26.24.1 Laevinus' campaigns in Greece are introduced by *per idem tempus*. This looks odd: the previous episode with which this is supposedly simultaneous was an end-of-year summary of miscellaneous annalistic material which was itself introduced simply with *eodem anno* (26.23.4, cf. 26.23.7; on this formula see below). But Livy anyway has a problem fitting his Greek narrative chronologically to the rest of the war; and in this case he needs specifically to deal with the fact that Laevinus has been appointed to the consulship in his absence.[111] So the *per idem tempus* formula expresses simultaneity with a generic 'end of year' narrative whose events may in fact have occurred earlier. This allows his account of Laevinus' doings to be linked implicitly to the end of the year without directly saying that the entire sequence implausibly took place in just a few weeks.[112] Also left ambiguous is whether or not the success in Greece that got Laevinus elected as consul at 26.22.12 is supposed to include his deeds here—an essential ambiguity, since Livy has said virtually nothing about the Macedonian war since 24.40, although Laevinus has been in command there the whole time. It then allows the very precise timing necessary for the narrative at the start of the following year, where Laevinus only learns of his election at the last minute—indeed, possibly even after he was due to take up office[113]—and then is delayed further by illness (26.26.4).

---

[111] Livy similarly inserts his Greek narrative between the end and the beginning of the year in Rome at 29.12. This is, not coincidentally, the second occasion when the commander in Greece is elected consul in his absence, though in this case he succeeds in returning to Rome in time to take up office (29.12.16). Note however Rich (1984: 137–43; *contra* Eckstein 2002: 285–6), who argues that Livy's chronology here is in error, and the Greek narrative belongs a year earlier.

[112] Livy's narrative assumes we are in late 211, since Laevinus refers to the recent capture of Capua (26.24.2). However, the Aetolian treaty negotiated here was alluded to in passing in the previous year as something the Romans were trying for even then (25.23.9), and some scholars have argued that we should date the treaty to 212 or early 211, and the campaign starting in 26.25 to that summer. Livy has, on this view, inserted the material in the wrong year (cf. below, 53–5). See Klaffenbach (1954: 4) and McDonald (1956: 157), though McDonald's reconstruction underestimates the artfulness with which Livy avoids overtly violating his basic chronology; see *contra* Badian (1958: 197–203) and Rich (1984: 156–7) for a defence of Livy's dating.

[113] At 26.26.1 Laevinus is still in Greece and unaware of his election *veris principio* ('at the beginning of spring'), which might imply the new year has begun—though these seasonal markers are not always so straightforward to interpret (see below, 52–63).

As a result he is not in Rome to take up the consulship in the new year (26.26.5), but receives the complaints of the Capuans and Syracusans on his way home (26.27.10–17), which in turn allows him to be the agent of their introduction into the Senate: the implication is that his long absence from Italy has left him unacquainted with the justice or otherwise of their grievances.

There are many other places where careful reading shows the artificiality of this apparently straightforward device. True simultaneity is transitive: if X is simultaneous with Y, and Y with Z, then X and Z must be too. However, in Livy such transitivity regularly breaks down. At 23.20.1–3 Hannibal takes Casilinum; then (1) *eodem tempore* (23.20.4) attempts to take Petelia. Then we are told (2) that *per idem fere tempus* (23.21.1) letters come to Rome from Sicily and Sardinia, and this leads into the account of the filling up of the Senate, the elections, and the death of Postumius (23.22–5 discussed above). Then (3) we move to Spain *dum haec in Italia geruntur apparanturque* (23.26.1: 'while these things were being done and prepared in Italy'), and we get the entire narrative of Spanish events of the year (23.26–9). After this (4) we return to Petelia: *dum haec in Hispania geruntur, Petelia . . . aliquot post mensibus, quam coepta oppugnari erat, ab Himilcone . . . expugnata est* (23.30.1: 'While these things were being done in Spain, Petelia . . . was stormed by Himilco . . . several months after the attack on it had begun'). All of these episodes are allegedly simultaneous with one another, yet (4) occurs 'several months after' (1).[114] Obviously one could construct a sort of justification: in (1) we are told that the Carthaginians 'were attacking' (*oppugnabant*) Petelia, so the attack could theoretically have begun a lot earlier; the phrase in (3) doubtless refers to the simultaneity between the entire Italian and Spanish campaigns of the year, whereas the phrase in (4) perhaps only covers the end-point of the Spanish campaign. But the similarity of the phrases in question and the absence of any earlier account of the attack beginning[115] suggests that this would be special pleading. Rather it seems that the reader can be satisfied that the story has moved on, simply because it is coming later in Livy's narrative sequence.[116]

This is not the invariable way in which the device is used, and sometimes one finds places where the expression of simultaneity must be taken more literally, such as 21.49–51: clearly Sempronius' campaign in Sicily is genuinely

---

[114] According to Polybius 7.1.3 the siege of Petelia lasted 11 months. That would be chronologically impossible in Livy's version, since the siege clearly began well after Cannae, and yet is completed within the same year. Livy accordingly gives no explicit length of time, although his season markers hint at the Polybian chronology (see below, 53–5).

[115] It is anyway more likely that the imperfect here is inceptive: 'began to attack'.

[116] We may compare in the same sequence 23.22.4, which explicitly states that the senatorial meeting occurs after the fall of Casilinum, two simultaneities earlier.

simultaneous with Hannibal's crossing the Alps and the battle of the Ticinus, because Scipio is awaiting his return from Sicily at 21.48.7, while he himself receives news of his recall at 21.51.5. He is thus able to join Scipio at the point at which the earlier narrative left off. But it is interesting that even here Livy seems to be accommodating the reader's sense that time is moving forward: the Sicilian episode is introduced with the words *cum ad Trebiam terrestre constitisset bellum, interim &c.* (21.49.1: 'When the land war had stopped at the Trebia, meanwhile &c.').[117] The Sicilian action is thus spoken of as if it all took place during a pause in the action in Italy, even though this is not literally the case in chronological terms.

In other words, while Livy uses phrases of simultaneity to connect adjacent events to one another, the mere progress of his narrative creates a sense of the forward movement of time which should not be there in terms of his strict chronological statements. In this respect (as well as in others) the sequence in which 'simultaneous' events are presented is essential,[118] and chronological and textual years are covertly diverging.

Another group of phrases that Livy regularly uses to introduce a new scene or set of events is *eo anno, eodem anno* and the like. These look superficially similar to the *per idem tempus* formulae that I have just been discussing, and sometimes can be used in a fashion that is effectively identical, as when the entire year's narrative for a particular theatre of war is about to be narrated: the phrase implies simultaneity with the entire year's events in the theatre of war that has just been recounted. However, the phrases can also be used of brief individual events rather than an entire narrative sequence, and here a crucial difference emerges. Instead of suggesting that the narrative is as far as possible mirroring chronology, these formulae leave open the possibility of narrating events overtly out of chronological sequence: here the textual year and the chronological one may be clearly distinct.[119] Such formulae are, for example, regularly used with brief annalistic notices at the end of the year (e.g. 24.9.6, 24.43.7, 25.2.1, 26.23.7, 27.6.15, 27.21.9, 27.36.6, 29.11.13, 29.38.6, 30.26.7, 30.39.6) or with prodigy lists (23.31.15, 24.10.6, 26.23.4, 29.10.4). It was clearly unlikely that all priests died and all temples were dedicated at the end of the year; likewise even if prodigies were all dealt with by the Senate at a single moment in the year, they were likely to have occurred at different times. This is most obvious when Livy includes dated events in them. It is unusual

---

[117] Cf. Händl-Sagawe (1995: 303–4).

[118] Compare the even greater looseness of expressions of simultaneity in epic (see e.g. Heinze 1915: 381–9, Reinmuth 1933), used of sequences whose detail often suggests that they are not literally taking place at the same time.

[119] Cf. Ginsburg (1981: 33–4).

for him to date events directly by the calendar: apart from the Ides of March for the start of the year, there are only four examples in the decade, three of which are giving dates for festivals (22.1.19–20, 27.23.7,[120] 29.14.14; also 25.12.1-2).[121] However, he frequently refers in his end-of-year summaries to two festivals with fixed dates: the *Ludi Romani* (around 13 September) and the *Ludi Plebeii* (around 13 November),[122] where he records that some days of the festival had to be repeated because of a religious flaw (23.30.16–17, 25.2.8–10, 27.6.19, 27.21.9, 27.36.8–9, 29.11.12, 29.38.8, 30.26.11, 30.39.6). There are also references to the *Ludi Apollinares* (13 July: 25.12.15, 26.23.3, 30.38.10–12; cf. 27.23.5–7 discussed above),[123] the *Quinquatrus* (19 March: 26.27.1), the *Cerialia* (19 April: 30.39.8), and the first day of the *Saturnalia* (17 December: 30.36.8). The great majority of these are associated with phrases like *eo anno*, and are placed anachronistically, out of their proper chronological sequence. And 22.1.19–20 and 27.23.5–7, which are not marked by *eo anno*-like phrases, are equally out of sequence: both come immediately after prodigy lists at the start of the year, but the first refers to events in December, the second to July.[124]

What does this suggest about Livy's attitude to calendrical chronology? One might feel that he was merely uninterested in it; but this would be far too simplistic a characterization. First, his very use of *eo anno* phrases in these situations suggests that he feels the need to cover himself for the occasions when he overtly departs from chronological order: he deliberately employs a phrase that does not make the precise time in the year explicit. It is noteworthy that one of the few places where he does not cover himself in this way, 22.1.19–20, is the last in a series of responses to prodigies, and the date is introduced *postremo Decembri iam mense* ('Finally, it being already the month

---

[120] In this case, moreover, the date is incorrect. Livy gives it as 5 July (*ante diem tertium nonas Quinctiles*), a slip for 13 July (*ante diem tertium Idus Quinctiles*).

[121] 25.12.1–2 is in fact also related to the introduction of a festival (it is the start of the sequence leading up to the first introduction of the *Ludi Apollinares*), but in this case the date given (26 April) is not the date of the festival itself. There are also a few examples of dates given as (near) future deadlines: 23.32.14, 25.1.12, 25.4.9.

[122] The *Ludi Romani* and *Ludi Plebeii* each lasted for several days, which were extended in the later Republic and early empire; it is unclear precisely how long they were thought of as lasting in this period. According to Habel (1931: 619; cf. Scullard 1981: 183), the former had reached ten days in 191, but this is based on Livy 36.2.4 and 36.36.2, which refer to special *ludi magni votivi*, not the regular *Ludi Romani* (for the distinction see Wissowa 1912: 452–4).

[123] In this case, however, there is the complication that according to 27.23.5–7, *ludi Apollinares* were then fixed in July for the first time: previously there was no fixed date, though admittedly the reader of Books 25 and 26 was unlikely to have been aware of that.

[124] The other two examples of precise calendar dates in the decade, on the other hand (25.12.1–2 and 29.14.14), are not obviously anachronistic, since they both are narrated near the start of the year and involve dates in April. Likewise 26.27.1 comes close to the beginning of the year and refers to a date just three days after the Ides of March, while 30.36.8 fixes 17 December as the date of a battle towards the end of the year's events in Africa.

of December')—the *iam* suggesting that although he is still close to the start of the year's narrative, he is aware that he is temporarily flashing forward in time.[125] Second, while it is true that references to festivals or games carry certain assumptions about dates, they are not as crudely apparent as the date itself would be, especially since the references are usually to the *repetition* of games (generally because of a religious flaw when they were first held): while it might be assumed that games would be repeated as soon as possible after they were originally scheduled, that may not have been inevitable.[126] Third, he rarely makes overt connections between the anachronistic events marked *eo anno* and other events that he narrates in their immediate vicinity. It is interesting to observe that the prodigy lists marked in this way are all short lists, where if anything Livy is actively avoiding a direct connection between them and surrounding events (above, 37–8).[127] Prodigy lists that directly foreshadow disaster, like 21.62, are introduced as matters that are occurring contemporaneously and have to be dealt with immediately.

But while all that is true, the 'textual' year is not left devoid of effect. The end-of-year summaries are used to show the year coming to its end, an effect that would be diminished if (for example) each death of a priest were narrated in its proper place. Indeed, it is interesting that one of the anachronistic

---

[125] This is the usual interpretation: see W-M *ad loc.*, supported by e.g. Vallet (1966: 36). Some historians of religion claim that it refers to the previous year: see e.g. Bayet (1969: 138), Bloch (1976: 35), and esp. Guittard (2004–5). However, this is an utterly unnatural interpretation of *postremo*, which, when attached to the last item in a list, has to mean that it is the last event in a chronological sequence (a point which Guittard (2004–5: 89–90) slides over in his paraphrase). It is of course possible that the reform of the Saturnalia which Livy is describing here really did take place in the previous year, 218, when Guittard suggests it would have made much more sense. But even if that is so, Livy is clearly presenting it as an event of 217, and expects the reader to take it as such. Guittard's main objection to reading it this way is that Livy could not have narrated something out of chronological sequence so lightly (Guittard 2004–5: 89: 'il s'agirait d'une anticipation audacieuse et injustifiable'); but the evidence that I have presented in this section shows that it is entirely in accord with his handling of chronology elsewhere.

[126] The Fasti of the *feriae Latinae* appear to record repetitions several months after their original celebration; however, see Mommsen (1879: 104–8), who argues that these should not necessarily be seen as true repetitions of the original games, as opposed to extra celebrations introduced for particular occasions. Dio 56.27.5 reports that when the *ludi Martiales* were repeated in AD 12, Germanicus laid on a show with 200 lions, the logistics of which suggest that a certain amount of time elapsed between the original games and the repetition.

[127] In 29.10.4 the prodigies are said to have occurred *eo anno*, but the panic they generate is *eo tempore* ('at that time'): the time in question being after the elections, so at the end of the year. The reason is that the panic sets in motion the sequence of events leading up to the introduction of the Magna Mater early in the following year: hence its timing is crucial. This thus still fits the pattern. The prodigies have no sinister effect (above, 38), but they do ultimately have positive consequences; so the prodigies themselves are not located closely in time, but their consequences are.

game-repetitions, at 23.30.16–17, is marked not by *eo anno* but by *exitu anni*. The reason in this case appears to be that Livy is marking the end of the year explicitly after several false closures (above, 39); the fact that he is still prepared to include game-repetitions out of chronological position shows that they *feel* like something that happens at the end of the year, even if they did not literally take place then. Likewise, while prodigy lists that are overtly connected to the surrounding narrative are usually explicitly linked with it, this does not mean that anachronism is absent in those cases, because the two most obviously anachronistic dates in the decade both occur in the aftermath of perhaps the two most ominous lists in the decade, 22.1.8-20 and 27.23.1-4. Chronologically speaking 22.1.19–20, though narrated at the very beginning of the year, occurs close to its end, long after the defeat at Trasimene and the dictatorship of Fabius Maximus. Although it concerns expiation for the prodigies and not the prodigies themselves, in terms of its narrative effect it clearly belongs here, just as other expiations usually follow closely on the prodigies themselves. When Fabius proposes a new set of expiations after Trasimene (22.9.7–10.10), the assumption is that new measures are needed because (thanks to Flaminius' impiety) the Romans are still out of favour with the gods despite the previous expiations, not that the previous expiations are still being worked through and might still prove successful.

An especially interesting example is 30.39.4–8, the end of the last full year of the war. Here the elections for 201 fail to be held at the end of 202, and so the new year begins with no consuls in place: *cum pridie idus Martias veteres magistratus abissent, novi suffecti non essent, res publica sine curulibus magistratibus erat* (30.39.5: 'when on 14 March the old magistrates left office and new ones had not replaced them, the republic was without curule magistrates'). Livy then proceeds in his usual fashion to report the deaths of priests and the repetitions of games *eo anno* (30.39.6–7)—this must refer to 202, and so involves a clear movement back in time. Then he reports that the election of the plebeian aediles was vitiated and so they resigned after holding games, and that the dictator put on the games for the *Cerealia* (30.39.8). Since the dictator was originally appointed to hold the elections at the end of 202 (30.39.4), and the *Cerealia* took place on 19 April, this must refer to the games in April 201: in other words the narrative is moving forward in time a month into the beginning of the (still consul-less) new year.[128] In this case, *eo anno*

---

[128] *Contra MRR* 318–19 n. 1, which claims that this refers to the games in 202, and that Livy is confused when he says that they were put on by the dictator. Against this construction, however, see Jahn (1970: 144–50); in any case, the main point for us here is that, even if Livy was mistaken, he apparently *thinks* he is concluding his annalistic notices with an event well into the new year.

involves events out of chronological sequence, but the textual position of these events is vital: they cover the movement between years at a time when the political situation does not allow the usual explicit markers to be used.

In other words, while Livy is aware of his calendrical anachronisms, and generally ensures that they do not overtly damage the main chronological sequence of his narrative, he is simultaneously prepared to allow them to maintain a narrative effect according to their place in his 'textual' year rather than according to when they actually occurred.

Another extremely common way in which Livy marks chronology is by seasons: references to something happening in winter, spring, summer, or (less often) autumn.[129] Very often this too is primarily an expression of simultaneity: instead of saying that the events in a particular area occurred 'during that time' or 'in that year', he may say, for example, that they occurred *eadem aestate* ('in the same summer'). Livy seems on the whole to assume that the seasons coincide with points in the Roman political year: the consuls' entry into office on 15 March is the springtime; it is then followed by military campaigns which take place over summer; and the onset of winter and the army's withdrawal into winter quarters are around the end of the year and are associated with the elections of new magistrates. So, for example, elections are sometimes juxtaposed with references to winter (e.g. 21.57.5, 22.32.4, 27.33.5, 29.10.3, 30.39.3) and the taking up of office with spring (e.g. 22.1.1, 28.11.12); conversely, nowhere in the decade do we see the change of magistrates associated with summertime. Consuls are chosen and provinces are distributed, apparently in time for everyone to leave for their armies to begin campaigning, and usually at least some of these campaigns are explicitly said to be happening in summer.

However, rather more than half of the years in the decade contain features that apparently contradict this picture. In particular, some years seem to contain more seasons than conventional meteorologists would think possible.[130] In 218 Hannibal sacks Saguntum after a siege of some length, and then withdraws into winter quarters in Spain (21.21.1). He then reassembles his troops in spring (21.21.8) and launches his invasion of Italy, which takes five months (21.38.1, cf. 21.15.3). The invasion culminates with the battle of the Trebia, by when we are once again in winter (21.54.7); Hannibal carries on fighting right through the winter. Only then do we reach the start of 217,

---

[129] In this he had a major predecessor in Thucydides, who famously structured his work around the annual change of seasons, itself a revolutionary revision to Herodotus, who used climatic phenomena for quite different purposes. See Bouvier (2000).

[130] Thucydides too is sometimes surprisingly cavalier about the limits of 'summer' or 'winter' (see Meritt 1962, 1964; Bouvier 2000: 129–31; *contra* Pritchett 1964: 21–9), but to nothing like the degree we find in Livy.

which comes in spring (22.1.1). Similarly in 216 Hannibal wins at Cannae and receives the defection of Capua, after which he withdraws to winter quarters there (23.18.9–16). He then leaves them *mitescente iam hieme* (23.19.1: 'with the winter now growing milder') in time for a siege several months long (23.30.1: cf. 47 above) to be completed before the end of the year. In 214 the Romans complete a full summer of campaigning in Italy by 24.20.15 (*aestas exacta erat*—'summer had been completed'), with Marcellus, then consul, apparently present until more or less the end (24.20.7). Marcellus is then sent to Sicily at 24.21.1 and arrives at 24.27.6, in time to carry out what is apparently a whole new set of campaigns before winter comes there too (24.39.13). There are a number of other similar if less dramatic examples.

One explanation for these anomalies is that they arise from Livy's problems in constructing his narrative out of different sources. These sources were not always consistent with one another, because some had themselves erroneously assigned material to the wrong year, as Livy sometimes has occasion to remark. And even when they were consistent, relating them to one another was not straightforward. It may not always have been clear even in Roman sources in which year an event occurred, especially if some authors were not meticulously narrating according to annalistic years. Polybius was even harder to incorporate, because he was not using Roman years but Olympiads, which had different beginning- and end-points,[131] and moreover were four-year periods with no standard and straightforward system of conversion to Roman consular years.[132] It is easy to see that even a careful historian might well sometimes fail to spot an existing inconsistency, or indeed create a new one, marrying material from one source to the wrong year (or wrong time of year) in another. And if Livy simply uncritically reproduced references to seasons that he found in (for example) Polybius, while placing them at the wrong point in his narrative, then the problems would be compounded.

This must be at least a partial explanation. Livy certainly sometimes presents clear inconsistencies of this sort, as when in 214 he records the Roman recapture of Saguntum in the 'eighth year under enemy control' (24.42.9 *octavum iam annum sub hostium potestate*). This is impossible

---

[131] On the Julian dates of Polybius' Olympiads see Pédech (1964: 449–61), who observes that Polybius himself often complicates the issue by narrating the events in certain countries on the basis of a non-Olympiadic year, but ascribing them to the nearest Olympiad.

[132] On the problem of relating consular years to Olympiads see Feeney (2007: 22). Clarke (2008: 116–17; cf. also Pédech 1964: 464–5) notes that while Polybius frequently refers to the Roman consuls of the current Olympiad, he does not do so systematically in a way that would allow his reader to make an easy equation—for example, he uses the election date and the accession into office interchangeably, although these usually happened in different consular years.

whenever one thinks Hannibal originally captured the city: Livy's source must have placed the episode is a later year. Slightly different is when Livy successively identifies 206 and 205 as the 'fourteenth year' of the Punic war (28.16.14, 28.38.12), which must result[133] from reproducing numbers from sources with different chronologies.[134] An extreme case comes with the notorious 'doublets', where Livy—or perhaps his source—mistakenly narrates events twice, because he has found similar stories in different sources and has not realized that they are actually describing the same events.[135] Livy is aware that such things happen (e.g. 29.35.2), but occasionally falls into the trap himself. Admittedly he does so less blatantly in the Hannibalic War than any other part of his surviving history (a sign of the care with which this part of his work was constructed). There are very few examples in the decade of Livy carelessly presenting a double sequence that literally could not have taken place twice.[136] One is the capture of Croton and Locri, reported briefly at 23.30.6–8 and then again in detail in the following year (24.1–3: see further below);[137] another is the restoration of Roman control over Clampetia and Consentia, mentioned in passing twice, in similar language but in successive years (29.38.1, 30.19.10).[138] Other possible doublets involve (for example) repeated battles where Livy is self-conscious about the similarity of the two

---

[133] Unless *quarto decimo* (= XIIII) at 28.16.14 is merely a scribal error for *tertio decimo* (= XIII). This was originally proposed by H. L. Glareanus in the 1530s, and is accepted by (*inter alios*) de Sanctis (1968: 482) and Scullard (1930: 306). But Livy is genuinely inconsistent often enough to make it unsatisfactory to preserve his consistency here by textual emendation.

[134] To do Livy justice, it should be pointed out that calculating periods of years is quite hard to do correctly when one is identifying years by consuls rather than by numbers. Moreover, the inconsistency in the second case depends on whether one regards the war as having begun in 219 or 218; as we shall see shortly, Livy in fact is less committed to one version of that than may appear at first sight.

[135] On doublets see above all Kraus (1998).

[136] There are quite a few apparent inconsistencies in Livy's narrative, some of which will be discussed in later chapters, but no others where unthinking duplication of the same event is the most likely explanation. For example, Kraus (1998: 274) refers to the vowing of the *ludi Apollinares*, which is twice done *in perpetuum* (26.23.3 and 27.23.5–7). This is probably not a true doublet, since the two vows were for different things—the first to hold the games every year, the second to fix a particular date on which they were to be held every year (27.23.7 *ii ludi in perpetuum in statam diem voverentur*: cf. n. 123 above). But in the second passage Livy wrongly describes the earlier vow as having been *in unum annum* (27.23.5: 'for one year'): in other words the problem is the inconsistency in his account of the first vow, not its duplication by a second vow.

[137] Kraus (1998: 275) suggests that the second account of the fall of Croton shows Livy self-conscious about the repetition, because the story itself contains numerous references to 'doubling'. However, such meta-textual symbols can be hard to pin down: after all, Croton 'doubles' also in the sense of repeating elements from other narratives of Carthaginian attempts on other Italian towns, such as Capua, Nola, and Tarentum. It is therefore hard to relate it specifically to the exceptional inconsistency here.

[138] Cf. Seemüller (1908: 45–8).

events,[139] such as Hannibal's fight against apparently different Gnaeii Fulvii in the same place but different years (25.21 and 27.1): Hannibal in the second battle refers explicitly to the first. Even though Livy may be wrong to treat the battles as separate,[140] it is not carelessness: he is fully aware of the narrative duplication.[141]

However, he appears less meticulous when it comes to finer chronological issues. The problem with Marcellus' arrival in Sicily is most naturally explained in terms of placing material in the wrong year. On Livy's chronology there is no Sicilian narrative at all for the (remarkably truncated) year 213; the story resumes in 212 at the point where it left off in 214. While it is theoretically possible that Marcellus sat doing nothing in Sicily for a year, it is unlikely.[142] The most likely explanation is that he went to Sicily late in 214 (or possibly early in 213), and that some or all of what Livy describes him doing there in 214 actually belongs in 213.[143] Something similar must also partially explain the problems in 216, where the (eventual) fall of Petelia at the end of the (textual) year is said to occur around the same time (23.30.6: *isdem ferme diebus*) as the fall of Croton and Locri, which Livy then goes on to narrate a second time as a doublet in the following year (24.1–3: cf. above, 47, 54).[144] Similarly with the problems in 218 (above, 52–3): Polybius gives a consistent narrative, in which the siege of Saguntum took place in 219, and then Hannibal retired to winter quarters prior to his invasion of Italy the following year (3.17.9, 3.33.5). Livy picks up the point about winter quarters, but retains the siege in 218: hence the inconsistency which has the year extending through multiple winters.

---

[139] For example, almost all of the alleged doublets discussed by Seemüller (1908) fall into this category.

[140] So de Sanctis (1968: 445–6), *contra MRR* (271 n.2), Rosenstein (1990a: 207–8).

[141] Kraus (1998: 276).

[142] Livy does, however, provide a retrospective though superficial explanation, since he points out that Marcellus could not capture Syracuse by conventional means and so needed to wait for internal dissension to provide him with an opportunity (25.23.1–4). Livy also uses the length of time that the Romans had been besieging the city to explain their lesser susceptibility to the climate when plague strikes (25.26.12: see below, 61–2).

[143] See de Sanctis (1968: 318–19), Seibert (1993b: 287–90). As de Sanctis notes, at 24.39.12 Marcellus sends Appius Claudius to Rome to seek the consulship, supposedly in late 214—but Appius was not consul until 212. This therefore likewise points to Marcellus' campaign being in 213, though Livy is not strictly speaking inconsistent here, since it is theoretically possible that Appius was defeated first time and stood again in the following year. For the precise chronology of events in Sicily see Eckstein (1987: 345–9).

[144] To confuse matters further, the fall of Consentia in the same sequence at the end of 216 (23.30.5) is said in 25.1.2 to have happened *anno priore*—i.e. in 214, so a year *later* than the (second) narrative of the fall of Croton and Locri. For an explanation of how the error arose see de Sanctis (1968: 354–5).

But this last passage also suggests that the explanation cannot be quite so simple, because Livy is himself perfectly aware of the chronological problem. Immediately after Saguntum has fallen, he refers to the issue in a well-known comment (21.15.3–6):

octavo mense quam coeptum oppugnari captum Saguntum quidam scripsere; inde Carthaginem Novam in hiberna Hannibalem concessisse; quinto deinde mense quam ab Carthagine profectus sit in Italiam pervenisse. quae si ita sunt, fieri non potuit, ut P. Cornelius Ti. Sempronius consules fuerint, ad quos et principio oppugnationis legati Saguntini missi sint et qui in suo magistratu cum Hannibale, alter ad Ticinum amnem, ambo aliquanto post ad Trebiam, pugnaverint. aut omnia breviora aliquanto fuere aut Saguntum principio anni, quo P. Cornelius Ti. Sempronius consules fuer-unt, non coeptum oppugnari est, sed captum. nam excessisse pugna ad Trebiam in annum Cn. Servili et C. Flamini non potest, quia C. Flaminius Arimini consulatum iniit, creatus a Ti. Sempronio consule, qui post pugnam ad Trebiam ad creandos consules Romam cum venisset, comitiis perfectis ad exercitum in hiberna rediit.

Some have written that Saguntum was captured in the eighth month after the siege began; then Hannibal retired from there to winter quarters in New Carthage; that then in the fifth month after leaving Carthage he reached Italy. If so, it was impossible that P. Cornelius and Ti. Sempronius both were the consuls to whom the Saguntine ambassadors were sent at the start of the siege, and who fought Hannibal during their magistracy, one at the River Ticinus, then both somewhat later at the Trebia. Either everything happened rather more quickly, or it was not the beginning of the siege of Saguntum that happened at the start of the year when P. Cornelius and Ti. Sempronius were consuls, but its capture. For the battle at the Trebia cannot have run over into the year of Cn. Servilius and C. Flaminius, because C. Flaminius entered his consulship at Ariminum, elected by the consul Ti. Sempronius, who went to Rome after the battle of the Trebia to conduct the consular elections, and who with the elections ended returned to his army in winter quarters.

This passage has achieved a surprising notoriety. It is often taken as a sign of Livy's incompetence: that although he had the evidence of the correct chronology, he failed to make proper use of it.[145] It is sometimes even taken to show something about his inadequate working methods:[146] that he wrote the opening of the siege on the basis that it happened in 218, and only now noticed that an alternative chronology was possible. Whereupon, instead of going back and making the requisite changes, he simply inserted an apologetic note and moved on.

However, this will hardly do. First, this argument fails to accord with other evidence for Livy's working methods: as Luce above all has demonstrated,[147]

---

[145] So e.g. de Sanctis (1968: 174): 'povero sempre nella critica, ma amico sincero della verità'—a remarkable mischaracterization on both counts.

[146] So e.g. Walsh (1961: 141–3, 1973: 32, 146–7), *contra* Händl-Sagawe (1995: 94).

[147] Luce (1977).

Livy's carefully balanced and structured books show that he was reading his sources and planning how to incorporate material well in advance. Second, it fails to take account of the rational clarity with which Livy presents the issue here:[148] he recognizes the two alternative possibilities and sets out correctly the implications of each one, and he further excludes a third possibility as inconsistent with well-established facts. Third, and perhaps most significantly, the argument overlooks how little Livy would have to change in order to make his version fit the Polybian chronology: he would simply have to change the names of the consuls at 21.6.3 to those of the previous year, and everything else could remain intact.[149] Admittedly he must already in Book 20 have narrated Roman events for 219 and the consular elections for 218, which he would not want to repeat here. But that matters little, since he has on any chronology begun Book 21 by moving considerably back in time (above, 13–14), and so using the Polybian chronology would simply mean that the Hannibalic story would catch up with his Roman sequence a few chapters later. Indeed, the very phrase which he uses to introduce the consuls' names in 21.6.3—*consules tunc Romae erant P. Cornelius Scipio et Ti. Sempronius Longus* ('the consuls at Rome then were P. Cornelius Scipio and Ti. Sempronius Longus')—shows that he does not expect the reader simply to assume that this is happening after the last consular elections: he has to set it out explicitly, and hence could easily have inserted other names instead.

So when Livy presents Hannibal attacking Saguntum and then moving into winter quarters apparently mid-year, he does so in full awareness of its implications (it is interesting that he twice in the passage explicitly mentions winter quarters as a chronological marker). In other words, he is deliberately presenting a narrative sequence that cannot make literal sense chronologically.

Nor is this the only place where seasonal anachronisms appear in a context where Livy clearly knows what he is doing. At 25.11.20 Hannibal succeeds in engineering the defection of Tarentum. He then retires into winter quarters (*regressus ipse in hiberna*). This does not fit Livy's usual assumption about the

---

[148] Observed by Hoffmann (1942: 105): 'Niemand kann beim Lesen dieser Stelle leugnen, daß dem Livius die Fähigkeit zu historischer Kritik gefehlt habe'.

[149] Such a change, while making the basic historical frame consistent with Polybius, would not by itself have brought Livy's account fully into line with his, since Polybius 3.15 has the Roman envoys visiting Hannibal and then moving on to Carthage before the siege of Saguntum even began, contrary to Livy's version (21.9.3–11.2). Seeck (1983: 83–4) suggests that Livy hints at the Polybian version when at 21.10.1 he says *ea quoque vana et irrita legatio fuit* ('That embassy too was empty and pointless'), and at 21.11.3 refers in the plural to the Romans 'sending out embassies' (*legationibus mittendis*), as if there were some earlier embassy that he had not himself mentioned; but see *contra* W-M *ad locc.*, who more plausibly interpret these phrases as meaning that the *legatio* to Hannibal and the one to Carthage are treated as two different 'embassies'.

year starting in spring, since it happens well after the entry of the consuls into office but before their departure for the summer's campaigns (the very next event in the narrative (25.12.1) is specifically dated to 26 April). But Livy goes on to comment on the timing: *ceterum defectio Tarentinorum utrum priore anno an hoc facta sit, in diversum auctores trahunt* (25.11.20: 'but authorities differ on whether the Tarentines' defection was in the previous year or this one'). Here too he is manifestly aware of the problem, but nevertheless reproduces a Polybian sequence according to which this happened at the end of the previous year,[150] while explicitly rejecting the chronology on which it is based. Once again he recognizes the difficulty yet seems happy to maintain a chronologically inconsistent narrative.

So how can we explain this? The first thing we need to remember is the problematic—not to say incompetent[151]—Republican calendar, which required an intercalation of a month every other year, but which even then left the years averaging 366 days. Intercalations were not always scheduled to the proper cycle, and even if they had been, the year would still rapidly lose track with the seasons. A dated eclipse in Livy 37.4.4 shows that what the Romans called 'July' in 190 was in fact March: in other words, the 'March' when consuls were taking up office was then not spring, but late autumn.

Now, it is true that the evidence for the Hannibalic War suggests that the dislocation of the calendar was then not nearly so marked.[152] But the issue for us is what Livy's assumptions about the relationship between the political calendar and the seasons would have been. Although he could not have calculated the precise dislocation at any time, he must have been aware of the *possibility* of dislocation. Julius Caesar's calendrical reform had taken place

---

[150] Polybius 8.34.13: παρεγένετο τριταῖος ἐπὶ τὸν ἐξ ἀρχῆς χάρακα, καὶ τὸ λοιπὸν τοῦ χειμῶνος ἐνταῦθα διατρίβων ἔμενε κατὰ χώραν—'He came on the third day to his old camp, and passing the rest of the winter there he stayed in that region'. On the correct chronology see de Sanctis (1968: 322–3).

[151] Though we should note the caution of Feeney (2007: 193–201), who argues that the Republican calendar only appears incompetent if we assume that the purpose of a calendar is to track the astronomical rhythms of the year. That assumption, he claims, is anachronistic, itself the product of Caesar's reforming the Roman calendar to match the solar year. Feeney's arguments are an important corrective to naïve modern assumptions, but are overstated, since there is some evidence to suggest that the Republican calendar was premised on at least a loose, if not a precise, relationship to the solar year. The existence of intercalation, however irregularly performed, makes little sense save as a device to track the sun, and not only agricultural festivals (which Feeney discusses), but also military campaigns (which he does not) seem to find their place in the Republican calendar according to solar years. In any event, Livy, admittedly from a post-Caesarian perspective, works from the basic assumption that the Republican calendar too was at bottom a solar one (above, 52), even if in practice it proves more flexible in his text.

[152] Derow (1976) argues that the Roman calendar in this period was dating events about a month early.

in 46/45 (so slightly more than a decade before Livy began working on his history), and had required him to extend one year to 445 days in order to realign it with the seasons. In other words, Livy spent the first part of his life in a world in which 'March', though theoretically associated with spring, had sometimes fallen in early winter, and where the relationship between the months and the seasons could change drastically in just three or four years. It is hardly surprising that, even while working from a core set of assumptions in which the political year correlated with the seasons, he did not find it difficult to include seasonal references which did not accord with those core assumptions.

This goes some way towards explaining why Livy seems to be relatively cavalier about seasonal anachronisms (unlike his attitude to anachronisms about calendar dates, where he generally covers himself cautiously, as we saw above). But it still does not explain how he could allow years to be extended to the point that he does. The Republican calendar may have been flexible, but it was not nearly flexible enough to allow eighteen-month years.

To understand this, we need to return to 21.15.3–6, and recognize that, far from attempting to cover up the chronological inconsistencies in his narrative, Livy is actually drawing attention to them. He could easily have corrected his earlier account to fit Polybius, as I said; alternatively he could have omitted Hannibal moving into winter quarters and continued his story on the assumption that this was all happening quite quickly in 218. Or else he could have inconsistently included elements from both, while keeping the inconsistency hidden from at least his less attentive readers. The analepsis that he had anyway introduced at the start of the book meant that he could have sent Hannibal to 'winter quarters' after Saguntum without readers assuming that Roman end-of-year annalistic material was imminent. Instead he chose to retain the inconsistency while actively pointing out the features that would alert readers to it.

It is clear that he regarded features of this inconsistent narrative as desirable: it is also not difficult to see why. Returning the siege of Saguntum to 219 would mean that the Romans could no longer be seen as focused exclusively upon it; they would manifestly be dividing their attention between it and other issues, as indeed they are in Polybius 3.16 and 18–19, where their response to Saguntum is interspersed with their campaigns in Illyria.[153] This is not to say that Livy is trying to exculpate the Romans from their

---

[153] Hoffmann (1942: 21–2, 105–6). Polybius 3.16.1 indeed suggests that the Romans deliberately (though mistakenly: cf. 3.16.5) pursued the Illyrian War first in order to pacify that region before turning to deal with the Carthaginians in Spain: cf. Rich (1976: 41–3).

failure to help their allies[154]—on the contrary he repeatedly draws attention
to their dilatoriness[155]—and if they were not distracted by other problems,
that if anything means their failure to do anything practical against Hannibal
looks all the worse. But the whole tenor of his narrative is that Hannibal is
from the start the essential and total threat, one the Romans know they *should*
deal with urgently, even if in the event they fail to handle it properly. That
impression could not be maintained were the siege in 219. But at the same
time Livy needed the account of Hannibal's winter after Saguntum as well, for
it allowed the introduction of key episodes relating to (for example) his
relationship with his troops and his preparations for his campaign, as well
as the dream that anticipates his (partial and temporary) future success
(21.21–22). Hence Livy included both.

The chronological discussion in 21.15.3–6 is thus significantly placed. It
comes at precisely the point where the move from one chronology to the
other is about to make a difference: where the Romans are allocating provinces to the consuls of 218 to deal with Hannibal (21.17.1),[156] but where
Hannibal is about to move to winter quarters as if at the end of 219. In other
words, by introducing the chronological question explicitly, Livy justifies his
juxtaposition of features that only make sense if one recognizes that they
depend on different chronologies.

So here too it would not be correct to claim that Livy does not care about
chronology. He manifestly does. But he does not seem to care about chronology in the way we would expect a modern historian to: deciding on a single

---

[154] This is a surprisingly common interpretation: see e.g. Händl-Sagawe (1995: 94), Cizek
(1995: 155), Jal (2001: 116); cf. Mineo (2006: 275–6), who suggests that Livy wants to show the
Roman delay as stemming from honourable attention to legality rather than culpable tardiness,
but overlooks the passages where Livy directly indicates that they are at fault: see n. 155 below.
The most that can be said is that it is possible that the sources from which Livy is drawing his
account of the war beginning in 218 had some such propagandist intention in making the
distortion, but Livy himself does not present the history in those terms.

[155] 21.6.6–7.1, 21.11.3, 21.16.2, 21.19.9–10; cf. 31.7.3.

[156] At 21.6.6 the choice of Spain and Africa as provinces had been presented as merely one
option among several; here it has already been decided. It looks as if Livy is smoothing over the
absence of provincial allocations at the start of the year, implying that they had been made
earlier but without specifying exactly when that 'earlier' might have been.

Livy's handling of the chronological complexities of this year shows other subtleties also. For
example, the Romans twice anticipate Hannibal's crossing of the Ebro (21.16.5, 21.20.9), but in
neither case is it clear whether this has yet happened. The first passage is a general statement of
Hannibal's overall war plans couched in the present tense, while the second is a report attributed
only to 'rumour' (*fama*). This might suggest that the latter is being framed as false, but it is
followed immediately (21.21.1) by the narrative returning to Hannibal at an earlier time,
explicitly marked as such by the pluperfect *concesserat*. Hannibal finally crosses the Ebro at
21.23.1 which may—or may not—be assumed to correspond to the time when the rumour of
his doing so reached Rome at 21.20.9.

chronological sequence and remaining with it consistently. Rather what matters to him is the incorporation of appropriate elements at appropriate points in his narrative. The sequence could not have literally occurred in the form in which he presents it, something that he admits and explains. But that does not prevent him from presenting it anyway,[157] at least when the primary points of inconsistency involve seasonal events which would not—because of the nature of the Roman calendar—be read as tied unequivocally to particular points in the year.

In these passages, then, we can once again see Livy creating a form of 'textual' or 'narrative' time—and in this case, the 'textual' year not only diverges from the chronological one but it actually takes it over. What matters is incorporating the appropriate material in the appropriate sequence.

And sometimes Livy combines these seasonal inconsistencies with the non-transitive simultaneities I discussed earlier, so as to create a single chronologically impossible but narratively desirable sequence. An example comes at the end of Book 25. As the Sicilian narrative for 212 draws to its close, we are told that the autumn climate is contributing to a plague (25.26.7), a plague that kills many on both sides, but particularly the entire Carthaginian force (25.26.14). Not long afterwards news from Spain comes to Sicily—from a soldier who we are specifically told had come from Spain not long before. The news is that *omnia Romanis ibi obtineri armis* (25.30.2: 'everything there is held by Roman weapons'). Shortly afterwards the Sicilian narrative ends, and the scene moves to Spain *eadem aestate* (25.32.1: 'in the same summer'); the Spanish narrative starts with the Romans moving from their winter quarters, so this is clearly simultaneous with the Sicilian narrative, which had begun in early spring (25.23.2). But before long disaster strikes the Romans: the Scipios are killed that summer, and Spain is therefore left on a knife-edge (25.39.18; cf. 26.18.1). Then the scene moves back to Marcellus in Sicily *dum haec in Hispania geruntur* (25.40.1), and it turns out that Hannibal has meanwhile had time to send Muttines as a replacement for one of the commanders who died in the autumn plague (25.40.5). We then get a series of new campaigns

---

[157] It may be relevant here to observe that Livy is not the only Roman author of the period to introduce chronologically impossible narratives. Catullus 64 notoriously centres on a series of time-markers which are inconsistent with one another. Admittedly this relates to mythical time, not historical time—or rather perhaps it relates to the moment when mythical time moves to historical time, incompatible views of which are presented to the reader. See Weber (1983), Feeney (2007: 123–7). Ovid's *Metamorphoses* are even more relevant, since there impossible chronologies extend across the whole poem, including the part dealing with purportedly historical time, as with Ovid's self-conscious play on Numa's alleged studies under Pythagoras at Croton: cf. S. M. Wheeler (1999: 117–39). See above all O'Hara (2007: esp. 34–44, 121–3), a fundamental study of the manner in which such inconsistencies in Latin literature can and cannot be interpreted.

involving Muttines before the end of the year comes (25.41.8 *iam ferme in exitu annus erat*). So there are multiple problems here: the hot news from Spain that arrives 'in autumn' does not seem to take account of Spanish events of 'the same summer', even though the end-point of those events is apparently simultaneous with a second set of Sicilian campaigns which anyway seem hard to fit in after 'autumn'.

Of course, one could once again try to construct a justification. Perhaps there is a way of timing everything very precisely so that the soldier from Spain could depart before the Scipios are killed but still arrive in Sicily in autumn, while leaving enough time for Hannibal to send a new commander and Marcellus to complete his campaigns before the end of the year. Or perhaps we are to see the Spanish soldier as blatantly lying (he is after all attempting to persuade his compatriot Moericus to defect to Rome). Or perhaps Livy has carelessly overlooked that he is drawing on sources employing different chronological frameworks:[158] the reference to Spain in the Sicilian episode depends on a version of the Spanish campaign in which the Scipios were killed in the following year,[159] when Marcellus' later campaigns likewise took place.[160] But in light of the arguments above, the simplest answer is that the primary issue that matters to Livy is his narrative sequence. The news from Spain reflects the position there at that point in his narrative (cf. 24.42.9, 24.48.1), not the position at that point in his chronology; and it

---

[158] A slightly different version of the same point would be to suggest that Livy's reference to the plague in Sicily occurring in autumn is his own invention, a detail that he has added as an allusion to the earlier sieges of Syracuse (in 413 and 396) which were likewise hindered by autumn plagues: see Thucydides 7.47.2 (cf. Plut., *Nic.* 22.2) and Diodorus 14.70.4–71.4. In the accounts of the earlier plagues, as in Livy, both the time of year and the location are identified as unhealthy. However, for it to be plausible that the autumn dating is merely an allusive detail, one would have to find other aspects of Livy's account that signalled an allusion to those earlier Syracusan plagues (cf. 98–9 below), and there is little to suggest that. There is nothing in Livy to indicate a direct allusion to Thucydides 7, and there are relatively few similarities with Diodorus. It is true that Diodorus has a lengthy account of the way in which carers caught the disease from their patients, which led to people abandoning the sick: Livy makes a similar point more briefly at 25.26.8–9. However, this particular similarity is more likely to be the result of Diodorus (or perhaps rather Diodorus' source) and Livy both drawing independently on Thucydides' far more famous account of the great plague in Athens (see Thucydides 2.51.2–5: cf. Walsh 1961: 182–3), which however struck in early summer, not autumn (Thucydides 2.47.2–3). It is possible that Livy dated the plague in Syracuse to the autumn in imitation not of Thucydides, but of some non-Thucydidean historian of one or other of the previous Syracusan plagues, such as Ephorus, but that must remain unprovable. See Villard (1994), who considers, but on balance rejects, the idea that Livy's plague is merely constructed in imitation of the earlier ones.

[159] This is fairly certainly the correct chronology of the Spanish campaign (see de Sanctis 1968: 354).

[160] Cf. de Sanctis (1968: 319–21), who argues that the final capture of Syracuse in fact took place in the following year; *contra* Lazenby (1978: 115).

has to be presented that way and in that order, because the good news from Spain enables Marcellus to complete his conquest of Syracuse. Marcellus' earlier campaigns have to last up to autumn, since the autumn climate plays a key role in killing off the Carthaginians; but that does not interfere with his ability to carry on a full campaign after that point. This enables Livy to end the book and the year (and thus the pentad: cf. 15–16 above) on a suitably decisive note.[161]

In short, for Livy, chronology is important, but it is also artificial. The true nature of events is governed partly by their chronological order, but also no less importantly by their order of appearance in his narrative. And when the two conflict, mere chronological possibility may under certain circumstances take second place to the sequence of events that his narrative requires if he is to explain the war in the most appropriate fashion.

1.3. NARRATIVE SEQUENCE

1.3.1 Keeping Up

One reason, perhaps, why (even among those not deterred by its length) Livy's remarkable narrative of the Hannibalic War has been less read and less regarded than it should be is that merely keeping track of the story feels bewilderingly difficult. We move from scene to scene, from theatre of war to theatre of war, sometimes picking up threads from a book or more earlier. Sometimes the characters are familiar ones like Hannibal or Fabius or Scipio; but just as often we are confronted by a large set of faceless Carthaginians, most of whom seem to be called Hanno, Mago, or Hasdrubal,[162] fighting against a varying cast of Romans who have a wider choice of nomenclature but scarcely anything more memorable in terms of attributes. They are fighting one another around a set of small towns whose location we may (if we are lucky) be familiar with, but more often are merely names to us, and whose topographical relationships may frequently be unclear. It is no surprise that modern editions of Livy tend to be liberally supplied with maps, tables, and indices. It is also no surprise that reading a work whose understanding apparently depends on repeated recourse to maps, tables, and indices can seem more of a chore than a pleasure.

---

[161] 25.41.7: *haec ultima in Sicilia Marcelli pugna fuit*—'This was Marcellus' final battle in Sicily'.

[162] 'It was a poor Carthaginian who didn't have at least one Hasdrubal in the family. They seemed to think this was a fine way to keep things straight' (Cuppy 1951: 48).

Yet there is an oddity about this that is rarely remarked; for the Romans themselves did not read Livy with maps and indices to hand.[163] Indeed, they were even more handicapped, because the ancient book-roll made it hard to check backwards to look up something one had encountered earlier. We may grant that the ancients were more used than we are to relying on memory, and so picking up a story after a gap might have felt less problematic to them; but we have already seen that at least some ancient readers could complain about the difficulty of following a fragmented narrative (above, n. 7).[164] We would moreover be unwise to assume that upper-class Romans had an encyclopaedic knowledge of minor officials from 200 years earlier, or that even the well-travelled minority would be personally acquainted with more than a handful of the towns and peoples that Livy alludes to, or indeed could locate them within 100 miles. Rather it must be the case that our expectations are misguided, and Livy is in fact presenting his story in a way that makes sense in the terms expected by an ancient readership, despite the handicaps that he seems to be putting in their way.

This should make us rethink how we address the issue of Livy's narrative comprehensibility. Instead of complaining about the work's failure to let us follow what we think we should be following, we need to ask what Livy's assumptions appear to be about the way his work is to be read. When he returns to a story or a person after an intervening gap, how much does he take for granted, and how far does he feel it is necessary to remind his audience of key facts? And where he does not remind them of something, is it because he is assuming that they will remember the details, or is it because those details are, despite appearances, actually unnecessary for understanding the significant points of the narrative?

Before I begin discussing these questions, it is worth raising one general caveat. We should not expect Livy to be adopting a single consistent practice, with clear boundaries between the things he assumes we know, the things he feels it necessary to remind us of, and the things he regards as unnecessary for

---

[163] Even Polybius, who is unusually insistent on the importance of geography for understanding history (below, 72), does not seem to envisage the use of maps either by himself or by his readers, and his geographical descriptions have little connection with cartography. See Janni (2003); also Pédech (1964: 590–6) and Prontera (2003), who note in particular how different Polybius' geographical conceptions are from the cartographic system of Eratosthenes. This is unsurprising, since such graphical representations of space as existed in antiquity were far removed from the modern idea of maps and were not formed in a manner likely to be illuminating for historical narratives (see Brodersen 2003).

[164] Small (1997: esp. 81–137, 177–201) discusses the ancients' heavy reliance on memory and their techniques for improving it, but also shows that one can greatly overestimate their capacity for accurate recall. As we shall see, the demands that Livy makes on his readers and the practical accommodations he offers to their fallibility bear out both aspects of Small's thesis.

our understanding. There are likely to be a number of salient considerations in each case, including how much text separates the different occurrences of the story, the fame (including the fame outside the text) of the people involved, the amount of time it would take to remind the reader of different things, and different levels of knowledge and attention that he is assuming within the readership. How much weight each of these considerations carries might vary on different occasions. For that reason the most one can do is point to some general trends and patterns within his practice.

Let us start, then, with some fairly obvious comments about what Livy does *not* feel it necessary to do when resuming the thread of a story. Though there are some exceptions, some of which will be discussed below, he will not as a rule offer any sort of explicit summary of previous episodes: for example, he will not tell us about earlier battles, or even remind us that they have happened. So, for example, when Livy at various points between Book 22 and Book 29 returns the narrative to Spain, he usually does not summarize exactly how the Romans and Carthaginians stood with regard to one another in the campaigns he had described previously. It appears to make no difference whether the previous events were decisive or not, or how closely they were juxtaposed in the narrative. 24.41.1 does not remind us of the perfunctory account of Roman successes a full book earlier (23.48.4–49.14), nor on the other hand does 27.17.1 recall for us the decisive victory Scipio achieved in the previous year (but less than half a book back) by capturing New Carthage at 26.41–51 (though we have had a reminder of it in the interim, when Laelius reported it to the Senate at 27.7.2). This suggests that on the rare occasions where Livy does explicitly offer such a summary, such as 28.12.10–15, he is not doing so primarily because he thinks the reader needs to be informed of the facts (in this case the events we are being 'reminded' of occurred just a few pages earlier, at 28.1–4), but for another purpose—in this case to make an explicit contrast between the situations in Spain and Italy (28.12.10: see 78–9 below for the significance of this). A good example of the demands Livy is making comes with the complicated story of the revolt of Syracuse and its eventual capture, which occurs in three distinct parts in Books 24 and 25, and where in each case the narrative is assumed to be able to continue more or less from where it had last been left. Or one might mention the Roman siege of Capua, begun in Book 25 and completed in Book 26. The narrative keeps leaving and returning: the Romans try to prosecute the siege, Hannibal tries various devices to distract them from it and help his Capuan allies, but each time we have to remember the situation in order to understand the point of the tactics that each side is adopting. There are many other examples.

So how is the reader expected to cope? Two basic points should be made immediately. One is that the mere identification of (as it might be) 'Spain' as the next sphere of action automatically gives us basic information that we can use, albeit not consciously, to orientate ourselves: it reminds us that a campaign is still proceeding there, so no absolute decision can have been reached. Similarly, even in the case of the more intricate actions at Syracuse, the introductory words of each episode provide us with some basic points of orientation. *Syracusarum oppugnatio ad finem venit* (25.23.1: 'the attack on Syracuse came to its end') reminds us of the fact of the unfinished siege from Book 24; 24.21.1 gives even more information, reminding us of the assassination of Hieronymus (*mors tyranni*), but also that the war had not yet involved Rome (*cum bellum . . . oreretur*—'since a war <u>was arising</u>'). Secondly, and more significantly, in many cases the action of a battle or season's campaign does not cease to be comprehensible if one does not remember precise details of the ones that preceded it: each sequence can proceed more or less independently of those that went before (though there are plenty of exceptions, including indeed Syracuse). Of course, in the case of major events Livy is certainly expecting it will be remembered. The taking of New Carthage, for example, has occupied a good proportion of the narrative, and he alludes to it in passing at 27.17.7 as if it is something we are expected to know. But in the case of minor events that he has only described cursorily, readers need to have retained only a general sense of the dynamic of the narrative: how the overall balance stands between the Carthaginians and the Romans, but no specifics of particular campaigns.

When it comes to reminding us of the past actions of people in the history, something similar seems to be going on. On the whole we do not get reminders of who people are or what they have done. This is obvious where the people are famous. We do not need to be told who Hannibal is each time he appears. Scipio is a slightly more complicated example, because in the first half of the decade he appears only intermittently, and so in each case he is distinguished from the other Scipios who feature in the narrative. But these prompts take the form not of reminding us what he has done, but drawing on our pre-existing knowledge of who he will be (21.46.8, 22.53.6, 25.2.6). This continues until he is ready to be established as the main 'Scipio' in the narrative at 26.18.7, after which no more identification is needed.[165]

More surprising is how far down the scale this appears to go. Most of the time Roman and Carthaginian commanders are simply reintroduced either

---

[165] An interesting example of the way Livy relies on the reader's possession of external information comes with Cato, who plays only a tiny role in the war. When he is introduced at 29.25.10 Livy comments *quaestor is tum erat* ('he was then quaestor'). The fact of commenting at all shows that this is the Cato who will later be famous as the Censor, especially since the quaestorship is normally too low-grade an office to rate Livy's attention. As with Scipio, it is his future rather than his past that qualifies him for the comment.

with no identification at all or identified by office alone: this includes a lot of apparently quite unmemorable figures where we might feel we would benefit from a quick reminder of their precise part in the war. This applies even to people whose positions do not appear obvious at first sight. If we look again at Sicily, the developing role of Epicydes is hard to follow unless we remember quite a lot of details from his prior appearances. When his role after Hieronymus' death is discussed at 24.23.5 we have to remember from 24.6–7 his Carthaginian orientation and his anti-Roman mission; when he is informed about the conspiracy to betray Syracuse at 25.23.7 the reader is presumably expected to remember his being in control there at 24.33.7–8. Or we might mention the Spanish princes Mandonius and Indibilis, who were first encountered as supporters of Carthage at 22.21.3, whose families are treated well by Scipio at 26.49.11–16 and who accordingly defect to Rome at 27.17, but then seek independence from her at 28.24.3–4, 28.31.5–7, and 29.1.19–3.5. In each case their prior stance and actions are simply assumed. The last passage is especially relevant, because while Indibilis is reintroduced at the beginning of the episode in an 'orienting' opening sentence (above, 66),[166] Mandonius is suddenly brought in towards the end in terms that make little sense unless we can recall his regular pairing with Indibilis (29.3.1).[167]

Clearly quite a lot of demands are being made on the reader's memory; but we can note aspects of Livy's narrative which can—up to a point—help to orientate us. The apparently endless string of apparently interchangeable Roman and Carthaginian commanders may in certain respects actually be viewed as helpful: in each episode we can at least spot the Latin and Punic names, and these alone imply things about their likely position in the war and their role in the coming narrative, even if we cannot recall the specifics of their earlier appearances. Paradoxically, with such a large number of participants in the war, it may in some respects be easier to follow the course of events if we are not searching for individual attributes but simply are looking for 'the Roman general' or 'the Carthaginian general' in each case (cf. below, 73–4)—and we can identify them from their names alone.[168] The 'annalistic' material at the start of each year is also worth mentioning in this context. One effect of it is

---

[166] 29.1.19 *in Hispania coortum ingens bellum, conciente Ilergete Indibili . . .*—'In Spain a great war arose, provoked by the Ilergitan Indibilis &c.'

[167] This pairing indeed may be Livy's own invention. Moret (1997: 158–9) argues that in reality Indibilis was the sole ruler of the Ilergeti, and that Livy has boosted the standing of Mandonius to create an artificial picture of a dual barbarian kingship with two recognizable leading actors.

[168] Plautus in the *Poenulus* called his sympathetic but fictional Carthaginian character 'Hanno', perhaps precisely because it was seen as a generic Carthaginian name (Maurach 1988: 35).

to provide a regular annual listing of the current Roman commanders and the regions where they are in command, and so when we then move to each region, we can at least do so in the awareness that the Roman armies in the region have had a commander explicitly assigned to them afresh not long before. Sometimes that is the same commander as in the previous year, sometimes it is a new one, but in practice that distinction rarely seems to make a difference, whether to the Roman soldiers or to us. The annalistic passages are an implicit guarantee that we can treat the commander in the campaign as someone fresh, unless his fame is such (as with Marcellus, Fabius, and Scipio) that we should remember his past actions anyway.

So far the discussion may have largely seemed to confirm our impression of the demands that Livy makes upon his readers, despite the various ways in which those demands may be softened. But there are also places where Livy does explicitly remind us of the background to some episode: we now need to examine those passages too.

One general place where we find reminders is at the start of books. Livy regularly begins a book with a phrase briefly recapitulating some aspect of the book before. So in Book 22 Hannibal's removal from winter quarters is accompanied by a reminder of his failure to cross the Appennines at 21.58 (22.1.1). Book 23 begins with a passing reminder of Cannae (23.1.1), while Book 27 refers to the capture of Salapia (27.1.1; cf. 26.38). Book 28 starts not only with a mention of Hasdrubal's crossing into Italy (28.1.1) but also a general summary of the current state of the war in Spain (28.1.2–4). Even Book 26, which begins 'annalistically' with the consuls entering office for the new year, repeats information from the last sentences of Book 25: the names of the consuls and the proroguing of the previous consuls' commands (26.1.1–2) have already been given in 25.41.11–13.

However, it is unlikely that these passages are there as reminders *per se*, although they doubtless incidentally can act as such. Other events of no less importance are not recalled explicitly, as I pointed out above, and the location at the start of the book is significant. It is an opening device that can be paralleled in poetry,[169] with the repetition both asserting the continuity with the previous book and emphasizing the break, by explicitly marking that this is a resumption of an earlier narrative. These passages are therefore not especially useful for working out what information Livy felt the reader needed reminding of.

There are other occasions, too, where one may feel that the point of the recapitulation is not primarily (or at least solely) as a reminder. For example,

---

[169] Cf. e.g. Maltby (1996: 96–101).

when Hannibal attempts to capture Nola in Books 23 and 24, he relies above all on internal divisions in the city between the pro-Roman leaders and the pro-Carthaginian population. Each time that Livy returns us to the story, he reminds us of this (23.39.7, 24.13.8). This is of course a key piece of information that the reader needs in order to understand what is happening; but one suspects that its repetition, when other equally key pieces of information are so often absent, has wider purposes. The theme of internal divisions in cities—and the anti-Roman instincts of their lower classes—is an especially prominent one in these books, exemplified above all at Capua and Syracuse (see below, 365–6). Repeating the point so often in the context of Nola keeps it in the forefront of the narrative.

There are, however, still other places where Livy provides reminders for the readers in contexts where the primary point must be to recall necessary background information; sometimes, indeed, he is absolutely explicit about the recapitulation by using a phrase such as *sicut ante dictum est* ('as was said previously').[170] An obvious criterion is if the events to be recalled occurred a considerable distance—a book or more—back in his narrative. Under those circumstances it is not unusual—though far from invariable even then—for him to give a brief summary. An example is 29.23.3, where an account of the alliance between Hasdrubal son of Gisgo and Syphax alludes explicitly to their meeting in the presence of Scipio at 28.18. So too the recapture of Saguntum and the defeat of the Turdetani at 24.42.9–11 are accompanied by a reminder of the fact that Saguntum had been the 'cause of war' in Book 21 (24.42.9 *causa belli*) and that the Turdetani had provided Hannibal with the excuse for his attack (24.42.11; cf. 21.6.1). Likewise when the Romans have the chance to retake Locri at 29.6.1 a brief clause reminds us of its defection—after all, it took place more than five books earlier, at 24.1, and Livy has hardly mentioned the town in the interim. Or we may mention the reintroduction of the Capuan Vibius Virrius at 26.13.2 as *defectionis auctor ab Romanis* ('the originator of the defection from the Romans')—reminding us of his role in the defection at 23.6.1–3.

Or sometimes Livy gives the information slightly more obliquely. An interesting example is at 29.15, when the question of the exemption of certain Latin colonies from military service is brought up in the Senate, resuming an issue from more than two books earlier (27.9–10). Livy has the senators who raise the question describe the situation in some detail (29.15.2–3), ostensibly for their listeners' benefit, but manifestly also for ours. Indeed, that memory is at issue is specifically assumed by his account of the Senate's response: *non*

---

[170] See in general Starr (1981).

memoria magis patribus renovata rei prope iam oblitteratae quam ira inritata est (29.15.4: 'The senators' anger was provoked no less than their memory renewed of a matter now almost wiped out'). There is however an additional irony to the senators' annoyance in this passage: when the matter was originally raised, the Senate's conclusion was merely that the offending colonies should not be mentioned, and Livy commented then that 'this silent reproof seemed most suited to the dignity of the Roman people' (27.10.10 *ea tacita castigatio maxime ex dignitate populi Romani visa est*). The Senate's 'forgetfulness' was thus deliberate (though it has already been undermined by Livy himself, who had carefully listed the colonies in question at the start of the Book 27 episode (27.9.7), and does so again here in Book 29 (29.15.5)).[171] The reader who took the Senate at its word earlier is the one most in need of the reminder here.

On a slightly different note, we sometimes—though again far from always—get an explicit recapitulation when something that was originally only mentioned in passing is now going to play a more substantial role in the story. At 25.5.10, for example, we are reintroduced to the troops who were punished for the defeat at Cannae (23.25.7, 23.31.4, 24.18.9), and who now make a long complaint to Marcellus. Similar recapitulations occur even when the events are fairly close together. For example, at 28.23.6–8 the Romans receive an offer from some people of Cadiz to betray the city; however, the story is then dropped for the account of Scipio's illness and the mutiny of his troops. When the Cadiz episode is resumed at greater length at 28.30.3–31.4, there is a brief but explicit recapitulation of the offer, even though, as it immediately transpires, the conspiracy in Cadiz had been a total failure (28.30.4). Here we need to know about the conspiracy if we are to understand the aftermath, and apparently the original description was so brief that it could easily have been overlooked or forgotten even in such a short time, were we not reminded of it.

Of course, what counts as 'recapitulation' is not always easy to recognize. An interesting example is at 26.21.10. Sosis and Moericus accompany Marcellus in his ovation for his Syracusan victory, *quorum altero duce nocturno Syracusas introitum erat, alter Nassum quodque ibi praesidii erat prodiderat* ('of whom one had led the entry into Syracuse by night, the other had betrayed Nassus and the garrison there'). Moericus' betrayal of Nassus had been described in 25.30, but this is the first time that we learn of Sosis' role in

---

[171] Cf. 40–1 above for another place where Livy plays with deliberate senatorial forgetfulness. More positively, in Book 27 he also makes a point of listing those colonies who stayed loyal 'so that even now they should not be left in silence after so many ages and be cheated of their praise' (27.10.7 *ne nunc quidem post tot saecula sileantur fraudenturve laude sua*); he thus uses his history to re-enact the honour which they received from the Roman state (27.10.5–6).

the entry into Syracuse. So while the description of Moericus is a reminder of something the reader has already encountered, the description of Sosis provides new information. Yet in Livy's language they are indistinguishable. Readers who remember Moericus (at least when prompted) may treat this as a useful reminder, and may indeed assume that the information about Sosis is likewise something that they have read but forgotten. Readers who have forgotten Moericus even when prompted will effectively treat both of these things as new information. The main point is that both kinds of readers now know that those who assisted Marcellus' victory are being rewarded.

There are other respects in which different groups of readers will gain information differently depending on their powers of recall. There are numerous places in Livy where, although the story appears to assume that we remember the relevant background from the earlier episodes, there are sufficient details given to ensure that, if we do happen to have forgotten, we can piece together a good deal and so make sense of the story anyway, even if with rather more effort. At 26.40 we continue the story of Muttines from 25.40–41. Ideally, no doubt, we will remember the relevant back-story: the energetic Muttines sent out by Hannibal to share in the Sicilian command, but resented by Hanno; Muttines being absent in order to deal with a mutiny, during which Hanno engages Marcellus in battle, only to be betrayed by Muttines' troops. But if we do happen to have forgotten this, all the necessary details are alluded to in the course of this episode: Muttines' success, Hanno's jealousy, the Numidians' prior mutiny and their willingness to betray Carthage to Rome. So too in many other episodes: enough oblique information can be acquired to allow us to replenish a good deal of our memories, though of course there are likely in all such cases to be additional resonances that will be accessible only to those who recall the story in more detail from the first time round.

So while it is true that Livy on the Hannibalic War makes considerable demands on our memories, those demands are not always absolute. Even while apparently working on the assumption that we will remember a good deal of the earlier narrative, he in various ways does accommodate and compromise to ensure that more fallible readers are not completely left behind. This conclusion is supported by a sense that there are certain things that Livy is actively *not* expecting us to remember or be interested in, even though modern readers can find this strange and uncomfortable. It seems unlikely, for example, that he expects his readers to have a very strong sense of the distance between various places. When at 26.42.6 Scipio reaches New Carthage (allegedly) seven days after crossing the Ebro, there is no indication that Livy saw this as a remarkable feat, let alone the impossible one that it was in reality.[172] The detailed geography is not something readers should for the most part be concerned about.[173] So when we leave a person in one place, and shortly after see him in another, there is no particular sense that we need to worry about how or when he went there. For example, Hannibal is among the Bruttii at Locri at 27.28.17, but more than 250 miles away in the territory of Larinum at 27.40.10[174] (admittedly in the following year); this is followed by a rapid retreat from Tarentine territory back to the Bruttii at 27.40.12.[175] Probably many Romans could have said little more about the relationship of Locri, Tarentum, and Larinum than that they are all in the southern half of Italy. This explains why Livy is unworried by problems that have vexed modern scholars, such as the inconsistency between 21.59.10, where Sempronius Longus retires with his troops to Luca, and 21.63.1 and 21.63.15, where Flaminius collects those same troops from Placentia. The discrepancy doubtless arises because Sempronius' entire winter campaign in 218/17 is fictional;[176] but Livy's failure to observe that there is a discrepancy at all is entirely of a piece with

[172] Livy draws this from Polybius 10.9.7, who appears to have made the same error with less excuse, since on his own showing (10.11.4), he had visited the site, which Livy may never have done, and at 3.39.6 he expressly states that the distance from the Ebro to New Carthage was 2,600 stades, which if anything overestimates the actual distance. See Scullard (1930: 67–9), Walbank (1967: 204–5). Gauthier (1968: 93–4) argues that Polybius meant only that Scipio took seven days to reach New Carthage from his winter quarters which (according to Gauthier) were well south of the Ebro (cf. de Sanctis 1968: 450 for a similar point). This seems a strained reading of Polybius, but even if it is correct, the main point here is that Livy has (mis)read Polybius in precisely the way most modern scholars have, and has transmitted the false information in all geographical innocence.

[173] Compare Polybius' complaint (3.36.1–5; cf. 5.21.4–10) about historians who merely provide bare geographical names with no further information; something which he suggests is all but meaningless for the readers. The complaint shows how even an ancient reader could be concerned about the absence of geographical information, but the fact that Polybius found it necessary to offer such an elaborate argument in support of his own practice suggests that most writers—and, we may assume, most readers—did not find it equally unsatisfactory (on Polybius' distinctive integration of geography and history see Clarke 1999a: 77–128). Polybius, of course, also has an ulterior motive, since he is emphasizing his own research that enabled him to provide such information at all: see e.g. 3.48.12, 10.11.4, 12.25e.1. Moreover, Polybius' own vagueness by modern standards of geography, even when he professes personal acquaintance with the area, is worth noting: see Walbank (1947: 162–8), Horsfall (1985: 198), and cf. n. 172 above.

[174] Reading, with the MSS, *per extremum finem agri Larinatis*. Madvig (followed by Walsh in the Teubner) emended *Larinatis* to *Tarentini*, which fits the implied movement at 27.40.12, but it is unsatisfactory methodology to attempt to save Livy's vague geography by correcting the text.

[175] On the geographical problems here see Lazenby (1978: 184–5).

[176] So de Sanctis (1968: 96–9).

the nebulousness of his own geography and (presumably) that of his readers also.[177]

Perhaps even more surprising is his treatment of certain individual characters. At the end of Book 25 the Roman position in Spain following the death of the Scipios is partly restored thanks to the emergency leadership of a certain L. Marcius (25.37–39); Marcius' success is reported to Rome at 26.2.1–6, and he hands over his army at 26.17.3, joining Scipio in a tour of the troops and allies at 26.20.3. We hear nothing more—but then in Book 28 there are a number of episodes involving an exceptionally active lieutenant of Scipio in Spain called L. Marcius. L. Marcius was (of course) a common Roman name. Is this the same person?

As it happens it is, and indeed Livy seems to have known this. In the middle of Book 28 Scipio makes a speech in which he refers back to the emergency leader from Book 25 as 'Septimus Marcius' (28.28.2).[178] No connection is made between this man and the lieutenant who has been acting just a few pages earlier; but in a much later book Livy gives the full name of the latter as L. Marcius Septimus (32.2.5). Clearly this is the same man; but nothing in Book 28 would encourage us to make the identification. As far as this narrative is concerned, they might as well be two different people, even though in fact they were not.

The same applies to various other characters in the narrative. A Capuan called Vibellius Taurea voluntarily and heroically offers himself up for execution and then commits suicide at 26.15.11–15. We have encountered a Vibellius Taurea before: at 23.46.12–47.8 someone of that name challenges a Roman called Claudius Asellus to a duel, only to be humiliated when it turns out that his courage does not live up to his braggadocio.[179] Again, this is presumably the same man, but again, nothing in Livy identifies him as such: 26.15.11 describes him as *Campanus*, an introductory formula which assumes that we would not recognize him from his earlier appearances.[180] Indeed, in

---

[177] Note especially Horsfall (1985). As he comments (Horsfall 1985: 199): 'What is so striking is that Livy's massive topographical confusions occur precisely in areas that he could reasonably be expected to know'. On Livy's geographical conceptions more broadly, see Girod (1982).

[178] In Book 25 he gave a slightly different version of the name: *L. Marcius Septimi filius* (25.37.2). See Briscoe (1973: 170–1). Jaeger (1997: 109) suggests that Livy calls Marcius *Septimi filius* on his introduction in order to provide his family background as a counterpoint to his natural talent and to the training that he is said to have received under Cn. Scipio.

[179] He had also been mentioned briefly at 23.8.5 as 'a man distinguished in war' (*insignem bello virum*).

[180] It is true that Cicero (*Pis.* 24) refers in passing to *Taurea illo Vibellio*, which suggests that he saw him as a familiar historical figure, at least in anecdote. If so, Roman readers might have recognized the name on each of his appearances, but it still seems unlikely that in Book 26 they were expected to recall specific details of his character or behaviour as they were represented three books earlier.

this case the two episodes make him look so different in character that we would be forgiven for assuming that they were different people, despite the names. Examples can be multiplied.

The lesson that we need to learn from this is the danger of what we might refer to as the *indexing fallacy*, the automatic response to a text that makes modern readers want to provide a unique identification for every figure in a narrative, with every occurrence recognized so that all occurrences can be related to one another. This instinct leads to some seriously misconceived ways of reading Livy—and, we may suspect, many other ancient writers also. It is not that Livy is never interested in watching a figure develop across an extended series of episodes, nor that he never presents people with varying and perhaps contradictory attributes while expecting the reader to recognize the identity of the person. As we shall see in later chapters, both of those are things that can at times form vital parts of his narrative. And sometimes, as we saw with Epicydes, readers can have considerable demands made on them to keep up with the changing position of a single minor character in the story. But this 'indexing fallacy' leads us to think that Livy is *always* going to be concerned about such things, or conversely if he appears not to be concerned about them it is a sign of his inattention to his own text. Neither of these is true. Sometimes the identification of certain figures is simply not relevant to what Livy is doing, and in those circumstances he is perfectly happy to regard connections with possible earlier occurrences of those characters in his narrative as an irrelevancy, and to leave the possible identity undetermined and opaque to his readers.

One reason, in other words, that many people find Livy on the Hannibalic War a hard text to come to terms with is that they work from an unstated belief that the text will contain a comprehensive network of identifiable and carefully separated characters, such as we find in the sorts of narratives that we are familiar with. As I shall explore further in Chapter 3, Livy's assumptions about the role of individual characters are manifestly quite different. In general, while certainly Livy 21–30 only fully makes sense if it is read as a whole, and while Livy's demands on readers are correspondingly considerable, our own manner of reading texts makes those demands appear even more extensive than in fact they would have been in antiquity.

1.3.2 Linking Up

The ancient book-roll, as I have said, hindered readers from referring back to earlier points in the narrative. But it also had the more positive effect of directly encouraging sequential reading. Reading selectively or skipping between separate parts of a narrative was cumbersome; most readers will have seen each episode in the context of the one that immediately preceded it. Livy's narrative strongly accommodates such readings: he regularly creates a sense of continuity by making overt connections or covert parallels between adjacent scenes.

When Livy introduces a new episode, he may simply do so with a temporal expression such as those discussed in Section 2 of the chapter, ostensibly relating it to the previous episode by nothing more than the relative time when they occurred. But very often there are more concrete connections as well. It is common for him, for example, to begin a new episode by describing someone moving into the location where the episode will take place. Now, it is true that this can be seen as part of a technique of rounding each episode into a distinct scene, setting it up as though beginning afresh in a place with new personnel or new information.[181] This is most obvious when the movement does not involve anyone involved in the previous episode. To give one prominent example, at 30.29.1–2 the scene of Zama is prepared by showing Hannibal's arrival there; he had last been seen arriving in Africa at the end of the previous year (30.25.12). Or we may note the scene in Carthage at 23.11.7–13.8, introduced by Mago's arrival there with news of the victory at Cannae. Lesser episodes are regularly marked in the same way: for instance 28.5.1, where the sequence of events in Greece begins with Sulpicius and Attalus moving to Lemnos to confront Philip.

So arrivals do not necessarily provide an actual link between adjacent scenes. But it is a natural corollary that Livy in practice often effects a transition between two scenes by having an individual move from the first place to the second.[182] For example, in Book 28 the extended narrative of Scipio's success in Spain ends with his departure (28.38.1). His return to Rome and report of his success to the Senate in turn leads into the regular end-of-year narrative centred (as usual) on Rome. Similarly Laelius' arrival with his African prisoners at 30.17.1 triggers the transition from Africa to Rome: he had been sent by Scipio at 30.16.1. Here too examples could be multiplied.

At times Livy adjusts the technique to suit particular circumstances. Sometimes he uses anticipation, where a character is said to be moving to a particular place, and the scene accordingly changes to that place even though the character has not yet arrived. Examples include Hannibal's march on

---

[181] The classic demonstration of Livy's technique of constructing his narrative by shaping individual scenes is Witte (1910).

[182] Noted by Walsh (1961: 180–1), who however seems to underestimate the flexibility of the technique.

Rome, which he decides to make at 26.7.3. This signals a move of the scene to Rome ahead of his arrival, as news of his march reaches the city at 26.8.1, well before he does (26.10.3). Sometimes, in an extension of the technique, the transition appears to involve a movement back in time. So, for example, Marcellus is sent to deal with Syracuse at 24.21.1; we are then told of earlier events in Syracuse even though Marcellus does not reach there until 24.27.6.[183] A further extension comes where the movement alluded to in the first scene does not actually occur at all, but the possibility of such a movement is enough to introduce the second scene. For example, when Gnaeus Fulvius is on trial, he writes to his brother Quintus to ask him to come to testify on his behalf (26.3.10–11). Quintus is at that point besieging Capua, and the Senate refuses to allow him to leave, so Gnaeus instead goes into exile (26.3.12). But the narrative now shifts to Capua, to recount the continuation of Quintus' siege. It appears that the mere allusion to a possible movement at the end of one scene is sufficient to effect the transition to the next.

With these and other examples we can see the trope of connecting episodes by movement being employed in a more extended way, but it is still fairly simple and straightforward. At times, however, Livy combines these to create a highly intricate narrative sequence. At 23.34.3–7 the Roman fleet in Calabria captures the Macedonians who have been negotiating with Hannibal, and the commander resolves to send them either to Rome or to wherever the consuls happen to be (23.34.8–9). The next episode accordingly moves to Rome, which has indeed received a message about an impending war on a new front – yet the message is not from Calabria, but from Sardinia (23.34.10). The Romans therefore send Torquatus to take command in Sardinia, while at the same time the Carthaginians are sending troops there, in response to a similar message they had received back in 23.32.7–12. However, the move to Sardinia is aborted when the Carthaginian ships are driven the wrong way by a storm, and accordingly Livy's narrative switches not to Sardinia but to Cumae, where Hannibal places the consul Gracchus under siege. Not until 23.38 do we find out what happened to the prisoners: they are indeed on their way to Rome (23.38.1), but are intercepted by Gracchus at Cumae, where we have just seen the siege lifted (23.37.8–9). Gracchus then sends them forward with his own message to the senate; effectively the two alternative possible movements at 23.34.8–9 are now united, since the ships come to both the consul and Rome. This returns us to Rome, where the Romans now prepare to cross to Macedonia to fight Philip. Accordingly the scene moves to

---

[183] See below, 321–6, for further discussion of the chronological complexities in this episode.

Macedonia—but it is not the Romans who take us there, but some escaped Macedonians who bring Philip news of the capture of his envoys: Philip is forced to waste time renegotiating the alliance (23.39.1–4). Then at last we return to the Sardinian story (23.40.1–41.7), where the Romans finally arrive in the island, and defeat the Carthaginians when they later appear.

The entire sequence thus involves two separate changes of scene to Rome, each anticipated by the movement of the captured envoys there, a planned move to Sardinia which is repeatedly alluded to but accomplished only at the very end of the sequence, as well as changes of scene to and from Cumae and Macedon, both once again anticipated by the movements of characters— though the characters who actually move are not necessarily the same ones whose movements were anticipated.

At least part of this ordering is forced on Livy by the need to unite the different threads at the appropriate point, since the siege of Cumae has to be completed before the captured envoys pass. But this could equally have been accomplished by finishing the entire Cumae episode before the narrative of the negotiations between Hannibal and Philip begins. Narrating it in that way would have solved a chronological problem which is only barely concealed by the complexity of the narrative arrangement: for Hannibal is involved in both the negotiations with Philip and the siege of Cumae. Livy begins his account of the siege only after narrating the negotiations, which seems to imply that the negotiations came first, but it is hard to see how that could be possible, if the envoys leaving Hannibal are to be met at Cumae after its liberation. And the interweaving with the Sardinian narrative also is hard to fit chronologically. As before (cf. 47–8 above), this may be related to Livy's non-transitive conception of simultaneity;[184] but in this case, unlike those I considered in Section 1.2, this can only be a partial explanation, since neither the beginning of the Cumae siege nor the arrival in Sardinia and its aftermath are put into direct chronological relationship to the preceding events.

The point seems rather to be that the sequence is governed by Livy's creation of a single overall narrative dynamic. Three events—the attempted revolt of Sardinia, the alliance of Philip and Hannibal, and the siege of Cumae—each involve the same general pattern: a hopeful development for Carthage which is aborted and ultimately turns out to the Romans' advantage. Rather than offering three short independent narratives with broadly this pattern, Livy interweaves them so as to create a single narrative in which one is presented with a series of attempts by Carthage to open new fronts,

---

[184] Compare 23.34.10 *per idem tempus*, 23.34.16 *sub idem fere tempus*, 23.37.10 *quibus diebus… isdem diebus*, 23.38.1 *dum haec… geruntur*, and 23.39.1 *dum haec Romani parant aguntque*.

each of which is successively scotched. And that interweaving is substantially facilitated by the creative use of scene-connecting movements, both anticipated and actual, which allow him to take the story to Rome twice while deferring the completion of events in Sardinia, to bring together the Cumaean and Macedonian threads, and to restore the story to Philip and show the hindrances to his planned alliance.

This sequence also suggests another aspect of the connections that Livy makes between successive episodes: that events that happen in one may affect our reading of another. In the case of Cumae and Macedon the two sequences are linked, albeit fairly late on. The Sardinian narrative is unconnected from the others in strict causal terms, and might have appeared anticlimactic were it presented as an independent sequence, since the arrival of the Carthaginian forces has been prepared for so heavily and anticipated so long (23.32.7–12, 23.34.16–17); but in the event they are massacred astonishingly easily (23.40.6–12). In practice, however, by the time the narrative finally moves to Sardinia the other checks to Carthaginian plans have established a general pattern, and the victory in Sardinia simply forms the culmination to the entire sequence (I shall discuss this issue further in Chapter 5).

There are many other points where narrative juxtapositions appear to govern Livy's handling of events. In my discussion of book-divisions (above, esp. 19) I have already alluded to the difference the order of scenes can make: the creation of climaxes and unified and balanced books was possible partly because of the licence Livy gave himself here. The effect of Livy's narrative would have been very different if (for example) Book 26 had ended on the messy defeat of Gnaeus Fulvius which currently stands at the start of Book 27, while Scipio's spectacular success at New Carthage had stood early in Book 27 instead of forming the climax to Book 26.[185] Likewise Book 25 would have appeared far more triumphant and far less balanced if the deaths of the Scipios and the capture of Syracuse had been reversed (assuming that were chronologically possible: cf. 61–3 above).

But we can also see places, even without marked structural significance, where we are invited to read one event in the context of another immediately before.[186] Sometimes the invitation is explicit, as at 28.12.10–15, where a

---

[185] Livy could indeed easily have done this merely by moving Scipio's capture of New Carthage to the following year, when some of his sources placed it (27.7.5–6) and when it is very likely that it really took place (de Sanctis 1968: 440).

[186] For the general approach cf. Hoch (1951: 22–6), though he chiefly confines his discussion to the relatively crude point that Livy will often balance a Roman setback with a juxtaposed success, so creating a less pessimistic impression of Rome's overall prospects. For a more sophisticated discussion of a single instance—the juxtaposition of the 'Shield of Marcius' (25.39.17) with the account of the spoils from Syracuse (25.40.1–3)—see Jaeger (1997: 124–31).

comparison is made between the position of Hannibal in Italy, which Livy has just described (28.12.1–9), and that of the Carthaginians in Spain. The ostensible point of comparison is that, while in both cases the Carthaginians have been forced into a tight position, the nature of both the terrain and the inhabitants in Spain makes counterattacks against the Romans far more likely. And indeed this observation is borne out by both the immediately succeeding narrative, where the Carthaginians rally under Hasdrubal son of Gisgo, and the broader history, where Spanish rebellions continue until the beginning of Book 29—and, as Livy tells us here (28.12.12), will not finally be suppressed until his own day. But the juxtaposition also invites a comparison in the other direction, since Livy has shown Hannibal, though trapped, as effectively invincible in Italy despite the lack of support from home. Yet Hasdrubal, *maximus clarissimusque eo bello secundum Barcinos dux* (28.12.13: 'the greatest and most famous general in that war after the Barcines'), falls so far short of him that he will be driven out of Spain by Scipio in a single battle despite the total concentration of Carthaginian efforts upon retaining their hold there (28.12.9). This accentuation of Hannibal's unique superiority provides in turn the essential context to the debate between Scipio and Fabius with which the book climaxes, and in particular to Fabius' determination that his own strategy of containment must be maintained, and Scipio's counter-claim that only by launching an invasion of Africa will Hannibal be dislodged from Italy.

Equally, sequential reading often suggests parallels even in places where Livy offers no explicit invitation to the reader to draw them. Such parallels are especially likely to be observed by the reader on occasions where the events are said to be simultaneous, since the Romans—like people in other cultures— were strongly conditioned to attach significance to and to see relationships between events merely because they chanced to take place at the same time.[187] These cases too can point to significant interpretative issues.[188] The narrative of Fabius' dictatorship (22.9.7–31.11) is marked by his disputes with his deputy Marcus Minucius, who opposes Fabius' avoidance of battle only to fall into disaster when he is given a command of his own and is trapped by Hannibal. In the middle of this sequence the narrative is broken by the simultaneous campaigns of the Scipio brothers in Spain (22.19–22). The mere placing of the Scipios' story here is not necessarily significant in itself, since Polybius likewise switches his narrative to Spain at precisely this point (3.95–99: I shall discuss this in more detail in the next chapter). But Livy's

---

[187] For fuller discussion of this tendency at Rome see Feeney (2007: esp. 43–52).
[188] So too Thucydides regularly invites certain interpretations of events by ordering them in a particular sequence: compare Rood (1998: 109–30).

version is slanted in such a way as to shed a particular light on the contentious points at issue in the Fabius–Minucius dispute. Minucius at 22.14.4–14 makes a speech advocating direct aggression, citing as examples Camillus, the Caudine Forks episode, and finally C. Lutatius' naval victory in the First Punic War brought about (according to Minucius) by his speed of action (22.14.13). When the scene switches to Spain, Cn. Scipio achieves a striking naval victory, which (in Livy) he achieves by attacking the Carthaginian fleet so rapidly that it is unprepared for battle (22.19.6–20.2): Livy describes at some length the confusion that the unexpected Roman onslaught engenders in the Carthaginians. In Polybius none of this is present: the Carthaginians are fully ready to meet the Romans (3.96.1), and the Roman victory is less the result of their aggressive attack than because the Carthaginian sailors have the opportunity to retreat onto dry land (3.96.3–5).

So Livy, by placing this slanted version of Cn. Scipio's victory within the narrative of Fabius' dictatorship, reinforces a point which is already implicit in Minucius' citation of historical examples.[189] Fabian tactics, though demonstrably superior to other possible responses to Hannibal at that time, are limited and fallible.[190] Indeed, directly prior to the narrative's move to Spain Fabius himself, despite his troops' numerical advantage, is defeated by Hannibal's Spanish cohort (22.18.2–4). Livy, unlike Polybius in the parallel passage (3.94.6), attributes this to the Spaniards' superior facility on precisely the sort of mountainous terrain whose occupation is a key part of Fabius' passive tactics (22.12.8–10). Cn. Scipio—fighting in Spain, though not here against Spanish opponents[191]—handles matters far more effectively. This then means that the subsequent narrative, where Fabius' position is undermined by the attacks of Varro, itself appears in a new light. The criticisms of Fabius, and the consequent decision that he should share the command with Minucius, are obviously misguided, indeed disastrously rash and foolish. But they are also part of a narrative sequence which appears to show us, if not the Romans (there is no direct suggestion that the success in Spain influences their decision over Fabius and Minucius), that an aggressive strategy such as that advocated by Minucius can be viewed as more desirable and successful than a passive one: the question is to determine the circumstances when it is

---

[189] Cf. Chaplin (2000: 45–6 and 114–15) on Minucius' misapplication of valid *exempla* in his speech.

[190] On this, as often, Catin is a more acute reader of Livy than are many later scholars: 'Tite-Live n'est pas sans voir ni laisser voir que le génie de Fabius est borné... Minucius, Varron, Scipion ne font souvent que développer ce que Tite-Live pense un peu' (Catin 1944: 182). I shall discuss this question further in Chapter 3 (below, 197, 228–36).

[191] Scipio does then proceed to defeat the Carthaginians' Spanish allies too, though the battle (which is not in Polybius) is described only summarily (22.21.4).

appropriate to adopt each. For the moment that question, as far as the Romans in Italy go, has a straightforward answer: abandoning Fabius' strategy will prove disastrous. But the narrative also shows us the potential for failure in that strategy, and we can understand better why the Romans are shortly to make so bad a misjudgement by abandoning it.

All this suggests that the fragmentation of the narrative of the Hannibalic War between different areas of conflict is not simply a hindrance to the reader's understanding compelled by the diffuse nature of the story, but forms an opportunity for Livy as well. By creating juxtapositions between apparently unrelated spheres of action he establishes a narrative sequence; by manipulating the order and by emphasizing particular details he allows significant parallels or contrasts to be drawn and issues to be raised overtly or covertly to affect the reader's reaction to the narrative. We saw in the discussion of chronology (above, 45–63) that the narrative sequence itself has causal implications that can sometimes override what is literally possible in chronological terms. We can see now that this is true more widely: even when they are not explicitly linked causally, the order of events as they are presented in the narrative is one way in which Livy communicates particular interpretations of the war. This is not, of course, to say that every juxtaposition is manipulated to significant effect or that all sequential events are implicitly paralleled or contrasted. As I have already pointed out (above, 22), Livy is constrained by the fact that the historical tradition could only be changed within certain limits, and there are occasions where one would be hard pressed to suggest that there is a marked significance to particular narrative orderings. But Livy had set himself up in these books to narrate a single war (above, 6–17), so in that sense a causal connection between different events, at least loosely defined, was a core underlying expectation of his presentation. Uniting disparate events into a meaningful sequence by creating parallelisms and contrasts was a primary way in which he could turn that expectation into a reality. This is not least among the factors that give these books their remarkable coherence of texture and theme.

2

Sources and Intertexts

No issue is more central to contemporary scholarship on Latin literature than the ways in which Latin authors allude to and rework their predecessors, and the consequences of this for how they are to be read. This topic takes its lead from ancient critics and commentators such as Servius and Macrobius, who regularly identify such allusions, and indeed work within a theoretical framework which explains, justifies, and assesses their value under the general heading of *imitatio*.[1] But in recent years, studies of the phenomenon have come to dominate the field as never before. This expansion of interest has by no means been confined to (or even led by) Latin studies, but Latinists have been especially keen to address such questions, no doubt because of the particular self-consciousness with which many Roman writers approached their relationship to their predecessors, and the consequent density of allusions to be discovered in many Latin texts. Accordingly, not only have innumerable studies sought to identify and explain particular allusions, but a large and influential literature has grown up which has attempted to place the study on a sound theoretical basis.[2]

One problem arising from this literature should be considered immediately. Theorists of allusion in classical scholarship have tended to fall into two camps, which one can broadly (if sometimes unfairly) label 'conservatives' and 'radicals'. 'Conservatives' examine the issue from a perspective not fundamentally unlike that of their ancient predecessors: they identify what appear to them to be deliberate attempts by authors to evoke particular earlier texts, and discuss in a more or less determinate fashion the significance of the implied comparison between the model text and the new one. 'Radicals' look for a much looser interplay between texts: every text (it is argued) is

---

[1] See Russell (1979). For a more nuanced account, emphasizing the differences between *imitatio* and other ancient attempts to conceptualize the practice, and allusion as it is nowadays generally conceived, see Pucci (1998: 51–108).

[2] For the general theoretical background see e.g. Piégay-Gros (1996), Pucci (1998), Allen (2000), Samoyault (2001), Gignoux (2005). Important contributions to the debate among classicists include Conte (1986: esp. 23–95), Thomas (1986), Farrell (1991: esp. 3–25, 2005), Wills (1996), Fowler (1997b), Hinds (1998), Laird (1999: 34–43), Edmunds (2001).

constructed and needs to be understood against a background of assumptions and language derived from the mass of texts that preceded it, whether or not the author actively had any of those earlier texts in mind, or indeed even had read them. The term 'intertextuality' was invented by Julia Kristeva precisely in order to have a word to describe the way texts relate to and build on their predecessors without suggesting that the effects were specifically intended by the authors, as would be implied by the term 'allusion'.

There is no reason—in theory—why both of these approaches should not reflect something that is genuinely present in the texts. It can be the case *both* that authors set up comparisons with earlier texts by deliberately and specifically alluding to them, *and* that those same texts relate to other texts through a web of linguistic relationships that go beyond anything that their authors intended.[3] However, in practice, many of those who argue for one of these modes of analysis regard the other as illegitimate. 'Conservatives' accuse 'radicals' of having no criteria that would enable them to distinguish genuine textual relationships from mere scholarly fantasy. 'Radicals' accuse 'conservatives' of seeking tacitly or explicitly to pin down a series of fluid connections to a specific but unprovable intention inside the mind of the author. Both groups can moreover point to practices of certain of their opponents that lend colour to these objections. It is indeed the case that old-style studies of 'allusion' often assume an implausible precision to the limits within which the allusion is held to operate; it is also the case that certain studies of 'intertexts' depend on producing increasingly far-fetched connections between texts, connections whose significance appears to lie only in the mind of the interpreter rather than any definable or coherent link. Moreover, each side can fail to do justice to the insights provided by the other. 'Radicals' too often make no substantial differentiation between those textual relationships which depend on obvious and easily recognizable linguistic repetition and those which are much looser and less apparent: and failing to allow that distinction is to fail to capture something very important. 'Conservatives' in their turn often fail to allow the significant point that even if one allows authorial intention as a legitimate object of study (something which many scholars would deny), texts can and regularly do have effects that are unintended by their authors. Moreover, even if one allows in principle that both approaches are acceptable, an additional problem is that there is a large fuzzy area where it is unclear which approach is most properly applicable. It is

---

[3] This point is recognized by various theorists who in their typologies treat allusion in its traditional sense not as an illegitimate alternative to intertextuality, but as a subset of the broader field of textual relationships (see e.g. Piégay-Gros 1996: 52–5; Samoyault 2001: 34–7; Gignoux 2005: 58–62).

difficult to decide in many instances whether we are dealing with a deliberate allusion introduced by the author or an incidental confluence of language or theme, and while both of these may be interesting, they are interesting in different ways and for different reasons, and accordingly require quite different modes of analysis.

These two approaches to textual relationships need not be divided as starkly as I have set them out here for expository convenience, and various forms of rapprochement have been proposed;[4] exploring them and their various ramifications lies, however, outside the scope of this book. For the moment I shall simply set out my own methodological stance. The study here falls towards the 'conservative' end of the spectrum, in that I am primarily interested in allusive effects which can plausibly be attributed to Livy's own intentions.[5] I do not deny that the 'radical' approaches can reveal important truths about texts, but those do not happen to be the truths I am currently interested in. However, it is necessary even for a 'conservative' student of allusion to be aware that finding criteria for the identification of allusions can be fraught, and that even apparently clear-cut examples of allusion frequently raise messy questions about the allusion's precise limits: I shall be discussing these questions further below (see esp. 99). The other point that I should mention is a terminological one. Although, as I said above, the term 'intertextuality' was developed in the context of a theory which I shall not be employing here, I shall often speak of 'intertexts' as well as 'allusions'. This is partly because such terminological interchangeability appears to have become accepted practice in literary scholarship; but more specifically because the language of 'intertexts' sometimes enables certain sorts of points to be made conveniently (for example about the salience of one text as a whole to another, as opposed to particular references) which would otherwise require clumsy circumlocutions.

One issue, however, requires more detailed consideration. It is noticeable that the classical scholarship on the theory of allusion and intertext, no matter which perspective the scholars adopt, overwhelmingly deals with verse rather

---

[4] For one influential example, see Hinds (1998).

[5] This of course assumes that one can legitimately discuss authors' intentions, something that has long been unfashionable in literary scholarship, not least because it is widely considered to rest on fallacious assumptions. This belief in an 'intentionalist fallacy' indeed has been one of the impulses behind the growth of more radical theories of intertextuality; it has also led to some remarkable contortions, as even relatively conservative critics seek to avoid intentionalist language in discussing matters which appear hard to conceptualize save in intentionalist terms. However, the problems of such critics appear to arise from mischaracterizations and indeed caricatures of intentionalism (see Heath 2002: 59–97).

than prose texts.[6] Of course, individual prose authors have quite regularly been subjected to intertextual analyses, and allusions to earlier texts in their own or other genres have been identified and interpreted. But there has been little attempt to provide a general framework for such allusivity; effectively the study has proceeded simply in the wake of the studies of verse literature. And this is unfortunate. It is unfortunate partly because one of the most influential theorists of allusion in Latin literature has argued that the phenomenon as found in verse is related to specific qualities of poetic language which we should not necessarily expect to be replicated in prose.[7] More importantly, however, it is unfortunate because historiography in particular has generic features that significantly alter the terms in which allusions need to be discussed. The defining feature of history is that it is—or purports to be—a representation of real events. In practice events in real life may show striking resemblances to other historical events, and people in real life may deliberately choose to model their behaviour or public image on earlier figures. Both can be true whether or not those resemblances happen to be recognized by the historians describing them. Moreover, even if the historian wishes to draw attention to the parallels, that can be done in different ways. It can appear in the form of a direct citation of the parallel without reference to any single source, for example, or the description of one set of events may be reworked in order to highlight features specifically associated with the other set—though again without any single source. Alternatively the parallel can be brought out via an imitation of a particular historian who has treated the other set of events. In addition, many historians draw much of their data closely from relatively small numbers of source texts, and these may or may not themselves have alluded to the resemblances between different past events and their representations in still earlier writers.

It is not that these phenomena are impossible to parallel in verse,[8] but in studies of verse allusion they have (reasonably enough) tended to be marginal. When considering allusion in historiography they need to be far more central; yet all too often they have been ignored or skated over. The most notable

[6] For two important recent exceptions, one broadly 'radical', the other broadly 'conservative' (but neither dogmatically so), see Riggsby (2006: esp. 2–8) and Kelly (2008: esp. 161–221). Neither, however, addresses the distinctive problems of historiographical allusion that I am considering here.

[7] Conte (1986: 40–95). In practice Conte accepts that a prose author may use 'poetic' language (e.g. 77–9), but his model strongly privileges features directly associated with verse. Cf. Edmunds (2001: 95–107), though Edmunds states more explicitly than Conte that, while intertextuality may have distinctive effects in poetry, this does not mean that it is confined to it (99).

[8] E.g. Fowler (1997b: 17–18) hints at some of these issues.

exception is A. J. Woodman, who in a couple of short but important articles centred his argument about ancient historians' capacity for invention on keeping a clear separation between genuinely repeated events and aspects of their representation that imitated earlier accounts of other events.[9] But although Woodman's first article in particular has often been cited, the careful distinctions that he makes have rarely been followed through systematically in this context,[10] nor have the additional issues raised by the historian's own source material been incorporated into that analysis.[11]

In the first part of this chapter I shall therefore provide a general account of the different styles of allusion that Livy in Books 21–30 makes to literary predecessors both within and outside the genre of historiography, considering among other questions the relationship between those allusions and the possible *realia* to which they correspond. In the second part of the chapter I shall specifically consider the question of Livy's sources in these books, both who those sources were and how they relate to the general complex of literary allusion in his work.

2.1. ALLUSIONS

We can begin with a unique occurrence in these books: an occasion when Livy directly and explicitly quotes a named earlier writer.[12] The occasion is the death of Fabius Maximus shortly before the final Roman victory (30.26.8–9):

vir certe fuit dignus tanto cognomine, vel si novum ab eo inciperet. superavit paternos honores, avitos aequavit. pluribus victoriis et maioribus proeliis avus insignis Rullus, sed omnia aequare unus hostis Hannibal potest. cautior tamen quam promptior hic habitus; et sicut dubites utrum ingenio cunctator fuerit an quia ita bello proprie, quod

---

[9] Woodman (1979, 1983). Admittedly, in the first article Woodman argues that Tacitus did not expect the imitation under discussion to be read as a specific allusion (Woodman 1979: 154). But *a fortiori* his points are relevant also in cases where such allusions are at issue, and indeed he elsewhere applies similar arguments to (e.g.) Herodotus' imitations of Homer (Woodman 1988: 3–4).

[10] Exceptions include the study of repetition and doublets in Livy by Kraus (1998).

[11] Woodman (1979: 147–8, 152, with n. 6 and n. 26) once again is the exception, though this is inevitably a minor feature of his argument, given that he is here arguing for self-imitation rather than imitation of an external source. Laird (1999: 141–2) is also suggestive, though working within a quite different theoretical framework.

[12] Livy also, of course, frequently cites historical sources by name when discussing alternative versions; but this is—at least on the face of things—a different phenomenon, which I shall be discussing in Section 2.2 below.

tum gerebatur, aptum erat, sic nihil certius est quam unum hominem nobis cunctando rem restituisse, sicut Ennius ait.

He was certainly a man worthy of so great a surname [sc. Maximus], even if it were newly beginning from him. He surpassed his father's honours, and equalled his grandfather's. His grandfather Rullus was distinguished in more victories and greater battles, but the one enemy Hannibal can equal them all. But he was regarded as more cautious than active; and while you may query whether he was a delayer by nature or because it was appropriate to the war in particular which was then being fought, nothing is more certain than that one man by delaying restored the state for us, as Ennius says.

The reference to Ennius is to his line *unus homo nobis cunctando restituit rem* (*Annals* 363 Sk.), a line more famous than any other in archaic Roman poetry, judging by the number of times it is quoted and imitated in Latin literature.[13] That very fact shows us something important: Livy could have relied on the allusion being recognized even had he not mentioned Ennius by name.[14] But naming Ennius superfluously is itself part of the effect: at Fabius' last appearance he finally receives his most famous eulogy from his most famous eulogist, much as Scipio is to receive his surname Africanus in the very last lines of the decade (above, 12–13). In the meantime Livy's more sophisticated literary credentials are on display too, since he is not above some teasing play on the quotation. As he leads up to it, he prepares us for the famous phrase: *omnia aequare unus ho . . .*,[15] which in context one would naturally expect to be a reference to Fabius' 'equalling' his grandfather's exploits (as with *aequavit* just a few words earlier), and to be completed with some adaptation of the Ennian line, which itself appears to have formed part of a general posthumous summary of Fabius' career, albeit not immediately on his death.[16] But in the event the word is *hostis*, and refers to Hannibal:[17] we must still wait for Ennius' version proper. And when it comes, it is not a direct quotation, but rewritten prosaically in the accusative and infinitive—except that Livy neatly repoeticizes it by reversing the order of the final two words, creating, if not quite a new hexameter, at least the last five feet of one.

  This passage is a clear and relatively uncomplicated demonstration of Livy's willingness to draw on the literary tradition. However, the quotation of

---

[13] See the list in Skutsch (1985: 529–30).

[14] Skutsch (1985: 27) notes of Cicero's numerous quotations of Ennius that 'with almost a third . . . he does not name Ennius as the author, knowing that his readers would not need to be told'.

[15] On the device ('sound allusion') see Wills (1996: 19).

[16] Skutsch (1985: 530–1).

[17] Santoro L'Hoir (1990: 231) notes the parallel between this phrase and the Ennius quotation, though not the consequent joke.

Ennius by name is, as I said, unique,[18] and other allusive material in Livy is not signalled so explicitly. A useful starting-point for understanding his technique is that there are certain places where he directly excludes literary quotations that he had before him in his sources. As I shall discuss in Section 2, one of his chief sources for the Hannibalic War was Polybius. There are four passages where Polybius directly quotes (or purports to quote) an earlier writer, where Livy follows Polybius quite closely, but does not incorporate the direct quotation. These passages are (a) Polybius 3.94.4 and Livy 22.18.1; (b) Polybius 9.21 and Livy 26.37.2-4; (c) Polybius 10.20.6–7 and Livy 26.51.7–8; and (d) Polybius 15.12.8–9 and Livy 30.34.1.[19]

Let us begin with the last of these:

ἐπειδὴ δ' ἐγγὺς ἦσαν ἀλλήλων, οἱ μὲν Ῥωμαῖοι κατὰ τὰ πάτρια συναλαλάξαντες καὶ συμψοφήσαντες τοῖς ξίφεσι τοὺς θυρεοὺς προσέβαλλον τοῖς ὑπεναντίοις, οἱ δὲ μισθοφόροι τῶν Καρχηδονίων ἀδιάκριτον ἐποίουν τὴν φωνὴν καὶ παρηλλαγμένην· οὐ γὰρ πάντων ἦν κατὰ τὸν ποιητὴν ὁ αὐτὸς θροῦς

> οὐδ' ἴα γῆρυς,
> ἄλλη δ' ἄλλων γλῶσσα, πολύκλητοι δ' ἔσαν ἄνδρες,
> καθάπερ ἀρτίως ἐξηριθμησάμην.

But when they were near to one another, the Romans, according to their native custom, shouted and clashed their swords against their shields in unison and attacked the enemy, while the Carthaginian mercenaries produced a confused and strange sound; for, as the poet says, the tongue of all of them was not the same,

> nor their speech one,
> but different people had different language, and men were called from many lands

as I recently enumerated.

ad hoc dictu parva sed magna eadem in re gerenda momenta: congruens clamor ab Romanis eoque maior et terribilior, dissonae illis, ut gentium multarum discrepantibus linguis, voces.

In addition to this was something small-sounding but in fact of great importance in action: the shout from the Romans was in unison, and therefore greater and more fearsome, but their opponents' voices were discordant, as expected from the differing tongues of many nations.

---

[18] It is worth observing that Ennius is twice quoted by name in the *Bellum Hispaniense* (23.3, 31.7), something unusual in classical Latin historiography (cf. below, 91), and especially surprising in the Caesarian corpus, given the relative plainness of its writing. The *Annals'* status as the iconic epic of Roman history, regularly taught in schools (until superseded in Livy's own day by the *Aeneid*), may be relevant here: cf. n. 14 above.

[19] In addition Polybius quotes Homer at 15.16.3: Livy 30.35.8–9 draws on that passage, but also reworks it in such a way that the point of the quotation is no longer relevant (see 240–2 below).

This passage comes from the opening phase of the battle of Zama, and is important if we are to understand the difference between Polybius and Livy's interpretation of that battle, as I shall discuss in Chapter 3. But for the moment we need simply to focus on Polybius' quotation, which is partly verbatim and partly paraphrased from the opening of the first pitched battle between the Trojan army and the Greeks in the *Iliad* (4.437–8, though Polybius has slightly altered it—the first half of his second line is from *Iliad* 2.804):[20]

οὐ γὰρ πάντων ἦεν ὁμὸς θρόος οὐδ' ἴα γῆρυς,
ἀλλὰ γλῶσσ' ἐμέμικτο, πολύκλητοι δ' ἔσαν ἄνδρες.

For there was not a common tongue to all of them, nor their speech one,
But their language was mixed, and men were called from many lands.

There are various different—indeed contradictory—explanations that we could give for Livy's omission. It might be that he was not interested in having literary allusions at all, but preferred his narrative to proceed without that sort of texture. Alternatively, it might be that he would in principle have been happy to have a literary allusion, but that he specifically shied away from alluding to a Greek text, much as Cicero in his speeches rarely alludes directly to Greek literature, though he is willing to incorporate references to at least some genres of Latin literature (below, 91). Alternatively, it might be that, while removing the overt quotation, he wished to retain a covert allusion to Homer which would be recognizable by at least some of his readers, though in that case one would still need to consider why he preferred his allusion to be covert rather than overt.

What may help us decide between these possibilities is that we have here something rare: namely a test-case for the existence and identifiability of a Homeric allusion where we can be certain that the author was aware of the possibility of relating this particular passage of Homer to his text—because he was reading the Homeric lines in his source, and had a direct decision whether or not to retain a reference to them. In this context, it may be relevant to do something which is usually frowned on in critical works, and offer anecdotal evidence from my own reading. When I first read Livy 30 some years ago, I was sufficiently struck by 30.34.1 to make a note of it as an allusion to that passage of *Iliad* 4. It was only long afterwards that I came to read Polybius 15, and realized that Livy demonstrably had those exact Homeric lines in front of him when writing this passage. Such anecdotes relying on the unattested word of a single individual are admittedly only of limited evidential value; but if the

---

[20] On Polybius' use of the quotation here see D'Huys (1990), who also shows how Polybius' account is part of a wider literary *topos* of battle cries.

honesty of the report can be accepted provisionally, one modern reader could recognize the Homeric background from Livy alone. It seems a reasonable conclusion that at least some educated Romans, whose knowledge of the *Iliad* is likely to have been superior to mine, would have done the same. It therefore also seems a reasonable conclusion that Livy was writing the passage in the expectation that at least some of his readers would view his narrative in the light of Homer.

What in the passage encourages that identification? The match between the situation in Homer and that in Livy is close in some respects, but not in others. This is a final battle, not an opening one; on the other hand it is the opening stage of the fighting in that battle. The contrast in Homer is between the silent Greeks and the discordant Trojans, whereas in Livy the Romans are not silent, but shouting in unison. But the Carthaginians are like the Trojans in being multi-ethnic and multilingual, and above all Livy's phrase *congruens clamor . . . dissonae, ut gentium multarum discrepantibus linguis, voces*, while not corresponding precisely to Homer's Greek, incorporates most of the elements from it: the use of the triple terms *clamor, lingua*, and *voces* to match θρόος, γῆρυς, and γλῶσσα, and *gentium multarum* equivalent to the πολύκλητοι . . . ἄνδρες. The activation of the allusion is perhaps helped by a general sense that Roman stereotypes would most naturally align the Carthaginians with the Trojans as barbarian Easterners,[21] a stereotype which at least by the time of the Greek tragedians had become commonplace,[22] and which was then passed to Rome, despite the potential for tension with the Romans' legend of their own Trojan origins.[23] I shall discuss these issues further in Chapter 3; but for the moment we can simply note that Livy's ethnically loaded antithesis—employed more prejudicially than in either Homer or Polybius—both encourages the recognition of the allusion and is further reinforced by that allusion.

So the Homeric allusion can be recognized from Livy alone, despite his avoidance of the direct quotation. This gives us reason to conclude that Livy's omission was not because he was averse to literary allusions to Greek texts,

---

[21] Hall (1989: 21–32) argues that the tendency among both ancient and modern Homeric scholars to interpret Homer's Trojans in those terms is anachronistic, stemming from a prejudiced and partial reading of the poem. However H. Mackie, in a wider study of the contrasts between Greek and Trojan modes of speech in the *Iliad*, argues that while in general the differences are not presented to the Trojans' detriment, the specific passage here does imply Trojan inferiority (Mackie 1996: 10, 15–17); cf. also Ross (2005: esp. 305–7).

[22] Hall (1989: e.g. 101–2).

[23] On the Roman perception of the Trojans as barbarians see Dauge (1981: 416–17, 546); however, note also Erskine (2001) on the shifting complex of attitudes in both Greece and Rome towards the legendary Trojan past.

but rather because, unlike Polybius, he preferred to keep such allusions covert. We now need to consider why.

A definitive answer is of course unlikely to be forthcoming, but one consideration that may guide us is the distribution of quotations in Latin literature more generally. Livy is far from unusual in the rarity with which he quotes overtly the literature to which he is alluding. The same is true of other historians, even Sallust and Tacitus, whose texts are if anything more densely allusive than Livy's, as I shall discuss shortly.[24] We may contrast prose texts in other genres, such as dialogues and treatises, in which direct quotations and citations are commonplace: indeed even in Cicero's speeches, which generally avoid most varieties of literary allusion, it is not uncommon to find quotations from and references to drama.[25] Roman historiography in this respect aligns itself more with verse, and particularly verse narrative such as epic, in which, though the network of allusivity is immensely dense, those allusions are rarely marked by explicit quotation of a named source.

But there is a further consideration that needs mentioning as well. While this Homeric allusion is sufficiently obvious to be recognized even by some modern readers, the intrinsic indeterminacy of the device and the variability of Livy's likely readership mean that it is also to be expected that the allusion was overlooked by many readers even in antiquity. But the existence of Livy's source material means that readers did—potentially—have another way to discover the allusion: for if they knew Polybius' text, they could read the overt reference to Homer there, and so be pointed to its covert relevance to the parallel passage of Livy. That might simply be an interesting accident: that an

---

[24] The major exception is Ammianus, who constantly quotes or alludes by name to his literary predecessors (cf. Kelly 2008: 182–4). This might be a function of the aesthetics of the time, where overt reworkings of the literary past were common: see the discussion in Kelly (2008: 214–20). Kelly wishes to mute the sense that Ammianus has broken with earlier literary aesthetics, arguing that the impression his work gives of a mosaic of allusion is largely the consequence of his being a late writer, and hence one whose sources survive in greater quantities. However, Kelly does not note that in his use of quotation Ammianus demonstrably marks a break from his surviving Latin predecessors. Ammianus' Greek background also may not be irrelevant here, since his practice conforms more closely to Greek than to Latin historiography, though we should also remember that much Latin historiography has been lost, and he may well have had Latin precedents of which we are unaware.

[25] On literary quotation in Cicero see Jocelyn (1973), who argues that its relative absence from the speeches was owing to its being felt incongruent with Roman dignity; the partial exception for drama was because it was more deeply rooted in Roman tradition; the density of quotation in the treatises and dialogues (he argues) draws on Greek practice. Roman historians manifestly do not follow Greek precedent in this respect; one might suggest that they too regarded overt literary references as out of keeping with the dignity of their genre, but the degree of covert allusion, which has no real parallel in oratory, suggests that they are seeking quite a different effect, one closer to poetic than to oratorical practice.

ancient scholar with a suitably equipped library could, like his modern counterpart, research the background to Livy's writing. But it is also worth observing the parallel between this and the common allusive technique in verse sometimes known as 'double allusion', where the author in the course of alluding to one source will also allude to the source of that source.[26] Were Livy actually assuming that some of his readers would be viewing his text in the light of Polybius, this parallel would be more or less exact. In Section 2.2 I shall be showing that this is indeed the case; for the moment the possibility simply needs to be borne in mind.

Bearing it in mind, let us move to look at Polybius 10.20.6–7 and Livy 26.51.7–8, where Scipio after his capture of New Carthage is preparing his troops for the next stage of their campaign:

λοιπὸν τῶν μὲν πεζικῶν στρατοπέδων κατὰ τοὺς πρὸ τῆς πόλεως τόπους χρωμένων ταῖς μελέταις καὶ ταῖς γυμνασίαις, τῶν δὲ ναυτικῶν δυνάμεων κατὰ θάλατταν ταῖς ἀναπείραις καὶ ταῖς εἰρεσίαις, τῶν δὲ κατὰ τὴν πόλιν ἀκονώντων τε καὶ χαλκευόντων καὶ τεκταινομένων, καὶ συλλήβδην ἁπάντων σπουδαζόντων περὶ τὰς τῶν ὅπλων κατασκευάς, οὐκ ἔσθ᾽ ὃς οὐκ ἂν εἶπε κατὰ τὸν Ξενοφῶντα τότε θεασάμενος ἐκείνην τὴν πόλιν ἐργαστήριον εἶναι πολέμου.

Furthermore with the infantry exercising and training in the area in front of the city, and the fleet practising and rowing on the sea, and the people in the city engaging in sharpening and forging and carpentry, and in short with everyone enthusiastically working on weapons, there is no one who, seeing this then, would not say (in Xenophon's words) that that city was a workshop of war.

haec extra urbem terra marique corpora simul animosque ad bellum acuebant. urbs ipsa strepebat apparatu belli, fabris omnium generum in publicam officinam inclusis. dux cuncta pari cura obibat. nunc in classe ac navali erat, nunc cum legionibus decurrebat, nunc operibus adspiciendis tempus dabat, quaeque in officinis quaeque in armamentario ac navalibus fabrorum multitudo plurima in singulos dies certamine ingenti faciebat.

These things outside the city by land and sea sharpened bodies and minds alike for war. The city itself resounded with the workings of war, with every kind of craftsman confined in public workshops. The general inspected everything with equal care. At one moment he was with the fleet and dockyard, at another he drilled with the legions, at another he spent time reviewing the works, and the things which every day the vast crowd of craftsmen made with tremendous rivalry in the workshops and in the armoury and docks.

---

[26] For the terminology see McKeown (1987: 37–45). Nelis (2001) provides an exceptionally comprehensive demonstration of the pervasiveness of this technique in Virgil with respect to Apollonius and Homer.

There is a significant difference between this and the Homeric allusion in Book 30 just discussed. Here, unlike in the Homeric case, the specific words that Polybius quotes from Xenophon are not taken over into Livy's text. This on the face of things makes it less likely that any reader would relate Livy's text to Xenophon's since, with or without Polybius, the relevant cues are not present in the Latin.

However, a closer examination of Polybius' use of Xenophon might lead to a different conclusion. The Xenophon passage is *Hellenica* 3.4.16–18 (*Agesilaus* 1.25–7 is similar), and describes the preparations of the Spartan king Agesilaus for his campaign against Persia:

ἐκ δὲ τούτου ἐπειδὴ ἔαρ ὑπέφαινε, συνήγαγε μὲν ἅπαν τὸ στράτευμα εἰς Ἔφεσον·
ἀσκῆσαι δ᾽ αὐτὸ βουλόμενος ἆθλα προύθηκε...ἐκ τούτου δὲ παρῆν ὁρᾶν τὰ μὲν
γυμνάσια πάντα μεστὰ ἀνδρῶν τῶν γυμναζομένων, τὸν δ᾽ ἱππόδρομον τῶν
ἱππαζομένων, τοὺς δὲ ἀκοντιστὰς καὶ τοὺς τοξότας μελετῶντας. ἀξίαν δὲ καὶ ὅλην
τὴν πόλιν ἐν ᾗ ἦν θέας ἐποίησεν· ἥ τε γὰρ ἀγορὰ ἦν μεστὴ παντοδαπῶν καὶ ἵππων καὶ
ὅπλων ὠνίων, οἵ τε χαλκοτύποι καὶ οἱ τέκτονες καὶ οἱ χαλκεῖς καὶ οἱ σκυτοτόμοι καὶ οἱ
ζωγράφοι πάντες πολεμικὰ ὅπλα κατεσκεύαζον, ὥστε τὴν πόλιν ὄντως οἴεσθαι πολέμου
ἐργαστήριον εἶναι. ἐπερρώσθη δ᾽ ἄν τις κἀκεῖνο ἰδών, Ἀγησίλαον μὲν πρῶτον, ἔπειτα δὲ
καὶ τοὺς ἄλλους στρατιώτας ἐστεφανωμένους ἀπὸ τῶν γυμνασίων ἀπιόντας...

After this when spring was appearing, he assembled the whole army at Ephesus; and wanting to train it he offered prizes...As a result it was possible to see all the gymnasia full of men exercising, the hippodrome full of men riding, and spearsmen and archers practising. He in fact made the whole city he was in into a spectacle. The agora was full of all sorts of horses and weapons for sale, and coppersmiths and carpenters and smiths and leather-cutters and painters were all preparing weapons for war, so that one would actually think the city to be a workshop of war. And one would be heartened by seeing this: Agesilaus first, and then his other soldiers, coming garlanded from the gymnasia...

We should first note that Polybius is drawing on Xenophon here in a way that goes beyond the short phrase he quotes. The broad organization of the passage is the same, moving from military training to the craftsmen preparing for war; and in particular Polybius' χαλκευόντων καὶ τεκταινομένων, καὶ συλλήβδην ἁπάντων σπουδαζόντων περὶ τὰς τῶν ὅπλων κατασκευάς is similar in both general structure and vocabulary to Xenophon's οἵ τε χαλκοτύποι καὶ οἱ τέκτονες...πάντες πολεμικὰ ὅπλα κατεσκεύαζον.

Livy does not take over this phrase, though he more or less reproduces Polybius' general organization. But more striking is that although Livy's account is less close to Xenophon's linguistically, a number of the changes that he makes to Polybius have the effect of aligning the situation here more directly with Xenophon's description. One of the points that Xenophon makes is that Agesilaus has pressed into service not only those like smiths or carpenters whom one would expect to be useful in war, but every craftsman available, even painters; Polybius drops that idea, but Livy reintroduces it with *fabris omnium generum in publicam officinam inclusis*. In Xenophon, the account of the craftsmen preparing for war is followed by a reference to Agesilaus himself engaging in military training. Polybius gives Scipio only a supervisory role, but Livy describes him participating directly, a description that comes at precisely the same point in the passage as Xenophon's. Livy's phrase 'sharpened bodies and minds at once for war' does not correspond to anything in Polybius, but is close to something Xenophon says slightly later in the passage: *Hellenica* 3.4.20 = *Agesilaus* 1.28 ὅπως ... τὰ σώματα καὶ τὴν γνώμην παρασκευάζοιντο ὡς ἀγωνιούμενοι ('so that ... they might prepare bodies and minds for fighting'). In other words, Livy neither quotes Xenophon nor reproduces the specific aspects of the imitation of Xenophon from Polybius, but rewrites Polybius in such a way that his Scipio looks more like Xenophon's Agesilaus than Polybius' did.

What makes this especially interesting is that in this case it would be more or less impossible to find the Xenophon parallel from Livy's text independently. While the situations described are not dissimilar, in the absence of any strongly distinctive linguistic markers there is nothing that would highlight that aspect of the passage and make it stand out as anything more than the incidental similarity of behaviour by two outstanding generals. We could call this another 'double allusion', but it is an unexpected variant on the technique—one almost might call it a 'parasitic allusion'. In the typical 'double allusion' it is possible to recognize both earlier passages alluded to from the final text alone. In this case the earliest passage, Xenophon, is on the face of things not alluded to in Livy's text at all. It is only by going back to Polybius that one discovers the significance of the Xenophon parallel, and only once it is discovered via Polybius can one recognize the additional elements from Xenophon that Livy incorporates.

If it is accepted that Livy is drawing ultimately on Xenophon here, what is the effect of that? It highlights the broader similarity between the situations of Scipio and Agesilaus: both inspirational leaders close to the start of their careers as generals, with their first significant victory behind them; Scipio is aligned with the (by now legendary) Spartan military training. More particularly, Agesilaus here is preparing for the next stage of his invasion of the Persian empire, just as Scipio is planning his campaign against the Carthaginians: once again, the Carthaginians are tacitly aligned with stereotypical Easterners. This is thus not dissimilar to the implications of the Homeric allusion in Book 30 discussed above. But the fact that in this case the allusion is to an historical source raises another possible consideration as well: the idea that, whether or not acting in conscious imitation, a commander of the quality of Scipio will repeat key features from Agesilaus' successful strategy, by mobilizing all available forces and by personally participating in the training he puts his troops through.[27] The connection between the two literary texts thus mirrors a similar connection in the real world—or rather, Livy encourages the reader to think that it does, since there is no evidence beyond Livy's description for Scipio engaging in so precise a set of Agesilaus-like activities at all.

The remaining two passages where Polybius' quotations are omitted by Livy can be dealt with more briefly. Polybius 3.94.4 describes Fabius' recognition of Hannibal's trick to escape him (tying torches to the horns of oxen so that they resemble an army), and once again quotes Homer;[28] once again the passage is imitated by Livy 22.18.1, with the Homeric words turned into part of Livy's direct narrative.[29] But in this case it does not seem as likely that the Homeric background could be recognized from Livy's Latin alone, since it is a short and unremarkable phrase. Here, as before, it is possible that the reader of Livy can discover the Homeric background from Polybius, and if so a certain parallel could be drawn between the situations. The Homeric phrase is from *Odyssey* 10.258 (= 10.232 in some MSS), and describes why Eurylochus does not fall into Circe's trap to transform Odysseus' sailors into pigs, and so we could note that Hannibal is broadly aligned with Circe, the archetype of the untrustworthy and tempting witch; we might also note that the trick that he is employing involves representing animals as humans, so bears a passing resemblance to Circe's transformation of Odysseus' sailors in the other direction. But in this case the parallels are far less close than either of the other examples we have considered, and in as much as there is any point of contact, the similarity is already implied more strongly in Polybius, who after all supplies the actual quotation, and there is nothing to suggest that Livy is drawing further on the Odyssean passage or highlighting it in any way.

Finally we come to Polybius 9.21, describing the positions of the Romans and the Carthaginians at the turning point of the war: κατὰ τὸν ποιητὴν ἄμα λύπην καὶ χαρὰν ὑποτρέχειν εἰκὸς ἦν τὰς ἑκάστων ψυχάς ('as the poet says, it was reasonable that grief and joy at the same time came over the souls of

---

[27] Compare Woodman (1979: 153).

[28] Φάβιος δὲ τὰ μὲν ἀπορούμενος ἐπὶ τῷ συμβαίνοντι καὶ κατὰ τὸν ποιητὴν οἰσσάμενος δόλον εἶναι . . . ἦγε τὴν ἡσυχίαν ἐπὶ τῷ χάρακι καὶ προσεδέχετο τὴν ἡμέραν—'But Fabius, confused by what was happening and (as the poet says) "thinking it a trick" . . . kept quietly within the palisades and waited for day.'

[29] *hunc tumultum sensit Fabius; ceterum et insidias esse ratus et ab nocturno utique abhorrens certamine suos munimentis tenuit*—Fabius noticed this confusion, but both thinking it a trap and in any case shying from a night-time battle, kept his men within the palisades.

each'). This passage is substantially expanded by Livy 26.37.2–4, though retaining the paradoxical combination of emotions:

nam Romanis et in provinciis hinc in Hispania adversae res, hinc prosperae in Sicilia luctum et laetitiam miscuerant; et in Italia cum Tarentum amissum damno et dolori tum arx cum praesidio retenta praeter spem gaudio fuit, et terrorem subitum pavoremque urbis Romae obsessae et oppugnatae Capua post dies paucos capta in laetitiam vertit.

After all, for the Romans and in the provinces on one side defeat in Spain, on the other success in Sicily had mixed grief and happiness, and in Italy while the loss of Tarentum was a source of damage and misery, the unexpected retention of the citadel with its garrison was a source of joy, and the sudden terror and panic of the city of Rome under siege and assault was turned to happiness by the capture of Capua a few days later.

My argument about the earlier passages indicates that we need to consider not only whether the quotation is recognizable from Livy alone, but also how Livy might reflect its wider context both in Polybius and the original author. This of course requires a clear identification of the original author. According to Walbank, the Polybius passage is 'an inaccurate recollection' of Homer *Odyssey* 19.471: τὴν δ' ἅμα χάρμα καὶ ἄλγος ἕλε φρένα ('joy and grief simultaneously took hold of her mind'), describing Eurycleia's recognition of Odysseus.[30] If so, it appears that little if anything survives of it in Livy. The bare reference to a person experiencing 'joy and grief' in combination is not at all distinctive: Sallust, *Cat.* 61.9 gives two such pairs, for example (*laetitia maeror, luctus atque gaudia agitabantur*), and three of these words appear in Livy here, though not sufficiently juxtaposed to suggest a Sallustian allusion either. And the situation in Homer is so far removed from that of the Romans and Carthaginians that the wider context seems irrelevant too. However, Walbank may well be wrong to suggest that Polybius is alluding to Homer here. It is true that the unqualified phrase κατὰ τὸν ποιητήν often marks a Homeric reference, but it does not inevitably do so: for example at Aristotle *EN* 1154b29 and Dio Chrysostom *Or.* 4.82 it is used to introduce quotations from Euripides. And in this case the fact that there is virtually no linguistic overlap makes any connection to Homer dubious, even granted that (as we have already seen) Polybius' quotations are not always accurate. It seems more likely that the quotation in Polybius is not from Homer, but some other, lost, work, and its appositeness to the current situation and the consequent possibility that Livy's version draws on it in greater detail are therefore issues that we cannot resolve.

[30] Walbank (1967: 149).

Livy's abandonment of direct quotations from Polybius thus illustrates the complexity of the issues raised by studies of allusivity in historians. Even while eschewing the quotations, he sometimes—but not always—builds them into a wider allusive network. We find direct allusions to earlier writers not unlike those in poets; but we also find allusions that can only be appreciated if we recognize them via the historian's source material. Sometimes the allusion is marked linguistically, but at other times it appears more from similarity of action[31] than any specifics of the language used. Some of the allusions are to verse, but others are to historical texts, and these can have extra implications, not merely indicating broad parallels between different historical situations, but suggesting that events in real life are organizing themselves according to certain set patterns.

These features make allusions in historians potentially richer than has often been appreciated, but it also raises difficult issues about how they are to be identified. We do not possess many of Livy's sources, so it is rare that we can expect guidance of the sort I have been discussing over the last few pages— and of course we should not expect that all, or even most, allusions would have been mediated via his sources anyway. Allusions marked solely by parallel historical circumstances have the problem that most historical events parallel a large number of other historical events in some respects but not in others, so even if a reader may note parallels, extra reasons are needed before those parallels could be regarded as relevant to the interpretation of the text (after all, readers will often spot historical parallels which the author certainly could not have been aware of, because the events occurred after the author was writing). If an allusion to a specific text is marked linguistically that is less of a problem (subject to the general caveat that some linguistic markers of allusion may be less clear than others, or less clear to some readers than to others). However, the style of many prose texts is not always conducive to dense linguistic allusion. Wills's important study of repetition as an allusive figure in Roman poetry bases itself on a discussion of 'markers': all texts are in some way marked with a variety of devices, but only rare devices or rare combinations of devices will be sufficient to activate an allusion linguistically.[32] Prose intrinsically has fewer such devices available to it, lacking the resources of, for example, metre and line-numbers; moreover, most prose writers tend to limit their uses of other devices because of their poetic associations. It is no accident that studies of allusion in Latin historiography have overwhelmingly focused on Sallust, Tacitus, and Ammianus, all three of whom are writers with

---

[31] I draw this phrase from Nelis (2001: e.g. 27–8).

[32] Wills (1996: esp. 15–41). Note Wills (1996: 33): 'In order to carry an allusion, a device cannot be too widespread or the point of reference is soon obscured and the boldness muted'.

highly anomalous styles, crammed with recondite vocabulary and eccentric locutions. Sallust's *Catiline* repeatedly and recognizably reworks material closely from (among others) Thucydides and Cato; in Livy on the Hannibalic War, a text more than fifteen times as long, there appear to be far fewer allusions with anything like that degree of linguistic recognizability.[33] This is not unconnected with the relative smoothness of his style:[34] as we have already seen with 22.18.1 (above, 95), even in a case when Livy has a Homeric passage in front of him that he is directly translating, the phrase he uses is bland enough to conceal the Homeric source rather than drawing attention to it.

If that is so, how can we expect a reader to identify meaningful allusions in Livy at all? First, although he rarely marks allusions linguistically by comparison with verse (or even with more linguistically adventurous historians), such allusions are sometimes present and recognizable. Second, Livy will sometimes encourage the selection of particular historical parallels out of the endless possibilities by directly referring to the parallel in a related context, so highlighting those particular events as especially pertinent. Third, sometimes the parallel is reinforced by structural features that he draws from an earlier source: for example, he may insert a speech on a similar topic at a similar point in his narrative.

Fourth, and most importantly, he may do more than one of these at once. For example, the possibility that a structural parallel signals an allusion is strengthened if there are phrases or sentences that are close to those of the parallel passage, while conversely a linguistic similarity which may appear relatively superficial or tentative if taken in isolation may be converted into a firmer allusion by its association with other allusive features, whether linguistic or structural. In particular, in cases where Livy has already drawn recognizably on a particular text, that text is now 'foregrounded', making it easier for it to be recalled again soon afterwards.[35] I have indeed already mentioned

---

[33] It is worth noting in this context the elder Seneca's report (*Contr.* 9.1.14) that Livy criticized Sallust for translating a phrase of pseudo-Demosthenes (though Seneca wrongly attributes the original to Thucydides)—both for translating the phrase at all and for translating it badly (*et tamquam translatam et tamquam corruptam dum transfertur*).

[34] This is a simplified statement of a complex and nuanced issue, since 'style' is a shorthand covering a large number of features, including vocabulary, word order, syntax, and sentence structure, and Livy uses any and all of these distinctively at different times. The difference between Livy's handling of them on the one hand, and Sallust's and Tacitus' on the other, is more in degree than in kind. It also appears that Livy may have to some extent changed his practice, since his earlier books have been argued to be more 'Sallustian' and 'poetic' than the later ones. Of the large bibliography on this question, Tränkle (1968) is fundamental; Oakley (1997: 128–51) gives the fullest recent analysis.

[35] Cf. Wills (1996: 26–9).

one example of this in a different context. The comparison between Livy's Carthaginians and Homer's Trojans at Zama (30.34.1) is reintroduced at 30.43.12, where the grief of the Carthaginians at the sudden sight of their ships burning is described as being 'as mournful to the Carthaginians as if Carthage itself were burning' (*conspectum repente incendium tam lugubre fuisse Poenis quam si ipsa Carthago arderet*: cf. above, 12). This recalls *Iliad* 22.410–11: τῷ δὲ μάλιστ' ἄρ' ἔην ἐναλίγκιον ὡς εἰ ἅπασα / Ἴλιος ὀφρυόεσσα πυρὶ σμύχοιτο κατ' ἄκρης ('And it was exactly as if all of towering Troy were being destroyed by fire from top to bottom'). Here the possibility of an allusion is signalled by the poetic register of *lugubre*[36] and by the simile (a relatively rare device in Livy); it is focused specifically on Homer not only by the parallel situations of the Carthaginians in defeat and the Trojans after the death of Hector, but also by the fact that the earlier Homeric allusion has already prepared us for the broad alignment between Carthage and Troy.

None of this, of course, is an exact science. Allusion, as has often been remarked, is frequently indeterminate to a greater or lesser degree.[37] It is indeterminate because there is no precise limit to how similar a phrase or linguistic usage or parallel situation has to be in order to be seen as meaningfully evoking another phrase or usage or situation, nor to how recently a particular model has to have been evoked in order for that text to be foregrounded for future allusions. Classicists have the additional problem that many of the texts to which ancient writers might be alluding no longer survive; so one is often faced with doubts whether a passage with a rare feature that might be allusive is primarily alluding to another passage which shares some aspect of it, or whether both passages might be more closely dependent on a lost original. The distinction between alluding to another historical event in general and alluding to a particular historian who related that event may also be hard to pin down firmly in many cases. So far my discussion has mainly confined itself to clear-cut cases: cases where the allusion is confirmed by explicit quotation of the passage either by Livy himself or by his Polybian source, but as we shall see, some of the most interesting examples of allusion in Livy 21–30 are less easily pinned down.

Perhaps the best-known example of an allusion in these books comes close to the opening: the character sketch of Hannibal (21.4.3–9):

numquam ingenium idem ad res diversissimas, parendum atque imperandum, habilius fuit. itaque haud facile discerneres, utrum imperatori an exercitui carior esset:

---

[36] Cf. Harrison (1991: 147).

[37] E.g. Hinds (1998: 17–51), Edmunds (2001: 150–4). It should be noted that this is not a problem for intentionalist understandings of allusion, since intentions are themselves frequently indeterminate: see Heath (2002: 66–8).

neque Hasdrubal alium quemquam praeficere malle, ubi quid fortiter ac strenue agendum esset, neque milites alio duce plus confidere aut audere. plurimum audaciae ad pericula capessenda, plurimum consilii inter ipsa pericula erat. nullo labore aut corpus fatigari aut animus vinci poterat. caloris ac frigoris patientia par; cibi potionisque desiderio naturali, non voluptate modus finitus; vigiliarum somnique nec die nec nocte discriminata tempora: id, quod gerendis rebus superesset, quieti datum; ea neque molli strato neque silentio accersita; multi saepe militari sagulo opertum humi iacentem inter custodias stationesque militum conspexerunt. vestitus nihil inter aequales excellens; arma atque equi conspiciebantur. equitum peditumque idem longe primus erat; princeps in proelium ibat, ultimus conserto proelio excedebat. has tantas viri virtutes ingentia vitia aequabant: inhumana crudelitas, perfidia plus quam Punica, nihil veri, nihil sancti, nullus deum metus, nullum ius iurandum, nulla religio.

Never was there a temperament more suited simultaneously for things that are utterly different: obedience and command. As a result, you would have found it hard to tell whether the general or the army was fonder of him. When anything needed doing that required courage and energy, he was Hasdrubal's first choice to be in charge of it, nor was there any other commander in whom the soldiers trusted more or for whom they showed more daring. He was the boldest at encountering dangers, but the finest strategist when in actual danger. No toil could weary his body or subdue his mind. He could endure heat and cold alike. He limited his eating and drinking to the requirements of nature, not pleasure. He held watch and slept without reference to day or night. He took his rest in the time left over from work, not when he had available a soft couch or a peaceful moment. Many people frequently saw him lying on the ground among the soldiers' guardposts and encampments, covered by a military cloak. There was nothing in his costume to mark him out from his contemporaries; it was his weapons and horses which were distinctive. He was without question pre-eminent both as cavalryman and infantryman. He led from the front in battle, and was the last to depart once battle had been joined. But these outstanding virtues were matched by the man's massive vices: his bestial cruelty, his treachery that even surpassed the typical Carthaginian. He had no regard for truth, none for sanctity, no fear of the gods, no respect for an oath, no religion.

It is not difficult to relate this long account of the chief antagonist at the opening of a work to Sallust's monographs. Both the *Catiline* and the *Jugurtha* contain character sketches of their key figures early in their narratives:

Sallust, *Cat.* 5.1–4: L. Catilina, nobili genere natus, fuit magna vi et animi et corporis, sed ingenio malo pravoque...corpus patiens inediae algoris vigiliae, supra quam quoiquam credibile est. animus audax subdolus varius, quoius rei lubet simulator ac dissimulator, alieni adpetens sui profusus, ardens in cupiditatibus; satis eloquentiae, sapientiae parum.

Catiline was of noble birth; a man of great mental and physical strength, but with an evil and perverted character...his body could endure incredible amounts of hunger, cold, and sleeplessness. His mind was bold, cunning and mobile; he could feign or conceal anything; he was greedy for others' property, extravagant with his own, burning in lusts; of adequate eloquence but too little wisdom.

Sallust, *Jug.* 6.1: qui ubi primum adolevit, pollens viribus, decora facie, sed multo maxume ingenio validus, non se luxu neque inertiae corrumpendum dedit, sed, uti mos gentis illius est, equitare iaculari, cursu cum aequalibus certare, et quom omnis gloria anteiret, omnibus tamen carus esse . . . plurumum facere, minumum ipse de se loqui.

When he first grew up, he was strong, handsome, but above all powerful of mind; he did not give himself to be corrupted by luxury or sloth, but, in the manner of his people, rode and shot; he competed at running with his contemporaries, and although he surpassed them all in glory, they all loved him . . . He did much, and spoke little of himself.

Sallust, *Jug.* 7.4-5: nam Iugurtha, ut erat inpigro atque acri ingenio, ubi naturam P. Scipionis, qui tum Romanis imperator erat, et morem hostium cognovit, multo labore multaque cura, praeterea modestissume parendo et saepe obviam eundo periculis in tantam claritudinem brevi pervenerat, ut nostris vehementer carus, Numantinis maxumo terrori esset. ac sane, quod difficillumum in primis est, et proelio strenuos erat et bonus consilio . . .

Jugurtha's mind was tireless and keen, and so, when he got to know the character of Scipio (who was then the Roman general) and the behaviour of the enemy, by his considerable hard work and considerable diligence, by his sensible obedience and willingness to go into danger, he soon became so famous that he was greatly loved by the Romans and feared by the Numidians. Indeed, he was that thing that is hardest to achieve: an energetic fighter and a good strategist . . .

The similarity between these passages and Livy's account of Hannibal is marked, despite the fact that there is little direct verbal overlap. The fact that they occupy similar positions in the narrative is obvious; slightly less obvious is that Livy here writes in a more Sallustian style than usual, with historic infinitives, brief sentences linked paratactically, and abrupt and pregnant phrases.[38] And thematically, rather than purely verbally, the match is very close: Hannibal appears to be a mixture of Catiline and Jugurtha. He has the physical endurance of Catiline (the same three areas of hunger, cold, and sleeplessness are mentioned), as well as his mixture of virtues and vices.[39] He is even closer to Jugurtha in his courage in battle, active powers as both

[38] Walsh (1973: 127).

[39] Cf. Clauss (1997: 170–2). Conceiving Catiline's character in these terms was admittedly not Sallust's invention: he is drawing on Cicero, who repeatedly refers in the *Catilinarians* to Catiline's exceptional endurance (Cic., *Cat.* 1.26, 2.9, 3.16), and in a later speech expounded at length on his paradoxical mixture of virtues and vices (Cic., *Cael.* 12–14). It is relevant to Livy, as we shall see, that this image of Catiline was historical, not merely a construct of Sallust's, and the Ciceronian background reinforces that key point. But the parallels between Sallust and Livy in the passage's position in the narrative and its linguistic manner make the Sallustian intertext particularly salient.

soldier and leader, his general popularity and the support he has from both his commander and his fellow soldiers. The fact that he, like Jugurtha, is an African is doubtless also relevant in establishing a link. As I showed in Chapter 1 (above, 10–15), Livy is setting up his narrative of the Hannibalic War as effectively a self-contained monograph, and the parallel that he introduces here with Sallust's monographs both reinforces that effect and is itself reinforced by it.

The further effect of the Sallustian imitation is more controversial. According to Clauss, the parallel between Catiline and Hannibal points to the threat Hannibal poses to *Carthage*, a threat analogous to the one that Catiline represented to Rome.[40] That Livy shows Hannibal as a threat to Carthage is clear, as I shall discuss below, and this may perhaps, as Clauss argues, form one part of the Catilinarian subtext. However, to treat this as the primary focus overlooks the even closer Jugurthan allusion interwoven with the Catilinarian one. Sallust set up his two antagonists as parallel iconic figures in relation to Rome, rather than in relation to their own states: in the case of Jugurtha, while he too incidentally destroys his own kingdom, it is his corruption of (and by) Rome that is at the centre of Sallust's narrative. Both Jugurtha and Catiline fundamentally threaten Rome, the former from the outside, the latter from within, and by uniting them in Hannibal Livy likewise places the primary focus on the parallel threat to Rome that he poses, especially since all three passages appear at the start of narratives which are predominantly Rome-centred.

What is the nature of Hannibal's challenge to Rome? Catiline and Jugurtha fight against the Romans, but the danger is not primarily military. The true threat comes because of their involvement with the vicious corruption which (Sallust claims) took hold of Rome after the fall of Carthage. Catiline is an aristocrat whose ancestry stretches back to the time of Rome's glory (cf. *Cat.* 31.7, 60.7); his virtues reflect that, but have been utterly perverted by the viciousness of the contemporary world which he both mirrors and encourages. Jugurtha comes to Roman society as a virtuous outsider and is himself corrupted by its venality, venality which he exploits in order to corrupt Rome further (*Jug.* 8.1).[41] Hannibal is likewise a fundamental threat to Rome, but on the face of things a more straightforwardly external one: a great general who comes close to destroying the empire through military victories.[42] However, as I shall be arguing in Chapter 3, the threat which in

---

[40] Clauss (1997: 175–81), followed by Rossi (2004: 376–8).

[41] This reading of Jugurtha's character and development has been questioned, e.g. by Vretska (1955: 29–30), but see Levene (1992: 59–60).

[42] Cf. Clauss (1997: 180–1).

Livy's view Hannibal represents to Rome goes beyond the simple question of military prowess: he is also a model that the Romans will have to copy if they are to defeat him—even though incorporating Hannibalic behaviour into Rome may endanger Roman morality. This issue will be discussed in much more detail later, but for the moment we simply need to observe that the Sallustian analogy raises the possibility that Roman morals as well as Roman power are at stake here.

This leads to a further issue. With the parallel discussed above between Agesilaus and Scipio, the allusive relationship between the texts corresponds, at least potentially, to a real-world relationship between the characters, since Scipio could theoretically have been imitating Agesilaus directly. The situation here is similar, but also reversed, because Jugurtha and Catiline are of course chronologically long after Hannibal, even though the texts in which they appear and which Livy is imitating here are necessarily prior to his own. In imitating Sallust Livy suggests Hannibal is not merely like Catiline and Jugurtha, but specifically is prefiguring them.[43] That of itself might not be more than a casual curiosity, were it not that both Sallust and Livy have a developmental model of Roman history: both see the disaster of the late Republic as the result of moral decline, as Livy indicated at the very start of his work. Livy's introduction of a Catiline/Jugurtha-like figure long before Catiline or Jugurtha existed points to a picture of that historical development that is interestingly different from the one assumed by Sallust. It does not—at least immediately—directly challenge Sallust, since the primary issue is Roman decline, and Hannibal is not a Roman; but if both Jugurtha and Catiline are replicating aspects of Hannibal's character, that fact alone significantly changes the terms in which Sallust's model of Roman history needs to be understood. How Livy ultimately worked that through is impossible to say in the absence of his own treatment of the Sallustian period, but, if we simply take his Hannibalic War narrative, we can see both obvious ways[44] and less obvious ones (as I shall discuss in Chapter 3) in which the programmatic hints offered here of his divergence from Sallust will be explored more thoroughly: moral problems are beginning earlier and develop more gradually and less schematically.

Even this relatively simple and long recognized allusion therefore contains a good deal of complexity. The significance of the Sallustian allusion is

---

[43] Cf. Clauss (1997: 180–2).

[44] To mention merely the most famous example, 25.40.1–2 identifies Marcellus' spoils from Syracuse as setting in motion a train of events that will lead to moral disaster for Rome herself (see below, 123–6, 208–9). By contrast, in all three of his works Sallust regards the period of the Second Punic War as a time of untrammelled virtue, and sees disaster setting in only with the destruction of Carthage in 146.

developed through intertwining allusions to two parallel Sallustian texts, rather than a single model, and the resulting passage has a complex relationship to the real world.[45]

Moreover, this is not the only place where we can see Livy responding to Sallust's moralistic reading of history. For example, his various narratives involving Capua repeatedly draw on Sallust—not surprisingly, perhaps, because his account of Capua explores the same themes of political and moral corruption which form the heart of Sallust's analysis (I shall discuss this further in Chapter 5). One can in particular note a number of verbal parallels between Sallust and Livy's description of the start of the Capuan revolt at the opening of Book 23.[46] The Capuan leader Pacuvius Calavius is described in the following terms: *senatum et sibi et plebi obnoxium Pacuvius Calavius fecerat, nobilis idem ac popularis homo, ceterum malis artibus nanctus opes* (23.2.2: 'Pacuvius Calavius had made the senate subservient to both himself and the people: he was a man at one and the same time noble and *popularis*, but who had obtained power by evil means'). This recalls the opening of Sallust's description of Catiline in *Cat.* 5.1 as *nobili genere natus . . . sed ingenio malo pravoque* ('born of a noble family . . . but of evil and perverted character'); the phrases *sibi obnoxium fecerat* and *malis artibus* are also Sallustian.[47] The Sallustian overtones are reinforced by the following sentence (23.2.3), where Pacuvius Calavius *plebem ratus per occasionem novandi res magnum*

---

[45] A harder issue to assess in this passage is that the phrase *cibi potionisque desiderio naturali, non voluptate modus finitus* has an unusually philosophical cast. The relationship between pleasure and fulfilment of need, and the limits that one should place on natural desires, were key issues in Hellenistic philosophical thought, and there is a surprisingly close parallel to Livy's wording here in Maximus of Tyre's attack on Epicureanism in *Oration* 33.3 (esp. μέχρι μὲν τούτων ἐστὶν λαβεῖν ὅρους ἡδονῶν, τὴν χρείαν αὐτήν—'up to this point it is possible to take one's limits on pleasures as need itself'; cf. also Clement of Alexandria, *Strom.* 2.20.118.6–7 = *SVF* III 405). Since we can discount the possibility that Maximus might have been reading Livy, the similarity of theme and language points to a common source, with Livy drawing on the extensive anti-Epicurean polemic that existed before his day (Seneca, *Ep.* 100.9 describes him as writing philosophically influenced dialogues, so he was presumably familiar with the literature). It is true that Epicureans would not have accepted the antithesis between 'pleasure' and 'need' found here, since they argued that pleasure was maximized if one limited oneself to the fulfilment of natural needs, but their opponents often misrepresented this point. Hannibal is thus represented as conforming—in this respect—to an Epicurean ideal, albeit one not characterized in precisely the terms that an Epicurean would use. See further Feldherr (2009) for a powerful and profound analysis of Livy's presentation of Hannibal in Book 21 through Epicurean language and imagery: Feldherr argues that Hannibal does not live up in all respects to Epicurean models, but that those respects in which he does live up to them are ones which expose the limits of Epicureanism as a philosophy.

[46] Several of the examples in this paragraph are drawn from a detailed discussion of the Capua episode in Glew (forthcoming). I am grateful to Professor Glew both for showing me his paper in advance of publication and for permission to cite it.

[47] *Cat.* 14.6; 3.4 and 13.5.

ausuram facinus ('thought that the people would use the opportunity for revolution to dare a great deed'). This once again appears to draw on the Sallustian account of Catiline, who tells his followers *animus ausus est maxumum atque pulcherrumum facinus incipere* (*Cat.* 20.3: 'my mind has dared to undertake the greatest and finest deed'); the phrase *novare res* is not itself Sallustian, but the related *res novae* is common in his work, and the topic helps focus the reader on the Sallustian theme of revolution. And more broadly, of course, the Capuans, with their soft and comfortable lifestyle (e.g. 23.2.1, 23.4.4), appear remarkably like the Romans in the state of corruption that Sallust describes in the *Catiline*, though here it is harder to see direct verbal parallels with Sallust. It is interesting to note that in a much later passage (25.13.7) the Capuans gather in supplies only *socordia neglegentiaque* ('with sloth and negligence'); Hanno accuses them of being worse than animals (*ne fames quidem, quae mutas accenderet bestias, curam eorum stimulare posset* – 'not even hunger, which fires brute beasts, could stimulate their concern'). *socordia* is a word Sallust likes, especially in pairings with other abstract nouns;[48] while the comparison with animals driven by hunger recalls the opening words of the *Catiline* (1.1–2, cf. 2.8), where animals are characterized as being driven by physical needs, which the human body shares, but which humans must seek to transcend. The allusion is signalled by a Sallustian theme combined with Sallustian phrasing, though with a certain irony, for the Capuans have not merely failed to transcend the limitations of their bodies, but have degenerated below them.

Here too none of this should suggest that Livy is imitating Sallust inertly: indeed, as I shall discuss in Chapter 5, the role played by the Capuans in general and Pacuvius Calavius in particular is more than a simple parable of luxury and corruption, and, as Glew argues, the interplay with the story of Catiline is more complex than might initially appear. But opening the narrative of Capua with that strong Sallustian colour provides a general framework within which the themes will be explored more intricately. We can observe further that Sallustian overtones in the context of the Capuans go beyond the corruption of their own state. Capua plays a central role in Livy's account of the war, because it is at Capua that Hannibal's troops are corrupted by luxury and thus sow the seeds of their defeat, a corruption famously described in 23.18.10–16: again the theme recalls the corruption of the Roman state through luxury in Sallust (e.g. *Cat.* 10–12), though here the language is not distinctively Sallustian. Less immediately obvious is that the Romans' reaction to the Capuan revolt itself recalls Sallust. At 23.35.5–9 Gracchus is in

---

[48] See e.g. *Cat.* 4.1, 52.29, 58.4; *Jug.* 2.4, 31.2, 70.5.

Campania with his newly enrolled army, an army that includes new recruits and volunteer ex-slaves purchased at public expense (cf. 22.57.11). In order to create an efficient force, he emphasizes to them their essential equality (23.35.7 *vetus miles tironi, liber voloni sese exaequari sineret*—'the veteran soldier should let himself be placed on a par with the recruit, the free man with the slave-volunteer'). The result is that (23.35.9):

ea non maiore cura praecepta ab ducibus sunt quam a militibus observata, brevique tanta concordia coaluerant omnium animi, ut prope in oblivionem veniret, qua ex condicione quisque esset miles factus.

This was followed by the soldiers no less carefully than it was instructed by the commanders, and soon everyone's minds had united with such concord that the class out of which each man had become a soldier was virtually forgotten.

The phrasing here is similar to two Sallustian passages. First, at *Cat.* 6.2 the coming together of the Trojans with the aboriginal Italians to found the city of Rome is described: *incredibile memoratu est quam facile coaluerint; ita brevi multitudo divorsa atque vaga concordia civitas facta erat* ('it is unbelievable to record how easily they united; so soon had a disparate and wandering mass become a state in concord'). Added to that, in *Jug.* 87.3 Marius forges an army out of veterans and new recruits to fight Jugurtha, and according to Sallust *sic brevi spatio novi veteresque coaluere, et virtus omnium aequalis facta* ('thus in a short space new and old united, and the virtue of all became equal'). The situation in Livy is obviously close to that faced by Marius, but it is verbally even closer to Sallust's description of the foundation of Rome in his earlier monograph, a foundation which the *Jugurtha* passage itself evokes,[49] and which in Livy's account (1.8.6, though the point is not explicit in Sallust) had itself involved uniting slave and free into a single city. Whereas their Capuan and Carthaginian opponents are in a state of corruption and decline, the Romans are effectively refounding their city and recreating the earliest stages of its virtue.

Naturally one should not overemphasize either the coherence or the solidity of the Sallustian allusions here. As I have already observed, the boundaries of allusion are indeterminate, and the evocation of Sallust here constantly fades in and out. In 23.18.10–16, for example, there is little that is directly Sallustian, but the similarity of subject matter, combined with the fact that we have already been alerted to the salience of the Sallustian intertext to Capua in the account of the revolt, means that for many readers he will be evoked somewhere in the background. The verbal similarities make the later passages 23.35.9 and 25.13.7 closer to Sallust—they would have to be if Sallust was to

---

[49] Cf. Koestermann (1971: 317).

be evoked at all, given how much later they appear and how much the context has changed. But for that very reason it is harder to unite them with the earlier allusions to create a single coherent picture of the way in which Livy is drawing on and responding to Sallust—or, at least, one could only do so by incorporating into the interpretation so many non-Sallustian passages that the Sallustian intertext would be pushed to the background. With a text the length of Livy's, an allusive relationship with a predecessor can only be maintained if the earlier text is constantly and repeatedly evoked. In the absence of that, each separate allusion is more likely to be interpreted in its immediate context, and without taking account of the implications of earlier evocations of the same author.

However, there may be occasions where there are reasons to unite allusions which are kept distant from one another.[50] I have already referred to the way in which the Carthaginians in defeat at the end of Book 30 are linked to Homer's Trojans (above, 98–9). As I discussed in Chapter 1, Book 30 in general repeatedly recalls Book 21, as part of the way Livy shapes this decade into a unity, and it is therefore not surprising that at the very start, also, we find the forthcoming war discussed in terms which appear to evoke the Trojan war, with Romans evoking Greeks and Carthage playing the role of Troy. An example of the first is 21.41.15, where Scipio encourages the Romans with the following words:

nec est alius ab tergo exercitus, qui, nisi nos vincimus, hosti obsistat, nec Alpes aliae sunt, quas dum superant, comparari nova possint praesidia. hic est obstandum, milites, velut si ante Romana moenia pugnemus.

Nor is there another army at our rear to block the enemy if we fail to win, nor are there other Alps, so that while they cross them, new garrisons can be raised. We must block them here, soldiers, as if we were fighting before the walls of Rome.

This has no counterpart in the speech of Scipio at Polybius 3.64, but is a clear imitation of the rallying cry of Ajax to the Greeks at *Iliad* 15.735-6: ἠέ τινάς φαμεν εἶναι ἀοσσητῆρας ὀπίσσω, / ἠέ τι τεῖχος ἄρειον, ὅ κ᾽ ἀνδράσι λοιγὸν ἀμύναι; ('Or do we think that there are some defenders behind us, or some better wall, which can ward off destruction from the men?').[51] The passages are close in both structure and sense. Livy, it is true, substitutes the Alps for Homer's walls, but that is itself pointed in light of the commonplace of the

---

[50] The general approach I take here, finding linguistic resemblances and parallel narrative structures which work together to set up a large-scale pattern of imitation, was famously pioneered in the study of Virgil's imitation of Homer by Knauer (1964).

[51] On this imitation see Doblhofer (1983: 146).

Alps being 'the walls of Italy', an image going back to Cato,[52] which Livy, probably following him, had employed directly at 21.35.9,[53] and had alluded to indirectly at 21.30.5, where Hannibal, before reaching the foot of the Alps, accuses his men of giving up 'at the very gates of the enemy' (*in ipsis portis hostium*).[54] The Alps function for Rome as a final line of defence, as the wall did for the retreating Greeks in the *Iliad*.

The imitation of Homer is pointed in another way also. While Livy aligns the Romans with Homer's Greeks, and hence implicitly the Carthaginians with the Trojans, he changes the circumstances. Ajax's point in Homer is that the Greeks are not fighting at home, so they have to rely on their own resources. Scipio claims the opposite: his army is the Romans' last line of defence for their own home.[55] However, it is even more important to see that Ajax is obviously wrong: the Greeks have not reached their last line of defence, because almost immediately Patroclus will sally out to rescue them. So too here Scipio's rallying-call will prove overdramatic. His army is not the Romans' final chance—indeed, not long after they are defeated at the Ticinus new troops arrive to reinforce them at the Trebia. Nor do the Alps prove the final physical barrier for Hannibal: before the end of the book he will attempt a similar crossing of the Appennines (21.58), only to be driven back when the conditions there 'almost surpassed the frightfulness of the Alps' (21.58.3 *Alpium prope foeditatem superaverit*; cf. below, 345–7). Not only the direct imitation, but also the parallel contexts implied by it, align the Romans with the ultimately victorious Greeks at Troy.

As for the equation of the Carthaginians with the Trojans, early in Book 21 Hannibal is opposed by the Carthaginian senator Hanno, who delivers a

[52] Cato, *Origines* fr. 85P = Servius, *ad Aen.* 10.13: *ipsas Alpes . . . quae secundum Catonem et Livium muri vice tuebantur Italiam* ('the Alps themselves . . . which according to Cato and Livy guarded Italy in the manner of a wall').

[53] *moeniaque eos tum transcendere non Italiae modo sed etiam urbis Romanae*—'and they were then crossing the walls not only of Italy but also of the city of Rome'. Polybius, himself perhaps reworking Cato, had used a slightly different image at this point: the Alps as 'the acropolis of all Italy' (3.54.2)—in other words, the Alps appear to be the stronghold rather than the outer defences (cf. Gärtner 1975: 165). Other examples of the image include Cic., *Prov. Cons.* 34, *Pis.* 81, *Phil.* 5.37; Strabo 6.4.1.

[54] Doblhofer (1983: 141–2).

[55] It is interesting in this context to note that Virgil, *Aen.* 9.782 imitates the same lines of Homer while transforming them in precisely the same way: *quos alios muros, quaeve ultra moenia habetis?* ('What other walls, what further bulwark do you have?'). The Trojans—here of course standing for Romans—are now citizens defending their home in Italy (Hardie 1994: 240). Unfortunately the precise chronology of Livy's and Virgil's writing is too uncertain to determine whether Livy might be alluding also to Virgil here, or Virgil to Livy, or whether both might be dependent on an earlier author who had transformed Homer in much the same way, or indeed whether it is merely a coincidence of two authors writing around the same time with similar interests.

speech warning the Carthaginians that allowing his aggression against Saguntum will lead to disaster for the Carthaginians themselves (21.10.10–11):

Carthagini nunc Hannibal vineas turresque admovet, Carthaginis moenia quatit ariete: Sagunti ruinae—falsus utinam vates sim—nostris capitibus incident, susceptumque cum Saguntinis bellum habendum cum Romanis est . . . hunc iuvenem tamquam furiam facemque huius belli odi ac detestor.

Now Hannibal is moving his mantlets and towers against Carthage; it is Carthage's walls that he is shattering with his ram. The ruins of Saguntum will topple on our heads (would that I might be a false prophet!), and the war begun against the Saguntines will inevitably be waged against the Romans . . . I loathe and abominate this young man as the Fury and torch of this war.

The poetic imagery here—the idea of Hannibal literally attacking his own city, the image of Hannibal as a Fury and a torch, and of Hanno himself as a *vates*—is unusually vivid for Livy. It also recalls vividly a famous mythological story: the story of the birth of Paris, when Hecuba dreamed that the child in her womb would destroy Troy itself.[56] According to most versions of that story, in her dream she imagined that she gave birth to a flaming torch that destroyed the city.[57] Livy speaks here about a 'Fury and torch', which might just be his own elaboration of the motif, since Furies and torches regularly go together.[58] But it is worth pointing out that there are other versions of the Hecuba story too. Pindar, *Paean* 8.11–12 (= B3.26–7 Rutherford) speaks of her giving birth to πυρφόρον ἐρι[. . . /ἑκατόγχειρα. The original editors, Grenfell and Hunt (*POxy* 841), restored the missing word as ἐρινύν—'a fire-bearing hundred-handed Fury'. Robert objected to this, mainly on the grounds that hundred-handed Furies are not otherwise attested in iconography, and proposed instead that ἐρι- is the beginning of an adjective like ἐρισφάραγον—'a fire-bearing loud-roaring Hundred-Hander'.[59] However, this is not a compelling argument, since fire-bearing Hundred-Handers do not seem to be attested iconographically either; in any case, the main point is that Pindar's version of Hecuba's dream has Paris represented not by a torch, but some sort of torch-bearing mythological creature. Also relevant may be Lycophron, *Alexandra* 86, a (typically) difficult passage in which Paris on his way to abduct Helen is described as γρυνὸν ἐπτερωμένον—'a winged torch'. The 'torch' clearly evokes Hecuba's dream; the scholiasts on the line suggest that 'winged' refers to the ship in which he is sailing to Sparta, but it carries

---

[56] Noted by Cipriani (1984: 78).
[57] So e.g. Euripides, *Tro.* 919–22; Ennius, *Alex.* (51–2 Jocelyn); Virgil, *Aen.* 7.319–20, 10.704–5; ps-Apollodorus 3.12.5.
[58] Cf. Horsfall (2000: 306).
[59] Robert (1914), followed by Rutherford (2001: 235–6).

strong overtones of the Furies, the beings whose regular attributes include both wings and torches. While obscure imagery is more or less par for the course in Lycophron, we should not discount the possibility that the description of Paris here is pointing to a version of Hecuba's dream in which he appears not as a torch, but as a winged being carrying one. One can further add into the mix Hyginus, *Fab.* 91, where Hecuba *vidit se facem ardentem parere, ex qua serpentes plurimos exisse* ('saw herself giving birth to a blazing torch, out of which came numerous snakes'). This is a bizarre image: one might guess that the text is corrupt, but no convincing emendation has been proposed. More likely is that Hyginus has (not for the only time) misunderstood something in his Greek source, in which case the combination of torches and serpents again points to a source using the iconography of the Furies.

None of these passages is conclusive, but if one puts them together, it looks reasonable to suggest that in an alternative version of the story Hecuba dreamed that she gave birth to a Fury (or some other mythological creature resembling one). If so, when Livy has Hanno describe Hannibal as a 'Fury and torch' the phrase is more than merely casual: in alluding to the famous story of Hecuba's dream, he artfully combines two different versions of it.

A further implication of the allusion is worth mentioning briefly. The role of Hanno in the story fits a common pattern that we find both within and outside historiography: the pattern of the 'tragic warner', who advises an overreaching character of the danger of his actions, only to be ignored. The device is a familiar one, but by the allusion in his speech to the story of Hecuba and Paris, and his description of himself as a *vates*,[60] Hanno is associated with the most famous 'tragic warner' of all: the prophetess Cassandra, who (in some versions)[61] unsuccessfully advised that the infant Paris be killed.[62] Not merely the specific allusion, then, but the entire context in which it is being introduced carries Trojan overtones.[63]

This passage thus provides some extra dimensions to our understanding of Livy's techniques of allusion. The most surprising thing to many readers may be the literary sophistication, of the sort that we would more usually associate with learned Alexandrian poets than with sober historians: his nod to the

---

[60] The word may also help mark the passage as an allusion in the first place, with its overtones of poetic as well as prophetic vision: compare Hinds (1998: 9).

[61] E.g. Euripides, *Andr.* 293–300. There is also an alternative version in which the warner was Aesacus (e.g. Lycophron, *Alex.* 224–5, ps-Apollodorus 3.12.5).

[62] The role of Hanno as 'tragic warner' is discussed at length by Mader (1993: 209–16), without however mentioning the Trojan dimension to his speech.

[63] On the complex of imagery in this speech that connects Hannibal to Paris, Hanno to Cassandra, and the doomed Carthage to the doomed Troy, see Cipriani (1984: 75–8).

multiple and indeed more obscure versions of a famous story. That style of allusion, though unexpected in Livy, is in fact not an unfamiliar one in Latin literature; Livy shows himself capable of appealing to those sensibilities, though one should not suggest that such intricate devices are a common feature of his writing. Another point is that the particular evocation of Troy shows once again his interest in providing his story of the Punic War with the iconic overtones of the central myth of the ancient world. This time, however, he does so via an allusion to the myth more broadly rather than to the specific version of Homer (or indeed any other single writer). This once again is a familiar style of literary allusion, though here it is interesting to note the overlap with the more specifically historiographical issue of alluding to historical events rather than to specific representations of those events, an issue I shall be discussing in more detail shortly (below, 119–21).

Finally we should note the point from which I began (above, 107): the way in which the allusions in Book 21 correspond to similar Trojan allusions in Book 30. It seems reasonable to suggest that the correspondence is not accidental: in both cases the Carthaginians are treated as Trojans specifically in the imminence and inevitability of their defeat, and their appearance as Trojans at the end both recalls and completes the narrative pattern raised by the allusion here, something recognizable despite the passages being separated by the space of more than nine books. As I discussed in Chapter 1, Livy in Book 30 repeatedly recalls episodes and themes from Book 21 (including indeed a reference back to Hanno himself), and so at the end of the decade the reader is being constantly reminded of the points which Livy introduced at the start. The pattern of allusion is linked to the structure of the work.

A further lesson we should learn from this is not to assume that allusions in Livy are simply to the most obvious sources. There is of course a constant and inevitable danger in the study of literary allusion that we will privilege those texts which are most familiar to us, rather than those read by the author and his audience; this danger is accentuated by the loss of so many key texts from the ancient world. An interesting example comes with the debate at the end of Book 28 between Fabius and Scipio over Scipio's proposed invasion of Africa. Rodgers argues that this debate, along with the actual launching of the invasion in Book 29, derives from the account of the launching of the Sicilian expedition in Thucydides Book 6, which centres on a similar debate between Nicias and Alcibiades (6.8–26).[64] She shows well some similarities in both the

---

[64] Rodgers (1986). That Livy modelled the Fabius–Scipio debate on Nicias and Alcibiades in Thucydides was originally suggested by Stübler (1941: 157–8); cf. Bonnefond (1982: 200–17), who however concludes that the similarities are governed by the comparable historical situations, and does not consider it in terms of Livy imitating Thucydides.

situation and in the arguments used. In both cases the primary mover of the expedition is a dynamic young man, and in both cases he is opposed by an older, more experienced general noted for his caution. In both cases the older man speaks first, and starts with a defence of himself before moving to arguments to show the folly of the policy, and concludes with an attack on the younger man; the younger man then successfully responds, initially by defending himself, and then argues for both the ease of victory and the likely advantages of his aggressive policy.

It may be objected, however, that Rodgers overstates the extent and recognizability of these parallels. Some of her argument depends on her applying particular labels to sections of the speeches, and once those labels are removed the parallels seem less compelling. For example, under the heading of *honestum* she parallels Alcibiades' discussion of the need for unity in the state (Thucydides 6.18.6) with Scipio's argument that Rome's *dignitas* and reputation require that she make Africa suffer rather than suffering herself (28.44.12–15).[65] The trouble is that the actual details of the arguments are far removed from one another: the sole similarity is in the label. What is worse in this case is that even the label looks problematic: it is not clear that Alcibiades' argument can properly be characterized as an argument from *honestum* at all. He is not advocating morality for its own sake, but making a practical argument that a state is more successful if composed of disparate but unified elements; Scipio by contrast does argue a moral case, explicitly saying that he would support invading Africa to maintain the Romans' *dignitas* and *fama* even if it were not a route to victory (28.44.12). The parallel that Rodgers draws here therefore seems strained and artificial. It is also uncomfortable for her case that while the arguments may be found in a broadly similar order in the two authors, the balance is often dramatically different; so, for example, Nicias' initial defence of himself is nothing more than a perfunctory phrase in passing (Thucydides 6.9.2), whereas Fabius' is lengthy, detailed, and elaborate (28.40.6–14).[66] Moreover Fabius ends this section of his speech with an acknowledgement of the importance of youth in obtaining the future victory over Hannibal (28.40.14), a point precisely opposite to the one that Nicias goes on to make later in his speech, when he argues that Alcibiades' youth is making him act against the interests of the state (Thucydides 6.12.2–13.1). This too makes reading them in parallel look less obvious. When we add to this the lack of any marked linguistic borrowings between the two speeches, one might wonder whether the parallels are

---

[65] Rodgers (1986: 348–9).

[66] The difference is acknowledged by Rodgers (1986: 340–1), but without considering the implications for the recognizability of the parallels.

anything more than an accidental coincidence, and moreover, even if Rodgers is right to hypothesize that Livy was partially modelling himself on Thucydides, whether he could expect that to be identified as a key intertext by any of his audience.

Against this, however, Rodgers's case is greatly strengthened by the fact that the example of the Sicilian Expedition is not merely something discovered by a modern scholar casting around for parallels. It is adduced explicitly by Fabius in his speech, with a direct comparison between Scipio and Alcibiades as author of the disastrous policy (28.41.17). A reader, thus alerted to the salience of that comparison in particular, would not find it difficult to extend it to encompass the situation more broadly, even if not in all of the details that Rodgers claims.[67]

But while that is true, would a comparison between the Sicilian Expedition and the Scipio-Fabius debate be enough to evoke Thucydides in particular? After all, we know of other important historians who had treated the Sicilian Expedition, such as Philistus, Ephorus, and Timaeus. Philistus was a Syracusan who was actually present during the Athenian attack,[68] and in that respect had a claim to historical authority which even surpassed that of Thucydides. He was regularly cited in tandem with Thucydides as a source for the events, or was associated with him more broadly, not least because he seems to have imitated the older historian's manner.[69] Ephorus and Timaeus, though writing later, were immensely influential writers who were widely read, admired, and quoted. The accident of survival by which we possess Thucydides and have lost Philistus, Ephorus, and Timaeus should not blind us to the fact that the ancients read the Sicilian Expedition through more than one author, and therefore that the mere mention of the expedition as an historical precedent could not automatically be tied down to Thucydides alone.

This is not to suggest that Rodgers's case should be dismissed: on balance it may be right to claim that Thucydides would be regarded as the key intertext here. Although, as I said, Philistus is regularly cited with Thucydides, those citations go hand in hand with a sense of his inferiority. Dionysius and Quintilian (above, n. 69) both explicitly say that Philistus, though imitating

---

[67] Cf. also Walsh (1961: 105–6) for the suggestion that other aspects of Livy's presentation of Fabius are modelled on Nicias, something that would make readers particularly receptive to finding elements of Nicias in his speech here.

[68] Plutarch, *Nicias* 19.5 (= Philistus *FGrH* 556 T 2).

[69] E.g. Cicero, *Brutus* 66 (= *FGrH* 556 T 21); Plutarch, *Nicias* 1.5, 19.5, 28.4 (=*FGrH* 556 FF 54–6); Theon, *Prog.* 63.25, 119.2 (Spengel) (=*FGrH* 556 FF 51–2). He is described as an 'imitator of Thucydides' by Cicero *Q.F.* 2.11.4, *De Or.* 2.57 (= *FGrH* 556 T 17), Dionysius of Halicarnassus, *De Im.* 208.14-209.12 (Usener-Rademacher), *Ep. Pomp.* 4.5 (=*FGrH* 556 T 16), and Quintilian 10.1.74 (= *FGrH* 556 T 15c). See Zoepffel (1965: 20-67), Bearzot (2002: 124–6).

Thucydides, was far weaker than him; Cicero calls him 'almost a miniature Thucydides' (*Q.F.* 2.11.4 *paene pusillus Thucydides*). He also seems to have been dependent on Thucydides for his account of Athenian affairs.[70] Most significantly, Plutarch, *Nicias* 1.1 begins his discussion of earlier historians of the Expedition by denying that he himself was seeking to rival Thucydides; only a little afterwards (*Nicias* 1.5) does he mention Philistus as another historian of the events. Clearly when one read a book about the Sicilian Expedition it was with Thucydides that one would immediately assume the author was competing.

But even though it is not unreasonable to see Thucydides as important here, it is likely that the parallels with the Expedition that Livy is raising include elements that readers could recognize as coming from other historians as well. One piece of evidence for this is the version of Nicias' speech in Diodorus 12.83.6. This is vastly abridged by comparison with either Thucydides or Livy, but in certain respects it parallels Fabius' speech in Livy more closely than Thucydides does. The two arguments that Nicias uses in Diodorus are, first, that the Athenians cannot complete the war (διαπολεμεῖν) against the Spartans if they divide their forces by sending a large-scale expedition to Sicily, and that Sicily will be too difficult to conquer, as shown by the failure of the Carthaginians to conquer it. Neither of these arguments is used in that form in Thucydides. His Nicias is concerned about the possibility of a *resumption* of war with the Spartans while the Athenians are distracted in Sicily (6.10.1–4), rather than about weakening the Athenians to prevent them from completing an existing war; nor does he cite historical precedents of failed attempts to conquer Sicily. But both of these points appear in the centre of Fabius' speech, who in quick succession raises the same two arguments in the same order (28.41.11–42.1): the lack of resources to fight a war on two fronts, and the bad precedents – including the Athenian one—for such an invasion. Diodorus' source here is generally assumed to be Ephorus,[71] and his general practice when handling speeches is to compress the material from his source, but to maintain the arguments faithfully.[72] It seems a reasonable deduction that these arguments appeared in a fuller form

---

[70] Theon, *Prog.* 63.25 (Spengel) (= *FGrH* 556 T 14 = F 51).

[71] E.g. Schwartz (1905: 681), Meister (1967: 61–2). However, identifying Diodorus' sources can be a tricky enterprise, especially since the passage in question could be considered part of the history of mainland Greece (for which Ephorus was demonstrably Diodorus' main source in Books 11–15: see Schwartz 1905: 679–81) or part of Sicilian history, where he may have used other material, with Timaeus overwhelmingly the most likely candidate (so e.g. Pearson 1987: 135–56, though see *contra* Stylianou 1998: 50–61). It is therefore just possible that the speech of Nicias comes from Timaeus (so Brock 1995: 215).

[72] Sacks (1990: 98–9, 1994: 229–30).

in (probably) Ephorus, and that Livy in creating Fabius' speech is expecting at least some of his readers to recognize that he is drawing not only on Thucydides, but also on Ephorus' anti-Thucydidean reworking of the story.[73]

This then leads to another consideration. As I said above, the main reason why it is reasonable to read Livy as alluding to the Sicilian Expedition in the first place is that it is explicitly cited in Fabius' speech. But when Scipio replies to that speech, he rejects the Athenian example, and instead offers a precedent of his own: that of the Sicilian tyrant Agathocles, who, when Syracuse was under siege by the Carthaginians in 310 BC, sought to draw them away by launching a counter-invasion of Africa (28.43.21). The example is obviously pertinent to the Romans' current situation—considerably more so, indeed, than the Sicilian Expedition. If Fabius' citation of the Sicilian Expedition alerts the reader to an allusion to the historians of that expedition, we should at least consider the possibility that Scipio's citation of Agathocles does the same.

To a modern reader, admittedly, the two cases can hardly be considered on a par. The Sicilian Expedition is familiar as one of the central episodes in one of the central periods of history as described by one of the central writers of the canon. Agathocles' invasion of Africa is merely one in a long list of obscure events from the period of Greek history between the death of Alexander and the rise of Rome, and an episode for which the only substantial surviving narratives are found in the emphatically (and deservedly) uncanonical Diodorus and Justin. But that was not the perception in antiquity. Agathocles was a great though contentious figure, whose deeds were described at length by some extremely famous and widely read historians.[74] Timaeus devoted the last five books of his history of the Western Greeks to a notoriously hostile account (he could perhaps be excused for his hostility, because Agathocles had sent him into exile);[75] Duris of Samos wrote a work (in at least four books) specifically devoted to him. (Both were outweighed in length, if not in fame, by Callias, whose history of Agathocles ran to twenty-two books.[76]) If Livy wished not merely to recall the events, but to allude to

---

[73] That Ephorus wrote in part challenging Thucydides is clear from his radically different account of the causes of the Peloponnesian War, which he blamed entirely on Pericles' desire to avoid prosecution for embezzlement (Diodorus 12.39.3–41.1 = Ephorus *FGrH* 70 F 196); cf. Barber (1935: 106–12). The same point would however apply even if Timaeus were Diodorus' source here, for he too, according to Plutarch, *Nicias* 1.1–4 (= Timaeus *FGrH* 566 T 18), directly sought to rival Thucydides' account of the Expedition.

[74] On the sources and historiographical tradition for Agathocles, see Pearson (1987: 225–55).

[75] Diodorus 21.17.1–3; cf. Polybius 8.10.12, 12.15 (= Timaeus *FGrH* 566 F 124).

[76] Diodorus 21.16.5 (= Callias *FGrH* 564 T 2).

specific texts in which they were described, he did not need to search out anything very recondite: familiar material was readily available to him.

Is there any evidence that he did so? Once again Diodorus supplies an interesting key. At 20.3.3 he gives an account of Agathocles' reasons for undertaking the invasion: that (a) the Carthaginians were living in peace, and hence would easily be defeated by the battle-hardened Syracusans; (b) the Carthaginians' allies had long resented them and would take the opportunity to revolt; (c) that the land was wealthy and ripe for plunder; and (d) that the invasion would draw the Carthaginians away from Sicily and take the war to Africa. Although this is not presented by Diodorus in a speech—Agathocles is deliberately keeping his intentions secret (20.4.1)—three of these four arguments closely correspond to points that Scipio makes in his speech. Indeed, the points come in the same order, and in the very section of his speech that directly follows after he has adduced Agathocles as a parallel, and so at the point when the possibility of an allusion is most immediately apparent to the readers (28.44.2–6). (c) is not among Scipio's arguments—plunder is a key part of Diodorus' narrative of Agathocles' campaign (e.g. 20.8.3–6), but is a far less significant theme in Livy, and certainly is not an argument that a Roman consul would be expected to raise in a speech before the Senate.[77] But the other three points all have their counterparts. Scipio argues that the Carthaginians will suffer because the invader has an intrinsic advantage over the defender—a slightly different idea to Diodorus', but recognizably in the same general vein. He goes on to note that the Carthaginians' allies in Africa resent their dominance and will support an invader, and finally makes the key point that this will draw Hannibal away from Italy, something to which he has not referred previously. This whole section of the speech is far closer to the arguments in Diodorus than to the very loose parallels that one might draw with Thucydides.[78]

It is not clear who Diodorus' source for his Agathocles narrative was: it may have been Duris, or it may have been Timaeus, or else it might have been a mixture of the two;[79] but both were well known. The similarity of the passages strongly suggests that Livy is here alluding to and reworking not Thucydides, but the historian of Agathocles who was Diodorus' source for this section, whether that was Duris or Timaeus.

---

[77] For the Romans' tendency—however disingenuous—to downplay plunder in presenting their motives, see Kostial (1995: 92–101).

[78] Set out by Rodgers (1986: 346–7).

[79] Schwartz (1905: 687–8) and Consolo Langher (1991, 1998, 2005) argue for Duris; Pearson (1987: 227–30) on balance prefers Timaeus. Meister (1991: 187–92) argues that he used both sources, with Timaeus supplying the greater bulk of the account; he had previously argued that Diodorus 20.3 is to be specifically attributed to Timaeus (Meister 1967: 143).

This leads to some interesting conclusions. Instead of a single model, what we have here is effectively two (or more) models being played off against one another—played off by Livy himself, but also, he implies, by Fabius and Scipio too. It is not merely that Livy imitates earlier historians: he simultaneously suggests that Fabius and Scipio modelled themselves on past history. Fabius, accusing Scipio of being a second Alcibiades, himself deliberately plays the part of Nicias, giving a speech that imitates Nicias' speech before the Sicilian Expedition—but intriguingly appears to use more than one version of the speech, as if he were not merely imitating Nicias, but were himself, like Livy, a historian reading and amalgamating the different texts in which Nicias' speech is described. Then in response Scipio changes the historical model from the Sicilian Expedition by citing the even better example of Agatho-cles—it may be worth observing that Scipio is recorded by Polybius 15.35.6 as having admired Agathocles, along with Agathocles' predecessor Dionysius, as the most efficient (πραγματικωτάτους) and daringly intelligent of all. Livy's Scipio implicitly shares the Polybian Scipio's judgement, but Livy frames it in a new context, with Scipio modelling his speech on Agathocles' thoughts as reported in Duris (or Timaeus)—but of course we can also see Livy himself alluding to the passage of Duris (or Timaeus) in writing the piece.

This whole section shows superbly how the terms in which allusion oper-ates are altered by the historical genre. A genuine (we are led to assume) competition over policy is framed in terms of the competing politicians modelling themselves on earlier characters, and accordingly modelling their speeches on earlier historical representations of their preferred *exempla*. But the whole debate is orchestrated by the historian, who is creating a single narrative by imitating, alluding to, and reworking the texts of a variety of his predecessors.

There is a further dimension to this also. Neither Fabius nor Scipio cites Greek examples alone. Both also adduce an earlier event in Roman history: Fabius refers to Regulus' failed campaign during the First Punic War (28.42.1); Scipio picks up the same example, but reinterprets it to suit his own ends as an *exemplum* of success, albeit temporary, and adds to it the Spartan Xanthippus, who had led the Carthaginians against Regulus in the same war (28.43.17–19). If the Greek examples mark allusions to texts, so too do these. However, the difference is that the text to which they refer is Livy's own: he had described these events in Books 17–18. This must necessarily work in a slightly different way, because Scipio and Fabius manifestly cannot be reading Livy. Rather Livy is relying on the privileged position and apparent transparency of his own text: its claim to represent reality, which therefore allows the characters within the text to know earlier events without worrying how they have learned them, or without awkward questions being asked about alternative versions of the events which might be found in historical rivals[80] (something of course also enabled by the fact that citation of historical examples without reference to particular texts was a standard rhetorical technique).[81]

This is thus a specific instance of the more general phenomenon of 'self-imitation': where an historian will write one episode on the model of an earlier episode in his history.[82] It is a common technique, but crucially distinct from the imitation of other authors which forms the main subject of this chapter, not least because the textual status of the text alluded to is usually less apparent: both the alluding passage and the passage alluded to are found within the same history as equal representations of real events. If Scipio models himself on Regulus or Xanthippus, he is replicating an event that has already been described and fixed within the world described by the author.[83] This technique thus shades into and is often (save sometimes in its self-consciousness) indistinguishable from the broader way in which historians—or indeed writers in any other genre—guide the interpretation of their works by patterns of repetition and alteration of themes within it.[84] That is apparent in Scipio's speech: for as well as Regulus, Xanthippus, and Agathocles, he cites other examples too, namely examples from the Hannibalic War itself. He offers the model of Hannibal (28.44.2–4), and indeed of his own campaigns in Spain (28.43.9–16). As I shall discuss in Chapter 3, patterns of generalship during the Hannibalic War, and the extent to which Hannibal should and should not be used as a model for Roman behaviour, is a key issue in Livy throughout the decade. It is, however, qualitatively different from the allusive techniques under discussion here.

---

[80] This needs slight qualification, because there are occasions where characters within Livy appear to cite non-Livian versions of events. The chief example is the ransoming of Rome from the Gauls: at 5.48.8–49.2 the Romans are saved by Camillus from having to pay any money, whereas some subsequent citations of the *exemplum* by characters in Livy seem to imply that money was in fact paid (9.4.16, 10.16.6, 22.59.7), which we know was the case in other versions of the story (for which see Ogilvie 1965: 736). However, the issue is complicated by the fact that those characters are adapting the case for their own purposes: Livy may actually be showing their tendentious misuse of the example. See Chaplin (2000: 39–41), and also the judicious comments of Oakley (2005a: 85).

[81] For Livy's technique of setting up his work as a source of *exempla* and having characters in the history cite and employ those *exempla* in a variety of ways, see above all Chaplin (2000).

[82] On self-imitation in historians, see esp. Woodman (1979). Kraus (1998) is particularly thought-provoking both on Livy's technique of 'self-allusion' and on the extent to which it may shade into inert repetition.

[83] Compare Catin (1944: 93–106) on the way in which Livy uses repetition of motifs to suggest the fundamental repetitiveness of history.

[84] Cf. West and Woodman (1979a: 195–6).

Livy's allusions to events he has described in his own work are a special case. When it comes to earlier historical events and persons beyond the boundaries of his history, we should not expect that all references to them signal allusions to specific texts containing those events or persons (cf. above, 84–6). We have so far seen Scipio modelling himself on two Greek generals, Agesilaus and Agathocles, and a further general, Alcibiades, is ascribed as a model to Scipio by Fabius. In all three cases the allusion appears to be simultaneously to the texts in which those generals were described. But the most famous Greek model that Livy provides for Scipio is harder to pin down so closely. At 26.19.6–8, in the course of his initial character sketch, Livy describes Scipio as follows:

hic mos, quem per omnem vitam servabat, seu consulto seu temere volgatae opinioni fidem apud quosdam fecit stirpis eum divinae virum esse, rettulitque famam in Alexandro Magno prius volgatam, et vanitate et fabula parem, anguis immanis concubitu conceptum, et in cubiculo matris eius visam persaepe prodigii eius speciem, interventuque hominum evolutam repente atque ex oculis elapsam. his miraculis nunquam ab ipso elusa fides est; quin potius aucta arte quadam nec abnuendi tale quicquam nec palam adfirmandi.

This custom [sc. of visiting the Capitol alone], which he kept up throughout his life, gave credence among some people to the idea (whether it was spread deliberately or casually) that he was a man of divine parentage, and recalled the story previously spread about Alexander the Great, a story equal in emptiness and fictionality, that he had been conceived from intercourse with a monstrous snake, and that an image of that portent had often been seen in his mother's bedroom, and when men came in it had suddenly slid away and disappeared. He himself never debunked belief in these miracles: on the contrary he increased it by a certain skill at never denying any such thing nor openly affirming it.

This story, which is found also in the sources for Alexander's life,[85] might not by itself have strongly invited a comparison between Alexander and Scipio, since similar stories were told of a number of other charismatic leaders.[86] However, Livy's explicit mention of Alexander highlights that as the point of comparison.[87] It is hard, however, to identify any particular historian of Alexander who might be alluded to here: the story is rather one which is assumed to be known widely

---

[85] E.g. Justin 11.11.3; Plutarch, *Alexander* 3.1–2.

[86] Note the stories of Aristomenes (Pausanias 4.14.7) and Aratus (Pausanias 2.10.3), both themselves doubtless created in imitation of Alexander.

[87] There may be a contemporary hint as well, since the same story was told of Augustus (Suetonius, *Div. Aug.* 94.4, citing Asclepiades of Mendes, *Theologoumena*). Weippert (1972: 248) suggests that Livy's dismissal of the legend of the birth of Scipio might be a criticism of those who applied it to Augustus, though this is complicated by the fact that Asclepiades' story was not only clearly invented on the model of Alexander, but may well have been intended to link Augustus to Scipio: see Lorsch (1997). More broadly on Augustus' attempts to link his own image to Alexander, see Kienast (1969), Weippert (1972: 214–59).

(cf. *volgatam*):[88] this is a case of a parallel between events (or in this case alleged events) rather than specific texts,[89] and a parallel that moreover appears to be deliberately created and fostered by Scipio himself. This points to a significant problem if we are trying to see how far the parallel in Livy extends. There is no doubt that the careers and images of Alexander and Scipio to a substantial degree paralleled one another.[90] In addition to their divine pretensions, both began their campaigns young, and in a brilliant series of victories conquered a great Oriental empire. Both made their mark with a spectacular victory by siege: Alexander at Tyre, Scipio at New Carthage, both cities surrounded by water which were attacked from sea and land, and the commander took his infantry across the harbour, personally leading the assault after claiming divine inspiration. Both Alexander and Scipio famously showed their continence and magnanimity towards the wives and daughters of their conquered enemies.[91] Both however were criticized by their own people for 'going native',[92] and had in addition to cope with a major mutiny among their own troops. However, one might question whether these parallels, close as they are, are really significant for Livy.[93] Polybius' narrative, which is one of Livy's main sources (below, section 2.2), appears to have contained much the same elements, and much of it may not be original to him either—it may well go back to Scipio's own propaganda and self-presentation.

But while all this is true, it does not prove that the Alexander connection is irrelevant to Livy's interpretation. After all, he alerts the reader to it early in Scipio's career, as we have seen, and he could therefore expect at least some

[88] Gellius 6.1.1–5, making the same comparison between the birth legends of Alexander and Scipio, attributes the Alexander story merely to *historia Graeca* (6.1.1: 'Greek history'). He attributes the version told of Scipio to Oppius (fr. 2P) and Hyginus (fr. 4P), the former writing slightly before Livy, the latter probably slightly after him: the implication is that they gave the story more credence than Livy does.

[89] Admittedly the historians of Alexander whom Livy might have read are lost, and identifying material deriving from them is notoriously problematic (see e.g. Pearson 1960, Hammond 1983). It is not totally impossible that Livy's language here allowed readers to recognize a more precise allusion to something that no longer survives. But the terms in which both he and Gellius describe the Alexander legend militate against that conclusion.

[90] Cf. Weippert (1972: 37–55), Bernard (2000: 325–30), Spencer (2002: esp. 172–6, 178–9).

[91] Alexander with the family of Darius, Scipio with the noble women of Spain: cf. 26.49. 11–50.14. The episode became a standard point of comparison between them: see Frontinus, *Str.* 2.11.5–6, Gellius 7.8, Ammianus 24.4.27.

[92] See especially 29.19.10–13. The issue is once again complicated by the fact that the 'Hellenizing' that Scipio is accused of engaging in here may have been part of a deliberate imitation of Alexander, though note the cautious comments of Weippert (1972: 52–3).

[93] Borzsák (2003) is an example of the problem. He briefly lists a number of parallels between material in the surviving Alexander historians and episodes in Latin literature, including several in Livy's Third Decade. Most of them, however, are far less close than those I have sketched in this paragraph, and Borzsák does little to show why they should be regarded as more than loose coincidences.

readers to retain memories of the parallel and draw appropriate conclusions even if he did nothing more to point to it directly. This is thus another good example of how the indeterminate boundaries of allusion may be exploited within an historical context. Once Livy has introduced the parallel, it will persist in the background as a potential point of comparison unless and until the careers or characters of the two men have diverged sufficiently, and there is of course no clearly defined point at which that will occur. It thus remains as a dimension of his narrative to which readers may be alert, although a dimension largely not of his own creation.

There is also some evidence that from time to time Livy may have re-inforced the comparison by introducing more specific allusions. For example, before the siege of New Carthage Scipio makes a speech to his troops (26.43.3–8). The last part of the speech is lost in a lacuna, but near the start Scipio says *in una urbe universam ceperitis Hispaniam* (26.43.3: 'in one city you shall have captured the whole of Spain'). In Arrian Alexander makes a speech before the siege of Tyre, in which he says the same thing: ἐξαιρεθείσης δὲ Τύρου ἥ ... Φοινίκη ἔχοιτο ἂν πᾶσα (2.17.3: 'with Tyre wiped out the whole of Phoenicia would be held'). This could be a coincidence. It is not clear on what Arrian is basing the speech (the only other source for a speech at this point is Curtius 4.2.17, which is entirely different): by his own account Ptolemy and Aristobulus were his main sources (*Praef.*; cf. 6.2.4), but it is hard to determine which he is using at any time.[94] Bosworth in fact argues that the speech did not even originally belong in this context: Arrian may have transferred here a speech that in his source appeared earlier in the narrative.[95] But the similarity is sufficient to make it possible that Livy in composing Scipio's speech alluded directly to a speech that (probably) either Ptolemy or Aristobulus supplied at the parallel moment in Alexander's career.

A more intriguing example comes shortly afterwards, when Scipio crosses the shallows to capture the city thanks to a quirk of the tide about which he had previously learned, but which he attributes to a divine prodigy (26.45.7–9). This parallels a slightly earlier moment in Alexander's career, when he was marching along the coast of Pamphylia: the sea was said to have receded, allowing him to pass. This is described in different terms in the sources: Callisthenes seems to have treated it as the sea prostrating itself before him;[96]

---

[94] For Arrian's sources and his techniques for handling them see Bosworth (1980: 16–34).

[95] Bosworth (1980: 238–9).

[96] *FGrH* 124 F 31 (= Eustathius, *ad Il.* 13.29). It should be noted that the extravagant image may represent Eustathius' gloss on the passage, rather than Callisthenes' own comment (Pearson 1960: 37): Callisthenes' version may have been closer to Arrian's than appears at first sight. But cf. *FGrH* 151 F 1.2, Josephus, *AJ* 2.348, Appian, *BC* 2.149; also Plutarch, *Alex.* 17.6–8, criticizing historians for their exaggerated and prodigious descriptions of the event.

for Arrian 1.26.1–2 it is simply that the path was only clear when the north wind blew (though Arrian still regards it as divine influence). Strabo 14.3.9 has an entirely different version: he says that on a calm day the path is 'exposed' (ταῖς μὲν νηνεμίαις γυμνουμένην), but that Alexander was prepared to tackle it on a stormy day before the water subsided, so that the soldiers had to wade through 'up to the navel' (μέχρι ὀμφαλοῦ βαπτιζομένων). Livy's account of Scipio is based on Polybius (10.14.7–11; cf. 10.8.6–7), but unlike him, he interestingly attributes the receding of the water not merely to the tide, but also to the north wind (26.45.8). Moreover, he describes the effect as 'exposing' the shallows such that in some places the water was 'up to the navel', in other places barely covering the knee (26.45.8 *adeo nudaverat vada ut alibi umbilico tenus aqua esset, alibi genua vix superaret*).[97] Neither of these points is in Polybius. The similarity to Strabo's account (and indeed language) is marked, but so too the role played by the north wind is remarkably like that in the otherwise contradictory account in Arrian. The most likely conclusion is that Livy is supplementing Polybius to make Scipio's feat appear closer to Alexander's[98]—but alluding simultaneously to different historical versions of Alexander's story.[99]

But when Livy alludes to historical figures who appear in particular texts, the texts in question are not necessarily other histories. When Scipio leaves his lieutenant Q. Pleminius in charge of Locri, Pleminius uses his authority to behave abominably towards both the Locrians and his fellow Romans. While it was not uncommon for Romans to mistreat provincials, a Roman official in a province engaging in quasi-legal violence against other Romans was much rarer. Its most obvious parallel was Verres. Cicero's famous series of speeches attacking him concluded (*II Verr.* 5.139–72) with a long account of the

---

[97] Appian, *Hisp.* 21 makes a comparable point, but unlike Livy his version has waves reaching the chest while receding below the knee.

[98] Scullard (1930: 85–6) recognizes that the wind is an addition to the Polybian original, and moreover notes the similarity to Arrian's account of the north wind assisting Alexander; but he regards it as improbable that the detail was merely added in imitation of the Alexander story, since north winds are recorded in modern times as lowering the water at New Carthage, albeit only by a foot or so, whereas there are in fact no strong tidal effects there (cf. Scullard 1930: 71–81). He believes that Livy is relaying an accurate detail, and the similarity to Alexander in Arrian is mere coincidence: so too e.g. Lazenby (1978: 136–7), Foulon (1989, 1998), Hoyos (1992). However, this argument overlooks the linguistic similarities to Strabo, which weights the argument more strongly in the direction of Livy incorporating allusive material which may coincidentally at one point have matched reality.

[99] Here too Arrian is presumably basing himself on Ptolemy or Aristobulus (above, n. 94); Bosworth (1980: 165–6) suggests that Strabo's source is Cleitarchus, whom he cites elsewhere. But that is unconvincing, since most of Strabo's citations of Cleitarchus are dismissive (7.2.1, 11.1.5, 11.5.4), and were it in Cleitarchus one might expect to find the story mentioned in Diodorus, Curtius, or Justin, who are generally accepted to employ him as a major source.

violence he inflicted on Roman citizens, the climax of which (*II Verr.* 5.158–70) is a lurid description of his treatment of a Roman citizen called Gavius. Verres begins by giving the order for him to be flogged: *repente hominem proripi atque in foro medio nudari et deligari et virgas expediri iubet* (*II Verr.* 5.161: 'he suddenly ordered the man to be rushed out and stripped and bound in the middle of the forum and for rods to be prepared'). When in Livy Pleminius unleashes his violence against the military tribunes who have sought to discipline a plundering soldier, remarkably similar language is used: *accensus ira domo sese proripuit, vocatosque tribunos nudari ac virgas expediri iubet* (29.9.4: 'fired by anger he rushed from his house, and ordered the tribunes to be summoned and stripped and for rods to be prepared'). The parallel circumstances might recall Verres in any event: the close similarity in wording, with *proripuit* transferred from the victim to Pleminius himself, is readily recognizable.[100] The uncomfortable implication is that Pleminius, acting of course under the aegis of Scipio, is prefiguring the most notorious excesses of the late Republic.

That allusion to Verres, while striking, is only a passing hint: earlier in the decade he has been recalled in a more complex fashion. Near the end of Book 25 Livy returns the scene to Syracuse, and famously discusses the effect of the spoils from that city on Rome (25.40.1–3):

Marcellus captis Syracusis, cum cetera in Sicilia tanta fide atque integritate composuisset, ut non modo suam gloriam sed etiam maiestatem populi Romani augeret, ornamenta urbis, signa tabulasque, quibus abundabant Syracusae, Romam devexit, hostium quidem illa spolia et parta belli iure; ceterum inde primum initium mirandi Graecarum artium opera licentiaeque huius sacra profanaque omnia vulgo spoliandi factum est, quae postremo in Romanos deos, templum id ipsum primum, quod a Marcello eximie ornatum est, vertit. visebantur enim ab externis ad portam Capenam dedicata a M. Marcello templa propter excellentia eius generis ornamenta, quorum perexigua pars comparet.

Marcellus, after capturing Syracuse and arranging everything else in Sicily with such honesty and integrity that he enhanced not only his own glory but also the majesty of the Roman people, transported to Rome the decorations of the city, the statues and pictures in which Syracuse abounded. Admittedly these were enemy spoils and obtained by right of war; but from this came the first beginnings of the fascination for Greek works of art and of this licence for despoiling far and wide everything sacred and profane, which in the end turned against the Roman gods, beginning with that

---

[100] Oakley (1998: 724) suggests (citing also 2.55.5, 3.36.5, 3.45.7, 8.32.10, 9.16.17) that wording such as *virgas . . . expediri iubere* is merely 'stock Livian phraseology'; but the resemblance of the phrasing in the passage here to Cicero goes well beyond anything in Oakley's other examples. Nor is there any other parallel for it in surviving Latin: the closest is Valerius Maximus 2.7.8 (*virgas expediri eumque nudari iussit*), who may be drawing on Cicero or Livy himself.

very temple which Marcellus decorated outstandingly. For foreigners used to visit the temples dedicated by M. Marcellus at the Porta Capena because of the outstanding collection of that sort of decoration; only a wretched proportion of these is now in evidence.

Polybius too (9.10) criticizes the Roman plundering of the artworks of Syracuse, but on quite different grounds: that it undermined the simplicity that made Rome great (9.10.4–5), and that it would incite the hatred of those whose wealth was appropriated (9.10.6–10). Neither of these ideas appears in Livy, at least in that form, though there is a possible hint at Polybius' arguments in the reference to the foreign visitors who once went to view Marcellus' temple: Polybius 9.10.8–9 refers to those who have been robbed going resentfully to see their former possessions in the hands of their conquerors.[101] But the idea that Marcellus' legitimate appropriation of the Syracusan artwork eventually turned back against the Romans themselves raises different issues.

More significant here, once again, is the man who was perhaps the most notorious plunderer of artwork in the late Republic, namely Verres. The mere mention of plundering art is admittedly unlikely to be enough to focus most readers' attention on Verres, but plundering in the context of Syracuse would make him appear an especially salient possibility. That is then strongly reinforced by the fact that the passage draws on themes and language from the *Verrines*. Notably, *sacra profanaque omnia vulgo spoliandi* closely recalls the opening sentence of the *Fifth Verrine*: *apertissime C. Verres in Sicilia sacra profanaque omnia et privatim et publice spoliarit* (*II Verr.* 5.1: 'C. Verres in Sicily quite openly despoiled both in private and public everything sacred and profane'). In other words, Marcellus' actions were the opening phase leading to a disastrous outcome, and the description that Livy offers of the latter relates it to the behaviour of Verres in particular.[102]

This then leads to a further consideration. That sentence from the opening of the *Fifth Verrine* is there to summarize the argument of the *Fourth Verrine* before Cicero moves on to the other issues that will form the topic of the new

---

[101] This passage is picked up more strongly by Livy at 26.32.4, where Torquatus and other senators, criticizing Marcellus for his plunder of Syracuse, have the conceit of Hiero rising from the dead and going to view his city despoiled and then Rome decorated with the spoils (cf. Jaeger 1997: 128–30). This passage, as well as the Syracusans' own complaints at 26.30.9–10, is oddly overlooked by Burck (1982: 1179–80), who claims that Livy's only concern about Marcellus' actions is their moral effect on Rome rather than the Syracusans' losses. The allusions to Cicero's speeches against Verres here likewise suggest that the sufferings of the victims are a matter of interest.

[102] There are also other places where Roman misbehaviour in Sicily recalls the *Verrines*, notably the massacre at Henna at 24.37–9, which repeatedly alludes to Verres' impiety at Henna in *II Verr.* 4.107–12. See Hinds (1982: 477), and cf. 341–3 below.

speech. The *Fourth Verrine* is the speech that centres on Verres' plundering of art: and that opening recalls one sentence of it in particular: *aedificiis omnibus, publicis privatis, sacris profanis, sic pepercit quasi ad ea defendenda cum exercitu, non oppugnanda venisset* (*II Verr.* 4.120: 'all buildings, public and private, sacred and profane, he spared as if he had come to defend them with his army, not to attack them'). That sentence obviously does not refer to Verres: it is in fact a description of Marcellus, and comes from an extended section of the speech (*II Verr.* 4.120–3) in which Cicero describes Marcellus' behaviour at the capture of Syracuse and contrasts it favourably with Verres'. It also includes other language which Livy appears to be drawing on here, though more loosely: for example *multa Romam deportare quae ornamento urbi esse possent* (*II Verr.* 4.120: 'to transport many things to Rome which could be a decoration for the city') resembles *ornamenta urbis... Romam devexit*. It does not recall it closely enough to be recognized in isolation, but once the relevance of the passage has already been established by the other verbal similarities and the fact that Verres and Marcellus are here compared, this reinforces the similarity, as does the reference in both passages to the temples of Honour and Virtue that Marcellus established in Rome at the Porta Capena. But Cicero explicitly says that the decorations of that temple are in his day there to be seen (*II Verr.* 4.121). In Livy that is no longer the case.

In other words, Livy presents the deleterious (though unintended) effects of Marcellus' actions in such a way as to recall not merely Verres, but the passage in which Cicero contrasted Verres unfavourably with Marcellus. As such his account can be seen as both an endorsement and a modification of Cicero's. Marcellus himself is no more culpable for his plunder than he was in Cicero: Livy, much as Cicero had done, notes that Marcellus' settlement in Sicily was done *fide et integritate* and that it worked to the credit of Rome,[103] and he also observes that even the artworks he took were legitimate prizes of war and used for religious purposes.[104] And, also like Cicero, he sees a contrast between this and the practice of his own day. But the difference is that he specifically connects the two: for him, Verres' behaviour may be unlike Marcellus', but it is also the ultimate consequence of it. And moreover even Verres will not form the end of the degeneration: for later (note *postremo*) the temples where, in Cicero's day, Marcellus' spoils were still available to be seen, by Livy's time had themselves been plundered. Livy's allusions to historical

---

[103] E.g. *II Verr.* 4.120 *non putavit ad laudem populi Romani hoc pertinere, hanc pulchritudi-nem... delere et extinguere* ('he did not think it was conducive to the praise of the Roman people to destroy and wipe out this beauty').

[104] Cf. *II Verr.* 4.121 *Romam quae adportata sunt, ad aedem Honoris et Virtutis itemque aliis in locis videmus* ('we see the things that were brought to Rome in the shrine of Honour and Virtue, and similarly in other places').

events here, as before, signal an historical connection and development
between and beyond two otherwise unrelated figures—even though in this
case the text through which the historical allusion is being made is not by an
historian.

From all of this we can get some sense of the range and flexibility of Livy's
practice of allusion. While it is certainly true that such allusions are less dense
than one might find in most poets and certain other historians, they are
still far more widely distributed and more complex than has usually been
recognized—and of course the examples I have discussed here form only a
small proportion of those we can identify, let alone those where the originals
are lost to us, since Livy demonstrably alludes not only to the texts we now
regard as canonical, but also to Greek historians of the Hellenistic age, little of
whose works survive. He alludes to orators as well as historians, to poets[105] as
well as prose writers. Sometimes an individual allusion is simply a passing
nuance given to the narrative, but at other times it links into a wider allusive
network, and sometimes one source alluded to is played off against another.
And most distinctive is that the allusions often carry specifically historical
implications about the behaviour of particular characters, the historical
models they adopted for themselves, and more broadly, the patterns of
historical change and decline that Livy is establishing for Roman history.

2.2. SOURCES

Perhaps the single question about Livy's Hannibalic narrative that has
received the most intense discussion is the issue of his sources. To some
degree this, like a lot of source-critical study, has necessarily been based on
limited evidence. Livy names a number of his sources, though usually only
when listing variant versions to his main narrative. The most frequently cited
is Coelius Antipater (21.38.6, 21.46.10, 21.47.4, 22.31.8–9, 23.6.8, 26.11.10,
27.27.13, 28.46.14, 29.25.3, 29.27.14, 29.35.2), followed by Valerius Antias
(25.39.14, 26.49.3, 26.49.5, 28.46.14, 29.35.2, 30.3.6, 30.19.11, 30.29.7). There
are also single citations of Cincius Alimentus (21.38.3), Fabius Pictor (22.7.4),

---

[105] Foucher (2000: 285–99) discusses allusions to poets in Livy, concluding that while he
often uses language with a poetic register, it is relatively rare for him to allude directly to poets,
with most examples being in the first pentad. However, Foucher oddly neglects to consider
allusions to Greek poetry, and so overlooks (e.g.) the Homeric passages I have identified in this
chapter.

Claudius Quadrigarius (25.39.12),[106] Piso (25.39.15), and Silenus (26.49.3).[107] What all of these historians have in common is that nothing of their work survives beyond what we can deduce from their occasional citations by Livy himself and a few brief notices or quotations in other writers. Though we may be certain that Livy used at least some, and possibly all, of these sources far more than his bare citations would indicate, the assignment of parts of his narrative to any of them in particular necessarily involves a good deal of speculation (though one would not always realize that from the confidence with which some scholars have drawn conclusions and others have subsequently cited them).

The complications come with the possible source who does substantially survive: namely Polybius. Contrary to what one might have expected, our possession of substantial quantities of hard data has not diminished controversy: if anything the opposite. Polybius too is cited by Livy only once in the decade, at the very end (30.45.5). The question is how much, if at all, he used him prior to that. A few people have suggested that he used him throughout.[108] Rather more, including most of the leading scholars to have considered the question, have argued that he did not use him (at least as a principal source) at the start, but adopted him for parts of the later books:[109] those scholars have generally held Books 21–22 to be entirely non-Polybian,[110] and suggest that their manifest similarities with Polybius Book 3 are the result either of Livy employing a source who might himself have used Polybius, such as Coelius,[111] or else of Livy's source and Polybius having a source in common.[112] Still other scholars have suggested that Livy did not use Polybius

---

[106] This identification is highly probable but not certain. Livy speaks here of 'Claudius, who translated the annals of Acilius from Greek into Latin'. He is identified with Claudius Quadrigarius by e.g. *HRR* (Claudius Quadrigarius fr. 57A), cf. Briscoe (1981: 165); also Chassignet (2004: xxx) with further bibliography; *contra* Zimmerer (1937: 10–14).

[107] In addition Clodius Licinus is apparently cited at 29.22.10; but that passage does not appear in all manuscripts and should probably be deleted as a later gloss (see Oakley 1992).

[108] E.g. Sontheimer (1934), Pianezzola (1969), Schwarte (1983: 18–22), Hoyos (2006: esp. 417–21).

[109] E.g. Nissen (1863: 83–5), de Sanctis (1968: 168–73), Klotz (1940–41: 111–99), Walsh (1961: 124–32), Burck (1971: 26–7), Luce (1977: 178–80).

[110] Sometimes this is extended to Book 23: this makes little practical difference to the argument, since the sections of Polybius 7 that must have corresponded to Livy 23 are almost entirely lost. The only real overlap is Polybius 7.1, a summary of the Capua and Petelia narratives taken from Athenaeus (7.1.1–3) and the Suda (7.1.4), neither of which can have stood in that form in Polybius' original text (if indeed the Suda passage is genuinely Polybian at all). In addition Polybius 7.9 is a verbatim record of the treaty between Philip and Hannibal which Livy summarizes at 23.33.10–12, probably inaccurately (see de Sanctis 1968: 393).

[111] So e.g. de Sanctis (1968: 168–73), Soltau (1897: 56–69, who identifies the intervening source as Claudius Quadrigarius).

[112] So e.g. Walsh (1961: 124–32), Burck (1971: 26–7), Schmitt (1991).

at all as a primary source in the Third Decade: here too similarities are explained by hypothesizing one or more intermediate sources. This last is the conclusion reached by the most comprehensive and powerful study of Livy's use of Polybius, by Tränkle, who seeks to demonstrate that Livy only adopted Polybius in time to use him as his major source for the Second Macedonian War, beginning in Book 31.[113] Tränkle's conclusions have certainly not been universally accepted,[114] but his arguments have received no systematic response, nor, if he is wrong, has any firm conclusion been reached on the question of how far Livy actually did use Polybius in Books 21–30.

Tränkle's argument is fundamentally based upon his analysis of Livy's use of Polybius in the Fourth and Fifth Decades, which occupies the bulk of his book. Having examined the various changes that Livy there made to his Polybian originals, he then takes a number of passages in the Third Decade where scholars have alleged that Livy used Polybius, which he examines in great detail, listing the points at which they differ from one another. He argues that in the Third Decade the differences between Livy and Polybius far exceed anything that one can parallel in the Fourth or the Fifth in either density and manner: if Livy were using Polybius here, he would be adapting him in ways entirely unlike his relatively faithful use of him in the later decades. It is methodologically unacceptable, he suggests, to postulate such a change: instead we should conclude that Livy was not making direct use of Polybius in these books at all.

Arguments like this, as Tränkle is aware,[115] run the risk of circularity. If our sole criterion for deciding whether Livy is employing Polybius as a source in the Third Decade is to see if his practice conforms to that of the Fourth and Fifth Decades, we exclude *a priori* the possibility that he did use Polybius but that his manner of handling his sources changed. Tränkle's answer to this is to place the onus on the person wishing to argue for such a change: we should assume that Livy's practice is constant unless we can see a good reason why it should not have been. This is a reasonable answer as far as it goes; but it leaves a number of issues unaddressed. First, the danger of circularity rests not only in our assumptions about the similarity between the Third Decade and the later decades, but also might arise from the way we have treated the later decades themselves. For example, there may be passages in Books 31–45

---

[113] Tränkle (1977: 193–241). A not dissimilar position had earlier been adopted by Soltau (1894a, 1894b), who argued that Livy began to use Polybius only while writing Book 30, but that he then went back and inserted a number of 'Polybian' episodes into Books 24–29. Cf. also Bornecque (1933: 82–3).

[114] He is followed by e.g. Hus (1979), Kukofka (1990: 164–8), Leidig (1994). Sceptics include Briscoe (1978), Rich (1978), Meister (1979: 181), Breebaart (1980).

[115] Cf. Tränkle (1977: 195).

where Livy differs from Polybius to much the same degree as in the Third Decade. If we have decided that those passages cannot be Polybian because of the degree of difference, then we cannot without circularity conclude that the use of Polybius in the Third Decade is anomalous; the same is true if we have overlooked substantial changes in avowedly Polybian passages. Second, we need to consider whether there might be other differences between the Third Decade and the later books that might correlate to a change in Livy's handling of his sources: if there are such differences, then it becomes distinctly less attractive to base our arguments on the assumption that he cannot have changed. Third, we need to consider not only the dissimilarities between Livy and Polybius in the Third Decade, but also the similarities: whether these can be plausibly explained without postulating a direct use of Polybius by Livy. If explaining such similarities via an intermediate source looks implausible on other grounds, then the idea that Livy changed his practice may prove a more economical explanation.

Let us start with the first of these issues. Is Tränkle's claim that Livy did not alter Polybius to this degree in the Fourth and Fifth Decades well founded? A comprehensive examination of the question is beyond the remit of this book;[116] but we may briefly note some instances where Tränkle may unreasonably have limited the scope that Livy allowed himself to alter a Polybian original. At 36.35.12–13 Livy reports an embassy from Philip to Rome; the same embassy appears in Polybius 21.3.1–3. Both versions of the embassy have the Romans freeing Philip's son Demetrius; Livy's version however has the ambassadors making an offering, which is not in Polybius; Polybius has the Senate proposing to remit Philip's tribute, which is not in Livy. Tränkle does not discuss the passage, presumably because (in common with some other scholars)[117] he does not regard it as deriving from Polybius. But that is hardly provable: Briscoe suggests that Livy has here combined Polybian material with other matter derived from Roman sources.[118] If so, he is altering Polybius to a very substantial degree, both adding and omitting material within a very short space.

A different issue arises at 37.55.4–56.10, describing the Senate's settlement in Asia following the battle of Magnesia. This corresponds closely to Polybius

---

[116] Note Briscoe (1993), comparing one passage from Livy Book 44 with its Polybian original. He shows the extent of Livy's alterations, and his aim in doing so (Briscoe 1993: 40) is to provide data for judging whether Tränkle's rejection of a Polybian origin for comparable passages in the Third Decade is justified. Briscoe never explicitly draws a conclusion, but his analysis supports the hypothesis that even in the later books, Livy's willingness to alter Polybius is substantially greater than Tränkle had indicated.

[117] E.g. Nissen (1863: 185), Walbank (1979: 91).

[118] Briscoe (1981: 273–4).

21.24.4–15—except that Livy inserts a passage (37.55.7–56.6) in which he gives the names of the commissioners that the Senate sent and their detailed remit: neither is in Polybius. Conversely at the same point he omits from Polybius 21.24.9 the specific notice of the commission's departure. Here Tränkle agrees that Livy used Polybius, but denies that he made such substantial changes to him: he claims that Polybius' original text had all of these details, but that they were omitted by the excerptor who preserves this fragment.[119] This argument however is implausible, since the additional details of the settlement do not fully concur with the rest of Polybius' description, which points to Livy incorporating material from a different source.[120] Here too Tränkle seems to have underestimated the degree to which Livy would alter Polybius.

One further example can be given. Livy 45.27.5–28.6 describes the tour of Greece made by Aemilius Paullus after Pydna. The passage corresponds to Polybius 30.10, which is universally agreed to be its source.[121] The Polybian passage unfortunately does not survive complete, but consists of a series of short extracts. However, those extracts point to a version of the tour quite unlike Livy's. In Polybius the focus is partly on the change in fortune represented by Aemilius replacing Perseus' statues with his own, and partly on Aemilius' interest in the layout of the cities. Nothing of this appears in Livy, whose primary focus is on Aemilius' historical interest and religious actions in the sites he visits, the latter of which, at any rate, seems unlikely to be Polybian, since it stands so far from his usual concerns.[122] This entirely changes the significance—and, in all likelihood, the specific detail—of what Aemilius is reported as seeing on his tour. Tränkle accepts the Polybian origins of the Livy passage, and makes a couple of brief comments on some of the alterations,[123] but fails to draw the general conclusion about Livy's radical reworking of his Polybian material across the passage as a whole.

So Tränkle, by underplaying the changes Livy was prepared to make to Polybius in the Fourth and Fifth Decades, lays his argument open to possible accusations of circularity when it comes to the Third. But this of itself is not sufficient to show that his conclusions are mistaken. He could reasonably object that (as he indeed explicitly states)[124] Livy in certain special instances in the Fourth and Fifth Decades was prepared to make more radical changes

---

[119] Tränkle (1977: 36–8); cf. Nissen (1863: 199–200).

[120] Briscoe (1981: 384–5).

[121] E.g. Nissen (1863: 276–7), Klotz (1940–41: 76), Eigler (2003: 254).

[122] See the various arguments of Levene (1993: 121–2), Eigler (2003: 259–60), Levene (2006a: 84–7).

[123] Tränkle (1977: 97, 99, 166–7).

[124] Tränkle (1977: 195).

to Polybius, but that if we think he used Polybius in the Third, we are faced with something of a quite different order, where radical reworking is the norm rather than the exception. Another way of putting the same objection would be that there are long stretches in the Fourth Decade where Livy has demonstrably used Polybius while making only minimal changes to him. There is nowhere in the Third Decade where we can see something comparable; and this, unless we can find some other explanation, should lead us to conclude that he did not use Polybius at all.

This brings us to the second issue (above, 129). Are we entitled to assume that Livy's use of his sources was uniform across his work? An objection to such an assumption could be raised even with the Fourth Decade alone, for one might point out that for the Eastern material where he primarily employed him, Polybius was a source of high (though not unchallengeable) reliability.[125] Livy does not seem to have regarded any of his Roman sources as superior to quite that degree, and one might plausibly hypothesize that he was, accordingly, prepared to adapt them more freely.[126] The same point can be made for the possible use of Polybius in the Third Decade, which deals with an area in which his authority was far less assured.[127]

One can go still further; for there are other respects in which the Third Decade diverges from the Fourth. In Books 21–30 Livy can be shown to have created a consistent religious subtext running across the entire decade. In Books 31–40 not only is there no such subtext, but Livy seems actively to avoid creating one, despite having plenty of possible material with which he might do so: the religious material thus looks relatively extraneous to much of the rest of the narrative. This gives those books an entirely different character, and one that appears to be at least in part due to changes in the way in which Livy approaches his source material in those books.[128] This suggests that one cannot legitimately extrapolate from the Fourth Decade to the Third when considering how Livy handles sources. And, more generally, the significant change in quality between the Third Decade and the Fourth needs acknowledgement: a subjective point, but one that has a great deal of force nevertheless. As I showed in Chapter 1, Livy organizes the Third Decade into a remarkable and consistent unity, by shaping individual books, by creating patterns and balances within and between those books, and by arranging his narrative to create striking and significant juxtapositions and arrangements. While there are many fine sustained pieces of writing in Books 31–40, and

[125] 33.10.10; but see Luce (1977: 145–50).
[126] Cf. Briscoe (1973: 9–11).
[127] Cf. Rich (1978).
[128] See Levene (1993: esp. 102–3, 124–5, 241–2).

even more in Books 41–5, and while it is demonstrable that Livy in many respects took great care to shape the overall structure of those decades, nevertheless they abound with clumsiness, lapses, and points of confusion.[129] Such problems are far rarer in the Third Decade, which engages with its material with a more consistent and single-mindedly dramatic sense. This too suggests that one should be wary of assuming that the relatively mechanical reproduction of significant portions of Polybius which we see in the Fourth Decade can legitimately be assumed to reflect Livy's practice in dealing with his sources in the Third.

Indeed, there is a certain amount of data to support this point directly. Cicero in *De Divinatione* records two stories from Coelius Antipater which correspond to episodes that Livy describes in Books 21–22. First, the dream of Hannibal after the fall of Saguntum is described in the following terms (Cicero, *Div.* 1.49 = Coelius Antipater fr. 11P):

Hannibalem, cum cepisset Saguntum, visum esse in somnis a Iove in deorum concilium vocari; quo cum venisset, Iovem imperavisse, ut Italiae bellum inferret, ducemque ei unum e concilio datum, quo illum utentem cum exercitu progredi coepisse; tum ei ducem illum praecepisse, ne respiceret; illum autem id diutius facere non potuisse elatumque cupiditate respexisse; tum visam beluam vastam et immanem circumplicatam serpentibus, quacumque incederet, omnia arbusta, virgulta, tecta pervertere; et eum admiratum quaesisse de deo, quodnam illud esset tale monstrum; et deum respondisse vastitatem esse Italiae praecepisseque, ut pergeret protinus, quid retro atque a tergo fieret, ne laboraret.

After Hannibal had captured Saguntum, he dreamed that he was summoned by Jupiter into a council of the gods. When he came there, Jupiter commanded him to invade Italy, and someone from the council was given to him as a guide. Following him he began to advance with his army. Then the guide instructed him not to look back; he could not do so any longer, and carried away by eagerness looked back, whereupon he saw a huge and monstrous beast entwined with serpents overturning all the trees, bushes, and buildings wherever it went. Hannibal was amazed and asked the god what so monstrous a creature was, and the god replied that it was the devastation of Italy, and instructed him to continue onwards and not be concerned about what happened behind him and in the rear.

Livy's version of this appears at 21.22.6–9:

ibi fama est in quiete visum ab eo iuvenem divina specie, qui se ab Iove diceret ducem in Italiam Hannibali missum: proinde sequeretur neque usquam a se deflecteret oculos. pavidum primo nusquam circumspicientem aut respicientem secutum; deinde cura ingenii humani cum, quidnam id esset, quod respicere vetitus esset,

---

[129] Luce (1977) examines systematically and sympathetically the ways in which Livy sought to shape these books, but clearsightedly acknowledges their failures and weaknesses as well.

agitaret animo, temperare oculis nequivisse; tum vidisse post sese serpentem mira magnitudine cum ingenti arborum ac virgultorum strage ferri, ac post insequi cum fragore caeli nimbum. tum, quae moles ea quidve prodigii esset, quaerentem audisse, vastitatem Italiae esse: pergeret porro ire nec ultra inquireret sineretque fata in occulto esse.

There the story goes that in the night he saw a young man of divine appearance, who said that he had been sent by Jupiter to Hannibal as a guide into Italy: he should therefore follow and not turn his eyes from him. In panic Hannibal initially followed without looking around at anything or looking back; then through natural human concern he began to wonder what he had been forbidden to look back at, and could not control his eyes. Then he saw behind him a serpent of amazing size proceeding with vast destruction of trees and bushes, and a cloud followed behind it with a thunderous sky. Then he asked what that monster was or what sort of prodigy it was, and heard that it was the devastation of Italy: he should continue forwards nor ask further and allow the fates to remain hidden.

We have already seen that Livy cites Coelius by name more than any other author, and it is manifest that he is drawing on him here. Even granted that Cicero may well be adapting Coelius' phrasing, the verbal overlap with Livy is remarkably close. But that close overlap goes hand in hand with significant changes to the actual substance of Coelius' version. Livy removes the whole opening section, in which Hannibal is invited into a council of the gods. A monster entwined with serpents in Coelius becomes a monstrous serpent in Livy. Likewise Livy's thundercloud does not appear to correspond to anything in Coelius (though that could admittedly be Cicero's omission). The primary reasons for the alteration appear to be to make the vision look more natural while diminishing the sense that the gods might actively be endorsing Hannibal's invasion.[130]

Even more striking is Cicero, *Div.* 1.77 = Coelius Antipater fr. 20P:

qui exercitu lustrato cum Arretium versus castra movisset et contra Hannibalem legiones duceret, et ipse et equus eius ante signum Iovis Statoris sine causa repente concidit nec eam rem habuit religioni obiecto signo, ut peritis videbatur, ne committeret proelium. idem cum tripudio auspicaretur, pullarius diem proelii committendi differebat. tum Flaminius ex eo quaesivit, si ne postea quidem pulli pascerentur, quid faciendum censeret. cum ille quiescendum respondisset, Flaminius: 'praeclara vero auspicia, si esurientibus pullis res geri poterit, saturis nihil geretur!' itaque signa convelli et se sequi iussit. quo tempore cum signifer primi hastati signum non posset movere loco, nec quicquam proficeretur, plures cum accederent, Flaminius re nuntiata, suo more, neglexit.

When he [Flaminius] had purified his army, moved his camp towards Arretium and was leading the legions against Hannibal, both he and his horse suddenly and inexplicably fell before the statue of Jupiter the Stayer; but he did not take this as a

---

[130] See e.g. Herrmann (1979: 82–4), Levene (1993: 45–6).

matter of religion, although a sign had been offered, the experts thought, to stop him from engaging in battle. When the same man took auspices with the *tripudium*, the chicken-keeper postponed the day of engaging in battle. Then Flaminius asked him what he would recommend should be done if the chickens refused to eat even later. He replied that one should be inactive, to which Flaminius said 'Splendid auspices indeed, if one can campaign with hungry chickens, but not at all with full ones!' So he ordered them to pull up the standards and follow him. At that point the standard-bearer of the first line could not shift the standard from its place, nor did it avail at all when more people came to help; it was reported to Flaminius, who as usual neglected it.

This takes place in the run-up to the battle of Lake Trasimene. In this case, admittedly, the wording does not overlap with Livy's account to such a degree (which may be a reflection of Cicero's summary rather than Livy's changes), but the narratives parallel one another closely enough that here too Coelius is reasonably assumed to be Livy's source (22.3.11–13):[131]

haec simul increpans cum ocius signa convelli iuberet et ipse in equum insiluisset, equus repente corruit consulemque lapsum super caput effudit. territis omnibus, qui circa erant, velut foedo omine incipiendae rei insuper nuntiatur signum omni vi moliente signifero convelli nequire. conversus ad nuntium 'num litteras quoque' inquit 'ab senatu adfers, quae me rem gerere vetant? abi, nuntia, effodiant signum, si ad convellendum manus prae metu obtorpuerit.'

With these taunts he ordered the standards to be pulled up swiftly and leapt onto his horse. The horse suddenly stumbled and threw the consul to the ground over its head. Everyone around was terrified by the apparently bad omen at the outset; and to crown this it was announced that, although the standard-bearer strove with all his might, the standard could not be pulled up. He turned to the messenger, and said 'Presumably you are not bringing me letters too from the senate forbidding me from campaigning? Go and tell them to dig up the standard, if their hands are too numb from fear to pull it up.'

The absence of Flaminius' last words from Cicero is not significant, since Cicero appears to be compressing the last part of the story. But simply looking at the general structure of the narrative, it is clear that Livy has altered Coelius substantially. It is obvious that he has missed out altogether the middle of the three omens; slightly less obvious, but even more significant, is that he has changed the entire circumstances under which they were received. In Coelius there are three events at different stages. First the fall of the horse, which appears to take place during the march rather than at the moment of setting out to battle; then the chicken omen, which must come later, since the commander himself is

---

[131] E.g. Soltau (1894b: 82–3), Klotz (1940–1: 137); *contra* Schmitt (1991: 101–12), whose elaborate argument however assumes an implausibly precise correlation between shared and distinct details in the surviving accounts of the episode (not only Coelius and Livy, but also Plut., *Fab.* 2.2–3.6) and the presumed sources for those accounts.

now taking the auspices; and finally the order to pull up the standard followed by the failure to do so. Livy conflates the whole series of omens into the last possible moment, with Flaminius ordering the standards to be pulled up at the start, then leaping onto and falling from his horse, and then receiving the news that the standards could not be moved. The whole occasion is rewritten in order to focus the events into a single dramatic moment.[132]

The limitations of our evidence only allow us this brief snapshot of Livy's handling of Coelius in Books 21–30, but it is enough to show that Tränkle's assumption that Livy handled his sources in the Third Decade in the same way as he did in the Fourth is ill-founded. Here we have precisely the same phenomena that we find in the allegedly Polybian passages of the Third Decade, and which Tränkle used as a reason to deny that those passages were Polybian at all: major and repeated changes of substance even within a small body of text. Much as we might have expected from a comparison of their general character, we may conclude that the Third Decade involved Livy reworking his source data to a degree that is rare in the Polybian sections of the Fourth.

But still, even showing that Tränkle's extrapolation from the Fourth Decade to the Third is based on flawed premises is not enough to prove that Livy actually did use Polybius in the latter. For that we need to go to the third plank of our argument (cf. above, 128–9) and examine the text itself, to show whether the hypothesis that Livy used Polybius is more plausible than the competing hypotheses of common and/or intermediate sources.

Tränkle's argument comprises fifty closely argued pages, with detailed analysis of a number of passages from Books 24–30 in which the use of Polybius is widely accepted, in order to show in each case that the differences from Polybius are too great for Livy to have used him directly. One might feel that ideally I should examine each passage anew in equal detail to show that the differences are not unacceptably large. However, the available space does not allow it, and even if space were not an issue, it would be both wearisome and repetitive for the reader, since many of the relevant arguments have already been made in pointing out the problems in Tränkle's general approach. Instead, therefore, I shall examine passages that Tränkle did not. Tränkle did not look at any passages from Books 21–22, relying on the wide acceptance that those could not be Polybian anyway.[133] I intend to revisit this question, and therefore will take my chief examples from those books. If it is accepted that even in these Livy is drawing directly on Polybius, it will, I hope, follow *a fortiori* that he is doing so in the later books as well.

---

[132] Herrmann (1979: 115), Levene (1993: 40–2).
[133] Tränkle (1977: 193); cf. n. 109 above.

Sources and Intertexts

In Table 2.1 let us look at one famous passage: the final stage of Hannibal's crossing of the Alps, as described in Polybius 3.54.4–56.4, corresponding to Livy 21.35.10–38.2:

Table 2.1. Polybius and Livy on Hannibal crossing the Alps

[3.54.4] τῇ δ' ἐπαύριον ἀναζεύξας ἐνήρχετο τῆς καταβάσεως. ἐν ᾗ ᾗ πολεμίοις μὲν οὐκέτι περιέτυχε πλὴν τῶν λάθρᾳ κακοποιούντων,	[21.35.10] procedere inde agmen coepit, iam nihil ne hostibus quidem praeter parva furta per occasionem temptantibus.
ὑπὸ δὲ τῶν τόπων καὶ τῆς χιόνος οὐ πολλῷ λείποντας ἀπέβαλε τῶν κατὰ τὴν ἀνάβασιν φθαρέντων.	[§11] ceterum iter multo quam in adscensu fuerat, ut pleraque Alpium ab Italia sicut breviora ita adrectiora sunt, difficilius fuit.
[§5] οὔσης γὰρ στενῆς καὶ κατωφεροῦς τῆς καταβάσεως, τῆς δὲ χιόνος ἄδηλον ποιούσης ἑκάστοις τὴν ἐπίβασιν, πᾶν τὸ παραπεσὸν τῆς ὁδοῦ καὶ σφαλὲν ἐφέρετο κατὰ τῶν κρημνῶν.	[§12] omnis enim ferme via praeceps, angusta, lubrica erat, ut neque sustinere se ab lapsu possent nec, qui paulum titubassent, haerere adfixi vestigio suo, aliique super alios et iumenta in homines occiderent.
[§6] οὐ μὴν ἀλλὰ ταύτην μὲν ὑπέφερον τὴν ταλαιπωρίαν, ἅτε συνήθεις ὄντες ἤδη τοῖς τοιούτοις κακοῖς·	
[§7] ἅμα δὲ τῷ παραγενέσθαι πρὸς τοιοῦτον τόπον, ὃν οὔτε τοῖς θηρίοις οὔτε τοῖς ὑποζυγίοις δυνατὸν ἦν παρελθεῖν διὰ τὴν στενότητα,	[36.1] ventum deinde ad multo angustiorem rupem atque ita rectis saxis, ut aegre expeditus miles temptabundus manibusque retinens virgulta ac stirpes circa eminentes demittere sese posset.
σχεδὸν ἐπὶ τρί' ἡμιστάδια τῆς ἀπορρῶγος καὶ πρὸ τοῦ μὲν οὔσης, τότε δὲ καὶ μᾶλλον ἔτι προσφάτως ἀπερρωγυίας,	[§2] natura locus iam ante praeceps recenti lapsu terrae in pedum mille admodum altitudinem abruptus erat.
ἐνταῦθα πάλιν ἀθυμῆσαι καὶ διατραπῆναι συνέβη τὸ πλῆθος.	[§3] ibi cum velut ad finem viae equites constitissent, miranti Hannibali quae res moraretur agmen, nuntiatur rupem inviam esse. [§4] digressus deinde ipse ad locum visendum.
[§8] τὸ μὲν οὖν πρῶτον ἐπεβάλετο περιελθεῖν τὰς δυσχωρίας ὁ τῶν Καρχηδονίων στρατηγός·	haud dubia res visa, quin per invia circa nec trita antea quamvis longo ambitu circumduceret agmen.
ἐπιγενομένης δὲ χιόνος καὶ ταύτην ἀδύνατον ποιούσης τὴν πορείαν, ἀπέστη τῆς ἐπιβολῆς. [55.1] τὸ γὰρ συμβαῖνον ἴδιον ἦν καὶ παρηλλαγμένον.	[§5] ea vero via insuperabilis fuit.
ἐπὶ γὰρ τὴν προϋπάρχουσαν χιόνα καὶ διαμεμενηκυίαν ἐκ τοῦ πρότερον χειμῶνος ἄρτι τῆς ἐπ' ἔτους πεπτωκυίας, ταύτην μὲν εὐδιάκοπτον εἶναι συνέβαινε καὶ διὰ τὸ πρόσφατον οὖσαν ἀπαλὴν ὑπάρχειν καὶ διὰ τὸ μηδέπω βάθος ἔχειν.	nam cum super veterem nivem intactam nova modicae altitudinis esset, molli nec praealtae facile pedes ingredientium insistebant;
[§2] ὁπότε δὲ ταύτην διαπατήσαντες ἐπὶ τὴν ὑποκάτω καὶ συνεστηκυῖαν ἐπιβαῖεν, οὐκέτι διέκοπτον, ἀλλ' ἐπέπλεον ὀλισθάνοντες ἀμφοτέροις ἅμα τοῖς ποσί, καθάπερ ἐπὶ τῇ γῇ συμβαίνει τοῖς διὰ τῶν ἀκροπήλων πορευομένοις.	[§6] ut vero tot hominum iumentorumque incessu dilapsa est, per nudam infra glaciem fluentemque tabem liquescentis nivis ingrediebantur.

[§3] τὸ δὲ συνεξακολουθοῦν τούτοις ἔτι δυσχερέστερον ὑπῆρχεν. [§4] οἱ μὲν γὰρ ἄνδρες οὐ δυνάμενοι τὴν κάτω χιόνα διακόπτειν, ὁπότε πεσόντες βουληθεῖεν ἢ τοῖς γόνασιν ἢ ταῖς χερσὶ προσεξερείσασθαι πρὸς τὴν ἐξανάστασιν, τότε καὶ μᾶλλον ἐπέπλεον ἅμα πᾶσι τοῖς ἐρείσμασιν, ἐπὶ πολὺ καταφερῶν ὄντων τῶν χωρίων·

[§5] τὰ δ' ὑποζύγια διέκοπτεν, ὅτε πέσοι, τὴν κάτω χιόνα κατὰ τὴν διανάστασιν, διακόψαντα δ' ἔμενε μετὰ τῶν φορτίων οἷον καταπεπηγότα διά τε τὸ βάρος καὶ διὰ τὸ πῆγμα τῆς προϋπαρχούσης χιόνος.

[§6] ὅθεν ἀποστὰς τῆς τοιαύτης ἐλπίδος ἐστρατοπέδευσε περὶ τὴν ῥάχιν, διαμησάμενος τὴν ἐπ' αὐτῇ χιόνα, καὶ μετὰ ταῦτα παραστήσας τὰ πλήθη τὸν κρημνὸν ἐξῳκοδόμει μετὰ πολλῆς ταλαιπωρίας.

[§7] τοῖς μὲν οὖν ὑποζυγίοις καὶ τοῖς ἵπποις ἱκανὴν ἐποίησε πάροδον ἐν ἡμέρᾳ μιᾷ. διὸ καὶ ταῦτα μὲν εὐθέως διαγαγὼν καὶ καταστρατοπεδεύσας περὶ τοὺς ἐκφεύγοντας ἤδη τὴν χιόνα τόπους διαφῆκε πρὸς τὰς νομάς, [§8] τοὺς δὲ Νομάδας ἀνὰ μέρος προῆγε πρὸς τὴν οἰκοδομίαν, καὶ μόλις ἐν ἡμέραις τρισὶ κακοπαθήσας διήγαγε τὰ θηρία.

καὶ τάδε συνέβαινε κακῶς ὑπὸ τοῦ λιμοῦ διατεθεῖσθαι· [§9] τῶν γὰρ Ἄλπεων τὰ μὲν ἄκρα καὶ τὰ πρὸς τὰς ὑπερβολὰς ἀνήκοντα τελέως ἄδενδρα καὶ ψιλὰ πάντ' ἔστι διὰ τὸ συνεχῶς ἐπιμένειν τὴν χιόνα καὶ θέρους καὶ χειμῶνος,

τὰ δ' ὑπὸ μέσην τὴν παρώρειαν ἐξ ἀμφοῖν τοῖν μεροῖν ὑλοφόρα καὶ δενδροφόρα καὶ τὸ ὅλον οἰκήσιμ' ἔστιν.

[56.1] Ἀννίβας δὲ συναθροίσας ὁμοῦ πᾶσαν τὴν δύναμιν κατέβαινε, καὶ τριταῖος ἀπὸ τῶν προειρημένων κρημνῶν διανύσας ἥψατο τῶν ἐπιπέδων,

[§7] taetra ibi luctatio erat via lubrica non recipiente vestigium et in prono citius pedes fallente, ut, seu manibus in adsurgendo seu genu se adiuvissent, ipsis adminiculis prolapsis iterum corruerent; nec stirpes circa radicesve, ad quas pede aut manu quisquam eniti posset, erant; ita in levi tantum glacie tabidaque nive volutabantur.

[§8] iumenta secabant interdum etiam infimam ingredientia nivem et prolapsa iactandis gravius in conitendo ungulis penitus perfringebant, ut pleraque velut pedica capta haererent in dura et alta concreta glacie.

[37.1] tandem nequiquam iumentis atque hominibus fatigatis castra in iugo posita, aegerrime ad id ipsum loco purgato: tantum nivis fodiendum atque egerendum fuit. [§2] inde ad rupem muniendam, per quam unam via esse poterat, milites ducti, cum caedendum esset saxum, arboribus circa inmanibus deiectis detruncatisque struem ingentem lignorum faciunt eamque, cum et vis venti apta faciendo igni coorta esset, succendunt ardentiaque saxa infuso aceto putrefaciunt.

[§3] ita torridam incendio rupem ferro pandunt molliuntque anfractibus modicis clivos, ut non iumenta solum sed elephanti etiam deduci possent.

[§4] quadriduum circa rupem consumptum iumentis prope fame absumptis; nuda enim fere cacumina sunt et, si quid est pabuli, obruunt nives.

[§5] inferiora valles apricosque quosdam colles habent rivosque prope silvas et iam humano cultu digniora loca.

[§6] ibi iumenta in pabulum missa et quies muniendo fessis hominibus data.

triduo inde ad planum descensum et iam locis mollioribus et accolarum ingeniis.

(continued)

Table 2.1. (Continued)

[§2] πολλοὺς μὲν ἀπολωλεκὼς τῶν
στρατιωτῶν ὑπό τε τῶν πολεμίων καὶ τῶν
ποταμῶν ἐν τῇ καθόλου πορείᾳ, πολλοὺς δ᾽ ὑπὸ
τῶν κρημνῶν καὶ τῶν δυσχωριῶν κατὰ τὰς
Ἄλπεις οὐ μόνον ἄνδρας, ἔτι δὲ πλείους ἵππους
καὶ ὑποζύγια.

[§3] τέλος δὲ τὴν μὲν πᾶσαν πορείαν ἐκ Καινῆς
πόλεως ἐν πέντε μησὶ ποιησάμενος τὴν δὲ τῶν
Ἄλπεων ὑπερβολὴν ἡμέραις δεκαπέντε κατῆρε
τολμηρῶς εἰς τὰ περὶ τὸν Πάδον πεδία καὶ τὸ
τῶν Ἰνσόμβρων ἔθνος,

[§4] ἔχων τὸ διασῳζόμενον μέρος τῆς μὲν τῶν
Λιβύων δυνάμεως πεζοὺς μυρίους καὶ
δισχιλίους, τῆς δὲ τῶν Ἰβήρων εἰς
ὀκτακισχιλίους, ἱππεῖς δὲ τοὺς πάντας οὐ
πλείους ἑξακισχιλίων, ὡς αὐτὸς ἐν τῇ στήλῃ τῇ
περὶ τοῦ πλήθους ἐχούσῃ τὴν ἐπιγραφὴν ἐπὶ
Λακινίῳ διασαφεῖ.

[38.1] hoc maxime modo in Italiam
perventum est, quinto mense a Carthagine
Nova, ut quidam auctores sunt, quinto
decimo die Alpibus superatis.

[§2] quantae copiae transgresso in Italiam
Hannibali fuerint, nequaquam inter auctores
constat. qui plurimum, centum milia
peditum, viginti equitum fuisse scribunt; qui
minimum, viginti milia peditum, sex
equitum.

[3.54.4] On the next day he broke camp and
began the descent. During this time he no
longer encountered enemies, apart from those
causing trouble by deception,

but because of the ground and the snow he
lost not far short of the numbers who died on
the ascent.

[21.35.10] Then the column began to move
forward, with even the enemy now attempting
nothing apart from minor and opportunistic
deceptions.

[§11] But the route was much more difficult
than it had been in the ascent, as most of the
Alps on the Italian side are both shorter and
steeper.

[§5] For the descent was narrow and steep,
and the snow made the footing unclear for
everyone, and anything that missed the path
and stumbled fell down the precipice.

[§12] For almost the entire road was steep,
narrow, and slippery, so that they could
neither keep themselves from falling, nor
could people who slightly stumbled keep
themselves firmly in their footing, and people
fell on top of each other and pack-animals fell
against the men.

[§6] But they endured this hardship, since
they were by now accustomed to such
problems;

[§7] but when they came to a place such that
neither the elephants nor the pack-animals
could pass because of the narrowness,

[36.1] Then they came to a much narrower
cliff and rocks vertical to the point that only
with difficulty could light-armed troops let
themselves down, feeling their way, and
holding shrubs and projecting stumps round
about with their hands.

something like one and a half stades of broken
land even beforehand, but then even more so
with it recently having broken off,

[§2] The place was naturally steep even
beforehand, but through a recent fall of earth
was something like a thousand feet deep sheer
drop.[134]

---

[134] For this translation see further below, 142–3.

here again the army came to lose heart and was deterred.

[§8] At first the Carthaginian general attempted to go around the difficult area.

But with snow having fallen on it making this road impossible he abandoned the attempt. [55.1] The situation was peculiar and extraordinary.

For on top of the preexisting snow remaining from the previous winter was snow newly fallen this year, and this happened to be easy to break through both because being recent it was soft and because of not yet having depth.

[§2] And when having trodden through this and walked on the snow congealed below, they no longer broke through it, but slipped, sliding along with both feet, as happens on the ground to those walking through surface mud.

[§3] The consequence was still more unpleasant. [§4] The men were not able to break through the snow below, and when they fell and helped with either knees or hands to support themselves to stand up, then all the more they slid along with all their supports, the area being very steep.

[§5] The pack animals, when they fell, broke through the snow underneath as they rose, and having broken through remained with their packs as if stuck because of the weight and the congealing of the pre-existing snow.

[§6] Consequently he gave up such hope and pitched camp on the ridge, having cleared away the snow, and after this set the army to build up the cliff with great trouble.

[§3] The cavalry stopped there as if they had reached the end of the road, and when Hannibal wondered what was delaying the column, he was told that the cliff had no path through it. [§4] Then he went around to see the place in person.

There seemed to be no doubt that he would have to lead the column around on a long detour through the pathless and previously untrodden area around.

[§5] Indeed, this road was impassable.

For since on top of old and untouched snow there was new and moderately shallow snow, the softness and lack of depth meant walkers could not set their feet easily on it;

[§6] indeed when through so many man and pack-animals treading on it it had melted, they were walking across bare ice below and the liquid slush of melting snow.

[§7] The struggle there was dreadful, since the slippery road did not take their steps and quickly deceived their feet on the slope, so that, if they helped themselves with either hands or knees in standing up, their very supports slipped from under them and they fell again; nor were there stumps or roots around on which one could lean with foot or hand; so they were floundering simply on smooth ice and melting snow.

[§8] The pack-animals cut through sometimes when walking even on the layer of snow underneath and falling thrust out their hoofs more vigorously in their struggle and broke right through, so that a lot of them were caught as if in a trap and stuck in the hard and deep-congealed ice.

[37.1] At last, when to no avail pack-animals and men had worn themselves out, they pitched camp on the ridge, after with the utmost difficulty clearing a spot for it: so much snow had to be dug out and extracted. [§2] Then he led the soldiers to build up the cliff, the only place through which a route was possible.

(continued)

Table 2.1. (Continued)

	Since the rock had to be cut away, they felled huge trees round about, lopped them and made a large pile of wood, and, once a wind powerful enough for making a fire had arisen, set it on fire, and poured vinegar on the heated rocks to crumble them.
[§7] For the pack animals and the horses he made an adequate route in one day; so he immediately led these through, encamped on places which escaped the snow and sent them out to pasture, [§8] and sent the Numidians in relays to the building work, and with difficulty in three days in a bad state <u>led the elephants through</u>.	[§3] They opened out with iron tools the cliff which the fire had scorched and alleviated the slopes by making the path wind to a degree, so that not only the pack-animals but also <u>the elephants</u> could be <u>led down</u>.
And these ended up in a terrible state <u>from hunger</u>. [§9] <u>For the peaks</u> of the Alps and the places near the passes are all completely treeless and <u>bare</u> because of <u>the snow remaining on it</u> continuously in both summer and winter,	[§4] On the fourth day spent around the cliff the pack-animals had almost perished <u>from hunger</u>; <u>for the peaks</u> are more or less <u>bare</u>, and <u>the snows cover</u> any fodder there happens to be.
but <u>the portions beneath the middle</u> of the mountains on both sides are <u>wooded</u> and treed and generally <u>inhabitable</u>.	[§5] <u>The lower portions</u> have valleys and some sunny hills and rivers near <u>woods</u> and places now <u>more suitable for human cultivation</u>.
	[§6] There the pack-animals were put out to forage and rest was given to men weary from building.
[56.1] Hannibal having gathered together his whole force <u>descended</u>, and <u>on the third day</u> from the aforementioned cliffs arrived at <u>the plains</u>,	<u>On the third day</u> they <u>descended</u> from there to <u>the plain</u> and now the places and the character of the inhabitants were softer.
[§2] having lost many of his soldiers at the hand of the enemy and at rivers along the whole march, and many, not just men but even more horses and pack-animals, in the cliffs and difficult terrain in the Alps.	
[§3] But in the end having made the whole march <u>from New Carthage in five months</u>, and <u>the crossing of the Alps in fifteen days</u>, he descended boldly into the plains around the Po and the people of the Insubrians,	[38.1] This is a general account of how they reached Italy, <u>in the fifth month from New Carthage</u> according to some authors, <u>with the Alps crossed on the fifteenth day</u>.
[§4] the surviving portion of his African army being 12,000 infantry, and of his Spanish army about 8,000, and no more than 6,000 cavalry in total, as he himself says clearly on the column at Lacinium which has the inscription about the size of his army.	[§2] As to the size of Hannibal's forces when he crossed into Italy, the authorities do not agree by any means. Those who give the maximum write of there being 100,000 infantry and 20,000 cavalry; the minimum, 20,000 infantry, 6,000 cavalry.

That there is some relationship between Polybius and Livy here is obvious: the question is what sort of relationship it is. There are three possibilities: (a) that Livy used Polybius directly; (b) that he used an intermediate source—perhaps Coelius—who had in turn used Polybius; or (c) that Livy's source—again perhaps Coelius—had used a source whom Polybius himself had used.[135] Can we decide between these?

The broad outlines of the story in Livy and Polybius are similar, but there are a large number of differences in detail, as the table above shows. The most striking point is that when Hannibal's crossing in Polybius is stymied, the problem is that the ground on the *side* of the path has fallen away, leaving it too narrow for the animals, and it has to be built back up before the army can pass through (3.54.7, 3.55.6–8). Livy on the other hand forms that part of his narrative around the assumption that the land in *front* of the path has fallen away leaving a steep cliff, and a zig-zagging path has to be cut down its side (21.36.1–3, 21.37.1–3). In the course of this he has an entire extra section corresponding to nothing in Polybius, in which the Carthaginians use fire and vinegar in order to render the rocks friable (21.37.2). There are a number of smaller differences also. These are the sort of things that have led most scholars to conclude that Livy could not be dependent on Polybius here, either directly or indirectly. Instead, it is argued, the similarities point to a common source, which Polybius and (probably) Coelius are drawing on with different degrees of fidelity, and Livy then takes the material over from (probably) Coelius. The most likely identity of the common source is reckoned to be Silenus, whom we know Coelius used elsewhere,[136] and who accompanied Hannibal on his march[137] and so would have given a first-hand account of it.[138]

However, as I pointed out above (129), such hypotheses have to account for the similarities as well as the dissimilarities; and there are a number of problems about doing so. First, there are a remarkable number of similarities

---

[135] A theoretical fourth possibility would be that Livy had used Polybius' source directly, rather than indirectly via (e.g.) Coelius. However, that would require there to be a pre-Polybian source, presumably someone with access to Carthaginian material, whom both Polybius and Livy had read and used extensively. While this is not entirely impossible, none of the predecessors that either of them cites would in practice seem to fit the bill; and in any case, the same arguments as I shall be using to exclude a joint source whom Livy accessed indirectly will equally work to exclude a joint source whom he accessed directly (below, 143–4).

[136] Cicero, *Div.* 1.48-9 = Coelius Antipater fr. 34P and fr. 11P = Silenus *FGrH* 175 F 2.

[137] Nepos, *Hann.* 13.3 = *FGrH* 175 T 2.

[138] So e.g. Meyer (1958: 232); Jumeau (1964: 327–8), Walbank (1972: 120), Luce (1977: 178–9), *contra* Schmitt (1991: 19–24).

in wording and sentence structure (underlined in the table above), including at places where the authors diverge in substance. So, for example, at Polybius 3.54.5 and Livy 21.35.12 the same ideas of steepness, narrowness, stumbling, loss of footing and falling appear, even though in Polybius the situation is people who fail to see the path and so fall off the precipice, whereas Livy envisages people slipping on the path and falling against one another. Polybius 3.55.6 and Livy 21.37.1 both have Hannibal having his troops 'build up the cliff', although what this means is entirely different in the two cases, as I have explained above. Polybius at 3.55.5 has a simile of 'sticking' to describe the animals caught in the snow. Livy 21.36.8 likewise has a simile—his only simile in the passage—to describe the animals caught in the snow. In this case the simile is one of a trap—but Livy retains Polybius' idea of 'sticking' too, using *haererent* directly.

The most striking point of similarity comes at the place at which the narratives diverge most substantially, because Livy's description of the point where Hannibal is held up at 21.36.1 seems remarkably close to the parallel moment at Polybius 3.54.2.[139] Polybius uses the phrase σχεδὸν ἐπὶ τρί᾽ ἡμιστάδια τῆς ἀπορρῶγος, which taken in isolation could perfectly well be translated 'something like one and a half stades of sheer drop'.[140] And a phrase with—apparently—that meaning appears in Livy: *in pedum mille*[141] *admodum altitudinem abruptus*.[142] However, that does not fit the broader context in Polybius, which shows that his phrase actually means 'one and a half stades of broken land'[143]—in other words, the one and a half stades is the breadth of

---

[139] Cf. de Sanctis (1968: 75–6).

[140] LSJ s.v. ἀπορρώξ I 2.

[141] One and a half stades is in fact 900 feet. Livy's 'thousand feet' may arise from rounding up, or from assuming a version of the Greek foot (the length of which was not standardized) longer than the Roman foot (see *OCD*[3], 942–3). But more likely is that the difference in length reflects the different stage that is being described, for in both authors there have been two landslides: Polybius' figure reflects the situation after the first, Livy's phrase describes the worsened state after the second.

[142] The situation is slightly more complicated than I have set out in the text, because Livy's Latin is ambiguous, and the sequence of thought is rearranged from that in Polybius. Livy's phrase describes the situation after the second landslide (see also the last note), and *abruptus* could, as I have translated it here, be an adjective ('steep'), corresponding to ἀπορρῶγος in the first Polybian phrase (so L&S s.v. *abruptus* A). But *abruptus erat* could also mean 'had been broken off' (so *TLL* s.v. *abrumpo* I 1; *OLD* s.v. *abrumpo* 4), the equivalent of ἀπερρωγυίας in the second phrase in Polybius. Hence Livy effectively represents both phrases at once. But on both meanings the general sense in Livy is fixed by *praeceps* earlier in the sentence, which confirms that we are talking about a 'sheer drop'.

[143] LSJ s.v. ἀπορρώξ II. Cf. Mauersberger (1956: 201).

the land that has fallen away, not the depth to which it has fallen. Livy's account is apparently based on a misunderstanding, but not an obscure or stupid one. It appears to be a reasonable mistranslation of the precise phrase found in Polybius.

None of this absolutely rules out Polybius and Livy depending on a common source, but it looks distinctly uncomfortable. We would have to assume that Polybius and Livy, as well as Livy's source, were all three reproducing the wording of their own sources with remarkable fidelity, despite diverging significantly from one another in actual substance, and doing so to the point that all three retained a simile at precisely the same moment, and that the description of the point where the march is held up was described so faithfully by all of them that Livy ended up with a mistranslation of the exact phrase that we find in Polybius, even though he was talking about something quite different. Obviously this is not an impossible scenario—after all, *someone* here is preserving wording quite closely in a variety of respects, and if one person can do it, then three can. But that so much would be preserved so precisely through so many iterations, where the actual substance of what is being described differs so extensively, might be felt to test our credulity.

There is an even worse problem with the hypothesis of joint sources, which can be seen if we look now not at the specifics of wording, but the more general way in which the passage is structured. Livy and Polybius follow the same structure point by point. One might feel that this simply follows from the fact that they are narrating the same events, but the shared structure covers not only the narrative, but also their comments on the narrative. Both Polybius (3.54.4) and Livy (21.35.11) comment on the difference between the ascent and the descent at exactly the same moment—even though their comments are actually different. Both Polybius (3.54.8) and Livy (21.36.5) affirm the impassability of the alternative route *before* launching into an extended explanation of why it was impassable. Both Polybius (3.55.9) and Livy (21.37.4–5) describe the topography of the lower Alps on the Italian side at exactly the same moment. And both Polybius (3.56.3–4) and Livy (21.38.1–2) conclude their accounts by commenting on, in the same order and at the same moment, the length of the total march, the length of the crossing, the number of infantry Hannibal brought in, and the number of cavalry.

Could these have been taken from a shared source? In theory, yes: but that overlooks something very important. Polybius specifically claims to have obtained this material in person: he says that he saw the size of Hannibal's army on an inscription (3.33.18, 3.56.4), and describes how he discovered the topography of the route by personal autopsy, as well as gaining information from eye-witnesses (3.48.12).[144] This hardly seems compatible with his mechanically inserting the information at precisely the same points as Livy's source just happened to insert his own version of that information.

Indeed, the whole hypothesis of the 'shared source' has the immense problem that it ignores what Polybius actually tells us about the method by which he researched and wrote this section. Doubtless he made some use of earlier written sources as well, but he never mentions the fact: he is highly critical of the only earlier accounts that he refers to, and instead emphasizes the extensive research by autopsy and questioning witnesses[145] that he did in person (3.47.6–48.12; cf. below, 150–1).[146] The claim that Silenus was the ultimate source is particularly poorly founded: Polybius never mentions Silenus, and the few brief fragments of his work that survive make him look more like the mythologizing historians Polybius criticized than an author on whom he would comfortably rely.[147] The willingness of scholars to dismiss Polybius' own account of what he actually did, and instead ascribe his narrative to a shared source he never mentions, is largely based on the assumption that Livy (or Coelius) could not be drawing on Polybius while changing and elaborating the narrative to such a degree. Once that assumption is abandoned, the need for this unlikely shared source likewise disappears. Polybius was—directly or indirectly—Livy's source for the section.

If Polybius was Livy's direct source, then that has some striking implications: that the substantial changes and additions that we see in this narrative are Livy's own. In particular, we would have to conclude that, having perhaps initially misunderstood Polybius' account of the landfall which held up

---

[144] Some scholars have argued, based on their reconstruction of Polybius' career, that this passage is a later insertion, and that he did not cross the Alps until after he had already written the description of Hannibal's crossing (see Walbank 1957: 382). But this can hardly be true of his questioning of eye-witnesses, which must have taken place earlier (Pédech 1964: 528), as must his examination of Hannibal's inscription, which informs a lengthy earlier passage also (3.33. 5–18). In any case the evidence for his precise date of writing and publication is sufficiently obscure (cf. Walbank 1972: 13–25) that it would be rash to claim that his account could not have been informed by his travels in the way he states.

[145] For the centrality of autopsy and cross-examining eye-witnesses in Polybius' methodology see also e.g. 12.4c–d, 12.27, 12.28a.

[146] It has occasionally been doubted (e.g. by Seibert 1988: 31, Schmitt 1991: 14–15) that Polybius was telling the truth about having consulted eye-witnesses, given that he was writing at least fifty years later. But we should not assume that research and writing were necessarily close to one another; and it is in any case unsatisfactory to go to the opposite extreme, and assume that Polybius' entire account was transferred from other sources rather than being governed by the research he claims to have done. Cf. de Sanctis (1968: 169–70); as Hoyos (2006: 418) comments, 'to regard Polybius as largely a copier is more than mildly implausible'.

[147] E.g. *FGrH* 175 FF 2, 3, 8.

Hannibal en route,[148] he then elaborated his account on the assumption of a cliff that needed descending rather than a path that needed widening. This would, however, not necessarily mean that it was entirely free invention on his part—he might well have incorporated some of the details (like the vinegar ploy) from other versions of Hannibal's march. There are other details in Polybian-looking narratives in Books 21 and 22 and which certainly must[149] come from other sources than Polybius—for example, where Livy mentions specific names of people or places which Polybius leaves anonymous.[150] But this should not be regarded as problematic, because even if we accept that Polybius was a source for Livy in these books, he was manifestly not his only source, since there are a significant number of episodes which find no counterpart in Polybius at all. Even in the Fourth Decade Livy was prepared to insert non-Polybian details from his other sources into Polybian episodes from time to time (above, 129–30): that he does the same thing more frequently in the Third should come as no surprise. Indeed, we have already seen in the first part of this chapter Livy's willingness to enhance his material by introducing new details to his narrative from entirely external sources such as the Alexander historians: this does not seem qualitatively different from what we are finding here.

But some may nevertheless be unhappy with this conclusion, and wish instead to hypothesize an intermediate source: that Livy is not drawing on Polybius directly, but is depending on someone else (Coelius, say) who had himself used Polybius. It is true that one might feel that this is an unnecessary multiplication: it is not clear how much we gain if, instead of Livy making substantial changes to Polybius, we conclude that it was Coelius doing so. But that it is an unnecessary multiplication does not of itself prove it false.

---

[148] An alternative possibility is that it is not a genuine mistranslation or misunderstanding, but that Livy, while aware of the real meaning of the Greek, deliberately played on the ambiguity of the phrase in order to keep a reference to Polybius while turning to a different view of events. This is perhaps a more attractive interpretation in the light of Livy's self-consciousness elsewhere about his use of Polybius (on which see further below).

[149] Unless Livy was the type of historian Bleckmann (2006) argues the *Hellenica Oxyrhynchia*, Ctesias, and certain others (including some of the Roman annalists) to have been: one who built his history on earlier accounts while seeking to give himself a spurious independent authority by adding fictional details such as names and places (cf. n. 155 below). But Bleckmann's account is controversial even for the historians he discusses; and he does not in any case include Livy in his list of fictionalizing historians (note Bleckmann 2006: 20–1). The broadly consistent prosopographical picture we can create from the names Livy records across many volumes of his history makes it in any case unlikely that they are merely fictional additions.

[150] For a list of examples see Jumeau (1964: 315–19). Jumeau uses this as the chief plank in his demonstration that these books are not Polybian at all, but rests his arguments on the same fallacies as Tränkle: overlooking comparable changes to Polybian narratives in the Fourth Decade, and ignoring the difference in character between the two sections of the work.

Can we see any reason to exclude an intermediate source? One reason may come if we look now, not simply at individual portions of the narrative, but at the organization of Books 21 and 22 as a whole. Livy here as elsewhere moves his narrative between different theatres of war. But more often than not he does so at exactly the same time as Polybius had made identical moves. Hannibal crosses the Pyrenees and moves his army into Gaul at 21.24. This is then followed by the account of the revolt of the Boii in 21.25.1–26.2 (concluding with the despatch of a praetor to deal with it), followed by Scipio's journey to Gaul at 21.26.3–5 (concluding with his sending out a squadron to reconnoitre). Exactly the same order appears in Polybius: Hannibal's move across the Pyrenees to Gaul at 3.35.7–8, the revolt of the Boii at 3.40 (concluding with the despatch of the praetor), and Scipio's journey to Gaul at 3.41 (concluding with sending out a squadron). Polybius also inserts a geographical digression at 3.36–39 which Livy does not have, but the basic narrative order is identical, even though the details of their accounts in some respects are not. Livy narrates the campaigns of Cn. Scipio in Spain in 218 at the end of the year (21.60–61), exactly as Polybius does (3.76), though he also surrounds it with a good deal of extra material which has no counterpart in Polybius. Most striking is 22.19–22, where the entire Spanish narrative for the year 217 is inserted directly following Fabius' departure for Rome leaving Minucius in charge. Polybius has the same move to Spain at exactly the same point (3.95–99).[151] Since the Spanish narrative covers the entire year, it could have been inserted anywhere at all. In fact, it is inserted at exactly the same moment in both authors.

The significance of this should be clear. Livy (on any account) is basing himself on more than one source and is moving between them at different points. The more sources that are shuffled in this way, and the more shuffling that takes place, the less we would expect the order of any particular source to be preserved. Indeed, at one point in these books he does not preserve Polybius' order: 22.31.1–7, a brief description of Servilius Geminus' raid on Africa, comes a few chapters later in the narrative than the corresponding Polybius passage (3.96.11–14), which appears in the middle of the Spanish narrative discussed above.[152] Occasional divergences of this sort are to be expected: the surprising

---

[151] Observed by Hoffmann (1942: 29), though he treats it as exceptional and so fails to appreciate its significance.

[152] A more complicated example is Livy 21.28.5–30.11 and Polybius 3.44.3–46.12, recounting the events between Hannibal's army crossing the Rhône and their setting off for the Alps. Polybius' order is (1) Hannibal sends off his cavalry to reconnoitre (3.44.3); (2) Hannibal orders the elephants to be taken across the Rhône (3.44.4), then addresses his troops (3.44.5–13); (3) the cavalry skirmish (3.45.1–2); (4) Hannibal takes the elephants over the Rhône (3.46). Livy appears to have the events in quite a different sequence: (4) Hannibal takes the elephants over the Rhône

thing is that they are not more common. That speaks to the closeness with which Livy in these books is keeping to Polybius in outline, if not in detail: he appears to be employing him in Books 21 and 22 as a baseline around which he can work his general narrative structure.[153] It is vastly less likely that the narratives would be so closely matched were there an intervening source who was himself moving between different sources: one would expect the double set of shufflings to produce something much more divergent from Polybius' original order.

This gives a strong positive reason for rejecting the hypothesis of an intermediate source, and arguing that Livy used Polybius directly. But there is a stronger reason still.

One problem with the way in which not only Livy's use of Polybius (and his other sources), but the whole issue of 'source-criticism' has traditionally been handled in classical scholarship, is that it has usually depended on making an artificial methodological distinction between identifying someone as a 'source' and identifying them as an 'allusive model' or 'intertext'. Identifying an 'intertext' implies that it was expected to be recognized by at least some of the readership: into one's own text resonances and nuances from an earlier text are incorporated, inviting comparisons or contrasts between them, as old themes are reworked and developed in new ways. A 'source', on the other hand, is not usually deemed to work like that. When scholars examine Livy's sources, and show how he is changing and adapting them, the usual implication is that we are, as it were, looking into Livy's workshop. We can see his adaptations as an expression of his

---

(21.28.5–12); (1) Hannibal sends off his cavalry to reconnoitre (21.29.1); (3) there is a cavalry skirmish (21.29.2–4); and (2) Hannibal addresses his troops (21.30). However, the divergence is more apparent than real: it is easy to see how Livy's rearrangement is actually based on Polybius. He reduces the number of scenes overall, as he often does (cf. Witte 1910), in this case by not recounting the sending out of the cavalry until the point when the skirmish actually takes place. Similarly, he describes the elephants being taken over the river at the point when Hannibal first raises the issue, rather than separating them as Polybius had done. The apparent displacement of Hannibal's speech is likewise based on Polybius, as will be explained below (149–52).

[153] For Books 23–30, on the other hand, the evidence strongly suggests that Polybius' structure was not followed. The *codex Urbinas* usually appears to preserve fragments of Polybius according to their order in his original text (Walbank 1967: 1), and its order in these later books is sometimes significantly different from the parallel passages of Livy: for example in Book 10 the fall of New Carthage (10.6–20: cf. Livy 26.41–51) comes after the recapture of Tarentum (10.1; cf. Livy 27.15–16), and the death of Marcellus (10.32: cf. Livy 27.27) before Scipio's victory over Hasdrubal in Spain (10.34–40: cf. Livy 27.17–20). This should not surprise us: Polybius Book 3 was anomalous, as he himself tells us (4.28.2–6, 5.31.4–7), in its virtually exclusive focus on the Punic War for the entire book. It was therefore easy for Livy largely to replicate its structure in Books 21 and 22. In Polybius' later books, where Roman and Carthaginian material is constantly interspersed with others, he was a less satisfactory structural model for Livy, even though he remains an important source for many individual episodes.

covert preferences or intentions, but this is our deduction as scholars from evidence that we happen to possess, a comparable process to (for example) the way scholars of more recent literature will compare an author's final product with early drafts or sketches. Modern authors do not usually write expecting their readers to be examining their processes of creation in this way—indeed, some might find it disquieting to have their rejected ideas laid open for public scrutiny. So too, it is tacitly assumed, Livy did not expect his Roman readers to be comparing his own version of history with Polybius' in the way Virgil clearly expected many of his readers to recognize the reworkings of Homer, Apollonius, and others, which loom so large in the *Aeneid*.

But such a division between source and intertext is not only unjustified: it is highly implausible.[154] I showed in the first part of this chapter Livy alluding not merely to one or two famous predecessors like Sallust and Thucydides, but to a range of authors, including a number of Hellenistic historians such as (probably) Ephorus and the Alexander historians. Livy is assuming that at least some of his readers are familiar enough with Ephorus to be able to spot an allusion to him: how likely is it, in that case, that he would be blind to the possibility that they would notice the infinitely more extensive similarities of wording and substance between his work and Polybius'? And if Livy knows that his readers will recognize Polybius underlying his text, then we might expect him to use that actively, exactly as he and others do with allusions in general, employing the intertextual relationship to signal interpretations of his own text and reinterpretations of his predecessors.[155]

---

[154] A similar argument has recently been made with respect to Ammianus by Kelly (2008: esp. 222–4). However, Kelly appears to regard this as a consequence of specific features of Ammianus, as a highly literary writer of contemporary history, rather than a sign of broader methodological problems with the entire approach.

[155] For Livy employing Polybius simultaneously as source and intertext see also Levene (2006a: 84–5); a comparable point was however made as long ago as Stübler (1941: 158–62: note especially Stübler 1941: 162: 'Gerade in der 3. Dekade ist Polybios für ihn mehr als nur Quelle, er ist sein Vorbild'). As for other historians, Pelling (1992, 2007; esp. 2007: 155) is unusual among scholars in recognizing the way in which Plutarch's use of Thucydides and Herodotus as sources goes hand in hand with an allusive critique of them. Recently Kelly (2008: 222–55) has addressed Ammianus in a similar fashion (though see n. 154 above).

An intriguing variant on the idea comes with Bleckmann (2006), who controversially suggests that there was a genre of ancient historiography according to which writers created apparently independent accounts not by doing new research, but instead via deliberate variations on and arbitrarily invented additions to a chosen predecessor. He claims this to be the case with (e.g.) Ctesias rewriting Herodotus, and the author of the *Hellenica Oxyrhynchia* (whom he identifies as Theopompus) rewriting Xenophon. However, Bleckmann does not make it entirely clear how far (on his theory) authors expected their readers to recognize the original underlying the new account, and whether readers in fact would have seen it as an allusive reworking rather than, like most modern scholars, thinking of it as an independent alternative source.

An especially interesting demonstration of this comes with the speech that Hannibal delivers to his troops to encourage them before they set off to cross the Alps. In Polybius 3.44.10–12 the speech is very short, and simply says that Hannibal encouraged his troops by reminding them of their previous successes. In Livy the speech (21.30) is rather different. First, he postpones it to a slightly later point in the narrative (cf. n. 152 above). Second, the speech is introduced differently: unlike in Polybius, the reason Hannibal chooses to address his troops at this point is because the soldiers are panicked by what they have heard about the Alps (21.29.7 *iter immensum Alpesque, rem fama utique inexpertis horrendam, metuebat* – 'they feared the unfathomable length of the march, and the Alps, of dread repute, at least among the ignorant'). Accordingly Hannibal, as well as listing their past accomplishments much as in Polybius (though in considerably greater detail), spends a good deal of the speech encouraging the soldiers by telling them that their fears are misplaced, arguments which have no counterpart in Polybius' version of the speech (21.30.1–31.1):

itaque Hannibal, postquam ipsi sententia stetit pergere ire atque Italiam petere, advocata contione varie militum versat animos castigando adhortandoque: mirari se, quinam pectora semper impavida repens terror invaserit. per tot annos vincentis eos stipendia facere . . . in conspectu Alpis habeant, quarum alterum latus Italiae sit, in ipsis portis hostium fatigatos subsistere—quid Alpes aliud esse credentes quam montium altitudines? fingerent altiores Pyrenaei iugis: nullas profecto terras caelum contingere nec inexsuperabiles humano generi esse. Alpis quidem habitari, coli, gignere atque alere animantes: pervias fauces esse exercitibus. eos ipsos, quos cernant, legatos non pinnis sublime elatos Alpis transgressos. ne maiores quidem eorum indigenas, sed advenas Italiae cultores has ipsas Alpis ingentibus saepe agminibus cum liberis ac coniugibus migrantium modo tuto transmisisse. militi quidem armato nihil secum praeter instrumenta belli portanti quid invium aut inexsuperabile esse? . . .

his adhortationibus incitatos corpora curare atque ad iter se parare iubet.

So Hannibal, after reaching the firm decision to continue on his march and make for Italy, called a meeting and swayed his soldiers' opinions with a mixture of reproof and encouragement. He was puzzled, he said, as to what had all of a sudden terrified hearts that were always undaunted. For years and years they had been campaigning victorious . . . Now, he said, they had in their sight the Alps, with Italy on the other side – and at the very gates of their enemy they were breaking down and halting. Did they imagine the Alps were anything except high mountains?[156] Suppose them higher than the peaks of the Pyrenees – but without question no lands touch the heavens; none is impassable to mankind. In fact the Alps were inhabited and cultivated; living creatures were born and nurtured there; their passes are traversable by armies. They saw the ambassadors before them – they had crossed

---

[156] Hannibal's argument here involves a teasing and learned pun, since Roman scholars believed that the word 'Alps' in fact meant 'high mountains' in Celtic: see Servius auct., *ad Aen.* 10.13; Scholia to Lucan 1.183. (I owe this point to Tony Woodman.)

the Alps, without being borne aloft on wings. Even the ancestors of these men were not natives to Italy: they had migrated there to till the land, and had crossed those very same Alps safely, frequently in massive columns accompanied, like nomads, by their children and wives. In that case, he asked, what was impassable or insurmountable to an armed soldier who carried no possessions with him save the tools of warfare? ...

This speech inspired the soldiers: Hannibal ordered them to refresh themselves and prepare for the march.

Where is Livy getting this material? It could be free invention; it could come from some other author. But looking at Polybius we can see a far more likely source. Between completing the crossing of the Rhône and setting off for the Alps – in other words, precisely the point at which Livy now introduces the speech – Polybius has a long digression in which he criticizes earlier historians of these events (3.47.6–3.48.12):

ἔνιοι δὲ τῶν γεγραφότων περὶ τῆς ὑπερβολῆς ταύτης, βουλόμενοι τοὺς ἀναγινώσκοντας ἐκπλήττειν τῇ περὶ τῶν προειρημένων τόπων παραδοξολογίᾳ, λανθάνουσιν ἐμπίπτοντες εἰς δύο τὰ πάσης ἱστορίας ἀλλοτριώτατα· καὶ γὰρ ψευδολογεῖν καὶ μαχόμενα γράφειν αὑτοῖς ἀναγκάζονται. ἅμα μὲν γὰρ τὸν Ἀννίβαν ἀμίμητόν τινα παρεισάγοντες στρατηγὸν καὶ τόλμῃ καὶ προνοίᾳ τοῦτον ὁμολογουμένως ἀποδεικνύουσιν ἡμῖν ἀλογιστότατον, ἅμα δὲ καταστροφὴν οὐ δυνάμενοι λαμβάνειν οὐδ᾽ ἔξοδον τοῦ ψεύδους θεοὺς καὶ θεῶν παῖδας εἰς πραγματικὴν ἱστορίαν παρεισάγουσιν. ὑποθέμενοι γὰρ τὰς ἐρυμνότητας καὶ τραχύτητας τῶν Ἀλπεινῶν ὀρῶν τοιαύτας ὥστε μὴ οἷον ἵππους καὶ στρατόπεδα, σὺν δὲ τούτοις ἐλέφαντας, ἀλλὰ μηδὲ πεζοὺς εὐζώνους εὐχερῶς ἂν διελθεῖν, ὁμοίως δὲ καὶ τὴν ἔρημον τοιαύτην τινὰ περὶ τοὺς τόπους ὑπογράψαντες ἡμῖν ὥστ᾽, εἰ μὴ θεός ἤ τις ἥρως ἀπαντήσας τοῖς περὶ τὸν Ἀννίβαν ὑπέδειξε τὰς ὁδούς, ἐξαπορήσαντας ἂν καταφθαρῆναι πάντας, ὁμολογουμένως ἐκ τούτων εἰς ἑκάτερον τῶν προειρημένων ἁμαρτημάτων ἐμπίπτουσι.

πρῶτον μὲν γὰρ ἂν τίς φανείη στρατηγὸς ἀλογιστότερος Ἀννίβου, τίς καὶ σκαιότερος ἡγεμών, ὃς τοσούτων ἡγούμενος δυνάμεων καὶ τὰς μεγίστας ἐλπίδας ἔχων ἐν τούτοις τοῦ κατορθώσειν τοῖς ὅλοις, οὔτε τὰς ὁδοὺς οὔτε τόπους, ὡς οὗτοί φασιν, οὔτε ποῦ πορεύεται τὸ παράπαν οὔτε πρὸς τίνας ἐγίνωσκε, τὸ δὲ πέρας, οὐδ᾽ εἰ καθόλου δυνατοῖς ἐπιβάλλεται πράγμασιν; ...

ὁμοίως δὲ καὶ τὰ περὶ τῆς ἐρημίας, ἔτι δ᾽ ἐρυμνότητος καὶ δυσχωρίας τῶν τόπων ἔκδηλον ποιεῖ τὸ ψεῦδος αὐτῶν. οὐχ ἱστορήσαντες γὰρ ὅτι συμβαίνει τοὺς Κελτοὺς τοὺς παρὰ τὸν Ῥοδανὸν ποταμὸν οἰκοῦντας οὐχ ἅπαξ οὐδὲ δὶς πρὸ τῆς Ἀννίβου παρουσίας, οὐδὲ μὴν πάλαι προσφάτως δέ, μεγάλοις στρατοπέδοις ὑπερβάντας τὰς Ἄλπεις ... πρὸς δὲ τούτοις οὐκ εἰδότες ὅτι πλεῖστον ἀνθρώπων φῦλον κατ᾽ αὐτὰς οἰκεῖν συμβαίνει τὰς Ἄλπεις, ἀλλ᾽ ἀγνοοῦντες ἕκαστα τῶν εἰρημένων ἥρω τινά φασιν ἐπιφανέντα συνυποδεῖξαι τὰς ὁδοὺς αὐτοῖς ...

Ἀννίβας γε μὴν οὐχ ὡς οὗτοι γράφουσιν, λίαν δὲ περὶ ταῦτα πραγματικῶς ἐχρῆτο ταῖς ἐπιβολαῖς. καὶ γὰρ τὴν τῆς χώρας ἀρετήν, εἰς ἣν ἐπεβάλετο καθιέναι, καὶ τὴν τῶν ὄχλων ἀλλοτριότητα πρὸς Ῥωμαίους ἐξητάκει σαφῶς, εἴς τε τὰς μεταξὺ δυσχωρίας ὁδηγοῖς καὶ καθηγεμόσιν ἐγχωρίοις ἐχρῆτο τοῖς τῶν αὐτῶν ἐλπίδων μέλλουσι κοινωνεῖν. ἡμεῖς δὲ περὶ τούτων εὐθαρσῶς ἀποφαινόμεθα διὰ τὸ περὶ τῶν πράξεων παρ᾽ αὐτῶν ἱστορηκέναι τῶν παρατετευχότων τοις καιροῖς, τοὺς δὲ τόπους κατωπτευκέναι καὶ τῇ διὰ τῶν Ἄλπεων αὐτοὶ κεχρῆσθαι πορείᾳ γνώσεως ἕνεκα καὶ θέας.

Some of those who have written about this crossing have desired to startle their readers with miraculous stories about the aforementioned places; but as a result have, unnoticed, fallen into the two faults most alien to the whole of history: they are forced into both falsehoods and inconsistencies. They introduce Hannibal as a general unparalleled in courage and foresight and demonstrably present him to us as totally irrational. At the same time, they are unable to create a denouement or conclusion to their falsehoods, and so introduce gods and the children of gods into practical history. They depict the steepness and ruggedness of the Alps as such as would cause difficulties even for light-armed infantry to cross, let alone horses and troops with elephants. Likewise they describe for us the country as so desolate that if a god or hero had not met Hannibal's men and showed them the way, they would all have perished in utter confusion. In this, they demonstrably fall into both of the aforementioned faults.

For first, what general would appear more irrational than Hannibal, or what leader more stupid? Someone who is leading so large a force, and with the greatest hopes of ultimate success resting on it, who, according to them, neither knows the roads nor the country, without the faintest idea where he is going or against whom, or in short if the whole enterprise he was engaged in was feasible? . . .

Likewise, their comments on the desolation and steepness and roughness of the place merely demonstrate their falsehoods. They failed to discover that the Gauls who live by the River Rhône crossed the Alps with large armies not just once or twice before Hannibal was there, and not long ago but recently . . . In addition, they are unaware that a substantial tribe of people live in the Alps themselves. In ignorance of everything I have said they say that some hero appeared and showed them the road . . .

Hannibal certainly did not do what these people write, but planned all this practically. He enquired closely and clearly into the quality of the land into which he undertook to descend, and the hostility of the people to the Romans, and for the intervening difficulties he employed native guides and scouts, who were going to share in the same hopes. I can speak confidently about this, because I have enquired about the events from people who were there at the time, and have reconnoitred the country and have crossed the Alps myself to learn and see about it.

There is a remarkable similarity of theme and approach between this passage in Polybius and the speech which Hannibal makes in Livy at precisely the same point.[157] Hannibal's soldiers are in the position of Polybius' predecessors: like

---

[157] The relationship between the digression in Polybius and Hannibal's speech in Livy—though not the critique of Polybius in Livy's aftermath—has often been noted: see e.g. Bruns (1898: 36–7), Girod (1982: 1206–8), Doblhofer (1983: 142); cf. Händl-Sagawe (1995: 196–7). The observation has however had surprisingly little influence on scholarly study of Livy's handling of his sources; however, Feldherr (2009) has independently come up with similar conclusions to mine about the passage and its significance for our reading of Livy and Polybius.

them, they imagine the Alps to be so vast and rugged as to be utterly impass-able. The arguments that Hannibal offers to show that they are wrong are the same arguments as Polybius uses to show the falsity of their accounts: that the Alps are inhabited, that the Gauls themselves have crossed them *en masse*, and that armed soldiers should certainly be able to do so. In addition we have been told directly before the speech that the ambassadors referred to here have offered to act as guides and share the danger (21.29.6 *se duces itinerum, socios periculi fore*): again, the same point is in Polybius.[158] In other words, Hannibal in Livy is acting with all the rationality and preparation that Polybius ascribed to him—the rationality indeed shown also by Polybius himself, who has by his own account tracked Hannibal's route, and who accordingly has interpreted the situation correctly. The soldiers, like the bad historians, have simply failed to understand the situation, though they are now reassured by the speech.

But there is a problem. When Livy's Carthaginians reach the Alps, they find something rather different from what Hannibal had led them to expect (21.32.7):

tum, quamquam fama prius, qua incerta in maius vero ferri solent, praecepta res erat, tamen ex propinquo visa montium altitudo nivesque caelo prope inmixtae, tecta informia inposita rupibus, pecora iumentaque torrida frigore, homines intonsi et inculti, animalia inanimaque omnia rigentia gelu, cetera visu quam dictu foediora terrorem renovarunt.

Previous information had come through rumour, which indeed tends to exaggerate the unknown. But now they saw close before them the height of the mountains, the snows all but mixed with the heavens, the shapeless structures crowning the crags, cattle and pack-animals shrivelled by the cold, men unshorn and unkempt, all things living and lifeless stiff with ice, and other things more appalling in sight than report: all these renewed their terror.

The relationship to Hannibal's speech is obvious. Hannibal had calmed the troops' fears by assuring them that the Alps did not touch the sky: now they see that they virtually do. He had assured them that people lived in the Alps: it now turns out that the people living there are wild and semi-human; he told them that there were animals there, but the only animals prove to be frozen with ice. And whereas the troops' original fears were based on mere *fama* (21.29.7), something proverbially unreliable, as Livy notes here, it now emerges that the *fama* if anything underplayed the reality.[159] In short, having shown Hannibal engaging in rational calculation and preparation of exactly

---

[158] This point had been made earlier in Polybius also, directly before Hannibal's speech, where the Gallic envoys make the same offer to the Carthaginian troops (3.44.6–7). Livy retains it as the prelude to Hannibal's speech, but with the speech in its new position both passages are alluded to simultaneously.

[159] Doblhofer (1983: 143–4).

the sort that Polybius advised, it now appears that he has wasted his time. Hannibal's—and hence Polybius'—rationalist debunking of the terrors of the Alps is shown to be false, and the rumours which so terrified his soldiers are true after all.

Needless to say, there is no counterpart to this passage in Polybius. But it is not a casual addition, nor a piece of sensational exaggeration by Livy for its own sake. It appears to be part of a systematic response to Polybius' declared rationalism. We can see the same thing emerging again and again through his description of the crossing: Livy increases the sense of the alien ruggedness of the terrain, the inability of the troops to deal with it, and accordingly points to the inadequacy of Hannibal's advance planning.[160] To give a few brief examples: Hannibal being forced to encamp *inter confragosa omnia praeruptaque* (21.32.9: 'among everything broken and precipitous': contrast Polybius 3.50.5); not only animals (as in Polybius 3.51.4) but also people falling over a precipice *in inmensum altitudinis* (21.33.7); the elephants delay the army *per artas praecipites vias* (21.35.3 'through the narrow and precipitous ways: not in Polybius 3.53.8). In the narrative of the descent (quoted above, 136–40) Livy omits the direct claim of Polybius 3.54.6 that the Carthaginians were able through familiarity to cope with the hazards of the path, and at 21.37.1 suggests that camping so as to build up a path could be done only with difficulty (*aegerrime*): the corresponding phrase at Polybius 3.55.6 (μετὰ πολλῆς ταλαιπωρίας) refers to the difficulties in subsequently building the path, not the difficulty of merely camping on the ridge in the first place.

What is more, the preparations which Hannibal did make are shown to be misplaced. Hannibal takes longer to reach the summit than he ought, *per invia pleraque et errores, quos aut ducentium fraus aut, ubi fides iis non esset, temere initae valles a coniectantibus iter faciebant* (21.35.4: 'through numerous pathless routes and mistakes caused by either the deceit of his guides or, when they were not trusted, by the valleys which were haphazardly entered by people trying to guess the road'). This too has no counterpart in Polybius 3.53.9, but is striking in view of the reliance which in both Polybius and Livy Hannibal is said to be placing on his guides, as well as Polybius' insistence on the rationality and good sense of that procedure. For Livy, relying on guides is worse than useless: either they deliberately lead the Carthaginians down the wrong path, or else the Carthaginians' belief that the guides are leading them down the wrong path causes them to choose the wrong path themselves.[161]

---

[160] Cf. Gärtner (1975: 158–65).

[161] One might also suggest that these false routes are themselves partly a metatextual symbol, marking the difficulties of finding a correct road through competing historical evidence whether or not one follows one's guides—guides indeed including Polybius himself. This might seem a

What is the significance of all this? First, it should be clear that the specific features of Livy's account that I have identified here only make sense if we recognize that they form a direct response to Polybius. This explains the new placing of Hannibal's speech, the overlap between the content of that speech and the polemical digression at that very point in Polybius, and the extra material found in Livy, which appears to be quite systematically referring back to and undermining the claims which Polybius made in his own voice and which Livy then replicated in the mouth of Hannibal. Livy is manifestly writing with Polybius' text directly in front of him, and moreover assuming that at least some of his readers will realize that he is doing so. Polybius is Livy's source. Polybius is also Livy's target.

Even more interesting are the further ramifications. Polybius' digression constitutes a critique of his own predecessors for their failure to recognize the proper rationality that Hannibal showed. Livy effectively engages in the debate on the side against Polybius, but does so by challenging the primacy of rationality itself. Polybius made two criticisms of his predecessors: that they showed Hannibal engaging in an operation without proper preparation, and that they exaggerated the dangers and difficulties of the route: these are of course linked, because he argues that Hannibal determined the feasability of the crossing in advance. Livy supports Polybius on the first point, but detaches it from the second. Hannibal plans in detail in exactly the way that Polybius suggests, but, although he does ultimately succeed in crossing the Alps, it is in spite of his planning rather than because of it. The Alps are a barrier such that even careful and reasoned plans will not cope with the reality. As I shall discuss further in Chapter 4, rationality, for Livy, is through-out the Third Decade a tool at best of limited value, and sometimes actively counterproductive. That conclusion is given a striking demonstration here.

The significance of Livy's critique goes further. Polybius noticeably con-flates himself and his own history with Hannibal's generalship. Like Hannibal, he has himself crossed the Alps (3.48.12); and his own rationalist approach to history is the thing that enables him to appreciate properly the similar rationality shown by Hannibal. Livy implicitly makes a similar comparison, for his Hannibal and the Carthaginian troops in some respects look remark-ably like historians, as I pointed out above. One of the issues with which historians in antiquity were concerned was the reliability of different sources of information. For Polybius, as for most other historians, *fama* – mere unquestioned report – came well down the list: autopsy where possible, or

---

far-fetched suggestion in isolation, but it is strengthened by the widespread metatextual use of journeys, false roads and labyrinths both elsewhere in Livy and in other authors. See Jaeger (1999), though she does not discuss this specific passage.

questioning eye-witnesses where not, was the primary mode one should adopt. Merely accepting transmitted material was likely to lead one astray.[162] The Carthaginian troops do the latter, but are corrected by Hannibal, who has eye-witness testimony to rely on. Yet in the event they are proved right and he wrong – and in this respect Livy vindicates not merely their stance, but his own, for he was himself (notoriously) an historian who wrote about events based largely on second- or third-hand material derived from books.[163] For all Polybius' self-advertised research he is, Livy implies, less likely to get the answer right than he would have done merely by sitting in his library. As to how Livy might have justified such a claim in this specific instance, it is worth noting 27.39.4–9, in which he claims that Hasdrubal's crossing of the Alps was much easier and swifter than Hannibal's had been, because the very fact of Hannibal's crossing had created routes which could be used by subsequent travellers,[164] and had also begun the process of civilizing the inhabitants. In other words, the conditions under which Polybius experienced the Alps were entirely unlike those faced by Hannibal, and were likely to lead him to underestimate the difficulties that Hannibal had to cope with.

The crossing of the Alps is not the only place where Livy appears to be responding directly to Polybius' criticisms of his predecessors. Another example comes with the reign of Hieronymus. Polybius 7.7 accuses earlier historians of exaggerating Hieronymus' tyranny, arguing that he was only a boy who reigned for just over a year, and so did not have time to persecute more than a few people, mostly close associates (7.3–4); he says that people would do better to focus on the virtuous lives of his grandfather and father Hiero and Gelo (7.7.7–8.9).[165] Livy's short account of Hieronymus' reign (24.4.1–7.9) has something of the rhetorical colour of tyranny that Polybius criticized, as when he talks about *libidines novae, inhumana crudelitas* (24.5.5: 'unprecedented lusts, inhuman cruelty').[166] Yet he frames it in a way that

---

[162] For an extended discussion of this issue, see Marincola (1997: 63–117).

[163] For a similarly 'metahistorical' episode in Book 45, in which Livy likewise vindicates the validity of *fama* against detractors like Polybius, see Levene (2006a: 77–87). Zadorojnyi (2005: 499–505) offers an interesting example of Plutarch likewise implicitly defending secondary history against Polybius' strictures, albeit along quite different lines from Livy.

[164] According to Varro (*ap.* Servius auct., *ad Aen.* 10.13), Hasdrubal had in fact used a different route from Hannibal. Livy selects a version which gives Hannibal's initial crossing the greatest influence on subsequent events.

[165] On Polybius' idealized picture of Hiero and the contrast he draws with Hieronymus see Eckstein (1985).

[166] Compare Diodorus 26.15.1, presumably reflecting the sorts of accounts of which Polybius disapproved: ἐξετράπη πρὸς τρυφὴν καὶ ἀκολασίαν καὶ τυραννικὴν ὠμότητα. ἐπετελεῖτο γὰρ γυναικῶνὕβρεις καὶ τοὺς παρρησίᾳ χρωμένους τῶν φίλων ἀπέκτεινεν καὶ πολλῶν ἀκρίτως οὐσίας ἐδήμευσεν καὶ τοῖς πρὸς χάριν ὁμιλοῦσιν ἐδωρεῖτο ('He turned to luxury and intemperance and tyrannical cruelty. For he performed outrages on women and killed those of his friends who

seems to be responding directly to Polybius' criticisms. He does not disagree
with Polybius on the substance: he does not, for example, suggest that
Hieronymus literally killed or persecuted large numbers of people. But instead he stresses the *image* of tyranny that Hieronymus instantly adopted,[167]
dressing on his first public appearance (24.5.2 *primo statim conspectu*) in the
manner of the tyrant Dionysius.[168] The vices simply follow on from the image
(24.5.5 *hunc tam superbum apparatum habitumque convenientes sequebantur
&c.*—'on such arrogant trappings and bearing there followed things matching
it &c.'). Although in Livy, as in Polybius, the direct victims of Hieronymus'
tyranny appear few, the terror it inspired was general (24.5.6 *tantus omnis
terror invaserat*—an idea that would perhaps be particularly pertinent to
someone who, like Livy, had lived through the proscriptions of the Second
Triumvirate.[169] In other words, Livy adopts a Polybian narrative while justifying the lurid colour of tyranny that he gives to it, for the tyranny rests in the
image that Hieronymus immediately and deliberately adopted and the perceptions of people at the time, rather than in his particular actions. We may
also note in passing 24.25.2, where Sopater makes a speech pointing out that
Hieronymus could not have done very much by himself, since he was a mere
boy and barely mature (*puerum ac vixdum pubescentem*): the same point as
Polybius had made. But Sopater uses it as an argument to whip up the
Syracusan mob to murder the women of the family, a crime which Livy
describes in dramatic terms and condemns outright (24.25.7–26.15).[170] Polybius' arguments against the significance of Hieronymus' tyranny become the
excuse for the unjust and brutal violence of others.

   More interesting still is Polybius' suggestion that the virtues of Hiero and
Gelo are better topics than the vices of Hieronymus for historical discussion.
Livy's account of Gelo was anyway different: at 23.30.11–12 he had prefigured
the Syracusan break from Rome with the suggestion that Gelo, far from being
the obedient son suggested at Polybius 7.8.9, despised his father (23.30.11
contempta . . . senectute patris) and attempted to undermine the Roman

---

spoke frankly and summarily confiscated the property of many and bestowed it on those who
cultivated his favour').

   [167] More broadly on images of tyranny in Livy's account of the accession of Hieronymus see
Jaeger (2003: 215–7).

   [168] Note also Bato of Sinope *FGrH* 268 F 4 = Athenaeus 6.251f, but Bato appears to have had
the episode later in his account of Hieronymus' reign. See Rizzo (1983–4), who suggests that
Bato was one of Polybius' targets in his criticisms of earlier historians of Hieronymus.

   [169] On the disjunction between the actual number of victims of the Triumvirs and the
reputation for brutality that they engendered see Syme (1939: 190–6).

   [170] Cf. Jaeger (2003: 225–7).

alliance, and that Hiero may have had him murdered (23.30.12, itself an interesting contrast to Polybius' claim at 7.8.2–4 of Hiero's virtues in power).[171] He is accordingly not compared favourably with Hieronymus here. Hiero is, but the main source of the comparison is, ironically, Hieronymus himself, who acts *velut suis vitiis desiderabilem efficere vellet avum* (24.5.2: 'as if by his vices he wanted to make his grandfather more desirable'). So one can, it seems, emphasize the remarkable virtues of Hiero much as Polybius wanted, but Hiero's virtues are brought out not by direct description, but by the contrasting behaviour of Hieronymus. And in fact Livy has directly beforehand shown Hiero as considerably less praiseworthy than Polybius thought him in the first place. Polybius says that Hiero wanted to give up his rule, but was persuaded to retain it by his citizens (7.8.5). For Livy the deterrent to giving it up was the control his daughters had over him: he was seduced by female coaxings (24.4.4 *muliebribus blanditiis*), because it was not easy for someone in his ninetieth year to act in the public interest – itself a correction to Polybius' suggestion that Hiero's retaining his physical and mental powers throughout his long life was a sign of his temperance (7.8.7–8). The virtues of Hiero in Livy are largely genuine, but Polybius' hagiographic description of them is itself, Livy implies, partly a false image derived from the contrast with Hieronymus' own deliberate display of tyranny.

A slightly different instance of Livy's self-conscious correction of Polybius may be discussed here. In Book 27 Scipio, after freeing his Spanish prisoners, is hailed by them as king (27.19.3–6):

circumfusa inde multitudo Hispanorum et ante deditorum et pridie captorum regem eum ingenti consensu appellavit. tum Scipio silentio per praeconem facto sibi maximum nomen imperatoris esse dixit quo se milites sui appellassent: regium nomen, alibi magnum, Romae intolerabile esse. regalem animum in se esse, si id in hominis ingenio amplissimum ducerent, taciti iudicarent: vocis usurpatione abstinerent. sensere etiam barbari magnitudinem animi, cuius miraculo nominis alii mortales stuperent, id ex tam alto fastigio aspernantis.

Then a crowd of Spaniards flocked round him, some who had surrendered to him previously, and some who had been captured the day before; with general agreement they called him 'King'. Then Scipio, calling for silence through the herald, said that for him the greatest name was the name of *imperator*, which his soldiers called him. The kingly name, great everywhere else, was unbearable at Rome. As for there being a kingly mind in him, if they considered that the grandest thing in human character, they should make the judgement silently: they should avoid assigning the word. Even though they were barbarians they realized his greatness of mind, which

---

[171] On the discrepancy between Polybius' and Livy's accounts of Gelo, see Deininger (1983).

rejected. from so lofty a height the name at the marvel of which other mortals were amazed.

This draws on Polybius 10.40.2–9:

τῶν δ' Ἰβήρων ὅσοι κατὰ τοὺς προειρημένους τόπους Καρχηδονίοις τότε συνεμάχουν, ἧκον ἐγχειρίζοντες σφᾶς αὐτοὺς εἰς τὴν Ῥωμαίων πίστιν, κατὰ δὲ τὰς ἐντεύξεις βασιλέα προσεφώνουν τὸν Πόπλιον. πρῶτον μὲν οὖν ἐποίησε τοῦτο καὶ προσεκύνησε πρῶτος Ἐδεκών, μετὰ δὲ τοῦτον οἱ περὶ τὸν Ἀνδοβάλην. τότε μὲν οὖν ἀνεπιστάτως αὐτὸν παρέδραμε τὸ ῥηθέν· μετὰ δὲ τὴν μάχην ἁπάντων βασιλέα προσφωνούντων, εἰς ἐπίστασιν ἤγαγε τὸν Πόπλιον τὸ γινόμενον. διὸ καὶ συναθροίσας τοὺς Ἴβηρας βασιλικὸς μὲν ἔφη βούλεσθαι καὶ λέγεσθαι παρὰ πᾶσι καὶ ταῖς ἀληθείαις ὑπάρχειν, βασιλεύς γε μὴν οὔτ' εἶναι θέλειν οὔτε λέγεσθαι παρ' οὐδενί. ταῦτα δ' εἰπὼν παρήγγειλε στρατηγὸν αὐτὸν προσφωνεῖν. ἴσως μὲν οὖν καὶ τότε δικαίως ἄν τις ἐπεσημήνατο τὴν μεγαλοψυχίαν τἀνδρός ... Πόπλιος δὲ τοσοῦτον ἠπερέθετο μεγαλοψυχίᾳ τοὺς ἄλλους ἀνθρώπους ὡς οὐ μεῖζον ἀγαθὸν εὔξασθαί τις τοῖς θεοῖς οὐ τολμήσειε, λέγω δὲ βασιλείας, τοῦτ' ἐκεῖνος πολλάκις ὑπὸ τῆς τύχης αὐτῷ δεδομένον ἀπηξίωσε, καὶ περὶ πλείονος ἐποιήσατο τὴν πατρίδα καὶ τὴν ταύτης πίστιν τῆς περιβλέπτου καὶ μακαριστῆς βασιλείας.

The Spaniards who were then allied to the Carthaginians in the places I mentioned beforehand came to place themselves under the Romans' protection, and when they met Scipio addressed him as 'King'. Edeco was the first person to do this and to prostrate himself, and after him the associates of Andobales. At that time Scipio passed over the term without noticing, but when after the battle everyone called him 'King', the matter gave him pause. Consequently he gathered the Spaniards and said that he wanted both to be called kingly by everyone and to be so in reality, but he neither wanted to be a king nor to be called king by anyone. After saying this he ordered them to address him as general. Perhaps even then one would justly applaud the man's greatness of mind ... But Scipio so surpassed other men in greatness of mind that he refused the thing greater than which no one would dare to pray for from the gods—I mean kingship—which was often offered to him by fortune, and he valued his country and his loyalty to her higher than the admired and blessed kingship.

Livy's version of this story clearly has contemporary resonances—the significant overtones of a young man turning down the title 'king' and instead preferring to be called *imperator* could hardly be missed, for all that the idea is already implicit in Polybius, if less pointedly phrased.[172] But his changes to Polybius go beyond that. The most obvious point is that Livy omits the idea that the appellation had already been applied to Scipio earlier: Edeco and Indibilis' men are presumably included in the 'some who had surrendered to him previously' (27.19.3), but neither here nor in his earlier account of their surrender to Scipio (27.17.1–3, 27.17.9–17; contrast Polybius 10.38.3) does he

---

[172] See Mineo (2006: 311–12).

suggest that they then either called him 'King' or prostrated themselves before him. Polybius explains Scipio's earlier lack of reaction by suggesting that he simply did not pay attention to it at the time; Livy conflates the acclamation into a single moment, and so suggests Scipio's greater sensitivity to a matter that was politically and culturally charged.[173] Polybius' account is reworked into something more suitable, and the self-consciousness of that reworking appears from the sequel, where Livy omits from Polybius Scipio's willingness to be called 'kingly' (βασιλικός), even if not 'king'—but in omitting it he appears to allude to it also, when Scipio describes the title he is turning down as a 'kingly name' (*regium nomen*), and adds that he is willing to be *thought*— but emphatically not *said* (unlike in Polybius)—to have a 'kingly mind' (*regalem animum*). Scipio in Livy carefully—if implicitly—excludes the version of the title which Polybius suggested he was willing to accept. And Livy has Scipio then make a specific reference to the unacceptability of the title at Rome—a point which not only is not in Polybius, but which Polybius' version of these events shows that he has failed to understand.[174] That lack of understanding is moreover hinted at by the sequel: for the Spaniards in Livy, being *barbari*, attribute Scipio's refusal not to the Romans' distaste for kingship, but to his personal qualities—his *magnitudinem animi*. The idea that the Spaniards admired Scipio's 'greatness of mind' is not in Polybius: the person who praises Scipio at great length for μεγαλοψυχία is Polybius himself. In other words, Polybius is, for Livy, acting as one of the *barbari*, and also proving by his own words that the title of king is indeed *alibi magnum*, exactly as Scipio says, and something at which *alii mortales* gape, as Livy comments: for even Polybius shows that he is seduced by its magic.[175]

Nor is Polybius the only one of Livy's sources who is the object of his critical reworkings. Our knowledge of his other sources, as I said earlier, is extremely limited, but one can occasionally find evidence for Livy adapting other writers on the Second Punic War in a comparable fashion. With regard to the ultimate responsibility for the war, Fabius Pictor (fr. 25P) claimed that Hannibal had launched the attack on Saguntum on his own initiative, without the support of any of the Carthaginian leadership, a version later followed by Dio fr. 54.11. Polybius 3.8.1–9.5 sharply criticized Fabius for this, arguing that his account was implausible in light of the subsequent

---

[173] Cf. Aymard (1954: 122–3).

[174] Or so it would have appeared to a Roman of Livy's day. Erskine (1991) argues that the Romans' ideological objection to kingship arose only in the second century BC as a response to their encounters with Hellenistic monarchies, and that at the time when Polybius was writing— let alone the time of Scipio—no such broad hostility to the term existed.

[175] Compare Foulon (1992), suggesting that Polybius constantly describes Scipio in terms associated with Hellenistic monarchies.

Carthaginian refusal to hand Hannibal over to the Romans, and Livy here follows Polybius, with no suggestion that Hannibal acted independently of Carthage.[176] However, the idea that the war was Hannibal's fault alone recurs in Book 30, where the Carthaginian representatives repeatedly, though disingenuously, attempt to deflect responsibility onto him and away from the state as a whole (30.16.5, 30.22.1–3, 30.42.13). The similarity between this and Fabius' analysis of the war has sometimes been noted, but the general tendency has been to assume the accuracy of Livy's account of the Carthaginians' arguments and to attempt to imagine why Fabius (a contemporary, after all) might have found them convincing.[177] But it is no less likely that the influence ran in the opposite direction: that Livy has created the arguments of these speeches himself[178] in allusion to but also as a criticism of Fabius' account. Much as we saw with Polybius' analysis of the crossing of the Alps, Fabius' account remains in the text, but is undercut by being attributed solely to the dishonest Carthaginians, in whose interest Fabius turns out to have been writing, albeit (perhaps) unwittingly.

Another example, though one a little harder to pin down, comes in the speech of Varro (23.5.12):

hunc natura et moribus inmitem ferumque insuper dux ipse efferavit, pontibus ac molibus ex humanorum corporum strue faciendis et, quod proloqui etiam piget, vesci corporibus humanis docendo.

This race [sc. the Carthaginians], brutal and fierce in their nature and customs, has been further brutalized by the general himself, building bridges and dams from a pile of human bodies, and, something shameful even to speak aloud, teaching them to feed on human bodies.

Livy nowhere shows the Carthaginian army either building bridges from corpses or engaging in cannibalism, and this accordingly looks like lurid exaggeration on Varro's part. However, the association of these things with

---

[176] Indeed, Livy is here more Polybian than Polybius. Unlike Polybius 3.15.12, the first Roman embassy (which in Livy arrives after the siege has begun: cf. Cic., *Phil.* 5.27) discovers that the attack on Saguntum is supported by 'almost all of the [Carthaginian] senate' (21.11.1 *prope omnis senatus*; cf. Händl-Sagawe 1995: 81); the sole exception is the anti-Barcid Hanno (21.10.2). Likewise, when the Romans later declare war in the Carthaginian senate, Polybius described 'a majority of the Senate' announcing their acceptance (3.33.4 πλείους τῶν ἐκ τοῦ συνεδρίου; cf. Diodorus 25.16)—for Livy it is 'all' of them (21.18.14 *omnes*; cf. Walsh 1973: 154).

[177] One possible reason for Fabius finding them convincing was that they were true: so e.g. Brizzi (2005: 33–4). The accuracy of Fabius' account is argued for by Gelzer (1933: 156–63 =1964: 81–8), who however does not note the similarity to the arguments in Livy Book 30. Fabius' picture is rejected as unhistorical by e.g. Walbank (1957: 310–11), who offers other reasons why Fabius might have accepted the Carthaginians' excuses.

[178] It is worth noting that Polybius 15.1.7–8 implies that the Carthaginians made exactly the opposite argument, accepting their collective responsibility but appealing for Roman mercy.

the Carthaginians is found in numerous other sources. The claim that Hannibal built a bridge of human bodies over the river Vergellus after the battle of
Cannae is relayed by Valerius Maximus 9.2 ext. 2, Silius Italicus 8.668–9,
Florus 1.22.18, and App., *Hann.* 28 (cf. *Pun.* 63). As for cannibalism, Polybius
9.23.4–8, in the course of a long analysis of the accusations of cruelty made
against Hannibal, records not that the Carthaginians literally ate human flesh,
but that Hannibal was advised by his friend Hannibal Monomachus to have
them do so, though he declined to act on it:[179] according to the version in Dio
fr. 57.3 his reason for declining was not a moral objection, but arose out of the
pragmatic fear that accustoming his troops to cannibalism would lead them
to practise it on each other. It is a reasonable presumption from this evidence
that one or more of Livy's predecessors told the story of the bridge of bodies,
and perhaps directly accused the Carthaginians of cannibalism as well. Livy,
however, implicitly rejects those who relayed such atrocity stories, not only by
not relaying them himself, but by damningly associating them with Varro's
speech, a speech which for other reasons appears dreadfully misplaced (below,
172, 359).[180]

There are odd occasions when Livy's allusions to Polybius are slightly more
underhand. A nice example comes at 21.57.6. This is directly after the result of
the Trebia has reached Rome, described by Livy in 21.57.1–4 and in Polybius
at 3.75. At this point Livy describes Hannibal's attack on a trading centre
(*emporium*) near Placentia (21.57.6), where he is wounded, followed by
another at Victumulae (21.57.10). Neither of these episodes is in Polybius:
instead Polybius moves the story at this point to Spain, where he begins by
describing Cn. Scipio landing at 'the place called Emporium' (3.76.1 τοὺς
κατὰ τὸ καλούμενον Ἐμπόριον τόπους). Livy's account must be taken from
some other source, but the specific idea that he is attacking *emporia* looks like
a sly nod to the reader who is expecting the Polybian narrative to continue.[181]
Livy is now going off in a different direction, though he will rejoin Polybius at
21.60, where indeed Cn. Scipio starts his campaign in Spain at 'Emporias'
(21.60.2). And Livy does make one explicit reference to Polybius in the
decade, as I said: namely in its very last lines (30.45.5), where he cites Polybius
haudquaquam spernendus auctor ('an authority not to be disregarded') for an
alternative view of Syphax being led in Scipio's triumph. Far from being a sign
that Livy has only recently discovered Polybius, as Tränkle's argument would

---

[179] Brizzi (1984: 7–29) argues that 'Hannibal Monomachus' was a fiction, an invention of
the Hannibalic historian Sosylos as a duplicate of Hannibal himself to whom he could ascribe all
suggestions of immorality in his hero: an ingenious but sadly implausible claim.

[180] As noted by Pomeroy (1989: 175).

[181] The only other account of this episode, in Appian, *Hann.* 7, describes the object of
Hannibal's attack here as a 'small harbour' (ἐπίνειον . . . τι βραχύ).

imply, if anything it signals the opposite. At the very end Livy acknowledges explicitly the thing we should have known all along: that Polybius is 'not to be disregarded' as the key authority underlying his work.

This returns us to the point at which I began the chapter, with Livy's teasing and closural play on the famous quotation from Ennius. Polybius is far more important to Livy than Ennius—or indeed any other writer mentioned in the first part of the chapter—appears to have been, yet his approach to them is in some very fundamental ways identical. Livy is a notoriously serious writer,[182] and the bulk of his allusive material inculcates points of comparison and criticism between his historical characters and other figures in history and mythology, as well as between himself and previous historians, but the more playful possibilities of such allusions are not entirely alien to him either, any more than they are to his poetic contemporaries. Nor are there any funda- mental differences between him and the poets either in the number of texts alluded to or in their presence within his narrative, ranging from a passing hint to a relationship across several pages.

But Livy's being an historian, as I have repeatedly noted, makes a consider- able difference to the terms in which allusions take place. One such difference, as I discussed extensively in the first part of the chapter, is the possibility that the allusion reflects a real-world imitation by one character of another, or else a real-world prefiguring of future events. But introducing Polybius into the mix adds still further issues. I said above (97–8) that Livy's style is not conducive to the sort of dense allusions that we associate with historians like Sallust, but we can now see that in one very important respect that is not true. Livy's language may not appear on the face of things to be sufficiently distinctive to mark allusions with great frequency, but in the case of Polybius he can engage in such an allusive relationship without needing to mark it stylistically, because the close narrative parallels alone are enough to fore- ground continuously the relationship between the texts. Livy's relationship to Polybius is thus as extensive as Virgil's to Homer, Sallust's to Thucydides, or any of the other famous examples of imitation from antiquity. And while in the last part of the chapter I have concentrated on occasions where Livy appears to be very self-consciously criticizing Polybius, one should not of course think that the allusions are limited to those passages alone. Any time that Livy uses Polybius he is effectively alluding to him. Any time that Livy changes Polybius he is effectively responding to him in an act of creative imitation.

---

[182] See e.g. Walsh (1961: 78–9), Ogilvie (1965: 4): 'no touches of humour are to be found in the history'—something of an overstatement. Catin (1944: 137–45) has a refreshingly different approach.

However, this allusive relationship is both less and more than the ones to which I have compared it. It is less, because its flexibility is so much more limited. Virgil can combine allusions to *Odyssey* and *Iliad*; he can combine multiple Homeric episodes into a single scene. Livy does not have that option with Polybius: he is largely limited by the sequence of events that he describes, since little in Polybius is written in a fashion that would strike a memorable chord out of context. On the other hand, he has advantages and opportunities as well. The systematic and linear nature of the relationship, which has few real parallels in verse, allows him to work through extended critiques and arguments with his predecessor. And, here too, the fact that his account represents—or purports to represent—an external reality makes a substantial difference to the nature of the relationship. When Livy improves on Polybius, or points to failings in Polybius' methods, he is not simply engaging in emulation for its own sake: he is making a claim about the true nature of the events of the Hannibalic War.

3

Persons and Peoples

3.1. CHARACTER

Perhaps the least interesting observation that one could make about Livy's history is that it centres on the actions of people, whether as individuals or as groups. History is written by human beings about the actions of other human beings. There have sometimes been historians who have wanted to see people as unimportant or essentially passive, at the mercy of vast impersonal forces, but it should come as little surprise that Livy was not among them. Although, as I shall discuss in Chapters 4 and 5, Livy has a more complicated and less transparent picture of historical causation than might appear from a superficial reading, it is not one that removes people from the centre of attention.

What gives the issue greater interest is that Livy generally does not appear to treat his characters in ways that are comfortable and attractive to modern Western readers. In simple terms, we have certain expectations of character-centred narratives. We have a strong liking for what one might call psychological depth: the sense that the intricacies of someone's interior thoughts and feelings are being explored. Connected with that is our preference for characters to be individuated: characters are not expected to be effectively interchangeable, but each should be portrayed in a way that reveals a unique personal identity. Consistency also matters: even if a character behaves in apparently contradictory ways, modern readers expect to be able to see these as deriving from different facets of the single personality being depicted. It is also, however, expected that characters are capable of changing and developing, and within a lengthy narrative a character, while recognizably the same person, may show evidence of being transformed by experiences.

Of course, even as an expression of modern preferences this is too crude. None of these criteria is an absolute requirement, and in particular genres, or for particular narrative purposes, all or any of them may be less prominent or disappear altogether. Nevertheless, there is a strong assumption that under most circumstances well-drawn characters will broadly conform to these expectations, and, conversely, that the absence of these features will represent a significant weakness. Hence (to mention one famous example) Dickens's characterization was frequently the object of criticism even in his own time for its apparent reliance on exterior tics and eccentricities to the exclusion of psychological depth or development, and for apparent discontinuities in the characters' behaviour. Recent critics have debated whether these are in fact flaws,[1] whether they may be founded in a consistent psychological theory,[2] or indeed whether they should be celebrated for undermining the assumptions of their day.[3] But for our purposes the point is that the criticisms, just or not, reveal the widespread assumptions of readers about the qualities required for effective literary characterization.

It can be seen immediately why Livy looks problematic if we judge him by such criteria. He rarely shows overt interest in presenting characters in ways that we might call psychologically profound. Of course, there are innumerable passages where he refers to an emotion experienced by a character, or to an idea that goes through a character's head. But it is rare for this to be explored in any detail: more often it will be nothing more than a passing word to explain why a particular course of action was undertaken, and will not be accompanied by any detailed description or discussion of inner thoughts or feelings. Nor are many Livian characters, at least on the face of things, clearly individuated. People are admittedly divided into crude categories, so one finds 'rash commanders' like Varro or Flaminius, or 'cautious commanders' like Fabius or Paullus.[4] But most rash commanders look much like most other rash commanders, and most cautious commanders look much like most other cautious commanders. The number of individuals who are clearly *sui generis* is small. Character development is almost entirely absent; even when we can watch someone over a number of years, there is rarely any sense that his experiences have changed him—something accentuated by the fact that few Livian characters are ever represented outside their public role, so we do not see them in the contexts of their childhood or families. And as I noted in Chapter 1, even these stereotyped characters sometimes do not maintain the desired consistency: so Vibellius Taurea can be a cowardly braggart in Book 23 and a self-sacrificing hero in Book 26. Both of these may be stereotypes, but they are different stereotypes, and there is nothing to indicate how we can connect one image to the other.

None of this is to say that Livy never introduces the sort of features that would be sought by modern readers. There are, for example, moments where

---

[1] E.g. Chase (1984: esp. 92–135).
[2] E.g. Vrettos (2000).
[3] E.g. Kincaid (1995: 75–87), Rosenberg (1996).
[4] On the 'rash commander—cautious commander' antithesis see Catin (1944: 42–53).

we can see a character emotionally torn and in distress, such as Masinissa after Scipio rebukes him over his marriage to Sophoniba (30.15.1–3). So too a character's actions are occasionally given a more private and personal context, as with the oath of hostility to Rome that the young Hannibal swears at his father's prompting (21.1.4), or when Adranadorus is encouraged by his wife to aspire to rule Syracuse (24.22.8–11, 24.24.1–2). But these are brief, rare, and exceptional. If one reads Livy expecting the intense engagement with individual characters' emotions and dilemmas that one would find in a modern novel or biography one is liable to be disappointed. Nor does this seem to reflect a clear-cut distinction between the ancient world and the modern, because there are many ancient writers – including indeed historians – who apparently present far more nuanced and detailed accounts of their characters' inner lives. It is true that, as I shall discuss shortly, there are substantial differences between ancient modes of character presentation and modern. But this does not always appear to result in deficiency: whether one takes Tacitus or Virgil, Plutarch or Euripides, one need not feel that they fall markedly short by our standards of effective characterization. The same is not true of Livy. To put it bluntly, by comparison with Tacitus (let alone Virgil or Euripides) his characters feel one-dimensional.

The explanation may of course simply be that Livy's strengths do not lie in effective characterization. But before we dismiss him so readily, we need to consider two other possibilities. One is that this immediate and superficial reaction to Livy's characters is mistaken, and that in fact a closer reading of his work will reveal the psychological nuances that seem at first sight to be missing. The other possibility is that the demands that modern readers make on Livy are anachronistic, and that ancient concepts of characterization were such that texts have to be assessed according to quite different criteria. Both of these approaches have been taken by modern scholars: I shall examine each in turn.

To begin with the first, this is, for example, the line adopted by the most recent systematic study of Livy's characterization, by Jacques-Emmanuel Bernard.[5] In the course of his extended typological analysis of Livy's character portrayals, Bernard makes it clear that he regards criticisms of Livy's characterization as unjust, the result of people examining only the relatively small number of extended descriptions, and overlooking the commoner but more indirect ways in which characters are given elements of individuality.[6] These

---

[5] Bernard (2000). The idea that Livy's characterization is largely conducted through such 'indirect' methods goes back to Bruns (1898: esp. 12–61), whose approach has for the most part been adopted unquestioningly in later Livian scholarship: see also e.g. Plöger (1975: 203–74), Burck (1992: 132–59).

[6] Bernard (2000: e.g. 15–17, 407–8).

include, for example, Livy distinguishing characters by the styles of their speeches,[7] or by the reactions of others to them. Although any particular point may not be enough to create a sense of an individuated character, such individuation emerges, Bernard argues, across a long series of episodes in which the character is viewed from a number of different standpoints and represented through a variety of means.[8] Bernard is naturally well aware of the prevalence of character types in Livy, and discusses these at considerable length.[9] But he treats them not as limiting features, but rather as counterpoints to the more complex and individual aspects of Livy's characters: a way of organizing them and placing them within the moral scheme of the history rather than reducing them to a succession of indistinguishable stereotypes.[10] Similarly he recognizes that some Livian characters are sketched in only superficially, but he makes a sharp distinction between those people who play a role in the narrative without being portrayed individually, and those actively characterized:[11] he counts 101 of the latter across the surviving work, more than a quarter of whom appear in the Third Decade, and most of whom he claims receive an extended and complex treatment.

Bernard's argument is not a negligible one. Certainly if we look at the more indirect ways in which characters are presented through their words and actions as well as through direct authorial comment we find a wider range of perspectives; and it is too crude simply to reduce all of Livy's characters to uncomplicated stereotypes.

As a single illustration let us look at the striking portrayal of M. Livius Salinator in Books 27–29, not least in his relationship to his consular and censorial colleague C. Claudius Nero. The chief aspect of Livius that emerges from Livy's initial account of him is his sense of resentment towards the Roman people for his condemnation following his earlier consulship in 219. We are told that he 'had borne this disgrace so badly' that he left the city for several years (27.34.4 *quam ignominiam adeo aegre tulerat*); when he is eventually brought back and offered the consulship he attempts to refuse it on the grounds of the people's previous treatment of him (27.34.12–13)—his bitterness appears in the words *accusans* (27.34.12: 'accusing') and *querentem* (27.34.14: 'complaining'). Moreover, we are given a direct description of the way he looked and dressed after he was brought back to the city, which

---

[7] Bernard (2000: 95–112).

[8] Bernard (2000: 16, 133–56, 370–2).

[9] Bernard (2000: 167–303).

[10] Bernard (2000: 163–5, 280).

[11] Bernard (2000: 131–2). However, it should be noted that Bernard provides no detailed criteria to explain how he has drawn this distinction, and it is hard in quite a number of cases to see why some figures are included in his list while others are excluded.

appears to correspond to his state of mind: 'his clothing was shabby, his hair and beard long, parading in his expression and his bearing the conspicuous memory of the disgrace he received' (27.34.5 *sed erat veste obsoleta capilloque et barba promissa, prae se ferens in voltu habituque insignem memoriam ignominiae acceptae*). There is something unusually and uncomfortably ostentatious about Livius deliberately reflecting his disgrace in his looks, an impression reinforced by the fact that he then has to be compelled by the censors to tidy up his appearance and to resume his role as senator (27.34.6), just as it is said to have been Marcellus' and Laevinus' initiative rather than his own desire which brought him back to the city in the first place (27.34.5). On leaving Rome he is 'still full of anger against the citizens' (27.40.8 *plenum adhuc irae in cives*) and is eager to fight even in the recognition that he may lose—on the appalling grounds that at least then he would have the pleasure of his fellow citizens' defeat (27.40.9). And when he holds the censorship a few years later and imposes a tax on salt, this too is attributed to his resentment and his hostility to the people over his condemnation (29.37.3–4). Livy does not directly endorse that interpretation, but it is given credence by Livius' behaviour immediately afterwards, when he attempts to disenfranchise virtually the entire populace on the basis of a quibble: they had inconsistently condemned him and then made him consul and censor, and either the condemnation or the election must have been wrong (29.37.13–14).

Livius' relationship with his colleague Claudius Nero is initially poisoned by the same state of mind: *inimicitiae autem nobiles inter eos erant, et acerbiores eas indignioresque Livio sua calamitas fecerat quod spretum se in ea fortuna credebat* (27.35.7: 'The enmity between them was notorious, which for Livius was made all the bitter and more undeserved by his disaster, because he believed that he had been scorned in his misfortune'); he also refuses Fabius' attempts at reconciliation before being persuaded by the Senate to put his enmity aside (27.35.6-9).[12] From then on, however, their consulship is marked by concord, something that Livy explicitly notes more than once (27.38.10, 28.9.4, 28.9.9–10, cf. 29.37.10), and which receives a striking symbolic illustration when Livius conceals Claudius' troops from Hasdrubal by mingling them with his own in the camp (27.46.1–2). But in their shared censorship the enmity returns. In this case Claudius more clearly takes the lead, when he attempts to degrade Livius because of his earlier condemnation 'whether because of the remnants of their old quarrel or because he was

---

[12] Contrast Valerius Maximus 4.2.2, where Livius' grounds for resentment against Claudius are more clearly justified, since it is said to have been Claudius' testimony that got him exiled (something that Livy does not mention until 29.37.10), and he is reconciled far more easily and spontaneously.

puffed up with a misplaced show of severity' (29.37.9 *sive ex residua vetere simultate sive intempestiva iactatione severitatis inflatus*), but Livius more than responds in kind, condemning Claudius' entire tribe and indeed virtually the whole population along with him (29.37.10, 13–15).

In some respects this portrait of Livius fits Bernard's model extremely well. The picture of the man burning with resentment and using every opportunity to take it out on those he blames for his degradation is vivid and memorable.[13] As Bernard suggests, Livy furthers that picture through a variety of techniques: direct description plays a role, but only a partial one, and Livius' character emerges even more from his own words and actions, as well as from the reactions and interpretations of other people. It is true that one might suggest that there is a certain element of stereotyping: that of the great man unjustly (as he sees it) rejected by his countrymen and repaying them with hostility of his own.[14] But Livius' character is not simply reducible to that stereotype, because his reaction is exceptional and distinctive, whether in his ostentatious adoption of squalor, or in his willingness to lead his countrymen to defeat in order to see them punished.

Yet, for all this, there is something strangely lacking here, something that Bernard does not seem to account for altogether satisfactorily. For one thing, it is a noticeably 'exterior' account, by which I mean not so much that we get a description of Livius' appearance (such visual descriptions of people in Livy are in fact relatively unusual),[15] but also that we are not given any real access to his thoughts and his emotions beyond the bare awareness of the resentment that we are told he is feeling. There is no attempt to analyse his state of mind in any detail, or to present it in terms that would invite an emotional engagement from the reader. Perhaps related to this, but even more immediately apparent, is the difficulty we have connecting what we see of Livius' character to much of his behaviour as consul. He totally drops his resentment against Claudius simply (it appears) on the Senate's say-so, and this new-found concord extends not merely to their actions as commanders, but to the mutual generosity with which they share the credit in the triumph.[16] His willingness to lead his army to defeat does not seem to have any obvious effect on his actual conduct of the battle against Hasdrubal. It is not that this is

---

[13] Compare Catin (1944: 73–5) on Livy's picture of Livius as 'une courte comédie de caractère'.

[14] The most famous example in Livy is Coriolanus in Book 2, but Athenian history furnishes a number of instances also.

[15] Note Bernard (2000: 63–9, 250–7).

[16] De Ravinel (1962) attempts to detect in Livy's narrative of the Metaurus and the subsequent triumph hints that Livius and Claudius maintained their mutual hostility through their consulship, but none of his examples are convincing.

completely inexplicable: one can imagine many possible reasons why Livius would not wish to conduct so vital a campaign while constantly sniping at his colleague and soldiers. But nothing in Livy tells us which reason is the right one: whether, for example, Livius genuinely (if temporarily) gives up his hatred of Claudius, or whether he chooses to act as if he had given it up for their period of office out of concern for the public interest. And there is no sense of what the chief motivation was that swayed him: whether it was mere deference to the *auctoritas senatus* (27.35.9), or whether he is now directly convinced by the arguments for the superiority of concord, despite his own earlier paradoxical claim that hostility between Claudius and him would actually benefit their conduct of the consulship (27.35.8). Indeed, nothing even invites us to consider these things as questions that might need answering. Livy's silence on such crucial issues makes Livius seem inconsistent and unmotivated. Rather than taking an easy opportunity to deepen our appreciation of the character by exploring a different facet to his behaviour, he ignores the question as if it were a matter without interest.

So even a character as striking and individual as Livius Salinator comes across as unsatisfactory to the modern reader. The same is even more obvious when we look at characters who conform more directly to stereotypes. Books 21 and 22 contain in quick succession four rash commanders who lead their armies to defeat against Hannibal: Sempronius Longus, Flaminius, Minucius, and Varro.[17] Each is described in a vivid episode which illustrates graphically his aggressive state of mind. So Sempronius is shown exulting in a minor victory, insulting and scornful towards his more cautious colleague Scipio, and taking every opportunity to promote a more active strategy (21.53.1–7). Flaminius is infuriated into action by the sight of Hannibal's ravages, and when his attempt to join battle is hindered by a sequence of bad omens, sarcastically attacks those who would be swayed by them (22.3.7–14). Minucius demonstrates his opposition to Fabius' passivity in a violent speech in which he contrasts at length Fabius' inaction with the heroism of earlier commanders (22.14.3–15), and arrogantly exults at his promotion to equality with him (22.27.1–4). Varro manipulates himself into power by exploiting lower-class resentment and attacking the upper classes (22.26.1–4, 22.34.2).

Thus, vivid description of these characters is not lacking; what is more, at least three of the portraits to some extent contain features that look more distinctive and individual. Flaminius' actions are governed by his memory of his

---

[17] Cf. Bernard (2000: 211, 262–4). On this sequence of commanders see Will (1983); also Rambaud (1980: 112–16), who notes some close parallels between Sempronius, Flaminius, and Caesar's portrayal of Sabinus in *BG* 5.26–37. On the portrayal of Minucius in particular see Bernard (2000: 135–9); on that of Varro see Vallet (1964), Bernard (2000: 139–41).

long-standing conflict with the main body of the Senate dating back to his tribunate in 232 and his earlier consulship in 223, which is part of what leads him to seek to circumvent them now (21.63.2–6, 22.3.3–4). Even more distinctively, he shows impiety and impatience with religious requirements, not only in ignoring the omens before battle, but also in his refusal to remain at Rome to perform the necessary rites as consul (21.63.5–11, 22.1.5–7). None of the others is actively irreligious: Varro comes closest, but on receiving a not dissimilar omen before Cannae remembers Flaminius' example and decides to obey it (22.42.7–9). Varro's accusations against the *nobiles* go well beyond those of the others, although his anti-senatorial stance aligns him politically with both Flaminius and Minucius; he is also set apart by his lower-class background (22.25.18–19) and his obviously calculated manipulations of class conflict for personal gain. Minucius' recantation and acknowledgement of Fabius' authority ultimately show him in a better light than any of the other three (22.29.7–30.6).[18]

Yet here too there is something not entirely satisfactory to the modern reader. Varro's demagoguery does not so much make him distinctive in his own right, but rather combines the 'rash commander' stereotype with the different stereotype of the manipulative demagogue, a stereotype familiar in the First Decade, but which has a wider history going back at least to Thucydides' Cleon, who similarly unites a strategy of aggression in war with self-serving demagoguery at home. The scenes in which the characters' reactions are described are vivid enough, and perhaps a little more involving than comparable episodes with Livius Salinator, as when the sight of Italy being ravaged prompts Minucius' infuriated response (22.14). Livy's actual description of the destruction is brief, but phrases like *exurebatur amoenissimus Italiae ager* (22.14.1: 'the loveliest territory of Italy was aflame') might be sufficient to evoke comparable outrage in a Roman audience familiar with the land, and hence identification with Minucius' reaction. But there is still relatively little to draw the reader to appreciate the characters' emotions and experiences from within, and the emotions that we are shown are simple and one-note. And, possibly as a consequence, for much of the time these four figures appear effectively interchangeable.[19] Even when there are differences

---

[18] Though, as Will (1983: 180–2) notes, Livy provides a measure of redemption for all of these commanders: not only Minucius' recantation fits this pattern, but also Sempronius' greater success against Hannibal after the Trebia (21.59), Flaminius' courage at Trasimene (22.6.1–2), and Varro's welcome at Rome for not having despaired of the state after Cannae (22.61.14–15). None of these are in Polybius.

[19] It is perhaps revealing (especially in the context of a book on characterization) that Bernard himself sometimes confuses Flaminius and Minucius, at one point making the former into Fabius' deputy (Bernard 2000: 370), and at another implying that Minucius was in command at Trasimene (Bernard 2000: 138).

between them they often feel the superficial result of particular circumstances rather than something intrinsic to the person. (Perhaps even Flaminius could have learned enough by his experiences to give at least the limited respect to omens that Varro does, had he survived Trasimene and been in command at Cannae.)

Moreover, as with Livius, inconsistencies in the characters' behaviour, which might under other circumstances have served to differentiate them, fail to do so because they are not strongly motivated. Minucius' recantation is effective enough as a dramatic resolution of the episode, but does not connect in any clear way with his character as it has appeared earlier. When Varro reappears at the beginning of Book 23 as the recipient of an embassy from Campania, he makes a speech which aims to encourage them to remain in the Roman alliance, but its despairing tone has precisely the opposite effect, leading them to accelerate their breach with Rome (23.5).[20] This is a masterly and subtle piece of writing by Livy, a speech whose effect is entirely misjudged by its speaker, and which can stand comparison with the finest pieces of self-undermining rhetoric in ancient literature. But there is little apparent connection with the aggressive and cleverly manipulative demagogue of the previous book.[21]

These and many other examples show that attempting to defend Livy's characters in terms of modern expectations is unsatisfactory. We should therefore examine the other possibility: that the ancients had different criteria for what makes effective characterization than we do, and that Livy's characters work well in those terms even if they may not always do so in ours.

One initial point that should be made is about verisimilitude. One basic criterion for success or otherwise in characterization is whether the characters come across to the reader as believable. In practice, as I have already indicated, for modern readers a major component of this is often the degree of psychological involvement that is induced in the reader: thus Lord Jim is a 'believable character' even though most people are unlikely to have encountered a sailor whose entire life has been blighted by a single moment of cowardice that he is attempting to live down, whereas Mr Micawber is not, even though we may well have known unreasonable optimists living a semi-respectable but hand-to-mouth existence. But believability is clearly not something independent of

---

[20] Cf. 23.5.2 *auxit rerum suarum suique contemptum consul nimis detegendo cladem nudan-doque*—'the consul increased their contempt for his situation and for him by excessively exposing and laying bare the disaster'.

[21] Vallet (1964: 709–11) would relate Varro's speech here to the cowardice that, he suggests, Livy hints at in his behaviour after Cannae. But even if true, that simply transfers the inconsistency a stage back, for Varro's aggressive desire to launch an immediate attack on Hannibal contained no hint of covert cowardice.

a particular culture: it is governed by expectations, first our expectations of what people actually are like, and second of how it is appropriate to represent that within a particular genre. Putting it bluntly, in a culture in which Arabs are uniformly believed to be cruel, deceitful, and violent, portraying an Arab as cruel, deceitful, and violent will inevitably increase the character's believ-ability. In a culture in which the 'cruel, deceitful, and violent Arab' is seen as an unpleasant racist stereotype, exactly the same elements of the portrait will diminish the believability. A society which expects every individual to be radically different from every other individual will regard it essential for believable characters to be portrayed in a manner which demonstrates their radical individuality. In a society in which people are assumed to fall into (for example) social or biological categories within which behaviour is entirely predictable, slotting people into the appropriate category and showing them to behave accordingly will be essential for their believability.[22] And there may well be variations between genres: characterization in a modern novel will necessarily proceed along different lines from that in a modern play, and the very features that increase believability in the former—for example, the explicit representation of a solitary character's thoughts and feelings—may in the latter appear a clichéd and implausible dramatic device.

It is therefore unsatisfactory to consider the apparent weaknesses in Livy's characterization in isolation from the evidence that we have for Roman ideas of character and of characterization more broadly. A comprehensive exami-nation of these lies well beyond the scope of this book, but we can at least sketch out some general points.

To begin with, we can consider a helpful distinction introduced some years ago in a series of articles by Christopher Gill: the distinction between what he calls 'character viewpoints' and 'personality viewpoints'.[23] 'Personality view-points', Gill argues, are psychologically focused and non-judgemental; they involve sympathetic engagement with the point of view of a particular individual. 'Character viewpoints' are evaluative and judgemental: people are described from an external perspective rather than explored from their own perspective, with the focus often on assessing them in moral terms. The former corresponds to what I suggested above was the typical expectations of modern readers; but it might seem that people in Livy fit much more naturally into the 'character' mould. It should of course be emphasized that

---

[22] Cf. Halliwell (1990: esp. 56–9).

[23] See esp. Gill (1986, 1990; also 1983, 1984: 165–6). As I shall explain shortly, it is hard to maintain quite as clear-cut a distinction as Gill does in these articles, and indeed in his more recent writings he has himself modified and to some degree retreated from the analysis here, but the distinction remains a useful way of thinking about ancient literature.

Gill is not suggesting anything as crude as the idea that 'personality view-points' are modern and 'character viewpoints' are ancient,[24] or indeed that authors can be divided neatly into 'character-authors' and 'personality-authors'. On the contrary, he explicitly rejects such a dichotomy, instead arguing that both 'character' and 'personality' may be found in different parts of ancient literature at different times, or indeed are often blended within a single work or a single character within a work. Nevertheless, one might suggest that, according to such a framework, Livy's characters are typically represented in a manner rather closer to the 'character' end of the scale, even if occasionally elements are included that remind one more of 'personality'; and one significant conclusion of Gill's studies is to show that ancient authors—and, by inference, ancient audiences—had a considerably greater tolerance for 'character viewpoints' than their modern counterparts do, and that the balance in many authors is therefore strongly weighted in the direction of 'character'.

Such an analysis would help explain why Livy's characters can appear to the modern reader relatively stereotyped and unengaging: his focus is on external, 'objective' analysis and on moral judgements based on that analysis rather than drawing the reader into subjective involvement with an individual's psychology.[25] But more needs to be said. I suggested above that Livy is unusual, even by the standards of ancient literature, in the relative absence of 'personality'-like features.[26] There is also the problem of the frequency with which his characters appear inconsistent. Gill argues that inconsistent behaviour is if anything associated more with 'personality viewpoints': it arises from the immediacy of the presentation of the vicissitudes of the character's thoughts and feelings. 'Character viewpoints', on the other hand, would more normally be expected to show someone whose behaviour is all of a piece.[27] The fact that Livy, while favouring 'character viewpoints', introduces the sort of inconsistency that we might associate with 'personality viewpoints', does

---

[24] Contrast the not dissimilar but far more simplistic formulations of Ginsberg (1983: 3–4, 14); also Gill's earlier and slightly more schematic division between ancient and modern approaches in Gill (1983: 471–3).

[25] Bernard (2000: 258) similarly refers to 'cette soumission de la psychologie à la morale' in Livy.

[26] Gill, focusing particularly on Plutarch, argues that not only does he overwhelmingly use 'character viewpoints', but that such a way of handling character is typical of historiography and biography of the Roman era more generally (Gill 1983: esp. 472–4). However, Pelling demonstrates that Plutarch makes considerably greater use of 'personality viewpoints' than Gill gave him credit for, albeit not always in a manner that a modern biographer would (Pelling 1990a: 224–35, updated in Pelling 2002: 307–15; also Pelling 2002: 321–9). One can make similar points about Tacitus (see e.g. Levene 1997).

[27] Gill (1986: 252–3).

not challenge Gill's analysis of the distinction: if anything our discomfort at the inconsistency tends to confirm it (it feels more natural and less disturbing when inconsistencies appear in someone presented as a 'personality'). But it does suggest that Gill's distinction, while taking us some way towards a comprehension of Livy's approach to character, is still inadequate to explain it.

We therefore need to delve a little deeper into ancient concepts of character, to see if there are other aspects which would mean that Roman readers would find Livy less problematic than we do. The most useful area of evidence is in rhetoric and oratory. There are discussions in Cicero and Quintilian (to mention only the two most obvious) of how characters are to be used in speeches; we also can see the underlying assumptions in the speeches themselves. One reason this is an especially promising source is that these works are especially likely to reflect assumptions found in Roman society more broadly, first because in order to be effective the speeches had to appear convincing to a wide audience, and second because anyone trained in rhetoric—effectively, any upper-class Roman man—would have these assumptions inculcated over a lengthy period of education.

This argument requires a certain qualification. 'Especially likely to reflect' does not mean that views of character other than those found in rhetoric and oratory are necessarily alien to Roman society; on the contrary, I shall be arguing shortly that some aspects of Livy's own techniques of characterization are incompatible with the assumptions of rhetoric but can be paralleled elsewhere in ancient thought. Rhetoric provides us with what Andrew Riggsby calls 'folk models of character';[28] but such 'folk models' can easily exist side by side with other contradictory attitudes that emerge in other contexts. What is reasonable to argue is that assumptions found repeatedly in rhetoric—especially if other contrary assumptions are not equally well represented—are reflecting not merely the needs of a particular case, but some fairly deep-seated attitudes in a fairly wide section of the society.[29] Moreover, the evidence of rhetoric is especially useful for understanding historiography, since the generic distinction between oratory and historiography was not drawn as sharply in antiquity as it is today, and prescriptions for the former in various respects applied also to the latter.[30]

In certain ways our rhetorical texts make it clear that aspects of Livy which seem problematic to modern audiences would have been far less so to ancient ones. Stereotyping, for example, appears both more acceptable and more

---

[28] Riggsby (2004: 166).
[29] Berry (1996: 275) would see attitudes to character in oratory as closely tied to the demands of each particular case; but see *contra* Riggsby (2004: 175).
[30] As argued by Woodman (1988: esp. 83–98).

nuanced than moderns would usually be prepared to credit. Stereotyping in modern Western thought is regarded (at least in polite and/or educated society) as something profoundly negative, not least because its primary associations are with racial and sexual prejudice and discrimination. But when Quintilian considers how an orator should use character to prove his case, he provides a large number of aspects of a person that he regards as relevant to determining that person's actions (5.10.23-27):

personis autem non quidquid accidit exequendum mihi est, ut plerique fecerunt, sed unde argumenta sumi possunt. ea porro sunt: genus, nam similes parentibus ac maioribus suis plerumque creduntur, et nonnumquam ad honeste turpiterque viven-dum inde causae fluunt: natio, nam et gentibus proprii mores sunt nec idem in barbaro, Romano, Graeco probabile est: patria, quia similiter etiam civitatium leges instituta opiniones habent differentiam; sexus, ut latrocinium facilius in viro, vene-ficium in femina credas; aetas, quia aliud aliis annis magis convenit; educatio et disciplina, quoniam refert a quibus et quo quisque modo sit institutus; habitus corporis, ducitur enim frequenter in argumentum species libidinis, robur petulantiae, his contraria in diversum; fortuna, neque enim idem credibile est in divite ac paupere, propinquis amicis clientibus abundante et his omnibus destituto (condicionis etiam distantia est: nam clarus an obscurus, magistratus an privatus, pater an filius, civis an peregrinus, liber an servus, maritus an caelebs, parens liberorum an orbus sit, plurimum distat); animi natura, etenim avaritia iracundia misericordia crudelitas severitas aliaque his similia adferunt fidem frequenter aut detrahunt, sicut victus luxuriosus an frugi an sordidus quaeritur; studia quoque, nam rusticus forensis negotiator miles navigator medicus aliud atque aliud efficiunt.

I do not have to examine everything that happens to characters, as many have done, but things from which arguments may be drawn. They are the following: family, for people are generally thought to be like their parents and ancestors, and sometimes this provides reasons for people living honourably or shamefully; nation, for even races have their own habits and the same things are not probable in a barbarian, Roman, and Greek; homeland, because similarly there are also differences between the laws, institutions, and opinions of states; sex, so that you would more readily believe in thuggery in the case of a man, poison in the case of a woman; age, because different things are more suited to different ages; education and training, since it makes a difference by whom and how everyone has been raised; physical character, because beauty is regularly adduced as a proof of lust, strength of aggression, and their opposites in the opposite direction; fortune, because the same thing is not credible in a rich man as in a poor, one with a wealth of relatives and friends and clients and one deprived of all these (there is also a distinction of position, since there is a great distinction between a famous and an obscure man, a magistrate and a private citizen, a father and a son, a citizen and a foreigner, a free man and a slave, a married man and a bachelor, a parent of children and someone childless); the nature of the mind, for avarice, anger, pity, cruelty, severity and suchlike regularly make things seem more or less likely—so it is asked whether a lifestyle is luxurious or frugal or mean;

occupation too, for a countryman, a lawyer, a businessman, a soldier, a sailor, a doctor all do things in different ways.

It is clear from this (and other examples also)[31] that one major way in which the Romans assessed a person was by placing the subject as precisely as possible within a social framework and seeing that as a major determinant of character.[32] It is not merely that people are expected to act in a particular way according to their race or sex, but also that people of the same family may be expected to behave in similar fashions to one another,[33] that fathers will behave similarly to each other and differently from the childless, that magistrates behave differently from private individuals, and so on; moreover, that different categories of people have set dispositions that likewise incline them to certain types of behaviour. The very complexity of this gives room for a good deal of variation in individual cases: after all, a magistrate may be a father or childless, a rich man may be a Roman or a foreigner, and any of these may be old or young and possess different emotional dispositions; I shall be exploring this point further below (184–6). Likewise Quintilian does not suggest that any of these are invariable determinants of behaviour, but treats them rather as general but not exceptionless predispositions (note phrases like *probabile est* and *facilius . . . credas*). But it is not surprising that a writer like Livy, brought up within a society and educational system within which it was normal to categorize behaviour according to such criteria, will find his characters falling into repeated patterns, especially if he tends to focus on a relatively narrow range of social relationships—most of Livy's characters are military commanders or political leaders, and are mostly seen only in relationship to their military and political roles. And a readership conditioned to expect such patterns is similarly likely to find characters plausible precisely because they fall into familiar categories, and is less likely to find them significantly deficient.

On the other hand, not all of the apparent limitations of Livy's characters are so readily defended. The strongly 'exterior' and evaluative approach he takes towards them—as 'characters', in Gill's sense—appears in some ways to fit well with the general role which Quintilian, like other rhetorical writers,

---

[31] Note, for example, the similar though briefer categorizations in Cicero, *Inv.* 2.29–30, *Part. Or.* 35. The specific idea of character being governed by age is expanded at length by Horace, *Ars* 153–78.

[32] Compare Heath (1987: 118–19) for the way in which individuality in Greek tragedy is achieved via the creation of characters who vividly and consistently conform to the expected behaviour of members of their social category.

[33] On the importance of this idea in Roman aristocratic culture, and the way it influenced historical representations by establishing stereotypical behaviour within families, see Walter (2004). In the Third Decade Livy indicates that Hannibal (21.4.2) and Scipio (26.41.24–5) resemble their parents both in looks and in character.

seems to assume for characters in oratory: that they are to be categorized and assessed according to their conformity with particular stereotypes. But rhetoric has an entirely separate dimension also, because as well as providing a framework for evaluating characters as evidence for one's case, it also offers techniques for presenting a character—whether the speaker, the client, or (less often) a third party—such that the audience is emotionally engaged with their experiences. This is not precisely identical to the sort of emotional engagement that one might find in narrative or dramatic literature—it is typically far more overt and the sympathy it seeks to evoke is narrowly focused on the requirements of the case—but there is an obvious overlap.[34]

Thus when Antonius in Cicero, *de Orat.* 2.194 describes his emotive defence of Aquilius, he revealingly refers to himself as *personae... auctor meae* ('author of my own character'): the representation of his own emotions is an aspect of his portrayal of his own character. Quintilian likewise, when discussing the arousal of emotions (6.1–2), partly does so in terms of presenting a character's thoughts and feelings in a vivid and 'internal' fashion. One example is his suggestion at 6.1.25–6 that the orator should speak as if in the persona of his client, 'for the judge seems not to hear someone lamenting another person's troubles, but to receive in his ears the feelings and voice of wretched people' (6.1.26 *non enim audire iudex videtur aliena mala deflentis, sed sensum ac vocem auribus accipere miserorum*). Another is his argument that the orator when speaking should himself be seen to experience the emotions that he seeks to arouse in the audience (6.2.25–36).[35] Likewise we should note the exercise of *ethopoeia* (which formed part of the standard rhetorical curriculum), by which one would have to compose speeches for assumed characters, an exercise in character creation which naturally often went hand in hand with the adoption of emotions appropriate for that person in that situation.[36] We may compare Longinus, *On the Sublime* 22, who

---

[34] Compare Kaster (2005b: 321–9) for a brief but useful account of how attempts to rouse passion in oratory merge with the representation of those experiencing passion, and how the effects found in rhetoric in turn mirror those in narrative and other literature.

[35] A commonplace of ancient criticism: see e.g. Cicero, *de Orat.* 2.189–94; Horace, *Ars* 102–3; cf. Wisse (1989: 257–69).

[36] Note in particular Aphthonius, *Progymnasmata* 35.1–10 (Rabe) (cf. ps.-Hermogenes, *Progymnasmata* 21.10–18 [Rabe]): τῶν δὲ ἠθοποιιῶν αἲ μέν εἰσι παθητικαί, αἲ δὲ ἠθικαί, αἲ δὲ μικταί. καὶ παθητικαὶ μὲν αἱ κατὰ πάντα πάθος σημαίνουσαι... ἠθικαὶ δὲ αἱ μόνον ἦθος εἰσφέρουσαι... μικταὶ δὲ αἱ τὸ συναμφότερον ἔχουσαι, καὶ ἦθος καὶ πάθος, οἷον τίνας ἂν εἴποι λόγους Ἀχιλλεὺς ἐπὶ Πατρόκλῳ κειμένῳ βουλευόμενος πολεμεῖν· ἦθος μὲν γὰρ ἡ βουλή, πάθος δὲ φίλος πεσών ('Of ethopoeias some are *pathetic*, some are *ethical*, some are mixed. The *pathetic* ones reveal emotion throughout... the *ethical* only introduce character... the mixed are those which have both emotion and character together, such as what Achilles would say over the dead Patroclus when resolving to fight: the deliberation is character, the friend having fallen is emotion'). See Heusch (2005: 19–22).

advocates using stylistic devices which accurately reflect the state of mind of speakers under emotional stress.[37] This evidence too, therefore, suggests that a Roman audience would be conditioned to respond well to characters presented in such a way, even if that audience did not regard it as a *sine qua non* for those characters' plausibility.

By this standard Livy falls markedly short.[38] One finds occasional examples of characters' thoughts and emotions vividly represented so that the audience can empathize with their experiences: one might mention the description of Heraclia and her daughters at the point of their murder (24.26.1–14), or Pacuvius Calavius' shocked speech when he learns of his son's plan to assassinate Hannibal (23.9.1–9). But these are exceptional. Not that Livy is uninterested in engaging the audience's emotions in general: on the contrary, he regularly presents vivid and moving scenes, and especially does so through the eyes of spectators in the text with whom the reader may identify.[39] So one often finds extended and powerful scenes of emotional drama: the brutal siege of Astapa, for example (28.22.1–23.5), or the long account of the response of the Roman populace to the threat from Hasdrubal and the battle of the Metaurus, with their apprehensiveness at the decisive struggle ahead (27.40.1–7, 27.44), their flocking in support of Claudius Nero as he makes his remarkable march north (27.45.7–11), and their wild celebrations at the victory (27.51.1–10). But these do not invite engagement with particular

---

[37] See Gray (1987: 468–72).

[38] *Pace* Quintilian 10.1.101: 'In speeches he [Livy] is eloquent beyond description, to such an extent is everything that is spoken suited both to the circumstances and the characters; and as for emotions, especially the sweeter ones, to speak briefly, no historian has done more to promote them.' ('in contionibus supra quam enarrari potest eloquentem, ita quae dicuntur omnia cum rebus tum personis accommodata sunt: adfectus quidem, praecipueque eos qui sunt dulciores, ut parcissime dicam, nemo historicorum commendavit magis.') Quintilian's judgement of Livy looks superficially at variance with mine, which would seem to undermine my suggestion that Livy's characterization would be seen as problematic even in ancient terms. However, what Quintilian says has little bearing on the particular features of Livy's characterization that I have been discussing here. In particular, Quintilian's focus on 'sweeter emotions' is revealing in the light of his discussion of emotion in Book 6, where he makes an interesting if confusing distinction, and speaks of gentler emotions as part of *ethos* rather than *pathos*, so contributing to the representation of character without inviting emotional involvement in the spectator (Quintilian 6.2.8–20, esp. 6.2.9; though see Gill (1984: esp. 158–60) for the suggestion that Quintilian's account may not be as confused as appears at first sight; also Wisse (1989) for a broader discussion of the *ethos/pathos* distinction). More importantly still, Quintilian's particular focus on the appropriateness of Livy's speeches to their particular circumstances and speakers leaves entirely open the question of whether the character of the speaker remains constant between speech and speech, or indeed speech and action. The problem of Livy's characters, as I have represented it, is that while they may speak or act appropriately in any *particular* set of circumstances, once one puts together the varied circumstances across which they are speaking and acting they do not behave consistently. See further below, 180–2.

[39] See e.g. Feldherr (1998).

individuals, and so do not contribute to characterization in the terms we are discussing here.[40]

We find a similar problem if we consider the question of the inconsistency of Livy's characters in the light of the rhetorical texts. The same texts that categorize people socially also indicate that those people are expected to act in a broadly consistent fashion: that just as their nature and position in life lead to valid inferences about their behaviour, so too does the fact that they have previously behaved in certain ways lead us to assume that they will continue to do so. Not only does the very fact that people are placed in these categories at all rely on this tacit assumption – that behaviour is regular and predictable from people's fundamental characteristics – but also it is suggested in related arguments that people behave consistently, such that (for example) past behaviour allows valid inferences about the present likelihood that they have committed a crime.[41] The sudden and unexplained lurches of character that we find in Livy do not fit easily into such a model. We can see the demand for consistency, in literature as well as in life, in other areas also. Horace, *Ars* 119–27 sets out his prescriptions for characterization as follows:

> aut famam sequere aut sibi convenientia finge,
> scriptor. †honoratum† si forte reponis Achillem,
> impiger, iracundus, inexorabilis, acer,
> iura neget sibi nata, nihil non arroget armis.
> sit Medea ferox invictaque, flebilis Ino,
> perfidus Ixion, Io vaga, tristis Orestes.
> si quid inexpertum scaenae committis et audes
> personam formare novam, servetur ad imum
> qualis ab incepto processerit, et sibi constet.

Either follow tradition, writer, or invent something consistent. If you happen to be representing honoured [?] Achilles, let him—unwearying, wrathful, inexorable, keen—deny his native laws and claim nothing save by arms. Let Medea be fierce and undefeated, Ino lacrimose, Ixion treacherous, Io wandering, Orestes sad. If you place anything untried on stage and dare to create a new character, let him be maintained to the end as he came forward at the start, and be consistent.

---

[40] For Livy's interest in the emotions of crowds see Catin (1944: 153–66), Walsh (1961: 183–6).

[41] E.g. *Rhet. Her.* 2.5, Cicero, *Inv.* 2.32–7, Quintilian 7.2.28–34; and note Riggsby (2004: esp. 165–75). Riggsby is primarily demonstrating that rhetorical theory and practice assume characters to be fixed across time; I am focusing on characters' consistency within a relatively short time rather than development over a longer period. But both conclusions follow equally from the same evidence, since inferences from character in courts assume both its long-term fixity and its immediate consistency. It should, however, be noted that, as I have already indicated, Riggsby's arguments do not preclude there being particular authors or texts in which characters change and develop over time: for discussion of some convincing examples see e.g. Gill (1983), Woodman (1989), Swain (1989).

Horace's prescriptions here are broad-brush, but it is nevertheless striking that his primary criterion for successful character invention is internal consistency, just as his primary criterion for the treatment of traditional characters is conformity with the monolithic qualities linked to those characters in the tradition.[42] It is also apparent from a later passage (*Ars Poetica* 312–18) that consistency is regarded as important not merely on abstract aesthetic grounds, but because it increases plausibility: people are expected to behave in consistent ways, and so a writer should represent them as consistent. Even more pertinent to Livy is an interesting passage of Polybius (4.8):

Ἄρατος γὰρ ἦν τὰ μὲν ἄλλα τέλειος ἀνὴρ εἰς τὸν πραγματικὸν τρόπον· καὶ γὰρ εἰπεῖν καὶ διανοηθῆναι καὶ στέξαι τὸ κριθὲν δυνατός, καὶ μὴν ἐνεγκεῖν τὰς πολιτικὰς διαφορὰς πρᾴως καὶ φίλους ἐνδήσασθαι καὶ συμμάχους προσλαβεῖν οὐδενὸς δεύτερος, ἔτι δὲ πράξεις, ἀπάτας, ἐπιβουλὰς συστήσασθαι κατὰ τῶν πολεμίων, καὶ ταύτας ἐπὶ τέλος ἀγαγεῖν διὰ τῆς αὑτοῦ κακοπαθείας καὶ τόλμης, δεινότατος ... ὁ δ' αὐτὸς οὗτος, ὅτε τῶν ὑπαίθρων ἀντιποιήσασθαι βουληθείη, νωθρὸς μὲν ἐν ταῖς ἐπινοίαις, ἄτολμος δ' ἐν ταῖς ἐπιβολαῖς, ἐν ὄψει δ' οὐ μένων τὸ δεινόν ... οὕτως αἱ τῶν ἀνθρώπων φύσεις οὐ μόνον τοῖς σώμασιν ἔχουσί τι πολυειδές, ἔτι δὲ μᾶλλον ταῖς ψυχαῖς, ὥστε τὸν αὐτὸν ἄνδρα μὴ μόνον ἐν τοῖς διαφέρουσι τῶν ἐνεργημάτων πρὸς ἃ μὲν εὐφυῶς ἔχειν, πρὸς ἃ δ' ἐναντίως, ἀλλὰ καὶ περί τινα τῶν ὁμοειδῶν πολλάκις τὸν αὐτὸν καὶ συνετώτατον εἶναι καὶ βραδύτατον, ὁμοίως δὲ καὶ τολμηρότατον καὶ δειλότατον. οὐ παράδοξα ταῦτά γε, συνήθη δὲ καὶ γνώριμα τοῖς βουλομένοις συνεφιστάνειν. τινὲς μὲν γὰρ ἐν ταῖς κυνηγίαις εἰσὶ τολμηροὶ πρὸς τὰς τῶν θηρίων συγκαταστάσεις, οἱ δ' αὐτοὶ πρὸς ὅπλα καὶ πολεμίους ἀγεννεῖς, καὶ τῆς γε πολεμικῆς χρείας τῆς κατ' ἄνδρα μὲν καὶ κατ' ἰδίαν εὐχερεῖς καὶ πρακτικοί, κοινῇ δὲ καὶ μετὰ πολεμικῆς ἐπ' ἴσον συντάξεως ἄπρακτοι ... ταῦτα μὲν εἰρήσθω μοι χάριν τοῦ μὴ διαπιστεῖν τοὺς ἀναγινώσκοντας τοῖς λεγομένοις, ἐάν που περὶ τῶν αὐτῶν ἀνδρῶν ἐναντίας ἀποφάσεις ποιώμεθα περὶ τὰ παραπλήσια τῶν ἐπιτηδευμάτων.

Aratus was in general a perfect man in practical affairs. He was able to speak and plan and keep his judgements secret, and was second to none in handling political differences amiably and securing friends and creating allies, and also was exceptionally skilled at contriving action, deceptions, and plots against the enemy, and at accomplishing them through his personal efforts and courage ... But this same man, when he wanted to engage in actions in open country, was sluggish in planning, cowardly in attacks, and unable to await danger publicly ... So people's natures have something complicated not only in their bodies, but also in their souls, so that it is not only differing activities to which the same man is partially well-suited, partially unsuited,

---

[42] Cf. Aristotle, *Po.* 1454a26–8: at 1454a31–2 he gives the example of Iphigenia in *Iphigenia at Aulis* as a character who fails through inconsistency. Aristotle also makes a revealing comment with broader implications: that while certain people may in fact act inconsistently, they are 'consistently inconsistent' (1454a27–8 ὁμαλῶς ἀνώμαλον), presumably meaning that inconsistency is a defined and predictable part of their personality. On this idea see Pelling (1990a: 237, updated in Pelling 2002: 315–16).

but even in some things of the same type the same man is often both exceptionally intelligent and dull, and likewise both exceptionally bold and cowardly. These things are not paradoxes, but normal and familiar to those who are willing to pay attention. Some people are daring at fighting animals in hunting, but the same people are ignoble against weapons and the enemy, and in military service some are cool and efficient in fighting alone in single combat, but inefficient in fighting jointly and in a uniform battle line . . . I have said this so that readers will not distrust what I say if I make opposite statements about the same men in related activities.

The most striking initial point about this passage is its explicit recognition of the possibility—indeed, the likelihood—of inconsistency in the behaviour of historical characters. To that extent it might appear to provide a model that Livy might be following when he introduces comparable inconsistencies in his own work. However, there are aspects of the passage that would point in a different direction. First, the very fact that Polybius feels it necessary to explain himself in this very elaborate way suggests that the automatic response of much of his readership, in the absence of such an explanation, would be to see such inconsistencies as implausible rather than arising from the complexities of the character. Second, it is noticeable that Polybius' way of accounting for the inconsistencies is simply to show that they are consistent when viewed over a narrower range of activity: one may be courageous in hunting (even if not in war), or courageous in single combat (even if not in a massed action).[43] This once again suggests that readers of Livy, in the absence of any specific acknowledgement of inconsistency such as we find in Polybius, or any specific account such as Polybius' that would encourage them to break them down into more coherent components, would find the lack of integration in his portrayals unsatisfying.

So while this evidence suggests that Roman readers would not find Livy's characters in all respects as unsatisfying as we do, it does not leave them looking unproblematic even in those terms. If we are to understand what Livy is doing with his characters, a different approach is needed.

One suggestion might be that the exteriority of characters in Livy—extreme even by the standards of ancient historiography—is connected with his strong ethical and didactic focus. It is true that presenting characters in an 'interior' and more psychological fashion is not incompatible with inculcating ethical

---

[43] This point is overlooked in the interesting comparison of Polybius' and Plutarch's account of Aratus by Pelling (1988: 264–7, updated in Pelling 2002: 288–9). Pelling sees Plutarch as turning Polybius' Aratus into an integrated character whose apparent inconsistencies are the result of a regular cluster of traits. He shows well that Plutarch does more to smooth over the inconsistencies into something more coherent, but underplays the extent to which Polybius' account is itself organized around categorizing the irregularities into predictable patterns; cf. Eckstein (1995: 239–40).

lessons.[44] Indeed, one major problem that a number of scholars have found with Gill's 'character–personality' dichotomy is that it associates moral evaluation exclusively with a 'character' perspective, and overlooks the extent to which 'personality'-like features may reinforce and indeed instil moral interpretations of the person in question.[45] That after all is the assumption underlying emotional appeals in oratory, that by engaging the audience emotionally with one's client or against one's opponent one encourages endorsement of the former's case and rejection of the latter's.[46] But while all this is true, it is also plausible to suggest that Livy's didactic focus might encourage him to concentrate more on those features of characters that invite evaluative responses in very direct ways.[47]

Suggesting that Livy's particular interest in moral issues lies behind his relatively narrow modes of character presentation may also help us to understand some of the reasons for his relative lack of interest in maintaining characters' consistency. In his most recent study of ancient views of character Gill has shown that certain philosophical schools of the Roman period—in particular the Stoics and Epicureans—share a notion of character which associates consistency with philosophical morality. The sage—the person who understands philosophical truth and has built his life around it—will be psychologically consistent. Everyone who is not a sage—in other words, virtually everyone in the world—will show their lack of moral virtue in their inconsistencies of character.[48] This idea is found even outside strictly

---

[44] Especially interesting from an historiographical perspective is the case of Theopompus (see Marincola 2003: 307–10), who was notorious for his attempts to cast aspersions on his characters, but whom Dionysius, *Pomp.* 6 defends by arguing that his reputation derives from his unique ability to present in depth their 'motives' (αἰτίας) and emotions (πάθη), which exposes them to public scrutiny.

[45] This is addressed from a variety of perspectives by (e.g.) Levene (1997), Pelling (2002: 310–11, 321–2); cf. also Marincola (2003). Gill's more recent work has likewise refined his earlier statements of the dichotomy in a way that allows a direct association between 'personality'-like features and moral evaluation. He now makes a distinction between what he calls 'objective-participant' and 'subjective-individualist' notions of the person, and argues that the latter itself invites certain sorts of ethical reflections. See Gill (1996: esp. 94–174).

[46] Quintilian 6.2.5 is especially pertinent here: *probationes enim efficiant sane ut causam nostram meliorem esse iudices putent, adfectus praestant ut etiam velint; sed id quod volunt credunt quoque* ('Proofs may doubtless make the judges think our case superior, but emotions make them also want it to be so; but that which they want they also believe').

[47] In Levene (2006a) I argue that Livy self-consciously presents himself as having a narrowly moralistic focus, even though that in many respects underplays and misrepresents other aspects of his own work.

[48] Gill (2006); as he observes, the idea is already partially prefigured in Aristotle: see e.g. *EN* 1159b7–9 οἱ δὲ μοχθηροὶ τὸ μὲν βέβαιον οὐκ ἔχουσιν· οὐδὲ γὰρ αὐτοῖς διαμένουσιν ὅμοιοι ὄντες ('the bad do not have firmness: for they do not even remain like themselves'), and note Gill (1996: 358–60).

philosophical works: so Plutarch's (unlike Polybius') explanation of Aratus' inconsistency is that in gifted people a lack of philosophy produces virtue without knowledge (*Aratus* 10.4).

It would be a considerable stretch to claim that Livy is following a comparably systematic mode of reasoning: that in introducing inconsistent characters he is working from a philosophical standpoint of which he never gives a single hint (let alone an explicit statement such as Plutarch's) and is seeking to show the philosophical incompleteness of such characters.[49] What is more important for our purposes is that Livy is writing within a cultural environment in which an inconsistent character is not self-evidently absurd or a sign of inattention on the part of the writer, and where such a character might hint at a loose if not precise association with a lack of proper ethics, especially given the way in which Livy repeatedly invites and insists on our evaluating his characters in moral terms. While the evidence from rhetorical and other texts shows that inconsistent characterization would be seen as disconcerting and counterintuitive by many readers, that itself has a destabilizing effect which can serve particular narrative ends. For all the apparent familiarity of the character types that Livy introduces, he is placing his readers in a world where people—and events—do not necessarily follow predictable patterns, and where our moral judgements on those people need to be comparably complex and provisional.

Moreover, these philosophical arguments intersect with the rhetorical texts to provide, if not a precise justification for inconsistency, at least a further framework within which the particular brand of inconsistency that we find in Livy can be understood. As I indicated above, the system of character types that we find in writers like Quintilian is so complex that it cannot merely be a way of placing each individual into a single pigeonhole. With so many axes of categorization any one person can fit multiple frameworks, depending on family relationships, social background, offices held, and indeed natural dispositions. Fathers and sons exhibit different characteristics, Quintilian implies; yet many adult men have been both fathers and sons, and in fact a good number are both simultaneously. Hence people will typically act in different ways depending which framework is most relevant to or dominant in their current situation. These ideas are articulated and systematized in philosophical writers. In particular, Stoic thinkers regularly suggest that ethical duties vary according to the individual's position in the

---

[49] Gill (2006: 408–61) argues that not only Plutarch, but the unstable characters of Senecan tragedy and the *Aeneid* can be interpreted in this way; but all three of those authors engage much more consistently with overtly philosophical issues than Livy does.

world;[50] this idea was systematized by Panaetius, from whom at least some of the later sources may be deriving their precepts. Cicero, *Off.* 1.107–16 sets out a 'four *personae*' theory (presumably derived from Panaetius), according to which each of us shares in four different characters: the character we all possess as rational human beings, the character which derives from our personal dispositions, the character which depends on aspects of our external circumstances (our family, our position in life, and so on), and the character arising from the life which we choose to lead.[51] Admittedly Cicero only briefly considers the possibility that these *personae* might in principle conflict (*Off.* 1.120), no doubt because his interest is in advising how one should ideally live in harmony with oneself, and the situation of people who lack such harmony is of secondary interest to him.[52] But the basic idea is implicit that the different aspects of our characters could potentially pull us in different directions.

Here too, of course, there should be no suggestion that Livy is systematically following a Panaetian model; but what appear oddities or discontinuities in his characters make sense within that general intellectual environment which in their different ways the Stoics and the rhetoricians both reflect. So if Livy shows the same person acting in ways that appear incompatible with earlier presentations of his character, one ready explanation may sometimes be that we are seeing him acting according to a different social perspective. When Minucius violently seeks battle against Hannibal, he is acting as one would expect a rash man to act under the provocation of Hannibal's destruction of Italy; when Minucius recants and submits to Fabius, he is acting as one would expect of a Roman magistrate. This multiplicity of perspectives does not of itself smooth over the sense of inconsistency, since Livy does not provide us with a sufficiently integrated explanation of the character in the first place such that these different aspects arise clearly from seeing one man in different lights. But it suggests ways in which we might frame our judgements of them. And at the same time the very fact of the inconsistency focuses the reader sharply on key issues. It is easy to see that Livius Salinator makes the right choice in co-operating with his colleague in his consulship: it is the right choice precisely because he is consul, and that is the way good consuls need to act. How that relates to his earlier sense of resentment is less significant than the fact that he was resentful in the first place, and so his

---

[50] The idea is common in Epictetus: see e.g. 1.2.5–11, 2.10.7–13, 3.23.4–5, 4.12.16–17; also Seneca, *Ep.* 94.1–4 (= Cleanthes, *SVF* I 582); *Ben.* 2.18.1–3. Cf. Brunt (1975: 12–16, 33–5), Long (1983).

[51] On this theory see De Lacy (1977), Gill (1988).

[52] Note Gill (1988: 180–6, 197–9) on the inherent tensions and inconsistencies in the theory that Cicero fails to explore.

co-operation is something that he needed to choose rather than arising as a matter of course.

But this in turn suggests that if we are to understand the role that Livy is creating for his characters, our analysis of them needs to proceed along quite different lines from the ones that we automatically take when reading modern texts. Rather than abstracting each individual, mentally assembling all the passages concerned with that person and trying to derive from them a single personality, we need to see each character according to the roles that he plays in a dynamic system of interactions with other characters, and more broadly against the progress of the war as a whole.[53] This is not to say that the characters are mere ciphers, whose actions may lurch according to the needs of Livy's dramatic scheme.[54] Characters matter for Livy precisely because the issues that he is raising are seen in terms of the actions of people who behave in certain ways and make certain choices at particular times. But it does not greatly matter whether those characters are starkly individuated from one another (though in practice some may be), nor whether we can appreciate the deeper roots of their personality which provide reasons for their actions (though we may occasionally be able to do so). Even stereotyped characters can play a vital part in the overall scheme, because each character may continue to have to address the same issues: indeed, the very stereotyping enables the same issues to be raised anew in a war that is constantly developing. The most important thing about the sequence of rash commanders in Books 21 and 22 is that they are more or less identical: this matters far more than the elements that might differentiate them. It is that similarity which leads to the escalating sequence of defeats despite the efforts of the (hardly any less stereotyped) commanders Publius Scipio, Fabius, and Aemilius to craft a strategy to counteract them. This is what brings Rome to the point of destruction by the end of Book 22: the question is how it can pull back from there. But the answer may well not be a simple one. Will a wholehearted adoption of a Fabian strategy now be sufficient, or, as circumstances subtly

---

[53] For a similar approach with regard to Greek tragedy, see Easterling (1990, esp. 88–9). Compare also the arguments of Walcutt (1966), who argues that the primary difference between characterization in pre-modern literature and that which developed in the nineteenth century is that characters were originally created through the events of the plot to which they responded. Only later did that come to appear inadequate, as writers sought to define characters independently of the circumstances of their stories. Walcutt provocatively claims that it is more often 'modern' novels that ultimately give a diminished and inadequate picture of human personality, which is better explored through depicting responses to action than via direct analysis independent of that action.

[54] That approach has sometimes been taken to explain supposed inconsistencies of characters in Greek tragedy: see e.g. Dawe (1963). However, it has regularly been criticized: see e.g. Easterling (1973).

change, may the approach represented by his rash and violent opponents in fact prove to have something to offer? And what might be the costs of either approach, or any combination of them? These are the sorts of questions that I shall be addressing in the remainder of this chapter.

To begin with, let us return to Livius Salinator and Claudius Nero, and note the terms in which they are introduced as candidates for the consulship (27.33.9–34.3):

ceterum cum duo consulares exercitus tam prope hostem sine ducibus essent, omnibus aliis omissis una praecipua cura patres populumque incessit consules primo quoque tempore creandi, et ut eos crearent potissimum quorum virtus satis tuta a fraude Punica esset; cum toto eo bello damnosa praepropera ac fervida ingenia imperatorum fuissent, tum eo ipso anno consules nimia cupiditate conserendi cum hoste manum in necopinatam fraudem lapsos esse.... cum circumspicerent patres quosnam consules facerent, longe ante alios eminebat C. Claudius Nero. ei collega quaerebatur; et virum quidem eum egregium ducebant, sed promptiorem acrioremque quam tempora belli postularent aut hostis Hannibal; temperandum acre ingenium eius moderato et prudenti viro adiuncto collega censebant. M. Livius erat, multis ante annis ex consulatu populi iudicio damnatus.

But since two consular armies so close to the enemy were without generals, everything else was set aside and the single primary concern that occupied the senators and people was to elect consuls as soon as possible, and in particular to elect men whose courage was adequately safeguarded against Carthaginian deceit; they felt that through that whole war the hasty and passionate characters of generals had been disastrous, and moreover in that very year the consuls had fallen into unexpected deceit through their excessive eagerness to come into combat with the enemy... When the senators searched for the men to make consuls, C. Claudius Nero was by far the outstanding candidate. They needed a colleague for him; they admittedly regarded him as an exceptional man, but also as keener and fiercer than was demanded at this moment of war and with Hannibal as the enemy; they thought that his fierce character should be tempered by having a moderate and sensible man as his colleague. That was M. Livius, condemned many years previously after his consulship by a popular vote.

This passage raises certain familiar-sounding themes. The danger of excessively aggressive generals reminds us of the type of commander who has been a perennial problem since the introduction of Sempronius Longus in Book 21: the commander who in his eagerness for battle falls for Hannibal's stratagems. Likewise the solution offered, to balance the aggressive commander with a cautious one, seems to be replicating the situation of 216 BC, where the more aggressive Varro is chosen first, and the more cautious Aemilius comes in as a counter-balance (22.35.2–4). In both cases, moreover, the more cautious man is reluctant to take office at all and has to be persuaded to do so (22.35.3, 27.34.14–15). That link is perhaps reinforced by the fact that

Aemilius and Livius had been consuls together in 219 and Aemilius had come close to sharing Livius' disgrace, as Livy observed at 22.35.3; however, in the absence of any information about how (or indeed whether) these events were treated in Book 20 or how much emphasis was placed on them,[55] it is unclear how far he would expect the earlier association of Aemilius and Livius still to be in the reader's mind in Book 27.

However, there is also a significant difference between these parallel situations. In Book 22 the primary reason for Aemilius' election was that he was *infestum plebei* (22.35.3: 'hostile to the people'), and his preference for a more cautious strategy only emerges later, from his speech before he leaves (22.38.8–13). Livius is chosen for his caution, and his hostility to the people is an irrelevancy—indeed, a hindrance. In other words, the division between Aemilius and Varro was primarily a political one—one indeed recalling the numerous class conflicts of the First Decade. Likewise the two previous 'rash commanders' in that sequence, Flaminius and Minucius, were both associated with popular and anti-senatorial politics (albeit in a less extreme fashion), and their aggressiveness is repeatedly linked to the popular support that such a strategy commanded (e.g. 22.3.14, 22.14.15, 22.23.3, 22.25–26, 22.34).[56] But with Livius not only is there no indication that his political division from Claudius Nero has any class component, but the Senate and people are now united in wanting cautious rather than rash commanders (27.33.9, cf. 27.34.11): the link between strategic and political stance no longer obtains. Livius' hostility to the people is so extreme as to look radically pathological— but that is as much a reflection of the anachronism of his stance as of his particular personality. For everyone else the needs of the war override class politics.

Livy's portrait of Livius and Claudius is thus governed by their relationship to the stereotypes he has established earlier: they are recognizably the same types, yet under these new circumstances look markedly different. But that is only the start of his manipulation of the theme. When Fabius Maximus seeks to reconcile the two consuls, Livius initially refuses, denying that hostility

---

[55] *Per.* 20 does not mention the prosecution and disgrace of Livius at all, though this is only weak evidence that Livy might have ignored it or played it down then, since the *Periochae* frequently fail to reproduce the emphases of his text. If the M. Livius and L. Aemilius who went on the embassy to Carthage at 21.18.1 are (or are assumed by Livy) to be the consuls of 219 (so e.g. *MRR* 241 n.8; Rich 1976: 31), that would imply that Livy had not described their fall from grace in Book 20. But Livy does not make the identification directly, and there were other possible Liviuses and Aemiliuses who might have been (or have been thought to be) on the embassy. See Händl-Sagawe (1995: 109).

[56] Catin (1944: 42) notes that the pairing of Claudius Nero and Livius is unusual in having the apparent 'rash commander' as a patrician and the 'cautious' one as a plebeian rather than *vice versa*.

between the consuls would be damaging at all: his claim is that *acrius et intentius omnia gesturos timentes ne crescendi ex se inimico collegae potestas fieret* (27.35.8: 'they would do everything more fiercely and more keenly out of fear that his hostile colleague would gain the power to advance because of him'). However plausible that argument might conceivably appear in the abstract, it is obviously radically counterintuitive by Livy's usual assumptions, where hostility between consuls is a source of weakness for the state rather than strength—once again, Varro and Aemilius provide a clear parallel.[57] No less surprising is that Livius implies that acting *acrius* is something that is desired, whereas the object of choosing him in the first place was that he was expected to temper the *acre ingenium* of Claudius—the word was used twice in quick succession (27.34.2–3). It now appears that the differences between him and Claudius are going to have precisely the opposite of the expected effect: rather than the 'cautious commander' keeping the 'rash commander' in check, they are going to exacerbate each other's ferocity.

But having shown that under the new situation in the war this old dual stereotype can no longer operate in the familiar way, Livy suddenly reverses our expectations yet again and draws us in an entirely different direction. First, Livius is persuaded almost immediately to set aside his quarrel with Claudius (27.35.9). Then, after a long and dramatic series of prodigies and expiations, which Livy narrates in an exceptionally heightened fashion to match the exceptional crisis (27.37),[58] the consuls prepare for the campaign (27.38.1–2):

dis rite placatis dilectum consules habebant acrius intentiusque quam prioribus annis quisquam meminerat habitum. nam et belli terror duplicatus novi hostis in Italiam adventu, et minus iuventutis erat unde scriberent milites.

With the gods duly appeased the consuls held a levy more fiercely and keenly than anyone remembered having been held in previous years. For both the terror of the war was doubled with the arrival in Italy of a new enemy and there were fewer young men to enrol as soldiers.

---

[57] Note in particular the paradoxical phrase at 22.35.4: *par magis in adversando quam collega datur consuli* ('the consul was being given more a rival in oppostion than a colleague'); also Fabius' words to Aemilius at 22.39.4–5: *erras... si tibi minus certaminis cum C. Terentio quam cum Hannibale futurum censes; nescio an infestior hic adversarius quam ille hostis maneat te, et cum illo in acie tantum, cum hoc omnibus locis ac temporibus sis certaturus* ('You are mistaken... if you think that you will be fighting less with C. Terentius than with Hannibal; I doubt that you are awaited with greater hostility by the latter opponent than by the former foe, and with Hannibal you are going to be in conflict only in the battle-line, with Varro at every place and time'). The suggestion that it is Varro who is the *hostis*, while Hannibal is merely the *adversarius*, is especially striking.

[58] Levene (1993: 65–6).

Almost exactly the same phrase[59]—*acrius intentiusque*—is used here to describe the levy as Livius had used shortly before to describe the advantages of maintaining his hostility to Claudius. It then appeared something paradoxical and undesirable; yet now it appears that it is a necessary approach to meet the new threat. So Livius had apparently been right about what was needed, even if not about the way in which it is to be achieved, since he has—apparently—given up the hostility towards his colleague that he earlier claimed would generate this ferocity. So the two consuls are indeed no longer antithetical figures, but united in ferocity, precisely the opposite of what was hoped at their election—yet that looks to be a good thing rather than bad.

This sense that the consuls are united in a desirably active rather than a cautious policy is reinforced by the sequel—which however contains a further twist (27.38.6–10):

cum omnes censerent primo quoque tempore consulibus eundum ad bellum—nam et Hasdrubali occurrendum esse descendenti ab Alpibus, ne Gallos Cisalpinos neve Etruriam erectam in spem rerum novarum sollicitaret, et Hannibalem suo proprio occupandum bello, ne emergere ex Bruttiis atque obviam ire fratri posset—Livius cunctabatur, parum fidens suarum provinciarum exercitibus: collegam ex duobus consularibus egregiis exercitibus et tertio cui Q. Claudius Tarenti praeesset electionem habere. intuleratque mentionem de volonibus revocandis ad signa. senatus liberam potestatem consulibus fecit et supplendi unde vellent et eligendi de omnibus exercitibus quos vellent permutandique et ex provinciis quos e re publica censerent esse traducendi. ea omnia cum summa concordia consulum acta.

When everyone thought that the consuls must go to war at the earliest possible moment—for they had both to confront Hasdrubal when he descended from the Alps to stop him causing disturbance in Cisalpine Gaul or Etruria, which was tense in the hope of sedition, and to involve Hannibal in a war of his own, so that he could not escape from the Bruttii and go to meet his brother—Livius delayed, mistrustful of the armies in his provinces: his colleague, he said, had a choice of two splendid consular armies and a third which Q. Claudius commanded at Tarentum. He also brought up the idea of recalling the slave-volunteers into the army. The senate gave the consuls absolute freedom to supplement their troops from any source they desired and to select and exchange out of all the armies they wanted and to transfer from the provinces any troops they thought were in the interests of the state. All this was done with the utmost harmony between the consuls.

---

[59] Moreover a relatively unusual one: these two passages are the only examples in Livy's surviving text. Wölfflin, followed by Gries (1951), treats this simply as a stylistic quirk. It is true that comparable repetitions can be found elsewhere with little apparent significance, but the fact that the language here is central to the themes of the entire episode makes it more pointed.

The beginning of the passage reaffirms the need for speed and direct confrontation of the enemy—but the plan is suddenly thrown awry when we are told that *Livius cunctabatur*. The verb is a pointed one in the context of a commander selected for his caution, because it is especially associated with Fabius, the most significant exemplar of the type;[60] the division between the commander and his troops is also a familiar theme in that context. But in this case the mistrust is all on Livius' side, and the delay proves to be not a healthy strategy but another opportunity for him to carp at the terms of his command. The senate accommodate him, as indeed does Claudius, and everything is harmonious—but by that point the moment has been lost. The result is that the consuls fail to make the immediate start they needed to, they have to accelerate their departure from Rome when they learn of Hasdrubal's imminent arrival (27.39.3), and even then they are too late. They are rescued from the consequences of their delay by errors of both Hannibal, who fails to anticipate the speed of Hasdrubal's crossing (27.39.4–6), and of Hasdrubal himself, who wastes time in a fruitless siege of Placentia (27.39.10–12). But this detracts little from the sense that Livius has hindered the campaign by his partial exhibition of the very stereotypical qualities for which he was elected, but which he seemed to have correctly abandoned.

If Livius is a 'cautious commander', then, he is an unexpected and off-key version of one: properly if surprisingly abandoning caution, but then exhibiting it in a most damaging fashion. And the scene of his departure for his campaign challenges the reader's expectations still further (27.40.8–9):

memoriae proditum est plenum adhuc irae in cives M. Livium ad bellum proficis-
centem monenti Q. Fabio ne priusquam genus hostium cognosset temere manum
consereret, respondisse ubi primum hostium agmen conspexisset pugnaturum. cum
quaereretur quae causa festinandi esset, 'aut ex hoste egregiam gloriam' inquit 'aut ex
civibus victis gaudium meritum certe, etsi non honestum, capiam'.

It is recorded that as M. Livius set off for war, still full of anger against his fellow-
citizens, Q. Fabius warned him not to join battle rashly before getting to know the
nature of the enemy. He replied that he would fight the moment he saw the enemy
column. When asked the reason for his hurry, he said 'Either I will get outstanding
glory from the enemy, or out of the defeated citizens I will get joy that is at least
deserved, even if not honorable'.

---

[60] The association of Fabius with *cunctatio* was of course eventually enshrined in the cognomen 'Cunctator', but that may well postdate Livy (see Stanton 1971). But the iconic line of Ennius, *Annals* 363 Sk. (which may indeed have generated the *cognomen*) in any case guaranteed his association with that particular attribute even before it was attached to him as a name (cf. above, 86–7), and Livy accordingly repeatedly uses *cunctari* and other cognate words of him, especially in Book 22 (22.12.12, 22.14.5, 22.14.10, 22.15.1, 22.23.1, 22.24.10, 22.27.4; cf. 28.40.6, 30.26.9).

The scene of the 'cautious commander' having his caution reinforced by Fabius' advice once again replays Book 22, with Fabius' long speech to Aemilius immediately before his departure (22.39). Here, however, the 'cautious commander'—at least if we are to believe the tradition reported here—fails once again to live up to his designated role. A self-confident emphasis on personal glory rather than the communal good has been the hallmark of the stereotypical 'rash commanders' in the decade:[61] Livius provides an unusual twist on it, recognizing that success may not in fact follow, but no less happy with the consequences of defeat than of victory. But the strategy he is adopting is not merely aggressive, but aggressive to a point that looks appallingly irresponsible, even given that a more active policy has been presented as desirable under the current circumstances. He fails to mention the inherent danger in his plan, familiar from so many Roman defeats earlier in the war: namely that an immediate attack may make victory less likely and defeat more so. If he has been a misguided version of a 'cautious commander', his disagreements with the people, which with Fabius and Aemilius went hand in hand with their more passive strategy, here lead him in exactly the opposite direction, to become an even more strikingly misguided version of a 'rash commander' too.

So what happens when Livius actually comes within sight of the enemy? Livy never tells us: the narrative remains with Claudius Nero and Hannibal until the point when Claudius has marched north and joined his army to Livius' (27.45.12). The implication of 27.46.4, where we learn that Livius and Hasdrubal had camped only a short distance apart, is that Livius cannot have literally attacked him immediately on sighting him, but it is left undetermined whether that is because he had no reasonable opportunity to do so, or because his statement to Fabius was hyperbolic, or indeed because Livy is doubtful about the reliability of the tradition he was reporting. Livy's account of Livius leaves our judgement of him in the balance: whether his unexpected adoption of an active military strategy is as dangerous as it had appeared. But in the meantime our attention has now shifted to his colleague, whose aggression Livius was chosen in order to restrain, but whose general attitudes he appears to have taken over.

But here too we find that events change our perspective of the stereotype. Claudius Nero was introduced in the familiar guise of the 'rash commander'; yet his actual approach in practice, unlike Livius', has not been presented as pathologically reckless. On the contrary, whereas previous 'rash consuls' had fallen into Hannibal's traps, he turns the tables and inflicts a defeat on

---

[61] E.g. 21.53.6, 22.27.1–3; cf. 27.2.2, 27.25.11–14 (on which see below, 203–6).

Hannibal by setting a similar trap for him (27.41.6–42.8).[62] So when he now, after discovering the plan to unite the Carthaginian armies, proposes *audendum ac novandum aliquid improvisum, inopinatum* (27.43.7: 'something unforeseen, unexpected must be dared and invented'), it appears a hazardous but perhaps necessary move, rather than the patent folly visible in comparable moves made by his predecessors. This is the occasion of his march the length of Italy to join Livius. The likelihood of its being successful is in the balance, as Livy memorably dramatizes through the apprehensions of the Roman citizen body on the one hand (27.44), followed by the optimistic speech of Claudius to his troops on the other (27.45.2–6).[63] Claudius fails to mention the obvious objection which had formed the main focus of the citizens' fears— the risk of leaving Hannibal unguarded without a full army to oppose him[64]—but against that the people have exaggerated the weakness of the Roman position, as Livy comments in his own voice.[65] This weights the balance if anything in Claudius' favour: he is taking a gamble, but a well-calculated one.[66]

On the other hand, the Romans' arguments remind us of a crucial fact: that this is not Claudius' first appearance in the war. While he has never before been the object of sustained attention, he was the protagonist of two earlier episodes (24.17.3–7 and 26.17), neither showing him to advantage, and in the latter of which he was beguiled by Hasdrubal in Spain: this is presented as an argument against his likely success now (27.44.9). Indeed, in as much as we have had any impression of Claudius' character prior to his candidature for the consulship this year, it is of a naïve incompetent: not particularly aggressive (despite his characterization by the senators at

---

[62] Note in particular 27.41.6 *ingenio hostis usus* ('using his enemy's ingenuity'); see also my discussion at 228–36 below.

[63] Note especially 27.45.2–3 *negat ullius consilium imperatoris in speciem audacius, re ipsa tutius fuisse quam suum. ad certam eos se victoriam ducere* ('He said that no other commander's plan was apparently more audacious, but in reality safer than his. He was leading them to certain victory').

[64] As they rightly observe (27.44.3), success crucially depends on Hannibal's failing to spot the deception of leaving the camp undermanned while the body of the army moves elsewhere. This key aspect of the plan had not been apparent from its initial presentation at 27.43.7–12, though Claudius does acknowledge it later (27.46.9). It appears especially risky in light of the fact that Hannibal had directly beforehand attempted an identical stratagem against Claudius (27.42.9–12), though this also shows again (cf. n. 62 above) Claudius departing from his stereotype by adopting Hannibalic techniques when needed.

[65] 27.44.10 *omnia maiora etiam vero praesidia hostium, minora sua, metu interprete semper in deteriora inclinato, ducebant* ('They exaggerated all the strength of the enemy and diminished their own: fear is an interpreter that always tends to pessimism').

[66] Livy's description of Claudius' careful logistical preparations prior to his march also supports that impression: see 27.43.10–11.

27.34.2),[67] but also far from the dynamic, canny, and confident commander here. Livy seems to be directly drawing our attention to an inconsistency of character which we might otherwise overlook—he will, of course, soon demonstrate that Claudius' earlier failures against Hasdrubal are no precedent for the likely outcome now, but does so through identifying him with a stereotype for which nothing in his earlier appearances had prepared us, but then adapting it in ways apparently compatible with neither the core stereotype nor the qualities that Claudius had exhibited earlier.

Once the commanders are together, Claudius is still the focus of attention, and his determination for immediate action is once again apparent. As in earlier battles, there is a debate over the relative merits of cautious and aggressive strategies (27.46.7–11). But, perhaps revealingly, the arguments for caution are not placed in the mouth of Livius, but are given to anonymous *multi* (27.46.7)—after all, the arguments are in part the same as Fabius made at 27.40.8 and that Livius had there rejected, that one should get to know one's enemy before engaging him in battle.[68] But whereas Livius' rejection appears to have been based primarily on spite, Claudius has clear and sensible arguments to show that aggression is the rational policy in their exceptional situation, for immediate battle gives him his only chance to secure victory and return to face Hannibal before he can act against them. But his arguments are presented with a paradoxical edge which once again plays with the 'rash' and 'cautious' stereotypes: *Nero non suadere modo sed summa ope orare institit ne consilium suum quod tutum celeritas fecisset temerarium morando facerent* (27.46.8: 'Nero insistently not merely advised but begged with all his might that they should not make his plan, which his speed had made safe, into a rash one by delaying'). Whereas a desire to fight immediately had often been one of the hallmarks of excessive rashness, under the situation here Claudius can plausibly present his own aggression as safe, and the ostensibly cautious approach as the rash one.

That is the decisive factor: from now on the right course is clear, and when the actual battle comes, while Claudius may be the first to engage the enemy (27.48.1), that is only because he is commanding the cavalry, and Livius with the infantry is not only close behind but ready for an immediate fight (27.48.3). The key moment in the battle comes when Claudius leads round a detachment to attack the Carthaginians from behind. In this manoeuvre Livy (unlike Polybius in the parallel passage at 11.1.7) stresses the speed with

---

[67] Rosenstein (1993: 327) notes the contradiction between the Senate's stated rationale for choosing Claudius and his actual career up to that point: he regards the choice as 'decidedly curious'. See also W-M *ad* 27.34.2.

[68] Cf. de Ravinel (1962: 8).

which Claudius moved (27.48.14): the same quality, indeed, as had brought him to the battle in the first place.[69] But here too Livy seems to remind his readers—or at least his most attentive readers—of Claudius' less distinguished earlier career: for on his first appearance in the war, as Marcellus' lieutenant at 24.17.3–7, he had been ordered to carry out a comparable move to the enemy's rear, but failed to accomplish it in time. Marcellus had berated him for the failure and accused him of preventing him from repaying the enemy for Cannae (24.17.7 *quo minus accepta ad Cannas redderetur hosti clades*). Here the Metaurus is directly said in similar language to repay the Carthaginians for Cannae (27.49.5 *redditaque aequa Cannensi clades*): Claudius' uncanny speed here has finally made up for his initial error, if error it was.[70] That Claudius' new guise enabled him to achieve such a reversal is the most important consequence of comparing the episodes. What in the hapless lieutenant's personality allowed him to turn into so stunningly dynamic a commander is an irrelevancy.

This analysis has demonstrated the importance and distinctiveness of Livy's characterizations once one sets aside presuppositions about the need for psychological explanation and engagement and we cease to worry that we are not looking inside the character's head. The features of Livius which we found hardest to explain in psychological terms—the sudden and poorly motivated lurches of behaviour—make perfect sense once one views him in the light of existing stereotypes and of the dynamic application of those stereotypes to a changing situation. Livius' behaviour cannot be understood except in terms of his notionally antithetical relationship to Claudius and *vice versa*. Livius and Claudius as a pair only make sense in the light of comparably antithetical pairs of commanders earlier in the war. And the particular dynamics of their actions in the particular situation which they face as consuls means that our attitude to the stereotype itself has to change—people do not always behave in the ways that we would expect from their typology. At the start of the episode it appears that caution here, as before, is needed, and aggressive policies are potentially dangerous. It soon becomes apparent that aggressive policies have now more to offer and that Livius' caution can be a potentially dangerous hindrance. Nor is this simply a lesson about the occasional need for active strategy, because there is a further dimension to the presentation. Livius' anti-popular stance, which in earlier incarnations of

---

[69] Claudius' *celeritas* is also exhibited on the march back south: see 27.50.1 and 27.50.7.

[70] Livy leaves open the actual responsibility for the failure, and hence the fairness or otherwise of Marcellus' criticism: *id errore viarum an exiguitate temporis Nero exsequi non potuerit, incertum est* (24.17.4: 'it is unclear whether Nero's failure to accomplish it was through mistaking the route or the lack of time'). If the first it was his own fault, if the latter it was presumably Marcellus' for not dispatching him in time (cf. 24.17.3).

the stereotype was a natural corollary of a cautious strategy, here leads him in the opposite direction, to aggression of a highly dangerous form.

It is true that aspects of this feel uncomfortable and destabilizing even in Roman terms. Our analysis of the theoretical texts led to the conclusion that Roman readers shared with modern readers a preference for consistency in characterization. The way that Livy presents Livius' (and, to a lesser extent, Claudius') inconsistencies via challenges to the readers' expectations of stereotypical behaviour does nothing to detract from that conclusion. Such reversals of expectation have their effect precisely because under most circumstances it is assumed that people will conform to type, and that conforming to type means behaving according to the general bundle of characteristics associated with that type, which are widely assumed to belong together, and so give plausibility to the character. Livy's treatment of Livius and Claudius uncouples those characteristics. The abandonment of features that would normally contribute to plausibility is especially surprising in an historian, the essence of whose work involves after all the representation of people who genuinely did exist. It might appear that Livy is undermining his own claim to represent reality, if he represents characters in ways that appear far from real.

But there is a difference between saying that Livy is a challenging writer and saying that he is an incompetent writer. The inconsistencies he introduces are not random, but make sense as part of his strategy of characterization through adaptation of familiar stereotypes. In other words, we can see Livy's handling of character as analogous to his handling of chronology, which I discussed in Chapter 1: there he is prepared even more overtly to abandon something that makes literal sense in order to foster a wider narrative scheme. If it alienates the reader on the one hand, it also makes broad sense on another (I shall be exploring the implications of this further in Chapter 5). In this case there is also, as I suggested, an undercurrent of ethical challenge as well. Inconsistency has at least a loose association with a lack of proper ethical harmony, and it is no accident that the character who exhibits inconsistency most directly, Livius, is also the one whom the reader is most likely to judge negatively for much of the narrative, as he lurches between dangerous if incompatible extremes.

Constraints of space have meant that this analysis of the characters of Livius and Claudius has had to be relatively self-contained. Their complex relationship does not reach its conclusion with the success at the Metaurus, or even with their subsequent triumph; as I noted above, they come into conflict once again in their censorship (29.37), which is treated by Livy in a complex and ethically ambiguous fashion—Livius' attack on the Roman citizen body there is explicitly said to be a mark of proper archaic virtue, yet it is equally a perversion of proper political action.[71] Nor is the issue of the correct relationship between aggressive and passive strategy resolved in Book 27: its true climax comes, if anywhere, at the end of Book 28, with the great debate between Scipio and Fabius over the right way to defeat Hannibal. Nor should we assume that even in Books 21 and 22 the issue was as one-sided as might appear from the hostile portraits of Sempronius, Flaminius, Minucius, and Varro. While those four characters are demonstrably misguided in their immediate decisions, the approach that they represent is one that, as we have already noted with Livius and Claudius, will form a component of the Romans' ultimate success. This is prefigured even as Livy damns them as 'rash commanders': I discussed in Chapter 1 (above, 79–81) a place where Minucius' criticisms of Fabius are significantly juxtaposed with Cn. Scipio achieving success in Spain by using the sort of aggression that Minucius advocates but Fabius eschews. Similarly, when Minucius ends his speech by saying that 'the Roman state grew by daring and acting, not these sluggish plans, which cowards call caution' (22.14.14: *audendo atque agendo res Romana crevit, non his segnibus consiliis, quae timidi cauta vocant*), his words are significantly echoed in the opening words of Scipio when he is dramatically reintroduced after Cannae: 'The young Scipio, fated leader of this war, said that it was not a matter for planning. He said that amidst such great evil one must dare and act, not discuss' (22.53.6–7 *negat consilii rem esse Scipio iuvenis, fatalis dux huiusce belli. audendum atque agendum, non consultandum ait in tanto malo esse*).[72] Scipio's successful strategy, it is implied, will be a version of Minucius'. Conversely, we may compare 22.39.9, where Fabius assures Aemilius Paullus before Cannae that *una ratio belli gerendi adversus Hannibali est, qua ego gessi* ('The one way of waging war against Hannibal is the way that I employed'). In the context of Cannae Fabius is clearly correct,[73] but as the debate in Book 28 will show, his approach is misguidedly narrow in the context of the war as a whole.

Moreover, Livy has made creative use of these stereotypes in the intervening books. One character who is central to that development is Marcellus.[74]

---

[71] See especially 29.37.16 *pravum certamen notarum inter censores; castigatio inconstantiae populi censoria gravitate temporum illorum digna* ('The censors' competition over black marks was perverse; but the censorial rebuke of the people's inconsistency was worthy of the seriousness of those times').

[72] Johner (1996: 33).

[73] Livy indeed repeatedly accentuates the success of Fabius' strategy in Book 22 by suggesting that in consequence Hannibal was left short of supplies (22.15.1–2, 22.32.2–3, 22.39.14, 22.40.8, 22.43.3). There is nothing of this in Polybius, who also has nothing of Fabius' decision to destroy supplies in Hannibal's path (22.11.4): these appear to be inventions, whether or not by Livy himself. See Erdkamp (1992: 129–36).

[74] On Marcellus in Livy see Carawan (1984–5), Mensching (1996).

He is (along with Fabius and Scipio) one of the three Romans who receive the most extensive attention from Livy in the Third Decade. He dominates much of the narrative on the Roman side between Book 23 and his death in Book 27. Indeed, his death is partly what generates the anxieties that led to Livius being selected as consul in the first place (27.33.10), and suggests that he too is being cast in the 'rash commander' mould, as one of those whose *praepropera ac fervida ingenia* were damaging to Roman interests. But as we will see, with Marcellus, even more than with Livius and Claudius, the stereotype is not applied so simplistically.

To start with, we should note that Marcellus, much as the figures we have been examining so far, might be seen as part of an antithetical aggressive/cautious pairing: with Fabius Maximus. Treating these two as iconically antithetical in that way predates Livy: it seems to have been part of the traditional perception of the Second Punic War. Posidonius' famous comparison of them as the 'shield' and 'sword' of Rome was, at least on his own account, not his own invention: he reports it as what they were called at Rome,[75] though he extends it into a further explanation of how they together saved the city.[76] Cicero, *De Re Publica* 5.8 (Powell) makes a similar comparison (though unfortunately the context is unknown): *Marcellus ut acer et pugnax, Maximus ut consideratus et lentus* ('Marcellus as fierce and aggressive, Maximus as cautious and slow'). Plutarch in particular expands on this in his lives of both figures (*Marcellus* 9.2-4, *Fabius* 19.1–4; cf. also *Marcellus* 24.2). Livy likewise had several opportunities to present Fabius and Marcellus in parallel in this way, since they held a consulship in tandem in 214, and campaigned in close proximity not only in that year but also in 209, when Fabius was consul and Marcellus proconsul.

When Livy first sets Fabius and Marcellus side by side, however, he does it in rather different terms (24.9.7–8):

quinto anno secundi Punici belli Q. Fabius Maximus quartum M. Claudius Marcellus tertium consulatum ineuntes plus solito converterant in se civitatis animos; multis enim annis tale consulum par non fuerat. referebant senes sic Maximum Rullum cum

---

[75] Posidonius F 260 (Edelstein–Kidd) = Plutarch, *Fab.* 19.3 (there is a briefer version in F 259 = Plutarch, *Marc.* 9.4): τοῦτον μὲν ὁ Ποσειδώνιός φησι θυρεόν, τὸν δὲ Μάρκελλον ξίφος ὑπὸ τῶν ʽ Ῥωμαίων καλεῖσθαικιρναμένην δὲ τὴν Φαβίου βεβαιότητα καὶ ἀσφάλειαν τῇ Μαρκέλλου συντονίᾳ σωτήριον γενέσθαι τοῖς ʽ Ῥωμαίοις ('Posidonius says that he [Fabius] was called by the Romans "shield", Marcellus "sword", and that the firmness and caution of Fabius tempered with the vigour of Marcellus became the salvation of the Romans'). συντονία is the emendation of Corais, accepted in Ziegler's Teubner. Edelstein–Kidd retain the MSS συνηθείᾳ ('friendliness'?), but that seems to make little sense in the context.

[76] Kidd (1988: 901) expresses himself misleadingly in saying that 'the Posidonian contribution is confined to the mot', since the subsequent comment also is grammatically part of what Plutarch attributes to him. But Kidd is clearly right in his main point: that the bulk of Plutarch's lengthy comparisons cannot be ascribed to Posidonius.

P. Decio ad bellum Gallicum, sic postea Papirium Carviliumque adversus Samnites Bruttiosque et Lucanum cum Tarentino populum consules declaratos.

In the fifth year of the Second Punic War, when Q. Fabius Maximus entered on his fourth and M. Claudius Marcellus on his third consulship, they had attracted the attention of the citizenry more than usual; there had not been such a pair of consuls for many years. Old men remembered that similarly Maximus Rullus[77] with P. Decius had been declared consuls in the Gallic war, and subsequently Papirius and Carvilius against the Samnites and the Bruttii and the Lucanian people along with Tarentum.

The focus here is less on Fabius and Marcellus as antithetical figures, and rather more on what they share. It might be felt that *tale consulum par* simply refers to their fame; but Livy does not state that explicitly, and the examples he gives point in a slightly different direction, since it is not obvious that Papirius and Carvilius in particular stood with Rullus and Decius as the most distinguished consular pair of the previous century.[78] What those pairs of consuls however exhibit, at least in Livy's presentation, is a remarkable degree of harmonious co-ordination. Not only did they hold repeated consulships in tandem,[79] but they campaigned side by side, and Livy's narrative constantly emphasizes their close co-operation:[80] indeed, the harmony of Rullus and Decius is described by Volumnius in terms of their shared

---

[77] This is Q. Fabius Maximus Rullianus, great-grandfather of the Fabius Maximus of the Third Decade. On the version of the name given here see Oakley (1998: 30–2, 600).

[78] While the loss of Livy's Second Decade makes the reputation of Romans of that period sometimes hard to determine, what evidence we have does not suggest that either Papirius or Carvilius would have stood out as exceptional figures in the historical memory of the late Republic and early Empire. One might feel that (e.g.) C. Fabricius Luscinus and Q. Aemilius Papus (coss. 282 and 278) were at least as remarkable in terms of straightforward distinction: the former in particular was endlessly cited as a classic exemplar of frugal virtue as well as military success. On the other hand Cicero never mentions Carvilius (unless he is the Sp. Carvilius of *De Or.* 2.249), nor indeed Papirius, even, revealingly, in his long discussion of the *gens Papiria* at *Fam.* 9.21.2–3. Another useful index of reputation is Valerius Maximus: Carvilius is not mentioned by him at all, Papirius appears just once (7.2.5), in the anecdote about the chicken-keeper at the battle of Aquilonia told at Livy 10.40.

[79] Rullus and Decius in 308, 297, and 295 (they also shared a censorship in 304); Papirius and Carvilius in 293 and 272.

[80] In both 297 and 295 Decius is elected because Rullus specifically requests him as a colleague (10.13.12–13, 10.22). Their final consulship is admittedly marked by a major dispute over the assignment of provinces (10.24). But Livy treats this as something highly anomalous and handles it with a great deal of circumspection. He attributes it more to class conflict than personal dissension (10.24.2–3), emphasizes the final consensus between them (10.25.17–26.4), and finally queries whether there was actually a quarrel at all (10.26.5–7). See Oakley (2005b: 271–4). Our loss of Book 14 means that we cannot tell how Papirius and Carvilius were treated at the time of their victory over Tarentum *et al.*, but it is worth noting that Livy's description of their first consulship likewise shows them working together unusually closely (10.39.7–10, 10.44.1–2).

character.[81] While the presentation of Fabius and Marcellus via this comparison as harmoniously united figures does not deny that they may have
different approaches to warfare (after all, the point of the comparison in
Posidonius and Plutarch is that, while contrasting figures, they provide
complementary service to Rome), it removes that aspect from the reader's
attention, and instead invites us to look for shared rather than antithetical
approaches.

The lack of a stark antithesis in those terms is perhaps less surprising when
we look at the details of their campaigns.[82] It is of course true that Marcellus
in the previous book had fought Hannibal successfully in the kind of pitched
battle that Fabius had advised eschewing, while Fabius avoided moving to
Campania until he knew Hannibal had left for Apulia (23.46.9). But Livy had
shown even Fabius confronting Hannibal in direct battle when rescuing
Minucius (22.29.1–6),[83] and actively storming the cities of Hannibal's allies
(23.39.5–8) much as Marcellus did shortly afterwards (23.41.13–14). At the
same time he makes a point of showing that Marcellus' active policy, even in
the absence of Hannibal, was marked by a level of circumspection and caution
that looks not altogether un-Fabian (23.43.7–8).[84] This is partly because the
antithesis between caution and active combat, which we saw Livy systematically undermining in Book 27 with Livius and Claudius, is already being
significantly qualified in Books 23 and 24 (it is worth noting, for example,
24.3.17, where the Romans become daily more cautious, while also gaining
increased success at the *levia proelia* in which they do engage).[85] But it is also

---

[81] 10.22.6 *Decium Fabiumque uno animo, una mente vivere; esse praeterea viros natos militiae,
factis magnos, ad verborum linguaeque certamina rudes* ('Decius and Fabius lived with one heart
and one mind; they were moreover men born for warfare, great in their deeds, inexperienced in
the contest of words and speech'). For the text see Oakley (2005b: 239–41).

[82] Noted by Carawan (1984–5: 133–4), though his confidence that Livy cannot be following
Polybius in this is misplaced: of the two Polybius passages he cites as evidence, 9.10 is on an
entirely different topic, while 10.32–33 relates specifically to the recklessness Marcellus showed
at his death (on which see further below) and says nothing about his earlier behaviour one way
or the other.

[83] See esp. 22.29.6 *ac iam prope una acies facta erat victi atque integri exercitus inferebantque
signa in hostem, cum Poenus receptui cecinit* ('and now the defeated and fresh armies had formed
more or less one line, and were advancing against the enemy, when the Carthaginian sounded
the retreat'). This represents a change to Polybius 3.105.5–7, who has no suggestion that Fabius
did anything more than cover Minucius' flight.

[84] 23.16.15–16 may also be relevant here: Livy queries the version of the earlier battle of Nola
that had turned it into a major victory for Marcellus, and sees his success primarily in the fact
that he was not defeated.

[85] This was already prefigured in 22.12.10, where Fabius' troops are helped to recover their
morale by *parva momenta levium certaminum ex tuto coeptorum* ('unimportant and minor
conflicts undertaken from positions of safety'); but there the stress is more strongly on the
precautions taken to avoid defeat.

the case that in his portrayal of Fabius and Marcellus Livy does not differentiate them especially strongly along that axis in the first place, in contrast to what one might have expected him to do in the light of the tradition that he inherited.

So too once they are paired as consuls, Fabius and Marcellus do not appear markedly different in terms of their caution or aggression. Marcellus fights and beats Hannibal at 24.17 near Nola, though his attempt to trap the Carthaginian fails. But even here he is not incautious: when Claudius Nero fails to complete the planned movement, Marcellus does not dare to pursue Hannibal's retreating troops (24.17.5), and while Livy had earlier commended his active approach—the commendation that we would expect in light of Marcellus' traditional reputation—it is not with Fabius, but with Hannibal himself, that he contrasted him: Hannibal had delayed and so failed to reach the town in time.[86] When Fabius is successfully storming towns at 24.20.3–7, Marcellus is inactive, albeit through illness.

Livy's presentation of Fabius' and Marcellus' actions at the siege of Casilinum does in some respects serve to differentiate them in the expected fashion, since it appears that Marcellus leads the assault while Fabius receives the surrender of the citizens (24.19.8–10; see further below, 209–10). But even there they appear less dissimilar than one might expect. Fabius argues against Marcellus' plan to prosecute the siege at 24.19.6–7—but, even though Livy tells us that rashness is what leads to the lack of success in the consuls' first attempts to assault the city,[87] he does not, as one might expect, have Fabius conduct the argument in those terms. Rather Fabius suggests that it is better to give up on a difficult but minor task when more important matters are pressing, whereas Marcellus argues that even if they should not have begun the siege, it would lead to a loss of face to abandon it. The argument appears a simple one, but its undercurrents are more nuanced, for the person who originally wanted to attack Casilinum was Fabius himself (24.14.1), and Marcellus' reply is thus a covert rebuke: his phrase at 24.19.7 *multa magnis ducibus . . . non adgredienda* ('many things should not be attempted by great generals') has an ironic edge, implying that it is Fabius who has recklessly overstretched himself, and Fabius is accordingly won over to continue the attack. In short, while Livy introduces elements into his portraits that might

---

[86] 24.13.11 *uti a consule omnia inpigre facta sunt ad praeoccupandam Nolam, ita Hannibal tempus terebat*—'just as everything was done vigorously by the consul to seize Nola first, so Hannibal was wasting time'.

[87] 24.19.6 *multa succedentes temere moenibus Romani milites acciperent vulnera neque satis inceptum succederet*—'the Roman soldiers received many wounds through approaching the walls rashly and the attempt was not proceeding satisfactorily'.

invite readers to recall previous versions of the Fabius–Marcellus antithesis, he repeatedly turns away from a full-blown comparison in those terms.

But when Fabius and Marcellus are once again campaigning in tandem in Book 27, the contrast between them is clearer and also in some respects closer to the tradition. Fabius achieves a major success in recapturing Tarentum (27.15.9–16.9), but does so via a betrayal by the Bruttians rather than a frontal assault. The Romans then massacre the Bruttians in order to—at least on one interpretation—cover up the fact that they won through treachery,[88] and they may have been successful. Livy comments subsequently that *Romae ... Fabio Tarentum captum astu magis quam virtute gloriae <u>tamen</u> esse* (27.20.9: 'At Rome ... the capture of Tarentum by cunning more than courage <u>nevertheless</u> was a distinction for Fabius'): the implication is that it is unexpected that such a victory should be to his credit, while leaving it unclear whether the glory that people ascribed to him was in full knowledge of the manner by which the capture was effected.[89] Fabius' capture of Tarentum, as we shall see shortly, is directly compared by Livy to Marcellus' capture of Syracuse in Book 25. Marcellus had not declined to make some use of treachery in his capture of Syracuse, but did so as part of a broader and sometimes more straightforward military campaign, and Livy's summary at 25.23.1 was accordingly more balanced: *Syracusarum oppugnatio ad finem venit, praeterquam vi ac virtute ducis exercitusque, intestina etiam proditione adiuta* ('The attack on Syracuse reached its conclusion, assisted not only by the strength and courage of the general and the army, but also by internal treachery'). Caution and treachery are not of course inevitable concomitants, but from the introduction of the 'Fabian strategy' in Book 22 it has been accepted that the avoidance of direct conflict went hand in hand with a more subtle strategic and tactical awareness, and conquest by treachery at the expense of military action appears an extension of that—albeit in some respects an uncomfortable one, as I shall discuss further below.

---

[88] 27.16.6 *Bruttii quoque multi passim interfecti, seu per errorem seu vetere in eos insito odio seu ad proditionis famam, ut vi potius atque armis captum Tarentum videretur, exstinguendam* ('Many Bruttians also were killed indiscriminately, either by mistake or because of the old ingrained hatred against them or to wipe out the report of treachery, so that Tarentum should seem to have been captured instead by force of arms'). It should however be noted that Livy gives no indication that Fabius himself orders the massacre, unlike Plutarch at *Fab.* 22.4. Plutarch also is unequivocal (a) that the reason was that Fabius' φιλοτιμία led him to try to conceal the treachery; and (b) that this plan failed. Livy's Fabius looks rather better; see further 208–9 below.

[89] It may be relevant that Livy has no mention of the fact that Fabius was awarded a triumph for his capture of Tarentum, as described in the *elogium* in the Forum Augustum (*ILS* 56) and Plutarch, *Fab.* 23.2.

Even the Syracuse–Tarentum comparison, then, seems to set Fabius and Marcellus to a certain degree apart; but the antithesis between them is accentuated by Marcellus' increasing level of confident bellicosity, which makes his version of active warfare look almost as uncomfortable as Fabius' current version of passivity. Fabius commissions him to involve Hannibal in 'the fiercest war possible' (27.12.2 *quam acerrimo bello*), something that Marcellus is keen to do not least because 'he had concluded that no Roman general equalled Hannibal in the way he did' (27.12.7 *in animum induxerat neminem ducem Romanum tam parem Hannibali quam se esse*). That judgement is, however, noticeably not endorsed directly by Livy himself, though it is entirely of a piece with Marcellus' behaviour shortly before. After Hannibal's victory over Cn. Fulvius at the start of the book, Marcellus had seen no reason to be downhearted and instead said that he would pursue him and 'make his joy short' (27.2.2 *brevem illi laetitiam . . . facturum*). But his confidence was not shared by the Romans (27.2.3), and in fact Marcellus does not fulfil either that boast or the one in 27.12.7, though on balance he comes out ahead both times. In the first episode Hannibal fights him to a draw,[90] and then largely evades Marcellus' attempts at pursuit (27.2.3–12). As for the second episode, in a pair of battles on successive days, Marcellus first loses, then, after rebuking his troops and shaming them into renewing the fight, wins, but on neither occasion decisively (27.12.8–14.15). So while Marcellus is clearly still presented as a fine general, he has only achieved limited success, and his claim of unique superiority looks arrogant and irrationally overconfident.[91] It appears particularly misguided in the context of the rise of Scipio and his victories in Spain at the end of the previous book. Readers after all know—and Livy has repeatedly reminded us—who the ultimate victor over Hannibal will be, and at 26.29.9–10 Livy has already ominously prefigured Hannibal's killing of Marcellus.

None of this is directly incoherent with the behaviour that we have seen for Marcellus earlier—this is not inconsistent characterization of the sort we saw with Livius, Claudius, Minucius, or Varro. Marcellus had shown his selfconfidence against Hannibal at 24.17.7, where he claimed that it was only Claudius Nero's failure that kept him from achieving the decisive victory.[92]

---

[90] See esp. 27.2.8 *nox incerta victoria diremit pugnantes* ('night separated the combatants with victory unclear'). It is true that in the brief summary by Frontinus, *Str.* 2.2.6, Hannibal is suggested to have won a decisive victory, something Livy does not allow. Livy gives Marcellus enough of a success to maintain the careful balance of his narrative: Marcellus is a more successful commander than other sources suggest, but not as good as he believes himself to be.

[91] Cf. Bernard (2000: 321–2).

[92] This in turn recalls the arrogant claim of Varro at 22.41.3 that Aemilius' caution prevented him from finishing Hannibal off.

His campaign at Syracuse in Books 24 and 25 had achieved its success at least in part from his willingness to take on the enemy actively, as at 25.27.9–10, when in order to avoid being trapped he challenges the Carthaginian fleet with a smaller force; while at 25.41.1 he gave battle primarily because he thought it *indignum* for the victor of Nola to decline a fight with an enemy he had previously defeated. But there at least one might also note, for example, 24.35.9–10, where he was cautiously avoiding battle with the Carthaginians after his speed proved inadequate to take Agrigentum, and he remains wary of potential traps even at the start of Book 27 (27.2.12). His confident aggression in Book 27 does not seem an inconsistency, therefore; but it is a marked intensification of certain aspects of his earlier behaviour.

The end of the year adds an interesting further dimension. Livy for the only time in the decade makes a direct comparison between the three leading Roman commanders (along with the other outgoing consul Q. Fulvius); but the main focus of his attention is Marcellus (27.20.9–21.4):

Romae fama Scipionis in dies crescere, Fabio Tarentum captum astu magis quam virtute gloriae tamen esse, Fulvi senescere fama, Marcellus etiam adverso rumore esse, superquam quod primo male pugnaverat, quia vagante per Italiam Hannibale media aestate Venusiam in tecta milites abduxisset. inimicus erat ei C. Publicius Bibulus tribunus plebis. is iam a prima pugna quae adversa fuerat adsiduis contionibus infamem invisumque plebei Claudium fecerat; et iam de imperio abrogando eius agebat . . . actum de imperio Marcelli in circo Flaminio est ingenti concursu plebisque et omnium ordinum. accusavit tribunus plebis non Marcellum modo sed omnem nobilitatem: fraude eorum et cunctatione fieri ut Hannibal decimum iam annum Italiam provinciam habeat, diutius ibi quam Carthagine vixerit. habere fructum imperii prorogati Marcello populum Romanum; bis caesum exercitum eius aestiva Venusiae sub tectis agere. hanc tribuni orationem ita obruit Marcellus commemoratione rerum suarum ut non rogatio solum de imperio eius abrogando antiquaretur, sed postero die consulem eum ingenti consensu centuriae omnes crearent.

At Rome Scipio's reputation grew daily, the capture of Tarentum by cunning more than courage nevertheless was a distinction for Fabius, Fulvius' reputation was waning, and Marcellus too was subjected to hostile rumours, apart from the fact that he had initially fought unsuccessfully, because he had led his soldiers to fixed quarters in Venusia in mid-summer while Hannibal was roaming through Italy. He had an enemy in C. Publicius Bibulus, the tribune of the people. Right from the first battle which had gone badly he had in constant public meetings made Claudius disgraced and unpopular among the people; and now he was moving to have his command abrogated . . . The question of Marcellus' command was heard in the Circus Flaminius at a large gathering of the plebs and men of all classes. The tribune of the people accused not only Marcellus but the entire nobility: because of their deceit and delay Hannibal had Italy as his province now for the tenth year—he had lived longer there than at Carthage. The Roman people (he said) had the fruits of having prolonged Marcellus' command: his twice-slaughtered army passed its summer in fixed quarters at Venusia. Marcellus recounted his deeds, and overcame the tribune's speech to the point that not only was the bill to abrogate his command rejected, but on the next day all the centuries overwhelmingly agreed to elect him consul.

Whereas Marcellus, as we have seen, now regarded himself as the leading Roman general, Livy shows his reputation at Rome quite differently: over-shadowed not only by Fabius, but most notably by Scipio. More striking still are the terms in which he is criticized. He is accused not merely of having been defeated—a true though partial account of his campaigns—but of retiring from the field to Venusia and allowing Hannibal a free run of Italy. Livy has not shown Marcellus retiring to Venusia, though he is clearly now there, since he comes from there to Rome (27.20.12; cf. also 27.25.10); nor, accordingly, do we know precisely why he did it[93] or the effect on Hannibal. His own self-exculpatory speech is successful, but Livy gives us no hint of how precisely he responded to these accusations.

The result is that Marcellus certainly does not look like the cowardly and negligent commander that he has been accused of being—the accusation fits nothing in the direct description of his behaviour—but he does look like someone whose reputation does not live up to his self-evaluation. More interesting still is that Publicius extends his attack to the entire nobility, and does so in terms that look remarkably similar to the accusations of Minucius and especially Varro in Book 22: that the nobility is effectively conspiring to keep Hannibal in Italy. The accusation restates the sharp division between 'rash' and 'cautious' commanders,[94] and—astonishingly—aligns Marcellus with the latter.[95] It clearly has little connection to reality—the only evidence is the unexplained retirement to Venusia, whereas in Livy's actual narrative, as I have already noted, Marcellus has been increasingly represented in the opposite fashion. But the mere fact that the antithesis is here set out so starkly is important: the distinction matters, and Livy has already made it clear to which side of it Marcellus' inclinations are taking him.

[93] Plutarch, *Marc.* 26.4 explains that it was because of the number of wounded in his army; but that is not supported by Livy—the number of wounded is used as an explanation for the failure to pursue Hannibal at 27.14.15, but there is no indication that it had any broader effect on Marcellus' ability to campaign.

[94] As with Livius (above, 190–1), it is worth noting the use of the pointed term *cunctatio* (27.21.2), linking Marcellus to Fabius in particular.

[95] The phrase *infamem invisumque plebei Claudium fecerat* (27.20.11) is also noteworthy. Livy never elsewhere refers to Marcellus by his *nomen* alone: the use of the name in so pointed a phrase seems to be a deliberate recollection of the stereotypical hostility between the *plebs* and the *gens Claudia* in the First Decade (on which see Wiseman 1979: 57–139), although the connection is strictly speaking spurious, since the Claudii Marcelli were not patrician (cf. 23.31.13–14) and indeed may not even have been blood relatives of the patrician *gens*.

It is against this background that we come to Marcellus' death.[96] Here, as before, his confident desire to confront Hannibal directly is explicit. Both he and Crispinus are described as 'fierce of character' and 'going out virtually daily into the battle line' (27.25.14 *ingenio feroces prope cottidie in aciem exire*); and Marcellus takes this to the point that in his eagerness to fight (27.27.1 *tanta cupiditas... dimicandi*) he ignores religious warnings from the *haruspices* after he receives first a bad omen and then an unusually good one which they advise him is still dangerous (27.26.13–14).[97] And when he is killed, Livy comments directly on his stupidity (27.27.11):

mors Marcelli cum alioqui miserabilis fuit tum quod nec pro aetate—iam enim maior sexaginta annis erat—neque pro veteris prudentia ducis tam improvide se collegamque et prope totam rem publicam in praeceps dederat.

The death of Marcellus was anyway wretched, but especially because he had so imprudently ruined himself and his colleague and almost the whole state in a manner appropriate neither to his age (he was now more than sixty years old) nor to the wisdom of an experienced general.

Livy is far from unique in noting that Marcellus' death was the result of his own folly:[98] there are comparable but longer discussions in Polybius 10.32.7–12 and Plutarch, *Marc.* 28.3 (cf. also *Comp. Pel. and Marc.* 3.3–4). But he frames the issue rather differently from them. For Polybius Marcellus' putting himself at risk in this way may have been 'more stupid than general-like' (10.32.7 ἀκακώτερον ἢ στρατηγικώτερον). But it is nevertheless a stupidity to which generals are regularly prone, rather than something specific to Marcellus in particular, and it leads Polybius into broader reflections about the inappropriateness of such conduct and thence to praise of the far less reckless Hannibal (10.33.1–7). Plutarch, like Livy, notes the potential inappropriateness of Marcellus' conduct to his age, but only in a roundabout way: that *if* he had not already been highly honoured, and *if* he had not already showed his exemplary good sense, Plutarch *would have* attributed his behaviour to his being overtaken by 'a youthful passion and one more ambitious than is

---

[96] On the scene cf. Bernard (2002); on the varied historical accounts of Marcellus' death see Caltabiano (1975).

[97] At Levene (1993: 64–5) I discuss the nuanced way in which Livy differentiates his characters via these omens. Marcellus is not actively irreligious like Flaminius, because the second omen is not bad *per se*. But he is still fighting against the gods' will, and as such is to be contrasted with Fabius, who was saved from Hannibal by his careful regard to a comparable set of omens a few chapters earlier (27.16.15–16). In Valerius Maximus 1.6.9, on the other hand, Marcellus is killed *because* he pays attention to the omens: that is why he decides on a scouting mission rather than a full battle immediately.

[98] Compare Flower (2003: 48–51).

appropriate for so great an age'.[99] The actual explanation that Plutarch gives instead is in terms of Marcellus' obsessive desire to fight Hannibal (*Marc.* 28.2–3; cf. 29.2); and while this is extreme and leads him to a misjudged end, Plutarch does not suggest that of itself it is something one would not expect in an old man.[100]

Livy on the other hand presents it starkly in terms of a stereotype, and hence draws attention to the incongruity: this sort of imprudence is expected of a young and inexperienced man, not an old and experienced commander.[101] But this does not make Marcellus' behaviour anomalous, because it is entirely of a piece with the picture that Livy has created over the earlier part of the book. It is thus a good example of the complexities of ancient stereotyping. Marcellus can be assessed according to more than one typology, and the types may sometimes draw an individual in different directions. An old and experienced commander is expected to be prudent; but Marcellus is also a man of impetuous and self-confident character, and in the events leading to his death the latter dominates. If we are philosophers we might note that a person in perfect psychological harmony would reconcile these countervailing tendencies without conflict, but even if we are philosophers we should not be surprised to find that Livy's Marcellus—like most other people in the world— falls short of perfect psychological harmony.

More, however, needs to be said. It would be possible to explain the dominance of Marcellus' more impetuous side here satisfactorily in psychological terms, using the information Livy has given us: that he fears that his reputation is being overshadowed by Scipio and Fabius,[102] that he has been stung by Publicius' accusations of sluggishness and cowardice, and is determined to prove his critics wrong by a decisive victory over Hannibal.[103] And this is not an interpretation that should be dismissed. Livy after all frequently hints at undercurrents to events that he does not discuss explicitly on the surface, and to wish to challenge an affront to one's *dignitas* in this way would

---

[99] εἰ μὴ πολλῆς μὲν ἤδη μεστὸς ὑπῆρχε δόξης, πολλὴν δὲ πεῖραν παρεσχήκει τοῦ παρ᾽ ὁντινοῦν τῶν στρατηγῶν ἐμβριθὴς γεγονέναι καὶ φρόνιμος, εἶπον ἂν ὅτι μειρακιῶδες αὐτῷ προσπεπτώκει καὶ φιλοτιμότερον πάθος ἢ κατὰ πρεσβύτην τοσοῦτον. Plutarch's phrasing here is noticeably close to Livy's: he appears to be alluding to but also correcting his characterization.

[100] The impression from the *Life* as a whole is that Marcellus' extreme bellicosity is rather to do with his lack of self-control, which in turn is the effect of his incompletely Hellenic education. See Pelling (1989: 205–8).

[101] Compare Johner (1996: 71–9) on the stereotypical impetuosity of youth in Livy.

[102] While this is not stated explicitly for Marcellus, his colleague Crispinus, who shares both his confidence and his death (27.25.14), attacks Locri at 27.25.11 because he remembers the reputation that Fabius achieved through capturing Tarentum; he only breaks off the attack because of the prospect of an even more prestigious victory over Hannibal.

[103] So e.g. Carawan (1984–5: 138).

make perfectly good sense in Roman culture. But we can see Marcellus' arrogant confidence against Hannibal growing from the very start of the book, even before the defeats that led to the decline in his reputation at Rome and the conflict with Publicius, and another way of viewing this is also available, one which fits the approach to character analysis outlined earlier in the chapter, by looking at it in terms of the development and dynamics of the stereotype itself. Marcellus was traditionally described via an antithesis with Fabius, yet when they first come together Livy does not present them in a markedly antithetical fashion. The antithesis is much more marked in Book 27, and increasingly so through the first half of the book, especially because of the increasing focus on Marcellus' belligerence. Effectively, he is growing into his traditional role—yet whereas for Posidonius that role, when combined with Fabius' caution, is something that preserved Rome, for Livy it all but brings the country to destruction. Marcellus moreover is in a perfectly harmonious relationship with his new consular colleague Crispinus—but that is something destructive rather than productive, since both are equally aggressive and so neither restrains the other. And this, along with Publicius' resurrection of accusations of general upper-class dilatoriness, then provides the context for the next major episode, in which those stereotypes are once again developed in surprising and counterintuitive ways: the election of Livius Salinator and Claudius Nero and the battle of the Metaurus.

This is, of course, by no means all there is to Marcellus' character, or indeed to the contrast with Fabius. As well as the issue of aggression and caution which I have primarily been discussing, there is a largely separate question: their behaviour towards their conquered enemies. As I have already noted, Fabius' behaviour at Tarentum is contrasted directly with Marcellus' at Syracuse (27.16.7–8):

triginta milia servilium capitum dicuntur capta, argenti vis ingens facti signatique, auri tria milia octoginta pondo, signa tabulae prope ut Syracusarum ornamenta aequaverint. sed maiore animo generis eius praeda abstinuit Fabius quam Marcellus; qui interroganti scribae quid fieri signis vellet ingentis magnitudinis—di sunt, suo quisque habitu in modum pugnantium formati—deos iratos Tarentinis relinqui iussit.

30,000 slaves are said to have been captured, a huge mass of wrought and coined silver, 3,080 pounds of gold, statues and paintings all but equalling the ornaments of Syracuse. But Fabius kept from spoil of that sort more magnanimously than Marcellus had; when a scribe asked him what he wanted done with the huge statues (they are gods, cast in the form of fighters, each in its own costume) he ordered that the angry gods should be left for the Tarentines.

This picks up a theme that has been recurrent in Livy's work since the end of Book 25: the justification or otherwise of Marcellus' plundering of Syracuse, an issue over which the account has been complex and ambivalent.[104] Livy at 25.40.1 had justified it as *hostium . . . illa spolia et parta belli iure* ('those were . . . enemy spoils and obtained by right of war')—but had almost immediately undermined that justification by observing the disastrous effects that it will have on Rome (25.40.2). He does not here indicate directly that Marcellus despoiled temples, but such despoliation is indicated by 27.16.7–8 as well as by the direct complaints of the Syracusans at 26.30.9; it is worth noting that even in Book 25 the despoliation of Roman temples was chief among the consequences of Marcellus' plunder that Livy gloomily foreshadows. More generally Livy's emphasis on the avarice exhibited at the sack of Syracuse makes it looks uncomfortable even if not illegal;[105] and although Marcellus tries to limit the soldiers' excesses (e.g. 25.30.12, 25.31.8), he is manifestly implicated throughout. Fabius' reliance on treachery rather than battle does not leave him looking unblemished (above, 202), but on the issue of plunder, and especially plunder of religious items,[106] he comes out considerably better from the comparison.[107]

This, however, leads to a further complexity, for it is still the case that Fabius' capture of Tarentum is marked by extreme brutality, albeit not at his orders (above, n. 88), and includes the massacre of those who had assisted in the capture of the town in the first place. The issue of the correct treatment of allies and vanquished enemies extends beyond the question of plunder: and here too Fabius is set against Marcellus, who reveals an uncomfortable degree of moral complacency which Livy's narrative persistently undermines. Here, however, the dynamic of the comparison has moved in the opposite direction. Whereas on

---

[104] For a fuller discussion of the issues raised here see Carawan (1984–5: 136–7), Pelling (1989: 204–5), Levene (1993: 55–7, 63–4).

[105] Esp. 25.31.9 *multa irae, multa avaritiae foeda exempla* ('many foul examples of anger, many of avarice'); also e.g. 25.25.5–9, 25.31.11, 26.30.9–10, 26.31.9, 26.32.3–4.

[106] Scrupulous regard for religion is in fact a consistent feature of Livy's portrayal of Fabius: e.g. 22.9.7–10.10, 23.36.9–10, 27.16.15–16. See Levene (1993: 42–3, 51–2, 63–5).

[107] As he certainly does not from a similar comparison in Plutarch, *Fab.* 22.4–6 (contrast *Marc.* 21.3–4, which is closer to Livy). In Plutarch the 'gods' that Fabius leaves behind are simply his ironic term for works of art, and he does in fact plunder a temple himself (cf. also Pliny, *NH* 34.40). Plutarch's comment is πολὺ Μαρκέλλου φανεὶς ἀτοπώτερος περὶ ταῦτα, μᾶλλον δ' ὅλως ἐκεῖνον ἄνδρα πρᾳότητι καὶ φιλανθρωπίᾳ θαυμαστὸν ἀποδείξας (*Fab.* 22.6: 'He appeared much odder in this than Marcellus, and instead made that man seem altogether admirable for gentleness and humanity'). Plutarch's interpretation of the plundering of Syracuse in *Marc.* had likewise been far less ambivalent than Livy's and far more to Marcellus' credit, with the focus more on introducing the Romans to culture and less on corrupting them with wealth (though the idea of corruption is placed into the mouths of the senators at *Marc.* 21.4–5). See Pelling (1989: 200–3), Swain (1990: 140–2), Duff (1999: 305–7). Cf. Bocci (1995), who argues— albeit on weak grounds—that this reading of Marcellus was taken over by Plutarch from Posidonius, in which case it may have predated Livy; but see *contra* Swain (1990: 141–2). Plutarch's broader contrasts between Fabius and Marcellus, which he extends systematically through the lives of both, are however not always to the latter's credit: see Beck (2002).

the issue of aggression the divisions between them look sharper in Book 27 than they had initially, on this question they have if anything converged.[108] When they jointly sacked Casilinum at 24.19.8–10, they played rather different roles:

vineae inde omniaque alia operum machinationumque genera cum admoverentur Campanique Fabium orarent, ut abire Capuam tuto liceret, paucis egressis Marcellus portam, qua egrediebantur, occupavit, caedesque promiscue omnium circa portam primo, deinde inruptione facta etiam in urbe fieri coepta est. quinquaginta fere primo egressi Campanorum, cum ad Fabium confugissent, praesidio eius Capuam pervenerunt: Casilinum inter conloquia cunctationemque petentium fidem per occasionem captum est.

Then, when mantlets and all other sorts of siege-works and devices were being moved up and the Campanians were begging Fabius to let them depart to Capua safely, after a few came out Marcellus seized the gate by which they were coming out, and first there was an indiscriminate massacre of everyone around the gate, then, after the soldiers broke in, the same began even in the city. Around fifty Campanians came out initially, and after fleeing to Fabius for refuge, they came under his protection to Capua. Casilinum was captured using the opportunity given during the negotiations and delay of those seeking terms.

The clearest conclusion of the narrative here is that Fabius is appealed to by and protects the Campanians while Marcellus massacres the inhabitants. A closer reading suggests that Marcellus has actively exploited the negotiations to complete a victory by deceit which he could not accomplish by main force, and this at least raises questions about Fabius' own responsibility, which Livy leaves ambiguous: he either has failed to rein in his less scrupulous colleague, or was complicit in Marcellus' action from the start.[109] But either way the narrative associates Marcellus directly with brutality towards a captured city, and this prefigures above all his behaviour at Syracuse, which Fabius, while less directly implicated here, then replicates at Tarentum.

It should be stressed, of course, that Roman attitudes to the massacre of enemy civilians were not identical with those now prevailing (at least for public consumption) in the West. This is clear not least from passages like Caesar, *BG* 7.28.4–5 (cf. also 7.47.5), where he describes in a matter-of-fact fashion his troops at Avaricum killing nearly 40,000 people—including elderly people, women, and infants—explaining it as revenge for an earlier massacre by the

---

[108] One may compare 27.12.5–6, where Fabius decides to unleash a force of violent irregular troops to attack the Bruttii and Caulonia, which they do with alacrity (*non impigre solum sed etiam avide*). The attempt on Caulonia however proves a failure, and the troops surrender to Hannibal (27.15.8, 27.16.9).

[109] The explanation that the town was captured *inter conloquia cunctationemque* looks pointed: while it is not directly said to be Fabius' *cunctatio*, it is with him that the people are holding *conloquia*, and *cunctatio* is of course his most familiar quality (above, n. 60).

Gauls, as well as the result of the effort the capture cost them.[110] The accepted rules of ancient warfare gave complete licence to those who captured cities without previously agreeing terms about the treatment of the inhabitants, and under certain circumstances, notably punishing rebellion, massacre was sometimes seen as the most appropriate action to take.[111] But, as with the issue of plunder, there is a distinction to be made between the legitimacy of the behaviour and its moral desirability. The suffering of captured cities—including enemy cities—was a standard literary and artistic motif by which to arouse audience sympathy:[112] this does not suggest that the Romans saw such things from a perspective of utter moral indifference. The same follows from the regular praise of the humanity and generosity of those commanders who spared the defeated, including indeed defeated rebels.[113]

And with Marcellus at Syracuse, Livy gives direct reasons to question his behaviour in this area, while not subjecting him to unequivocal condemnation. He certainly appears concerned to moderate his troops and to treat the Sicilians well.[114] Most famous is the scene of his weeping as he sees the city laid out before him, remembers Hiero's friendship for Rome, and consequently determines to negotiate a surrender rather than sacking the town (25.24.11–15). Accordingly he orders his soldiers when taking the districts of Neapolis and Tyche to refrain from massacre and arson, while allowing them plunder (25.25.6–9).[115] Before he takes the remaining portion of the city, he also assures the Syracusan ambassadors that the penalty paid by the leaders of the revolt had been greater than the Romans wished, and that his aim in besieging the town was to free the Syracusans from oppression (25.31.4–5).[116]

---

[110] On Caesar's frequent willingness to attribute unashamedly to himself and his troops what we would nowadays regard as atrocities see Collins (1972: 933–42).

[111] See e.g. Ziolkowski (1993), Gilliver (1996).

[112] On this motif (the '*urbs capta* topos') see e.g. Paul (1982), Rossi (2002: esp. 232–6).

[113] Gilliver (1996: 219–22, 231–4) argues that merciful behaviour was often a pragmatic tool on the general's part, but also notes that certain writers (e.g. Cicero, *De Imp.* 42 and *Off.* 1.34–6, 1.82) set up such humanity as an ideal across the board. The fact that Cicero expressed such sentiments in a popular speech suggests that they would have had a great deal of resonance in theory, no matter how often they were compromised in practice. With regard to Livy, it is worth noting the capture of Iliturgi (28.19–20), where, even while showing the sack as justified, he condemns the descent into massacre of women and children as *ira crudelis* (28.20.6): see further below, 347–8.

[114] He had sometimes shown such concern earlier too: most notably at 23.15.7–16.1, where he wins over a potential traitor in Nola by matching Hannibal's earlier generosity to him.

[115] Though even here one might contrast Plutarch, *Marc.* 19.2, who gives a rather different impression from Livy, saying that the concession about plunder was forced on Marcellus unwillingly. Plutarch also fails to distinguish clearly the different stages in Marcellus' capture of Syracuse, implying that the orders here applied to the entire city, not just two districts of it.

[116] Marcellus' ambassador had said much the same when addressing the Syracusans before the siege (24.33.5–6). On this point it is worth comparing the not dissimilar comments of

When Archimedes is killed by a soldier Marcellus is annoyed, ensures him a proper burial, and protects his relatives (25.31.9–10). After the capture of the city Livy praises the justice of Marcellus' Sicilian settlement (25.40.1). None of this is negligible; but at the same time Marcellus directly countenances a level of brutality that undermines these merciful tendencies. The statement that he was fighting to liberate the Syracusans is immediately followed by a more double-edged comment: that capturing Syracuse was not much recompense for the effort and dangers the siege cost him (25.31.7).[117] He then immediately acts on the implication of this: instead of explicitly ordering the protection of the populace, as he had with Neapolis and Tyche, he merely takes steps to secure the royal treasure (25.31.8), to which he was agreed even by the Syracusans to be entitled (25.28.3), but the quantity of which he has overestimated (25.30.12)—a further indication of his lack of proper priorities. He leaves the rest of the town to the troops, who accordingly commit *multa irae, multa avaritiae foeda exempla* (25.31.9: 'many foul examples of anger, many of avarice'). The killing of Archimedes in the course of it may be against his will, but is a not unlikely consequence of the violence he has permitted.

The clearest sign of Marcellus' moral flexibility comes with his response to the massacre perpetrated by L. Pinarius at Henna (24.39.7–9):[118]

ita Henna aut malo aut necessario facinore retenta. Marcellus nec factum inprobavit et praedam Hennensium militibus concessit ratus timore fore deterritos a proditionibus praesidiorum Siculos. atque ea clades, ut urbis in media Sicilia sitae claraeque

Manlius Torquatus at 26.32.2—except that Torquatus is speaking against Marcellus there, and arguing what he thinks *should* have been done to the Syracusans. Likewise his emotive appeal to the memory of Hiero at 26.32.4 recalls Marcellus' own words as he wept before the city at 25.24.13. Torquatus expresses in a more highly coloured fashion what was already implicit in the narrative of Book 25: that Marcellus' actual treatment of Syracuse has not matched his stated aims. See also below, 331–4.

[117] This interpretation is admittedly controversial, since the text is probably corrupt. The MS reading is *nequaquam tantum fructum esse, quod capere Syracusas potuisset*. This is retained by Dorey in the Teubner, but it is hard to make sense of the consecutive clause here, and most editors have preferred to emend. The simplest emendation is to replace *tantum* by *tanti eum* (Harant, accepted by W-M) or *dignum* (Crevier), which presumably means ' . . . the recompense was by no means an adequate return for having being able to capture Syracuse'. This gives the double-edged meaning: but it too seems quite a difficult reading, and other scholars have understandably posited a lacuna, in which case the interpretation of the sentence cannot be determined in a non-circular fashion: the lacuna is filled according to one's assumptions about what Marcellus might be saying. Thus Madvig hypothesized the much less threatening *quod capere Syracusas <potuerit quantum si servare> potuisset*, which has the opposite implication: that Marcellus saw the true reward as saving Syracuse, with capturing it as a second best, and plundering it not even on the agenda. No definite conclusion can be reached, save to note that even if Madvig is right about the general sense, the inconsistency between Marcellus' words and the Roman behaviour at the sack becomes all the more marked.

[118] On this see Levene (1993: 55–6), and cf. further below, 341–3.

vel ob insignem munimento naturali locum vel ob sacrata omnia vestigiis raptae quondam Proserpinae, prope uno die omnem Siciliam pervasit. et quia caede infanda rebantur non hominum tantum sed etiam deorum sedem violatam esse, tum vero qui etiam ante dubii fuerant defecere ad Poenos.

So Henna was retained by a deed either evil or necessary. Marcellus did not condemn the action and allowed the soldiers to have the booty of the Hennans, thinking that the Sicilians would be deterred from betraying their garrisons. And that disaster, happening to a city right in the middle of Sicily and famous both because it was a place with outstanding natural defences and because of its general sanctity from the traces of the ancient rape of Prosepina, in virtually a single day was known in the whole of Sicily. And because they reckoned that the unspeakable massacre had violated not only the home of men but also of the gods, then in fact even those who had previously been doubtful defected to the Carthaginians.

Livy himself is equivocal about the morality of the massacre, but not about its consequences. There is no indication that Marcellus knew about it in advance, but he certainly condones it after the event—but on reasoning that is disastrously misjudged and indeed achieves precisely the opposite result of the one he intended. While this is not identical to his behaviour at Syracuse in the following book, the practical condoning of violence is much the same in both cases. It is little surprise that when the Sicilians in Book 26 believe that Marcellus may be assigned to them again, they react with genuine shock and dismay (26.29.2–4), even if the arguments that they then use against him in the Senate (26.30.1–10) are partly tendentious.[119]

   All of this shows that simply categorizing Marcellus on a rash–cautious axis is far too simplistic: there are other aspects of his character that are not readily captured by such a continuum (and of course one should not think that all aspects of Livy's presentation are exhausted even once we add his treatment of Syracuse to the mix). But one should also note how strongly in this area characterization shades into moral judgement: the key question about the treatment of Henna or Syracuse is whether and why it is right or wrong (or, more accurately, how right and how wrong it is). It is not that this cannot be seen in terms of a particular person's character – as Gill noted and I discussed earlier, one brand of character portrayal does have a highly moralistic edge. Cruelty and avarice against gentleness, magnanimity against cynical expediency or petty revenge – these are issues that would certainly serve to characterize individuals in ancient eyes as in modern, and Marcellus possesses a combination of them that looks moderately distinctive, just as (in its very different way) Scipio's spectacular magnanimity and generosity to the Spaniards after the fall of New Carthage do (esp. 26.49–50). But what makes these passages interesting seems to be less what they reveal about Marcellus as an

---

[119] See Pelling (1989: 204–5; esp. n. 8).

individual, and rather more how they feed into Livy's complex and intricate moral picture of the Second Punic War, in which the question of the treatment of defeated enemies is raised repeatedly, a question to which many people on both sides respond in different ways. To Livy the particular character of each person contributing to the moral argument is less important than the argument itself and its development across the decade as a whole. Marcellus—like Fabius, Scipio, Hannibal, and many others—has a distinctive role to play in that; but to abstract his role and look at him in isolation is to miss the most significant dimension of the work in which he appears. The fact that Marcellus behaves in these ways towards the Sicilians is important. But more important still is the relationship between that behaviour and (for example) Fabius at Tarentum, Scipio at New Carthage, or, even more strikingly, Q. Fulvius Flaccus and Ap. Claudius Pulcher at Capua in Book 26. Here, although the Romans in question do not appear to be 'characterized' in any very marked fashion,[120] the issue of the morality of their treatment of the captured city is explored by Livy in even more complex and balanced ways, and is juxtaposed with Marcellus at Syracuse even more sharply when, in a lengthy scene, the Syracusans and Capuans jointly appeal to the Senate about their treatment (26.26.5–34.13). I shall be returning to this comparison when I discuss Livy's account of the recapture of Capua in Chapter 5; but for the moment it should simply be recognized that examining such issues primarily in terms of 'character', while sometimes illuminating, is often liable to distort the meaning of Livy's work.

3.2. ETHNICITY

The mistreatment of foreigners in Livy is thus often a problem. But there is an additional reason why one might suspect that the particular foreigners mistreated here and elsewhere in the Third Decade would generate anxieties in Livy's day, because the people so mistreated are not unproblematically foreign. The expansion of the empire in the 200 years up to Livy's time had swept virtually every group mentioned in these books under Roman sway, and was indeed increasingly granting them the rights of Roman citizens. Most striking for Livy is that his own home town, Padua, was itself a beneficiary of this: it was in Cisalpine Gaul, which at the time of his birth was only partially enfranchised; it was then fully enfranchised in 49 and incorporated into Italy in 42. We do not know how closely Livy was affected by this personally (he could well have been a Roman citizen from

---

[120] One may note, for example, that neither of them is so much as mentioned in Bernard's book.

birth), but these changes were dramatic, and he retained at least a residual interest in Padua, as his occasional references to it show—indeed the entire history begins with its foundation (1.1.2–3).

It is of course possible that Livy regarded all this as irrelevant, and that he was prepared to ignore the interests of those of his readers to whom it might not have seemed irrelevant. Indeed, Livy's perspective seems so patently Romanocentric that the general tendency among scholars has been to take that as a given, and accept that he wholeheartedly if narrowly saw the world from the standpoint of the Romans, with 'Romans' defined according to whatever happened to be constructed as 'Roman' at the particular time about which he was writing.[121] Romulus' foundation of Rome was from people of mixed origins (1.8–9); but thenceforward the 'Romans' are essentially the descendants of those at the time of Romulus. The exceptions are a few Italians who are assimilated completely into Rome over the next centuries, but they are effectively treated as Romans, with their Italian identity ignored. All other Italians are merely non-Roman allies or (no less often) enemies, which is what makes them potentially vulnerable to Hannibal's blandishments. Nowhere (on this view) does Livy incorporate into his account an awareness of the changes that would bring these Italians to full Roman citizenship. Virgil, from the same region and writing at almost exactly the same time, produced an epic about a Trojan–Italian conflict which constantly explores the idea that both sides would eventually come together into a single but complex Roman–Italian identity. There is apparently nothing in Livy to match this. And as for non-Italians, there is not even a hint that their alienness might be mitigated by eventual Roman conquest and incorporation. Whether good or bad, noble or corrupt, allies or enemies of Rome, they remain foreign. Even if this could not possibly have been maintained in Livy's narrative of the first century,[122] we have little evidence for how he treated the first century. As far as the surviving text goes, there is an unproblematic division between Rome and all others.

However, there are good reasons to think that this may not be satisfactory as an analysis. The entire question of the construction of ethnic identity in the late Republic and early Empire has been significantly reconsidered in scholarship of the last ten years, both from the perspective of the 'Romanizing' provincials and in terms of the categories of Roman and foreign ethnicity that are set out in literature, and the perennial problems and complications of pinning down a univocal identity in either reality or ideology have been

---

[121] For an especially clear and eloquent statement of this position see Luce (1977: 276–88); see also e.g. Paschoud (1993: 129).

[122] So Syme (1958a: 139–40).

repeatedly exposed.[123] If Livy, born in a non-Roman city, was indeed exclud-
ing not merely non-Roman but even future Roman perspectives as utterly as
is often thought, that itself would be something remarkable and noteworthy.
But the exclusion may not be so complete: I noted in Chapter 1 (40–2), for
example, an instance in Book 23 where a debate over the incorporation of
Latins into the Senate appears to be narrated with an ironic eye on the issue's
future recurrence. The relationship between Romans and non-Romans in
Livy 21–30 requires some reconsideration.

  The most obvious aspect of the treatment of non-Romans is admittedly the
degree to which they are overtly stereotyped,[124] and stereotyped moreover in
terms which assume their distance from proper (Roman) values.[125] In describing the actions of a foreigner, Livy will often provide a few words of explanation
in terms of their ethnic type. So, most notoriously, from the opening description
of Hannibal, deception is seen as a quintessentially Carthaginian trait—Hannibal
has *perfidia plus quam Punica* (21.4.9: 'a treachery more than Carthaginian'), a
phrase which assumes that the type is already familiar. When Maharbal promises
to free Roman prisoners after Trasimene, *Punica religione servata fides ab Hannibale est, atque in vincula omnes coniecti* (22.6.12: 'the agreement was kept by
Hannibal with Punic religion, and they were all thrown into chains');[126] the false
deserters who trap the Romans at Cannae are acting with *Punica... fraude*
(22.48.1: 'Punic deceit'),[127] a phrase that regularly recurs (26.17.15, 27.33.9,
30.22.6). One can find equally sweeping comments attached to other groups as
well; Numidians are lascivious,[128] Campanians luxury-loving and arrogant,[129]
Gauls primitive[130] and greedy (21.20.8, 27.36.1–2), incapable of enduring

---

[123] From a vast bibliography I can mention e.g. Dench (1995), Webster and Cooper (1996),
Woolf (1998), Keay and Terrenato (2001), Webster (2001), Williams (2001), Dench (2005),
Farney (2007).

[124] See Walsh (1961: 108–9).

[125] Livy shows little sense that moral premises might not be universally shared, or that other
societies might have sets of values different from but no less valid than Roman ones. In this he is
admittedly in the mainstream of Roman thought: the cultural relativism exemplified by Nepos,
Prologue 1–7 is the exception. See Pfeilschifter (2000).

[126] Cf. also Livy's play on the motif in the mouth of Hannibal at 30.30.27: *haud negaverim...
suspectam esse vobis Punicam fidem* ('I do not deny... that Punic faith has been suspected by you').

[127] In both cases Livy is drawing partly on Polybius (3.85.2–3 and 3.116.5), but neither is
seen by Polybius in terms of ethnic stereotypes, though Polybius is certainly not averse to such
stereotypes in other contexts (e.g. 6.52.10, 9.11.2, 14.1.4). Hannibal's retraction of Maharbal's
agreement is primarily, for Polybius, because Maharbal was not authorized to make such an
agreement in the first place.

[128] 30.12.18 *ut est genus Numidarum in venerem praeceps*; cf. 29.23.4.

[129] 23.5.1 *superbis atque infidelibus, ut erant Campani*; 23.8.6 *civitate... diti ac luxuriosa*; 25.18.2
superbae suopte ingenio genti. Cf. 7.31.6 *luxuria superbiaque clarus* and 9.6.5 *superbiam ingenitam*.

[130] 21.25.6 *gens ad oppugnandarum urbium artes rudis*. There is nothing of this in the parallel
passage of Polybius (3.40.8): it does fit the picture of Gallic society that he provides at 2.17.9–11,

hardship[131] but ferocious (21.20.8).[132] Ligurians are tough (27.48.10 *durum in armis genus*), Spaniards fierce (21.5.12; cf. 28.12.11), Aetolians 'fiercer than the usual Greek character' (27.30.5 *ferociore quam pro ingeniis Graecorum*).[133] Perfidy is a trait found more widely than in just the Carthaginians: it is also present in Numidians (25.41.4 *gens fallax*; 28.17.6; 28.42.7, 28.44.5),[134] Spaniards (25.33.2, 28.19.7),[135] and Gauls (21.25.7, 21.52.7).[136] Moreover, people regularly live up to these traits even when they are not overtly characterized in those terms: hence much of the Carthaginians' campaign is marked by deceit and disloyalty, and Gauls consistently show themselves unable to cope with the rigours of warfare.

Nevertheless, it would be a mistake to regard this as a reason to dismiss Livy's picture of non-Romans as the uninteresting product of mere prejudice.[137] I have already considered one point in the context of the portrayal of individual characters: that the use of stereotypes, in a society in which those stereotypes are accepted as true, is a major way in which verisimilitude may be supplied to one's work. And it is clear that the broad repertoire of ethnic stereotypes that Livy presents is not specific to him. The 'deceitful Carthaginian' was a Roman type of long standing;[138] so too, for example, the arrogant and luxurious

but in practice Polybius often describes Gallic life as considerably more civilized (see Foulon 2001: 35–8).

[131] 22.2.4 *ut est mollis ad talia gens*. In this case Livy's comment is based closely on Polybius 3.79.4 τῆς τῶν Κελτῶν μαλακίας καὶ φυγοπονίας; Livy here makes the generalization more explicit, but this is in accordance with the stereotype that Polybius, too, regularly relays (see Foulon 2000: 352–4). Cf. 27.48.16 *itinere ac vigiliis fessi, intolerantissima laboris corpora, vix arma umeris gerebant*; the corresponding passage of Polybius (11.3.1) has the Gauls caught off-guard while drunk. See also the summary of the Gallic type which Livy later placed into the mouth of Manlius Vulso (38.17.6–7; cf. 5.33.2–3): and note Kremer (1994: 31–7). On Livy's picture of the Gauls more broadly see Kremer (1994: 17–80).

[132] See Kremer (1994: 46–9).

[133] On Livy's attitude to Greeks generally see Moreschini (1984); Achard (2002). On his characterization of Aetolians in particular see Hoch (1951: 49–52).

[134] On Livy's overlapping stereotypes of Africans cf. Texier (1979).

[135] As Mineo (2006: 27) observes, the Saguntines are the exception that prove the rule: they are Spaniards who remain loyal to Rome, but are not true Spaniards, since they are partly of Italian origin (21.7.2–3).

[136] See Kremer (1994: 39–43).

[137] As does e.g. Walsh (1961: 108): 'These judgements are not distinguished by subtlety or insight; some reflect Roman insularity at its most biased, and others achieve a unique level of banality'. Cf. Mineo (2006: 31): 'cette faiblesse de l'oeuvre livienne'.

[138] Polybius describes Hannibal's changing costume to protect himself from assassination as a 'Punic stratagem' (3.78.1 Φοινικικῷ στρατηγήματι): Livy's version (22.1.3) does not this time describe the behaviour explicitly in terms of the stereotype, although it is certainly congruent with it. See Molin (2003: 285). See also e.g. Plautus, *Poen.* 113; *Rhet. Her.* 4.20; Cicero, *Inv.* 1.71, *Leg. Agr.* 2.95; *Scaur.* 42; *Off.* 1.38 (perhaps quoting Ennius: see Skutsch 1985: 781–2); Sallust, *Jug.* 108.3. On the type see Burck (1943); also Prandi (1979), who traces it back to earlier Greek stereotypes of Phoenicians, and Waldherr (2000), who argues that the stereotype became more marked in later periods, as the Punic Wars vanished into the past and Carthaginians ceased to be

Campanians,[139] and tough Ligurians[140] are found elsewhere. A second point is also relevant: that with ethnic stereotypes, as with stereotypes of other sorts (above, 177), holding to them as generalizations does not preclude qualifying or rejecting them in particular cases.[141] So at 25.41.4 Livy's characterization of the Numidians as a *gens fallax* is specifically designed to give the context for a particular instance when they kept their word, while at 22.22.15 Bostar is described as *homini non ad cetera Punica ingenia callido* ('a man whose cunning did not match the character of other Carthaginians).[142] A third point is also of interest: that Livy, like many other ancient writers,[143] sometimes explains these ethnic types in terms of environment as well as—or sometimes instead of— inherited characteristics.[144] Admittedly the distinction between 'racial' and 'environmental' stereotyping is less significant in a Roman context than it may appear to a modern,[145] burdened as we are with the legacy of the 'race-science' of the mid-nineteenth to mid-twentieth centuries, which sought to justify anything from segregation to mass murder by reference to supposedly inherited and inalienable racial traits. But even in the Roman context 'environmental' explanations highlight the possibility that ethnic stereotypes, while true, may in certain circumstances change.[146] Most notably in Livy, it is the luxury of

---

identifiable. Both Prandi (1975: 91–2) and Waldherr (2000: 217–18) treat Livy merely as an extreme example of an anti-Carthaginian writer, which hardly reflects the complexity of his account, as I shall show.

[139] E.g. C. Gracchus *ORF* fr. 59 (from Val. Max. 9.5 ext. 4), Cicero, *Leg. Agr.* 2.95, *Red. Sen.* 17, Gellius 1.24.2. Cf. Lomas (1997); Oakley (1998: 305); Briquel (2002: 150–4).

[140] E.g. Cicero, *Leg. Agr.* 2.95.

[141] This fundamental point is overlooked in the recent study of ancient racism by Isaac (2004). Isaac defines racism as the belief that individuals' characters possess 'collective traits . . . which are constant and unalterable by human will, because they are caused by hereditary factors or external influences, such as climate or geography . . . It is assumed that they cannot change these traits individually' (Isaac 2004: 23). He distinguishes this sharply but somewhat tendentiously from 'ethnic or group prejudice' (Isaac 2004: 37), which he claims to be less deterministic. But Isaac fails to observe how often in practice not only Livy, but many other writers, indicate that individuals do not match up in all respects to the inherited or environmentally influenced stereotype of their ethnic group. Hence Isaac's overall conclusion that 'racism' as he defines it was prevalent at Greece and Rome is largely a consequence of the superficiality of his readings.

[142] The comment does not appear in the parallel passage of Polybius (3.98.11).

[143] See Borca (2003).

[144] E.g. 23.4.4, 29.25.12; cf. 9.13.7, 38.17.9–12, 45.30.7 (though the contrary view is put into the mouth of the Rhodians at 37.54.18–21). On this cf. Luce (1977: 279–84), Girod (1982: 1222–9).

[145] Note Dench (2005: 222–7), and cf. Stok (1993), Mineo (2006: 22–8). As Stok (1993: 79– 86) observes, 'environmental' stereotyping at Rome was itself used to justify Roman domination, since Rome was treated as having the climate that made for an ideal national character: see e.g. Vitruvius 6.1, and cf. also Borca (2003: 69–88). This point lies at the heart of the account of Isaac (2004), who treats 'environmental' stereotyping as functionally indistinguishable from 'genetic'; however the differences are more marked and of greater significance than he allows.

[146] Cf. Mineo (2006: 27–8).

Capua which leads to the corruption of Hannibal's hardened soldiers when he winters there after Cannae (23.18.10–16). As we shall see, this issue has wider ramifications.

There is a further complicating factor that we need to take into account: the notion of the 'barbarian'. Yves Dauge's classic structuralist study of the Roman concept of the barbarian subsumes the particular ethnographic stereotypes of individual non-Roman peoples within a more general account of the non-Roman as the antithesis of the Roman.[147] Or perhaps I should rather say, the antithesis of what the Roman should be, for on Dauge's model Romans themselves often reveal barbarian traits, and Romans have to struggle constantly against the barbarian within themselves: I shall be exploring this issue further below. But for the moment we need only consider the relationship between the barbarian as a general category and the stereotypes of separate groups. Dauge does of course recognize that the Romans distinguished between foreigners—he is particularly interested in their differentiation between the uncivilized barbarians of 'primitive' societies like the Gauls and the barbarism connected with the luxurious lifestyle of hypercivilized peoples like those of the East. But both of those, on his argument, are merely different parts of the same ideological field. For him, although people may be more or less 'barbarian', or 'barbarian' in different ways, nevertheless 'barbarian' and 'Roman' are clearly antithetical categories.

Dauge's model is in general a powerful one. I referred above to the way in which an apparently quintessentially Carthaginian trait like treachery turns out to be no less applicable to other non-Roman groups, even if explicitly adverted to less often; the same (as Dauge extensively documents) is true of many other qualities, like ferocity, brutality, or arrogance.[148] Likewise Livy will sometimes characterize 'barbarians' *en masse* as being undisciplined (e.g. 28.1.8) or fickle (e.g. 22.22.6,[149] 28.17.6). All of these traits stand in contrast to the truly Roman qualities of *humanitas*, loyalty, and self-restraint. Livy, with his overwhelmingly Roman focus, is apparently less inclined than almost

---

[147] Dauge (1981).

[148] See e.g. Dauge (1981: 450–66); cf. Riggsby (2006: 55–8).

[149] *qualia plerumque sunt barbarorum ingenia, cum fortuna mutaverat fidem* ('as is usual with barbarian characters, he had changed his loyalties with fortune'). Cf. the not dissimilar sentiments in the parallel passage of Polybius (3.98.3 συλλογισμὸν Ἰβηρικὸν καὶ βαρβαρικόν), but there the barbarian quality exhibited by the Spaniard is not changing sides with fortune *per se*, but his attempt to use the change of sides in order to promote himself. It is perhaps worth observing that Polybius himself was someone who changed sides with fortune: Livy's allusion to the Polybian motif while refocusing it on the issue of disloyalty ironically hints at that (cf. Chapter 2 above, 157–9, for another place where Livy slyly assimilates Polybius to 'barbarian' attitudes).

any other author to make significant distinctions between or within non-Roman groups.[150]

Nevertheless, he does make more distinctions than Dauge's picture might lead one to expect, and sometimes revealing ones.[151] In particular, the Carthaginians, while clearly in Dauge's sense 'barbarians' in terms of their stereotypical attributes, are never called such by Livy himself in the Third Decade, though he has Roman speakers occasionally use the word of them in polemical contexts (22.59.14, 24.47.5; cf. n. 155 below). On the contrary, Livy repeatedly distinguishes the Carthaginians from the *barbari*: for example at 28.18.6, where Scipio charms *non Syphacem modo, barbarum insuetumque moribus Romanis, sed hostem etiam infestissimum* ('not only Syphax, a barbarian unaccustomed to Roman ways, but also his most hostile enemy [sc. Hasdrubal son of Gisgo]'). The implication is that Hasdrubal himself is not a 'barbarian unaccustomed to Roman ways'. At 28.1.8 the Celtiberian camp is described as *soluta neglectaque, ut barbarorum et tironum* ('casual and ne-glected, typical of barbarians and raw recruits')—but this is contrasted directly with the Carthaginians' own camp, which is *stationibus, vigiliis, omni iusta militari custodia tuta et firma* ('safe and solid with outposts and watches and all the proper military protections'). Or one can mention 29.23.6, where Hasdrubal knows *quam vana et mutabilia barbarorum ingenia essent* ('how empty and changeable the characters of barbarians are') and so acts to reinforce the Carthaginian alliance with Syphax,[152] or 25.33.2, where Hasdrubal the brother of Hannibal is said to be *peritus omnis barbaricae et praecipue omnium earum gentium, in quibus per tot annos militabat, perfidiae* ('knowledgeable about all barbarian treachery, and especially that of those people, among whom he had campaigned for so many years'). The last is particularly striking, because *perfidia* is, as I said, a quintessentially Carthaginian trait, yet Hasdrubal appears to know of *barbarica perfidia* as an experienced outsider, not because he himself is a 'barbarian' of that sort,

---

[150] Note especially Dauge (1981: 172–3): 'Tite-Live insiste jusqu'à satiété sur leur *feritas*, leur *ferocia*, leur *perfidia*, leur *temeritas*, leur *superbia*, etc.: quelle différence, en somme, entre un Samnite et un Gaulois? Sabins, Éques, Volsques, Étrusques, Campaniens, Samnites, Lucaniens, Ombriens présentent en effet les mêmes défauts que Rome retrouvera chez les Espagnols, les Celtes, les Germains, les Illyriens ou les Puniques: ce sont donc bien les barbares, et si l'on ne va pas jusqu'à les déclarer tels explicitement, c'est à cause de leur qualité d'Italiens, les premiers à avoir été assimilés par Rome.' Dauge's final concession here is, however, revealing, as I shall discuss further below.

[151] Cf. Rüger (1965: 72–4), Kremer (1994: 76–7).

[152] Cf. Scipio's account of the fickleness of Carthage's African and Numidian allies at 28.44.5, here too implicitly distinguishing them from the Carthaginians themselves. Johner (1996: 53) notes that Hasdrubal's judgement of Syphax mirrors Scipio's at 28.17.7, but fails to observe that it is part of Livy's broader pattern of uniting Rome and Carthage on the side of civilization.

and indeed, despite that experience, he to some extent underestimates the treachery of these particular barbarians, as I discuss below (244–5).[153] Similarly Varro, in an admittedly partial description (23.5.11), characterizes the Carthaginians themselves as 'not even natives of Africa' (*ne Africae quidem indigena*,[154] a pointer to their Phoenician roots), but their troops as 'from the ultimate margins of the earth, the strait of Ocean and the Pillars of Hercules, without knowledge of any human law, constitution, or virtually language' (*ab ultimis terrarum oris, freto Oceani Herculisque columnis, expertem omnis iuris et condicionis et linguae prope humanae*)—although the word *barbarus* is not used here, the connotations of the description are unmistakable and unambiguous, and they are not applied to the Carthaginians.[155] It is true that Livy sometimes shows Numidians and Carthaginians treating one another as 'Africans', as if in a mirror-image of the shared 'Italian' sensibilities of Romans and Italians (see below, 236).[156] But like the Romans and Italians, that identification is inconsistent and shifting, and the Carthaginians never cross explicitly into the category of 'barbarian' associated with other Africans.

This suggests that it is rather too simplistic to examine Livy's narrative merely in terms of a Roman/barbarian antithesis; nor indeed, for the same reason, is it adequate to look at it merely in terms of a Roman/Carthaginian one. Both Carthaginians and 'barbarians' are present in the narrative, and both are presented as possessing stereotypical qualities, qualities indeed that overlap; both moreover are in some sense presented as the antithesis of Rome. Yet while the Carthaginians remain anti-Roman, in terms of the Roman/ barbarian antithesis they are implicitly aligned with Rome rather than with the barbarians. And this is a striking conclusion. Roman ethnography is often read in terms of creating an antithesis between Romans and 'others', an antithesis supported either by playing down differences between the 'others',

---

[153] Along similar lines we might note 25.40.12, where Hanno scorns Muttines as a *degenerem Afrum* ('degenerate African')—though in this case, while it clearly points to Hanno's perception of a distinction between Carthaginians and Africans, his particular formulation is misguided, since Muttines is demonstrably the superior commander: see below, 247.

[154] So the reading of the archetype, accepted by the Teubner and W-M. Some late MSS correct to *indigenam* and so refer it to the non-Carthaginian soldiers alone, and this reading is followed by Madvig and the Oxford text. But even apart from the weak manuscript support this is less plausible, since even Varro is unlikely to be denying the presence of African soldiers in Hannibal's army.

[155] The phrase *ab ultimis terrarum orbis* picks up 22.14.5, where Minucius refers to 'the Carthaginian stranger, from the extreme limits of the earth' (*Poenus advena, ab extremis orbis terrarum terminis*). Here it is applied to the Carthaginians themselves, but in applying it to their allied troops alone Varro turns it into a far more pointed description of the typical 'barbarian'.

[156] E.g. 29.23.10 (esp. *pro terra Africa*); 29.34.2 *universae Africae*; 30.12.15. See the brief but provocative arguments of Huss (1989), though he implausibly treats this as historical reality rather than merely Livy's construction.

or else by assimilating some non-Romans to Rome.[157] But when it comes to Livy's Carthaginians—and indeed, as we shall shortly see, his Africans, Spaniards, and Italians—this appears a caricature.[158] The Carthaginians' distance from Rome is usually maintained,[159] but so too is their distance from their non-Carthaginian allies.

Similarly, it is over-simplistic to see Livy's Italians merely as non-Roman allies of varying reliability. As an historical fact, of course, many Italians at the period of the Hannibalic War did not have Roman status, and moreover the individual Italian communities maintained—as indeed they continued to do much later— an independent culture and identity. When Livy repeatedly describes Italians not as Romans but as allied peoples who might waver in their loyalty, and who in some cases turn against Rome and go over to Hannibal, as with the long list of defecting communities he provides at 22.61.10–12, his analysis is not unreasonable historically: it is noticeable in that passage that beyond the bare identification he makes no material distinction between Italic nations, the cities of Greek Italy, and the people of Cisalpine Gaul. And yet throughout the decade Livy constantly pushes at the boundaries of Italian identity. That very list is revealing in a different way, for it consists solely of Italian communities by the definition of 'Italian' at the time when Livy was writing. Cisalpine Gaul, which was Italian under Augustus but not at the time of Hannibal, is listed. Roman allies in Transalpine Gaul or Sicily, for example, are not, although some of those certainly defected too. Defectors who are by later definition 'Italian' matter to Livy in a way that 'non-Italian' defectors do not.[160] We can compare the way in which Sempronius before the battle of the Trebia refers to 'the Carthaginians' camp in Italy and almost in view of the city' (21.53.4 *castra Carthaginiensium in Italia ac prope in conspectu urbis*), and the Romans' own army as being 'in the middle of Italy' (21.53.5 *in media Italia*).[161] Livy has in fact explained in the previous

---

[157] So e.g. O'Gorman (1993: 147): 'The discourse of barbarian representation in the ancient world is very much a discourse of duality, polarity, of being either one or the other, although this is often masked by the assignation of otherness to elements of one's own society. Three-way splitting does not in practice occur. If two types of barbarianism are represented, one will be assimilated to the Roman'.

[158] Note Riggsby (2006: 47–71; esp. 65–7), who similarly argues that Caesar's tripartite picture of Romans/Gauls/Germans likewise conflicts with the standard model. He suggests that this is an exception to the rule, but the fact that Livy too cannot easily be confined within such a framework may indicate that the framework itself has not been accurately characterized.

[159] But not uniformly: see e.g. 30.7.6, where the Carthaginians in refusing to despair in crisis are said to show 'Roman constancy in adversity' (*Romanae in adversis rebus constantiae*).

[160] Mahé-Simon (2003) shows that Livy, especially in the Third Decade, regularly thinks of 'Italy' in terms of the Augustan definition current in his own day, though she also suggests that certain details of his language point to a narrower definition from the period of the Hannibalic War, which have survived into his account from his sources.

[161] Cf. Bonjour (1975: 21–2).

chapter that 'the territory between the Trebia and the Po was <u>then</u> inhabited by Gauls' (21.52.3 *quod inter Trebiam Padumque agri est Galli tum incolebant*), and he has set out in some detail how the inhabitants wavered between Rome and Carthage until Hannibal sent troops to ravage their land (21.52.3–6). Sempronius' statement is an exaggerated misrepresentation, albeit one that fits his articulated policy (in opposition to the suspicious Scipio) of tying the allies as closely to Rome as possible by defending them from attack (21.52.8–9). But even if a misrepresentation, it is one that would resonate with Romans of Livy's day, for whom the land in question was unequivocally Italian, even while they retained the awareness that it was not so at the time about which Livy was writing.

It is true that this still seems to maintain a firm division between 'Italy' (however defined) and Rome,[162] a division that is clear in many other passages also, as for example at 22.13.11, where Italian loyalty to Rome is defined in terms of their submission to superior authority.[163] But elsewhere that division is rather less stable. One striking episode is the attack on Hanno's camp near Beneventum by Q. Fulvius at 25.13.11–14.14. Fulvius decides to abandon the attack after receiving heavy losses, but the soldiers refuse to obey *tam segne imperium* (25.14.3: 'so passive a command'); the prefect of a cohort of Paelignians hurls the military standard over into the camp and then leads his soldiers to break into the camp to recover it (25.14.4–6). The Romans are provoked by rivalry to do the same, with the military tribune Valerius Flaccus *exprobrante Romanis ignaviam qui sociis captorum castrorum concederent decus* (25.14.6: 'upbraiding the Romans with their cowardice in conceding to allies the glory of capturing the camp'). The result is that the camp is captured despite the consul's attempt to retreat, and the Paelignian prefect is rewarded (25.14.13). Here the differentiation between Romans and allies is certainly present, since it generates the rivalry that leads to the victory; but the point at issue is that the Paelignians here are leading the attack in the manner that Romans would be expected to – more so, indeed, than the Roman consul himself had done.[164] Along similar lines one might note Scipio's praise of his

---

[162] Cf. Mahé-Simon (2003: 247).

[163] *iusto et moderato regebantur imperio nec abnuebant, quod unum vinculum fidei est, melioribus parere* ('they were ruled by a just and moderate power and did not refuse—the one bond of loyalty—to obey their superiors'). The sentiment is taken from Polybius 3.90.14, though Livy makes the point about Roman superiority more direct.

[164] The Paelignians and other people of the central Apennines were celebrated in the early imperial period as possessing the qualities of the ideal Roman soldier: that image is reflected by Livy here. See Dench (1995: 68, 105–7). It is perhaps revealing that Valerius Maximus' version of this story (3.2.20), though drawing on Livy, has Flaccus characterize the Paelignians as *Latini* rather than simply *socii*. This is historically inaccurate, but reinforces the sense of their closeness to Rome already implicit in Livy's story.

army at 28.32.6 as *omnes cives aut socios Latinique nominis* ('all citizens or allies and people of Latin status') who had been brought from Italy by his father and uncle: a shared Italian background effectively characterizes their unity; we can compare the way in which the Sibylline oracle at 29.10.5 speaks of 'Italy' under threat from a 'foreign enemy' (*hostis alienigena*), with Rome simply assumed to be part of the former.[165]

Another example is more sinister. Livy's Campanians defect to Carthage and are apparently stereotyped as non-Roman as firmly as any group in the decade—certainly a far from sympathetic portrayal. Yet they are described as being bound up with the Roman polity:[166] their upper classes have inter-married with the Romans (23.4.7) and Varro in his (admittedly misjudged) speech refers to the citizenship rights awarded to them (23.5.9),[167] and encourages them to defend Rome as their 'common homeland' (23.5.10 *communem patriam*); the same point is raised by Decius Magius in his attempt to forestall the defection (23.7.6) and by the Capuan ambassadors in their appeal to the Senate after the recapture of the city (26.33.3; cf. 26.33.10).

Naturally, none of this is to suggest that Livy presents the Capuan associa-tion with Rome as something desirable.[168] On the contrary, not only by their dissolute behaviour, but also by their perfidious willingness to abandon Rome, the Capuans show the extent to which their claims to Romanness are

---

[165] See Urso (2003: 83–5). Note also the way both the elder Scipio (21.41.14) and Fabius (22.39.11) speak of Italy as the Roman homeland (cf. Mahé-Simon 2003: 246).

[166] Cf. Briquel (2002: 147–50).

[167] The technical status granted to them was *civitas sine suffragio*, as Livy had explained originally at 8.14.10–11. It is controversial how far this actually conferred a degree of equality: Sherwin-White (1973: 39–58, 200–14) sees it as offering reciprocal citizenship rights between communities, at least in its origins, whereas Humbert (1978; cf. Oakley 1998: 544–59) argues for it being a fundamentally oppressive move by the Romans against actually or potentially recalcitrant neighbours. As far as Livy is concerned, there are passages that support both readings (he may well himself not have had a clear picture of the institution, which was after all obsolete in his own day), but for our purposes the main point is that he regularly treats the Capuans as having legal equality with Roman citizens in the Hannibalic War narrative (cf. Sherwin-White 1973: 41, Oakley 1998: 549).

[168] Interesting in this context is 23.10.2, where Hannibal promises to subordinate Rome to Capua as 'the capital of Italy' (*caput Italiae*). Cf. 23.11.11, where Mago uses the same phrase in his speech to the Carthaginian senate, and 23.6.1, where Vibius Virrius suggests that an alliance with Hannibal will leave *Italiae imperium* ('rule over Italy') in the hands of the Campanians. The close connection between Rome and Italy is here reaffirmed, but only as a shocking reversal of the proper order, albeit a reversal that certainly is not Livy's invention, since the idea of Capua as a rival to Rome predated him (e.g. Cicero, *Leg. Agr.* 1.24, 2.86, *Phil.* 12.7; Horace, *Epod.* 16.5). See Pobjoy (1996: 124–38), Briquel (2002: 155–9); also Fronda (2007: 96–103), who argues that it was Capua's claim to Italian hegemony which led to her revolt during the Second Punic War. However, it is worth observing that the topos of the 'counter-Rome' was a much broader one, applied to many potential rivals through Roman history and literature: see Ceausescu (1976).

inappropriate and their true nature is far from that expected of a Roman.[169] Indeed, he shows the Capuans themselves as determined to reinforce their separateness from Rome, as at 25.18, where the Campanian Badius dramatically renounces his Roman friend Crispinus and challenges him to a duel. Only in defeat do the Campanians seek to mitigate their punishment by recalling their Roman connections. But the places where they are identified with Rome carry particular resonances. A key part of their punishment by Rome is the permanent removal of any rights to Roman or Latin citizenship (26.34.7); yet those rights were ones that they had possessed before and were later restored to them.[170] When Livy repeatedly refers to the close relationship between Campania, he is recognizably describing something that was even more true in his own day than it had been in Hannibal's, even if it was not for some of the intervening period. He does not present the relationship sympathetically, but that very fact points to something else: a certain anxiety. Livy alludes to the Campanian kinship with Rome more often than he does with any other Italian people in the Third Decade, and yet the Campanians are stereotyped most emphatically with non-Roman characteristics.

The problem emerges not least from Varro's appeal to the shared *patria* of Romans and Capuans. That very word exposes an intrinsic tension in Roman ideas of ethnic identity.[171] Cicero, *Leg.* 2.5 speaks of people having two *patriae*—their hometown, which is their natural *patria*, and Rome as their legal one. But Cicero's statement is a response to a challenge by Atticus as to how it was even possible to have two *patriae*: the suggestion would have sounded paradoxical to most Romans,[172] and in practice epigraphic evidence throughout the imperial period demonstrates that even people with Roman citizenship continued to regard their hometown alone as their *patria*.[173] Accordingly, in Livy the Capuans themselves—even those loyal to Rome— invariably speak of their *patria* as Capua, not as Rome (23.9.10–12, 23.31.11, 25.18.10, 26.13.15, 26.15.14), a natural locution, but one which nevertheless reinforces the sense of their separateness from Rome despite Varro's jarring attempt to assert the contrary, as well as the genuine legal and familial bonds between Capua and Rome which are constantly alluded to.

The strain on Roman–Italian identity appears in the opposite direction also. At 27.9.1–6 objections to conscription are raised among 'Latins and

---

[169] See Mineo (2006: 25–6), who observes the ways in which Livy distances the Capuans from Rome in the Third Decade, but fails to note how this is set against affirmations of their kinship and citizenship.

[170] On the later restoration of Campanian citizenship rights see Frederiksen (1984: 247–50).

[171] On this issue see especially the extended study by Bonjour (1975).

[172] Cf. Bonjour (1975: 83–5), Dyck (2004: 255–60).

[173] See Le Roux (2002).

allies' (27.9.2 *Latinos sociosque*), and twelve of the thirty *coloniae populi Romani* refuse to supply either soldiers or money (27.9.7).[174] Livy gives a full list of them, as well as a list of the eighteen which stood by Rome (27.10.7–8), and which therefore enabled the 'rule of the Roman people' (27.10.9 *imperium populi Romani*) to survive. The interest here, however, is the way in which Livy uses this episode to challenge assumptions about Roman and Italian identity. The consuls appeal to the offending colonists in terms of their Romanness (27.9.10–11):

admonerent non Campanos neque Tarentinos esse eos sed Romanos, inde oriundos, inde in colonias atque in agrum bello captum stirpis augendae causa missos. quae liberi parentibus deberent, ea illos Romanis debere, si ulla pietas, si memoria antiquae patriae esset.

They [sc. the colonies' ambassadors] should remind them [their people] that they were not Campanians or Tarentines, but Romans, from Rome in origin, sent from Rome to colonies and to land captured in war in order to increase the national stock. The things that children owe to their parents, they owed to the Romans, if they had any respect and memory for their homeland of old.

These colonies are apparently uncomplicatedly Roman—certainly from the perspective of Livy's own day the Roman identity of towns like Ardea or Interamna would rarely be questioned; and the consuls not only point to their Roman ancestry, but differentiate them sharply from the inhabitants of Greek Italy and Campania whose loyalty has been so problematic. Yet in practice their behaviour aligns them with other Italians against Rome: the complaints had come from 'allies and Latins', and when they refuse to be persuaded the fear in the Senate is that this will be a precedent not only for other colonies but for the allies as well (27.9.14). In the event the effects are less damaging than was feared, but this was because the other colonies stayed loyal, as Livy celebrates by listing them in full (27.10.7–8); as it later transpires, the allies did as well (29.15.3; cf. 28.45.14–20). In this case, therefore, some—but not all—towns that are 'Roman' have appeared less Roman than those who are merely 'Italian'. At 23.12.16 Hanno had used the failure of Latins and Romans to defect as a demonstration of the resilience of Roman power; here Roman colonies are engaging in an act described by the consuls as 'open defection' (27.9.9 *apertam defectionem*) and seen by the Senate as an effective betrayal of Rome to Hannibal

---

[174] In fact, most, and probably all, of the colonies in question were Latin colonies, not 'colonies of the Roman people'. Livy correctly calls them *colonias Latinas* at 29.15.2, but here and elsewhere (e.g. 8.3.9) treats them as Roman: for him the two appear to be effectively interchangeable, perhaps because even 'Latin' colonies were often substantially populated by people of Roman origin. See Sherwin-White (1973: 36–7, 76–118); cf. Oakley (1997: 341–4).

(27.9.14).[175] The incorporation of non-Roman Italians into Rome, from Livy's perspective, is potentially dangerous; but so too those originally Roman can easily meld into the problematic behaviour of their Italian neighbours.

Hence in Livy, as in Virgil, there is an awareness of the future in which Roman and Italian identities will blur together; but for Livy far more than for Virgil this appears something problematic and dangerous, to be feared as much as celebrated. Livy is certainly not unique in adopting such a perspective: one can find similarly ambivalent play on Roman–Italian relationships in Catullus,[176] Cicero,[177] and many other places also. But as an historian Livy has a more uniform (or perhaps more narrow) focus on the political aspects of the relationship, and one which has a strong contemporary charge in the light of the propagandist use of the idea of a unified Italy (*tota Italia*) in particular by Augustus.[178] Livy certainly does not challenge this in any direct way, but for him it has far more ambivalent and nuanced overtones than one finds in Catullus or Cicero: differences between Rome and Italy are less a source of rich cultural variation within a single broad identity, and more a political phenomenon whose positive and negative elements are surprisingly balanced.

All of these matters that I have been discussing demonstrate that the role Livy ascribes to ethnic identity during the Second Punic War is more difficult and challenging than a superficial reading might imply. But the issue does not end here. If Livy sees the future incorporation of Italians into Roman citizenship as a basis for troubled exploration of the boundaries of identity, what of the future incorporation of non-Italians, whose Romanness is necessarily many times more problematic? Conversely, if the Romans' Carthaginian enemies are not merely part of the 'barbarian' community, what does that imply about their own relationship with Rome?

---

[175] One may compare 28.24.13, where C. Albius, who is a citizen of one of the 'defecting' towns, Cales, is a leader (along with the Umbrian C. Atrius) of the mutiny against Scipio. Scipio in his rebuke to the soldiers repeatedly and scathingly refers to their ethnic background (28.27.5, 28.28.4, 28.29.7)—a point oddly overlooked by Salmon (1986: 82–4), who claims that Livy does not suggest anything derogatory about Albius' and Atrius' ethnicity.

[176] See Dench (2005: 330–42); also more broadly Dench (2005: 152–221).

[177] Connolly (2007: 82–117) gives an especially thought-provoking account of Cicero's representation of the ideal citizen in works like *De Oratore*, *De Re Publica*, and *De Legibus*. She argues that the broad expansion of Roman citizenship in Italy after the Social War undermined definitions of the Roman community in purely ethnic terms, and that Cicero is seeking to craft a natural basis for a citizen community which does not depend on blood relationships, but is instead rooted in the practice of rhetoric.

[178] Esp. *RG* 25. See Syme (1939: 284–8), Dench (2005: 182–6). One should, however, note that (as observed by Polverini 1998) Augustus' division of Italy into eleven regions—albeit probably after Livy wrote these books—followed broadly ethnic lines, and as such reinforced the individuality of the separate Italian peoples even while their unity was insisted upon; cf. also Dench (2005: 200–4).

Let us begin by considering the second of these questions. The central Carthaginian focus in Livy's account of the Second Punic War is of course on Hannibal himself, named as the key figure in the very opening sentence (21.1.1);[179] and he is the source of the crisis that Rome faces in these books. His attributes, as his opening character sketch makes clear, draw on the stereotype of the Carthaginian; however, they appear in a form—a bold strategic insight combined with a reliance on deceit and treachery that is exceptional even by Carthaginian standards—which bring Rome to the verge of defeat. The question for the Romans is what qualities they need to possess in order to recover their position—and, notably, how far the qualities that they need are those already possessed by Hannibal himself. As I discussed in the first section of the chapter, Livy's approach to character typically involves the development of patterns of behaviour across several different individuals. Hannibal becomes a model for the Romans—if a dangerous one—in precisely that way.[180] But because his qualities as an individual are also a refraction of the qualities of a foreign community, looking at Roman commanders' adoption of Hannibalic models simultaneously also raises the issue of Roman adoption of Carthaginian qualities.

The 'Hannibalic model', in this context, is not a clear-cut or an uncontroversially bad one. The Romans, like the Greeks before them, had an ambivalent reaction towards the use of strategic devices in battle rather than a straightforward head-on conflict. In many contexts one finds the two placed in sharp antithesis, and very often with the implication that the use of stratagems is deceptive and morally inferior to fighting directly without them. But there is also a regular sense that deliberation and wisdom in fighting is superior to merely rushing in head-long, and terms like *consilium*, which may be used of deceptive stratagems, tend even in those contexts to have positive rather than negative overtones.[181] Livy

---

[179] Cf. Burck (1962: 60–1) on Livy's unusual emphasis on Hannibal personally in his account of the opening of the war.

[180] It may be revealing that, as noted by Harris (2005: 467–9), Hannibal is the chief exception to Livy's general practice of not assigning *virtus* to foreign enemies in his own voice. Admittedly he does so only after Hannibal's defeat (30.35.10, 31.1.6, 35.43.1), but he and his soldiers are also assumed by their Roman enemies to possess *virtus*, which is hardly more common in the work (22.29.2, 23.45.4—though the latter passage attributes it to them only after they are said to have lost it in Capua).

[181] The key study of this question is Wheeler (1988). Wheeler demonstrates that despite frequent Roman disavowals of trickery, or their association of it with the degenerate present rather than the heroic past, they (unsurprisingly) in fact employed such devices throughout their history. More contentiously he argues that the Latin terms denoting such trickery are largely neutral (though he does concede that some of them acquired negative overtones by the imperial period); some of his evidence is strained, but on *consilium* in particular its positive overtones are clear (Wheeler 1988: 53–6). For the complexities of the *virtus*/trickery antithesis compare Riggsby (2006: 83–105; esp. 101–2). An interesting sidelight on the question is provided by Leigh (2004: 24–56), who argues that the Plautine stereotype of the 'cunning slave' was created on the model of Hannibalic trickery.

throughout his surviving work, like other Roman writers, tends to treat the antithesis in terms of 'traditional Roman courage vs. reprehensible deceit',[182] but this clearly does not preclude him from criticizing headstrong commanders such as those of Books 21 and 22 when they lead to disaster, or from praising the alternative strategy associated especially with Fabius Maximus. The problem for Livy is how to handle Fabius' approach, since it was demonstrably successful and arguably essential, yet it appeared to fall on the wrong side of the traditional antithesis that opposed straightforward Roman fighting to foreign-influenced stratagems. The way Fabius fights looks potentially—and uncomfortably—like Hannibal himself. Livy could of course have covered up that similarity, by drawing on the more positive terminology to describe the Fabian approach, and backing away from any overt comparisons with Hannibal. But in fact, as we shall see, he does the opposite.

This is apparent in the criticisms of Fabius by Minucius at 22.14.4–14 which, however misguided in these particular circumstances, nevertheless raise precisely these issues of traditional and untraditional ways of Roman fighting, when he contrasts Fabius' passivity unfavourably with the aggressive approach taken by the heroes of the past like Camillus, whom he revealingly describes as 'a man and truly Roman' (22.14.11 *vir et vere Romanus*). Granted that we are to see Minucius as wrong (cf. above, 79–81), he strikes a chord in his listeners (22.14.15), and the overlap with the Romans' sense of their own traditional values suggests that he would strike one in Livy's readers as well.[183] When Livy shows Minucius criticizing Fabius by 'ascribing to him vices close to virtues' (22.12.12 *adfingens vicina virtutibus vitia*; cf. 22.14.14), calling him 'sluggish' (*segnis*) instead of 'delaying' (*cunctator*), 'cowardly' (*timidus*) instead of 'cautious' (*cautus*), he draws attention to the difficult position that Fabius occupies in Roman terms, where the qualities that lead to his success are indeed close to those which would traditionally be seen as faults.

Moreover, this is not only a problem raised by Fabius' critics. As soon as Fabius is chosen general Hannibal fears that the Romans have chosen a general equal to himself (22.12.5 *Romani parem Hannibali ducem quaesissent*),[184] a

---

[182] The most extended statement of this is at 42.47.4–9, where the 'older senators and those mindful of ancient custom' say that the use of deception and ambushes are not 'Roman skills' (*Romanas . . . artes*), but belong to Carthaginians or Greeks; but one can find various other examples also, such as 1.53.4 or 26.39.11.

[183] Note Goldsworthy (1996: 246–7) on the way that Roman military culture and techniques tended to favour aggressive tactics; also Lendon (2005: 206–8). Polybius 3.105.9, unlike Livy, loads the debate between Fabius and Minucius more strongly towards the former, treating it not as the conflict of two styles of generalship, but as Fabius' true rational generalship in conflict with the empty aggression of a common soldier.

[184] Cf. also 22.27.3, where Minucius refers ironically to the same point.

theme which recurs, for example, at 24.8, where Fabius, opposing the election of Otacilius, centres his argument on the need for 'a consul equal in generalship to Hannibal' (24.8.2 *Hannibali imperatori parem consulem*; cf. 24.8.6), and the consuls accordingly elected are Marcellus and Fabius himself, the only Roman commanders at that point of whom such a claim could plausibly be made; we have seen Marcellus later making a similar claim for himself at 27.12.7. Equality does not of course necessarily imply parallel methods, but Roman success often depends on using methods that are described in ways that make them appear functionally indistinguishable from Hannibal's own. At 22.15.11–16.4 Fabius manoeuvres Hannibal so that he cannot break through without exposing his army to attack in an inferior position—on which Livy's comment is *nec Hannibalem fefellit suis se artibus peti* (22.16.5: 'nor did it escape Hannibal's notice that he was being attacked with his own methods').[185] Hannibal does not fall into the trap, but instead outmanoeuvres Fabius in his turn;[186] but the principle that a Roman may adopt a Hannibalic approach has been established. I have already referred to the brutal stratagem by which Marcellus and Fabius capture Casilinum at 24.19; but Fabius' recapture of Tarentum at 27.15–16, relying as it does on treachery rather than assault, looks even more uncomfortably similar to the technique that Hannibal used to take the city in the first place at 25.8–11; and if Hannibal, unlike Fabius, directly orders the massacre of the defeated (25.9.16), he at least confines the killings to the Romans and spares the townspeople, whereas Fabius' troops slaughter everyone indiscriminately, including their own allies (27.16.6: cf. above, 202). Of course, Livy did not invent these episodes, but the comparison is one that he explicitly places into the mouth of Hannibal, who on hearing of the fall of Tarentum '*et Romani suum Hannibalem*' inquit '*habent. eadem qua ceperamus arte Tarentum amisimus*' (27.16.10: '"The Romans too have their Hannibal," he said. "We have lost Tarentum by the same method by which we had captured it"'); this moreover provides the context for the ambivalent

---

[185] This theme is prefigured at 21.34.1, where Hannibal is attacked in the Alps *non bello aperto sed suis artibus, fraude et insidiis* ('not in open war, but by his own methods, trickery and traps'). Both passages look back to Sallust, *Jug.* 48.1, where Jugurtha, under threat from Metellus, 'realized that he was being attacked by his own methods' (*se suis artibus temptari animadvortit*). Sallust, too, shows how Romans win through the adoption of foreign methods (compare Koestermann (1971: 189), Levene (1992: 61); also more generally Kraus (1999a) on the way in which the Romans are infected by Jugurthine characteristics), though the fact that Hannibal was a far more direct threat to Rome than Jugurtha was, and the need to defeat him accordingly was much more urgent, makes Livy's account more ambivalent than Sallust's had been.

[186] Livy also soon afterwards shows that the dynamic of imitation goes in both directions: for when faced with Minucius Hannibal is explicitly said to adopt 'Fabian tactics, sitting and delaying' (22.24.10 *artibus Fabii, sedendo et cunctando*).

recognition accorded to Fabius' victory (27.20.9; cf. above, 202).[187] So too other Roman successes are attributed explicitly or implicitly to their adoption of Carthaginian tactics. We have already seen Claudius Nero employing Hannibal's own methods to trap and defeat him (27.41.6; see above, 192–3). Another example is the victory of Marcius in Spain following the deaths of the Scipio brothers (25.39), a victory which involves not merely the attack on the unguarded Carthaginian camps, but also concealing troops to ambush those who might escape—Livy explicitly calls the latter a 'Carthaginian method' (25.39.1 *arte Punica*),[188] and it resembles the similar ambushes that Hannibal had used earlier, for example at the Trebia (21.54.1–4), Trasimene (22.4.3), and against Minucius (22.28.5–8). Another example is 27.28.13, where Hannibal is unable to capitalize on killing Marcellus by sending a false message in his name, because the Salapians see through the trick and turn it back against him: Livy comments that he was 'caught in his own deceit' (*suamet ipse fraude captus*).

But the Roman who most systematically draws on the model of Carthaginians in general and of Hannibal in particular is Scipio. If Livy was presenting him in terms of a straightforward choice between active and passive strategies one would expect him to be Fabius' antithesis, and hence also Hannibal's; but in fact he is no less 'Hannibalic' than Fabius is. His adoption of a Hannibalic approach to war is presented as conscious and deliberate. One key moment is his debate with Fabius at 28.40–44, where a central argument that he uses in favour of his plan to invade Africa is that it is the strategy that had successfully been employed by Hannibal himself, to fight on the enemy's territory rather than one's own (28.44.2–4; cf. 28.18.11); one may compare his prayer at 29.27.4, where he brings out the symmetry in another way, asking to be allowed to do to Carthage what Carthage sought to do to Rome. But Scipio's Hannibal-like behaviour extends beyond broad strategy, and beyond the imitation of Hannibal's dynamism. It had already appeared, for example, shortly before, when he completed the conquest of Spain (28.33.2–6), where it looks somewhat more problematic:

in eam vallem Scipio cum pecora rapta pleraque ex ipsorum hostium agris propelli ad inritandam feritatem barbarorum iussisset, velites subsidio misit, a quibus ubi per procursationem commissa pugna esset Laelium cum equitatu impetum ex occulto facere iubet. mons opportune prominens equitum insidias texit; nec ulla mora pugnae

---

[187] On the way the recapture of Tarentum mirrors Hannibal originally taking it see Chlup (2004: 91–4).

[188] In this context it is also worth noting 25.38.21, where Marcius argues that the Romans can obtain victory by attacking their opponents while divided, exactly as the Carthaginians had done to them, and comments *alia belli gerendi via nulla est* ('there is no other way of waging war').

facta est ... ancepsque pedestre certamen erat ni equites supervenissent. neque ex adverso tantum inlati obvios obtrivere, sed circumvecti etiam quidam per infima clivi ab tergo se ut plerosque intercluderent obiecerunt.

Scipio ordered cattle plundered (mostly from the enemy's own fields) to be driven into that valley to provoke the barbarians' ferocity. He sent light-armed infantry in support, and ordered Laelius, when they had started the battle by rushing forward, to attack with his cavalry from hiding. A convenient spur of a mountain concealed the trap the cavalry set, and battle began without delay ... The infantry battle was equally matched—had not the cavalry appeared. They not only attacked and crushed the enemy head-on, but also some rode around the bottom of the slope and engaged them in the rear so as to cut most of them off.

This is based on Polybius 11.32.2–4—but with some striking changes:

τῇ δ' ἑξῆς εἰς τὸν προειρημένον αὐλῶνα προσέβαλέ τινα θρέμματα τῶν παρεπομένων τῷ στρατοπέδῳ, συντάξας ἑτοίμους ἔχειν τοὺς ἱππεῖς τῷ Γαΐῳ, τοὺς δὲ γροσφομάχους ἐπέταξε τῶν χιλιάρχων τισὶ παρασκευάζειν. ταχὺ δὲ τῶν Ἰβήρων ἐπιπεσόντων ἐπὶ τὰ θρέμματ' ἐξαφῆκε τῶν γροσφομάχων τινάς ... τοῦ δὲ καιροῦ παραδιδόντος εὐλόγους ἀφορμὰς πρὸς ἐπίθεσιν, ἔχων ὁ Γάιος ἑτοίμους τοὺς ἱππεῖς κατὰ τὸ συνταχθὲν ἐπεβάλετο τοῖς ἀκροβολιζομένοις, ἀποτεμόμενος ἀπὸ τῆς παρωρείας, ὥστε τοὺς πλείους αὐτῶν κατὰ τὸν αὐλῶνα σκεδασθέντας ὑπὸ τῶν ἱππέων διαφθαρῆναι.

On the next day he sent some of the cattle that followed the army into the aforementioned valley, ordering Laelius to keep the cavalry ready, and instructed some of the tribunes to prepare the skirmishers. Soon the Spaniards fell on the cattle, and he dispatched some of the skirmishers against them ... The occasion now presented a good opportunity for an attack; Laelius had been holding the cavalry ready as ordered, and charged the skirmishers, cutting them off from the hillside, so that most of them were scattered through the valley and were killed by the cavalry.

In Polybius there is no explicit indication that Laelius' troops are concealed in an ambush—there is certainly no equivalent of the loaded word *insidias*,[189] or of Livy's specific note about the terrain that made such concealment possible. And likewise, while Livy's comment about Laelius going around the bottom of the hill to cut the Spaniards off draws on Polybius' wording (ἀποτεμόμενος ἀπὸ τῆς παρωρείας), nothing in Polybius suggests that sort of flanking movement—for him the cavalry act as one. But both are familiar tactical ploys in Livy—familiar as ploys used regularly by Hannibal to trap and defeat the Romans.[190] Similarly, in the battle on the following day (28.33.7–17;

---

[189] On the significance of the word see Wheeler (1988: 84-7). Burck (1962: 136-7, 148), discussing Scipio's campaigns earlier in Book 28 and at the end of Book 29, notes the similarity to Hannibal's tactics, but claims that Livy never uses the words *dolus, fraus,* or *insidiae* in this context, overlooking that the last is indeed used of Scipio here.

[190] It is remarkably similar to the device at Trasimene, for example, note 22.4.2–4.

compare Polybius 11.32.5–33.6) Scipio once again has Laelius take his cavalry around to engage the enemy from the rear (28.33.11). In this case Polybius 11.33.2 has a similar stratagem, but Livy emphasizes that this is specifically designed for trickery, since Scipio orders Laelius to go by 'the most concealed route possible' (*quam occultissimo itinere*) and accordingly states that the Roman cavalry was not noticed by the Spaniards until they appeared in their rear (28.33.13): neither of these points is in Polybius. Scipio continues to pursue such tactics in his invasion of Africa: at 29.34 he defeats Hanno by using a small cavalry detachment to provoke him and draw him out, while leaving the main body of his army concealed by the hills in order to attack the enemy with fresh troops when they are tired by pursuing the detachment: here once again he is replicating tactics used by Hannibal at the Trebia in Book 21.

Or one might mention the attack on the Numidian and Carthaginian camps at 30.3–6. As Livy presents it, Scipio engages in negotiations over a peace treaty which he has no intention of concluding, merely to give an opportunity for his men to spy out the enemy camp; when the negotiations are eventually broken off, Scipio first distracts the enemy with a feint against Utica, and then attacks and burns their camps at night. In this case, though the episode is closely based on Polybius 14.1–5, Livy 'corrects' Polybius' account by making some changes which together have the effect of sparing Scipio's character. Scipio does not make his preparations against Utica until after he has formally broken off negotiations (30.4.10–11; contrast Polybius 14.2.1–4), and while his negotiating was merely a ploy that he never intended to act on (30.3.7), he is able to withdraw with clear conscience (30.4.10 *libera fide*) when the Carthaginians attempt to insert unfair conditions into the proposed treaty (30.4.8; contrast Polybius 14.2.10). But even there, although Scipio has acted formally correctly, Livy makes it clear that it is only chance that has enabled him to do so,[191] and his plan from the start was to win through deceptive stratagems rather than open battle:[192] there is a remarkably close overlap with the Carthaginian behaviour at 30.16.14–15, where they deliberately use the interlude provided by peace negotiations to bring Hannibal back to Africa (see below, 326–31). It is little surprise that Livy removes the high praise that Polybius awards Scipio for the entire episode: ἦ καὶ πολλῶν καὶ καλῶν διειργασμένων Σκιπίωνι κάλλιστον εἶναί μοι δοκεῖ τοῦτο τοὔργον καὶ παραβολώτατον τῶν ἐκείνῳ πεπραγμένων (14.5.15: 'Therefore of the many fine things accomplished by Scipio this seems to me the finest and

---

[191] Note especially 30.4.8 *quae peropportune cupienti tollere indutias Scipioni causam praebuere* ('Scipio desired to end the truce, and this very opportunely provided him with a reason').

[192] Note 30.4.3, where Scipio instructs his spies to find out *nocte an interdiu opportuniores insidianti essent* ('whether they could more suitably be ambushed by night or day').

boldest that he did').[193] Livy's Scipio may not engage with treachery in the manner that Polybius has him do, but he is verging closer to it than might be expected in a Roman commander.

But Scipio follows a Hannibalic model in broader and in some respects even less positive ways. Their entire careers in a sense have moved in parallel, as is stated explicitly by Hannibal in his speech at 30.30.12–15, as part of his argument to warn Scipio not to rely too confidently on his current success:

quod ego fui ad Trasumennum, ad Cannas, id tu hodie es. vixdum militari aetate imperio accepto, omnia audacissime incipientem nusquam fefellit fortuna. patris et patrui persecutus mortem, ex calamitate vestrae domus decus insigne virtutis pietatisque eximiae cepisti. amissas Hispanias reciperasti, quattuor inde Punicis exercitibus pulsis; consul creatus, cum ceteris ad tutandam Italiam parum animi esset, transgressus in Africam, duobus hic exercitibus caesis, binis eadem hora captis simul incensisque castris, Syphace potentissimo rege capto, tot urbibus regni eius, tot nostri imperii ereptis, me sextum decimum iam annum haerentem in possessione Italiae detraxisti. potest victoriam malle quam pacem animus. novi spiritus magnos magis quam utiles; et mihi talis aliquando fortuna adfulsit.

What I was at Trasimene and Cannae, you are today. I/you[194] received command when I/you had barely reached the military age, I/you entered into everything most boldly and fortune nowhere deceived me/you. You avenged the death of your father and uncle and from the disaster of your house received the glorious distinction of outstanding virtue and piety. You recovered Spain after its loss and drove four Carthaginian armies from there; you were elected consul, and when no one else had heart enough to defend Italy, you crossed to Africa, slaughtered here two armies, captured and burned two camps at once in the same hour, captured Syphax, that most powerful king, seized so many cities of his kingdom and so many of our empire, and dragged away me, who was now for the sixteenth year clinging to the possession of Italy. A heart may prefer victory to peace. I know great spirits better than expedient ones: and such fortune once shone on me too.

The parallels implied by this passage have recently been explored by Andreola Rossi;[195] she shows numerous respects, going well beyond the points Hannibal lists here, in which Livy presents events of Scipio's life mirroring those of Hannibal. However, the main thrust of Rossi's argument is that Scipio,

---

[193] Eckstein (1995: 86–7) argues that Polybius' praise for Scipio here relates only to the action itself, and says nothing about his view of the deception leading up to it. This, however, seems to assume a finer distinction than Polybius' text justifies; in any case, for our purposes the chief point to note is that even if Polybius intended such a distinction, Livy is unlikely to have read the sentence so narrowly.

[194] The Latin leaves it for the moment undetermined whether this refers to Scipio or Hannibal (*contra* W-M *ad loc.*, who believe it refers to Scipio alone): this accentuates the point that their careers have proceeded in parallel.

[195] Rossi (2004).

though mirroring Hannibal, does so as his antithesis, and things that Hannibal gets wrong Scipio gets right—though she also argues that Hannibal represents the decline which Rome will herself undergo in the future. This underplays the extent to which Scipio himself is already presented by Livy as a problematic figure.[196] For example, Rossi contrasts the corruption of Hannibal's troops at Capua in Book 23 with the allegations of excessive Hellenization levelled against Scipio and his troops at Syracuse in Book 29 (especially 29.19.11–12), but sees this resolved entirely in Scipio's favour.[197] In fact Livy presents it less straightforwardly. He has Scipio clearing himself primarily through a specious show (29.22.1–6), and the implication is that he may genuinely have 'Hellenized' in this way,[198] something potentially suspect in Roman eyes even if its consequences are less immediate and less disastrous than what happened to Hannibal at Capua. Even worse, the allegations are bound up with the complaints by the Locrians over their treatment by Scipio's lieutenant Pleminius (29.17–18), behaviour for which Scipio may not be directly responsible, but which he effectively condoned (cf. 29.9.8–12, 29.19.1–2). This may not be as bad as the worst of Hannibal's behaviour,[199] but it hardly constitutes a marked antithesis with it either. Because the issue of corruption has been highlighted, as I said, Hannibal at Capua is the most natural parallel; yet as far as his treatment of the Capuans goes, the comparison is if anything in his favour. He had angrily demanded the surrender and punishment of the pro-Roman Decius Magius (23.10.1–10; cf. 23.7.7–8) contrary to the agreement that he had concluded with the Capuans at 23.7.1; but there is nothing there to match the unjustified brutality inflicted on the Locrians *en masse*.

So when Livy presents the Carthaginians as being in certain senses more Roman than 'barbarian', he does so in the context of a war in which victory comes to Rome, but only at a severe price. The Carthaginians are implicitly a sort of counter-Rome, as they are in the *Aeneid* or in Sallust: the empire that rivals Rome for world dominion. Accordingly Livy, from the very first lines of

---

[196] On Livy's ambivalent treatment of Scipio, not least over his behaviour in Syracuse and Locri, see Scott (1986: 174–8), Levene (1993: 72–4, 83–4), Johner (1996: 34–7). Rossi does recognize one or two points where Livy presents Scipio in a less flattering light (Rossi 2004: 378–80), but fails to appreciate how broadly this extends.

[197] Rossi (2004: 372–3); a similar conclusion is reached at greater length by Burck (1969).

[198] Note especially 29.20.1, where the allegations against Scipio are not said to be false, but are *partim vera partim mixta eoque similia veris* ('partly true, partly mixed and thus similar to truth')—and Livy noticeably declines to tell the reader which are which.

[199] Note e.g. 26.38.3, where Livy characterizes Hannibal's behaviour as *praeceps in avaritiam et crudelitatem animus ad spolianda quae tueri nequibat, ut vastata hosti relinquerentur, inclinavit* ('a mind plunging into avarice and cruelty inclined him to despoil what he could not preserve, so that things should be left devastated for the enemy').

the decade, places the two states in parallel with one another (21.1.2, 23.33.1, 28.18.1, 29.17.6, 30.13.3, and especially 30.32.1–4).²⁰⁰ It is interesting to note 28.19.6–7, where Scipio exhorts his troops to fight with more hostility against the Spaniards than against the Carthaginians—with the Carthaginians they were fighting *sine ira de imperio et gloria* ('without anger for empire and glory'), whereas the Spaniards are to be punished for *perfidia* and *crudelitas*— in other contexts these might be seen as typically Carthaginian traits. At such times the Carthaginians are, like the Romans, differentiated from their actual or potential 'barbarian' subjects; and similarly are just enough like the Romans to make them a plausible model for Romans to follow. Yet Carthaginians are also sometimes characterized via a stereotype that is antithetical to the self-image of Rome, such that following a Carthaginian model of behaviour appears uncomfortable even if necessary. Livy is not doing anything as crude as showing the Romans as uncomplicatedly behaving in Carthaginian ways—the boundaries are more or less maintained—but Scipio, as also other Romans before him, comes extremely close to the dividing line and at times appears to be crossing it.

Non-Italians offer to Rome another challenge than simply the possibility that Romans might have to (or choose to) behave like them. One recurring issue in Livy's account of the Carthaginian army is its composition out of different ethnicities. This first emerges as Hannibal makes arrangements for his invasion of Italy at 21.21.9–22.4: he deliberately decides to garrison Spain with African troops and Africa with Spanish, but both groups are far from homogeneous. The Spaniards in Africa include Balearics and cavalry *mixtos ex multis gentibus* (21.21.12: 'mixed from many nations'); the troops in Spain include Ligurians, Balearics, Numidians, Moors, the Spanish tribe of the Ilergetes, and the Libyphoenices, 'a Carthaginian race mixed with Africans' (21.22.3 *mixtum Punicum Afris genus*). As for the troops Hannibal is leading into Italy, these include Spaniards (21.21.2), but Livy characterizes them more generally as 'the auxiliaries of all nations' (21.21.9 *omnium gentium auxilia*). Much of this derives from Polybius 3.33.5–16, but Polybius has no equivalent of the *multis gentibus* (he simply lists four specific Spanish tribes at that point—3.33.9) or the *omnium gentium*; nor does he explicitly characterize

²⁰⁰ Cf. Rüger (1965: 72–3). Carthage and Rome mirror each other in certain other ways too; for example Carthage is governed by a senate which appears to operate not unlike the Roman one, and at 29.34.2 Hasdrubal appeals to Syphax in the name of *universa Africa* rather as Romans had earlier appealed to Italians on behalf of Italy (e.g. 24.47.5). It is true that Livy is far from unusual among ancient (and indeed modern) writers in modelling his picture of Carthage on Rome (see Crouzet 2003). But he goes beyond other writers in his willingness to extend that into comparisons which are not uniformly to Carthage's detriment.

the Libyphoenices as being of mixed race (3.33.15).[201] Livy's account makes the Carthaginians appear all the more more heterogeneous. This theme then reappears before Cannae, where the disaffection among Hannibal's troops is explained in terms of their being *mixtos ex conluvione omnium gentium* (22.43.2: 'mixed from the sewage of all nations'), which leads them to complain about the lack of pay and food (22.43.3); at the battle itself Livy (22.46.4-6) reproduces closely Polybius' detailed account of the appearance of the different troops on Hannibal's side (3.114.1–4). At 26.20.9 the Carthaginian fleet before Tarentum is handicapped through being composed of 'a mixed crowd of sailors of every race of mankind' (*turba navali mixta ex omni genere hominum*: cf. below, 303). Later Scipio in arguing for the likely success of his plan to invade Africa refers to the Carthaginians, unlike the Romans, as having no citizen army, but only African and Numidian mercenaries of dubious reliability (28.44.5); the Carthaginians themselves make the same point at 29.3.11–13.

But the two most important places where the mixed composition of the Carthaginian armies is discussed are, first, the 'second character-sketch' of Hannibal at 28.12.1–9, and second at the battle of Zama.

Let us begin with the first of these (28.12.2–5):

ac nescio an mirabilior adversis quam secundis rebus fuerit, quippe qui, cum in hostium terra per annos tredecim, tam procul ab domo, varia fortuna bellum gereret, exercitu non suo civili sed mixto ex conluvione omnium gentium, quibus non lex, non mos, non lingua communis, alius habitus, alia vestis, alia arma, alii ritus, alia sacra, alii prope di essent, ita quodam uno vinculo copulaverit eos ut nulla nec inter ipsos nec adversus ducem seditio exstiterit, cum et pecunia saepe in stipendium et commeatus in hostium agro deesset, quorum inopia priore Punico bello multa infanda inter duces militesque commissa fuerant.

And I think he may have been more remarkable in failure than in success; he was waging war in enemy territory for thirteen years, so far from home and with varying success, with an army composed not of his fellow-citizens but from the mixed sewage of all nations, who did not have law, custom, language in common, different manner, different clothing, different weapons, different rituals, different rites, virtually different gods. Yet he united them with a single bond such that there was no disaffection among themselves or against their general, although both money for pay and supplies on enemy soil were often unavailable, the lack of which had led to many unspeakable atrocities among generals and soldiers in the First Punic War.

---

[201] Livy also explicitly characterizes the Ilergetes as Spanish, which reinforces the sense of mixture (21.22.3). Polybius simply mentions them by name, and it is not even clear that he is referring to the Spanish tribe rather than an African tribe with a similar name (cf. Walbank 1957: 363–4), though if the latter is what Polybius intended Livy admittedly is unlikely to have known it.

This is partly based on Polybius 11.19.3–5:

συνεχῶς Ἀννίβας ἑκκαίδεκα πολεμήσας ἔτη ʿ Ρωμαίοις κατὰ τὴνἸταλίαν οὐδέποτε
διέλυσε τὰς δυνάμεις ἐκ τῶν ὑπαίθρων, ἀλλὰ συνέχων ὑφʾ αὑτόν, ὥσπερ ἀγαθὸς
κυβερνήτης, ἀστασίαστα διετήρησε τοσαῦτα πλήθη καὶ πρὸς αὑτὸν καὶ πρὸς ἄλληλα,
καίπερ οὐχ οἷον ὁμοεθνέσιν, ἀλλʾ οὐδʾ ὁμοφύλοις χρησάμενος στρατοπέδοις. εἶχε γὰρ
Λίβυας, ʾ ἼβηραςΛιγυστίνους, Κελτούς, Φοίνικας, Ἰταλούς, ʿ Ἕλληναςοἷς οὐ νόμος, οὐκ
ἔθος, οὐ λόγος, οὐχ ἕτερον οὐδὲν ἦν κοινὸν ἐκ φύσεως πρὸς ἀλλήλους. ἀλλʾ ὅμως ἡ τοῦ
προεστῶτος ἀγχίνοια τὰς τηλικαύτας καὶ τοιαύτας διαφορὰς ἑνὸς ἐποίει προστάγματος
ἀκούειν καὶ μιᾷ πείθεσθαι γνώμῃ, καίπερ οὐχ ἁπλῆς οὔσης τῆς περιστάσεως, ἀλλὰ καὶ
ποικίλης, καὶ πολλάκις μὲν αὐτοῖς λαμπρᾶς ἐπιπνεούσης τῆς τύχης, ποτὲ δὲ τοὐναντίον.

Hannibal warred constantly with the Romans in Italy for sixteen years, but never dissolved his forces from the field, but kept them under him, like a good helmsman, and maintained that vast army free from sedition both towards himself and towards each other, although they were organized in units not only not of single nations, but not even single races. For he had Libyans, Spaniards, Ligurians, Celts, Phoenicians, Italians, and Greeks, who did not have law, custom, language, or anything else naturally in common with each other. But nevertheless the intelligence of the commander made such vastly different groups listen to one command and obey one judgement, although the circumstances were not straightforward but complex, and often fortune blew brightly on them, but sometimes the opposite.

Livy draws a number of themes in this passage quite closely from Polybius, indeed translating whole phrases directly from the Greek. But he also refocuses the emphasis. He increases the sense of diversity by greatly lengthening the number of points on which the nations in Hannibal's army differ. By contrasting the 'sewage of all nations' with a citizen army he implicitly makes the same contrast as Scipio later makes explicitly: between the mercenary troops serving the Carthaginians and the homogeneous army of Rome, not a comparison which seems to matter to Polybius here.[202] And he removes the statement that they 'heard a single command': this may seem a minor issue, but as we shall see shortly, has surprisingly serious ramifications.

There is a subtler point here as well. Livy begins by suggesting that Hannibal may have been 'more remarkable in failure than success'; the broad idea is from Polybius, but while Polybius says that Hannibal kept his troops together through thick and thin, he does not indicate that times of

---

[202] See, however, Polybius 6.52.3–9 for a suggestion that the Carthaginians' reliance on mercenaries was a problem for them, albeit for a different reason from Livy's: that people fighting for their own country have better morale (cf. also 1.67 for Polybius' assessment of the advantages and disadvantages of mercenary troops at times of mutiny). On Polybius' broadly negative characterization of mercenaries see Eckstein (1995: 125–9).

adversity were specifically what showed Hannibal to his best advantage.[203]
But that comment by Livy is not a casual one, but very carefully worded,
because his narrative has shown it as true in a very strict sense. The phrase
mixto ex conluvione omnium gentium alludes to an earlier point in his own
narrative—22.43.2 (quoted above), where almost exactly the same phrase
appeared. But there Hannibal's troops were doing exactly what Livy here
claims they did not: they are disaffected, indeed disaffected over the very
issues of pay and supplies cited in this passage. If we put these two passages
together—and the close parallel in wording invites us to put them together—
the implication is that it is *only* in the sort of adversity that Hannibal now
faces in Book 28 that he is able to maintain his disparate troops' loyalty. In the
run of success in the opening books they are far more vulnerable to temporary
setbacks such as the ones they faced before Cannae. The idea that success
breeds misbehaviour is of course a Roman commonplace,[204] but it is particularly pointed in this context, because (as I shall shortly discuss) Hannibal's
army is in some very important respects a model for Rome as a whole.

The mixed ethnic composition of Hannibal's army plays an even more
dramatic and significant role at Zama. In Chapter 2 (above, 88–90) I discussed
the way in which both Polybius 15.12.8–9 and Livy 30.34.1–2, both drawing
on the *Iliad*, contrast the dissonant noise of the Carthaginian army with the
unified shouts of the Romans. In Polybius this appears to be little more than
an interesting ethnographic observation, but Livy turns it into a significant
military factor,[205] prefacing his description with the words *ad hoc dictu
parva sed magna eadem in re gerenda momenta* (30.34.1: 'in addition to this
were influences small to relate, but great in the battle itself'): Livy does not
indicate directly how the shouting influences the battle, but the implication is
that it is connected with the inability of the Carthaginian front line to hold
the Roman advance shortly afterwards (30.34.3). The idea that apparently
minor circumstances can have major consequences is a recurrent one in
Livy's narrative of the Hannibalic War, as I shall be discussing more fully in
Chapters 4 and 5: in the specific case here he clearly shows the lack of a

[203] Moreover, the phrase seems to refer back to Hiero's description of the Romans (22.37.3 *magnitudinem populi Romani admirabiliorem prope adversis rebus quam secundis esse*—'the greatness of the Roman people was almost more admirable in failure than success'): a further indication that Hannibal's and Rome's qualities and fates mirror one another.

[204] It is indeed encountered in a quite similar context later in the book, where in their *otium* after the Roman victory in Spain the troops are disaffected and mutiny against Scipio—and here too the lack of pay and plunder is a key issue (28.24.6–8). See below, 349–53.

[205] Cf. Rossi (2004: 373–4). D'Huys (1990: 283–4) suggests that Livy's adaptation shows that he read Polybius too as giving an implicit military significance to the scene, but this seems to give Livy too little credit for being able to provide his own interpretations of events even against the grain of his sources.

congruens clamor as one respect in which fighting with an army of mixed nationalities is a serious military handicap.

Nor is this the only respect in which Livy makes a significantly different use of the ethnic composition of Hannibal's army from that of Polybius. After the battle Polybius admires the skill with which Hannibal organized his battle order; Livy has a similar eulogy at the same point, but shows Hannibal doing something substantially different, and so changes the entire nature of the battle. Polybius first (15.16.2–6):

τὸ μὲν γὰρ τῶν ἐλεφάντων πλῆθος ἐξ αὐτῆς παρεσκευάσατο καὶ τότε προεβάλετο χάριν τοῦ συνταράξαι καὶ διασπάσαι τὰς τάξεις τῶν ὑπεναντίων· τοὺς δὲ μισθοφόρους προέταξε καὶ τοὺς Καρχηδονίους ἔθηκε μετὰ τούτους ἕνεκα τοῦ προεκλῦσαι μὲν τῷ κόπῳ τὰ σώματα τῶν πολεμίων, ἀχρειῶσαι δὲ τὰς ἀκμὰς τῶν ὅπλων διὰ τὸ πλῆθος τῶν φονευομένων, ἀναγκάσαι δὲ τοὺς Καρχηδονίους μέσους ὄντας μένειν καὶ μάχεσθαι κατὰ τὸν ποιητὴν

> ὄφρα καὶ οὐκ ἐθέλων τις ἀναγκαίῃ πολεμίζοι.

τοὺς δὲ μαχιμωτάτους καὶ στασιμωτάτους τῶν ἀνδρῶν ἐν ἀποστάσει παρενέβαλε χάριν τοῦ προορωμένους ἐκ πολλοῦ τὸ συμβαῖνον καὶ διαμένοντας ἀκεραίους τοῖς τε σώμασι καὶ ταῖς ψυχαῖς σὺν καιρῷ χρήσασθαι ταῖς σφετέραις ἀρεταῖς. εἰ δὲ πάντα τὰ δυνατὰ ποιήσας πρὸς τὸ νικᾶν ἐσφάλη τὸν πρὸ τούτου χρόνον ἀήττητος ὤν, συγγνώμην δοτέον· ἔστι μὲν γὰρ ὅτε καὶ ταὐτόματον ἀντέπραξε ταῖς ἐπιβολαῖς τῶν ἀγαθῶν ἀνδρῶν, ἔστι δ᾽ ὅτε πάλιν κατὰ τὴν παροιμίαν 'ἐσθλὸς ἐὼν ἄλλου κρείττονος ἀντέτυχεν'.

He at once prepared the mass of elephants and then put them in front in order to confuse and break apart the ranks of their opponents. He then put the mercenaries in front, and placed the Carthaginians behind them in order to weaken the enemies' bodies by the fighting, and to blunt the points of their weapons by the mass of people being slaughtered, and to force the Carthaginians to remain and fight in the middle, as the poet says:

> 'So that even the unwilling man may make war through necessity'.

The most warlike and steadfast of the men he drew up a distance in the rear in order that they should anticipate from afar what happened and their bodies and spirits should remain fresh, and then should use their courage at the appropriate moment. If someone previously undefeated did everything possible to win, but lost, he should be pardoned: sometimes bad luck works against the plans of good men, and also sometimes, as the proverb says, 'a good man encounters another better one'.

Now Livy's version (30.35.5–9):

confessione etiam Scipionis omniumque peritorum militiae illam laudem adeptus, singulari arte aciem eo die instruxisse; elephantos in prima fronte, quorum fortuitus impetus atque intolerabilis vis signa sequi et servare ordines, in quo plurimum spei ponerent, Romanos prohiberent; deinde auxiliares ante Carthaginiensium aciem, ne homines mixti ex conluvione omnium gentium, quos non fides teneret sed merces, liberum receptum fugae haberent, simul ut primum ardorem atque impetum hostium excipientes fatigarent, ac si nihil aliud volneribus suis ferrum hostile hebetarent; tum, ubi omnis spes esset, milites Carthaginienses Afrosque, ut omnibus rebus aliis pares, eo quod integri cum fessis ac sauciis pugnarent superiores essent; Italicos incertos socii an hostes essent, in postremam aciem summotos, intervallo quoque diremptos.

Also, Scipio and everyone with military expertise admit that Hannibal is to be praised for the singular skill with which he drew up the battle line on that day. He placed the elephants in the very front, so that their haphazard attack and unendurable violence should prevent the Romans from following their standards and keeping their ranks, in which they placed the greatest hope. Then he put the auxiliaries in front of the Carthaginian line so that men mixed from the dregs of all nations, held by payment not by loyalty, should not have a free line of flight, and also to take the enemy's initial ardour and force and weary it and, if nothing else, to blunt the enemy's blades with their wounds. Then he put the Carthaginian and African soldiers in whom he had all his hope; they were equal to the Romans in all other respects, and could then be superior by fighting fresh against the tired and wounded. As for the Italians, it was unclear whether they were allies or enemies, so he removed them to the final line, also separated by a gap from the other troops.

Once again we have a version of that loaded phrase—*mixti ex conluvione omnium gentium*. Livy corrects Polybius via an allusion back to his own version of Hannibal's control of his army in Book 28, and thence to the disaffection of the soldiers before Cannae. For Polybius it was the Carthaginians themselves who were the weak point and who needed to be held in place; for Livy the ethnically mixed mercenaries are placed in the front because they are fickle and liable to flee: the strongest troops are the Carthaginians and Africans in the centre. This sense that the Carthaginians themselves are the best troops, and thus the ones most closely analogous to the Romans themselves, is reinforced by Livy's final transformation of Polybius' battle order, according to which the troops left in the rear are there because of their potential disloyalty, rather than because of their superior force. Livy's suggestion that one would place potential traitors in the rear is an unlikely piece of military strategy and is accordingly often mocked;[206] but it has the effect of focusing attention on the

---

[206] So De Sanctis (1968: 636: 'ridicola spiegazione'), Walsh (1961: 157–8). Livy's account may derive partly from a misinterpretation of Polybius: when Polybius 15.11.2 describes the last line of troops as τοὺς ἐξ Ἰταλίας ἥκοντας μεθ' αὑτοῦ ('those who had come from Italy with him'), he presumably means Hannibal's veteran army who served with him in Italy, not (as Livy assumes) the Italian allies he brought back; Appian, *Pun.* 40 makes the same mistake (see Walbank 1967: 458). But whereas Appian nevertheless accepts Polybius' characterization of these as his best troops (arguing that the Italians would fight the best for fear of being punished as traitors on defeat), Livy dramatically challenges Polybius' judgement, and instead switches his praise to the Carthaginians themselves, about whose fighting qualities Polybius was distinctly cool.

Carthaginian centre as the core troops whom the Romans had to beat. This is also apparent from Livy's description of the battle itself, where the Carthaginian centre is described as follows (30.34.12–13):

ad veros hostes perventum erat, et armorum genere et usu militiae et fama rerum gestarum et magnitudine vel spei vel periculi pares. sed et numero superior Romanus erat et animo, quod iam equites, iam elephantos fuderat, iam prima acie pulsa in secundam pugnabat.

They had reached the true enemy, equal both in type of weapons and military experience and fame of their deeds and greatness whether of hope or of danger. But the Romans were superior in numbers, as well as in spirit from having routed now the cavalry, now the elephants, and from now fighting against the second Carthaginian rank, the front rank having been driven back.

Livy turns the battle into a fundamental struggle between two existential enemies;[207] here, as we saw before, the Carthaginians themselves are surprisingly close to the Romans. He is deriving his version from Polybius, who says ὄντων δὲ καὶ τῷ πλήθει καὶ τοῖς φρονήμασι καὶ ταῖς ἀρεταῖς καὶ τοῖς καθοπλισμοῖς παραπλησίων ἀμφοτέρων (15.14.6: 'both sides being nearly equal in number and spirit and courage and weaponry'). But he has changed two of Polybius' points of near-parity (number and spirit) into areas where the Romans are superior. For Polybius the battle is still to some extent in the balance, until it is swayed by the intervention of Masinissa and Laelius (15.14.7). For Livy Roman superiority is already assured by the earlier events of the battle, which mean that the Carthaginians are now fighting at a disadvantage.

The 'mixed multitude' contributes to the Carthaginian defeat in Livy in a further, perhaps even more fundamental way. At the very start of the battle, the Carthaginian elephants turn on their own side: as we have just seen, Livy regards this as one of the factors that mean that the Carthaginians are subsequently unable to match the Romans in the fight. This is Polybius' version (15.12.1–2):

ἐπειδὴ δ' ἑκατέροις ἦν εὐτρεπῆ τὰ πρὸς τὸν κίνδυνον, πάλαι τῶν Νομαδικῶν ἱππέων πρὸς ἀλλήλους ἀκροβολιζομένων, τότε παρήγγειλε τοῖς ἐπὶ τῶν ἐλεφάντων Ἀννίβας ποιεῖσθαι τὴν ἔφοδον ἐπὶ τοὺς ὑπεναντίους. ἅμα δὲ τῷ πανταχόθεν τὰς σάλπιγγας καὶ τὰς βυκάνας ἀναβοῆσαι τινὰ μὲν διαταραχθέντα τῶν θηρίων ἐξ αὐτῆς ὥρμησε παλίσσυτα κατὰ τῶν βεβοηθηκότων τοῖς Καρχηδονίοις Νομάδων.

When everything on both sides was ready for the fight, the Numidian cavalry had for some time been skirmishing, and then Hannibal ordered the commanders of the

---

[207] In this, moreover, he contradicts what the Carthaginians said earlier: that their own people were 'unwarlike' (29.3.13 *imbellem*); but it fits the broader indications he has given since the opening lines of the decade of Carthaginian and Roman equality (cf. above, 235–6).

elephants to charge the enemy. At the same time some of the beasts were confused by the trumpets and bugles ringing out on all sides and immediately charged backwards against the Numidians who had come to help the Carthaginians.

Livy, however, once again transforms the whole dynamic of the narrative (30.33.8–13):

varia adhortatio erat in exercitu inter tot homines quibus non lingua, non mos, non lex, non arma, non vestitus habitusque, non causa militandi eadem esset…cum maxime haec imperator apud Carthaginienses, duces suarum gentium inter populares, pleraque per interpretes inter immixtos alienigenis agerent, tubae cornuaque ab Romanis cecinerunt, tantusque clamor ortus ut elephanti in suos, sinistrum maxime cornu, verterentur, Mauros ac Numidas.

There was a variety of encouraging speeches in Hannibal's army, among so many men who shared neither language nor custom nor law nor weapons nor costume and manner nor a reason for fighting…At the very time when the general was saying these things to the Carthaginians, and each nation's leader was doing likewise among his people, mainly through interpreters because of the number of foreigners mixed in, trumpets and horns rang out among the Romans, and such an uproar arose that the elephants turned against their own troops, especially the Moors and Numidians on the left wing.

So whereas Polybius has the battle beginning when both sides were ready, and the trumpets that panicked the elephants were sounding on all sides, Livy rejects that: for him it is clear that it is Roman trumpets alone that are panicking them, because the Romans are attacking when the Carthaginians are not ready for battle—not ready because they have been fatally delayed by the mixed ethnic composition of the Carthaginian army. Because of that they are not fighting with a single aim, and so have to be addressed and encouraged in different terms and indeed in different languages: they are certainly not (as Polybius put it) 'hearing a single command' in any literal sense (cf. above, 238). For Livy, the Carthaginians' multi-ethnic army, faced with the linguistically homogeneous Romans,[208] has doomed their chances even before the battle begins.

But this has striking and disturbing implications. In Livy's day, the most obvious and familiar example of a multi-ethnic and multilingual army was not the Carthaginians: it was the Romans themselves. The Roman army in the early imperial period employed numerous auxiliary regiments recruited in the provinces; it also recruited numerous non-Latin speakers into the

---

[208] Habinek (1998: 41–2) observes that throughout the Hannibalic books Livy repeatedly emphasizes Hannibal's linguistic difficulties compared with the easy communication enjoyed by the Romans and their allies. However, Habinek fails to see that this is a construct of the racial politics of Livy's narrative rather than a reflection of the actual linguistic conditions of the time (cf. n. 209 below), and so creates an unlikely story in which linguistic difference suddenly becomes more politically charged in second-century Italy than it had been in the third.

legions.[209] While Latin certainly remained the language of prestige in the army, and was regularly learned by soldiers who were not native speakers, there were plenty of soldiers, especially in the auxiliaries, whose Latin was rudimentary and who would accordingly be addressed by their commanders in their native tongues, with interpreters used as necessary.[210] Livy's version of Zama, with the Carthaginians doomed because of the extent to which they have incorporated foreigners into their forces, is not merely a celebration of Roman success. It is also a pessimistic warning: Rome has already gone down the route that brought the Carthaginian empire to ruin.[211]

This point has particular force in Livy's narrative of the Hannibalic War, because he has already shown the Romans taking some early steps down that apparently disastrous road. The Scipio brothers recruited Celtiberian mercenary auxiliaries to support them in their attempt to defeat the Carthaginians in Spain—and Livy specifically observes that this was the first time the Romans had employed soldiers for hire (24.49.8;[212] cf. 25.32.3). They are placed under the command of Cn. Scipio, who has with him a third of the Roman army proper (25.32.7: the other two-thirds are with Publius). However, the Celtiberians are immediately bribed by Hasdrubal to betray the Romans, using his knowledge of the people and also the ease of

---

[209] On the increasing tendency in the early imperial period for legionaries to be non-Italian see Forni (1974). Forni focuses particularly on the first centuries AD, after these books of Livy were written, but his data show that the tendencies he documents were already visible in the Augustan period, though Italians at that point still formed a substantial majority. See also Keppie (1997), who notes that already in the middle of the first century BC the legionaries whom Caesar recruited in Gaul contained many non-Romans (Suetonius, *Div. Jul.* 24).

[210] On the limits of the penetration of Latin in the early imperial army see Adams (2003: 20, cf. 275); for the extent and limits of Roman acculturation within auxiliary regiments see Haynes (1999). In fact ethnic mixing in the Roman army went back well before the first century, indeed to the time of the Hannibalic War itself, when non-Roman Italian regiments (and even some Gallic) served side by side with Rome: according to Polybius (3.72.11 (cf. Livy 21.55.4), 3.107.12, 6.26.7) over half of the Roman army at this time was not Roman. We may presume that for many of these their native languages would not have been Latin (see Jehne 2006: esp. 245–8). But these are still mostly Italians, and Livy, as I discussed earlier, tends to assimilate them to Rome, albeit often in complex and ambivalent ways: certainly he rarely points to any linguistic differences between Romans and Italians (though cf. 10.4.8–10).

[211] Dench (2005: 222–64) has a useful discussion of ancient views on 'race-mixing' in the context of the Roman empire, though in her (justified) criticisms of twentieth-century scholars for analysing the decline of the Roman empire in racial terms, she seriously underplays the range of comparable views in the ancient world which may have influenced them. As far as Livy goes, she discusses him primarily in the context of his account of the racially mixed foundation of Rome in Book 1, and has little to say about the considerably more nuanced and critical attitudes in the rest of his work. Likewise Lendon (2005: 257–8) denies that the Romans ever saw problems in their increasing reliance on foreign troops, but he makes no reference to Livy in this context.

[212] *mercennarium militem in castris neminem ante quam Celtiberos Romani habuerunt.* These are the very final words of Book 24: a closural device emphasizing it as a key thematic point.

communication given by the Spaniards serving in his own camp (25.33.1–4). The Celtiberians accordingly withdrew, leaving a numerically smaller Roman army vulnerable to the Carthaginian attack which resulted in the death of Cn. Scipio, followed shortly afterwards by the defeat and death of his brother. Livy's comment when the Celtiberians withdrew is as follows (25.33.5–6):

simul ne metus quidem ab Romanis erat, quippe tam paucis, si vi retinerent. id quidem cavendum semper Romanis ducibus erit, exemplaque haec vere pro documentis habenda, ne ita externis credant auxiliis, ut non plus sui roboris suarumque proprie virium in castris habeant.

At the same time there was not even anything to fear from the Romans if they tried to keep them back by force, given how few in number they were. Roman commanders will always have to take care, and will really have to treat these examples as lessons not to trust in foreign auxiliaries to the point of failing to keep a greater force of their own and strength of their very own in their camp.

Livy's sudden switch to the future tense and to a direct lesson to be drawn from the episode is unusual and blunt. But its implications are even starker than a superficial reading might imply. Livy's warning focuses on the question of allowing foreigners to outnumber the Romans: the assumption underlying his argument is that such auxiliaries are intrinsically unreliable and prone to defect, and Roman troops are therefore needed in significant numbers in order to keep their disloyalty in check. Moreover, given Livy's account of the Celtiberians, the betrayal is to be expected in another sense too. The reason they joined the Romans in the first place was for money: they had switched sides for the same pay that they had previously been given by the Carthaginians (24.49.7). So too it is money that persuades them here (25.33.3–4)—so large a sum, indeed, that Livy ironically hints that Hasdrubal has underestimated its effect (they would have fought for the Carthaginians for such money, but he merely requires them to withdraw from the fight).[213]

Yet despite all this Livy does not warn against the use of auxiliaries as such: after all, the Scipios are plainly at a disadvantage without them, and Livy does not suggest that they could have made up the numbers with Roman troops instead. The depressing conclusion to which he seems to be pointing is that the Romans still in his own day are in a position where intrinsically unreliable troops are necessary, and the best one can do is mitigate the worst of their effects. This is indeed what Scipio later does. In an episode narrated by Livy

---

[213] 25.33.4 *nec atrox visum facinus; non enim ut in Romanos verterent arma agebatur, et merces, quanta vel pro bello satis esset, dabatur, ne bellum gererent* (25.33.4: 'nor did that seem so dreadful a crime; for the issue was not one of turning arms against the Romans, and the payment, which was quite enough to fight a war, was being given them not to wage war'). Livy's irony here is of course also directed at the limited scruples of the Celtiberians.

directly after the character sketch in which Hannibal was praised for his control of his multi-ethnic army, Scipio too decides that he needs Spanish auxiliaries to face a larger Carthaginian army, 'at least for show' (28.13.1 *in speciem saltem*). The idea is taken from Polybius 11.20.7, but Livy adds an allusion back to Book 25: *neque in iis tantum virium ponendum ut mutando fidem, quae cladis causa fuisset patri patruoque, magnum momentum facerent* (28.13.2: 'he thought that so much strength should not be placed in them that they would have a significant influence by changing sides, the thing that had caused disaster for his father and uncle'). Hence he not only implicitly contrasts Scipio with Hannibal, but reframes him as someone who has effectively acted as a good reader of Livy, taking his direct advice to minimize the problems of using foreign troops. Scipio, like Hannibal, avoids the inherent problems with foreign troops, but does so in quite a different way, minimizing their practical role. The main use of the Spanish auxiliaries that Scipio makes in the subsequent battle is as a feint: he pretends to place them on the wings against their fellow countrymen serving the Carthaginians, only to exchange them with the Romans, so that the Romans can sweep the Carthaginians' Spanish troops aside and then concentrate on attacking the main body of the army (28.14.8–15.16).

But here too, as we saw with the question of the Romanness of the Italians, Livy sometimes presents the issue differently: non-Italian foreigners, also, may be more than allies who are perhaps necessary but always unreliable. This indeed appears with the Scipios' initial recruitment of the Celtiberians, which comes at the end of a sequence of relationships between Romans and foreigners which are more complex and far less unequivocally negative. When the Romans sought to retake Arpi from the Carthaginians (24.46.1–47.11), they were assisted not only by the townspeople, who were persuaded to turn on the Carthaginians in the heart of the battle (24.47.3–7), but also by a cohort of Spaniards, who arrange to hand the town over to the Romans on the condition of safe conduct for the Carthaginians in it (24.47.8). The Spaniards remain with the Romans, are rewarded, and Livy comments *opera eorum forti ac fideli persaepe res publica usa est* (24.47.11: 'the state very often made use of their brave and loyal assistance'), contrasting them with the treacherous Arpian Dasius Altinius (24.47.10; cf. 24.45), who had turned to Carthage after Cannae and now sought to return his town to Rome (for a price) in the light of the revival of their fortunes: the Romans had not taken him up on his offer, and the town was retaken without his help. Here Spaniards show the consistency and loyalty that an Italian lacked: and in the light of that the Scipios' recruitment of more Spaniards immediately afterwards does not appear an unreasonable strategy, though in the event it is to prove disastrous.

Another, more straightforward, example is Muttines.[214] He is described on his first appearance as a 'vigorous man' (25.40.5 *vir inpiger*), whose successes lead him to victory against Marcellus (25.40.9–11)—a victory which is however undermined when Hanno engages Marcellus in Muttines' absence and promptly loses to him (25.40.12–41.7). Hanno is inspired by jealousy at the success of a 'degenerate African' (25.40.12 *degenerem Afrum*), whom he wants to deprive of the glory of a victory (25.40.13). Hanno's jealousy moreover continues into the following book, where he deprives Muttines of his command, despite his continuing successes against the Romans (26.40.3–6; cf. 26.21.15). Muttines' response is to defect to Rome and to help Laevinus to capture Agrigentum (26.40.7–13); he is rewarded with Roman citizenship (27.5.6–7). Here, then, a foreigner not only becomes Roman, but is someone who exhibits the finest military qualities, qualities that would appear to qualify him for that citizenship. Moreover, this is a foreigner whose background might appear unpropitious: he is closely associated with Hannibal, by whom he was trained (25.40.5), and Hanno's racial slur against him, while clearly unjustified given Muttines' superior generalship, would appear to strike a chord in terms of Livy's suspicions about 'mixed multitudes', since Muttines is specifically identified as a 'Libyphoenician' (25.40.5), the most obvious symbol of the ethnic mix that characterizes the Carthaginian army (cf. 21.22.3 and above, 236–7). His support of Rome and his personal qualities appear to trump any doubts about his desirability as an ally or indeed a citizen, even though those doubts are based on issues that Livy himself has highlighted.

Muttines is, as I said, a straightforward case. However, the model that he provides of successful assimilation into Rome may not be as positive as this episode in isolation would make it appear. The same issue is explored at greater length by Livy with two other Africans who are introduced at the end of Book 24, between the recapture of Arpi and the recruitment of the Celtiberians (above, 244–6): Syphax and Masinissa (24.48.1–49.6). Here, as with the characters I discussed in the first part of the chapter, they are effectively treated as an antithetical pair, with their qualities being developed in tandem—but with the additional point, as with Hannibal, that they are not merely individuals, but play a significant role as representative foreign enemies and allies of Rome.[215] Syphax is the unreliable 'barbarian' who veers

---

[214] On his career see Lengrand (1993): apart from the evidence in these books, and 38.41.12–13 (where Muttines commands a squadron with the Roman army in Thrace), he is recorded by Varro, *De Vita Populi Romani* Book 3, fr. 96 Riposati (*ap.* Asconius, *In Pis.* 13C) as having received Roman citizenship; cf. also *SIG* 585.87.

[215] See Chlup (2004: 94–109) on Livy's exploration of the Syphax–Masinissa contrast.

between the two sides, Masinissa the quintessentially loyal ally.[216] And as I shall show, between them they illustrate in a variety of ways both the advantages and the difficulties that the Romans face with regard to their foreign allies—and ultimately the advantages and difficulties of incorporating foreigners not merely as allies, but as Romans.

The immediate surprise, to anyone who is aware of their future actions, is that they are introduced on the 'wrong' sides: Syphax as someone seeking an alliance with Rome, Masinissa as a steadfast supporter of Carthage. On the other hand, their 'proper' roles are prefigured in a variety of ways. Masinissa is *iuvenem ea indole, ut iam tum appareret maius regnum opulentius, quam quod accepisset, facturum* (24.49.1: 'a young man of the sort of character that it even then was clear that he would make his kingdom greater and wealthier than when he had received it'), and he defeats Syphax in a massive battle (24.49.4)—Syphax's alliance with Rome has not apparently brought lasting advantage to either side. Syphax, on the other hand, is described as *rex Numidarum, subito Carthaginiensibus hostis factus* (24.48.2: 'king of the Numidians, who suddenly became an enemy to the Carthaginians')—the *subito* is marked and unexplained, which in turn hints at the instability of Syphax's support, and also draws on the stereotype of the 'deceitful Numidian' which I discussed above. A more sinister point emerges from his initial exchanges with Rome: he realizes the inferiority of his own troops to the Romans' (24.48.4–7), and so persuades one of the Roman envoys to stay to train his troops in the Roman manner (24.48.9–12). This is a remarkable and double-edged episode: the Romans are training the army of their future enemy, but also anticipating a time when non-Romans will regularly be drilled in Roman military techniques.

So too Masinissa's next appearance occurs in much the same context. Immediately after the defection of the Celtiberians, he is described as attacking P. Scipio, and we are reminded more directly of his future story: *eo tempore socius Carthaginiensium, quem deinde clarum potentemque Romana fecit amicitia* (25.34.2: 'at that time he was an ally of the Carthaginians; subsequently his friendship with Rome made him famous and powerful'). His role is ambivalent from the Roman perspective: his future friendship with Rome is alluded to, yet as its counterpoint he is described as a 'new enemy' (25.34.1 *novo hoste*). And more specifically his attack forces Scipio, *dux cautus et providens* (25.34.7: 'a cautious and circumspect commander') to attempt

---

[216] Syphax is frequently referred to as *barbarus*, including in his introduction here (24.48.4, 28.17.6, 28.17.8, 28.18.6, 29.23.4, 29.23.6, 30.11.3, 30.28.3); Masinissa never is, although in purely ethnic terms they are not far apart (e.g. 30.12.13). Syphax and Masinissa were already implicitly contrasted in Sallust, *Jug.* 5.4–5.

the 'rash plan' (*temerarium . . . consilium*) of marching to attack Indibilis before he can join the Carthaginians, in the course of which he is caught and killed (yet another twist on the 'rash/cautious commander' motif I discussed in the first part of the chapter). When Masinissa joins Scipio Africanus, he effectively has Scipio's father's blood on his hands.

Masinissa and Syphax are likewise juxtaposed at 28.16.11–18.12. Syphax is courted by Scipio at 28.17.4–9 as a prelude to his plan to invade Africa. The oddity is that Livy introduces him not only by informing the reader that he is king of the Masaesulii (28.17.5), almost as if he had not mentioned him previously,[217] but also by observing that *foedus ea tempestate regi cum Cartha-giniensibus erat, quod haud gravius ei sanctiusque quam volgi barbaris, quibus ex fortuna pendet fides, ratus fore* (28.17.6–7: 'The king had a treaty at that time with the Carthaginians, which Scipio thought would be no more serious or holy to him than such things usually are to barbarians, whose loyalty depends on fortune'). The mere fact that Livy does not appear to assume that we remember Syphax from the earlier episodes is admittedly not a surprise. As I explained in Chapter 1, he varies greatly in the demands he makes on readers and in what he assumes we will remember from earlier in his narrative, and in fact in this case he provides new information that is relevant even for a reader who does remember Syphax, namely his proximity to Spain and New Carthage. But more surprising is the assumption that Syphax is currently an ally of Carthage and needs to be won over by Scipio. In Book 24, as we saw, Syphax had already abandoned the Carthaginians and allied himself to Rome; he had moreover reasserted his support for Rome in an embassy at 27.4.5–9 in which he had described himself as *nec inimiciorem ulli populo quam Carthaginiensi, nec amiciorem quam Romanis* (27.4.6: 'neither more inimical to any people than to the Carthaginians, nor more friendly to any than to the Romans').[218] Nothing indicates why he is now apparently back on the Carthaginian side, albeit still ready for an alliance with Rome.[219] It is possible that Livy has

---

[217] *Syphacem primum regem statuit temptare. Masaesuliorum is rex erat; Masaesulii, gens adfinis Mauris, in regionem Hispaniae maxime qua sita Nova Carthago est spectant* ('First he decided to try out King Syphax. He was king of the Masaesulii; the Masaesulii, a people near the Moors, look across in particular to the region of Spain where New Carthage is sited.').

[218] This passage once again juxtaposes Syphax and Masinissa; for shortly after the embassy the Romans receive information about Masinissa's position in the Carthaginian forces (27.5.11). It is worth noting that Muttines' receipt of citizenship appears in the same sequence (27.5.6–7): we hear of the model African ally at the same time as the unreliable present one and the famous future one.

[219] Gerhold (2002: 97–8) claims that there is no inconsistency on Livy's part save a terminological one: that Syphax had a formal treaty with Carthage, but only 'friendship' (*amicitia*) with Rome, and Scipio now wishes to convert the friendship into an actual treaty and detach him from his alliance with Carthage. But Syphax's actions earlier in the war, as reported by Livy, are not compatible with the suggestion that he was formally allied to Carthage.

himself overlooked the inconsistency; but that would perhaps be surprising with a figure as significant as Syphax (if one whose role in the story has hitherto been limited), and moreover Livy alludes to the earlier episodes when he refers to Syphax having 'already experienced the Carthaginians themselves in war' (28.17.10 *bello iam expertus ipsos Carthaginienses*; cf. 24.48.12 and 27.4.5). It is more likely to be deliberate: the destabilizing effect on the reader who has recalled Syphax's earlier position is effective in the context of Livy's overall presentation. Syphax's (typically barbarian) unreliability as an ally is stated explicitly as the grounds for Scipio's thinking that he will be able to detach him from his current alliance with Carthage, but it also suggests the risks inherent in the plan, and indeed the same fickleness that leads Syphax to abandon Carthage for Rome here will a little more than a book later lead him to abandon Rome again for Carthage. That portrait of instability is reinforced by the reader's sense that Syphax had 'suddenly' formed an alliance with Rome before and protested his loyalty at some length—and yet has unaccountably ended up back on the other side.

This portrayal is further complicated by being juxtaposed to the defection of Masinissa. Here we might expect a picture of loyalty to contrast with the intrinsic fickleness of Syphax. Instead Livy is hardly any less ambivalent (28.16.11–12):

Masinissa cum Silano clam congressus, ut ad nova consilia gentem quoque suam oboedientem haberet, cum paucis popularibus in Africam traiecit, non tam evidenti eo tempore subitae mutationis causa quam documento post id tempus constantissimae ad ultimam senectam fidei ne tum quidem eum sine probabili causa fecisse.

After Masinissa secretly met Silanus, he crossed to Africa with a few of his countrymen in order to have his own people also obedient to his new plans. The reason was not clear for his sudden change at that time, but his solid loyalty until extreme old age subsequently proved that even then he had not done it without an acceptable reason.

As before, we get a reminder of Masinissa's later position as a Roman ally; but from the perspective of the time he appears virtually indistinguishable from Syphax, whose support for Rome is likewise sudden and unexplained.[220] In fact, even in retrospect Livy refuses to identify a reason for Masinissa to have changed sides here. The best that he can say is that he must have had a good one—better, presumably than the fact that the Romans have just emphatically destroyed Carthaginian power in Spain (28.16.14) and so Masinissa is favouring the winning side: that would merely suggest that, as with Syphax, 'loyalty depends on fortune' (28.17.6). Yet no other explanation is offered, and the juxtaposition of Masinissa's defection with the Roman victory makes that

---

[220] Cf. Johner (1996: 241–2).

seem the most natural conclusion, even though it certainly does not explain his sustained support in the future. Once again Livy seems to be drawing on the stereotype of Numidian unreliability—but in an unexpected way, for Masinissa will eventually prove loyal, even if Livy cannot explain why.

Nor indeed, as a superficial reading might have led us to expect, is Masinissa even now clearly with Rome. Livy has not said in so many words that he has gone over to the Roman side, as opposed to planning secretly for such a shift; and when he next reappears at 28.35.1 it transpires that *incohata res iam ante de Masinissa aliis atque aliis causis dilata erat* ('the matter begun previously concerning Masinissa had been postponed for one reason after another'). It turns out that Masinissa—remarkably like Syphax at 28.17.8—has refused to confirm the alliance except with Scipio in person and, again like Syphax, is strongly affected by Scipio's personal bearing (28.35.5–7; cf. 28.18.6). At this point Masinissa is still serving with Carthage, and he has to trick Mago into allowing him to cross to the mainland (28.35.2–3; cf. 28.35.13); he is not described as an open supporter of Rome until 29.3.14, and even that leaves it unclear when and how his open break took place.

Masinissa does now offer an account of his desire to join Scipio—that it is in gratitude for Scipio having freed his nephew (28.35.8; cf. 27.19.8–12). He also says *cupere se illi populoque Romano operam navare ita ut nemo unus externus magis enixe adiuverit rem Romanam* (28.35.9: 'he desired to devote his efforts to Scipio and the Roman people in such a way that no one foreigner would serve Rome more strenuously'), a claim whose sincerity is apparently guaranteed by the reader's knowledge—and Livy's explicit reminder—that it will be borne out in reality. And Scipio's reaction to Masinissa is described in terms that assume the latter's sincerity—that Masinissa's external appearance was a reflection of his inner character.[221] Yet his further claim that he had wanted to help Rome for a long time but was unable to because he was in the 'alien and unknown' land of Spain (28.35.10 *terra aliena atque ignota*) does not quite ring true (being in Spain had apparently not prevented him from helping Carthage); it also does not quite fit the suggestion that his primary motivation was the relatively recent release of his nephew,[222] a suggestion which not only does Livy not support in his own voice, but which his studied agnosticism on the subject earlier has implied cannot be quite so simple. This is not to say that Livy is presenting Masinissa as untrustworthy, but it leaves a sense of something slightly disquieting about his protestations.

---

[221] 28.35.12 *ipse iuvenis specimen animi prae se ferret* ('the young man himself had a demeanour that showed his mind').

[222] On Livy's chronology this had happened three years earlier, but there had been little Spanish narrative between then and the point where Masinissa began to negotiate his defection.

So Syphax and Masinissa, though contrasting figures, have joined Rome in tandem; and if Syphax's stereotypically Numidian slipperiness is marked repeatedly by Livy, Masinissa, his apparent antithesis, shares something of it too. The Romans are acquiring an exceptionally good ally and a notoriously bad one. The concern is not that there is no difference between them, but that it is remarkably difficult to identify what that difference consists in. The general danger inherent in such alliances is stated explicitly by Fabius at 28.42.7–9,[223] where he not only treats Masinissa and Syphax as equally untrustworthy, but associates both with the Celtiberians who had betrayed the Scipio brothers in Book 25; Scipio responds by accepting that characterization, but assuring the listeners that he will guard against their treachery even while relying on their loyalty (28.44.7).[224] Here too there is apparently nothing to distinguish one potentially treacherous African ally from another.

Book 29 complicates the question further. When Laelius raids Africa at the start of the book, Masinissa meets him and complains about Scipio's failure to invade immediately *perculsis Carthaginiensibus, Syphace impedito finitimis bellis* (29.4.8: 'with the Carthaginians beaten down and Syphax hindered by border wars'). That formulation is a surprising one: Syphax is supposedly a Roman ally, as we have been repeatedly reminded (most recently at 29.3.14), and hence his being otherwise occupied might appear a reason for Scipio to postpone his invasion rather than accelerate it. Masinissa's explanation is that *si spatium ad sua ut velit componenda detur, nihil sincera fide cum Romanis acturum* (29.4.8: 'if Syphax were given time to arrange his affairs as he wanted, he would not deal with the Romans with honest loyalty'). This is a fair description of Syphax's unreliability in general, as events prove, since Syphax's next appearance has him transferring his loyalty to the Carthaginians after his marriage (29.23), but the convoluted reasoning is still uncomfortable, the more since Masinissa's entire speech raises other unanswered questions. There is no indication what these wars are in which Syphax is engaged, and moreover Masinissa suddenly introduces the information that he has himself been driven from his kingdom, although he claims still to have a 'far from negligible force' of infantry and cavalry to contribute to Scipio (29.4.9 *haud contemnendis copiis*)—nothing earlier has prepared us for this, and the last time Masinissa's kingdom was mentioned was in terms that implied he was in

---

[223] Cf. Rüger (1965: 60); however, he regards Fabius as simply wrong in the case of Masinissa, overlooking the extent to which Livy's account gives colour to Fabius' fears.

[224] Scipio's confident claim to have taken their potential disloyalty into account is moreover not obviously borne out by what actually happens when Syphax eventually defects—Scipio is manifestly not expecting it, sees it as a substantial blow against him (29.24.2), and has to lie to his troops in order to prevent them from being disheartened (29.24.4–7). Cf. Chlup (2004: 99–100), who notes that Hasdrubal has read Syphax's character better than Scipio has.

control of it (28.16.11). Masinissa may be a reliable ally, but that is still to be proved, and Livy's account of his speech suggests that he is not telling the Romans the whole story.

That story eventually appears in the long digression at the end of the book (29.29.6–33.10)—but is introduced in terms that appear to challenge Masinissa's earlier claims. The Romans are said to be overjoyed at Masinissa's arrival (29.29.4)—but Livy immediately questions the size of the forces he brought with him, whether it is no more than 200 cavalry, as some of his sources claim, or whether it is 2,000, as most do. The dispute is significant. Two hundred cavalry is hardly the substantial force of cavalry and infantry that Masinissa had promised,[225] yet that is the version which Livy eventually endorses: at the end of the digression he concludes (29.33.10) that the smaller figure must be correct, since an exile would not be able to supply the larger number. Thus Masinissa may not have lied, but he has certainly raised expectations that he appears unable to fulfil. Yet the Romans are delighted to see him (29.29.4), and Livy's initial justification for his digression supports that: Masinissa 'was by far the greatest of all kings of his time, and gave the most help to Rome' (29.29.5 *longe maximus omnium aetatis suae regum hic fuerit plurimumque rem Romanam iuverit*). Once again Masinissa's remarkable value as an ally is emphasized, even at the point where the practical help he is offering appears questionable and his earlier promises apparently deceptive.

The digression moreover fills in an extremely significant gap. Masinissa and Syphax have, as I have shown, been presented by Livy in tandem, and episodes in which they appear have regularly been juxtaposed. Yet they have only once been shown in direct contact: on their very first appearance, when Masinissa had fought successfully on the side of the Carthaginians against Syphax (24.49.1–6). Now we are given a back-story in which the vicissitudes of their relationship are shown in detail. Masinissa, it now transpires, had contested the throne in a complex dynastic struggle, with Syphax supporting his chief rivals Mazaetullus and Lacumazes (29.29.13, 29.30.5–8); after he had achieved the throne Syphax had attacked him again and defeated him (29.31.4–8), then sent troops to harry and kill him and his remaining followers (29.31.12–32.10); Masinissa had moved to recover his kingdom and built a new army (29.32.11–14), but Syphax had defeated and expelled him yet again (29.33.1–8).

All of this gives a rather different perspective on Masinissa's warnings against Syphax and his advice to the Romans earlier in the book. Syphax is

---

[225] Livy had discussed the total size of Scipio's invasion forces at 29.25.1–2; the minimum figure he quoted for the cavalry is 1,600, so on the smaller figure for Masinissa's contribution it would at best add barely 12 per cent to one branch of the force.

indeed having problems with border wars, as Masinissa had said—but the person with whom he is having problems appears to be Masinissa himself (cf. 29.31.5, 29.32.14). It is likewise true that Syphax's loyalty to Rome is not to be trusted—but Masinissa is assessing that from a more partial position than appeared at first sight, and his slightly odd reasoning for an immediate Roman invasion makes more sense when seen in terms of that partiality: for Masinissa, whom Syphax has deprived of his kingdom, has a strong interest in having Rome enter Africa on his side as soon as possible. Rome's most loyal ally is apparently allowing his advice to be driven by his own best interest, and paying less regard to what will benefit Rome. And moreover he has been successful: Scipio's response to his advice was to try to accelerate the invasion exactly as Masinissa had wanted (29.6.1), though in the event he is deflected by the desire to retake Locri, and postpones the attack on Africa until the following year. Rome's alliance with Masinissa means that, if only to a limited degree, the Romans are dancing to Masinissa's tune.

But the digression gives occasion for another, more positive assessment of Masinissa's support for Rome as well. It is remarkably hard to fit Masinissa's campaigns in the digression chronologically with Masinissa's and Syphax's earlier appearances in the Third Decade: to see, for example, at what point in the narrative of Masinissa's struggles for his kingdom he had fought against the elder Scipios, or had approached Rome about the possibility of defection, or had encouraged Scipio to launch an immediate invasion of Africa.[226] But a consistent if underlying theme is the hostility between Masinissa and Carthage, a hostility which in the absence of a clear chronology appears something intrinsic and fundamental. When Masinissa first gains the throne he secures his position by reconciling himself with his rivals Mazaetullus and Lacumazes, but that reconciliation is opposed by the Carthaginians (29.30.13), even though there is no obvious reason for them to do so—it is true that they had given support to Mazaetullus and Lacumazes (29.29.12–13, 29.30.10),

---

[226] The only direct chronological indications are, first, that his father Gala had died while Masinissa was fighting for Carthage in Spain (29.29.6), and second, that Masinissa left Spain to claim his kingdom after his uncle died (29.30.1). The implication of the subsequent narrative is that he does not then return to Spain, since he seems to be fully occupied in Africa. But in Livy's main narrative Masinissa was last in Spain at 28.35, less than two years earlier, and it is hard to see how so extensive a series of events as described in the digression, with Masinissa twice gaining and losing his kingdom, could have taken place in less than two years. For an attempt to construct a clear sequence of events from the digression and Livy's main narrative while accepting their overall outlines see Thompson (1981); however, he does not address the chronological problem directly. De Sanctis (1968: 504) solves the problem historically by suggesting that one of Masinissa's losses of his throne is a doublet; Walsh (1965: 150) regards the meeting with Scipio at 28.35 as unhistorical, and argues that Masinissa left Spain for good in the previous year, leaving enough time for the events of the digression.

but the last we had heard Masinissa himself had also been fighting on their side. Likewise, when Syphax is inclined to be unconcerned about Masinissa (29.31.1), he is prompted into action by Hasdrubal's warning that Masinissa's remarkable qualities, which he had exhibited in Spain, would not let him be content with his kingdom, and that Syphax and the Carthaginians needed to crush 'that growing flame' (29.31.3: *orientem illum ignem*) while his hold on the kingdom was still insecure (29.31.2–4).

It is not clear what prompts the Carthaginians and Hasdrubal here—whether Masinissa has already by this point revealed himself as a supporter of Rome, or whether they indeed believe him to represent an independent threat to Carthage—but either way it aligns Masinissa firmly and fundamentally against Carthage in a way that goes beyond any particular cause that might have brought him to the side of Rome. The enmity between Masinissa and Carthage emerges no less from the subsequent narrative. Masinissa, driven to banditry, concentrates his attacks on Carthaginian territory, as being richer and safer to plunder (29.31.10), 'and more Carthaginians were killed and captured than often happens in regular warfare' (29.31.11 *pluresque quam iusto saepe in bello Carthaginienses caderent caperenturque*; cf. 29.32.14); accordingly, when the (false) news of Masinissa's death reaches Carthage, it is a 'huge joy' (29.32.10 *gaudium ingens*). Hence Masinissa in some very fundamental ways justifies the faith that Scipio places in him: he is shown as being intrinsically on the Roman side in their fight against Carthage, even if in terms of his detailed dealings with Rome his behaviour is uncomfortably paralleled to the unreliable Syphax.

But one further episode shows how problematic for the Romans Masinissa can be: the famous account of his relationship with Syphax's wife Sophoniba (30.12–15). This episode is well known and has often been discussed:[227] Masinissa meeting Sophoniba, her appeal to him to keep her from becoming Scipio's prisoner and their consequent marriage, Syphax's jealous denunciation of the pair to Scipio, Scipio's rebuke to Masinissa, and Sophoniba's suicide. But a close reading suggests that more is going on than appears at first sight.

One point that emerges from this episode is that Scipio does not seem to be fully aware of the nature of the passions that he is dealing with. Sophoniba actively works on both Masinissa and Syphax (29.23.7, 30.7.8–9, 30.11.3, 30.12.17)[228]—and part of what enables her to do so is the intrinsic lustfulness

---

[227] E.g. Martin (1941–42), Catin (1944: 83–6), Rüger (1965: 61–3), Toppani (1977–8), Haley (1989, 1990), Johner (1996: 86–8), Kowalewski (2002: 219–39), Chlup (2004: 104–8).

[228] This is less prominent in other sources, and may reflect the contemporary image of Cleopatra, with the anxieties that her (alleged) seductiveness generated: see Haley (1989: 178–81); also Kowalewski (2002: 239).

of Numidians.[229] Yet Scipio persistently misreads that. At 30.3.4 he had hoped that Syphax would have tired of his wife, a statement based on Polybius 14.1.4, but which Livy has changed. In Polybius Scipio's reasoning is based on the intrinsic fickleness of Numidians—a stereotype to which Livy too has often appealed, but which he does not mention here.[230] Conversely, Polybius seems to have laid less stress on Sophoniba's sexual appeal to Syphax. Although much of his account is lost, at 14.7.6 she merely begs him not to abandon the fight: the corresponding passage of Livy emphasizes that though she appeals for pity here, she had previously done so *blanditiis, satis potentibus ad animum amantis* (30.7.8: 'with coaxings, which are powerful enough for the mind of a lover'). The result is that the Numidian stereotype that is to the fore in this part of Livy is the one of sexual passion,[231] and Scipio's hope of Syphax's defection is accordingly misguided. Likewise with Scipio's rebuke to Masinissa: he contrasts at length the latter's susceptibility with his own mastery of sexual passion (30.14.5–7, cf. 30.14.3), and regards the key issue as their shared youth (30.14.3, 30.14.6; cf. 30.15.9)—as indeed Syphax had encouraged him to do, when warning him jealously that Masinissa was likely to be more susceptible than Syphax himself was (30.13.14). The rebuke is to that extent misplaced and ineffective, since it assumes a common ground between Scipio and Masinissa such that Masinissa could be persuaded in much the terms that Scipio himself could: the latter's 'African' character in fact sets him apart. Masinissa may blush and cry (30.15.1), but he nevertheless continues to act as Sophoniba rather than Scipio wanted.

But a greater concern is that Scipio appears to be actively manipulated by Masinissa. His intention in rebuking him is to persuade him to give Sophoniba up to the Romans: she is 'booty of the Roman people' (30.14.9

---

[229] Livy comments on Masinissa about 'the impetuosity of the Numidian race towards sex' (30.12.18 *genus Numidarum in venerem praeceps*); similarly he had said of Syphax that 'the Numidians above all barbarians are uncontrolled with regard to sex' (29.23.4 *sunt ante omnes barbaros Numidae effusi in venerem*). This aspect of the story is less apparent in the alternative version found in Diodorus 27.7, Appian, *Pun.* 10, and Zonaras 9.11, 9.13 (cf. also Dio fr. 57.51), according to which Masinissa and Sophoniba had been married (Diodorus) or betrothed (Appian, Zonaras) before Hasdrubal had married her to Syphax. Although Diodorus and Dio/Zonaras also comment explicitly on her seductiveness, the longer relationship means that Masinissa's behaviour towards her appears less the product of an immediate and uncontrolled sexual impulse than it does in Livy: see Haley (1989: 174), Johner (1996: 243–4).

[230] At 29.23.6–7, on the other hand, Hasdrubal had worried about the same point explicitly as Scipio does later in Polybius—that the *vana et mutabilia barbarorum ingenia* ('the empty and changeable character of barbarians') might send Syphax back to Scipio's side despite his marriage, if Scipio actually appeared in Africa. In the event Hasdrubal too has underestimated Syphax's passion (cf. above, 220–1): even when Scipio is in Africa Sophoniba keeps Syphax with the Carthaginians.

[231] Cf. also 30.11.3, where Syphax is described as *aegrum amore* ('lovesick').

praeda populi Romani), and must be sent to Rome to be judged for alienating Syphax from his alliance (30.14.10). Masinissa responds in the following form (30.15.1–2):

cum se quidem in potestate futurum imperatoris dixisset, orassetque eum ut quantum res sineret fidei suae temere obstrictae consuleret—promisisse enim se in nullius potestatem eam traditurum—ex praetorio in tabernaculum suum confusus concessit.

After saying that he would indeed be in the general's power and begging that, as far as the matter permitted, he might have regard to the promise that he had rashly bound himself to—for he said that he had promised that he would not hand her over into anyone's power—he withdrew in consternation from the headquarters into his own tent.

Masinissa here describes his promise to Sophoniba as being 'not to hand her over', and asks to be allowed to keep that promise as far as possible. But he is suitably vague about what *quantum res sineret fidei suae . . . consuleret* might actually mean in practice, and he carefully does not say that the promise which she actually extracted from him was in two parts—first, that he would keep her out of the hands of the Romans, and second, that failing all else he would ensure that she died (30.12.16). Accordingly, having failed at the first, he now keeps the second, as he says explicitly in his message to her (30.15.5). Sophoniba commits suicide (30.15.7–8); and Scipio's response on hearing the news is as follows (30.15.9–10):

quod ubi nuntiatum est Scipioni, ne quid aeger animi ferox iuvenis gravius consuleret, accitum eum extemplo nunc solatur, nunc quod temeritatem temeritate alia luerit tristioremque rem quam necesse fuerit fecerit, leniter castigat.

When this was announced to Scipio, so that the passionate young man in his distress would not do something worse, he summoned him immediately and consoled him, while gently rebuking him for atoning for his rashness with another rashness and making the matter sadder than it needed to be.

Scipio's interpretation of the episode still does not appear to recognize the point at issue: while certainly Masinissa is grief-stricken (cf. 30.15.3), it was not, as he implies, merely an act of passionate impulse when he allowed Sophoniba to commit suicide. He did so in fulfilment of his promise to her—the promise which he told Scipio he intended to keep, while not informing him of its precise content. Hence he has succeeded in taking Sophoniba out of the power of Rome, exactly as she wanted and as he had promised, and in direct contravention of Scipio's instructions to him.[232] And Masinissa has

---

[232] Walsh (1961: 87: Rossi 2004: 373 is similar) exculpates Masinissa by spectacularly misreading this episode: 'At Scipio's command, he controls his wayward passions by administering poison to Sophoniba'. Scipio had commanded the opposite.

come out of it remarkably well, at least as far as his relationship with the Romans goes. Not only has his deception allowed him to maintain a good relationship with Scipio while keeping his promise to his wife, but he is actively rewarded (30.15.11–12):

postero die ut a praesenti motu averteret animum eius, in tribunal escendit et contionem advocari iussit. ibi Masinissam, primum regem appellatum eximiisque ornatum laudibus, aurea corona, aurea patera, sella curuli et scipione eburneo, toga picta et palmata tunica donat. addit verbis honorem: neque magnificentius quicquam triumpho apud Romanos, neque triumphantibus ampliorem eo ornatum esse quo unum omnium externorum dignum Masinissam populus Romanus ducat.

On the next day, to divert Masinissa's mind from its current emotional state, he ascended the tribunal and ordered a meeting to be called. There Masinissa was first called king and celebrated with exceptional praise; he then presented him with a golden crown, a golden dish, a curule chair and an ivory sceptre, an embroidered toga and a tunic decorated with palms. He added honour in words: that among the Romans nothing was more splendid than a triumph, and no decoration for those triumphing was grander than that which the Roman people thought Masinissa, alone of all foreigners, was worthy of.

Livy has regularly referred to Masinissa's future as the ideal ally, and that alone would make the honours that he receives here appropriate; indeed, they are subsequently endorsed by the Senate (30.17.12), and his envoys promise, in another foreshadowing of his future loyalty, that he will live up to them (30.17.9). Yet the specific trigger for his receiving them now is a combination of Scipio's misunderstanding and Masinissa's manipulation: Scipio's belief that the death of Sophoniba was an error of youthful passion rather than a fulfilment of a promise.

But there is a further dimension to this passage. As Scipio notes, the honours are specifically ones that are given to Romans; the same is true of the additional gifts that the Senate gives him at 30.17.13, which include tunics with the *latus clavus* and *tabernacula militaremque supellectilem qualem prae-beri consuli mos* ('tents and the sort of military furnishings that are customar-ily supplied to a consul'). Masinissa, though a foreigner, is being received not merely into the Roman world, but into the highest status within that world.[233] But that highlights Livy's double-edged attitude towards what Masinissa represents. He is unquestionably an outstanding candidate for

---

[233] Rossi (2004: 373). In practice these honours, though certainly Roman in form, had a more complex significance. As Rawson (1975: 155–6; = Rawson 1991: 181–3) observes, they also carry overtones of royalty, with an implied equation of Roman magistrates with kings: hence they may not have been perceived as distinctively 'Roman' by their recipients. But Livy here explicitly treats it as giving Roman status to a foreigner.

such honours, yet he receives them partly through behaviour that was distinctly un-Roman and indeed stereotypically Numidian, from the sexual passion that led to his entanglement with Sophoniba in the first place to his manipulation and deception of Scipio. Nor does that behaviour appear an aberration in the light of the ambivalent representation of Masinissa's support for Rome in the previous books. Masinissa is constantly paralleled with Syphax, a parallel which frequently invites us to contrast them, but almost as often shows the uncomfortable similarities, especially as viewed from the perspective of their own time rather than with hindsight: it is worth noting that Syphax too had received similar gifts from the Senate at a time when he was assumed to be a reliable ally (27.4.8–9).

Hence, with Syphax and Masinissa, Livy bases himself on national stereotypes; yet he does not merely accept those stereotypes passively, but explores their limits. Numidian sexual passion and Numidian fickleness may sometimes pull in opposite directions, as Syphax's lust for Sophoniba keeps him loyal to Carthage contrary to Scipio's and Hasdrubal's expectations. And, as I discussed in the first part of the chapter, a person may conform to multiple stereotypes, and different aspects of a person's character may be at odds with one another. Masinissa is both a Numidian and a Roman military ally of exceptional personal qualities. He shows himself a 'deceitful Numidian' even as Livy celebrates his fidelity.

And Masinissa, though apparently unique in his day, and an indispensable support for the Roman empire over fifty years, is the predecessor of many more foreigners who will be incorporated into Rome, not only as allies as he is, but as subjects and indeed in some cases citizens.[234] The road of Roman expansion will increasingly lead them down the route that Carthage followed before them, to the acceptance into Rome of people who may have outstanding qualities as Masinissa does, but whose native characters appear in various respects un-Roman and indeed dangerous. Masinissa is in almost all respects a fine and desirable ally, but he represents another step towards the multiethnic empire that doomed Carthage at Zama.

Livy's account of non-Romans is thus far from the caricature of his attitudes that is sometimes presented. While he recognizes the historical limits to 'Romanness' at the time about which he is writing, he also is constantly aware of the instability of Roman identity when viewed across time, and regularly hints at the future when many of Rome's current enemies and allies will be part of the empire, acquiring citizenship, serving in the army, and

---

[234] The honours Masinissa (and, earlier, Syphax) received were standard gifts to allied rulers throughout the late Republic and early empire. See Rawson (1975: 155–6 = Rawson 1991: 181–3).

indeed occasionally becoming candidates for senior office.[235] And his attitude to this is complex and ambivalent. Even Italians, whose claims to Romanness in Livy's own day were widely accepted, sometimes appear alien and threatening to Roman identity. Non-Italians are often viewed from an even more negative perspective, yet they offer both models of behaviour and military support which Rome will find indispensable. The problem for the Romans is how they can take on the benefits without compromising themselves irrevocably. Even Masinissa conforms—in part and in unexpected ways—to a national stereotype, with a dangerously alien side which can baffle such a skilled tactician and diplomat as Scipio. And for every Masinissa there may be a Syphax, someone who appears effectively identical, even though he is likely to provide a lifetime of betrayal instead of a lifetime of loyalty. To these dilemmas Livy offers no answer: he may have thought them unanswerable.

One final point should be made. Livy's constant awareness of Roman expansion may additionally explain an interesting phenomenon about his work. He goes against the standard Roman historiographical convention in never[236] referring to Roman troops in his own voice as *nos* or *nostri*. Leeman suggests that this is connected with Livy's own marginal status as a Paduan, which meant that he presented himself as a sympathetic outsider rather than identifying fully with Rome.[237] But in the light of what I have argued here, it seems more plausible to suggest that this reflects not the personal status of the historian, but the assumptions about the relationship of Rome and other nations underlying his work. Rome at any time may be fighting others, but those 'others', for all their alienness, will themselves one day be part of Rome.

---

[235] Riggsby (2006: 129–30) argues something similar for Caesar: that unlike other late-Republican writers, who assimilate Italy to Rome but maintain a firm boundary between Italy and the non-Italian provinces, Caesar sees the boundary between Gaul and Rome as fluid. Livy's fluidity is similar, but is given a broader historical perspective and articulated with far greater pessimism.

[236] Kraus (1994a: 9) offers two Livian instances, but neither is a true counterexample to the generalization made here. 7.14.6 refers to *contemporary* Roman generals, not those of the period about which he is writing, while 28.1.3 simply names the Mediterranean *mare nostrum* (cf. *OLD* s.v. *noster* 7c).

[237] Leeman (1963: 194–6); for the device in general see Marincola (1997: 287–8).

4

Winners and Losers

4.1. BATTLES

Most ancient historiography centres explicitly or implicitly on war. The earliest surviving historians, Herodotus and Thucydides, announce the Persian and Peloponnesian Wars respectively as their theme, and even if in practice Herodotus in particular introduces a great deal of other material, it is ultimately ancillary to the narrative of the war. They are followed by numerous other historians who write the history of wars, from Caesar's memoirs of his own campaigns to Arrian and Curtius narrating the campaigns of Alexander.[1] Moreover, even those who, like Livy, purport to be providing a more comprehensive narrative of events over a period of time, in practice find war looming large in much of their narrative: this is as true of Xenophon and Polybius as it is of Velleius and Ammianus. Livy's choice to devote a lengthy segment of his history to the Hannibalic War was a natural one.

The attraction of war to the ancient historian and (presumably) the ancient reader was multiple. It partly stemmed from the literary prestige of the war narrative, associated with epic, and above all with the epic that stood at the head of the entire Greco–Roman literary tradition, namely the *Iliad*.[2] It was partly the consequence of an aesthetic which set a great store in the representation of violence and emotion,[3] in narratives where victory or defeat depended on a single complex action, with death, destruction, rape, enslavement, and plunder the potential lot of the losers. It also partly arose from the prestige of the warrior and of martial virtues within Greek and Roman culture, where political leaders and ordinary citizens alike were expected to be able to demonstrate their true qualities on the battlefield.[4] And of course these factors were not separate but interdependent. The prestige of the *Iliad* and the war narrative lay beneath the

---

[1] Cf. Campbell (2002: 12–13).

[2] On historiographical battle narratives as an imitation of epic themes see Foucher (2000: 358–432).

[3] Note D'Huys (1987) for ancient views of the appropriate method for historians to represent violence.

[4] On the centrality of martial virtues within Roman culture see e.g. Harris (1979: 9–53).

aesthetic of violence, and both can be argued to have influenced the praise given to actual warriors and indeed the conduct of actual wars.[5]

But the historian's narrative of war was expected to go beyond excitement and pathos. History as a genre centred as much on the 'why' as on the 'how', and questions of causation and explanation are often highlighted directly.[6] From his very first pages Herodotus raises the question of why the Persian Wars were fought at all; and for all the manifest influence of the *Iliad* on Herodotus, that focus instantly sets his work apart from his epic predecessor, since the *Iliad* shows little concern for tracing the true origins of the Trojan War, let alone seeking its aetiology in a chain of causes extending centuries into the past as Herodotus does. And not only the beginnings of wars, but also their results were regularly the object of explanation. Naturally this did not preclude any particular historian from narrating any particular battle with a focus on pathetic narrative to the exclusion of explanatory material; but it is noteworthy that such historians were the object of criticism. Most famously— and most importantly for our purposes here—Polybius criticizes Phylarchus for his excessively pathetic and dramatic narratives, and one of his chief points of criticism is that Phylarchus has abandoned any causal explanation but simply offers a pathetic narrative for its own sake (2.56.13–16). We do not, of course, have Phylarchus' side to this debate, so we do not know whether he would have claimed that Polybius was misrepresenting him and that he did in fact show the causal structure underlying events, or whether he would have proudly accepted Polybius' characterization of his method but argued that Polybius had too narrow a view of what was appropriate to history. But the fact that Polybius took this stance is relevant here, since even if Livy disagreed with him, he was, as I showed in Chapter 2, writing against the background of Polybius' narrative and Polybius' assumptions.

That Livy had a particular interest in narrating at least some of his battles with an eye on explaining their outcomes was argued many years ago in a classic study by Heinz Bruckmann.[7] Bruckmann analysed Livy's accounts of Roman defeats, including the defeats inflicted by Hannibal in the opening books of the Third Decade, and showed that typically he is keen to provide excuses to explain the defeats away. The underlying implication is that in a

---

[5] See Lendon (2005), who argues powerfully if controversially for the conduct of Greek and Roman warfare being strongly dependent on literary and legendary models.

[6] Cf. Momigliano (1966).

[7] Bruckmann (1936). See *contra* Plathner (1934: 37–8), who suggests that Livy, unlike Polybius, is more interested in narrating battles than explaining them. But, at least in the Third Decade, this is contradicted by Livy's repeated and careful interest in the conditions that may have contributed to defeat, which are no less prominent than they had been in Polybius—although Livy, as I shall demonstrate, handles them in odd and counterintuitive ways.

straight fight the Romans would always win, so Livy offers reasons why it was not a straight fight. Either the Romans were handicapped by a rash and over-confident general (as happened at the Trebia, Trasimene, and Cannae), whose religious errors alienate the gods (Trasimene), or they were caught by Hanni-bal's stratagems which made it something less than a fair fight (Ticinus, Trebia, Trasimene, Cannae), or they were hindered by the terrain (Trasimene) or by exhaustion (Trebia) or betrayal by allies (Trebia, Cannae). Or, most commonly, several of these applied simultaneously, so as to protect the Roman army completely from any suggestion of intrinsic inferiority to their enemies. These excuses were not invented by Livy—for example, Polybius refers also to the problem of exhaustion at the Trebia or the difficult terrain at Trasimene—and doubtless sometimes reflect what actually happened in the battle (for example, there is little reason to doubt that Hannibal's tactical manoeuvres played a role in his victories). But Livy highlights these issues in a way that goes well beyond Polybius: notably, he spends much more time than Polybius does in recounting the personal deficiencies of rash commanders like Sempronius, Flaminius, and Varro.[8]

Bruckmann's analysis of Livy's battle scenes is in many respects a powerful one, most notably in its demonstration that for Livy, as for Polybius and other historians, the outcome of a battle is something that is not merely accepted and narrated, but is something which is explained; his demonstration of the way Livy slants his account away from any hint at intrinsic Roman inferiority is also important. But in certain crucial respects, as I shall show, he fails to recognize how revolutionary Livy's presentation of the causal structure of battles, the explanations he offers for defeat or victory, actually is.

Let us take as an example one of Bruckmann's central illustrations, the defeat at the Trebia at the end of Book 21.[9] In some ways Livy's and Polybius' accounts of this battle run quite closely in tandem. For both of them one significant feature of the battle is the terrain on which it was fought, which gave Hannibal the chance to entrap the Romans by setting an ambush in their rear (Polybius 3.71, Livy 21.54.1–5). Another aspect of the battle which they both emphasize is the difference between the condition of the Romans and that of the Carthaginians when they enter the battle: the Romans left camp without breakfast, forded the river in extreme cold, and (in Livy) were

---

[8] Contrast, for example, Polybius' relatively restrained account of Sempronius' argument with Scipio (3.70.1–8; cf. 3.72.1–2), focusing as much on the latter's objections as on the former's aggressiveness, with Livy's vivid and dramatic characterization of Sempronius' mis-placed elation at 21.53.1–6 (cf. Burck 1962: 75); or the short description of Flaminius' rashness and incompetence at Polybius 3.82.1–8 with the much fuller account of his violence and irreligiosity at Livy 21.63 and 22.3.

[9] Bruckmann (1936: 59–65).

consequently exhausted before even starting to fight, whereas the Carthaginians had eaten and prepared themselves (Polybius 3.72.3–6, Livy 21.54.8–55.1). Both Livy and Polybius attribute Sempronius' willingness to engage in battle under such unfavourable conditions as being due to his overconfidence, though that looms much larger in Livy than it does in Polybius (above, n. 8).[10] For both writers, then, the essential preconditions for the Romans' being worsted in the battle are more or less identical.

However, when it comes to the actual narrative of the battle they diverge more sharply. In the opening section Polybius presents a complex series of movements, with the Roman spearsmen retreating before their Carthaginian counterparts, the Carthaginian cavalry then pressing on the wings, the Roman cavalry then retreating, and the Numidians then advancing through the lines to attack the Roman wings (3.73.1–7). The corresponding portion of the battle in Livy is simpler, and more in the Romans' favour: the Roman light-armed troops are superior to the Carthaginians, and so the latter move to join their cavalry in attacking the Roman cavalry on the wings, with the additional support of the elephants (which are not described in Polybius at this point in the battle): the Roman cavalry suffer accordingly (21.55.5–7).

At this point we reach the central narrative of the battle, as described by both authors: the fight between the heavy infantry on both sides. First, Polybius 3.73.8–74.6:

οἱ δ᾽ ἐν τοῖς βαρέσιν ὅπλοις παρ᾽ ἀμφοῖν τὰς πρώτας ἔχοντες καὶ μέσας τῆς ὅλης παρεμβολῆς τάξεις ἐπὶ πολὺν χρόνον ἐμάχοντο συστάδην, ἐφάμιλλον ποιούμενοι τὸν κίνδυνον. ἐν ᾧ καιρῷ διαναστάντων τῶν ἐκ τῆς ἐνέδρας Νομάδων καὶ προσπεσόντων ἄφνω κατὰ νώτου τοῖς ἀγωνιζομένοις περὶ τὰ μέσα, μεγάλην ταραχὴν καὶ δυσχρηστίαν συνέβαινε γίνεσθαι περὶ τὰς τῶν ῾Ρωμαίων δυνάμεις. τέλος δ᾽ ἀμφότερα τὰ κέρατα τῶν περὶ τὸν Τεβέριον πιεζούμενα κατὰ πρόσωπον μὲν ὑπὸ τῶν θηρίων, πέριξ δὲ καὶ κατὰ τὰς ἐκ τῶν πλαγίων ἐπιφανείας ὑπὸ τῶν εὐζώνων, ἐτράπησαν καὶ συνωθοῦντο κατὰ τὸν διωγμὸν πρὸς τὸν ὑποκείμενον ποταμόν. τούτου δὲ συμβάντος οἱ κατὰ μέσον τὸν κίνδυνον ταχθέντες τῶν ῾Ρωμαίων οἱ μὲν κατόπιν ἐφεστῶτες ὑπὸ τῶν ἐκ τῆς ἐνέδρας προσπεσόντων ἀπώλλυντο καὶ κακῶς ἔπασχον, οἱ δὲ περὶ τὰς πρώτας χώρας ἐπαναγκασθέντες ἐκράτησαν τῶν Κελτῶν καὶ μέρους τινὸς τῶν Λιβύων καὶ πολλοὺς αὐτῶν ἀποκτείναντες διέκοψαν τὴν τῶν Καρχηδονίων τάξιν. θεωροῦντες δὲ τοὺς ἀπὸ τῶν ἰδίων κεράτων ἐκπεπιεσμένους, τὸ μὲν ἐπιβοηθεῖν τούτοις ἢ πάλιν εἰς τὴν ἑαυτῶν ἀπιέναι παρεμβολὴν ἀπέγνωσαν, ὑφορώμενοι μὲν τὸ πλῆθος τῶν ἱππέων, κωλυόμενοι δὲ διὰ τὸν ποταμὸν καὶ τὴν ἐπιφορὰν καὶ συστροφὴν τοῦ κατὰ κεφαλὴν ὄμβρου. τηροῦντες δὲ τὰς τάξεις ἀθρόοι μετ᾽ ἀσφαλείας ἀπεχώρησαν εἰς Πλακεντίαν, ὄντες οὐκ ἐλάττους μυρίων.

---

[10] Bruckmann (1936: 59–60), Händl-Sagawe (1995: 321).

The heavy-armed troops on both sides were at the front and centre of the battle-order; they fought for a long time in close combat, but the hazard was even. At this point the Numidians arose from their ambush, and suddenly fell on the rear of those fighting in the centre: this caused great confusion and distress in the Roman army. In the end both of Sempronius' wings, pressed at the front by the elephants and all round and on the outside of their flanks by the light-armed troops, turned and were forced towards the river behind by those pursuing. But now, in the middle of the danger, those Romans in the rear were being defeated and cut down by the attack from the ambush; but those in the front lines, under extreme pressure, defeated the Celts and some of the Africans, killed many and cut through the Carthaginian line. They saw that their own wings had been forced away, and so despaired of helping them or of returning to their camp, being suspicious of the number of cavalry, and hindered by the river and the violent storm of rain beating on their heads. They maintained close ranks and got away safely to Placentia—their total number was at least 10,000.

The parallel narrative in Livy is not only fuller, but also revealingly slanted (21.55.8–56.3):

pedestris pugna par animis magis quam viribus erat, quas recentis Poenus paulo ante curatis corporibus in proelium attulerat; contra ieiuna fessaque corpora Romanis et rigentia gelu torpebant. restitissent tamen animis, si cum pedite solum foret pugnatum; sed et Baliares pulso equite iaculabantur in latera et elephanti iam in mediam peditum aciem sese tulerant et Mago Numidaeque, simul latebras eorum inprovida praeterlata acies est, exorti ab tergo ingentem tumultum ac terrorem fecere. tamen in tot circumstantibus malis mansit aliquamdiu immota acies, maxime praeter spem omnium adversus elephantos. eos velites ad id ipsum locati verutis coniectis et avertere et insecuti aversos sub caudis, qua maxime molli cute vulnera accipiunt, fodiebant. trepidantesque et prope iam in suos consternatos e media acie in extremam ad sinistrum cornu adversus Gallos auxiliares agi iussit Hannibal. ibi extemplo haud dubiam fecere fugam, eoque novus terror additus Romanis, ut fusa auxilia sua viderunt. itaque cum iam in orbem pugnarent, decem milia ferme hominum, cum alia evadere nequissent, media Afrorum acie, quae Gallicis auxiliis firmata erat, cum ingenti caede hostium perrupere et, cum neque in castra reditus esset flumine interclusis neque prae imbri satis decernere possent, qua suis opem ferrent, Placentiam recto itinere perrexere.

The infantry were evenly matched in spirit, but not in strength. The Carthaginians were fresh for battle, having taken care of their bodily needs shortly before; but the Romans' bodies were hungry, tired, and frozen with cold. Even so, had the battle been confined to the infantry, their spirit would have enabled them to resist; but the Baliarics, now that the cavalry had been routed, hurled weapons at their flanks, and the elephants had now launched themselves against the central infantry position; and Mago and the Numidians, as soon as the army had in ignorance passed their hiding place, arose suddenly in the rear and created huge confusion and terror. Nevertheless, surrounded by all these difficulties, the Roman line for a considerable time held its position unmoved, especially (what no one expected) against the elephants. The

Roman light troops, who had been positioned for precisely that purpose, hurled their javelins and turned them aside, pursued them, and wounded them from behind beneath their tails, where the skin is soft and particularly vulnerable. The beasts were terrified, and were close to turning against their own side in panic; so Hannibal ordered them to be taken out of the centre to the furthest left wing against the Gallic auxiliaries. There they instantly caused a clear rout; hence a new terror was added to the Romans when they saw their auxiliaries in flight. The Romans were now fighting in a circle; around 10,000 men, having no other mode of escape, broke through the centre of the African line, which had been reinforced by Gallic auxiliaries. They killed many in the process, but were unable to return to camp because of the river blocking their route, and the rain prevented them from seeing properly where to bring aid; so they made straight for Placentia.

The same basic outline of events appears in both Livy and Polybius, save that Livy, as before, has more to say about the Carthaginian elephants. But the narrative is slanted quite differently. In Polybius we see the Roman and Carthaginian heavy infantry fighting evenly, until the Romans are worn down and forced into defeat by a combination of the ambush from their rear and the pressure applied on their flanks once their own troops had been forced out by the fresh and well-fed Carthaginians. But Livy appears as eager to discount the effect of the Romans' disadvantageous position as to use it to explain the outcome. He followed Polybius in setting up a situation in which the Romans appear destined to lose; but at every point they appear able to overcome the disadvantage. They are (Livy reminds us) tired, cold, and hungry: but they could have held out in spirit despite those difficulties. They are also under attack from the flanks and from the ambush in the rear: but these are not the disaster one might have anticipated, for the Romans continue to hold out for a considerable time (*aliquamdiu*). Even the elephants are less formidable than they appear: the single aspect of the fight that Livy gives in the fullest detail is the Roman method of handling them. So Hannibal moves the elephants against the Romans' Gallic allies, who flee, causing a 'new terror' to the Romans—but the consequence of that terror is not described, since the focus is still on the solid Roman centre which survives intact.

The effect of Livy's slant is to change the way in which the result of the battle is explained. If one considers the question of why, in Polybius and Livy, the battle is won or lost, both provide the same reasons—excuses, if one likes—for the Roman defeat. The Romans are poorly led, they are cold and hungry, they are caught in an ambush. They are faced by the 'shock tactics' of Hannibal's elephants. Yet Livy, unlike Polybius, having set those up, systematically knocks them down one by one, showing that the Romans hold out despite all of these disadvantages.

But this leaves Livy with what one might call an 'explanatory gap'. Having demolished all of the clear explanations for the Roman defeat that he himself, following Polybius, had carefully described, the defeat, when it comes, is underdetermined, not fully explained by the evidence that Livy has presented.

One might suspect that Livy is attempting to minimize the impression of a serious Roman defeat; but that is clearly not the tenor of his narrative. It is true that he places far more emphasis than Polybius on the Carthaginian losses to the weather,[11] but this does nothing to undercut the magnitude of the Roman defeat. He says more than Polybius does about the Romans killed in flight (21.56.4; contrast Polybius 3.74.7). More significantly, the effect of the news of the defeat at Rome is that *Romam tantus terror ex hac clade perlatus est, ut iam ad urbem Romanam crederent infestis signis hostem venturum* (21.57.1: 'This disaster brought such terror to Rome that they believed that the enemy and his army was about to approach the city of Rome'); Polybius 3.75.4 is much more low-key.[12] This cannot be the reason for the lack of explanation.

Another possibility would be to suggest that Livy's undermining of his own explanations for the defeat is not a desire to avoid explanation, but is rather a by-product of his praise of the Roman soldiery.[13] He so emphasizes their ability to overcome disadvantage that he ends up unable to explain why they lost at all. Taking his account of the Trebia in isolation that might seem a reasonable explanation: the patriotic praise of the soldiers' success even in defeat is manifest, and it is noticeable that the rout in Livy is precipitated by the Romans' Gallic allies, whom Polybius does not mention at all, and who panic before the elephants as the Romans themselves do not.[14] However, the Trebia does not appear in Livy's narrative in isolation; and looking at the wider context of his narrative we may reach a different conclusion about the odd omission of a full explanation for the defeat here.

Livy's self-conscious correction of Polybius' causal sequence is even more marked at Trasimene at the start of Book 22.[15] Here, as with the Trebia, he generally follows Polybius in the way he sets up the conditions that led to the

---

[11] Burck (1962: 76–7): for Livy the Carthaginians' losses are so great 'that they barely felt the joy of victory' (21.56.7 *vix laetitiam victoriae sentirent*)—a direct correction to Polybius, whose Carthaginians are 'overjoyed' (3.74.10 περιχαρεῖς), and it is only later that the weather damages them (3.74.11; contrast Livy 21.56.6). Cf. Händl-Sagawe (1995: 350–1).

[12] Walsh (1973: 228), Händl-Sagawe (1995: 353–4). As is noted by Davidson (1991: 13–14), in Polybius Book 3 the Romans take a long time to come to terms with the fact that Hannibal is genuinely beating them: the dynamic in Livy's account is quite different.

[13] Cf. Händl-Sagawe (1995: 344). For Livy's regular formula of near defeat followed by reasserted Roman superiority see Hoch (1951: 19–20).

[14] Händl-Sagawe (1995: 347).

[15] Cf. Bruckmann (1936: 65–70).

defeat: both authors highlight the trap that Hannibal lays, luring the Romans into a position where they are encircled from above (Polybius 3.83.1–4, Livy 22.4.2–3). Both emphasize the rashness of Flaminius in allowing himself to be led into the trap, though they expound on this in different ways, Polybius engaging in a long abstract disquisition on the dangers of rashness in a general and the advantages of being able to spot weaknesses in one's opponent (3.81), Livy focusing on the specifics of Flaminius' behaviour as he rejects not only the advice of his officers (22.3.4–10; cf. Polybius 3.82.1–8), but also divine signs (22.3.11–14). And accordingly, when the Romans enter Hannibal's trap, Polybius and Livy set out their predicament in almost exactly the same fashion: the fog that reduces their vision, combined with an unexpected attack from all sides with the enemy descending on them from above (Polybius 3.84.1–5, Livy 22.4.5–7).

But at this point Livy's narrative and Polybius' sharply diverge. Polybius merely has a brief notice of Flaminius' death: 'At this time, while Flaminius himself was in distress and dejection about the whole situation, some of the Gauls fell on him and killed him' (3.84.6 ἐν ᾧ καιρῷ καὶ τὸν Φλαμίνιον αὐτὸν δυσχρηστούμενον καὶ περικακοῦντα τοῖς ὅλοις προσπεσόντες τινὲς τῶν Κελτῶν ἀπέκτειναν). This then leads to a lengthy account of the behaviour of the Romans in defeat, but the defeat itself is a forgone conclusion, even if some groups of Romans manage to force their way to safety (3.84.7–14).

Livy, on the other hand, between the Polybian opening of the battle described above, and the account of the final rout, which likewise mirrors Polybius closely (22.6.5–11), incorporates a long central episode (22.5.1–6.4) which has no counterpart in Polybius at all. It is likely that it comes, at least in part, from Coelius Antipater,[16] but the transition between the Polybian and the (probably) Coelian material once again looks like Livy's own correction of Polybius, since it draws on his themes and indeed language while saying exactly the opposite of what he does: 'The consul, with everything overcome,[17] was himself quite as unpanicked as one could be in a terrifying situation' (22.5.1 *consul perculsis omnibus ipse satis, ut in re trepida, inpavidus*). So for Livy Flaminius is not despairing, but remains in control of himself, and, correspondingly, the battle goes far better for the Romans than one might have expected. First Flaminius himself acts to rally the troops (22.5.1–2), but the chaos persists despite his efforts (22.5.3–5). But then the

---

[16] Cf. below, 269–70 with n. 20. The earthquake at 22.5.8, which is not in Polybius, was described in Coelius fr. 20P (= Cicero, *Div.* 1.77–78); likewise Coelius gave the duration of the battle as three hours, exactly as at Livy 22.6.1. The earthquake appears also in Pliny, *NH* 2.200, Plutarch, *Fabius* 3.2, Florus 1.22.14, Zonaras 8.25.

[17] Or 'with everyone downcast': the Latin is ambiguous, but both interpretations reflect aspects of Polybius at this point.

Romans rally, albeit not in proper battle order (22.5.6–8). Flaminius acts vigorously (*inpigre*) to bring help wherever necessary (22.6.1–2), but then is killed (22.6.3–4), after which the Romans are routed much as in Polybius.

Here too, then, much as with the Trebia, the Romans, though caught at what appeared a hopeless disadvantage, succeed in coping with the situation, only ultimately to be defeated anyway.[18] For that reason the same question arises as at the Trebia. Livy sets up the same factors that lead to the defeat as Polybius did, only to show the Romans overcoming them: so why, in Livy, do the Romans end up defeated?

The answer on the face of things appears clearer than at the Trebia. Flaminius commands effectively in the battle line, but is killed, and his death leads to the rout (22.6.5 *magnae partis fuga* <u>*inde*</u> *primum coepit*—'the flight of the majority first began <u>from that point</u>'). But there is an odd twist to Livy's narrative which undermines that explanation. The bulk of his account emphasizes the lack of perception of their surroundings that the Romans had throughout the battle. He, like Polybius (3.83.1–2) had described the fog over the battlefield: unlike Polybius he claimed that it affected the Romans disproportionately, since it settled on the plain and the Carthaginians were attacking from higher ground (22.4.6).[19] And in the centre of his narrative he emphasizes the effect that this had on the Romans: they had to rely more on their hearing than on their sight (22.5.3; cf. 22.6.8). But this is only one part of the theme of lack of perception; because in fact he suggests that hearing too was of little help to the Romans. Flaminius' orders to them cannot be heard because of the noise (22.5.3), noise which increases the chaos as people turn in all directions to face it (22.5.4). The Roman rally begins when they cease to look to the general or rely on anything except themselves (22.5.7 *tum sibi quisque dux adhortatorque factus ad rem gerendam, et nova de integro exorta pugna est*—'then each became his own general and encourager to action, and a new battle arose afresh'). The most extreme—not to say bizarre—demonstration of their lack of perception comes with the statement that they did not even notice the earthquake that took place while they were fighting.[20] In the rout

---

[18] Bruckmann (1936: 67).

[19] The implication of Polybius 3.84.1 and 3.84.13 is that the fog affected the low and high ground equally: the escaping Romans in the latter passage are able to look down from a hill and see the defeat since the fog had now dispersed, not because their elevated position placed them above it (cf. Livy 22.6.9).

[20] Coelius fr. 20P does not mention that the earthquake went unperceived: admittedly this may be because Cicero has simply omitted the point when paraphrasing him, but it is no less possible that it represents Livy's own elaboration. Pliny, *NH* 2.200, Plutarch, *Fabius* 3.2, and Zonaras 8.25 describe the battle in those terms, but they may themselves have drawn on Livy. Pliny lists both Coelius and Livy among his sources for Book 2: according to Münzer (1897: 242–3), 'Livius kann nicht die Quelle des Plinius sein': but this depends on his broader but

itself the Romans are 'all but blind' (22.6.5 *velut caeci*), and even those who escape are initially unable to see what is going on until finally the fog lifts (22.6.8: Polybius 3.84.11 is similar but less forthright).

Yet having centred so much of his account on the Romans' inability to perceive their surroundings, Livy then states that the consul's death led to the rout. In a battle in which the commander was playing a significant (or at least visible) role in leading the troops, that is easily explained. In a battle where we have already been told that the commander's exhortations have no effect, where we are explicitly told that every soldier 'became his own general', and where indeed the entire tenor of the narrative is that most of the Romans have little sense of the commander or of anyone else save their immediate surroundings, it seems odd.[21] And the contradiction is accentuated by the fact that Flaminius is said to be 'distinguished by his weapons' (*insignem . . . armis*), and hence at the centre of the struggle, immediately after which his face is recognized by his eventual killer (22.6.3; see further below, 289–91). It is not that it is an absolutely impossible scenario, but it is significantly at variance with the way in which Livy has constructed the bulk of the narrative. Hence the outcome at Trasimene in Livy, like that at the Trebia, is hard to explain, and for much the same reason. Livy has taken a Polybian narrative in which there is a clear connection between the conditions in which the Romans entered the battle, their conduct in the battle, and the ultimate outcome, and has rewritten the battle in such a way that the ultimate outcome ceases to be dependent on the initial conditions that left the Romans at a disadvantage.

Prior to the defeat at the Trebia, the Romans had suffered another defeat, at the Ticinus. Here the Roman defeat is not excused in advance in quite the way that it was at the Trebia or Trasimene. The commander this time is the far-from-rash elder Scipio, and while Hannibal's tactical acumen plays a key role (the Romans are outflanked by his cavalry), there is no sense that this involves a deceptive ambush as it did in the later battles. The Romans, however, are defeated: and here too Livy changes Polybius' account of that defeat in a way that revealingly alters the emphasis.

First let us look at Polybius 3.65.5–11:

---

questionable argument (227–31) that Pliny generally obtained his material for the Second Punic War from Varro who had himself used Coelius. See the critique of Münzer by Ramosino (2004: 18–19); also 232–3, where she suggests that Pliny's account of the Trasimene earthquake is drawn from Livy. Klotz (1936: 72–4) claims that Dio (and hence Zonaras) took his account from Coelius, but his reasoning is likewise weak; cf. also Schmitt (1991: 101–12). None of the later authors can be assumed to provide independent access to the pre-Livian tradition.

[21] At 22.6.1–2 Livy describes Flaminius as supported by his strongest men (*robora virorum*) and bringing help to others when he found them in trouble, but does not contradict his earlier statement that he was invisible to most of the army.

ὁ μὲν οὖν Πόπλιος προθέμενος τοὺς ἀκοντιστὰς καὶ τοὺς ἅμα τούτοις Γαλατικοὺς ἱππεῖς,
τοὺς δὲ λοιποὺς ἐν μετώπῳ καταστήσας προῄει βάδην. ὁ δ᾽ Ἀννίβας τὴν μὲν
κεχαλινωμένην ἵππον καὶ πᾶν τὸ στάσιμον αὐτῆς κατὰ πρόσωπον τάξας ἀπήντα τοῖς
πολεμίοις, τοὺς δὲ Νομαδικοὺς ἱππεῖς ἀφ᾽ ἑκατέρου τοῦ κέρατος ἡτοιμάκει πρὸς
κύκλωσιν. ἀμφοτέρων δὲ καὶ τῶν ἡγεμόνων καὶ τῶν ἱππέων φιλοτίμως διακειμένων
πρὸς τὸν κίνδυνον, τοιαύτην συνέβη γενέσθαι τὴν πρώτην σύμπτωσιν ὥστε τοὺς
ἀκοντιστὰς μὴ φθάσαι τὸ πρῶτον ἐκβαλόντας βέλος, φεύγειν δ᾽ ἐγκλίναντας εὐθέως διὰ
τῶν διαστημάτων ὑπὸ τὰς παρ᾽ αὑτῶν ἴλας, καταπλαγέντας τὴν ἐπιφορὰν καὶ περιδεεῖς
γενομένους μὴ συμπατηθῶσιν ὑπὸ τῶν ἐπιφερομένων ἱππέων. οἱ μὲν οὖν κατὰ πρόσωπον
ἀλλήλοις συμπεσόντες ἐπὶ πολὺν χρόνον ἐποίουν ἰσόρροπον τὸν κίνδυνον· ὁμοῦ γὰρ ἦν
ἱππομαχία καὶ πεζομαχία διὰ τὸ πλῆθος τῶν παρακαταβαινόντων ἀνδρῶν ἐν αὐτῇ τῇ
μάχῃ. τῶν δὲ Νομάδων κυκλωσάντων καὶ κατόπιν ἐπιπεσόντων, οἱ μὲν πεζακοντισταὶ τὸ
πρῶτον διαφυγόντες τὴν σύμπτωσιν τῶν ἱππέων τότε συνεπατήθησαν ὑπὸ τοῦ πλήθους
καὶ τῆς ἐπιφορᾶς τῶν Νομάδων· οἱ δὲ κατὰ πρόσωπον ἐξ ἀρχῆς διαμαχόμενοι πρὸς τοὺς
Καρχηδονίους, πολλοὺς μὲν αὐτῶν ἀπολωλεκότες, ἔτι δὲ πλείους τῶν Καρχηδονίων
διεφθαρκότες, συνεπιθεμένων ἀπ᾽ οὐρᾶς τῶν Νομάδων, ἐτράπησαν, οἱ μὲν πολλοὶ
σποράδες, τινὲς δὲ περὶ τὸν ἡγεμόνα συστραφέντες.

Scipio put in front his spearsmen and the Gallic cavalry that was with them, and the
rest in a line facing forward, and advanced. Hannibal arranged his bridled cavalry and
all the heavy part in front, and prepared the Numidian cavalry on both wings to
encircle the Romans. Both commanders and both cavalry were zealous for danger—so
much so that when the first assault came the spearsmen could not get in their first
cast, but immediately turned and fled through the gaps behind their own squadrons,
terrified at the sudden attack and frightened of being trampled by the charging
cavalry. The cavalry met head on, and the hazard was for a long time evenly balanced;
for it was simultaneously a cavalry and infantry battle, thanks to the number of men
who dismounted in the course of the actual fight. But when the Numidians encircled
the Romans and fell on them from behind, the spearsmen on foot who had fled the
attack of the cavalry at the start were trampled by the numbers and the violent
onslaught of the Numidians. The Roman cavalry had been fighting the Carthaginians
head on from the start, had sustained heavy losses, but had killed still greater numbers
of Carthaginians. Now, however, when the Numidians attacked their rear, they turned
in flight, most scattering, but some crowding round the general.

Livy 21.46.5–7 essentially presents the same sequence of events, but describes
them in a way that changes the whole account of the battle's outcome:

Scipio iaculatores et Gallos equites in fronte locat, Romanos sociorumque quod roboris
fuit in subsidiis; Hannibal frenatos equites in medium accipit, cornua Numidis firmat.
vixdum clamore sublato iaculatores fugerunt inter subsidia ad secundam aciem. inde
equitum certamen erat aliquamdiu anceps; dein, quia turbabant equos pedites inter-
mixti, multis labentibus ex equis aut desilientibus, ubi suos premi circumventos vidis-
sent, iam magna ex parte ad pedes pugna abierat, donec Numidae, qui in cornibus erant,
circumvecti paulum ab tergo se ostenderunt. is pavor perculit Romanos.

Scipio placed his spearsmen and Gallic cavalry in front, and his Roman troops and the pick of the allies in support. Hannibal put his bridled cavalry in the middle, and strengthened the wings with the Numidians. Almost at the first shout the Roman spearsmen fled among the supporting troops to the second line. The cavalry battle that ensued was in the balance for a considerable time; then, because the infantry who had mixed themselves in disturbed the Romans' horses, many cavalrymen fell from horseback or dismounted where they saw their comrades surrounded and in trouble. The battle had largely turned into an infantry one, until the Numidians on the wings moved around and appeared just behind. That caused panic among the Romans.

There are two key differences here. Whereas in Polybius the reason for the Roman spearsmen retreating into their own lines at the start is that the charge began too quickly for them to use their weapons, in Livy no explanation at all is given.[22] And the consequence of that initial retreat is more serious than it had been in Polybius. In Polybius the retreating spearsmen do not cause any problems for anyone except themselves, and the fight remains evenly balanced until the Numidians attack the Romans from the rear. In Livy the fight is initially even (*anceps*), but *then* (*dein*) the spearsmen get in the way of their own cavalry, and it is that which forces them to dismount and turns the battle into a partially infantry one: the implication is that this already has turned the tide against the Romans even before the Numidians attack from the rear.[23] So Livy's explanation for the Roman defeat is ultimately quite different: the key event is now the initial retreat by the Roman spearsmen, yet that retreat is not given a clear explanation as it is in Polybius.

It is however possible to explain it in a different way. Directly before the battle in both Livy and Polybius there is an elaborate account of the preparations made by the commanders: speeches made by both sides, and also a practical encouragement to his troops made by Hannibal in the form of a fight to the death arranged among his Gallic prisoners, with freedom offered to the victors. But the sequence is different in the two authors. Polybius begins with Hannibal's arranged duel (3.62.2–11), moves on to his speech (3.63), and then to Scipio's speech (3.64.1–10), at the end of which the Roman troops are said to be 'enthusiastic for danger both because of their trust in the speaker and because of the truth of what was said' (3.64.11 καὶ διὰ τὴν τοῦ λέγοντος πίστιν καὶ διὰ τὴν τῶν λεγομένων ἀλήθειαν ἐκθύμως ἐχόντων πρὸς τὸ κινδυνεύειν). Livy begins with Scipio's speech (21.40–41), moves then to the arranged duel (21.42) and Hannibal's speech (21.43–44), at the end of which both sides are said to be fired up for battle (21.45.1). But then he adds

---

[22] Sontheimer (1934: 91–2), Bruckmann (1936: 106).

[23] Cf. Sontheimer (1934: 92–3), who however merely attributes it to Livy's misinterpretation of Polybius.

something further: Hannibal makes a series of extra promises to encourage his troops, which he guarantees with a prayer and sacrifice: the Carthaginians demand battle with the sense that the gods are supporting them (21.45.4–9). The Romans, on the other hand, are terrified by bad omens and so are less eager (21.46.1–2): this then leads directly into the account of the battle.

The most striking feature about this is that the material added to the Polybian sequence changes the motivation of the Romans and Carthaginians. Whereas in Polybius the two sides go into battle equally encouraged (3.63.14, 3.64.11), and accordingly begin the battle with the enthusiastic charge that causes the Roman spearmen to flee, in Livy the Romans' enthusiasm for the battle is considerably lower than the Carthaginians'. That diminution in morale, though not explicitly commented on in the actual fight, forms the background to it, and hence gives a possible explanation for the Romans' otherwise incomprehensibly fleeing before the battle has even begun.[24]

But while it is possible to read Livy's account in this way, it is still not entirely satisfactory. After all, it is unusual in ancient battle narratives for troops to turn and flee before even joining battle, even when their morale is low.[25] The combination of this exceptional behaviour in Livy's Romans with the absence of any explicit attribution of their lower morale in order to explain their actions makes it harder to read morale alone as the explanation for their flight.[26] Here too, as with the Trebia and Trasimene, while Livy provides a possible explanation for a crucial feature of the battle—more crucial than it was in Polybius, as set out above—he does not seem to offer quite enough to account for it adequately. Once again there is a gap between the event that is being explained and the explanation that one might give for it.

So the Trebia does not stand in isolation in its failure to give a full explanation for the result of the battle. In all three cases, Trebia, Trasimene, and Ticinus, Polybius provides a much more neatly mechanistic account which explains things clearly and satisfactorily. Livy is dependent on Polybius for his account of the Ticinus, as well as for the bulk of his account at the Trebia (though with the incorporation of extra material concerning the role of

---

[24] Cf. Rambaud (1980: 110–12).

[25] Sabin (1996: 73–7) discusses various reasons why soldiers in the Second Punic War broke and fled in the battle. Perhaps revealingly, he does not discuss this flight at the Ticinus, and none of his examples involves flight before combat has been joined.

[26] Rambaud (1980: 111–12) suggests that the spearmen were lower class, and hence that Livy's intention is to exculpate the Roman aristocracy. This is, however, implausible: Livy does not mention such a class differentiation in this context. It is true that (on his account) poorer citizens formed the spearmen under Servius Tullius' constitution (1.43.6), but it is unlikely either that this reflected military organization during the Hannibalic War, or that Livy expected his readers to assume that it did: see Ogilvie (1965: 166–70).

the elephants). But, as I showed in Chapter 2, Livy's dependence on Polybius often goes hand in hand with correcting and criticizing him, and it is not hard to see that happening here as well: the reader who knows Polybius will recognize both the dependence and the criticism implicit in Livy's alterations. At the Ticinus Livy offers the same sequence of events in the battle as Polybius, but entirely changes both the motivation and the significance for those events in the battle. At the Trebia and Trasimene he identifies what appeared to be the same basic reasons for the defeat as Polybius did, and yet he systematically demonstrates that none of them is actually a sufficiently crucial factor to explain the defeat. And in all three cases, having undermined Polybius' explanation for the defeat, he does not—at least on the face of things— offer any satisfactory substitute in its place.

All of this shows that interpreting Livy's battles primarily in terms of his provision of patriotic excuses for defeat, as Bruckmann does, is not satisfactory. Livy's position is more complex—more opaque, indeed—than that. The excuses that he provides are largely derived from Polybius, and far from accepting them as the primary explanation for Roman losses, he rewrites the battles in order to minimize their actual effect on the sequence of events. The reader is invited to recognize Polybius' account underlying Livy's, but also to reject it. The problem is that Livy's battle narrative, once the Polybian causal sequence has been rejected, appears to offer no substitute. The outcome of the battle thus remains ostentatiously underexplained.

Moreover, this is true not only with Roman defeats, but also with various of the Roman victories. Let us take, for example, Silanus' victory over Hanno and Mago in Spain at the opening of Book 28 (28.1–2), a victory which Livy presents as vital for the eventual Roman conquest of the Carthaginians in Spain (28.2.13). This battle is structured very similarly to the Carthaginian victories in the early books. Here, as there, the battle is set up in such a way as to offer explanations for the outcome, but here too the narrative of the battle undermines the significance of those explanations.

The Carthaginian army is composed partly of their own troops, and partly of their Celtiberian allies, who are in a separate camp: Silanus' plan is to attack the latter, since he has discovered that their camp is not properly defended (28.1.7–8). He keeps his troops concealed from the Carthaginians, and moves towards the Celtiberians until he reaches a spot near the camp where they can rest and eat safely (28.1.9–2.2). The plan appears clear: the attack on their camp will catch the Celtiberians off-guard and wipe them out before the Carthaginians can come up in their support, depriving the enemy of half of their army at a stroke.

But in fact that is not exactly the way the battle works out. The Romans deploy themselves in battle line (*iusta acie*) and are seen by the Celtiberians when they are a mile away (28.2.3). The Celtiberians are initially in confusion (*trepidari*), but Mago is able to draw them up in a battle line and face the Romans on apparently equal terms (28.2.4–6). The Romans are admittedly advantaged by the terrain, which favoured a style of fighting that relied less on rapid mobility (28.2.7)—but they too, it emerges, are hampered, because their battle line is broken up by it (28.2.8). Nor is it clear that the plan of detaching the Celtiberians from their Carthaginian allies has worked. The Carthaginians are present at the battle, as emerges from 28.2.10: *iam ferme omnibus scutatis Celtiberorum interfectis, levis armatura et Carthaginienses, qui ex alteris castris subsidio venerant, perculsi caedebantur* ('now more or less all of the heavy-armed Celtiberi had been killed, and the light-armed troops and the Carthaginians, who had come in support from the other camp, were overcome and were being cut down'). The pluperfect *venerant* leaves it unclear at what point these Carthaginians arrived, but it was clearly in good time to join the fight, since the Romans are engaging them at the same time as the light-armed Celtiberians, who had been placed in the rear as part of Mago's initial deployment of his army (28.2.4). There are other Carthaginians who arrived too late for the battle (28.2.11), but these are captured alive along with their general Hanno, and so are clearly not the same as the ones who are killed along with the light-armed Celtiberians.

So the apparently clear-cut advantages which would lead the reader to expect that the Romans would win the battle do not appear to be the decisive factors when the battle actually comes to be narrated. Yet the outcome of the battle never seems to be in doubt, a point that is brought home at the very end of the narrative, when it emerges that Mago, along with 2,000 of his infantry and all of his cavalry, had fled as soon as it had begun (28.2.11 *vix inito proelio*); likewise a major effect of the terrain on the Celtiberians is the fact that it prevents them from fleeing and so 'delivers them to slaughter as if they were bound' (28.2.9 *ad caedem eos velut vinctos praebebat*). So the enemy's flight is a feature of the battle from the very start: yet little is offered to explain why they flee. Much as we saw in reverse in the early Roman defeats, the initial advantages that Livy showed for the Romans are systematically shown to have less effect in the battle than we had been led to expect. But that leaves open the question of why, in that case, the Romans actually do win.

One could multiply examples, but this should be enough to demonstrate that, when it comes to battle narratives, Livy's tendency is to detach the outcome of the battle from the factors which his own account had suggested would be decisive. It is true that not every battle is narrated in this way, and one can certainly find plenty of examples where there is a clear link between the conditions of the battle that Livy describes and the final outcome. But battles described in the manner set out above are no less numerous, and far more puzzling. It is not merely that Livy appears to be narrating the battles in a way that does not entirely make sense—that might merely suggest that he was ignorant.[27] The problem is rather that he is setting the battles up so as to lead the reader to expect them to make sense, only then to undermine his own explanations in a systematic and apparently self-conscious manner.

We therefore need to adopt a different approach if we are to understand Livy's battle narratives. One possible alternative is offered by an important current strand of scholarship on military history. I shall begin by giving a brief general summary of the relevant theories, since they may not be familiar to many readers; I shall then show how these may be used to shed light on the problems I have identified in Livy—albeit, as I shall also show, the light is only going to be shed quite obliquely.

The single most significant contribution to the theory of military history in the last forty years was provided in a groundbreaking book by John Keegan.[28] Keegan argued that most battle descriptions found in military historians are misleading, because they approach the narrative from the point of view of the commander moving people around the field *en masse*. But a consideration (he argued) of the actual circumstances of warfare would show that in order to explain what happened in a battle one would need to pay primary attention to the experience of the individual soldiers participating in it: for example their relationship to their fellow soldiers, the practical constraints created by their (often heavy) weaponry, the experience of men on both sides trying to remain alive in the battle. Only by examining those fundamentally individual experiences can one make sense of the actual result of the battle. In order to demonstrate the difference between the misleading history writing he decries and the more accurate writing he endorses Keegan offers two contrasting examples from the ancient world: Thucydides' account of the battle of Mantinea (5.68.1–72.2), and Caesar's of the defeat of the Nervii (*BG* 2.25).[29] Caesar, he argued, ignored the experience of his individual soldiers almost completely, whereas Thucydides focused on it; whereas Caesar simply treated his men as automata obeying his commands, Thucydides' soldiers were individuals with a wide range of motiva-

---

[27] It is often claimed that Livy's narrations of warfare are unsatisfactory in consequence of his (presumed) lack of military experience. See e.g. Walsh (1961: 157–63, 191–204), who suggests that Livy not only misunderstands various key military points, but also stylizes his accounts to make them much neater than any battle could be in practice; also Foucher (2000: 402–9). See however the careful analysis of Plathner (1934): he focuses chiefly on the battles of the First Decade, few if any of which are likely to depend on reliable historical sources, and demonstrates that even these are far more individual, less formulaic, and indeed more plausibly realistic than is generally assumed. More recently, Roth (2006) similarly argues that Livy's accounts of sieges are less stylized and show more awareness of historical realities than he has been given credit for.

[28] Keegan (1976).

[29] Keegan (1976: 61–7).

tions for their actions. But it was Caesar, he suggested, whose approach dominated subsequent military history.

Keegan's account of the difference between Thucydides and Caesar is oversimplistic as a characterization of those specific historians. The description of Mantinea is exceptional within Thucydides' work—and indeed unusual in ancient historiography—for its detailed account of the constraints of hoplite warfare (and as such forms a major piece of evidence for hoplite fighting in general),[30] while Caesar sometimes shows himself less schematic and more aware of individual soldiers' responses than he does in the battle with the Nervii.[31] But this is not to deny the importance of Keegan's essential insights into the nature of battle, which have become immensely influential among military historians, including ancient military historians: histories of both Greek and Roman warfare have now been written from the perspective of individual soldiers, and centre on an awareness of the practical constraints on them.[32]

One key conclusion that emerges from Keegan's work is the crucial link that he detects between the mode of narrative chosen by the military historian and the causal sequence within a battle. The problem that he detects in Caesar is not that the events that he describes did not happen, but that the description omits the crucial features of those events which allow us to understand why exactly a particular tactical movement was successful, or why a group of soldiers broke and fled at a particular moment. Understanding a battle properly, for Keegan, goes hand in hand with narrating it from a particular perspective, namely the perspective of the actual fighters, whose primary aim is less to 'win' than to stay alive.[33]

Keegan's account, though influential, is not altogether uncontroversial, especially when it comes to ancient writers. Kimberley Kagan has recently argued that Keegan's model fails to recognize that Caesar's technique offers a feature which is no less important in explaining a battle: namely a synoptic, commander's-eye view of the events.[34] She contrasts Ammianus' account of battles in which he participated as a soldier with Caesar's account of the battles where he acted as commander, arguing that the limitations of perspective in the former prevent any proper understanding of the outcome, whereas Caesar, contrary to what Keegan argues, is able to amalgamate a large number of disparate

---

[30] On the exceptional features of Thucydides' account of Mantinea see Hanson (1989: 44–5); though see *contra* Hunt (2006: 392–4).

[31] Note Campbell (2002: 167–8).

[32] For Greece, see e.g. Hanson (1989); for Rome, Goldsworthy (1996), Lee (1996), Sabin (2000). These focus on the experience of battle in general rather than giving an analysis of specific battles as Keegan does: for an attempt to use Keegan's approach within a detailed account of one battle see e.g. Daly (2002).

[33] Keegan (1976: 45–7).

[34] Kagan (2006).

experiences into a narrative which makes sense of the whole. Kagan shares with Keegan the perception that our understanding of the causal sequence of a battle is bound up with the manner of its narration, but wishes to return to an understanding of warfare in which the commander's strategic and tactical plans and manoeuvres are the central key (though she does recognize various limitations on the commander's own perspective, which she suggests sets her—and Caesar's—method apart from 'traditional, command-centered approaches').[35]

Kagan's critique of Keegan does not always hit its target, though she does score some useful points. Keegan has never failed to recognize that the commander, with his synoptic oversight and his ability to manoeuvre groups of men, plays a more significant role in battles than does any other individual: he makes the point explicitly in *The Face of Battle*,[36] and in a subsequent book focused directly on the art of generalship as exemplified in leading commanders across the ages.[37] His argument is rather that the central features of a battle—and in particular its result—cannot be understood without appreciating the varying practical constraints on the soldiers whom the commander expects to carry out his orders, and that is largely absent from Kagan's 'eye of command' viewpoint, except in a misleadingly reduced and stylized form.[38] She argues for the limitations of a 'face of battle' approach through an analysis of Ammianus' accounts of battles in which he fought, which leave a great deal that is important unexplained.[39] But to say that Ammianus' particular version of such battle narratives is inadequate to explain the outcome of the battle is not sufficient to show that a better focused version (such as Hanson, Goldsworthy, Sabin, or Daly offer for the ancient world, or as Keegan did for more recent conflicts) is equally unsatisfactory.

But Kagan still provides a central insight: namely that Keegan's focus on individual soldiers is effectively a reductionist account, and as such would, if taken to its logical conclusion, leave a battle incapable of being narrated in any way that could make useful sense of the overall concatenation of events. If it is really true that battles are governed by the experiences of individual soldiers on the battlefield, one would appear to set oneself the impossible task of tracing every individual movement and every individual piece of motivation, which is clearly impossible to do in practice, and would make the battle

---

[35] Kagan (2006: 200).

[36] Keegan (1976: 50–1).

[37] Keegan (1987).

[38] For example, Keegan's analysis highlights the occasions where a general's interests and the interests of his troops directly collide, as when a commander in pursuit of victory deliberately sacrifices a unit by placing it in extreme danger. Kagan (2006: 182–3) glosses over the question, despite its obvious pertinence.

[39] Kagan (2006: esp. 91–5).

incomprehensible if *per impossibile* one were to make a good attempt to do it. Keegan himself, indeed, does not do this: in his discussions of battles he, like other historians, amalgamates groups of soldiers and summarizes aspects of their (often presumed) experiences in order to produce a meaningful narrative. Kagan's 'eye of command', which looks at the commander's view of the battle and his expectations of his troops, provides one way—albeit too limited a one—of justifying that amalgamation.

This brings me to another aspect of Kagan's argument, and one which has roots in much earlier theory: the role of the unpredictable in battles. The significance of this has been recognized at least since Clausewitz, with his famous and much-discussed concept of 'friction'—the unpredictable behaviour of individuals which may work against the commander's plans: Kagan analyses Caesar's account of Gergovia in similar terms.[40] But Clausewitz's account has also been reinterpreted in terms of 'chaos theory', a mathematical discipline which shows how in complex systems wildly differing patterns can arise from minor variations in initial conditions. This was applied to Clausewitz in an important article by Alan Beyerchen, who argued that Clausewitz—rightly—perceived war as a non-linear system, in other words a system where there is not a simple relationship of cause and effect, but where different effects interact with and feed back into one another in a way that is effectively unpredictable.[41] The implications of this are more controversial: for Beyerchen it means that war intrinsically resists rational analysis, whereas for critics such as Kagan this still allows a significant domain for rational strategic thinking, even if one has to take account of chance elements that defy prediction.[42] But either

[40] Kagan (2006: 155–80).
[41] Beyerchen (1992–3); cf. also Culham (1989) for an interpretation of ancient warfare in those terms (n. 42 below).
[42] Kagan (2006: 99–106); also e.g. Gray (2002: esp. 5–8, 90–116). Gray and Kagan, however, approach the issue very differently. Gray accepts the unpredictability of non-linear phenomena in warfare, but argues that there are entire domains of explanation (such as the political and economic) which swamp the unpredictable elements in many instances: an army can equip and prepare itself so as to make defeat against a lesser force vanishingly unlikely. Kagan on the other hand (e.g. 155 and 180) specifically argues that even in areas where unpredictable and non-linear phenomena hold sway (such as the outcome of a battle between reasonably matched forces) the 'eye of command' approach allows unpredictable elements to be understood within an overall causal system in a way that Keegan's reduction of war to the level of the individual participants does not. However, Kagan's argument seems to take no account of the central insight into the role of chaos theory in war offered by Beyerchen (1992–93: e.g. 79): that an immeasurably (and, from the point of view of the commander, imperceptibly) small cause can have vast consequences which will change the entire outcome in ways that are intrinsically unpredictable. For a more measured account see Culham (1989), who argues that while ancient warfare was conducted in such a way as to seek to minimize such chaotic effects, in practice battles were often decided by them.

way, a strong case can be made that battles in practice are not reducible to a clear and predictable chain of cause and effect.

This general theoretical background may at first sight appear tangential to the issue that I am addressing here: namely Livy's apparent failure to explain the outcomes of his battles. However, two elements in particular emerge from it which may be relevant for our problem. First is the question what sort of description of a battle can best explain its outcome—whether it is best understood from a synoptic, commander's perspective, or from understanding the influences on individual soldiers. The second question is whether battles, seen from either point of view, are non-linear phenomena which are radically unpredictable, or whether it is in fact possible to identify a clear chain of causes within them that will explain their outcome. What is Livy's attitude towards these issues?

With regard to the first, Livy's accounts of battles are clearly synoptic ones. He pays relatively little attention to the specific constraints on the soldiers, except in a highly general way which amalgamates their experiences into a very simple and uniform set of motivations: indeed, he looks rather more vulnerable to Keegan's critique of 'command-centred narratives' than Caesar, Keegan's actual example, does.[43] It is true that sometimes, as both at Trasimene and in Spain at 28.1–2, he describes soldiers fighting more as individuals than in massed units, and in the latter he discusses the variable effects of the terrain combined with different weaponry on the different sides. But even here the soldiers on the different sides behave in an essentially uniform fashion: the perspective is still a synoptic one that takes the entire battle into account simultaneously. It is not synoptic in the sense of providing the 'commander's-eye view' that Kagan discusses for Caesar, since Livy rarely shows the specific limitations on his perceptions that the commander experiences in the course of a battle—the exceptions being the times when, as at Trasimene and indeed Cannae, the commander is caught in the same trap as the troops are and so is unable to command them effectively at all.[44] Rather it is an attempt to narrate a battle in terms of the 'big picture' that centres on the grand strategic vision and a clear picture of the soldiers' movements *en masse*.

So it would appear that Livy, judging by his preferred mode of narrative, broadly favours a picture of warfare which centres on the overall strategic plans that the commander develops and the mass movement of sets of troops:

[43] Keegan (1976: 63–4) summarizes the weaknesses that he finds in Caesar under four headings: 'disjunctive movement' (i.e. the implication that different groups of soldiers move at discrete times); 'uniformity of behaviour'; 'simplified characterization'; and 'simplified motivation'. I do not think that I need to demonstrate in detail that most of Livy's battles illustrate the same features.

[44] Cf. Sabin (1996: 68).

he implicitly rejects the reduction of battles to the level of the individual soldier that Keegan would later advocate. It is, admittedly, not surprising that Livy would adopt this narrative perspective, which is widespread in the ancient historiographical tradition, despite the occasional treatment of battles by writers such as Thucydides and Ammianus from the point of view of individual fighters directly engaged in combat (see also below, 311). But what is more surprising is that Livy, in adopting that perspective, breaks the connection between narrative and explanation. Although the adoption of a command-centred narrative perspective would seem to imply that he regards that as the mode which best enables the narrator to explain the outcome of the battle, in practice the outcome is often left unexplained in those terms.

This brings us to the second point: the question of whether Livy considers battles rational and predictable in principle. The bare fact that his synoptic narratives often fail to provide adequate explanations for the outcome is compatible with two alternative explanations. The first (a) is that he regards battles as fundamentally unpredictable, as (on at least one interpretation) Clausewitz later would; the other (b) is that he regards them as explicable and predictable in some terms other than the macrocosmic strategic ones that are the only things that his narrative ostensibly offers.

Let us consider (b) first. Does Livy in fact offer any alternative modes of explanation than simply the strategic one? One possibility is offered by a recent study of Caesar by J. E. Lendon.[45] Lendon notes a mismatch in Caesar between the strategic terms in which he describes his victory at Pharsalus and the rhetorical emphasis that he places on the key role of morale in explaining the superiority of his own troops over Pompey's. He argues that this is because Caesar is drawing on two separate traditions of understanding battle, one (exemplified by Polybius) in which the commander's strategic acumen played the key role, set against another (represented by Xenophon) which gives a central part to the troops' morale. He further argues that Caesar gave a central role to a third feature as well, namely *virtus*, or the troops' intrinsic courage over and above the specific morale they showed on that occasion, and this was something that was not strongly represented in Greek writing on warfare, but which he drew from a specifically Roman understanding of the nature of combat.[46] Lendon concludes by suggesting that one reason that modern historians find it hard to reconstruct Caesar's battles is that modern readers

---

[45] Lendon (1999). Note also Lee (1996: 203–12) for the genuine importance of morale in Roman warfare; Goldsworthy (1996: 248–64) examines in greater detail the way in which Roman soldiers' morale was maintained.

[46] Cf. Rosenstein (1990a: 92–113) on the central role that Romans ascribed to the *virtus militum* in explaining the outcomes of battles.

instinctively conceptualize battles in materialist terms like those of Polybius, seeing them governed by tactical movement of forces, whereas Caesar often presents such matters in a simplified and stylized form; conversely, we tend not to recognize the significance of the psychology and character of the troops that loom so large in Caesar.

If Lendon is right to see these features of battle narratives as not specific to Caesar, but as rooted more broadly in Roman cultural understandings of warfare, we might expect Livy to follow a similar pattern. And indeed he often does give far greater play to questions of morale and courage than Polybius did.[47] There are battles which turn entirely on these issues. A good example is the fight between Gracchus and Hanno at Beneventum (24.14–16). Here there is no clear ethnic expectation that either side is intrinsically superior in warfare: the bulk of the Carthaginian troops are in fact Italian (24.15.2), whereas Gracchus' troops are mainly slave volunteers (24.14.3; cf. 22.57.11), so of unspecified national background—though with the understanding that, under Rome's regular disposition, they are potential Romans, since they will obtain citizenship on achieving freedom. Nor does anything in Livy's account of the battle suggest any tactical ploys on either side: Gracchus promises his troops at the start that the fight will be 'on a clear and open field, where the issue can be conducted through true courage without any fear of traps' (24.14.6 *dimicaturum puro ac patenti campo, ubi sine ullo insidiarum metu vera virtute geri res posset*), and the account of the battle bears this out. Gracchus' problem is not a tactical one, but how to give his troops the appropriate incentive. His first idea is to promise freedom to anyone who brings back an enemy head (24.14.7); but this has the (predictable) consequence that the best slave soldiers spend too much time cutting off heads and then are handicapped by having to carry them around (24.15.3–4): the fight thus remains in the balance. When Gracchus discovers this, he changes the plan—they can throw away the heads, since 'their courage is sufficiently clear and apparent' (24.15.6 *claram satis et insignem virtutem*). But even with that the fight proves balanced: this is presumably, at least in part (though Livy does not make the point explicitly), because there is no longer an incentive for each individual to contribute to the victory, since they will now obtain freedom no

---

[47] This, however, is not invariable: there are places where Polybius interpreted events in terms of morale and Livy turns it in a more material direction. For example, Hannibal after capturing Tarentum traps the Romans in the citadel into a futile attack. According to Polybius 8.32.4 he does so in order that the Roman defeat will terrify them and hearten the Tarentines, which is indeed what happens (8.33.1–3). In Livy's reworking of the episode Hannibal has the more practical intention of reducing the Romans' numbers to the point where the Tarentines will no longer need Carthaginian support to contain them (25.11.3). On Polybius' use of morale in his battle narratives see Davidson (1991: 21).

matter what. So Gracchus changes the rule again: the slaves will only be given freedom in the event of a Roman victory (24.15.8). This instantly turns the course of the battle, and the Roman side routs the enemy (24.16.1)—though Gracchus then has to deal with the problem of the appropriate treatment for those slaves who did not in fact fight courageously, a problem he solves by awarding them freedom but compelling them to eat standing until they complete their military service (24.16.11–13)—something they immediately put into practice at the celebratory banquet (24.16.18). Gracchus' limited competence here is worth noting, as he lurches between different ways of creating the appropriate level of morale: I shall be discussing this in more depth in the second half of the chapter. For our purposes now, however, the chief point is that the various swings in the battle essentially turn on the commander's ability to give the greatest morale to his soldiers and the greatest play to the intrinsic courage of the best of them.

The same thing is relevant to the more problematic battles that I discussed earlier. We already saw that for Livy the Romans at the Ticinus enter the battle with their morale lowered, as they do not in Polybius. At the Trebia (21.55.8–56.3 quoted above) part of the reason that the Roman soldiers are able to hold out despite everything that is against them is their 'spirit' (*animi*: the standard word to reflect soldierly morale), and the eventual loss is triggered by the flight of the Gauls causing *terror* among the Romans, just as at Trasimene it is triggered by the killing of Flaminius: Polybius does not analyse the battle in those terms. And attributions of *virtus* to the Romans in particular are too frequent to require detailed illustration.

To some extent, then, Livy certainly does point the reader to morale as an issue that could make a difference in a battle. One might therefore wonder whether a Roman, who might (unlike a modern reader) already be geared up to understand warfare in those terms, would naturally 'read in' morale as the key factor leading to defeat even at points where it is not directly stated as being at issue. But this, while perhaps underlying some of Livy's failure to set out the reasons for victory or defeat explicitly, can only be a small part of the explanation. With the battles analysed above, the problem is not merely that no direct explanation is given, but that the battle is narrated in terms that seem to defy explanation altogether. At the Ticinus and Trasimene there are certainly pointers in the direction of morale being a critical factor, but the actual narrative goes beyond what could naturally be explained in terms of morale: the exceptional flight of the Roman spearmen at the Ticinus despite the fact that battle has not yet even been joined, and the routing of the Romans at Trasimene after Flaminius' death despite the fact that the battle has been so narrated to imply that the commander was invisible and inaudible to the majority of his troops. The Trebia, where the Romans are described as maintaining morale until the flight of their allies causes *novus terror*, would be a more straightforward candidate for seeing largely unexpressed psychological factors as the key issue beneath the surface—except that at the Trebia the only Romans who are described are the ones who maintain their formation and escape. Poor morale may be an issue, but we are not offered any soldiers on which it appears to be working.

So while Lendon is certainly right to emphasize the significance of morale and intrinsic courage in Roman understandings of warfare, the puzzling features of Livy's battles are not explicable in those terms without some strain.

Let us therefore consider possibility (a) outlined above (281): that Livy regards battles as fundamentally unpredictable. Here the relationship to Polybius may offer us some guidance. Livy, in self-consciously rewriting Polybius' sequence of events at Ticinus, Trebia, and Trasimene, is clearly offering a critique of his rationalist account of battles, in which effect typically follows cause mechanically and where the tactical abilities of the commanders play the central role.[48] This could be because he regards Polybius as overlooking some key but non-mechanistic factor such as morale that Livy sees as crucial. But, as I have just shown, while it is certainly the case that morale and the like plays a smaller role in Polybius' battles than it does in Livy's, the tenor of Livy's alterations of Polybius does not seem to point us to morale or any other comparable factor as the key. Livy does, as I said, rewrite Polybius' battles to give a bigger role to psychology, but he does not highlight it in a way that would suggest that it was the key to understanding defeat or victory.

Could Livy then be suggesting, contrary to Polybius, that battles are governed by no definable factor, but merely by random chance? Although Polybius was far from averse to attributing events to 'chance'—τύχη, or sometimes τὸ αὐτόματον—he largely confines its scope to places where an outcome is unexpected or a sudden and dramatic reversal takes place,[49] and in the context of warfare he frequently stresses that a good commander achieves his successes through his own rational control of events. He provides a long general discussion of the rational tactical behaviour required of commanders in 9.12–20; in the specific context of the Hannibalic War he has a lengthy account of Hannibal's

---

[48] Cf. Hoffman (2002: esp. 193–201) on the way in which Polybius tends with hindsight to attribute thoughts and motivations to his characters, precisely in order to draw a close link between people's actions and their consequences.

[49] This is admittedly a simplification of a complex question, since τύχη has a wide range of uses in Polybius and appears in a significant number of different contexts. His most detailed discussion of it comes in a passage late in his history (36.17), which limits it to a relatively small number of things which genuinely defy rational explanation; but it is unlikely that this is to be seen as a master-key that applies to all earlier uses of the concept in the work. See Walbank (1957: 16–26), Pédech (1964: 331–54), Walbank (1972: 58–65), cf. also Hoffman (2002: 201–7).

success through reliance on rational calculation at 3.47.6–48.12 (one which Livy systematically challenges in his reworking of this episode: see above, 149–54). At 10.2.5–6 and 10.5.8 he similarly attributes Scipio's success to his rational ability to assess a situation rather than to fortune: here too, as with Hannibal, he criticizes historians who failed to appreciate this.

So one might anticipate that Livy's rejection of Polybius' rationalistic account of battles would go hand in hand with attributing them explicitly or implicitly to mere chance. However, while it is true that 'chance'—*fortuna*—is an extremely common concept in Livy,[50] who from time to time reflects on its vagaries in a manner familiar not only from Polybius but from much ancient literature, in fact it plays a considerably smaller role in Livy's account of the battles of the Hannibalic War than one might have anticipated, at least if one judges by his willingness to attribute a key feature of a battle to it explicitly. Indeed, it plays a much smaller role than it does even in Polybius. *fortuna* rarely appears in battles as a meaningful causal agent.[51] It is often spoken about by characters as if it were something that could or does make a major difference to the outcome of a battle, but Livy's narrative rarely bears that out directly.[52] The only suggestion of a significant role for chance at Cannae, for example, is at the very start, when the fact that neither side had the sun in their eyes is said to be 'whether they were deliberately placed that way or because they stood that way by chance' (22.46.8 *seu de industria ita locatis seu quod forte ita stetere*)—but it is noticeable that not only is 'chance' only offered as one possibility, it also is in reference to something that makes the battle equal[53] rather than something that sways it in one or other direction.[54] The Romans were (according to Livy, though not

---

[50] The word appears more than 500 times in Livy's surviving text, and that leaves out of account related terms like *fors*. My brief account of Livy's use of *fortuna* at Levene (1993: 30–3) (itself following Kajanto 1957: 53–100) has been superseded by Davies (2004: 115–23). I still regard Livy's use of the term as less coherent than Davies does, but he shows successfully how many of the apparently disparate elements of Livy's usage fall within the broad framework of Roman ideas about the workings of the gods, of which Fortuna was one.

[51] One exception is 22.41.1–2, where a minor Roman victory is directly referred to as something that happened by *fortuna*. In this case the chief point appears to be that it was indeed effectively a random result: the soldiers are not acting under direction of their generals, and the battle is described as 'chaotic' (22.41.1 *tumultuario*). But this is clearly atypical of the battles of the Hannibalic War.

[52] Cf. Kajanto (1957: 92–5); also Erkell (1952: 162–73).

[53] Compare 26.39.7–8, where 'by chance' (*forte*) the Roman commander is under sail unprepared for battle, but then—equally 'by chance'—the wind drops and allows the Romans to prepare themselves and enter the battle on equal terms. See further below, 309–10.

[54] An alternative version had the Romans disadvantaged through having the sun in their eyes, as at Valerius Maximus 7.4 ext. 2, Seneca, *NQ* 5.16.4, and Florus 1.22.16, though they attribute this to Hannibal's tactics rather than mere bad fortune. (Ennius, *Ann.* 265 Sk. may be describing the same thing, but note the doubts of Skutsch 1985: 444–5.) Livy follows Polybius 3.114.8, who may be polemically rejecting the other version as a Roman excuse (so Walbank 1957: 436).

Polybius)[55] additionally disadvantaged by having the wind blow dust in their eyes, but this is attributed not to bad luck, but to Hannibal's deliberate design (22.43.10–11, 22.46.9), however implausible that may sound.[56]

The character who most prominently attributes events to *fortuna* is Hannibal, especially in his speech to Scipio before Zama (30.30.3–30), in which he warns him against placing too much reliance in it (30.30.10–12, 15–23). This speech is based on Polybius 15.6.4–7.9, which likewise has Hannibal warning Scipio against τύχη in very similar terms (15.6.8–7.4). In both authors, moreover, Scipio in his reply accepts the basic point about the fickleness of fortune that Hannibal makes (30.31.6; cf. Polybius 15.8.3), while denying that this is sufficient reason to come to terms before the battle as Hannibal had wished. But Livy has significantly changed both the balance and the context of Hannibal's argument.[57] He expands the whole speech, and specifically the point about fortune, giving many further examples. The word *fortuna* appears no fewer than eleven times in this speech,[58] which is more than 6 per cent of all its occurrences in the entire decade; Livy even inserts it into the beginning of the speech (30.30.5), as part of an additional argument which has no parallel in Polybius.[59]

Yet in some crucial ways Hannibal appears to be wrong. When it comes to the battle, 'fortune' is given even less play than it received in Polybius. In discussing Hannibal's final defeat at Zama (15.15–16), after praising his decisions in command Polybius gives two possible reasons why a good commander may nevertheless be defeated: one is chance, but the second is that he meets his superior, and Polybius is of the opinion that it was the latter that applied at Zama (15.16.6). This is imitated by Livy (30.35.5–9 discussed above, 240–2), though the praise of Hannibal is in the voice of Scipio 'and everyone with military expertise' rather than the narrator: the people with

---

[55] Ennius, *Ann.* 264 Sk. appears to have referred to the effect of dust at Cannae, though that line does not directly suggest the Romans were disadvantaged by it (see Skutsch 1985: 443). It then became a popular feature of later accounts; apart from Valerius Maximus, Seneca, and Florus (n. 54 above), it is referred to by Plutarch, *Fabius* 16.1; Appian, *Hann.* 20, 22; Zonaras 9.1.

[56] Walbank (1957: 438) doubts the story altogether; Daly (2002: 43) argues that the dust is an authentic feature of the battle, despite its absence from Polybius, but that it was unlikely to have been either Hannibal's deliberate design or as significant a factor in the Roman defeat as the ancient sources imply.

[57] Stübler (1941: 164–8).

[58] τύχη appears just three times in Polybius' (admittedly shorter) version of the speech.

[59] Hannibal's emphasis on the role of fortune is something of a leitmotif in Livy's representation of him. In his speech at 21.43–44 (a speech which parallels in important ways the one he gives before Zama: see above, 16–17) he likewise mentions the word six times; cf. Stübler (1941: 97–8). He also uses it in direct speech or has it attributed to him in a passage of indirect speech at 21.45.6, 22.23.2, 26.7.5, 26.11.4, 27.14.1, 27.51.12, 30.37.9.

military expertise may be presumed to include Polybius.[60] However Livy, unlike Polybius, does not go on to ask why Hannibal lost at Zama despite his tactical acumen, and this is presumably because of his rejection of Polybius' neat antithesis. As I discussed in Chapter 3, the key factor for Livy in the Carthaginian defeat at Zama was neither Scipio's superior tactics (though they were obviously not irrelevant), nor 'fortune', at least in the sense in which Polybius seems to conceive it and which Hannibal argues for in his speech, but something more fundamental than either: the multiracial structure of the Carthaginian army itself, which was the consequence of a far larger and longer historical process than any individual could control.[61]

This is not the only place where Livy parses the role of 'fortune' in a battle differently from the way Polybius had. When Hannibal is about to attack the city of Rome in Polybius he is put off by what Polybius refers to as 'an unexpected and <u>fortunate</u> occurrence to save the Romans' (9.6.5 παράδοξόν τι καὶ <u>τυχικὸν</u> σύμπτωμα πρὸς σωτηρίαν τοῖς ʿΡωμαίοιǯ: the Romans happened to have enlisted new troops in the city at the precise point when he arrived. Nevertheless Polybius regards Hannibal as praiseworthy for his rational handling of the situation despite the 'chance reversal' (9.9.3 τὰς ἐκ ταὐτομάτου περιπετείας; cf. 9.9.10), comparing him to Epaminondas, who did everything right and was 'superior to his enemies, but inferior to fortune' (9.8.13 τῶν μὲν ὑπεναντίων κρείττω, τῆς δὲ τύχης ἥττω). Livy likewise has a reverse for Hannibal at that point, but for quite a different reason— something indeed that might look more like pure chance than the parallel sequence does in Polybius. Instead of the unexpected troops, the attempt on Rome by Hannibal is thwarted by a rainstorm (26.11.1–4). Here, as at Zama, Hannibal himself speaks of *fortuna* thwarting him (26.11.4), and this is clearly something that was unpredictable in any normal terms. But Livy does not speak of *fortuna* in the narrative voice, and it is apparent from his description that he does not regard the storm as merely a normal phenomenon of the weather: he describes it in a way that makes it appear miraculous.[62] The rain occurs twice on consecutive days, and corresponds precisely to the Carthaginians' appearing on the field: when they return to camp the weather turns to 'amazing serenity and calm' (26.11.3 *mira serenitas cum tranquillitate*). At 26.8.3–5 Fabius, opposing the withdrawal of the army from Capua to protect

---

[60] De Sanctis (1968: 636). Apart from his history, Polybius was the author of a treatise on tactics (9.20.4; it is also cited by Arrian and Aelian); for Polybius as a theorist of war see Poznanski (1994).

[61] Compare Koselleck (2004: 115–27) on the way in which historians' sense of historical contingency summarized in the term 'chance' is at odds with—and in later historical thought was largely superseded by—a sense of a broad historical meaning and direction.

[62] Levene (1993: 59–60).

Rome, had assured the Romans that 'Rome . . . would be defended by Jupiter, witness to the treaties broken by Hannibal, and the other gods' (26.8.5: *Romam . . . Iovem foederum ruptorum ab Hannibale testem deosque alios defensuros esse*). The connection between the sky god and the miraculous weather conditions is obvious—Livy is writing the battle so as to prove Fabius correct.[63] For Livy, Hannibal is defeated not by mere chance, but by a divine hand. Nor does Livy suggest that Hannibal's abilities as a general enabled him to overcome this setback.

Livy is here, as elsewhere, challenging Polybius' focus on superiority in command as the key factor in victory or defeat; but he also appears to be declining to attribute victory or defeat to mere chance, which in Polybius seems to be the only alternative. Admittedly here, unlike with Zama, it does not look as if Livy is actively making a contrast between Hannibal's obsessive focus on 'fortune' and the actual conduct of the battle. The fact that he introduces Hannibal's view by saying that the Carthaginians 'attributed the matter to religion' (26.11.4 *in religionem ea res apud Poenos versa est*), combined with the fact that (as Davies has shown) *fortuna* at Rome regularly had overtones of divine action, means that Hannibal's suggestion that *fortuna* has thwarted him would be likely to be seen more as a sign of divine disfavour than of mere blind chance working against him, and this is the tenor of Livy's description of the battle also. Even in his speech before Zama Hannibal, while talking primarily about 'fortune', equates it with the result of the battle being 'in the hands of the gods' (30.30.19 *in deorum manu*). But it is still significant how rarely Livy in his own voice attributes the outcome of battles to the direct workings of *fortuna*, and this is doubtless because, though *fortuna* certainly had overtones of divine control, it presents the workings of the divine as if it were something capricious.[64] But Livy is not presenting these battles in those terms. The reason Hannibal fails to take Rome in Book 26, as also the reason he loses at Zama, is not, for Livy, something beyond reason, but it also is not primarily to do with the decisions and tactics of the commanders—even

---

[63] Gärtner (1975: 42). In this, Livy reflects the common opinion among Roman writers, although the precise nature of the divine intervention varied. Ennius (*ap.* Propertius 3.3.11) had, like Livy, described Hannibal's repulse from Rome in divine terms, but had attributed it to the Lares; Varro, *Men.* 213, attributed it to Tutanus (or Hercules Tutanus), who drove away the army 'by night' (*noctu*), while according to Festus p. 282M (cf. Pliny, *NH* 10.122) a shrine to Rediculus was dedicated on the spot where Hannibal had retreated 'terrified by certain visions' (*quibusdam visis perterritus*). It is unclear whether these gods might have been identified with one another (note Skutsch 1985: 271).

[64] Cf. Davies (2004: 121–3). It should, however, be observed that while Hannibal does cite the gods as well as *fortuna*, and is not actively impious here, he has little sense of a divine concern for justice, a point which Scipio emphasizes in his reply (30.31.4–5). See Levene (1993: 75), and below, 339–53.

though those decisions and tactics form the perspective from which he narrates his battles.

So in terms of the antithesis set out above (281), it appears that after all (b) may have been correct. Livy does not simply regard battles as unpredictable, but there is indeed an alternative mode of explanation to the tactics adopted by the commanders, an explanation which is, however, not merely the morale of the troops. As I showed above, at both the Ticinus and Trasimene the crucial flight of the Romans is associated with lower morale, but the lower morale does not seem sufficient given the way the battle and the flight are described. But with both of these battles a broader examination of the context allows an explanation in quite different terms. Both battles are preceded by a series of omens (21.46.1–2, 22.3.11–14)[65] which suggest that the gods are not on the Romans' side. The first of those passages was mentioned in the context of the Romans' loss of morale at the Ticinus, but I argued that one cannot adequately explain the initial flight at the Ticinus merely in terms of loss of morale, while at Trasimene the soldiers' morale is actually increased by Flaminius' willingness to ignore the omens (22.3.14). But if we think of the omens not in terms of their effect on the participants in the battle, but rather in terms of the indications of future defeat that they offer, a different and more fruitful interpretation emerges. The troops' flight at the Ticinus may not make sense in terms of their morale; still less does it make sense in terms of any strategic or tactical considerations. But it makes a great deal of sense if we see it in the context of a picture of the world in which the gods have determined that the Romans will lose. The flight of the spearsmen at the start of the Ticinus is from this perspective exactly parallel to the miraculous rainstorm before Rome in Book 26. And from the perspective of the reader, it is the very incongruity of the flight, just as it is the stunning miraculousness of the storm, which alerts them that defeat or victory is to be attributed to some pattern other than the rational and mechanistic one which Livy drew—but corrected—from Polybius.

Nor is Livy merely showing us a crude connection between a generalized divine disfavour and the Romans' defeat. At Trasimene the oddities of his account point to something more complex. It is the death of Flaminius in the battle that leads directly to the Roman rout—although the narrative of the battle suggests that Flaminius was not visible or audible to most of his

---

[65] The omens before Trasimene are in fact the culmination of a series of supernatural events which point to the gods' disfavour with Flaminius' command: the prodigy list at 21.62, the omen at 21.63.13–14, the further prodigy list at 22.1.8–20; and Flaminius accentuates the divine displeasure by actively ignoring the warnings, an impiety he had also shown earlier, when he failed to carry out the appropriate ceremonies on his accession to the consulship (21.63.5–11, 22.1.5–7). See Levene (1993: 38–43).

soldiers. But the way Flaminius is killed is significant. Whereas in Polybius his death at the hands of 'certain Gauls' is described only summarily (3.84.6 τινèς τῶν Κελτῶν),[66] Livy gives a full account of his killer: a specific Gaul, Ducarius the Insubrian, who, despite the fact that (as we have been told: above, 269–70) the soldiers are unable to see each other properly or receive orders, recognizes Flaminius not only by his armour but also by his face as the general who had defeated their armies and ravaged their lands (22.6.3–4).[67] This refers to Flaminius' earlier consulship in 223, in which he fought against the Insubrians. Our loss of Book 20 means that we cannot tell precisely how Flaminius' treatment of the Gauls was handled by Livy (*Per.* 20 is, as often, far too laconic to be informative); but the references to his earlier consulship in the surviving portions of Livy have a strongly negative cast, relaying accusations of impiety which match his impiety directly before Trasimene (21.63.7, cf. 21.63.2–4, 21.63.12, 22.3.4).[68] Flaminius' behaviour in his second consulship is of a piece with that in his first. When Fabius suggests after the battle that 'the consul Flaminius offended more in his neglect of ceremonies and auspices than through rashness and ignorance' (22.9.7: *plus neglegentia caerimoniarum auspiciorumque quam temeritate atque inscitia peccatum a C. Flaminio consule esse*), while the immediate reference is naturally to his actions that year, the broad statement has a wider scope. Flaminius is trapped and defeated through his failure to heed divine signs, but the specific trigger for his death and hence defeat within the battle has its roots in his wrongdoing years earlier. It makes sense morally that he should die in this way; it also makes sense morally that this should in turn trigger the Roman defeat, since the Roman state as a whole has been implicated in his behaviour.[69] But the

---

[66] Note Urban (1991: 147–57), arguing that Polybius, unlike Livy, slants his account of the Gauls in the Hannibalic War in order to give them a fundamentally anti-Roman role: see further n. 69 below.

[67] Cf. Catin (1944: 46), who also suggests that Hannibal's inability to find Flaminius' body and provide it with funeral rites (22.7.5) is to be seen as the final punishment for his impiety.

[68] Levene (1993: 39–40).

[69] Compare Johner (1996: 170–1) on the unusually close assocation Livy draws between Flaminius as an individual and the army as a whole at Trasimene. Moreover, the Romans' recent treatment of the Gauls has already caused them problems against Hannibal. At 21.20.6 it is cited by the Gauls as a reason for their being unwilling to support Rome to block Hannibal's march, while at 21.25.2 the foundation of Roman colonies on Gallic territory is the reason for an uprising by the Boii. This latter is a reworking of Polybius 3.40.3–8, in which resentment over the colonies is merely an excuse, and the real reason is the Gauls' long-standing antagonism to Rome—an interpretation which Livy explicitly rejects (*nec tam ob veteres in populum Romanum iras*): for him it is the Romans' own behaviour towards the Gauls that stands at the root of their difficulties (see Urban 1991: 149–50; cf. 154–5). It has a further consequence also, for in Livy 21.29.6, unlike Polybius 3.44.5, it is specifically the Boii who offer support to Hannibal in his planned crossing of the Alps—although in the event that support is less useful to Hannibal than initially appeared (above, 152–3).

fact that it makes sense morally is given a crucial significance in interpreting the battle, which is deliberately written so as to make less sense in any other way, a point which Fabius' comment reinforces. Livy visibly changes Polybius' rational account into something that does not quite work in Polybius' rationalist and commander-centred terms (as when Flaminius apparently becomes visible specifically in order to be killed); but he also adds moral and religious material which suggest alternative terms in which it does work.

'Working' does not always imply a straightforward relationship of cause and effect even if one takes divine action into account. It is hard to construct an explicit picture of divine intervention which would lead to precisely the sequence that Livy presents in many of these battles, nor is there any indication that Livy expects the reader to construct such a picture. At Zama the crucial causal sequence that Hannibal (and Polybius) overlooks is not overtly divine, but connected with the structure of the Carthaginian army and the Carthaginian empire. There is, however, also a more general sense of moral endorsement on the divine level that appears through not merely Scipio's reply to Hannibal before the battle, but also the quasi-prophetic terms in which he predicts victory to his troops (30.32.9–11), though it is very hard to see that working in direct causal terms.

Indeed, sometimes the apparent cause and effect are chronologically out of sequence. Immediately on Hannibal's retreat from Rome Livy shows him plundering the temple at Feronia (26.11.8–13): the close juxtaposition with his being miraculously thwarted invites the reader to connect the two events.[70] The natural connection that one would make would be that Hannibal's impiety, especially when combined with his original treaty-breaking alluded to by Fabius at 26.8.5 (quoted above) and the Roman piety at 26.9.7–8, makes the gods hostile to him. Yet, at least on the face of things, the effect precedes the cause, since this particular impious act comes after the divine intervention. But the precise sequence is something that Livy instantly shows is in doubt: he cites the alternative view of Coelius Antipater, under which the plundering of the temple was indeed prior to Hannibal's arrival at Rome (26.11.10–11), and offers no conclusion as to which version is correct (26.11.13). The point he emphasizes is that either way Hannibal definitely carried out the plundering (26.11.10, cf. 26.11.13)—in effect, the chronological sequence is irrelevant to the implied connection that Livy is drawing.

Or sometimes the apparent cause and effect are so closely intertwined as to be effectively inseparable. The very first time that Roman and Carthaginian troops encounter each other is a clear example. In Polybius this encounter, though abridged, is straightforward (3.45.1–2):

---

[70] Levene (1993: 60); more generally see above, 287–9.

ἧκον τῶν Νομάδων οἱ προαποσταλέντες ἐπὶ τὴν κατασκοπήν, τοὺς μὲν πλείστους αὐτῶν
ἀπολωλεκότες, οἱ δὲ λοιποὶ προτροπάδην πεφευγότες. συμπεσόντες γὰρ οὐ μακρὰν ἀπὸ
τῆς ἰδίας στρατοπεδείας τοῖς τῶν ʽΡωμαίων ἱππεῦσι τοῖς ἐπὶ τὴν αὐτὴν χρείαν
ἐξαπεσταλμένοις ὑπὸ τοῦ Ποπλίου τοιαύτην ἐποιήσαντο φιλοτιμίαν ἀμφότεροι κατὰ
τὴν συμπλοκὴν ὥστε τῶν ʽΡωμαίων καὶ Κελτῶν εἰς ἑκατὸν ἱππεῖς καὶ τεττεράκοντα
διαφθαρῆναι, τῶν δὲ Νομάδων ὑπὲρ τοὺς διακοσίους.

The Numidians who had been sent out to scout earlier returned, with most of them lost,
and the rest fleeing headlong. For they had encountered near their camp the Roman
cavalry sent out on the same mission by Scipio. Both sides had shown such zeal in the
struggle that the Romans and Celts lost about 140 cavalry, the Numidians over 200.

The implication in Polybius is thus that the Numidians' flight was triggered by
their greater loss of troops in a hard-fought battle. But when Livy reaches the same
episode, he rewrites Polybius in a startling and significant fashion (21.29.1–4):

Hannibal Numidas equites quingentos ad castra Romana miserat speculatum, ubi et
quantae copiae essent et quid pararent. huic alae equitum missi, ut ante dictum est, ab
ostio Rhodani trecenti Romanorum equites occurrunt. proelium atrocius quam pro
numero pugnantium editur; nam praeter multa vulnera caedes etiam prope par utrimque
fuit, fugaque et pavor[71] Numidarum Romanis iam admodum fessis victoriam dedit.
victores ad centum sexaginta, nec omnes Romani sed pars Gallorum, victi amplius ducenti
ceciderunt. hoc principium simul omenque belli ut summae rerum prosperum eventum,
ita haud sane incruentam ancipitisque certaminis victoriam Romanis portendit.

Hannibal had sent 500 Numidian cavalry to the Roman camp to spy out the position,
strength, and plans of the army. As was said before, 300 Roman cavalry had been sent
from the mouth of the Rhône: they encountered the Numidian cavalry squadron. The
ensuing battle was bloody out of proportion to its scale; apart from the many
wounded, approximately equal numbers were killed on each side, and the Numidians'
flight and panic gave the Romans victory when they were all but exhausted. The
winning side lost about 160, some Gauls as well as Romans, the losers more than 200.
This was simultaneously the start of the war and an omen of it: it portended that the
ultimate result would be favourable, but that the war would be close, and the Roman
victory an especially bloody one.

Livy not only makes the battle closer (the Romans lose 160 troops here to the
Carthaginians' 200; in Polybius it is 140), but he rewrites the sequence of events.
Whereas in Polybius the flight of the Numidians appears to be triggered by their
greater losses in the battle, in Livy it is the reverse. In the fight itself the Romans
and the Numidians are explicitly said to have had more or less equal losses, and if
anything the Romans are doing worse, since it is they who are described as 'all
but exhausted'. Yet it is the Numidians who flee. Just as we saw in other battles,

---

[71] The Teubner here reads *fuga pavorque*, but the asyndeton is awkward, and the more usual
reading is to be preferred.

no reason for their flight is given, and it appears more or less inexplicable given the way that the battle is described. But the explicit moral Livy draws from it provides an explanation of a different sort. This is an omen of the war, not merely in the Roman victory, but in the closeness that the Romans came to defeat prior to that victory: in the opening lines of the book Livy had characterized the war in similar terms to the skirmish here, as one where the ultimate victors were also the closest to destruction (21.1.2). Livy rewrites the narrative to make the parallel more apparent; but reconstructs the events into a sequence which makes less rational sense as an account of a battle than Polybius' did, and so indicates that it needs to be understood in other terms. What 'causes' the Numidians to flee, in Livy's version, is nothing more or less than the fact that this skirmish *is* an omen of victory. To attempt to address the question of why the Romans won on a material level is to miss the point.

Hence, as I said above, it should be clear that Livy does not see battles as being governed by mere chance. Every battle, even ones which turn on unexplained events, makes sense in broader terms, and indeed it is precisely because of the introduction of those unexplained events that the reader is encouraged to think in those broader terms. But the fact that they are not governed by chance does not mean that they are determined by the general's strategy either.[72] While it is true that sometimes a stark dichotomy is made between generals who rely on 'reason' and those who rely on 'luck' (with the implication that the former is more likely to lead to success),[73] in the broader context of the battles in the Hannibalic War this is a false dichotomy. Although 'chance' is rarely at issue, Livy's commanders—even in victory— look less in control of events than Polybius' do (I shall discuss this further in the second half of the chapter). Livy's battles are not reductionist, in the sense that they do not turn on the experience of each individual soldier but rather on a synoptic picture which is not reducible to individuals; but that is not to say that the commander, who is better placed to see the synoptic picture, is the person on whom all depends.[74]

---

[72] Cf. 27.44.1–2, where Livy comments on the unfairness of judging a commander simply by the success or otherwise of his strategy: the implication, of course, is that even the right strategy may lead to the wrong result.

[73] So, for example, at 22.23.2 Fabius worries Hannibal, because he sees him as a general 'who wages war by reason, not chance' (*qui bellum ratione, non fortuna gereret*); cf. 22.25.14, 22.39.21– 2, and also 28.42.15, where Fabius ironically suggests that one can attribute Scipio's successes to his *consilium*, but his failures to *casibus incertis belli et fortunae*.

[74] This is not altogether surprising: as Rosenstein (1990a) shows, within Republican political culture Roman defeats were rarely ascribed to the commanders' incompetence, but rather to the interplay of broader factors. See further below, 311–16.

So battles in Livy are not won or lost through 'mere chance': victory or defeat appears to happen for a reason. Yet although 'chance' is not at issue, the battles do not appear to depend on a clear sequence of cause and effect either—they are not 'linear' in the sense discussed above (279–80). While the battles as a whole may not be unpredictable (since victory and defeat happen for a reason), they certainly contain unpredictable elements within them, tiny things which no one in the battle could possibly have taken account of or predicted in advance. And these tiny things seem to matter. Livy regularly sees battles turning on small events which have effects out of all proportion to their apparent importance. The idea that minor events can have large consequences is admittedly a commonplace of ancient literature,[75] but Livy insists on this point explicitly to a far greater degree than any other author does,[76] and does so above all in the Third Decade.[77] At 25.18.3 he makes the following generalization about war: *in bello nihil tam leve est, quod non magnae interdum rei momentum faciat* ('in war nothing is too trivial to bring about an important consequence at times'). He repeats the generalization at 27.9.1, and offers further explicit illustrations of it at 26.11.6–7, 27.15.9, 29.6.2, and at Zama in 30.34.1 (above, 239–40); it is also alluded to in Claudius Nero's speech to his troops at 27.45.3–5. What is significant is not merely that he repeats the point so regularly, but also that he focuses it especially on battles. Moreover, Livy's battles regularly turn on apparently minor circumstances even when he does not explicitly draw the reader's attention to the fact:[78] here too the Ticinus is a good example, where the initial (and unexplained) flight of the Roman spearsmen has seriously deleterious effects on the broader conduct of the battle.

That interest in the trivial events that can turn battles should remind us of Beyerchen's argument that Clausewitz, who centred much of his theory around comparable observations, saw war as a non-linear phenomenon (above, 279–80).[79] It is typical of such phenomena that effects are magnified

---

[75] Examples include Caesar, *BC* 1.21.1, 3.68.1, 3.72.4, Cicero, *Phil.* 5.26, Pliny, *Letters* 1.20.12, Tacitus, *Ann.* 4.32.2, 5.4.1.

[76] Cf. Ducos (1987: 134–7). Note however van der Veen (1996), who persuasively argues that a similar recognition of the importance of the trivial is central to Herodotus' historical world-view, though rarely explicit; cf. also Harrison (2003: 244–51) and Węcowski (2004: 152–4), who both argue that this is connected with Herodotus' picture of divine government of the world, with the gods using trivial events to sway history in the appropriate direction. Livy is more explicit than Herodotus about the importance of trivial matters, but unlike him never directly attributes those trivial events to divine intervention, although the role of the divine is relevant to his overall understanding of the workings of history (cf. below, 339–53).

[77] The observation is rarer in other parts of his work, but note 3.27.7, 6.34.5, and 32.17.9. See Dutoit (1946).

[78] Cf. van der Veen (1996) on Herodotus' similar technique.

[79] Beyerchen (1992–93: 79–80).

out of proportion to their apparent causes, and while of course Livy does not theorize this mathematically, or even in a systematic but non-mathematical fashion as (on this interpretation) Clausewitz later would, the essential insight is very similar. Small events feed back into larger ones in ways that cannot be predicted. But Livy's account of battles, while non-linear, is also radically different from Clausewitz's: for his battles' non-linearity (the unpredictably magnified results of small causes) is combined with non-reductionism. Livy's narration of battles so that they make sense in terms of the religious and moral order sets his work apart from most other writers who recognize the large effects of apparently minor events. For Livy those minor events, however they are working, and whatever reason they have the effects they do, are part of a system which can only be understood in macrocosmic terms, and those macrocosmic terms are not merely reducible to the unpredictable combinations of small-scale happenings.

It is that combination which makes much of Livy's analysis of battles so original but at the same time so difficult to interpret, because these two perspectives—non-linearity and non-reductionism—appear contradictory, in practice if not in strictly formal terms. Non-linearity implies that any explanation of defeat or victory would have to look for the imperceptibly small events which could sway the battle unpredictably in either direction. Non-reductionism implies that the result of the battle is decided by terms of grand structures which are not merely reducible to those tiny events. In other words, Livy indicates that battles are to be understood *both* through a causal system which operates intrinsically at a microscopic level *and* through a macroscopic structure which cannot be reduced to the microscopic. Looked at in the first way the battles are utterly unpredictable, yet from the second perspective they are utterly predictable and make perfect sense to the reader who sees them against the wider narrative background. The reader can understand that the way battles are lost and won fits closely the broad moral structure of the narrative, while simultaneously observing how slight a change is required to sway them.[80] But the precise way one is supposed to reconcile these different perspectives remains opaque.[81]

---

[80] Hunt (2006: 400) similarly suggests that Thucydides can be read partly as a deterministic historian, but also presents a world that is 'profoundly undetermined'. However, on Hunt's reading Thucydides is far less systematic in offering these apparently contradictory perspectives than Livy is here.

[81] Ducos (1987: 137–8) observes the double perspective, and suggests that Livy is leaving open the possibility of different types of causation, and in particular is rejecting a purely deterministic system by showing that human decisions hold sway. I shall be discussing issues of causation in Livy at greater length in Chapter 5; for the moment I shall simply note that not all of the small events on which major events turn appear to be the consequence of human free will.

Livy occasionally presents the causes of victory and defeat in a manner that is more radical still. Just as he sometimes employs alternative and incompatible chronologies in order to suggest a sequence of events that he is aware could not literally have occurred, as I demonstrated in Chapter 1, so too he occasionally invites us to interpret battles in the light of versions of events which he does not appear to accept. An example is at Scipio's decisive victory at Silpia[82] over Hasdrubal son of Gisgo, which destroys Carthaginian power in Spain. Before the battle Livy debates the numbers of troops involved on the Carthaginian side (28.12.13–14):

ibi tum Hasdrubal Gisgonis, maximus clarissimusque eo bello secundum Barcinos dux, regressus ab Gadibus rebellandi spe, adiuvante Magone Hamilcaris filio dilectibus per ulteriorem Hispaniam habitis, ad quinquaginta milia peditum quattuor milia et quingentos equites armavit. de equestribus copiis ferme inter auctores convenit; peditum septuaginta milia quidam adducta ad Silpiam urbem scribunt.

There at that time Hasdrubal son of Gisgo, the greatest and most famous general in that war after the Barcas, having returned from Cadiz in hope of renewing the war, with the help of Mago son of Hamilcar held levies throughout Further Spain, and put under arms around 50,000 infantry and 4,500 cavalry. My authorities more or less agree about the cavalry forces: some write that 70,000 infantry were brought to the city of Silpia.

The 'some' who speak about 70,000 infantry include Polybius 11.20.2, who also gives a figure of 4,000 for the cavalry, within sufficient distance of Livy's to justify the statement that his sources were 'more or less' (ferme) in agreement on this point. Scipio then collects an army of his own, including Spanish allies, to counter this: according to Livy (28.13.5) his total force consisted of 45,000 in total, including both infantry and cavalry, which is similar to (though slightly below) the numbers given by Polybius 11.20.8, who gives him 45,000 infantry and 3,000 cavalry.

So what was the actual size of the Carthaginian force? It makes a significant difference, since on the one view Scipio is fighting from a position of near equality, whereas on Polybius' figures he is grossly outnumbered.[83] Livy does not explicitly state his view, but he weights the argument in favour of the smaller force,[84] since he offers that version as a fact in the indicative, whereas the larger

---

[82] This is the name in Livy (28.12.14). The town was actually called Ilipa (cf. *CIL* II 1085, 1091); the MSS of Polybius 11.20.1 refer to it as ʼΙλίγγα or ʼΗλίγγα corrected to ʼΙλίπα by Schweighaeuser. See Walbank (1967: 296).

[83] Not as grossly as he is in Appian, *Hisp.* 25–26, however, whose Scipio has 'less than a third' of the Carthaginians' numbers, though admittedly Appian may be deliberately ignoring Scipio's Spanish allies, whom he does not mention at all, but whom Polybius 11.20.7 and Livy 28.13.1–2 agree Scipio was using primarily for show.

[84] Cf. Wiehemeyer (1938: 27–9).

force is ascribed only to 'some' authorities. And indeed he appears in the main body of the battle to accept the smaller number. In describing the deployment of the two lines he says explicitly (28.14.5) that both sides described the strength of the Roman troops and Carthaginians in the centre as being equal, and he at least implies that the strength of the Spanish allies on each side was approximately equal as well when he describes how each side drew them up on the wings facing one another (28.14.4: Polybius has neither of these points, although his general picture of the deployment is similar (11.22.2–3)).

Yet his account of the preparations for the battle makes it less clear. Immediately after noting the dispute over the numbers of troops, Livy continues (28.13.1–2):

Scipio, cum ad eum fama tanti comparati exercitus perlata esset, neque Romanis legionibus tantae se fore parem multitudini ratus ut non in speciem saltem opponerentur barbarorum auxilia, neque in iis tamen tantum virium ponendum ut mutando fidem, quae cladis causa fuisset patri patruoque, magnum momentum facerent...

When report reached Scipio of so great an army that had been raised, he neither thought that he with his Roman legions would be a match for so great a multitude that he should not put barbarian auxiliaries against the enemy at least for show, nor did he think that so much strength should rest on them that they would make a major difference by changing sides, which had been the reason for the defeat of his father and uncle.

Coming just after Livy has raised the possibility that the Carthaginians might have had as many as 70,000 troops, the repeated references to the vast size of the Carthaginian army (*tanti... exercitus, tantae... multitudini*) strongly suggest that this larger number represents the forces against which Scipio will in fact be fighting. Accordingly, when Scipio's full army is collected and proves to be considerably less than 70,000, the implication is that he may well after all be grossly outnumbered, which leaves it open how far his plan not to rely on the strength of the Spanish allies lest they betray him as they did his father and uncle is a feasible one.

The battle itself then commences with the Carthaginian cavalry attacking the Romans while they are in the process of fortifying their camp, only to be repulsed by cavalry whom Scipio had placed there for this purpose (28.13.6–7). The account is drawn from Polybius 11.21.1–5, with an important omission—but also an even more significant addition. Livy leaves out Polybius' explicit comment (11.21.2) that Scipio's cavalry equalled the Carthaginians' numerically—and unlike Polybius he had earlier only given the total size of the Roman forces, not the number of cavalry specifically. He thus continues to leave the balance of forces open. Moreover, in Livy, unlike in Polybius, the Roman cavalry attack does not succeed in turning back the Carthaginian cavalry: it is only when the Romans are reinforced by successive waves of infantry, ultimately adding up to a *magnum . . . agmen armatorum* (28.13.8: 'a great column of armed men') that they repel them.[85] In other words, Livy in presenting Scipio's initial success in the battle slants the narrative away from the idea that the Romans and the Carthaginians are approximately evenly matched: even with surprise on their side, the Roman cavalry require substantial infantry support to drive their Carthaginian counterparts off.

In the main body of the battle (which took place after several days of further skirmishing), as I observed above, Livy implies (though does not explicitly state) that the two sides were approximately evenly matched, which fits his initial presentation of the Carthaginian numbers as being approximately equal to the forces that Scipio then collected to confront them, contrary to what Polybius explicitly states the balance of forces to have been. This picture fits other aspects of his presentation of this battle: as he says explicitly at 28.14.5, the Romans and the Carthaginians see themselves as evenly matched, as appropriate for those 'between whom was the reason for the war' (*quos inter belli causa esset*)—a suggestion of an existential struggle which will ultimately be played out more fully at Zama (30.32.1–3), but which is no less appropriate here, since this is the battle which drives the Carthaginians from Spain (28.16.14–15; though note below, 349–50). But while doing this, Livy also changes the slant of his narrative to keep the Polybian numbers in play and to imply that Scipio is winning against massive numerical odds—even to the point of rewriting Polybius in order to make the odds against Scipio appear greater. Faced with two incompatible accounts, Livy effectively constructs his narrative around both simultaneously, not only the one that he ostensibly supports, but also the one that he apparently rejects.

There is an intriguing variant of this technique with the battle between Minucius and Hannibal at Gereonium (22.24).[86] Livy gives two versions of this: in the first (22.24.4–10) the Carthaginians and Romans compete for control of a hill between their camps, with the Romans ultimately gaining control. They then use that as a base to attack the Carthaginian foragers; Hannibal refuses to engage in a pitched battle he is likely to lose, but instead remains Fabius-like within his camp. According to the second version (22.24.11–14), however, which Livy attributes to *quidam auctores* (22.24.11), there is a pitched battle, which the Carthaginians appear to be winning until Numerius Decimus appears in Hannibal's rear with new troops, leading Hannibal to withdraw; the Romans then capture two forts. Livy's handling of the episode has, as Vallet shows, a complex relationship with Polybius 3.101–2: Livy's first version appears to

---

[85] Cf. Scullard (1930: 129), who regards this as Livy's misunderstanding of Polybius, but does not show any point where Polybius' Greek would be susceptible to such a (mis)interpretation.

[86] For the following discussion see Vallet (1961).

correspond to Polybius in most respects, but in Polybius Hannibal does not avoid a pitched battle, but fights one, as in the second version offered by Livy. But the second version is not identical with Polybius' either, because in Polybius Minucius' victory is straightforwardly to his credit, not an accidental by-product of the arrival of Numerius Decimus. Livy has, it appears, reworked Polybius' material into two separate versions (though with the addition of some further details, presumably taken from another source), which share the feature of giving less credit to Minucius, who emerged rather better from Polybius' account.[87]

Livy structures his account so as to give weight to the first version, which he narrates without qualification, whereas the second is confined to a variant offered by 'some authorities'. But the subsequent narrative generally assumes that Minucius achieved an actual victory in a pitched battle, as he does only in the second version: it is the second version alone that generates the 'rumour' (*fama*) and letters which lead to Minucius' success being celebrated and Fabius' caution damned at Rome (22.24.14; cf. 22.25.1–2, 22.25.9). It is true that Fabius himself expresses doubts about this second version: he 'believed neither the rumour nor the letters at all' (22.25.2 *nihil nec famae nec litteris crederet*), but those doubts are presumably addressed more to their empty claims of over-whelming success rather than to the existence of a pitched battle at all. Moreover, Hannibal's retreat to his earlier camp at the end of the first version (22.24.10) is itself hard to explain; it appears a more natural consequence of a defeat such as the one he suffers in the second version than of the stalemate in the first.[88]

Hence here too, as at Silpia, Livy creates his account out of two competing versions: the one he apparently rejects as well as the one he accepts. But the difference in this case is that not only the process that created victory or defeat, but the actual existence of a victory is at issue. In the first version there is no victory at all; in the second there is a victory for Rome, albeit a less impressive one than Minucius made it out to be. The reader can trace the thread of the story only by rejecting a straightforward linear sense of cause and effect: the sequel depends on a version of events in which Minucius achieved a victory, yet Livy gives us reason to doubt that such a victory even took place. And the sequence of the events in the first version is itself not fully explained in terms of that version. Once again things in a Livian battle are ostentatiously presented as happening for no reason, if we judge reason in terms of a precise sequence of cause and effect. Only if we look to the wider meaning of the narrative—in this case the equivocal treatment of Minucius' aggression set against Fabius' cautious successes, but the greater regard accorded at Rome to

[87] Vallet (1961: 191–2).
[88] Cf. Vallet (1961: 188–9).

the former than to the latter—can we see how the battle makes sense. Battle was engaged through the sort of activity which is often commendable, but may not be here (cf. above, 79–81, 197); it leads to a victory which may not even have happened, and which was exaggerated if it did happen; and this gives Minucius a reputation that on any account he certainly does not deserve.

4.2. COMMANDERS

A corollary to the opacity of causation in Livy's battles is the regular inadequacy of commanders, both Roman and Carthaginian. This is not only true in the obvious ways, with plainly incompetent commanders like Flaminius or Varro who rashly fall into Hannibal's traps. A common feature of Livy's battles is that even apparently effective commanders are unable to predict the course of events and in consequence fall into defeat.

Scipio's battle at Utica at 30.10 is an example. In Livy's version he had focused his attention on the town because of what appeared an overconfident assumption that the war was over after his destruction of the enemies' camps. He was then forced to abandon the siege in a hurry when the Carthaginians and Syphax renewed their alliance.[89] He took the bulk of his troops away, leaving only a token force to besiege the city, enough to present 'merely the appearance of a siege' (30.8.2 *ad speciem modo obsidionis*). Neither the initial error nor the deceptive stratagem are in Livy's source, Polybius 14.8.1, who has Scipio dividing his forces between the siege of Utica and the rest of his campaign. Livy's version immediately changes the dynamic of the fight, and does so in a way that is not obviously to Scipio's credit. The plan does not work, since the Carthaginians do not appear to be deceived, and recognize the Romans' vulnerability;[90] hence Scipio has merely increased the hazard to his own troops in the subsequent counterattack, and he has to dash back to protect them. He does return in time, but is faced with a further problem: his ships are equipped for a siege and not therefore ready to fight a naval battle (30.10.2–3). The basic idea is taken from Polybius 14.10.9, but Livy has adapted it so as to suggest not merely that the ships were prepared for siege rather than for battle, but that their lack of preparation for battle is precisely

---

[89] *Scipionem, velut iam debellato quod ad Syphacem Carthaginiensesque attineret, Uticae oppugnandae intentum iamque machinas admoventem muris avertit fama redintegrati belli* (30.8.1: 'Scipio was concentrating on the siege of Utica and was already moving his engines against the walls, as if the war was at an end as far as Syphax and the Carthaginians were concerned: but he was diverted from it by news of the renewal of the war').

[90] Note *levi praesidio* (30.9.6): this too is absent from the source passage (Polybius 14.9.7).

because they were laden with the material for conducting a siege.[91] What is more, that appears to be Scipio's fault, since his plan (in Livy) depended on the ships giving the impression that they were focused on a siege that they could not in practice prosecute effectively. In other words, the Roman lack of preparation for battle in Polybius is something that happened despite Scipio.[92] In Livy it happens because of him.

What is more, even when Scipio returns, he has given himself inadequate time to prepare for the Carthaginian attack. Livy describes the innovative plan he adopts, of lashing his ships together into a protective line, with gaps for the Roman scouting ships to be able to advance between them and retreat securely (30.10.4–7). Yet on Livy's account, if the Carthaginians had attacked immediately, they could have overwhelmed the Romans while they were still in a state of panic: they were deterred from doing so only by their own lack of confidence after their earlier defeats, and so they delay the attack until the following day (30.10.8–9). When the battle finally starts, Scipio's plan appears initially successful, since the Carthaginians are unable to deploy their missiles effectively against the taller ships of the Roman line (30.10.12–13). But the Roman scouting ships which Scipio sent out to attack the Carthaginians are easily sunk at the beginning of the battle, and their presence among the Carthaginian fleet moreover inhibits the Romans from firing at the Carthaginians, in case they hit their own people (30.10.14–15)—an unanticipated consequence of Scipio's plan. Finally the Carthaginians throw grappling-hooks against the Roman ships and tow them out of the line: they capture sixty Roman ships (30.10.16–20).[93]

Livy does emphasize that the defeat at Utica was not of major significance to the Romans in the context of the overall war: he says that the Carthaginians' 'happiness was out of proportion to the event' (30.10.20 *maior quam pro re laetitia*), and later refers to it as 'joy that was not only brief but almost empty'

---

[91] 30.10.3: 'For how could ships, carrying artillery and siege engines and either adapted for use in transport or driven up to the walls so as to be able to provide an ascent in place of using a rampart and bridges, resist a mobile armed fleet fitted with naval equipment?' (*qui enim restitissent agili et nautico instrumento aptae et armatae classi naves tormenta machinasque portantes et aut in onerariarum usum versae aut ita adpulsae muris ut pro aggere ac pontibus praebere adscensum possent?*).

[92] Polybius refers to Scipio 'finding' (καταλαβών) the ships unprepared, and accordingly deciding against battle on the spur of the moment (14.10.9–10). Livy's Scipio knows the situation even before he arrives—after all, it is his own decisions that have created it—but is more culpable in taking those decisions in the first place.

[93] Polybius' account of the actual battle does not survive. Appian, *Pun.* 25 has a version which is similar to Livy's in its opening, but with a dramatically different result: the Romans have the better of the battle, with the scouting ships capturing a Carthaginian ship. It is conceivable that this derives from Polybius, and that Livy has adapted the final part of his version from a different source, but this is hardly demonstrable.

(30.16.2 *non brevi solum sed prope vano gaudio*), which was then dashed by the capture of Syphax. But nevertheless it is a Roman defeat, albeit a minor one, and Livy also observes how close it came to being a major one, because it was only the Carthaginians' own delay and Scipio's arrival to take charge that prevented it from being considerably more serious (30.10.21). Moreover, it is a defeat that is presented as being the consequence of Scipio's own inadequate planning and his inability to foresee or forestall the course of events.[94]

Hannibal's planning is sometimes no less fallible than Scipio's. An example can be given from the account of his taking of Tarentum in Book 25. After he has captured the town but the Romans have retreated to the citadel, he surveys the site and concludes that, defended as it is by a wall and a ditch, it is 'impregnable by force or siege-works' (25.11.1 *nec vi nec operibus expugnabilem esse*), and so instead blocks it off with a wall of his own in order to protect the Tarentines while he is gone; in the course of this he lures the Romans into an unsuccessful sortie (25.11.3–7). He then surveys the site again after the siege-work has gone ahead somewhat faster than he expected (25.11.9 *aliquantum opinione eius celerius creverat*) and decides that the citadel can after all be taken, since it is 'only' defended by a wall and ditch, and not by superior height. However, his attempted assault fails when the Romans receive reinforcements and by night unexpectedly (*ex inproviso*) destroy the siege equipment (25.11.10). The main sequence of Hannibal's building the wall, the Roman sortie, his attempted assault on the citadel, and the Roman night attack that thwarts him are all taken from Polybius 8.32.2–34.1. But Livy adds to Polybius Hannibal's two surveys of the layout of the town and the radically different conclusions to which they lead him; nor does Polybius suggest that Hannibal conceived the assault after he walls off the town quicker than expected. The implication in Polybius is that Hannibal's plans are fully coherent if not entirely successful: he begins by protecting the Tarentines by a wall, and then moves to an assault (which however is thwarted). In Livy Hannibal's plans are not coherent: he builds the wall to protect the Tarentines only on concluding that an assault was not likely to work, and then apparently changes his mind about the assault after his second survey of the site. Livy does not explicitly tell us what led Hannibal to change his mind, but the implication is that the fact that the wall was built quicker than he anticipated makes him overconfident: he now believes in the possibility of an assault that he had previously rejected as impossible. Admittedly the question of whether the citadel was impregnable is never tested in practice, since the Romans destroy the siege engines before Hannibal can use them. But Livy's language implies

---

[94] On Scipio's general incompetence in this battle compare Thiel (1946: 165–8).

that Hannibal was right the first time round to regard attacking the citadel as pointless, and wrong when he comes to believe that the assault could work: at the first survey of the citadel he 'saw' (*videret*) that it was impregnable, but later only 'came to hope' (*spem cepit*) that it could be captured.

Moreover, the Romans' destruction of the siege engines is enabled by their receiving reinforcements.[95] Hannibal could presumably have anticipated this (but did not), since the Romans currently control the sea, as Livy (and Hannibal) then goes on to discuss at some length (25.11.11–19). In order to counter this Hannibal institutes a blockade (25.11.19). That blockade itself, however, proves less effective than he claimed it would, since the Romans are immediately able to bypass it and bring in supplies (25.15.4–5). What is more, in the following book (26.20.7–11) it emerges that the blockade has damaged the Tarentines more than it has the Romans, since the Romans have enough food stockpiled, whereas the Carthaginians cannot import enough to feed their fleet, and so, far from being a support for Tarentum, run short of food themselves.[96] Livy explains the fleet's need for food by saying that it was composed of a 'mixed crowd . . . of every race of mankind' (26.20.9 *turba . . . mixta ex omni genere hominum*). The connection of thought here is unclear: there is no obvious reason (even in terms of Roman racial stereotypes) why an ethnically mixed fleet should require more food than an ethnically homogeneous fleet would.[97] But Livy sees the ethnic mixing of the Carthaginian army as a major weakness in their empire, as I discussed in Chapter 3 (236–44), and it makes sense—in general terms—that this should cause them a problem at Tarentum as it does at other times, even though the mechanism by which it does so is never explained. The consequence is that the fleet has to be withdrawn—but this then means that the Tarentines still run short, since they can no longer import food in the absence of the protection offered by the Carthaginians (26.20.11). Hannibal's blockade thus has failed to achieve its aim, and has indeed made the situation worse than it would have been if he had simply left well alone.

[95] These reinforcements, however, come from Metapontum, and the town promptly defects to Hannibal once the garrison is removed (25.15.6). It is not only Hannibal whose planning over Tarentum is defective.

[96] Polybius 9.9.11 appears to describe the same episode in rather different terms: the Carthaginian fleet there runs out of food, but it is not suggested that this led the Tarentines themselves to run short, or that this was paradoxical given that the aim was to deprive the Romans of food. However, that passage has been seriously garbled by the excerptor (see Walbank 1967: 133–4), and it is impossible to be sure that Livy's slant was not paralleled in Polybius.

[97] It is theoretically possible that an ethnically mixed force would require a greater *variety* of food in order to accommodate national diets. But those are not the terms in which Livy presents the problem, and it is in fact unlikely that there was a great diversity in the basic diets of the different components of the Carthaginian army (Klingbeil 2000: 20).

A common feature of both of Scipio at Utica and Hannibal at Tarentum is
that they not only fail to plan properly, but that the things that they do plan
prove to be self-defeating: the consequences of the stratagems that they
employ are precisely what the stratagems were designed to avoid. This
theme regularly recurs in Livy's account of the Hannibalic War. One example
is at the recapture of Arpi at 24.47.2–7, where the Carthaginians place the
Arpini in the forefront of the battle because of doubts about their loyalty—
but the consequence is that individual Romans recognize acquaintances
among their former allies and start challenging them over their defection,
and these mid-battle conversations lead to the Arpini deciding to return to
the Roman side.[98] Another is the way in which the Carthaginians' use of
elephants to attempt to shock the enemy troops often backfires, as the
Romans succeed in turning the animals back against the Carthaginians
themselves, when they are effectively uncontrollable and trample down their
own side.[99] This happens at Zama, as we have already seen (30.33.13: cf.
above, 242–3); and it comes close to happening at the Trebia (21.56.1) and at
the Metaurus, where the drivers are forced to kill their elephants themselves in
order to prevent it (27.49.1–2). It also happens in Scipio's victory at Silpia,
where the elephants are initially described as 'looking from afar like fortresses'
(28.14.4 *castellorum procul speciem praebebant*), but whose only role in the
battle itself is be panicked by the 'chaotic nature of the fighting' (28.15.5
tumultuoso genere pugnae) and to move from the wings to cause problems for
their own infantry in the centre.[100] But the most dramatic example is in the
fight between Hannibal and Marcellus at 27.14, where the fight is doubtful

---

[98] Moreover, the Romans' success is itself contrary to expectations, as has emerged earlier
(24.46.4–5), where Livy comments that a rainstorm that seemed as if it would hinder them in
fact assisted them (24.46.4 *quod impedimentum agentibus fore videbatur, id maxime ad fall-
endum adiuvit*), because it made the guards leave their posts, and also covered up the noise of
the assault on the city.

[99] This was a recognized problem with elephants. 'If history had taught any one thing up to
that time, it was never to use elephants in war. Don't ask me why Hamilcar did not see this. The
Carthaginian elephants were trained to rush forward and trample the Romans, but only too
frequently they would rush backwards and trample the Carthaginians. If this happened to you,
wouldn't you notice it? And wouldn't you do something about it?' (Cuppy 1951: 49). For a more
sober analysis along not dissimilar lines, see Charles and Rhodan (2007: 368–72). It should,
however, be observed that Livy emphasizes the point beyond any other ancient writer.

[100] This latter point is based on Polybius 11.24.1, who is more explicit about the havoc the
elephants caused among the Carthaginians, but has nothing of Livy's earlier comment about their
appearance, with its misleading implication that the elephants will give a solid backing to
the Carthaginian army. Nor does Polybius suggest that the Carthaginian centre was affected
by the elephants: he describes their panic earlier in the battle, before describing the problems facing
the centre of the Carthaginian army. Livy transfers it to the point where he is relating the collapse
of the Carthaginian centre, and so makes the self-destructive consequences of the elephants' rout
more far-reaching.

(*anceps*) until 'Hannibal ordered his elephants to be moved to the front line to see if that could introduce some chaos and panic' (27.14.6: *Hannibal elephantos in primam aciem induci iussit si quem inicere ea res tumultum ac pavorem posset*). But Livy's phrasing here is more ironic than a superficial reading would suggest: he does not say in whom the chaos and panic might be introduced. And indeed Hannibal does introduce chaos and panic, initially in the Romans (27.14.7), but then the elephants—'a doubtful species' (27.14.9 *genus anceps*)—are wounded and driven back, and cause greater havoc among the Carthaginians than they had among the Romans: Livy's explanation for the elephants' behaviour (27.14.10) is that 'panic' (*pavor*) is a more powerful motivator than the instructions of their driver. The linguistic repetitions underline the extent to which Hannibal loses control of events and indeed achieves the precise opposite of what he intended.

The phenomenon of commanders failing to predict the sequence of events or understand the consequence of their plans is not confined to defeats. Even in victory one often finds that people are presented as winning for reasons that are only partly connected with the plans that they have adopted. A straightforward example is at 24.35.9–36.1, where Marcellus defeats a Syracusan army which he did not believe even to be in the vicinity:[101] the reason he defeats it so easily is that he expected to encounter a much larger Carthaginian force, and so had his troops ready to meet that eventuality. The implication is that if he had actually known that he had only the Sicilians to deal with, he would have been less well prepared: his easy victory is actually the consequence of an error.

Another example is where Hannibal at the beginning of Book 27 attacks Cn. Fulvius and defeats him in battle. Here Hannibal is explicitly said to be the superior general (27.1.7; cf. 27.1.5), and he readily outmanoeuvres the Romans, outflanking them so as to attack them from behind. Yet that was not the plan with which he initially launched the battle. His intention was to catch Fulvius unawares (*incautum*), and moreover approached with his army drawn up for battle 'so as to strike more terror into the enemy' (27.1.6 *quo plus terroris hosti obiceret*). But the second part of the plan manifestly fails, since the Romans enthusiastically enter the battle 'equal in boldness' (27.1.7 *par audacia*), and the first part does not seem to have achieved its intended effect either. Hannibal's march is said 'almost to outstrip the report' (27.1.6 *ut famam prope praeveniret*), but 'almost' is not enough for a surprise attack, and despite 'the negligence ingrained in his character' (27.1.5 *neglegentiam insitam ingenio*)

---

[101] Note especially 24.35.9 *nihil minus ratus quam illo tempore ac loco Syracusanum sibi exercitum obvium fore*.

Fulvius' troops do not seem to be fighting unprepared.[102] Hannibal appears to be at an advantage in any case—even before the Romans are encircled from behind, 'many' of them fall in what appears to be a straightforward infantry battle (27.1.10); no comparable Carthaginian losses are mentioned. No reason for this is given—another example of the phenomenon I discussed earlier, where Livy leaves key events in battles without an explanation in normal material terms. But here, as before, another sort of explanation is on offer, because Hannibal himself notes that the battle is following a predetermined pattern (27.1.9): he defeated another Cn. Fulvius two years earlier on the same spot (25.21; cf. above, 54–5). In the terms in which Livy constructs battles, the Roman defeat follows from that pattern, and in the absence of another clear explanation for their fighting at a disadvantage even before Hannibal's strata-gem can take effect, the reader is pointed to the pattern itself as being the key issue that makes the difference between victory and defeat. The Romans lose because they have to.[103] Hannibal's initial plan is an irrelevancy, and his later stratagem less important than one might have expected.

Precisely the same pattern appears at Nola in Book 23, where Marcellus is encouraged into battle because he sees that Hannibal has split his forces by sending some out to plunder (23.44.5–6). But Livy tacitly points to this being a miscalculation, because some of the troops engaged in plunder are able to return on hearing the noise of battle and join in the fight (23.44.8).[104] So Marcellus is left fighting with equal forces (23.45.1)—but he encourages his troops not only by reminding them of their earlier victories (including one on the very same spot) and that they are not facing the full enemy force (23.45.1–2), but argues at some length that the Carthaginians have been enervated by their stay in Capua (23.45.2–4), something which Livy has already described in his own voice (23.18.10–16) and which Hannibal acknowledges in his own reproaches to his troops (23.45.6). And accordingly the Carthaginians prove him right: the tide instantly turns in the Romans' direction. This time Livy does describe this in

---

[102] Contrast the version of the battle found in Appian, *Hann.* 48 (cf. also Frontinus, *Strat.* 2.5.21), in which Hannibal's cavalry launches a surprise attack on the Romans under the cover of mist, catching them unawares and in disarray, while the Carthaginian infantry attacks from behind.

[103] Compare Kraus (1998: esp. 267–72) on the way in which Livy draws attention to repeated events within his history in order to underscore the repetitive nature of history itself: her examples include not only Fulvius here (276) but also Marcellus at Nola (268–9), which I discuss below. However, the pattern by which Livy shows victory and defeat governed by the wider significance of the narrative rather than the immediate actions taken in the particular battle extends well beyond cases of repetition.

[104] Contrast Plutarch, *Marc.* 12.2, where Hannibal likewise sends out part of his troops to plunder, but here Marcellus catches him unawares, and there is no indication that the plunder-ing troops return in time to reinforce the Carthaginians.

terms of the increase in Roman morale, here as often a significant factor in the Roman conception of battles (23.45.5, 23.46.1–2; cf. above, 281–4), but the implication is that it is more than Marcellus' superior ability to encourage his troops that is at issue. The Carthaginians lose because the Carthaginians have been ruined by Capua, and in spite of the fact that Marcellus' plans for the battle have in fact failed.[105]

Even Scipio's attack on New Carthage shows something of the same disconnection between the commander's reading of the situation and the actual conduct of the battle. His victory is presented as something remarkable and all but miraculous,[106] and yet it does not follow the pattern that he planned for it. He sees that the walls have lost their defenders, and so orders the soldiers to use ladders to climb them (26.44.6–7). This comes from Polybius (10.12.10–11), as does the Roman failure at 26.45.2–4, when the walls prove too high for the ladders to be used effectively (cf. Polybius 10.13.6–8). But Livy changes a number of details which significantly alter the tenor of Polybius' account. He explicitly says that the walls were remanned by the time the Romans sought to scale them (26.45.1)—and the implication is that one reason for this is because of the Romans' enthusiasm which leads them to get in one another's way (26.44.11). Neither of these points is in Polybius, and the overall effect is to imply that Scipio miscalculated in his belief that he could attack the walls while they were lacking defenders. Moreover, Livy also subtracts from Polybius in a significant fashion. In Polybius the Romans persist enthusiastically in their attempt to scale the walls even after they meet with difficulties, though Scipio decides to withdraw his troops anyway (10.13.10–11); in Livy the attack has more clearly failed, and Scipio's withdrawal is hence more obviously a response to that failure, a failure which is primarily due to his own inability to assess the situation properly. The failure is, it is true, only temporary, since he then launches the attack across the lagoon which enables him to capture the city; but Livy's rewriting of Polybius has demonstrated a fallibility in Scipio even at the point of his first great victory.

One further feature of several of these examples is that it is not only the commander who is misled about the likely consequences of his actions: it is also the reader who is liable to misinterpret them. When commanders make mistakes, Livy's general practice (except in the case of egregious incompetence such as that of Minucius or Varro) is not to draw attention to the fact that it is a mistake—one reason, presumably, why critics have usually failed to

---

[105] Here too we may contrast Plutarch, *Marc.* 12.2–3, who attributes Marcellus' victory at Nola simply to superior weaponry: his troops have longer spears than the Carthaginians.

[106] Levene (1993: 61).

appreciate that he is presenting such things as mistakes at all.[107] Much more commonly he narrates the episode in such a way as to seduce the reader into thinking that the plan is a sensible one which might well prove effective—only for events to demonstrate that this reading is mistaken. In effect, he encourages the reader to make the same mistakes that the participants did. A typical example is the Roman recapture of Locri at 29.6–7, where the battle swings through many phases which point successively to Roman or Carthaginian victory. At each point Livy appears to be suggesting that a decisive juncture in the battle has been reached, only then for it to emerge that some further factor is present which will turn the tide once again. So at 29.6.10–11 the Roman force secretly enters the citadel, and Livy repeatedly emphasizes the preparations they had made for the operation: they have gone there with 3,000 troops (29.6.9), they have 'ladders constructed for the exceptional height of the citadel' (29.6.10 *scalas ad editam altitudinem arcis fabricatas*); they have allies within the citadel who themselves let down 'specially made ladders' (29.6.11 *scalas ad id ipsum factas*); the allies are 'ready and alert' (29.6.11 *parati intentique*). They accordingly take the Carthaginian guards by surprise and kill them in their sleep. At this point, however, the other Carthaginians wake up, and the Romans prove to be outnumbered and 'would have been crushed' except that the noise of those outside the citadel increases the chaos, and the Carthaginians assume that the citadel is in fact full of the enemy and retreat (29.6.12–13). So the Romans have the advantage—but not for the reasons we were led to expect, since they were in fact outnumbered despite their preparations, and they are saved only by confusion of a sort that there is no suggestion they could have anticipated.[108] The reader is seduced into accepting an impression of Roman competence and foresight that the actual narrative does not bear out.

But the battle does not end there: it suddenly emerges that there are two citadels at Locri, and the Carthaginians take refuge in the other one (29.6.14). Now the conflict is described in terms that imply equality: 'the townspeople controlled the city, set in the middle as the reward for the victors: from the two citadels every day there were conflicts with minor battles' (29.6.15 *oppidani urbem habebant, victoribus praemium in medio positam; ex arcibus duabus proeliis cottidie levibus certabatur*). Hannibal is summoned, and the Romans 'would not have held out' had it not been for the fact that the

---

[107] So e.g. on the death of P. Scipio at 25.34, Hoyos (2001: 86) comments: 'What Livy predictably does not admit, but what is obvious to the reader, is the poverty of P. Scipio's military judgement'. Livy does in fact refer to Scipio's 'rash...plan' (25.34.7 *temerarium...consilium*), but even if he had not, the evidence of this chapter is that what is obvious to the reader was also obvious enough to the author that he had no need to 'admit' it.

[108] Compare Hunt (2006: 396–401) on Thucydides' regular use of such counterfactuals.

Locrians supported them, because they were angered by the Carthaginians' arrogance and avarice (29.6.17). Hannibal's arrival is presented as something that swings the battle in the Carthaginians' direction, though the Locrian support for Rome acts as a counterbalance.

But Hannibal's intervention is in fact less decisive than Livy's initial presentation had implied, and for reasons that interestingly are the mirror image of the Romans' failure earlier—a mirroring reinforced by the oddity of the double citadel, which allows a stronger parallel between the earlier attack by the Romans and the current one by Hannibal. The Romans had prepared ladders but had arrived with an inadequate force to support their attack. Hannibal appears to have an adequate force, but unlike the Romans has prepared no ladders, so is unable to carry out his plan of attacking the city from behind while the Romans are distracted; and his very numbers mean that he does not want to remain in the Carthaginian citadel (29.7.3–4). He attempts to compensate for this by preparing ladders while riding round the city in search of the right place to launch an attack, but is almost hit by a missile and so retreats (29.7.5–6). In the meantime Scipio arrives and enters the city without Hannibal's knowledge (29.7.7; cf. 29.7.9); the Romans launch an attack, and Hannibal is forced to retreat and abandon the defence of the city (29.7.8–10).

Nothing in the sequential presentation of this battle prepares the reader for the ultimate outcome. Even the possible conflict between Scipio and Hannibal which is prefigured at 29.7.1–2, when Scipio comes to support the Romans in the city precisely because he has heard of Hannibal's arrival, is defused when Hannibal retreats before he can engage with Scipio directly. Indeed, not only are readers left unprepared, they are actively misled. What appears to be a representation of careful advance planning by the Romans in fact turns out to be a dangerous miscalculation which would have proved disastrous were it not for considerations that were not previously mentioned as part of the Roman plan. What appears to be a decisive intervention by Hannibal fizzles to nothing when it turns out that he too—in precisely the opposite way to the Romans—has not anticipated what is needed for the attack. Effectively, readers are lured into sharing the commanders' mistakes about the appropriate plans to adopt and their likely outcome.

One can multiply examples of such induced misperceptions: indeed they are sometimes present even when we have been led to distrust the commander's abilities—but to distrust them for the wrong reasons, in ways that appear unconnected with the actual defeat. At 26.39 the Roman fleet coming to relieve Tarentum is led by D. Quinctius, who is described as 'born from an undistinguished family, but renowned in military glory because of many brave deeds' (26.39.3 *obscuro genere ortus, ceterum multis fortibus factis militari gloria inlustris*). This immediately marks Quinctius as a contentious figure: not that a Roman reader would necessarily see a commander of undistinguished family background as a bad one (Marius stands as an obvious counterexample),[109] but to introduce him in those terms suggests that we are being alerted to someone who is potentially suspect, the more so since it associates him above all with Varro, the only major Roman commander in the the Second Punic War of (allegedly) lower-class background (22.25.18–19; cf. 22.34.2). And indeed, like Varro, he appears imprudent: he sails to Tarentum *improvidus futuri certaminis* (26.39.7: 'failing to anticipate the coming contest'). But in fact—through good fortune (cf. n. 53 above)—Quinctius is able to prepare himself in time and enter the battle on equal terms (26.39.8). His lack of prudence does not seem—unlike Varro's—to have brought him to a strategic disadvantage.

Quinctius is not, however, the only person who is introduced misleadingly in this battle. On the opposing ship is Nico Perco, 'hated by and hostile to the Romans with not only public but also private loathing' (26.39.15 *non publico modo sed privato etiam odio invisus atque infestus Romanis*): the highlighting of personal Roman hostility to him as a traitor suggests that he will become the focus of the battle, as the Romans recognize and attack him. But in fact Roman hostility to him is irrelevant: there is no suggestion that the Romans recognize him, here or later, and it is he who attacks Quinctius rather than vice versa. And what enables him to do so is in fact Quinctius' lack of caution, which recurs in an unexpected context: his courage places him in the front line; there Nico attacks him and strikes him *incautum* (26.39.16: 'unawares'), and the Romans lose their flagship and consequently the battle. Quinctius' failure to take proper precautions has indeed led to the Roman defeat, but not through the strategic lack of foresight that his initial actions indicated: rather it is the by-product of the courage that led him to obtain the command in the first place. And the private bad feeling between Nico and the Romans, far from being an encouragement to the Romans to attack further, merely gives extra point to his subsequent actions, where he assaults the Roman flagship all the more aggressively (26.39.17). The terms in which Livy narrates the battle systematically point the reader to expect the trajectory of the conflict to be quite different from the one that actually occurs.

It is not solely in the context of battles that Livy employs this deceptive technique of inducing the reader into a judgement which he then shows to be mistaken. In an important study Andrew Feldherr showed how Livy employs

---

[109] Note also Valerius Maximus 3.4, devoted to the praise of those who rose from humble origins, including indeed Varro (3.4.4), though admittedly Valerius' praise in this case is rather back-handed.

internal audiences within his history to inculcate ethical lessons by, effectively, encouraging readers to identify with people who were ethically misguided and then showing the limitations of their perspective[110]—what one might call a 'surprised by sin'[111] approach to writing history. I shall be exploring Livy's ethical vision further in Chapter 5; for the moment we simply need to observe that he manipulates his readers both ethically and also in his presentation of the process of historical causation. Things do not happen as we are led to expect, nor do they happen for the reasons that we are led to expect, nor are their ethical implications what we would expect.

Livy's picture of battle and warfare, as I have explored it in this chapter, emerges as something that runs radically counter to the way in which battles are often thought to work, and indeed were often thought to work in antiquity. However much some modern scholars may question the central role played by the commander in making a difference between defeat and victory, a primary focus of most ancient writers on warfare was on the commander and the decisions he made. This is unsurprising. Most ancient writers on war came from an extremely narrow class, the same class, indeed, which supplied the generals in command of armies. Many ancient historians either had commanded armies themselves, as is certainly the case for (for example) Thucydides, Xenophon, Caesar, and Josephus, or had served on the staff of those commanding armies, as had (for example) Sallust and Velleius. Even those who, like Livy, are known or presumed never to have held high military office, nevertheless formed part of the social circle of people who had held such offices. That such people and their plans and decisions should be the overwhelming object of attention would appear to follow virtually auto-matically. Prestige and power within the upper classes came from a successful military command: it was natural that the commanders and their peers examined minutely the behaviour of those commanders and the strategies they adopted, and made the connection between the strategies and their successes.

That Livy should, like others, narrate the battles of the Hannibalic War primarily in terms of the commanders' actions is simply to be expected. But what is less predictable is how often he undermines the idea that these actions were the ultimate determinate of victory or defeat. The most distinctive aspect of Livy's portrayal of commanders in battle is how often he shows them not to be

---

[110] Feldherr (1998: esp. 105–11).

[111] I take the phrase from Stanley Fish's classic book on *Paradise Lost* (Fish 1967), which argues that Milton deliberately presents Satan as attractive and persuasive in the early books so that readers will be seduced into agreement with him, and so will themselves experience the Fall of Adam and Eve that the poem recounts.

fully in control of events.[112] They fail to understand the forces that they are facing or what they need to do to counter them; they make plans which are not followed through or which are positively counterproductive when they are followed through; they win battles in spite of their tactics rather than because of them.

In presenting his commanders—even his best commanders—as so limited, Livy is reflecting something genuine though often underappreciated about Roman generalship. On the whole, at least in the Republic and early Empire,[113] Roman generals were not chosen primarily because they were felt to be well qualified for the positions that they were thrust into.[114] Although one can obviously find consistently successful commanders like Caesar or Marius, or indeed Fabius and Scipio, and while such people might be singled out for a major post in critical times, they were exceptional, and there was certainly no guarantee that those making the appointments would confine their choice to candidates of proven ability.

Indeed, Livy presents this very issue as a major source of contention in the Hannibalic War, most strikingly when Fabius opposes the election to the consulship of T. Otacilius (his own nephew by marriage) on the grounds of his lack of military accomplishment (24.7.10–9.3). While Fabius is successful on this occasion at ensuring the election of himself and Marcellus, the two

---

[112] One may contrast the reported statement of Scipio Aemilianus: *turpe esse aiebat in re militari dicere 'non putaram'* ('he used to say that it is shameful in military affairs to say "I had not thought of it" '). The quotation comes from Valerius Maximus 7.2.2, but it appears from Gellius 13.3.6, who cites a further statement of Scipio reported by Valerius in the same chapter, that it may go back to Sempronius Asellio (fr. 5P).

[113] Birley (e.g. 1950, 1954) and Syme (e.g. 1957: 134–5, 1958b) argued that in the high empire there was a group of *viri militares*, military specialists who were fast-tracked to the consulship. This has been challenged by, among others, Campbell (1975, 1984: 325–47) and Mattern (1999: 14–20), who *inter alia* emphasize how many factors entered into consideration for such appointments apart from proven military qualities; cf. more generally Saller (1982: 94–111) for the way in which in the early empire general virtue entirely outweighed proven skill when men were selected for positions of responsibility. Whatever the situation in the high empire, however, it seems unlikely that military specialization was current either in Livy's own day or in the period about which he is writing. Syme (1958b: 2–3) argues that it only emerged under the Flavians, and was not fully systematized until the second century AD; Birley (1954) wished to date it back to the time of Augustus, but little of his evidence relates to the period before the middle of the first century AD.

[114] It is true that in the middle Republic upper-class Romans would almost invariably have had several years of military service behind them prior to their taking on any command, including service as one of the six *tribuni militum* in a legion. This is explicitly stated as a rule by Polybius 6.19.4–5, and is emphasized by Harris (1979: 10–15). But one may question how effectively such service prepared one for independent command (see Campbell 1975: 18–19, 1987: 20), and more importantly, it does not seem that incompetence in it acted as an impediment to further promotion—indeed, even failure in command was rarely a bar to holding further commands (see Rosenstein 1990a, 1990b). In general, see Campbell (1987), arguing that, in the absence of systematic military training at Rome, surviving military manuals such as those of Onasander or Arrian served to give practical advice for generals who lacked relevant military experience.

leading Roman generals before the rise of Scipio, most commands in the war are held by people of rather less distinction. Fabius indeed presents this as not merely an accident, but a problem endemic in the Republican system, arguing that the constant turnover of commanders allows no individual enough time to gain the requisite experience (24.8.7–8): a point that is heavily politically charged in the context of the early principate when Livy was writing. But even more important for our purposes is that Livy, while raising in this passage the issue of the selection of competent generals, undermines Fabius' arguments, because he shows him grossly misrepresenting Otacilius' achievements. Fabius claims at 24.8.14–16 that Otacilius' command of the fleet that year had accomplished none of the things that the Senate had instructed him to do; but Livy's brief narrative of the successes of Otacilius' command (23.41.8–9) proves Fabius' attack on him to be an outright lie.[115] This does not mean that Livy is presenting the opposition to Otacilius as entirely misguided, since Fabius and Marcellus are recognizable to readers as obviously good choices in the light of their past successes and what people knew of their future accomplishments. But even so, Fabius does not emerge well from the dispute either.[116]

Moreover, the problems raised by Otacilius' election recur in Book 26. Here a remarkably similar election is run to that in Book 24 (26.22.2–15). Yet again Otacilius is chosen by the younger members of the first century to vote, here again the election is opposed and the voting is run again on the grounds of the lack of competence of those initially selected—the twist in this case being that the person whose competence is questioned is not Otacilius, but his colleague Manlius Torquatus, and the person who challenges it is Torquatus himself on the grounds of his short-sightedness (26.22.5–6). But Torquatus' arguments go beyond his own infirmity: he repeatedly reminds the people, just as Fabius had done, of the danger that Hannibal poses and the need to select a general

---

[115] According to Fabius, Otacilius had been given three tasks: to ravage Africa, to guard the shores of Italy, and to prevent supplies from reaching Hannibal. He performed the first, and arguably the second when he defeated a Carthaginian fleet around Sardinia. It is true that the Carthaginians did succeed in getting supplies to Hannibal (23.41.10–12), but, at least on Livy's account, this was because the crossing 'by chance' (*forte*) was made while Otacilius was occupied with the fighting around Sardinia, and Livy seems to place the primary blame for allowing them through on Appius Claudius in Sicily. Brennan (2000: 140) endorses Fabius' criticisms, but this appears to be because he has conflated the two sets of Carthaginians, treating the fleet which Otacilius defeated near Sardinia as identical with the one which supplied Hannibal.

[116] Otacilius in response accuses Fabius of merely wanting to continue in the consulship himself (24.9.1): in the light of Fabius' lies and the fact that he was indeed re-elected the accusation has some force. Livy goes on (24.9.10–11) to note that no one accused Fabius of personal ambition, but instead he was praised for his selfless magnanimity in risking *invidia* for the sake of the state. But he noticeably does not endorse this judgement in his own voice, and the passage is better read as Livy's ironic comment on the naivety of the citizenry rather than as a sign that he shared that naivety.

who would be his equal (26.22.8–9; cf. 24.8.2). The matter is then given over to the senior members of the voting century, and they too tacitly drop Otacilius from consideration as unqualified, recommending instead that two out of the three most successful commanders, Fabius, Marcellus, and Laevinus, be chosen instead: the last two are indeed selected.

Once again this does not seem a bad decision. Livy emphatically praises the Romans of the time for being so concerned for the public good, and the younger Romans for being so willing to defer to their seniors (26.22.14–15)— he compares them favourably with the idealized cities of the philosophers and directly contrasts their behaviour with the degeneration of his own day, when parental authority was no longer respected.[117] And, as before, one might feel that the choice is validated by events. Otacilius dies almost immediately after the election (26.23.2), apparently a chance (*forte*) occurrence, but one which suggests that Rome lost nothing through his failure to be elected. Moreover, Marcellus does well that year against Hannibal, though the fact that he ends up facing Hannibal at all is only the result of the objections to his candidacy by the Syracusans, which lead to his command being changed, and something which also leaves him ultimately in a position to be killed by Hannibal two years later, a connection that might seem a loose one were it not that Livy makes it directly himself at 26.29.9–10. But this time the limitations of the argument that experience is required in commanders appears in a different way also. Directly before the election, the unqualified and inexperienced Scipio has been selected to command in Spain (26.18–19). The people have no practical alternative, since there are no other candidates; but his youth is repeatedly alluded to as a cause for worry (26.18.11, 26.19.1, 26.19.9)—and he has of course in consequence had no experience at all in command.[118] Scipio quells the people's worries, but Livy emphasizes that this was more through his self-promotion than a reasoned assessment of his likely success in the post (26.19.2; cf. 26.18.11). The opposite conclusion is reached to the one that twice prevailed in the case of Otacilius, yet again it seems to be the right one, since Scipio will be the ultimate victor not only in Spain but also over Hannibal. These cases suggest that for Livy the line which divides a successful from an unsuccessful general is a finer one than might superficially appear, and is not reducible to proven military experience of the sort on which Fabius and Torquatus demand that the Romans base their election.

---

[117] On Livy's self-conscious presentation of the gap separating the present from the past see Heuss (1983: esp. 197 on this passage).

[118] As one of the four *tribuni militum* who escaped to Canusium after Cannae he shared with Ap. Claudius Pulcher the *summa imperii* (22.53.3), but that is far short of actual command of an army.

Now it is true that there was considerably more to being a Roman general than simply making tactical decisions. Indeed, Adrian Goldsworthy has argued that modern complaints about Roman generals' 'amateurism' depend on an anachronistic understanding of ancient battles, in which complex tactical movements played a relatively minor role, and a lot more depended on the general's wider qualities of leadership, including his ability to direct small-scale movements of troops at short notice on the field, his acquisition of intelligence, and the like.[119] Accordingly, Roman accounts of desirable qualities in a general regularly placed other possible issues such as moral behaviour or family background at least on a par with military expertise.[120] But in practice not all Roman generals had the requisite experience or qualities to allow them to be effective even in the broader terms that Goldsworthy identifies: and certainly Livy regularly shows even good generals as surprisingly ill-equipped at various points where their choices might be thought to matter. Their failures relate not only to tactics, but also to intelligence, to the decisions when and where to fight, and to much else.

So the way in which Livy regularly introduces fallibility into his generals does reflect something real about Roman warfare, albeit something that is usually absent from writers like Polybius, whose good commanders are more consistently effective, or at least rarely fail for reasons which reflect badly on their decisions.[121] But, as I showed in the first part of the chapter, Livy's battle narratives do not merely undermine his commanders. It is not simply that individuals are less competent than one might expect, but that the competence of the commander is not the thing that ultimately makes the

---

[119] Goldsworthy (1996: 116–70); a similar argument was put forward more briefly by Rosenstein (1990a: 332–4).

[120] See e.g. Cicero, *De Imp.* 28–48, Onasander 1–2, Tacitus, *Ann.* 4.6.2; cf. Campbell (1987: 22–3), Mattern (1999: 19–20).

[121] On Polybius' view of the ideal general who is victorious through his superior rationality and tactical acumen, see Poznanski (1994: 24–31), and in particular the important article by Podes (1990). Podes explores Polybius' theory of human action, arguing that for him the paramount consideration is the state of mind and intentions of the actors. The difference between success and failure rests in the actor's prior assessment of the situation: if done with full rationality success will follow, whereas less effective actors reason less thoroughly, sometimes because they are swayed by non-rational considerations. Cf. the broadly similar though less systematic account of Polybius' thought by Eckstein (1989), who argues that Polybius presents Hannibal's decision to go to war (as opposed to his conduct of the war once it has started) as fundamentally irrational, and thus bound to lead to disaster.

Podes' account sheds an important light on the contrasts between Polybius and Livy that I have explored in this chapter and elsewhere in the book. Livy does have a major predecessor in Thucydides, however, who frequently demonstrates the ways in which strategies and plans tend to go awry in practice. See Stahl (2003: esp. 37–101, 173–88).

greatest difference.[122] Despite focusing on generals, Livy shows that generals
matter rather less than one might expect. The things that generals fail to
predict are sometimes things that are fundamentally unpredictable, tiny
things which make a vast difference in the battle: and many of Livy's battles
turn on such apparently minor considerations. But Livy's battle narratives
challenge expectations more radically, because sometimes it is not clear that
battles are turned by any defined cause at all—indeed, as I showed, he presents
a battle in a way that suggests that all of the causes that one might think led to
victory or defeat failed to be decisive. Yet he does not attribute it to blind
chance either, which one might think would be the obvious alternative.
Victory and defeat happen: and they appear to happen in ways that make
sense, in that they fit the wider moral significance of Livy's narrative, yet they
ostentatiously do not appear to be capable of being analysed in any causal
terms that we would think normal.

We therefore cannot understand Livy's account of war and battles in the
Third Decade in isolation from his broader picture of the world. If battles can
be determined by something other than a straightforward sequence of causes
and effects, what of other events within the Second Punic War? The question
of why battles are won and lost is merely a specific instance of a wider
question: why does Livy think that anything in history happens the way it
does? That will be the subject of my final chapter.

---

[122] In this, too, Livy is not outside the broad expectations of Roman culture. Note Rosenstein (1990a), arguing that a major reason why Roman generals were rarely punished for their
defeats was that battles were held to have been lost because of the intervention of other factors
(cf. above, 311–12). Livy's emphasis on this point in the context of victories as well as defeats is
more noteworthy.

5

Causation

What in Livy's opinion causes things in history to happen?

There are two possible ways of understanding this question. One is to see it as a request to set out what categories of things Livy sees as relevant to explaining[1] historical events and what categories he sees as less relevant—whether, for example, he sees events as primarily the result of the activities of individuals, or whether he would prefer to ascribe primary responsibility to nations acting *en masse*, or to the gods, or (less plausibly) to changes in the environment or to economic forces. This is obviously a question of some interest, even if with Greek and Roman historians the answers tend to vary only within fairly narrow parameters.[2]

---

[1] I am here treating 'cause' and 'explanation' as interchangeable concepts. This is more controversial than may appear at first sight. In certain contexts it is clearly possible to have explanations which do not imply a causal relationship—mathematical explanations are an obvious example, as are other relationships between abstract terms. Nor is it necessarily the case that all causes simply qualify as explanations, since changing the terms in which something is described may arguably remove its explanatory value but make no difference to its causal value (cf. Mackie 1974: 248–69).

But for our purposes there is no compelling need to distinguish 'cause' from 'explanation'. It is not clear that in the physical world it is valid to abstract explanation from causation: for various defences of understanding explanation in causal terms see e.g. Lewis (1986), Strevens (2004, 2008). Certainly not all ancient thinkers differentiated causes and explanations. Aristotle, *Physics* 2.3 and 2.7, speaking of αἴτια, famously classifies them into four categories, and, as is often noted, it is misleading to translate Aristotle's αἴτια by 'causes', since they include reasons for things happening—for example teleological ones—which people nowadays would often feel uncomfortable referring to as 'causes': 'explanation' would here be closer (cf. e.g. Hocutt 1974). But for Aristotle the concepts run into one another. Admittedly later Greek philosophers, under the influence of Stoicism, narrowed the term to things which are more like 'causes' in the modern sense, things which actively produce a result, but even here the older terminology was sometimes maintained (see Frede 1980).

And most importantly for our purposes, in historical contexts, as opposed to scientific or abstract reasoning, one can make an especially strong case that 'causes' and 'explanations' run together, since history involves people whose reasons for actions are also chief among the causes of those actions. It is true that some philosophers (e.g. Gardiner 1952; cf. Collins 1984) have denied that explanations in terms of human motivation are 'causes', but this depends on an artificial restriction of the notion of causation (cf. Dray 1957: 150–5; Davidson 1963). Under most normal circumstances we would expect historical 'explanations' to qualify as 'causes'.

[2] Note e.g. Reinhold (1985), or the analysis of Hecataeus, Herodotus, Thucydides, and Polybius by Derow (1994); for Livy see e.g. Ducos (1987).

But the question can also be understood in another way. Instead of asking what particular things Livy sees as causing particular events, we can ask something more abstract and more fundamental: what is his concept of an historical cause in general? How does Livy conceive events in history are to be interpreted in relation to other events? In other words, what is it that makes something a 'cause' rather than (for example) a mere concomitant of an event with which it may be associated?

These two versions of the question are naturally not unrelated to one another. The type of answers we give to the second may well affect the possible answers that are given to the first. So, for instance, if a particular historian sees a concrete material connection as essential if one thing is to 'cause' another, then it is unlikely that he will see the immaterial activity of a divine spirit or the workings out of a grand and impersonal Fate as relevant causal factors. But this is not to say that we should not consider the second version of the question in its own right, since it may well raise issues which are not simply reducible to the specific question of what sort of causes the historian tends to identify as operating.

Admittedly, with some historians there would appear to be little point in raising so abstract and so philosophical a question.[3] Historians, like most people in everyday life, tend to take the concept of 'cause' as a common-sense given, and when trying to explain an event they simply search for the 'causes' of the event within that common-sense framework. Moreover, there is some reason to think that the commonsense understanding of 'cause' is one that is not culture dependent, but rather is basic to the way humans perceive the world.[4] Of course, cultures may differ in the things to which they attribute causal efficacy: in many cultures, for example, witches are deemed able to have powerful effects on things remote from them, and to achieve these effects by connections between objects that to a Western eye appear entirely unrelated. But even in these cases 'causes' still work in familiar ways, though applied to different domains. Hence there is little reason to think that the Romans in

---

[3] An important exception is Pédech (1964: 54–98), who explores Polybius' concept of causation against the background not only of earlier historiography, but of Aristotelian and Stoic philosophy. On earlier historians cf. also Brown (1989) on Thucydides, and especially the fundamental work of Hunter (1982: 117–296), whose powerful insights into Herodotus' and Thucydides' understanding of causation have still not been fully appreciated.

[4] Some anthropologists (e.g. Needham 1976) have argued that (e.g.) magical practices in non-Western cultures show that members of those cultures have a concept of cause quite alien to Western understandings. Against this, however, see the arguments of Boyer (1994: 125–54), suggesting that it is an error to see any generalized 'principles of causation' underlying either Western or non-Western belief systems, but rather that people in all cultures develop broadly similar ideas about causes from a collection of distinct and largely empirical understandings of how the world works, which then are applied to different ontological domains.

general had a different notion of cause from our own, although, as one would expect, the systematic accounts of causation given by philosophers could vary radically from intuitive conceptions.[5]

But the very fact that we expect the Romans generally to understand causation in much the same terms as we do makes Livy's Third Decade seem all the stranger. Previous chapters have already thrown up a number of oddities. In Chapter 1 I showed that Livy sometimes employs inconsistent chronological schemes, apparently in full awareness that they are inconsistent, and moreover draws them together into what appears to be a single linear narrative, each event connected with the one before. This would appear to make no sense in a narrative representing actual historical events in the world—unless Livy's concept of an acceptable historical connection is such as to accommodate what to us seems so impossible a sequence. I also showed how adjacent events in Livy sometimes appear to influence one another, even in cases where there does not seem to be any identifiable causal sequence to connect them. In Chapter 4 I similarly demonstrated that Livy appears to allow the outcomes of battles to be governed by things which do not precede them, but are either intertwined with or sometimes even occur after them: this too appears highly counterintuitive according to our everyday understanding of causation, especially when one adds that Livy at the same time is ostentatiously rewriting his battle narratives so as to undermine any sense that their outcomes are decided by everyday material factors. And in Chapter 3 I discussed his representation of individual characters in the Hannibalic War, and showed that Livy presented characters who did not conform to the usual Roman standards of believability, but whose behaviour appeared to be governed by their wider role in the narrative at any particular point. This last is not directly an example of causation failing to work in expected terms, but has clear connections with it, since the behaviour of individuals is a strong motivating force in Livy's history, yet that behaviour is not always straightforwardly explicable. These anomalies in Livy do not fit normal causal patterns, nor are they likely to arise merely from his adherence to some philosophical school with distinctive views about causation. Although Livy is attested as having written works about philosophy,[6] there is little in his

---

[5] On ancient philosophers' concepts of causation see e.g. Sorabji (1980: esp. 3–88), Hankinson (1998). Causation is of particular interest in Stoicism because of its relationship to the much-discussed issue of determinism and free will. However, fewer scholars have considered the Stoic concept of causation as a topic in its own right: for exceptions see e.g. Frede (1980) and Bobzien (1999). See further below, 376–82.

[6] According to Seneca, *Ep.* 100.9, Livy 'wrote both dialogues, which you could count as historical as much as philosophical, and books expressly containing philosophy' (*scripsit enim et dialogos, quos non magis philosophiae adnumerare possis quam historiae, et ex professo philosophiam continentis libros*).

history to suggest that he was writing it from a dogmatic philosophical stand-point[7]—although, as I shall suggest later in the chapter, philosophical accounts of causation do provide part of the intellectual framework within which Livy's anomalous picture may be interpreted.

I shall begin my discussion by examining more systematically some of these ways in which Livy handles causation in apparently eccentric terms, and I shall do so under three main headings: first, the relationship between causation and time; second, narrative causation; and third, moral causation.

5.1. TIME AND CAUSE

One of the most fundamental aspects of our everyday conceptions of causation is that it is strictly temporal. For causation to make sense, one generally assumes that whatever is identified as a 'cause' temporally precedes, or at most is simultaneous with, its 'effect'; if that is not the case one would hesitate to identify them as 'cause' and 'effect' at all.[8] Hence the expectation is that the chronological sequence an historian adopts will be reflected in the causal sequence that he identifies.

In Livy's case, however, that expectation is not always fulfilled in practice, and even when it is fulfilled it sometimes leads to odd consequences. In Chapter 4 I briefly referred to a case where Livy appears to be prepared to countenance 'backwards causation': where Hannibal's miraculous defeat when he attacked Rome is implied to be caused by his plundering of a temple, even though the plundering of the temple, in the version of the story that Livy appears to favour, occurred after he lost the battle. In that case the causal sequence is not aligned with the chronology. Conversely, as I discussed

---

[7] The main proponent of the idea that Livy endorsed a particular philosophical school—Stoicism—is Walsh (1958, 1961: 49–64); but see *contra* e.g. Liebeschuetz (1967: 51–3), Levene (1993: 30–3).

[8] I am stating here a commonsense position. From a philosophical perspective the possibility that causation may operate backwards in time is not necessarily to be ruled out (see e.g. Dummett 1954, 1964), though many philosophers reject the idea (e.g. Flew 1954; Black 1955–56; Gorovitz 1964); likewise there have been suggestions (though this too is controversial) that certain aspects of the behaviour of subatomic particles may amount to backward causation (see e.g. de Beauregard 1977: esp. 49–50; Dowe 1996). But certainly no ancient writer on causation explicitly allows it to operate backwards (note Sextus Empiricus, *Outlines of Pyrrhonism* 3.26: τὸ μὲν οὖν λέγειν, ὅτι τὸ αἴτιον εἰς ὑπόστασιν ἄγεται μετὰ τὴν γένεσιν τοῦ ἀποτελέσματος αὐτοῦ μὴ καὶ γελοῖον ᾖ—'saying that the cause is brought into existence after the creation of its own effect would be laughable'), although, as I shall discuss later, backward causation may not appear as strange within the ancient conceptual universe as it has subsequently come to do.

in Chapter 1, there are places where the causal sequence apparently is tied to the chronology, but where the chronology is avowedly impossible—for example, when Livy has combined incompatible frameworks into a single narrative sequence—and where it would accordingly seem to follow that the causal sequence that the narrative identifies is equally impossible. Neither of these phenomena is by any means uniformly present in Livy's narrative— indeed, one can plausibly argue that it would be more or less impossible to construct a meaningful narrative at all if most of the time both chronology and the connection between chronology and causation were not working in expected terms. But they are nevertheless more common than is comfortable in an historian, whose works are presumed to be written in such a way as to reflect a series of events that genuinely did occur (or at the very least could have occurred).

Moreover, Livy, even at times when he does not overtly violate ordinary expectations, manipulates the relationship between temporal and causal sequences in sometimes counterintuitive ways (compare also my account of the Masinissa digression above, 253–5). An example is the opening of the Roman campaign in Syracuse in Book 24. At 24.21.1 Marcellus is sent to Syracuse, an event described as follows:

Romani, cum bellum nequaquam contemnendum in Sicilia oreretur morsque tyranni duces magis inpigros dedisset Syracusanis quam causam aut animos mutasset, M. Marcello alteri consulum eam provinciam decernunt.

Since a far from negligible war was arising in Sicily, and the tyrant's death had done more to give the Syracusans vigorous generals than to change their reasons or their minds, the Romans decreed that province to Marcus Marcellus, one of the two consuls.

The next sentence then moves into the pluperfect—*secundum Hieronymi caedem primo tumultuatum in Leontinis apud milites fuerat* (24.21.2: 'following the murder of Hieronymus there had initially been rioting among the soldiers in Leontini'). This links the episode with the last moment at which events in Syracuse had been narrated, which was indeed the assassination of Hieronymus (24.7.1–7), and implies that the Syracusan narrative here follows directly from that, and that this is accordingly earlier than the assignment of Sicily to Marcellus. Marcellus does not arrive in Sicily until 24.27.6, and the intervening narrative presumably brings events in Sicily up to date. Livy thus has a clear and consistent chronology which keeps the Sicilian events aligned with the Italian narrative that has occupied 24.8–20. As I noted in Chapter 1 (above, 53–5), there is a problem with the year-breaks here, but there are no problems with its internal consistency.

The problem however comes when one attempts to relate this chronology to Livy's account of the Sicilians' actions and the Romans' motivation. The

Syracusans' changing their alliance from Rome to Carthage had appeared earlier, when Hieronymus executed his pro-Roman adviser Thraso (24.5.13). He then (prompted by his pro-Carthaginian advisers Adranodorus and Zoippus) negotiated a treaty with Hannibal and Carthage and rejected that with Rome, insulting the envoys whom Appius Claudius had sent to try to renew the Roman alliance (24.6). Indeed, it is while he is campaigning actively against Roman holdings in Sicily that Hieronymus is assassinated by members of his own army (24.7.1–2).

Hence the break from Rome that Hieronymus represents is clear:[9] the oddity is the Romans' apparent response to his assassination. It is true that Livy constructs his picture of Syracusan politics in such a way that Thraso is the only force for maintaining the Roman alliance—'the one bond holding the alliance with the Romans' (24.6.1 *unum vinculum cum Romanis societatis*). Polybius had identified several others of Hieronymus' advisers with the same views (7.5.3), whom Livy simply wipes out of the picture. It is also true that the conspirators who assassinate Hieronymus appear to be objecting to his tyranny rather than his pro-Carthaginian slant. But they are described as acting not only against him but against Adranadorus (24.7.7), and the only policy Adranodorus had been associated with is the alliance with Carthage (24.5.7–8): the conspirators, by killing the anti-Roman Hieronymus and challenging the anti-Roman Adranodorus, are certainly acting in Rome's interests, even if their own intentions towards Rome are left unclear.[10] So when Livy concludes this initial account of Syracusan events by saying, immediately after Hieronymus' assassination, that 'in the uncertain state of things Appius Claudius saw from close hand war arising' (24.7.8 *incerto rerum statu Ap. Claudius bellum oriens ex propinquo . . . cerneret*), he is of course right to identify war with Syracuse as imminent, but strangely attaches it to exactly the wrong moment.[11] That conclusion would clearly have been justified by Livy's narrative earlier, before the assassination; it could be justified later also,

---

[9] Polybius is more complex and has more stages to the break: even after Hieronymus insults Appius' embassy and makes a treaty with Carthage, a further Roman embassy comes to him to appeal for the maintenance of the alliance, and the final break comes only when Hieronymus stupidly insults them by demanding ludicrous terms (7.5).

[10] It is perhaps worth noting that one of the conspirators against Hieronymus, Sosis, later reappears acting on the Romans' side (25.25.3; cf. 26.21.9–10, 26.30.6, 26.31.4), though Livy is admittedly not likely to be expecting the reader here to be interpreting events in the light of that information.

[11] Eckstein (1987: 142–3) observes the mismatch, but merely attributes it to Appius' misjudgement. In Livy's presentation, at any rate, the judgement is correct (as implied by *cerneret*), despite not fitting the actual circumstances. Marchetti (1972: 10–13) solves the problem by dating Appius' letter before Hieronymus' assassination, which likewise goes against Livy's direct statements, and his attempt to explain the displacement in Livy is very strained.

once the Syracusans slip back into war with Rome, but at this precise point in the narrative it makes far less sense.[12] In one way the claim obviously justifies itself by its ultimate truth, but that truth appears to be independent of the development in Syracuse that Livy has established.

Looking at this passage in isolation, of course, it is possible to see other reasons for Livy to have set things out in this order; most obviously, by concluding the Syracusan episode with Appius sending a message to Rome, he allows a transition back to his Italian narrative—as I noted in Chapter 1, such transitions are often mediated by characters' movement and the like. But the content of the message did not need to be expressed in terms which failed to match the actual situation in Syracuse at that moment; and, no less importantly, the passage does not stand in isolation, but the same issues recur once the Syracusan narrative resumes. The introduction to the episode at 24.21.1 (quoted above, 321) with the words *bellum . . . oreretur* looks back to the judgement of Appius Claudius in the previous year about 'war arising'; yet chronologically it must relate to a later period, at some point during the ensuing Sicilian narrative which (as I said) is a flashback filling in the gap between Appius' letter in late 215 and Marcellus' dispatch in 214.[13] But it is remarkably difficult to find the precise point in that narrative too where it would be apparent that 'war was arising' or which would have shown the Romans that 'the tyrant's death had done more to give the Syracusans vigorous generals than to change their reasons or their minds'. We are given a long account of the complex power struggle that succeeded Hieronymus' assassination: the assassins taking power with the (eventual) support of Adranodorus (24.21.2–23.4), the attempted coup by Adranodorus and Themistius, its betrayal and their murder along with their families (24.23.5–26.16), and a new election at which the pro-Carthaginian Hippocrates and Epicydes replace Adranodorus and Themistius as praetors (24.27.1–5). But how this relates to a possible war with Rome is less apparent. Anti-Roman feelings at Syracuse are described at 24.23.10–24.1,[14] when Hippocrates and Epicydes return there

---

[12] Compare also 24.11.7 *cum increbresceret rumor bellum in Sicilia esse* ('since rumour was growing that there was a war in Sicily'). On Livy's narrative sequence, rumour is wrong on this occasion, since there was not actually a war in Sicily at that time—although there would be one eventually, and so the Romans' assignment of their forces there turns out for the best.

[13] Eckstein (1987: 140–1) argues that it was indeed Appius' letter that prompted Marcellus' dispatch: he accordingly dates the former, along with the assassination of Hieronymus, in the summer of 214, and sees the events of 24.21.2–27.6 as occurring in just a few weeks in late summer (cf. Eckstein 1987: 348–9). However plausible this may be as a reconstruction of the actual history, it is clearly incompatible with Livy's explicit chronological statements.

[14] In addition, the Syracusans take weapons dedicated by the Romans from the shrine of Jupiter at 24.21.9–10. At Levene (1993: 55) I argued that this lowers their moral standing; however, it is actually less pointedly anti-Roman than I suggested there, since the ostensible and

after the death of Hieronymus. Their own antagonism towards the Romans is apparent: they seek permission to return to join Hannibal, which the Syracusan leaders are happy to allow them (24.23.8–9), but before it can be put into effect, they start accusing the leaders of wanting to renew the treaty with Rome only as a pretext, and claim that the secret plan was for the Romans to control the state (24.23.11). Moreover, they appear to have a ready audience of (mainly Roman allied) deserters and 'people of the lowest class' (24.23.10 *infimae plebis homines*), and 'every day a greater mass of people primed to hear and believe this was flowing to Syracuse' (24.24.1 *his audiendis credendisque opportuna multitudo maior in dies Syracusas confluebat*). So there is a large number of Syracusans who oppose renewing the Roman alliance—but Livy instantly shows their failure to put this into practice. It is this influx of people opposed to Rome that leads Adranodorus to attempt his coup (24.24.1–2); but it is instantly betrayed and he is killed. And Sopater persuades the masses that the killing was justified, which is what leads them to demand the killing of his family too (24.25). Only after that do the people elect Epicydes and Hippocrates praetors (24.27.1–5).

Where in this is the Syracusans' move against Rome determined? The answer is that it is not determined in any clear fashion. Certainly Epicydes and Hippocrates are shown as having increasing support for their anti-Roman agenda, but that is hardly stable: the people in the first instance elect leaders with no such agenda, and who indeed, it is implied, are seeking to renew the alliance with Rome. When Adranodorus seeks to mount a coup of his own on the back of that anti-Roman feeling he is killed and popular sentiment is whipped up against him and his family. It would be reasonable to conclude that the election of Epicydes and Hippocrates shows that power has finally swung towards support for Carthage— but on Livy's account, that election cannot have been the motivation for the Romans assigning Marcellus and his forces to Sicily, since according to Livy's presentation of the chronological sequence that had already happened by that point.[15] At the time of the election (so it appears) the Syracusans were negotiating a new treaty with Rome, and Marcellus is party to those negotiations (24.27.6)— the back-story has now reached the point it left in 24.21.1, when he was assigned to Sicily. Moreover, even after the election of Hippocrates and Epicydes and Marcellus' arrival war is far from inevitable. Immediately prior to Marcellus reaching Sicily, the Roman fleet is described as awaiting the outcome of events in

---

immediate use of the arms is not against Rome but rather to defend the people against a resumption of tyranny.

[15] Marchetti (1972: 15–19) correctly identifies the problem, but solves it merely by rejecting Livy's chronology: he sees the events following the election as the trigger for assigning Marcellus to Sicily. See *contra* Eckstein (1987: 141).

a way that implies that the outcome is still undetermined.[16] And the very next event in the sequence is that the Syracusan assembly votes to seek peace with Rome (24.28), though those efforts are then derailed by a combination of sabotage and misunderstandings—misunderstandings which are in fact prompted in part by the Romans' own activities, since their capture of Leontini is falsely reported as having been accompanied by atrocities (24.30.3–14, 24.31.6–32.2).[17]

In other words, Livy's narrative of the Syracusans' break with Rome offers no precise point at which one might have grounds for believing that war was imminent, even though the Romans act on the basis that it is imminent. Indeed, the sequence is still more counterintuitive: for the Romans are led to campaign in Sicily by the (correct) perception of imminent war, yet their presence in Sicily is one of the chief factors that enables the war.

None of this suggests that Livy is presenting the Romans as overreacting or failing to read the evidence properly. Livy endorses their perceptions with his own voice, and, as I have said, they are proved right by events, since war between Syracuse and Rome does (eventually) arise. Much of the problem in Syracuse is the anarchic nature of the freedom that they acquire on Hieronymus' assassination: every time a wise leader manages to control the mob something intervenes to derail the move to moderation.[18] And such a chaotic move to freedom is associated by Livy with anti-Roman feeling:[19] immediately after the Syracusans attempt to come to terms with Marcellus he directly compares the Syracusan state to a diseased body, which suffers worse relapses at every point it appears to be recovering (24.29.3). This is a common historiographical image for a state whose political structures are fundamentally awry:[20] here Livy ties this specifically to the ability of Hippocrates to continue to provoke the Syracusans into conflict with Rome. But the identification of imminent war on which the Romans base their actions appears to require something more precise than a generalized sense of political instability in Syracuse: it seems to be based on a real sense of movement towards conflict. But there is no point in Livy's Syracusan narrative where one can see such a clear movement towards conflict—except after the time when the Romans

---

[16] 24.27.5: *ad Murgantiam tum classem navium centum Romanus habebat, quonam evaderent motus ex caedibus tyrannorum orti Syracusis, quove eos ageret nova atque insolita libertas, opperiens* ('The Romans then had a fleet of a hundred ships at Murgantia, waiting to see how the disturbances created by the killing of the tyrants would turn out, and what direction their new and unaccustomed freedom would take them').

[17] Cf. 26.30.4 for the persistence of the false report when the Sicilians complain to the Senate about Marcellus' behaviour.

[18] On this point see Jaeger (2003: esp. 219–29).

[19] As it is elsewhere also, most notably at Capua in Book 23 (which however presents complications of its own: see below, 354–66).

[20] Cf. Woodman (forthcoming).

have already acted on that future conflict, and where their own consequent presence in Syracuse is part of the causal sequence that enables it.

So what we have here is two separate causal sequences superimposed on each other. One sequence is the chronological narrative of events in Syracuse, which is clear and consistent in its own terms, and where every point leads naturally to the next. But floating above that is a clear and accurate judgement by both the narrator and the characters that there is an imminent war: where the characters act on that judgement of imminent war, but where the imminence of war appears to be entirely outside the events of the chronological narrative. We readers too—like Livy—know that Syracuse is moving to war with Rome, because war is the eventual outcome. That knowledge does not derive from any identifiable events in the main chronological sequence. Yet it does not appear to be simply due to the narrator's or readers' privileged position either, since the Romans within the narrative reach the same conclusion. It appears to reflect a real causal sequence in the world, yet one which, though eventually intertwined with the main sequence, is initiated independently of it, and in particular is independent of the precise chronology of events in Syracuse.

The negotiations between the Romans and the Carthaginians in Book 30 are more complex, yet in some crucial respects similar to the account of the Syracusan revolt. The first point where the possibility of a truce is mentioned is at 30.7.6–7, where the Carthaginians debate three courses of action: to negotiate peace with Scipio, to recall Hannibal from Italy, or to reconstitute the army and encourage Syphax to continue the war. The third view prevails, since it is supported by Hasdrubal and the Barcids, and Livy appears to approve the decision, referring to it as a mark of 'Roman constancy in adversity' (30.7.6 *Romanae in adversis rebus constantiae*).[21] However, unlike the Romans' strategy in similar straits after Cannae, with which this is implicitly compared,[22] the plan fails: the Romans almost immediately defeat the combined army of Hasdrubal and Syphax (30.8) and now the threat to Carthage appears imminent: the debate is therefore renewed (30.9.4–9). Once

---

[21] This is derived from Polybius 14.6.9–12, who is however much more dismissive. For him the mere fact of debating appears to be a mark of weakness and indecision (14.6.9 ἦν τὸ συνέδριον ἀπορίας καὶ ποικίλων καὶ τεταραγμένων ἐπινοημάτων πλῆρες). He neither explicitly endorses the eventual outcome nor compares it to Roman behaviour in similar exigencies, nor does he associate it with the Barcids.

[22] On *constantia* as a distinctively Roman virtue in Livy see Moore (1989: 66, 158). Livy had laid great emphasis in Book 22 on the Romans' resolve and refusal to surrender in the aftermath of Cannae, comparing them favourably with the Carthaginians at comparable times: note in particular 22.54.10–11 and 22.61.11–15.

again they have three courses of action open to them,[23] and those courses are similar to the ones before: make moves to peace, recall Hannibal, or launch a counterattack against the Romans at Utica. They prefer the last option, but decide to recall Hannibal as well, since even if they win at Utica (as in fact they do: see above, 300–2) they foresee that they will still need Hannibal's army to defend the city. As for peace, they are still not ready to countenance the idea. Livy reports that 'peace was rarely referred to' (30.9.5 *rara mentio est pacis*), a significant and pointed reworking of Polybius, who not only lists the option to pursue peace among those that the Carthaginians were considering (14.9.10), but concludes by noting that they decided to adopt all of them.[24] The Carthaginians in Livy are still single-mindedly pursuing the war; those in Polybius are exploring peace options even as they continue to fight.

So, in Livy, the Carthaginians, even in adversity, are not initially seeking peace. The change in their attitude comes after the defeat and capture of Syphax: here the Carthaginians, according to Livy, 'giving no further hearing to any advocates of war, sent thirty leading elders as advocates to seek peace' (30.16.3 *iam nullo auctore belli ultra audito, oratores ad pacem petendam mittunt triginta seniorum principes*). They hear Scipio's terms, and decide, as he suggested (30.16.13), to agree a truce with him while sending envoys to Rome to make peace. However, at this point it appears that they have an ulterior motive (30.16.14–15):

ita dimissi Carthaginienses nullas recusandas condiciones pacis cum censuissent, quippe qui moram temporis quaererent dum Hannibal in Africam traiceret, legatos alios ad Scipionem ut indutias facerent, alios Romam ad pacem petendam mittunt.

The Carthaginians, dismissed in this fashion, were of the view that no terms of peace should be rejected, since they were looking for a delay until Hannibal might cross into Africa; they sent some envoys to Scipio to make a truce, and others to Rome to seek peace.

With these final comments Livy offers a new version of the Carthaginians' motivation which is not entirely consistent with what he stated at the start of

---

[23] Polybius 14.9.6–11 constructs the debate a little differently, setting out four options, not three, the fourth being 'preparing the city for a siege'. Livy moves this point slightly earlier (30.9.4), so that it does not appear to be part of the discussion, but is something the Carthaginians do at the start as a matter of course without even debating the topic. One effect is to increase the sense of pressure on the Carthaginians in Livy, since defending the city is presented as a necessity, not an option.

[24] 14.9.11 γενομένων δὲ καὶ πλειόνων λόγων περὶ ταῦτα, πάσας ἐκύρωσαν ἅμα τὰς γνώμας ('After several discussions of these matters, they decided to follow all of the opinions simultaneously'). Walbank (1967: 433, following Scullard 1930: 213) suggests that Polybius did not count a peace agreement as one of the options that the Carthaginians decided to pursue at this point. But that is an implausible reading of Polybius' text, in which pursuing peace is the last option mentioned before he concludes that the Carthaginians decided to follow them 'all'.

the paragraph. There it appeared that peace was being sought as an alternative to war, and that the more aggressive options that had been outlined in the previous internal debates in Carthage had been rejected. Now the Carthaginians look, at least on the face of things, like hypocrites, since their primary object is to give Hannibal sufficient time to return. Admittedly that does not necessarily mean that Livy is presenting their negotiations to date as having been conducted entirely in bad faith, since they might be preparing for alternative contingencies; but the implication of what is stated here is that they are prepared to appear to endorse terms which they have no intention of accepting in the long run.[25] But Livy's account of the Carthaginians' behaviour is more ambivalent and inconsistent than Polybius' appears to have been. For Polybius the double strategy of pursuing peace while recalling Hannibal to defend Africa was central to the Carthaginians' approach from the moment Syphax and Hasdrubal were defeated.[26] Livy has them veering between different strategies, while himself veering between different interpretations of their strategy. In Livy the Carthaginians begin by preparing for war with no mention of peace, but then abandon all talk of war in favour of pursuing peace alone. Only at the end does Livy synthesize these, implying that the two were part of a single strategy much along the lines that Polybius had implied from the start, even though that is not fully borne out by his account of their deliberations.

This final interpretation, however, is the one that appears to dominate when the Carthaginian envoys come to address the Senate in Rome (30.23.2–8). The Romans are in doubt how to respond to their appeals. Metellus recommends that they should follow the advice of Scipio, as being the actual victor and the person on the spot who was in a position to assess their sincerity (30.23.3–4). Scipio had, of course, endorsed the Carthaginians' appeal for peace (30.16.9, 30.16.13), so this would imply that his peace terms should be ratified. Laevinus responds by accusing the Carthaginians of merely being spies, and says that no peace agreement should be made (30.23.5). Laelius and Fulvius support this by claiming that the Carthaginians were being disingenuous: that they were merely waiting for Hannibal to be recalled from Italy and were planning to

---

[25] It is worth noting in this context Livy's account of the Carthaginian envoys prostrating themselves 'in the style of flatterers' (30.16.4 *more adulantium*) before Scipio. He attributes this to their Eastern heritage (unlike Polybius 15.1.7, who implies that even other Carthaginians would have found it 'unseemly' (ἀγεννῶς)), but adds that 'their speech matched such debased flattery' (30.16.5 *conveniens oratio tam humili adulationi fuit*), a phrase which implies the speakers' dishonesty (cf. Mantel 1991: 123).

[26] Compare Polybius 15.1.10, where the Roman ambassadors accuse the Carthaginians of adopting precisely that strategy. Appian, *Pun.* 31 similarly shows this double strategy as intrinsic to the Carthaginians' peace negotiations.

violate any terms they agreed once that had happened; they add that Scipio's support for peace was premised on Hannibal not being recalled (30.23.6–7). As a result of these arguments Laevinus' opinion prevails, and no peace agreement is made.[27]

However, in terms of the chronology of events that Livy has presented, these Roman arguments do not seem to make sense. First, Laelius was not in any position to report Scipio's assessment of the Carthaginians' sincerity with regard to the peace agreement, since he had left Africa prior to the Carthaginian peace initiatives, something which Livy has emphasized by inserting his account of those initiatives precisely in the interval between Laelius' departure at 30.16.1 and his arrival there 'many days before' the negotiations between Scipio and the Carthaginians were concluded (30.17.1 *multis ante diebus*). It is true that Scipio's legate Q. Fulvius Gillo is also present, and that he arrived with the Carthaginians and so (hypothetically) could report Scipio's final thoughts on the negotiations (30.21.12). But even if we are meant to assume that Laelius was relying on Fulvius' account of Scipio's interpretation of events (something that Livy nowhere suggests),[28] there is a further problem. On Livy's account the Carthaginians had already sent for Hannibal well before they began thinking of peace and negotiating with Scipio, so Scipio could hardly have made his acceptance of the peace terms conditional on their not doing so.

We could perhaps argue that Laelius and Fulvius are to be seen as lying in order to scuttle the peace negotiations, but that too does not fit the tenor of Livy's account. We can begin with the general unlikelihood that Laelius in particular would be presented as undermining a treaty that Scipio has favoured: at every point since his introduction in Book 26 he has been presented as operating in unquestioning harmony with Scipio's plans. Moreover, whereas Laevinus' claim that the Carthaginians are merely spies appears tendentious, Laelius and Fulvius are right that the Carthaginians were being

---

[27] Livy's account of the Romans refusing the treaty is found in no other source (cf. below, 330–1), and its historicity is generally rejected (see e.g. Scullard 1930: 222–3, Mantel 1991: 125–8, Hoyos 2003: 167–70). *Contra* Gerhold (2002: 111–40), who offers an elaborate but implausible defence of Livy's basic reliability. Seibert (1993a: 453–5) likewise more briefly argues that Livy is reliably reporting an earlier stage of the debate, but not the final decision: his grounds are that Roman historians would not have invented something that justified the Carthaginians' renewal of war—a revealing failure to recognize how Livy regularly and deliberately slants his account in the direction of moral complexity rather than the mere provision of patriotic excuses.

[28] The implication of the Senate's insistence on Laelius' presence when peace was discussed (30.17.2, 30.21.11) is that he personally is recognized as Scipio's particular intimate, something that Livy's narrative repeatedly bears out. The closeness of their relationship is explicitly remarked at 27.17.8, but Scipio's reliance on him appears constantly.

disingenuous in their negotiations with Scipio, at least according to the report of their intentions at 30.16.14–15. We can add that the entire Carthaginian appeal to the Senate is presented as duplicitous, both in their denial of responsibility for Hannibal's actions (30.22.1–2)—an argument they had made to Scipio as well, as Livy remarks (cf. 30.16.5)—and in their inability to defend their claim that they had kept faithfully to previous treaties (30.22.3–6).[29] The problem is that the actual sequence of the negotiations does not justify the correct interpretation that the Romans draw from them, since they are manifestly not in possession of the relevant information, and such information as they may be assumed to possess points largely in the opposite direction.

In this respect, then, the account of the abortive peace treaty is very similar to the account of the Syracusan revolt. In both we have a sequence of events in which the non-Roman party is moving towards war, where the Romans and Livy alike recognize that they are moving towards war, and yet where there is no point in the narrative where the detailed account of their behaviour would justify the Romans drawing the conclusion that they do. The peace negotiations in Book 30 are admittedly more complicated in ways that are especially morally challenging to the reader, since Livy's account of the Carthaginians' motivation is ostentatiously inconsistent even in its own terms, something that he draws attention to by changing the sequence described in Polybius, where (as far as we can tell from the surviving portion of his account) the Carthaginians consistently followed the double strategy of recalling Hannibal while pursuing peace. That inconsistency also makes Scipio's position harder to determine: he has manifestly approved the Carthaginians' peace proposal, contrary to what Laelius and Fulvius state in the Senate, but Livy leaves it unclear whether he has merely been duped (as the final account of the Carthaginians' intentions would imply) or whether his push for peace is reasonable (which would fit Livy's account of their initial sincerity). There are also additional moral complications in the aftermath, where the Carthaginians, prior to learning from Rome that their peace proposal had been rejected (30.25.1), break the truce by capturing a Roman fleet and then almost assaulting the ambassadors that Scipio sends to complain and attacking their ship on their return. Though the truce is certainly broken,[30] none of these is morally unambiguous, since the Carthaginians appear at first at least to be

---

[29] We might note the pointed ambiguity in the Romans' anger that the Carthaginian ambassadors 'did not remember' the previous treaty (30.22.6 *non meminissent*). They did not 'remember' it because they were too young (30.22.5)—but the word also has the sense of 'failing to pay heed to' those treaties (*OLD* s.v. *memini* 3): a persistent, and, on Livy's account (cf. 21.19.1–5), justified complaint against the Carthaginians from the beginning of the war.

[30] Note especially 30.25.9 *haud dubie indutiae ruptae essent* ('the truce had unquestionably been broken').

attempting to act in a way that will preserve their agreements, and the ships captured are unmanned (30.24.11–12); the near assault on the ambassadors is without the authorization of the Carthaginian leadership, who in fact protect them (30.25.3–4);[31] and the attack on the Roman ship may likewise be unauthorized (Livy leaves the matter open).[32] Polybius' rather different account had placed the Carthaginians in a far less morally tenable position.[33] But even through these complications the double picture of causation works much as it had at Syracuse. Carthaginian violations and bad faith are understood to occur, yet that understanding is independent of the actual sequence of events.

Prior to the capture of Syracuse in Book 25, Livy creates a causal sequence that is chronologically anomalous in a different way. The relevant section of the narrative begins at 25.28.1: at this point Bomilcar and the Carthaginians have sailed away, abandoning any hope of fighting off the Romans, and Epicydes has left the city. The Sicilian soldiers in the field decide to negotiate with Marcellus (25.28.2–6):

legatos de condicionibus dedendae urbis explorata prius per conloquia voluntate eorum, qui obsidebantur, ad Marcellum mittunt. cum haud ferme discreparet, quin, quae ubique regum fuissent, Romanorum essent, Siculis cetera cum libertate ac legibus suis servarentur, evocatis ad conloquium iis, quibus ab Epicyde creditae res erant, missos se simul ad Marcellum, simul ad eos ab exercitu Siculorum aiunt, ut una omnium, qui obsiderentur quique extra obsidionem fuissent, fortuna esset, neve alteri

---

[31] Polybius has nothing of this near assault and rescue; Diodorus 27.12.1 has a briefer but more lurid version, in which it is not merely that the ambassadors are 'almost assaulted', as in Livy (30.25.3 *prope violati*), but 'the mob almost killed them' (οἱ δὲ ὄχλοι παρ' ὀλίγον αὐτοὺς ἀνεῖλον). In Appian, *Pun.* 34 the mob's plan appears to be to hold them as hostages.

[32] 30.25.5 *seu clam misso a Carthagine nuntio ut id fieret, seu Hasdrubale qui classi praeerat sine publica fraude auso facinus* ('whether a messenger had been secretly sent from Carthage to bring this about, or whether Hasdrubal, the commander of the fleet, dared to commit the deed without state involvement in the violation').

[33] In Polybius (Diodorus 27.11–12, Appian, *Pun.* 34, and Dio 57 fr. 57.74–5 are similar) the Romans agreed to the treaty that in Livy they rejected, and moreover the Carthaginians were informed of the fact by Scipio's ambassadors (15.1.3–4; cf. 15.4.8, 15.8.8–9), so all subsequent actions by them are in direct violation of a treaty that had been agreed by both sides. What is more, the decision to violate it is the result of a considered policy by the Carthaginians (15.2.1–3), and the Carthaginian leadership deliberately arranges for the attack on the ambassadors' ship (15.2.4–8). Scipio then constantly harps on the violation (15.4.2–3, 15.8.8-12, 15.17.3; cf. 15.3.2, 15.4.7, 15.4.11). Livy's Scipio is less forthright in his accusations (30.25.2, 30.25.10, 30.31.1–4, 30.31.9), which is appropriate, since those violations could have been acceptable had the news of the Senate's decision arrived earlier, and were not clearly intentional anyway. Scipio does imply at 30.31.1 that the violation was deliberate and done in the knowledge of Hannibal's imminent arrival, but that appears to be his misinterpretation. Polybius 15.2.3 had described it that way, but Livy's account was quite different: his Scipio wrongly interprets events according to a Polybian model.

proprie sibi paciscerentur quicquam. recepti deinde ab iis, ut necessarios hospitesque adloquerentur, expositis, quae pacta iam cum Marcello haberent, oblata spe salutis perpulere eos, ut secum praefectos Epicydis Polyclitum et Philistionem et Epicyden, cui Sindon cognomen erat, adgrederentur. interfectis iis &.

They sent envoys to Marcellus about the terms of surrender for the city, after previously finding out through conferences the preferences of the people under siege. Since there was hardly any disagreement that all the kings' property, wherever it was, should be Roman, and everything else should be kept for the Sicilians along with their liberty and their laws, after summoning to a conference those whom Epicydes had entrusted with control, they said that they had been sent simultaneously by the Sicilian army to Marcellus and to them, so that everyone, those under siege and those who had been outside the siege, should share in a single fortune, and that neither side should make any private agreement for themselves. Then they were welcomed by them so that they could talk to their relatives and friends, and after they set out what they had already agreed with Marcellus, through the hope of safety that was offered they induced them to join in an attack on Epicydes' prefects Polyclitus and Philistio and Epicydes surnamed Sindon; when they were killed &c.

The chronology of the events described in these few lines is surprisingly difficult to disentangle. The first sentence suggests that it was only after coming to an agreement with those in the town that the Sicilian army began negotiations with Marcellus, and the following sentence appears then to record the aftermath of that agreement and those negotiations. But that does not appear possible, since in the following sentence the Sicilians appear to be discussing the matter with the people in Syracuse for the first time. This might imply that the first sentence was a general summary of the Sicilian army's actions, which is then expanded upon in the remainder of the passage, an interpretation apparently supported by the repetitions *conloquia/conloquium, qui obsidebantur/qui obsiderentur,* and *ad Marcellum mittunt/missos . . . ad Marcellum*—the discussion here with the Syracusan leaders is the same one described in the first sentence, in which their views are determined prior to their going on to discuss the matter with Marcellus.[34] But that too cannot be right, since it is contradicted by the next part, in which the army's envoys inform the Syracusans of what they have *already* agreed with Marcellus: they have apparently spoken to him before coming to Syracuse, contrary to what was stated in the first sentence, where the Sicilians present a position to Marcellus that they have previously agreed jointly among themselves. This then is the premise of the next part of the subsequent narrative, in which the representatives of the Sicilian army give the Syracusans an apparently authoritative statement of the Romans' goodwill towards the city (25.28.7–9). But the

---

[34] *Contra* W-M *ad* 25.28.3, who overlook the repeated language and suggest that the *conloquia* referred to in 25.28.2 were informal discussions that had taken place earlier.

problems do not end there. After the townspeople have been persuaded to come to terms, the Syracusans send representatives to Marcellus (25.29.1–7), and they appear here to be negotiating with him for the first time. This apparently returns us to the earlier version, in which Marcellus is only contacted subsequent to the agreement between the Sicilians themselves.

We effectively appear to have two contradictory sequences of events interwoven with each other: one in which all the Sicilians agree among themselves first and then go to Marcellus, and one in which terms are agreed with Marcellus first and only then with the Syracusans. The inconsistency has the consequence that the relationship between Marcellus' proposed terms and the Syracusans' willingness to accept those terms may be read in two incompatible ways: each one appears to be both the cause and the consequence of the other. This chronological—and hence causal—circularity may remind us of the impossible chronological sequences that I described in Chapter 1, though this is a much tighter and narrower example.

But the problem is not only in the sequence of the negotiations, but also in their content. When the Sicilians appeal to Marcellus at 25.29.1–7 they offer to surrender to Marcellus on whatever terms he chooses to impose (25.29.4); they simply argue that his future reputation for the magnitude of his victory would be more secure if he were to leave the city visibly intact with the trophies of its past victories rather than destroying it, an argument which Marcellus apparently accepts (25.29.8). But when the terms were discussed earlier—the terms which, on one reading, encouraged the Syracusans to negotiate the surrender in the first place—something much more specific was implied (25.28.3): that the Sicilians should retain not only their liberty but everything else except for the property previously belonging to the kings.

The question then is who is implied to have accepted those earlier terms—and that is a matter which Livy, crucially, presents ambiguously. He says that 'there was hardly any disagreement' (*haud ferme discreparet*) on the acceptable terms of a settlement—but the impersonal verb leaves it unclear who precisely was agreeing. Is it only the Sicilians among themselves who have agreed this prior to contacting Marcellus, as in the first version of the story, or have both the Sicilians and Marcellus accepted this as the terms under which the surrender will be conducted, as implied on the second version? The reason this matters is that Marcellus clearly violates those terms in the manner in which he eventually plunders the city. Admittedly he is given a measure of legal justification by subsequent events, in which Syracuse is briefly taken over by the deserters and mercenaries who fear (rightly in the former case, wrongly in the latter) that any agreement with Rome will lead to their punishment (25.29.8–10), and Marcellus eventually completes the capture by persuading one of their leaders, Moericus, to betray his colleagues (25.30). But, as

I discussed in Chapter 3, Livy constantly highlights Marcellus' moral failures in the capture of Syracuse even while defending his legal right to have acted as he did, and he especially points to the gap between his stated aims and the actions that he tacitly fosters and permits. Livy's double picture of events here, where two separate and inconsistent chronological sequences with two separate and inconsistent outcomes are inextricably intertwined, reinforces that moral ambiguity. On one version Marcellus has from the start been given carte blanche by the Syracusans to act as he will; on the other he has already conceded to them that he is seeking nothing more than the royal treasure, and indeed it is that concession which persuades the Syracusans to agree to the surrender. The causal loop created by the circular chronology is reflected at the moral level, where Marcellus' stated sympathy for the Sicilians and his violation of personal commitments each appears to generate the other.

While very different in form from the narratives that we examined in Books 24 and 30, where cause was detached from chronology, this episode thus has one fundamental similarity with them as well. In all three cases Livy presents a world that makes sense, but does so only on some other level of understanding than that of mechanical causation. The Syracusans will break from Rome, and that future break from Rome is identifiable even independently of their specific actions. The Carthaginians will violate the terms that they have negotiated with Rome, and that violation is likewise identifiable independently of their specific actions, though it is also treated in a way that highlights its moral complexity. The even more morally complex double picture of Marcellus, as someone with scrupulous respect for the Sicilians in theory but who allows disastrous outcomes in practice, is consistent and clear, but it is generated from a chronological sequence that is inconsistent and impossible.

5.2. NARRATIVE CAUSATION

Connected with but separate from the issues I have been considering in the previous section are cases where Livy implies a causal sequence that is purely a function of his own construction of his narrative. I discussed this issue in Chapter 1: the case, for example, where the ease of the Romans' defeat of the Carthaginians in Sardinia (23.40.6–12) appears to be because it forms the climax to his description of a long series of interconnected Roman successes (above, 76–8). Similarly there are cases where Livy's 'textual' years—the order in which he presents things happening in the narrative—are explicitly shown by him to diverge from the chronological year, but where it is the narrative order rather than the actual chronology which is suggested to have the primary effect on the action (see the discussion above, 50–63). But it may be useful to give a few further brief examples here as well. A straightforward case is the revolt of the Boii in 21.25. Here we are explicitly told that there has been no news of Hannibal in Italy except for the fact that he has crossed the Ebro (21.25.1), but the Boii nevertheless revolt 'exactly as if he had already crossed the Alps' (21.25.2 *perinde ac si Alpis iam transisset*). This surprising prescience on their part is a direct change to Polybius, for whom the Boii's revolt is prompted by specific messages informing them of the Carthaginians' immi-nent arrival (3.40.7: 'elated from the messages sent to them and trusting in the presence of the Carthaginians'—μετεωριζόμενοι καὶ πιστεύοντες ἐκ τῶν διαπεμπομένων τῇ παρουσίᾳ τῶν Καρχηδονίων). Livy retains the connection that Polybius made between the revolt and the imminent Carthaginian invasion, while simultaneously removing the explanation that Polybius gave of how the Boii knew about the imminent Carthaginian invasion. From the point of view of providing a rational explanation for their actions this makes little sense. But from the point of view of Livy's narrative it makes perfect sense, because directly prior to the narrative of the revolt of the Boii we have been informed that Hannibal has in fact not merely crossed the Ebro but also the Pyrenees, and is currently in Transalpine Gaul, where he has assured the locals that he is their friend, that he is heading for Italy and promises to do no harm to anyone before he reaches there (21.24). Livy, in other words, has the Boii revolting on the basis of something that he is clear that they do not know, and where indeed he has emphasized their lack of knowledge by changing Polybius' account in which they do have the relevant information. But their revolt nevertheless is understandable, simply because it is juxtaposed to the relevant information in his text, even though the people in the narrative do not know it.

It is admittedly rare to find quite so clear an indication that events are being influenced by their proximity to certain other events in Livy's narrative rather than by more mundane historical connections, but it is not uncommon for him to provide a looser sense that narratively juxtaposed but not necessarily chronologically adjacent events are nevertheless causally connected with one another. One might, for example, consider the campaign in Greece that follows the treaty between the Romans and the Aetolians that is struck at 26.24.[35] As I noted in Chapter 1, Livy maintains a studied ambiguity in the chronology of this episode, since he implies that it is to be placed at the end of the year, even though the length of the Greek narrative in this and the following chapter would appear to be hard to fit into so short a period, and

---

[35] A fragmentary inscription recording this treaty was discovered in 1949 (see Klaffenbach 1954).

indeed Livy has already implied that Laevinus' successes in Greece had occurred much earlier (26.22.12; cf. above, 46–7). But more important for our purposes here is that, whenever the narrative is presumed to have occurred chronologically, Livy invites the reader to see how this episode has been influenced by the events that he has described in the previous chapters. Laevinus begins the negotiations over the treaty by reminding the Aetolians of the recent capture of Syracuse and Capua (26.24.2): his ostensible reason for doing so is to prove that the Romans are currently enjoying success and that they are therefore in a position to be powerful allies for the Aetolians,[36] but it is hard not to relate it also to the point that he immediately goes on to make, namely the Roman traditions of dealing with their allies (26.24.3):

adiecit se sequi iam inde a maioribus traditum morem Romanis colendi socios, ex quibus alios in civitatem atque aequum secum ius accepissent, alios in ea fortuna haberent ut socii esse quam cives mallent.

He added that he was following the custom of cultivating allies that had been handed down to the Romans ever since their ancestors: they accepted some into citizenship and equal rights with themselves, while they kept others in a position such that they preferred to be allies rather than citizens.

This digression on Roman alliances does not seem entirely pertinent to the case of the Aetolians, since there is no suggestion that they should be given Roman citizenship. But it is entirely pertinent to the cases of Capua and Syracuse that Laevinus has just cited, since the former had been granted Roman citizenship,[37] the latter had remained as favoured allies. The juxtaposition of the capture of Capua and Syracuse with a reference to alliances of precisely the sort that Capua and Syracuse had formed sounds pointed: Laevinus is effectively giving a covert warning to the Aetolians that while an alliance with Rome may have its benefits, they should be wary of breaking that alliance.[38]

But introducing Capua and Syracuse at the start of the episode implies a connection of a different sort as well. The capture of Capua by the Romans earlier that year is facilitated by the unwillingness of Hannibal to support his allies: he attempts a diversionary march on Rome, but when that march fails he is unwilling to return to defend the city, which is what allows it to be captured

---

[36] 26.24.2 *Syracusas Capuamque captas in fidem in Sicilia Italiaque rerum secundarum ostentasset.*

[37] See above, 224–5.

[38] As in fact the Aetolians eventually will do, by making a treaty with Philip independently of the Romans at 29.12.1 (compare 26.24.12), to the Romans' fury (29.12.4)—though that fury is misplaced, since (at least on Livy's presentation) that breach of the treaty is entirely the Romans' fault for abandoning the Aetolians to Philip. Nevertheless the Senate subsequently cites it at 31.1.9 as a major ground for their willingness to go to war against Philip again.

(see the discussion below, 367). This is oddly paralleled by the actions of Philip in 26.25; although he is aware of the imminent Aetolian attack on his own supporters in Acarnania, he goes in the opposite direction in order to subdue the tribes of Thrace first (26.25.6–8), which encourages the Aetolians to pursue their assault on Acarnania. However, the Aetolians have miscalculated, despite being able to rely on their own superior strength and Roman support (26.25.10).[39] Unlike Hannibal, Philip rushes back from Thrace with the intention of supporting his allies (26.25.15), and indeed the Acarnanians themselves under pressure respond far more aggressively than the Capuans had, taking an oath not to return from battle unless victorious, and prescribing penalties for anyone who retreated (26.25.10-11). This combined opposition forces the Aetolians to retreat (26.25.16). It is of course possible that Livy here is simply reproducing a series of events from (presumably) Polybius, though that is unknowable:[40] we have seen elsewhere how substantially he is prepared to change Polybius for his own purposes, including indeed specifically rewriting campaigns in order to make them look closer to other campaigns which are adjacent in his text (see above, 79–81). But even if in this case Livy is reproducing Polybius closely, Laevinus' pointed citation of Capua, combined with Livy's pointed verbal association of Rome with the attack on Acarnania (n. 39 above), indicates a motivating force for events which is likely to be his own. Philip acts as a superior imitation of his ally Hannibal in the episode earlier in the book, leaving the Acarnanians at the mercy of Rome, yet returning to defend them at the proper time. But there is no particular indication that Philip has consciously learned from Hannibal's mistakes, and still less that the Acarnanians are responding to the negative *exemplum* of Capua. The connection is simply in the juxtaposition of events, which is foregrounded when Laevinus cites Capua at the start of the episode for apparently quite different ends.

An especially interesting occasion where Livy's narrative juxtapositions appear to have causal force is the appeal by the veterans of Cannae at 25.6. They ask to be allowed to serve in the main Roman army—they explicitly say that they are not attempting to expunge their penalty for the involvement in the defeat

---

[39] The phrase that Livy uses to describe that Roman support moreover reinforces the parallel between Acarnania and Capua: *Romanaque insuper arma ingruere. ingruo* in a military context tends to connote a direct attack (*OLD s.v. ingruo* 1) at least as often as a more remote threat (*OLD s.v. ingruo* 3). The word here stands out: it is choice (cf. Oakley 1997: 413–14), but also slightly odd in this context, given the Romans' actual lack of involvement in the attack on Acarnania. It however suits well Livy's general sense that the Acarnanians here are responding to something closely analogous to what the Capuans had had to endure.

[40] The only part of the Polybian narrative that survives is 9.40.4–6, two brief accounts of the Acarnanian resistance taken from the Suda, which are broadly similar to Livy (26.25.10 and 26.25.12), though with the extra feature that the Epirots also were warned against accepting deserters from the battle.

(although in fact many of their arguments are addressed to the unjustifiability of that penalty), but are merely asking for the opportunity to redeem themselves in battle (25.6.19). This is an appeal that could have been made at any time, but Livy inserts it here at a significant moment. Directly prior to this, the Romans have levied new troops, but only after some difficulty. The levy is hindered first by a near riot over an attempt to prosecute corrupt tax agents (25.3.8–4.11), then, more crucially, by the lack of potential recruits: the Senate is forced to enlist boys below the usual age for military service (25.5.5–9). It is at this point that we are told that a letter from Marcellus is read in the Senate asking for advice on the appeal from the Cannae veterans (25.5.10). The appeal thus could not have come at a more pertinent moment: the veterans are offering themselves as soldiers at precisely the point when the state most needs them—yet the Senate firmly (not to say perversely)[41] turns the request down, allowing only that Marcellus may use the troops in Sicily if that is his choice.

That timing is not on the face of things connected with the failure of the levy. Marcellus' letter may have arrived in the Senate at this point, but the actual appeal, Livy implies, took place rather earlier: he refers to the soldiers delivering it to Marcellus 'in winter quarters' (25.6.1), and the soldiers refer to this being the 'second year' of the Sicilian campaign—in other words, in 213 (25.6.20).[42] This implies that Livy in his account of the speech is moving back in time, and that he is envisaging the appeal to Marcellus as having been delivered at the end of the previous year. But he simultaneously shows that the soldiers have the Senate in mind: even though they are in theory speaking to Marcellus alone (as is absolutely clear at both its beginning and its end), the bulk of the speech is a direct address to the Senate, who are appealed to in the second person as *patres conscripti* (25.6.4, 25.6.9; cf. 25.6.22 *vobis*), and most of the arguments are ones that can only carry their point if they are addressed to the senators who had endorsed the soldiers' disgrace in the first place. This

---

[41] At least some of the veterans' arguments are manifestly justified, notably their observation that the officers of the army appear to have been rehabilitated and indeed praised while their troops are punished (25.6.7–9): Livy at 22.61.14–15 had singled out the Romans' refusal to punish their guilty commander as a mark of their superiority over Carthage. Likewise their citations of the past examples of the rehabilitation of troops after the Allia, Caudium, and Heraclea seem powerful and appropriate. We may note that Scipio eventually draws on these troops as a key part of his invasion force of Africa (29.24.11–14), and part of his reason for doing so is that 'he knew that the disaster at Cannae was not the result of their cowardice' (29.24.12 *neque ad Cannas ignavia eorum cladem acceptam sciret*). See Chaplin (2000: 45–6, 90). Livy is of course conscious that Scipio had first-hand knowledge of this: he had himself served at Cannae (22.53), and was in fact one of the very *tribuni militum* who the soldiers here complain was pursuing a political career despite his presence at the defeat (25.6.8: note 25.2.6–7).

[42] This is assuming that the Sicilian war began in 214, as on Livy's chronology: for reasons to question that chronology see above, 55.

is clearly not a mistake on Livy's part, since he has the speakers (rather awkwardly) justify their language by explaining that when looking at Marcellus they imagine that they are looking at the entire Senate (25.6.5). But it makes little sense in terms of a speech to Marcellus, since at the point when they are presumed to be speaking it is not clear that Marcellus is not willing to rehabilitate them on his own authority, and so they have no rhetorical reason to slant their arguments towards the Senate rather than him: it is only after their speech that he informs them that he has no power in the matter and intends to refer it to the Senate (25.7.1).[43] Nor is there even any indication that Marcellus' letter to the Senate reproduced their arguments.[44] Rather Livy appears to be writing the speech on the basis of when and where it will appear in his narrative, rather than when he explicitly indicates that it was delivered. Its arguments are addressed to an audience who will not hear it, against a context of a Roman shortage of manpower which has not become apparent at the point when the speech is presumed to have been given.

It is worth noting the parallel between this and the well-known phenomenon of a character in an historian delivering a speech which answers another speech which he could not have heard: an example in Livy 21–30 is the speeches of Scipio and Hannibal at 21.40–44, where many of Hannibal's arguments are in direct response to points that Scipio has made in his speech, but the technique goes back at least to Thucydides. Livy's handling of the speech in 25.6 is more extreme in its self-conscious dislocation between the stated circumstances in which the speech was delivered and the content of its arguments, but it is recognizably of the same general type. What Livy is doing with the speech of the Cannae veterans not only is easily aligned with his techniques of invented responsion in other speeches in his work, but both of these are part of a wider technique of manipulating his account of the events of the war to produce causal connections from mere narrative sequence.

5.3. MORAL CAUSATION

The third area I wish to discuss is the connection Livy often draws between events and the moral position of the characters involved in those events: this is

---

[43] It is also noticeable that Marcellus makes no comment on the merits or otherwise of their appeal, unlike in Valerius Maximus 2.7.15c and Plutarch, *Marcellus* 13.4–5, in which he directly requests from the Senate permission to use them in his forces: Plutarch emphasizes that he regarded their treatment as unjust.

[44] *Contra* Chaplin (2000: 90): Livy says only that the letter 'was on the subject of the soldiers' requests' (25.5.10 *de postulatis militum*).

perhaps the most far-reaching of all the topics in this chapter, but also the most familiar and easiest to comprehend. I have already discussed something of this in Chapter 4, when, for example, Livy implies that the Roman rout at Trasimene was precipitated by the death of Flaminius. In the terms in which Livy has described the battle, this death should not have been able to have such an effect; it appears to do so because of its association with Flaminius' earlier mistreatment of the Insubrians in his first consulship, as well as the wider association of Flaminius with impiety which culminates in the omens prior to the battle. In other words, the primary reason why the Romans lose to Hannibal at Trasimene is that they have placed themselves at least partly in the wrong.

The simplest way in which Livy connects lack of morality and lack of success is admittedly not one that of itself suggests anything anomalous in causal terms. He often sets out such a connection as a straightforwardly psychological one: treating other people with manifest injustice leads to the victims themselves or others who learn of the crime to act in ways detrimental to the perpetrators. A clear instance is at 26.38.1–5, where Hannibal, following the Roman capture of Capua and the consequent abandonment of his cause by many of his allies,[45] acts increasingly aggressively towards them. Part of his reasoning is that maintaining garrisons in so many locations would involve splitting and so weakening his army (26.38.2), but Livy implies that his approach is rooted more fundamentally in his character: 'his mind, which tended to rush into avarice and cruelty, inclined him to plunder the things he was unable to defend, so as to leave it ravaged for the enemy' (26.38.3 *praeceps in avaritiam et crudelitatem animus ad spolianda quae tueri nequibat, ut vastata hosti relinqueretur, inclinavit*). Livy immediately continues that 'this was a revolting plan both in its beginning and also in its outcome' (26.38.4 *id foedum consilium cum incepto tum etiam exitu fuit*); *foedum* might naturally lead us to expect that the *exitus* to which Livy refers is the effect of Hannibal's brutality on his victims. But in fact he immediately reverses that expectation—the worst effect is on Hannibal himself,[46] since he alienates not only the victims but also the other Italians. Hannibal's cruelty backfires instantly.[47] Similarly at 22.13.11 Hannibal's ravaging of the Italians'

---

[45] Something which Livy moreover indicates to be his own fault (26.38.1–2; cf. 26.16.13): he was not sufficiently assiduous in the Capuans' defence.

[46] This is signalled also by the echo of *Praef.* 10: *foedum inceptu foedum exitu* ('revolting in its beginning, revolting in its outcome'). Livy is here talking about the use of history as providing models of immoral behaviour to avoid, and it is the consequences for the readers themselves (were they to fail to draw the appropriate lesson) which are primarily at issue.

[47] It is worth contrasting the Romans' behaviour earlier in the book (26.16.12), where they carefully combine punishment of the guilty Capuans with a refusal to alienate the Capuans' neighbours by devastating the city itself: Livy praises this, though that clear-cut judgement is set against a sense that the Romans' behaviour over Capua more broadly is far more morally problematic, as I shall discuss later in the chapter (367–74).

territory fails to detach them from their alliance with Rome, 'presumably because they were governed by a just and moderate rule and did not refuse to obey their betters—the one bond of loyalty' (*videlicet quia iusto et moderato regebantur imperio nec abnuebant, quod unum vinculum fidei, melioribus parere*). As I noted in Chapter 4, Livy is anyway intensely interested in the failure of plans and cases where actions are self-defeating: it is not surprising that he regularly observes similar patterns in cases where people's behaviour may be impugned morally as well as merely tactically.

Sometimes the self-defeating side to immorality in Livy is not because of its effect on others, but rather because it leads one to act contrary to one's own best interests. A simple example is at 21.48.5–6, where the Numidians sent by Hannibal in pursuit of the fleeing Roman army fail to inflict significant damage on them because, 'through eagerness for plunder' (21.48.5 *aviditate praedae*), they waste time rifling through the abandoned Roman camp, despite the fact there was nothing to be found there. Livy is here following Polybius 3.68.2–4, where the Numidians allow the Romans to escape in a similarly counterproductive way, but where there is no suggestion that it is cupidity that has led to this—their mistake is to burn the camp, presumably to prevent it from being used in future, rather than to search for plunder in it.[48] Livy 21.48.6 also makes it explicit that the only losses to the Romans were a few stragglers (*paucos moratorum*): Polybius 3.68.4 suggests something rather greater, though he does acknowledge that most of the Roman army got away.[49] Livy challenges Polybius' account by providing a moral dimension that Polybius had lacked, and puts greater emphasis than Polybius had on the extent of the Numidians' failure.

In these examples the connection between morality and outcome is straightforward and relatively mechanical—it is clear how in these specific instances Hannibal's or the Numidians' misbehaviour leads to their failure, even if there is no explanation in broader terms of why immorality might be expected to meet with such conveniently just results. At other times, however, the connection appears to operate at more than a single level. One such case is the Romans' massacre of the local population at Henna, which I discussed briefly earlier (above, 32–3, 212–13). The Romans here certainly have good reason to fear that they are about to be betrayed (24.37.5; cf. 24.37.1–3), but in fact the Hennans, once their plan for betrayal appears not to be feasible, determine on a negotiated transfer of the city instead (24.37.6). Pinarius nevertheless is distrustful and decides on killing the population—something which he himself recognizes in his speech to his troops to be morally

---

[48] Cf. Pianezzola (1969: 26–8).
[49] Händl-Sagawe (1995: 298).

problematic,[50] but which he insists is unavoidable. It is true that the Hennans have not given strong reasons to trust them—their first instinct was certainly to treachery—but Livy nevertheless does not endorse Pinarius' reading of the situation. He never supports in his own voice the claim that the Hennans' negotations are not being carried out in good faith; Pinarius' observation at the end of the speech that the Hennans will be 'unarmed' (24.38.9 *inermes*) places his plan in a less attractive light, since it undermines his earlier suggestion that Hennans will massacre the Romans at the handover of the city unless the latter pre-empt them; and Livy's description of the massacre itself not only confirms this but highlights its questionable basis: 'the soldiers' fury was no less intense, because they were slaughtering an unarmed crowd, <u>than if</u> they were being spurred on by an equal danger and eagerness for the fight' (24.39.6 *nihilo remissiore militum ira, quod turbam inermem caedebant, quam si periculum par et ardor certaminis eos inritaret*). Livy sums up the episode by saying that 'Henna was retained by a deed either evil or necessary' (24.39.7 *Henna aut malo aut necessario facinore retenta*), but he has weighted the argument in favour of the former.[51] And accordingly, Pinarius' actions backfire against the Romans themselves, exactly as we saw with Hannibal after the capture of Capua—for while Marcellus believes that the effect of the massacre will be to deter future defections, and so is prepared to condone it (24.39.7), its actual effect is exactly the opposite. The Sicilians are so outraged that even those who were previously wavering decide to defect to the Carthaginians (24.39.8–9).

There is, however, a further dimension to the episode, because it is not only the massacre itself that has outraged the Sicilians, but also the fact that it has violated a sacred place, since Henna was the spot where Proserpina was abducted (24.38.8–9). The connection between this violation and the Romans' loss of Sicilian support is set out explicitly in much the same terms as we have already seen: the Sicilians react against the Romans' immorality. But underlying this is a sense that the religious violation in and of itself is something which is expected to cause problems for the Romans over and beyond its psychological effect on other people. Livy reports 'that disaster... in virtually one day spread over the whole of Sicily' (24.39.8 *ea clades...prope uno die omnem Siciliam pervasit*). The speed is remarkable,

---

[50] Note, for example, his prayer that the gods recognize that they are acting 'in order to avoid treachery, not perpetrate it' (24.38.8 *vitandae, non inferendae fraudis causa*); also the moral equivalence suggested by phrases like 'Henna will be drenched in either your blood or that of the Hennans' (24.38.5 *aut vestro aut Hennensium sanguine Henna inundabitur*) and 'neither by suffering nor doing unspeakable things' (24.38.2 *nec patiendo infanda nec faciendo*).

[51] Compare Levene (1993: 55–6).

though not unique,[52] but Livy's language here implies more than merely a report. *ea clades... pervasit* could of course merely be taken to mean '[the news of] the disaster spread', but the literal meaning is that the disaster itself pervaded everywhere[53]—Pinarius' religious violation at the very heart of Sicily (24.39.8 *in media Sicilia*) has effectively polluted the whole island.

This in turn fits the hints throughout the episode that the massacre at Henna is to be seen in divine terms and is liable to be punished accordingly. The only explicit mention of the gods earlier is in Pinarius' speech (24.38.8), where he appeals to them for support—the implication is that this action is one that they might react against were they not satisfied of its justifiability. But from the start Livy has alluded to another occasion when Henna was sacrilegiously violated: namely Verres' plunder of the shrine of Ceres, as described by Cicero in an exceptionally famous passage, *II Verr.* 4.106–15.[54] Cicero is evoked at the very start of the story, where the description of Henna as set on a 'lofty place and steep' (24.37.2 *excelso loco ac praerupto*) recalls Cicero's *loco perexcelso atque edito* (*II Verr.* 4.107); 'you inhabit lakes and groves' (24.38.8 *lacus lucosque colitis*) in Pinarius' appeal to Ceres and Prosepina recalls *lacus lucique* in *II Verr.* 4.107, as well as *lacus lucosque incolitis* in Cicero's own final invocation of these gods at *II Verr.* 5.188; the 'traces of the stolen Proserpina' (24.39.8 *vestigiis raptae... Proserpinae*) reminds us of the 'traces... of the gods' in Cicero (*II Verr.* 4.107 *vestigia... deorum*). More broadly, the sense that not only Henna but the whole of Sicily is consecrated to these gods, so that Verres' crime affects the entire island, is implicit throughout the Cicero passage (esp. *II Verr.* 4.106 *insulam Siciliam totam*, 4.107 *tota Sicilia*, 4.113 *omnium Siculorum*), which gives particular colour to Livy's account of the whole of Sicily reacting against the Henna massacre. In Cicero the reaction is on the divine level as well as the human, at least in the Sicilians' eyes: the island is suffering from a mass failure of crops, though Cicero carefully offers the alternative naturalistic explanation that this is the result of Verres driving the farmers from the land (*II Verr.* 4.114). Livy is himself not explicit that the Sicilians' reaction against the Romans has a divine cause, but the evocation of the sacrilege of Verres, combined with the language in which he describes the universal consequence of the disaster, makes such an interpretation a natural if not inevitable one.

---

[52] Compare Caesar, *BG* 7.3, in which it is suggested—perhaps implausibly—that the Gauls' method of shouting news to one another allows a report of an attack on the Romans to travel 160 miles in a little more than twelve hours.

[53] Compare the similar expression at 42.5.7; cf. e.g. 24.2.8, 28.29.3, also Sallust, *Cat.* 36.5.

[54] On Livy's systematic allusions to Cicero here see Hinds (1982: 477); as he notes, the fame of the Cicero passage is demonstrated by the fact that it is repeatedly singled out by Quintilian (4.2.19, 4.3.13, 9.4.127, 11.3.164).

Divine favour and anger towards humans' moral and religious behaviour, and the consequent divine reward and punishment, is indeed a regular subtext against which many of the events of the Third Decade need to be understood. I set out much of the evidence for this in an earlier work,[55] in particular demonstrating how Livy manipulates his reports of supernatural events, changing (for example) their position and length in order to ensure that they correlate to people's moral and religious actions. The gods respond to immorality with anger, and this in turn leads to punishment, especially in the form of defeat; conversely moral behaviour is rewarded. I will not recapitulate this material in detail here. For our purposes at the moment the main thing to note is that while Livy regularly structures his narrative in order to imply such connections, he is rarely explicit, at least in his own voice, about the link between immorality and punishment. The only exception is 29.8.9–11, where Pleminius' plundering of the temple of Proserpina at Locri is compared to Pyrrhus' earlier plundering of the same temple, and both are suggested to have been punished by the gods; the same comparison is made at much greater length by the Locrian ambassadors to the Senate at 29.18, who warn that the entire state may similarly be liable to disaster if restitution is not made. While an unfamiliar mode of reasoning to modern historians, it is neither surprising nor difficult to understand in the context of an ancient writer, many of whom interpret events in comparable terms,[56] nor does the suggestion that a divine hand is at work necessarily indicate an anomalous conception of causation. As I noted at the start of the chapter, one can perfectly well regard the gods as historical causes while seeing their causal agency as operating in modes closely analogous to the standard ones we understand in the case of human agents. Effectively, one could—and in practice most ancients did—see the gods (at least in this respect) simply as more powerful versions of humans, who act on more reliable information and to more efficient ends, but who basically affect things in much the same fashion as humans do.

But the boundaries of divine action are hard to establish, and where no direct indication of divine action is given it is not clear how far we are meant to see it beneath the surface. Certainly Livy provides constant accounts of supernatural events through the Third Decade, above all in prodigy lists, and he treats those lists in ways that allow them to be correlated to both the moral behaviour and the success or failure in the surrounding human actions; the implication is that the

---

[55] Levene (1993: 38–77).

[56] Indeed, Diodorus 27.4.2–3 makes precisely the same point about Pleminius and precisely the same comparison with Pyrrhus as Livy does here; Dionysius, *Roman Antiquities* 20.9–10 likewise narrates the Pyrrhus episode in those terms.

gods are constantly reacting to human misbehaviour by punishing transgressors. There is also a sense, albeit a vaguer one, that the gods are controlling events in the longer term as well, not least in the implication that the defeat of Carthage is in retribution for their original crime of launching the war, something they did in clear violation of treaties (according to Livy in 21.19.1–5).[57] Livy never makes that connection directly in his own voice, but he repeatedly places the idea into the mouths of others, notably Hanno at 21.10, the elder Scipio at 21.40.11, Fabius at 26.8.5, Scipio Africanus at 28.44.7 and 30.31.4–5, and Hasdrubal Haedus at 30.42.21; this too can be paralleled elsewhere in ancient literature.[58]

But there are also a good number of cases in Livy where immorality appears to be closely juxtaposed with failure, but where there is no indication of any direct connection between the two in terms of divine action or punishment. In these cases one could certainly see an instance of a divine hand at work— one could easily imagine a Roman like Valerius Maximus drawing a moral of precisely that sort—but there is nothing in Livy to make that interpretation inevitable.[59] In some cases he describes the failure in terms which could invite us to see divine justice exacting retribution, whereas at other times, even if one recognizes the connection, there is little that would indicate specifically divine action. But in either case the connection between morality and outcome is more clearly apparent than the mechanism by which that connection is formed: it matters more that one should see that immorality is followed by failure than that one should attribute it specifically to the gods at work.

An example at one end of the scale is at the end of Book 21. Hannibal after his victory at the Trebia engages in a series of minor campaigns in the region, culminating (21.57.9–14) with a successful attack on the town of Victumulae.

---

[57] Livy here endorses in his own voice the Roman arguments against the claims of the Carthaginian senator at 21.18.7–11, arguments that on his account (21.19.1) the Romans have rightly disdained to make for themselves. Indeed, for Livy, the very fact that they have refused to make the arguments is a sign of the strength of their case (cf. Hoffmann 1942: 19). As is often observed, he weights the argument still further in the Romans' direction by misrepresenting the treaty with Hasdrubal, which appears from Polybius 2.13.7 not to have specified that the Saguntines should be immune from attack, contrary to what Livy stated at 21.2.7. However, both the precise terms of the treaties and the validity of the case against the Carthaginians have been the subject of huge scholarly dispute: among key recent treatments are e.g. Schwarte (1983), Rich (1996), Hoyos (1998: 150–259); for a different approach, centring on the role these treaties played in the historiographical sources, see Mantel (1991: 19–104).

[58] To pick one particularly striking example, Valerius Maximus 1.1.14 sees the ultimate destruction of Carthage in the Third Punic War as divine punishment for the execution of Regulus in the First Punic War a 100 years before; but the idea of long-delayed divine punishment is an ancient commonplace (for further examples see Wardle 1998: 131).

[59] Compare Feeney (1998: esp. 12–31) on the way in which Roman religious discourse regularly allowed multiple and competing interpretations of a single phenomenon, even by a single individual.

The people attempt to go out to confront Hannibal but are easily defeated (21.57.11–12), and the town agrees to surrender. But Hannibal treats the surrendering town 'as if it were a city captured by force' (21.57.13 *tamquam vi captam urbem*) and allows his troops to plunder it, and Livy comments (21.57.14):

neque ulla, quae in tali re memorabilis scribentibus videri solet, praetermissa clades est; adeo omne libidinis crudelitatisque et inhumanae superbiae editum in miseros exemplum est.

And none of the atrocities which writers tend to think memorable on such occasions was overlooked: to such a degree was every instance of lust and cruelty and bestial arrogance unleashed upon the wretched people.

Livy at the start of the book referred programmatically to Hannibal's 'bestial cruelty' (21.4.9 *inhumana crudelitas*), as well as to his treacherous disregard for pledges and lack of religion, but this is the first time that he has actually lived up to this—his earlier behaviour has been (if perhaps cynically) humane and pious. Even at Saguntum, where he orders all the males to be killed, Livy partially justified him: 'a cruel order, but it was recognized in the event to be almost essential' (21.14.3 *imperium crudele, ceterum prope necessarium cognitum ipso eventu est*), since the people refused to surrender and either killed themselves or continued to fight to the last. Appian, *Hisp.* 12 has a far more lurid account of him torturing the survivors to death. In the Gallic duel that Hannibal sets up at 21.42 Livy emphasizes the willingness of the fighters, and removes Polybius' suggestion (3.62.4) that he had maltreated them. After his victory at the Ticinus he not only warmly welcomes the deserters (21.48.2) but is merciful to his prisoners, 'in order to garnish a reputation for clemency at the start of his campaign' (21.48.10 *ut fama clementiae in principio rerum colligeretur*: cf. Polybius 3.67.4, 3.69.3). And as for his purported irreligion, his actions throughout the book have been surprisingly pious, fulfilling vows to Hercules (21.21.9) and making vows and sacrifices before the Ticinus (21.45.8–9).[60] Victumulae is thus the first time when Hannibal's behaviour matches what Livy has advertised as his essential character.

And accordingly it appears to have immediate consequences, because the very next episode is the first time in the book where Hannibal meets with a substantial setback. He is induced by the 'first doubtful signs of spring' (21.58.2 *prima ac dubia signa veris*) to attempt to cross the Apennines (21.58).[61] Livy describes in lurid terms the reasons for his failure: 'a storm

---

[60] Compare Levene (1993: 45–7).

[61] Neither this nor the Victumulae episode is in Polybius. It is sometimes claimed (e.g. by Lazenby 1978: 59–60; Burck 1992: 120, 224; *contra* Miltner 1943; Seibert 1993a: 138–9) that the failed crossing of the Apennines is a duplication of the successful crossing in 22.2, but it should

so dreadful assaulted him that it almost surpassed the frightfulness of the Alps' (21.58.3 *adeo atrox adorta tempestas est, ut Alpium prope foeditatem superaverit*); there is wind and rain, thunder and lightning which terrify the army (21.58.5), snow and hail (21.58.8).

It is not hard to relate this dramatic and lurid account of Hannibal's failure to his brutality directly beforehand: the close correlation between his morality and his success earlier, and his lack of morality and his lack of success now, seems too pointed to ignore, especially when the earlier morality has contradicted not only Livy's initial sketch of his character, but has directly challenged Polybius' account, in which Hannibal's behaviour conformed more closely to what Livy led us to expect. Yet while the connection appears clear, the causal mechanics are less so. Though the weather is described in grandiose terms, nothing here is presented in language that evokes the divine. It is true that exceptional weather might be felt to be intrinsically the sort of thing that has divine connotations, and so it is not a great stretch to see the divine at work here, nor, by extension, is it difficult to see a divine hand underlying Hannibal's earlier successes and rewarding him for his surprisingly good conduct: the Ticinus indeed is preceded by omens which make that connection immediately apparent, as I discussed above (289). But that interpretation, even though a natural one in Roman terms, is not foregrounded here. In its absence we are left with a vaguer sense that morality and immorality may—at least some of the time—be causally connected with success and failure. But the nature of that connection is opaque.

This applies even more strongly in those cases where divine activity appears more remote. An example occurs in the campaign of Scipio in Spain in Book 28. At 28.19–23 the Romans engage in a series of campaigns to reduce recalcitrant Spanish towns, beginning with Iliturgi. Livy begins here by emphasizing the justice of the Romans' case against the town: they had not only defected but murdered refugees who had fled to them (28.19.2). Scipio's explicit motive in the attack is to punish them for this (28.19.3–5), a point he emphasizes to his troops before the assault—that 'they had to pay the penalty for treachery and cruelty and crime' (28.19.7 *ab his perfidiae et crudelitatis et sceleris poenas*

---

be noted that Livy, following Polybius 3.78.6–79.12, does not treat the latter as a mountain crossing at all, focusing entirely on the difficulties caused by the marshes of the River Arno. In practice there is no plausible way in which Hannibal could have reached the Arno marshes from his winter quarters in Cisalpine Gaul (Polybius 3.77.3) save by crossing the Apennines (on the probable route see de Sanctis 1968: 101–5, Walbank 1957: 413), but as I discussed in Chapter 1, there is good reason to doubt that either Livy or his readership had a clear idea about the precise geography involved in Hannibal's movements, or had a synoptic picture of northern Italy which would allow them to consider all possible routes. If we leave our knowledge of geography aside, Livy's account is entirely consistent in its own terms: Hannibal fails to cross the Apennines at the end of Book 21, and then takes another, marsh-ridden route into Etruria without attempting a mountain crossing in Book 22.

expetendas esse; cf. 28.19.8). However, this leads the people to defend them-selves all the more strongly, suspecting that the Romans will give them no quarter (28.19.10–14). They are both right and wrong: when the town is captured, the Roman soldiers' desire for revenge overrides all else (28.20.6–7):

nemo capiendi vivos, nemo patentibus ad direptionem omnibus praedae memor est. trucidant inermes iuxta atque armatos, feminas pariter ac viros; usque ad infantium caedem ira crudelis pervenit. ignem deinde tectis iniciunt, ac diruunt quae incendio absumi nequeunt; adeo vestigia quoque urbis exstinguere ac delere memoriam hostium sedis cordi est.

No one thought of capturing anyone alive, no one thought of booty even though everything lay open to plunder; they slaughtered the unarmed as much as the armed, women no less than men; their cruel anger extended to the slaughter of infants. Then they threw fire onto the buildings and tore down what could not be consumed by burning; so keen were they to extinguish the very traces of the city and destroy the memory of the enemy's abode.

As I noted in Chapter 3 (210–11), one should beware of anachronism in responding to this. The modern West regards such massacres as criminal to the highest degree, whereas in Roman eyes the victors' behaviour here could certainly be justified both legally and in customary practice. Nevertheless, Livy regularly praises those who do not mete out the full measure under such circumstances, and in this particular case the sense of a degree of moral disorder is created not only by the sympathetic portrayal of the desperate townspeople holding the Romans off (28.19.13–14), but also by the fact that the Romans' revenge actually surpasses the worst that the Spaniards had feared—they had expected the women and children to be spared, as would indeed have been normal (28.19.12)—and above all by the phrase *ira crudelis* to describe the motivation for the massacre of the children,[62] which recalls the *crudelitas* for which the Iliturgi were being punished (28.19.7).[63]

The immediate effect is positive: Castulo, the other rebellious town which Scipio is targeting, is sufficiently horrified by the fate of Iliturgi to negotiate a surrender, and is treated more leniently in consequence (28.20.8–12). The people of Astapa, however, draw a different lesson from the Ilurgitans' appar-ently similar model.[64] Like the Iliturgi, they are conscious of their guilt and

---

[62] Cf. Mineo (2006: 29). In Appian, *Hisp.* 32 the soldiers' motivation is primarily loyalty to Scipio, who has been wounded in the fight; Appian also emphasizes that Scipio himself did not order the massacre. Conceivably (but far from certainly) this reflects a pre-Livian version which Livy is altering in order to make Scipio partially responsible.

[63] Cf. Mueller (1999: 183–5), who shows how Livy slants his account to indicate that the Romans' behaviour at Iliturgi met Roman criteria for unjustifiable cruelty.

[64] Livy moreover deliberately misleads the reader over Astapa: he begins by remarking that Marcius 'received the surrender of two wealthy states without a fight' (28.22.1 *duas opulentas*

believe that they will not be spared (28.22.2–5; cf. 28.19.10–11, although with Astapa, unlike Iliturgi, Livy provides no direct evidence that their fears will be justified). The Astapans, like the Iliturgans, set before themselves the alternatives of battle or capture (28.22.9–10; cf. 28.19.11–12). But their response is quite different: they arrange for their families to be murdered by their own citizens in the event that they lose the battle. The consequence for Astapa is thus the same as for Iliturgi, in that the entire population is killed and the entire town destroyed (28.23.1–5). The difference is that it is their own act rather than the Romans' which has accomplished this: their argument is that it is better for their families to be killed by 'friendly and faithful hands' (28.22.10 *amicae ac fideles . . . manus*), but Livy presents this as a horrific perversion[65]—he refers to it as a 'foul and bestial crime' (28.22.5 *facinus . . . foedum ac ferum*), and a 'fouler massacre' (28.23.2 *foedior . . . trucidatio*), 'so foul a thing' (28.23.3 *tam foedae rei*) and 'a wretched slaughter of their own people' (28.23.2 *caede misera suorum*). The Astapans are clearly the ones responsible for this, but the parallel with the massacre earlier carried out by the Romans is apparent too, not least when those killed are described as an 'unwarlike and unarmed crowd of women and children' (28.23.2 *turbam feminarum puerorumque imbellem inermem*; cf. 28.20.6 quoted above), and the burning of the town and the lack of plunder for the soldiers is described in similar terms (28.23.4–5; cf. 28.19.6–7)—admittedly in this case the soldiers do attempt to plunder the town out of 'characteristic human greed' (28.23.4 *aviditate ingenii humani*), but they suffer themselves as a result, since they are caught in the fire. The Romans, in other words, are not presented as directly guilty at Astapa, but their indirect responsibility is apparent through the parallels drawn between their own earlier massacre at Iliturgi and the Astapans' mass suicide here, and the indications that the former has prompted the latter. The Romans may have been justified in the abstract in punishing rebels, but the approach they have taken is morally compromised.

And immediately following this problems turn back on Rome herself. First, it appears that the Carthaginians have not in fact been driven out of Spain, contrary to Livy's direct statement at 28.16.14:[66] there is a garrison still in

---

civitates sine certamine deditionem accepit), and immediately continues 'Astapa was a city which was always a supporter of the Carthaginians' (28.22.2 *Astapa urbs erat Carthaginiensium semper partis*), as if that were one of the cities that surrendered—which accentuates the shock of what the Astapans eventually do instead of surrendering.

[65] A point overlooked by Eckstein (1995: 48–50), who argues both that Livy's account is closely based on Polybius' lost version, and that Polybius highly admired the mass suicide. It is hard to see how both of these claims can be maintained in light of the actual tenor of Livy's narrative.

[66] 'In this way above all under the leadership and auspices of Publius Scipio the Carthaginians were driven from Spain in the fourteenth year after the war began, and the fifth after

Cadiz, and indeed a significant force of auxiliaries supporting it (28.23.6–8). Then Scipio is struck down by illness (28.24.1), which gives space to both the Spaniards and the Romans to cause trouble. The Spaniards react in a disturbing but perhaps not unexpected fashion, by taking the opportunity to renew their rebellion (28.24.2–4); they abandon this rapidly, however, once Scipio reappears on the scene (28.25.11), though this does not spare them from a measure of eventual retribution (28.32–34). The soldiers, as Livy recounts at far greater length, mutiny (28.24.5–29.12).

It is the latter that is most interesting for our purposes. Livy begins by linking their response, like the Spaniards', to the vacuum created by Scipio's illness: he describes the way in which rumours multiply under such circumstances, and concludes with the blunt comment that 'allies did not remain loyal, nor the army dutiful' (28.24.2 *non socii in fide, non exercitus in officio mansit*). The implication is that for the Romans, like the Spaniards, it is the absence of Scipio that has led to their moral collapse. But when he moves to describe the events of the mutiny in detail, he gives it a different aetiology (28.24.6–8):

motae autem eorum mentes sunt non tum primum cum de vita imperatoris rumores dubii allati sunt, sed iam ante licentia ex diutino, ut fit, otio collecta, et nonnihil quod in hostico laxius rapto suetis vivere artiores in pace res erant. ac primo sermones tantum occulti serebantur: si bellum in provincia esset, quid sese inter pacatos facere? si debellatum iam et confecta provincia esset, cur in Italiam non revehi? flagitatum quoque stipendium procacius quam ex more et modestia militari erat.

The first time their minds were disturbed was not when doubtful rumours reached them about the commander's health, but even before that licence had accumulated from long leisure, as tends to happen, and it was also significant that, for men accustomed to live more expansively on enemy plunder, circumstances were more straitened in peacetime. And first they merely exchanged private conversations: if there was war in the province, what were they doing among those who were pacified? If war was now over and the province was under control, why were they not returning to Italy? They also demanded their pay more insolently than would be expected from the usual military moderation.

The theme of *otium* leading to moral breakdown is of course a traditional one at Rome, associated especially with Sallust; but Livy offers an unusual twist on

---

Publius Scipio received the province and the army' (*hoc maxime modo ductu atque auspicio P. Scipionis pulsi Hispania Carthaginienses sunt quarto decimo anno post bellum initum, quinto quam P. Scipio provinciam et exercitum accepit*). The statement is moreover a politically charged one, since (as noted by Mineo 2006: 312–13) it refers back to the wording that Livy had used shortly before to describe Augustus' final conquest of Spain in Livy's own day (28.12.12 *ductu auspicioque Augusti Caesaris perdomita est*). Livy draws an implicit analogy between Augustus and Scipio, but also undercuts the latter's success. Whether that undercutting is meant to suggest an analogy or a contrast with Augustus is left open.

the theme. While he shares with Sallust the general sense that the mere presence of peace allows licentiousness to flourish, another part of the problem for these soldiers is almost exactly the opposite of the Sallustian one. Whereas for Sallust untrammelled peace led directly to luxurious excess, for Livy here it is warfare itself that has accustomed the soldiers to high living.

The significance of this double picture is that it associates the mutiny with the actual conduct of the war just as closely as it does with the movement from war to peace. The mutiny is implied to be rooted in behaviour similar to that which the troops exhibited in the campaigns earlier that year,[67] and in particular the problematic avarice which the soldiers had showed immediately beforehand at Astapa (discussed above), and which they now continue by plundering the neighbouring countryside even though there is no longer a war to justify it (28.24.8). Yet the connection with the arrival of *otium*, which fits the narrative sequence, simultaneously relates it to the ending of those campaigns, as the connection with Scipio's illness had also implied. Moreover, the dilemma the soldiers present in their complaint, while not perhaps a compelling argument in itself (these troops are a garrison [28.24.5 *praesidium*], who might reasonably be argued to be preventing the local population from defecting as other Spaniards were doing),[68] strikes a chord in another way, since it reinforces Livy's suggestion immediately beforehand that the question of how far Spain is genuinely under Roman control is more open than he had previously suggested.

Livy thus employs inconsistent chronological schemes not unlike the ones I discussed in Section 5.1. The mutiny is linked both to Scipio's illness and to earlier events, and those earlier events themselves are not fully stable, since it has become unclear how far Spain actually is pacified. But for our current discussion the most important point to observe is that even though there appears to be a connection between the troops' earlier behaviour at Iliturgi

---

[67] The connection between the mutiny and those earlier events is argued for by Aranita (2009), although she draws a closer connection with the revolt of Iliturgi itself, rather than the Romans' response to that revolt: on her account the Romans are infected by the defections of the Spaniards. This reading—itself implying an anomalous causal picture whereby juxtaposed events influence one another, as I discussed in Section 5.2—is supported by the direct connection that Livy draws between the mutineers and the concurrent revolt of Mandonius and Indibilis, and in general Livy's tendency, which I discussed in Section 5.2, to see juxtaposed events as causally connected makes it easier to read the revolt in those terms. But the specific motivation given to the soldiers here is a very Roman one: it bears little resemblance to anything said of the treacherous Spaniards and is more closely related to the earlier descriptions of the Romans themselves.

[68] However, the fact that Livy—probably incorrectly (see n. 69 below)—places the garrison north of the Ebro gives their argument some extra force, since the assumption of the entire decade is that Spain north of the Ebro had accepted Roman hegemony before the war even began, and has remained securely under their control ever since (see e.g. 22.20.10, 26.20.2, 26.51.11). Hence a garrison there does not seem to serve so obvious a purpose.

and Astapa and their mutiny here, that connection is not simply one of a group of people continuing on an immoral path, because these mutinous troops are at Sucro, which is, according to him, north of the Ebro (28.24.5),[69] and are thus not the same ones as were involved in the campaigns in 28.19–23. The moral parallel appears to invite us to read a causal connection between the two sets of events, even though these are different people, and no direct line is shown to link them to the soldiers earlier beyond the fact that they are both ultimately under Scipio's command in Spain. It is easy to read the mutiny as the consequence of the earlier actions, but only in moral terms.

It should be emphasized that the moral judgements the reader is invited to make here—as so often in Livy—are not simple ones. The Roman troops at Iliturgi and Astapa are not merely vicious. In the former case they are responding to genuine crimes and are doing so in a fashion which may appear brutal but was accepted within Roman military practice, even if in this case they take it to unacceptable extremes. In the latter case the primary crime is committed by the Astapans themselves—even if it is fear of the Romans that has generated it—and the troops are mainly onlookers. But this does not change the essential point that moral failings, even if complex and tempered, have broader consequences within Livy's picture of the world.

Indeed, those consequences may be broader still than I have so far indicated. The other trigger that Livy identifies for the mutiny is Scipio's absence through illness. There is no specific indication of why Scipio might have become ill at that moment. But it is worth noting that the mutiny itself is described in terms of a disease:[70] Livy initially refers to it as 'madness... arising' (28.24.5 *furor... ortus*; cf. 28.24.12), and shortly afterwards speaks of the *contagio furoris* (28.24.10 'contagion of madness') through which it spread; the language of disease recurs constantly throughout the passage.[71] Scipio's illness and the troops' mutiny are effectively given an identical

---

[69] In fact Sucro lay south of the Ebro: see Walbank (1967: 148–9), Lazenby (1978: 152–3) for a discussion of the error. Even though the mistake is presumably inadvertent, it does allow Livy to make a firm division between the mutinous troops and those campaigning earlier.

[70] In describing the mutiny in those terms Livy is in part drawing on Polybius 11.25.2–7, who has an extended comparison of the measures that Scipio needed to take with his army and those which need to be taken in the case of disease. Polybius does not connect this even by juxtaposition to Scipio's own illness, although such a juxtaposition may have been lost in the excerptor's abridgement at the opening of the passage; more importantly, there is no indication in the surviving text of any connection to the troops' moral behaviour earlier in the campaign.

[71] E.g. 28.25.7, 28.25.11, 28.25.12, 28.27.11–12, 28.28.8, 28.29.3, 28.29.8. On disease metaphors in this passage, and their relationship to Scipio's own illness, see Aranita (2009). On descriptions of mutiny using the language of disease see Woodman (2006), arguing not only that disease metaphors pervade Tacitus' account of the mutinies early in Tiberius' reign, but that Tacitus' account is specifically imitating this section of Livy with its own extensive metaphors of illness.

pathology: both occur around the same time and are described in similar terms. And if, as I have suggested, Livy implicitly links the mutiny to the troops' earlier behaviour, it might be that Scipio's illness is to be understood in similar terms. In the abstract that might appear a far-fetched idea, but there are two reasons to think that Livy might be expecting this to be seen as a plausible reading of the sequence of events. The first is that there is a long literary tradition of seeing disease as a very specific response to human misbehaviour: this ultimately descends from the ancestor of all classical literary plagues, namely that sent by Apollo at *Iliad* 1.43–52, but there are many later examples, including ones where the connection between disease and misbehaviour is merely assumed rather than needing to be spelled out.[72] The second, related point is that in Livy, as in Roman culture more broadly, diseases are often treated as prodigies[73]—in other words, there is an implied supernatural mechanism that would allow a ready connection between disease and moral behaviour. In this case, however, there is no actual indication of the supernatural either here or in any other part of the Spanish campaign in Book 28. As before, what is foregrounded is the connection between the morality of the actors and the outcomes of events; the mechanism that could connect them is left far in the background.

The last three sections have shown various ways in which Livy presents events as causally connected in ways that appear anomalous, whether in their detachment from a clear chronological relationship, or in their dependence on juxtapositions in Livy's own narrative, or finally in their highlighting a relationship between morality and events even in the absence of any clear account of how that relationship might be thought to be operating. We can add to this the examples discussed in previous chapters, notably the handling of unpredictable events in battles and the discontinuities Livy describes in people's characters. All of these together contribute to the sense that history, for Livy, works in a very different fashion from the terms in which we are accustomed to understand it.

---

[72] Woodman (1988: 32–3) summarizes a number of early examples, concluding that 'there was an established connection between war, plague and ὕβρις' (33). The most famous historiographical plague, Thucydides 2.47–54, is admittedly more difficult. It too might perhaps be understood as a reaction to the *hybris* shown in Pericles' Funeral Speech, which it immediately follows. However, see Woodman (1988: 36–7), who argues that Thucydides sets up his account so as to reject that position, and that his point is rather that Pericles' wise policy is undercut by chance events (as Woodman 1988: 65 acknowledges, this reading was partly anticipated by Parry 1981: 173–5). Woodman's reading is persuasive, but it should be emphasized that on this account Thucydides is undermining what would be the expected interpretation of a plague: indeed, he shows the Athenians themselves (wrongly) interpreting it as Pericles' fault (2.59.2).

[73] E.g. 3.6.2–8.2, 4.21.5, 4.25.3–4, 4.30.7–11, 5.13.4–5, 6.20.15–16, 7.1.7–2.3, 7.3.1–4, 41.21.5–11.

However, these discussions of anomalous causation have in one respect been seriously misleading. Because each section of this book has been devoted to a separate aspect of Livy's writing, the oddities of his handling of (for example) chronology or characterization have been considered largely in isolation from one another. This was necessary in order to highlight the distinctive features of his work, but it has also involved an artificial abstraction of particular elements from his narrative which are in practice generally intertwined. Every individual episode in Livy involves characters acting in particular ways; each one necessarily also involves, explicitly or implicitly, chronological sequences and juxtapositions with other episodes, as well as military narratives or other descriptions of causally connected events; virtually every event is described in such a way as to foreground its moral implications. Any strange or counterintuitive feature in one aspect of the narrative is likely to have ramifications which extend into another, and these cannot be fully understood except in the context of the narrative as a whole.

5.4. CAPUA

To illustrate the ways in which different issues are interwoven in Livy's narrative, a useful exemplary episode is the Capuan sequence with which he opens Book 23, as well as its ultimate resolution with the capture of Capua in Book 26. Capua plays a vital role in Livy's account of the war, as the leading community in Italy that defected to Hannibal, but also as the place where the seeds of Hannibal's ultimate defeat were sown, when his troops are corrupted by their stay there (23.18.10–16). The story of the defection, as Livy sets it out, falls clearly into three sections. First there is the account of the internal strife at Capua in which Pacuvius Calavius took control of the state (23.2.1–4.5). Then there is a central episode where the Capuans send an embassy to the Roman consul, and in consequence of what he tells them abandon Rome and instead form an alliance with Hannibal (23.4.6–7.12). Finally there is the party at which Pacuvius' son plans to assassinate Hannibal, only to be deterred by his father's appeals; following this Hannibal has Decius Magius arrested, the leading opponent of the Carthaginian alliance (23.8–10).

Pacuvius is the central character in the initial narrative of the Capuan defection, and he is often spoken of by scholars as being the prime mover in the revolt.[74] And this might on the face of things appear to be supported by

---

[74] As he certainly is in Diodorus 26.10 (in which, however, he is called 'Pancylus Paucus'). Pacuvius' central role is accepted by (*inter alios*) Reid (1915: 112) 'the arch-plotter', Briscoe

Livy's account. Towards the end Pacuvius' son refers to him as 'the originator of the defection from the Romans' (23.9.11 *defectionis ab Romanis . . . auctor*),[75] and that appears to fit with the words with which Livy reintroduced him at 23.8.2: 'leader of that party which had taken the state to the Carthaginians' (23.8.2 *princeps factionis eius, quae traxerat rem ad Poenos*). But this does not seem entirely of a piece with the actual narrative of the revolt and of Pacuvius' role.[76] He does not appear at all in the central section, in which the defection actually occurs: the chief advocate of defection there is Vibius Virrius (23.6.1–3), and it is Vibius, not Pacuvius, who in Book 26 is described—though in remarkably similar language—as 'the originator of the defection from the Romans' (26.13.2 *defectionis auctor ab Romanis*). Pacuvius is not mentioned in either passage. What is more, the narrative of Pacuvius' seizure of power in Capua skirts oddly around the connection between that seizure and the defection from Rome. Pacuvius certainly has personal motives for his actions: he wants power for himself. But Livy is surprisingly ambiguous about suggesting that he objects to Roman rule or favours Hannibal. On the contrary, the prospect of defection is raised as part of a sequence of events that he is seeking to avert (23.2.3–7):

iam diu infestam senatui plebem ratus per occasionem novandi res magnum ausuram facinus, ut, si in ea loca Hannibal cum victore exercitu venisset, trucidato senatu traderet Capuam Poenis, inprobus homo, sed non ad extremum perditus, cum mallet incolumi quam eversa re publica dominari, nullam autem incolumem esse orbatam publico consilio crederet, rationem iniit, qua et senatum servaret et obnoxium sibi ac plebi faceret. vocato senatu cum sibi defectionis ab Romanis consilium placiturum nullo modo, nisi necessarium fuisset, praefatus esset, quippe qui liberos ex Appii Claudii filia haberet filiamque Romam nuptum M. Livio dedisset; ceterum maiorem multo rem magisque timendam instare: non enim per defectionem ad tollendum ex

---

(1989: 72) 'the leader of the revolt of Capua'; Briquel (2002: 189–90, 192), Hoyos (2003: 123); cf. also the slightly more nuanced version of Frederiksen (1984: 239). More recently Fronda (2007: 86–7, 96–103), noting Livy's ambiguous treatment of Pacuvius, has argued that he was originally pro-Roman and only belatedly came over to support the Carthaginians. This too, however, depends on taking parts of Livy's description entirely at face value while skating over other details which do not fit the picture.

[75] The text here is problematic: the MS reading is corrupt (*defectione inissa*), and other emendations have also been proposed. But the general sense of the sentence certainly requires that the son is accusing his father of taking the lead in the defection.

[76] Cf. Ungern-Sternberg (1975: 29–31), who sees this as the consequence of combining a 'Pacuvius Calavius tradition' with an incompatible 'Vibius Virrius tradition'; he attributes the combination not to Livy, but to his source, whom he takes to be Coelius (Ungern-Sternberg 1975: 44–5). Even if we leave aside other doubts about the methodology Ungern-Sternberg employs here, however (cf. above, 126–7) Glew (forthcoming) points to a number of respects in which the story as constructed in Livy reflects the political events of the end of the Roman Republic, which makes it unlikely that it could be a product of Coelius.

civitate senatum plebem spectare, sed per caedem senatus vacuam rem publicam tradere Hannibali ac Poenis velle.

He reckoned that the people had now been hostile to the Senate for a long time and given the opportunity for revolution would dare to commit a great crime, so that they, if Hannibal came to that area with his victorious army, would massacre the Senate and hand Capua over to the Carthaginians. He was an immoral man, but not utterly corrupt, and since he preferred to rule in a state that was intact rather than one that had been overturned, and believed that no state was intact if bereft of its deliberative council, he formed a plan to both save the Senate and make it subservient to himself and the people. He called the Senate and began by saying that he would not approve/have approved of the idea of defecting from the Romans, unless it proved necessary/if it had not proved necessary,[77] speaking as someone who had children by the daughter of Appius Claudius and had given his own daughter to be married to Marcus Livius at Rome; but a much greater and more frightening thing was at hand, for the people were not looking to remove the Senate from the state by means of their defection, but wanted to hand over to Hannibal and the Carthaginians a state made empty by the murder of the Senate.

Livy is remarkably oblique in his account of Pacuvius' motives. He is described as objecting to the people's plan to massacre the senate and give the state to Hannibal, but the grounds given for his objection (that he wanted to rule a state that was intact) relate entirely to the first part of the plan, and tell us nothing about his attitude to the second. When Livy describes him raising the prospect of defection at the opening of his speech to the Senate, he does so in a convoluted indirect statement, which leaves the key phrase ambiguous. *sibi ... consilium placiturum nullo modo, nisi necessarium fuisset* is capable of being construed with two different grammatical constructions. We can understand *esse* with *placiturum*, representing *placebit* in direct speech, in which case the passage is about a possible but indeterminate future in which defection might be necessary but was not so yet ('he would not approve ... unless it proved necessary'—the *fuisset* representing an original future perfect *fuerit*). Alternatively we can understand *fuisse*, representing *fuisset* in direct speech, which turns the sentence into a past counterfactual conditional—'he would not *have* approved ... if it *had not* proved necessary. Commentators and translators generally read the passage in the former way,[78] but the latter is equally acceptable grammatically,[79] and gives rather a different picture: it implies that Pacuvius is (disingenuously) presenting defection to the Senate as

---

[77] For the interpretation of this phrase see below.

[78] E.g. Macaulay (1885: 138), W-M *ad loc.*; de Sélincourt (1965: 168) 'unless it proved necessary ... would by no means have his support'; Yardley (2006: 136) 'would find no favour with him, unless it proved essential'.

[79] Cf. Weissenborn (1872: 286); for parallels for the omission of *fuisse* see Kühner and Stegmann (1955: 15), though they query whether that is the correct interpretation of this particular passage.

something already inevitable. The significant thing to note here is that the ambiguity is entirely in Livy's presentation: it would have been unambiguous in Pacuvius' (presumed) original statement.[80] It is not that he is presenting Pacuvius as someone concealing his true intentions, rather that Livy is leaving them opaque to the reader. All one can do is gather hints, and those hints, if anything, point more to Pacuvius' being a supporter of Rome than inclined to hand Capua to Hannibal. By his own account he is connected by marriage to the Roman aristocracy (23.2.6), which seems to associate him with those Capuans whose personal ties to Rome make them want to maintain the alliance (23.4.7). Yet in the second half of the story he is an uncompromising supporter of the Carthaginian alliance, who is described by his son as its prime mover in a statement that gains force from its closural position as the episode draws to its close; he moreover scotches the one chance the Capuans have to reaffirm their support of Rome by assassinating Hannibal.

What we thus have with Pacuvius is a double picture not unlike the character portraits I discussed in Chapter 3, where the same person at different times exhibits contradictory features, depending how they fit into the developing and dynamic contrasts of certain character-types. The account of Pacuvius certainly makes sense within this framework: he is both a leading example of an anti-Roman provincial—Capua is, after all, just one of a series of defections in the years after Cannae—and a model of a certain sort of anti-senatorial politician, with counterparts both at Rome and elsewhere. The Syracusan revolt in Book 24, which I discussed earlier in the chapter, both parallels and develops the themes of the Capua narrative, including a number of figures playing partially analogous roles to Pacuvius here, including Adranodorus, Hippocrates, and Epicydes.

But the way Livy sets up the contradictory elements in his portrait of Pacuvius appears more pointed, because the narrative of the Capuan revolt is so structured as to throw particular emphasis on those contradictions. The two halves of the story are strongly paralleled: in both Pacuvius is faced with the prospect of violence against other people, and in both he persuades the potential assassins to abandon their plans.[81] But that very parallel invites a comparison between the two episodes which exposes the extent to which Pacuvius' character in each is quite different—so different, indeed, that we would assume that they were in fact different people were it not that Livy

---

[80] Here too we may contrast Diodorus 26.10: his 'Pancylus' likewise speaks of it being 'necessary' to defect (ἀναγκαῖον εἶναι), but in this case it is unambiguous that he endorses the claim of necessity. The arguments are similar enough to make it conceivable that Livy is alluding to Diodorus' source, but has altered it enough to leave other possibilities open too; but that is certainly not provable.

[81] I owe this point to Robert Maltby.

assures us that they were a single man. In the first half he is devious, manipulative, amoral and self-seeking. Almost the first thing we are told about him is
that he 'acquired power through evil means' (23.2.2 *malis artibus nanctus
opes*), his refusal to countenance the massacre of the Senate is qualified by
the comment that he was 'an immoral man, but not utterly corrupt' (23.2.4
inprobus homo, sed non ad extremum perditus), and it is explained that his
protection of the Senate is tied to his personal desire for control. His ingenious
method of achieving this is engaging and entertaining, but here too ultimately
self-serving, since it puts the Senate in his power (23.4.1).

But Pacuvius looks nothing like this in the second half of the story. Here he
is an impassioned, sentimental, and apparently sincere family man, a man
who achieved Hannibal's pardon for his son and is now horrified by that son's
proposed actions. His pleas to Hannibal on his son's behalf depend on no
deception or device, but are a simple, tearful appeal for Hannibal's mercy
(23.8.4); his reaction to learning of the planned assassination is to be 'insane
with fear' (23.9.1 *amens metu*); his emotional speech reduces his son to tears
until he prevails on him to abandon his plan (23.9.9). It is hard to see any
connection between this man and the cynical manipulator of the first section.

But there is another aspect to this also. Pacuvius in his second incarnation
is not only surprisingly ingenuous, he is also surprisingly focused on issues of
morality. His argument with his son does not, as one might expect, focus
primarily on either the unfeasability of the plan or the potential danger
(though these issues are briefly raised at 23.9.6–7), but on the immorality of
the violation of hospitality and treaties if his son were to assassinate Hannibal
(23.9.2–5)—an argument which he reinforces with his final threat to protect
Hannibal at the cost of his own life (23.9.7–8). And the moral considerations
he raises are real ones:[82] after all, Hannibal genuinely has signed a treaty with
Capua and the Pacuvii genuinely are guests in another man's house. Yet this
focus on morality seems if anything to work against other aspects of Livy's
presentation of the character. When Pacuvius appeals to morality here, he is
(as his son observes) doing so against the interests of both Rome and (as it
transpires) his own people, and he is identified as the leader who broke the
alliance with Rome. When on the other hand he was amoral and self-serving,

---

[82] Though not decisive ones: as often, Livy leaves the moral issue carefully balanced.
Pacuvius had appealed not only to hospitality and treaties, but also to his own claims on his
son's respect (23.9.2), an argument that carried strong weight within Roman patriarchal culture.
But the son used other arguments which Pacuvius does not address: that in destroying the
alliance with Hannibal he would be reinforcing the earlier alliance with Rome (23.8.9–11; his
mentor Decius Magius had made a similar point at 23.7.6). On the other hand the son does not
address the question of hospitality or the treaty with Carthage; he gives up the assassination only
out of respect for his father, but says that by doing so he is effectively betraying his country
(23.9.10–12). The symbolic action by which he does not merely throw his sword away, but does
so *in publicum* as a patriotic dedication, is also worth noting (23.9.12–13).

he was associated (albeit ambiguously) with support for Rome, and he saved the Capuans from their worst instincts by deflecting the populace from their murderous rage against the Senate.

Taking the portrait of Pacuvius Calavius in isolation from the rest of the story, it is easy enough to conclude that Livy, as he often does, is engaging in complex moral explorations. Pacuvius is a morally challenging figure precisely because he sometimes—but not always—exhibits moral instincts, but his intermittent exhibition of morality does not correlate to clearly moral outcomes. But while this is certainly the case, it is far from the whole explanation. Pacuvius does not appear in isolation: his portrait is bound together with the picture of Capua as a whole and their defection from Rome. And an analysis of the exact sequence of events that leads to the defection reveals puzzling features of its own.

If we ask the simple question 'Why do the Capuans defect', the immediate trigger, as I said above, was not Pacuvius but Vibius Virrius, who in Book 26 appears as the *auctor* of the defection: it is he who, after leaving the Roman consul Varro, persuades first his colleagues on the embassy and then the people as a whole that it is in the best interests of Capua to abandon Rome for Hannibal (23.6.1–3). The implication is that he has been prompted to this by Varro's appallingly misjudged speech,[83] which leaves the impression that Roman power is on the verge of collapse. But while Vibius may be the man who triggers the defection, he is certainly not the root cause: the Capuans were already prepared to reject Rome before the embassy, which was merely a last-ditch attempt by those Capuans with strong Roman connections to delay the break (23.4.7–5.1). The reason that the Capuans were ready to defect was, according to Livy (23.4.4–6):

prona semper civitas in luxuriam non ingeniorum modo vitio sed affluenti copia voluptatium et inlecebris omnis amoenitatis maritimae terrestrisque, tum vero ita obsequio principum et licentia plebei lascivire, ut nec libidini nec sumptibus modus esset. ad contemptum legum magistratuum senatus accessit tum, post Cannensem cladem, ut, cuius aliqua verecundia erat, Romanum quoque spernerent imperium.

The community was always prone to luxury, not only because of a flaw in their temperaments, but because of a superabundance of pleasures and the seductions of every delight of sea and land. But now it ran riot because of the leading men's subservience and the licence of the populace, so that there was no limit to their lusts or their expenditure. And to their disdain for laws, magistrates, and senate was now, after the disaster at Cannae, added their contempt for Roman power as well, which had previously held some respect/restraint.[84]

---

[83] Note especially 23.5.2: 'And the consul increased their contempt for his situation and for him by revealing and laying bare too much of the disaster' (*et auxit rerum suarum suique contemptum consul nimis detegendo cladem nudandoque*).

[84] For the meaning of *verecundia* here see below.

The Capuans' revolt is partly generated by their natural character, partly by the availability of a sybaritic lifestyle, which attracted them to luxury; this then was taken to excess by the overturning of the natural political order, with the Senate being subservient to the people;[85] after Cannae that popular disdain for authority was extended to Rome. To that extent Pacuvius Calavius might be seen as indirectly responsible for the defection, since he had been a key part of the movement which had led to this fatal lack of respect for traditional power: his intention from the start had been to 'make the Senate subservient to himself and to the people' (23.2.4 *obnoxium sibi ac plebi faceret*; cf. 23.2.2), and he indeed is said to have accomplished this even more comprehensively than Livy had originally suggested, with himself more than the people holding the power: 'he made . . . the senate <u>much more</u> subservient to himself than to the people' (23.4.1 *obnoxium . . . senatum <u>multo</u> sibi <u>magis</u> quam plebi fecisset*). This makes sense, in as much as the people are an incidental part of his plan: he is admittedly described as a *popularis* (23.2.2), but his primary aim is personal domination (23.2.4 *dominari*; cf. 23.4.1), and he accepts the centrality of the Senate to the stability of the state (23.2.4). However, it does not make sense in terms of the subsequent explanation of the defection.[86] Here Pacuvius vanishes from sight, although he is said to be dominant: the people whom he has empowered over the Senate become the centre of attention, and it is the complaisance of the Senate towards them that generates their lack of respect for authority and hence their willingness to hand power over to Hannibal.

But Livy's explanation for the revolt has another side to it as well. Before Pacuvius even takes power, and before the Roman collapse at Cannae (though after Trasimene) he already suspects that the people will want to hand the state over to Hannibal (23.2.3-7 quoted above, 355–6).[87] But here the reasons given are quite different: it is not because of the complaisance of

---

[85] Compare also the preamble to the whole episode, where Capua is described in very similar terms as 'luxuriating through long success and the favour of fortune, but above all among the general corruption through the licence of the people who enjoyed liberty without restriction' (23.2.1 *luxuriantem longa felicitate atque indulgentia fortunae, maxime tamen inter corrupta omnia licentia plebis sine modo libertatem exercentis*). The luxury of Capua was a standard feature of the Roman image of the region: note Cicero, *Leg. Agr.* 2.95–9, who likewise associates it with the collapse of traditional political structures; and cf. above, 216–18.

[86] I owe this point to Ellen O'Gorman.

[87] This was already prefigured at 22.13.2–4, where three Campanian knights captured at Trasimene assure Hannibal that if he went to Campania he would get control of Capua. Perhaps revealingly, Hannibal does not trust them, and asks them to return with other leaders of their country. The account in Book 23 of the complex political dynamics in Capua after Trasimene suggests why Hannibal was right to be distrustful, and also (perhaps) explains why the extra supporters he sought do not immediately materialize.

the Senate to the people, but because of the people's hostility towards the Senate. In both cases it is assumed that the breakdown of political authority will bring the state to Hannibal, but the mechanism by which this is assumed to happen is reversed: an excessive hatred of the authority of the Senate would take them to Hannibal directly, but Pacuvius Calavius' manipulations instead lead to the people's despising all authority, including that of Rome, which leads them to Hannibal by another route.[88]

The amoral Pacuvius of this section is not directly implicated in the defection, but the defection is a consequence of his policies—though, as I observed above, Livy carefully leaves it ambiguous how far these consequences were intended by him. But the time-frame leaves the ultimate impetus for the revolt opaque.[89] The Capuans are said to defect because they despised Rome after Cannae, but that itself is only an extension of their general lack of respect for authority in the wake of Pacuvius' subordination of the Senate. Yet (it appears) they were considering defection even in the previous year and before Pacuvius had set them over the Senate. There it was for quite different reasons, in which taking sides for or against Hannibal was merely a convenient vehicle for their domestic hatreds rather than because of their attitude to Rome, and we are not yet at the stage described in 23.2.1 and 23.4.4-6, in which the people have abandoned themselves to *licentia*: that is implied to have arrived only with Pacuvius' coup. The one consistent feature is the actual or threatened breakdown of the traditional hierarchy of the state, but, rather as with the battle narratives that I examined in Chapter 4, we lack a single line of causation that would explain the connection between that breakdown of authority, the desire to join Hannibal, and the consequent defection. Rather what we have are two lines which are not entirely congruent with each other, and it is far from clear how we should see them as operating. Pacuvius is interwoven with both, but it is also not clear how far his responsibility extends—certainly it appears more indirect and ambivalent than one would guess from his description on his reappearance.

The other complicating causal factor is Capuan 'luxury'. This is clearly implicated in the defection at both 23.2.1 and 23.4.4, where the people's tendency to luxury is extended through their contempt for authority. But here too the causal sequence is not quite clear. What Livy says explicitly at 23.4.4-5, and had earlier implied at 23.2.1, is that the people were already prone to luxury, but this was exacerbated once there were no authorities to limit them: in other words the excess of luxury is the consequence, not the

---

[88] We may contrast Zonaras 9.2, where Pacuvius is not mentioned (the man who saves the Senate is a random and anonymous member of the crowd) and the whole episode takes place after Cannae: Livy's different stages of the move to Hannibal are conflated into one.

[89] Cf. Ungern-Sternberg (1975: 26–8).

cause, of the political breakdown which after Trasimene had led the people to favour the Romans. But the direct move from the account of the growth of luxury to despising Rome in 23.4.6 seems rather to suggest that the luxury is itself implicated in the lack of regard for Roman authority,[90] a point which is accentuated by the word *verecundia*, the connotations of which include a generalized sense of self-restraint, but with a specific focus on showing respect to other people, especially (though not only) one's social superiors.[91] A loss of *verecundia* leads to the people despising Rome: and that covers both the specific lack of respect for their superiors and the general collapse into lust which is engendered by that. In effect, Livy successively treats being prone to luxury and an excessive licence in one's behaviour towards traditional authority as both the cause and effect of each other.

Luxury's precise causal role in the story is thus not fully determined, but that lack of clarity only emphasizes its centrality, because it pervades the narrative in a way that it could not if it appeared only at a specific point in the causal sequence. Luxury was of course part of the standard stereotype of Campania in general and Capua in particular well before Livy (see above, 217–18); but it forms the centre of his account not only of the revolt, but also of its aftermath. It is Capuan luxury that eventually corrupts Hannibal's troops (23.18.11–16) and so (as Livy explicitly indicates at 23.18.13)[92] is the fundamental cause of the ultimate Carthaginian defeat in the war,[93] and that corruption through luxury is prefigured from the start. As Hannibal enters the city he is greeted by an invitation to leave off serious business and have a

---

[90] This appears also to be the direction of causation in Polybius 7.1.2 (from Athenaeus 12.528b): οὐ δυνάμενοι . . . φέρειν τὴν παροῦσαν εὐδαιμονίαν ἐκάλουν τὸν Ἀννίβαν ('Not being able to endure their present prosperity they called in Hannibal'). However, the mechanism by which an 'inability to endure' luxury led to defection is unclear, and the passage has in any case clearly been heavily abridged by Athenaeus and may reflect his interpretation as much as Polybius': it is part of a long list of stereotypically luxurious states, many of which are shown to have come to disaster as a consequence.

[91] On this complex of ideas subsumed within *verecundia* see above all Kaster (2005a: 13–27).

[92] Cf. also 23.35.1, where the failure of the Carthaginians to prosecute the war effectively in the following year is attributed to their 'softened minds' (*mollitis animis*), and in particular 23.45.4–6, where both Marcellus and Hannibal at Nola note the difference between the troops now and those who won at Cannae.

[93] This idea predated Livy: it is found already in Cicero, *Leg. Agr.* 2.95 *ea luxuries quae ipsum Hannibalem armis etiam tum invictum voluptate vicit* ('that luxury which through pleasure defeated Hannibal himself who was even at that point unconquered militarily'); cf. *Leg. Agr.* 1.20. Note also Livy 7.29.5, 7.31.1, 7.31.6, and especially 7.38.5–10, where Roman troops stationed in Capua are induced to mutiny: Livy here anticipates the later corruption of the Carthaginians with his comment that Capua was '*even then* utterly unhealthy for military discipline' (7.38.5 *iam tum* minime salubris militari disciplinae). On the persistent theme in Livy of the corrupting influence of Capua, stretching back to her original foundation (4.37.1–2), see Pobjoy (1996: 230–4).

celebratory tour of the city, which he engages in despite his own inclinations.[94] The dinner party where Pacuvius protects Hannibal from his son's assassination plot 'was not conducted according to Carthaginian habits or military discipline, but—typically for a state and moreover a house of wealth and luxury—with all the seductions of pleasures' (23.8.6 *non ex more Punico aut militari disciplina esse, sed, ut in civitate atque etiam domo diti ac luxuriosa, omnibus voluptatium inlecebris instructum*). By contrast, Livy in this episode puts far less emphasis on the even more typical Campanian trait of *superbia*,[95] though this stereotype is alluded to directly at 23.5.1 and is implicit in their contempt for Rome at 23.4.6. The one thing that is clear is that Capuan luxury is at the heart of their problems and the problems of those who would associate with them. But any attempt to try to construct a precise causal connection between the luxury and the wider problems collapses on close examination.

The eventual Carthaginian collapse that luxury engenders introduces similar complications. As I discussed in Chapter 1 (above, 53), this is during a stay in winter quarters which seems incongruously to take place in the middle of the year. The consequence is that it is impossible to identify precisely when in the war this key Carthaginian collapse actually occurs. It might be suggested that Livy was simply unaware of the problem—that he was not conceptualizing the chronology of the war in terms of an abstract time-line into which one might slot particular events: there are strong grounds for saying that the Romans tended to view time in this way less than moderns do (above, 34–5, n. 80). But I demonstrated that Livy elsewhere shows himself self-conscious about his apparent chronological incongruities, and here too he carefully covers himself with the ambiguous phrase with which he describes the end of Hannibal's stay in Capua: 23.19.1 *mitescente iam hieme* ('with the winter now becoming mild'), which could refer to the seasonal change from winter to spring,[96] or could simply refer to a temporary alleviation of the winter weather.[97] The first interpretation fits better the direct statement at 23.18.10 that the Carthaginians spent most of the winter in Capua; the second is better suited to the length of the

---

[94] 23.7.11–12: the business he is temporarily putting off is the punishment of the recalcitrant Capuan Decius Magius, as is made clear by the reference to Hannibal's *ira* which he would have preferred to indulge immediately (cf. 23.7.7 and 23.10.3).

[95] It is revealing that Cicero, *Leg. Agr.* 2.95 cites *superbia* even before luxury as the quintessential Campanian attribute; cf. also e.g. *Leg. Agr.* 2.93, *Red. Sen.* 17, Gellius 1.24.2, and Livy 9.6.5. See Oakley (1998: 305), Briquel (2002: 150–2).

[96] Cf. Horace, *Odes* 4.7.9, Silius Italicus 15.502.

[97] Cf. Curtius 8.4.13. Note also Columella 11.3.22, where the reference is to the winter regularly turning milder in January, long before spring proper sets in.

subsequent narrative before the new year is finally marked. But either way the chronology is hard to make sense of in literal terms.

The collapse through luxury is even odd in terms of its place in the narrative sequence. The emphasis placed on the winter in Capua as a watershed in Carthaginian success does not entirely fit the events that surround it. After taking Capua, Hannibal seeks to capture various other towns in the region, but with little success. In particular, he suffers his first significant defeat, against Marcellus at Nola (23.16): Livy debates the precise scale of the Roman victory, but hails it as perhaps the most important action of the war, since Marcellus fought off Hannibal at the height of his success (23.16.15–16). Moreover, he fails to take Casilinum despite his considerable numerical superiority (23.18.1–9)—he does better when he returns to the siege after leaving winter quarters at 23.19, taking the town, albeit through terms rather than an outright assault. It appears that Hannibal's problems have begun from the moment of his encounter with Capua and its luxury, though how precisely he has been affected by it is not clear. The general imprecision of the chronology and the reversal of the expected sequence of Carthaginian corruption and Carthaginian defeat once again suggest the pervasiveness of Capuan luxury in the story, which transcends any precise causal role that one can identify that it is playing.

As can be seen from this analysis, the difficulty of interpreting the sequence of events at Capua is the consequence of a variety of separate but linked problems. The causal issue is tangled into an apparently impossible chronology and counterintuitive narrative sequence, in which Hannibal suffers his expected defeat, but does so before the formal notice of the corruption of his troops. The impetus for the original Capuan defection both exists in the period after Trasimene, where it is the consequence of the people's hatred of the Senate, and is dated to the period after Cannae, where it is the consequence of the breakdown of political authority. The latter is connected with the malign influence of luxury, but it is not entirely clear how far luxury is the cause and how far the consequence of the breakdown. And the whole story is bound up with the double picture of Pacuvius Calavius, who plays two distinct roles. In one he appears to be directly responsible for the defection despite not behaving like someone who is responsible for a defection, in the other he appears to oppose the defection despite behaving with the amorality of a supporter of defection, and the defection is at most an unintended by-product of his policies rather than his deliberate decision.

It is hard to make sense of this in any normal terms of cause and effect. But in another way it all makes perfect sense. The central role is given to *luxuria*, and it has strong moral overtones: it is a marker here as elsewhere in Latin literature of a society collapsing under its own success. Pacuvius Calavius' role may be contradictory in terms of his character, actions, and motivation, but in terms of his effect on the narrative it is entirely consistent. Although he is never directly implicated in that luxury himself, in both halves of the story he (apparently unwittingly) enables it to have its maximum effect, by first establishing the conditions that allow it to run riot before the defection, and then by welcoming Hannibal at the sybaritic party and protecting him there. Both are moreover connected to his moral failures, whether (as in the first half of the story) because he is an immoral man acting to moral effect, or (as in the second) he is a moral man acting to immoral effect: either way the consequences of his actions are ruinous for his country and for the Carthaginians. The inconsistencies in the causal sequence of the story appear to be a deliberate aspect of Livy's presentation: if one is looking for straightforward explanations in terms of mechanical causation they are not to be found. But the absence of straightforward causal explanations throws the emphasis onto something else, namely the precise correlation between Capuan luxury, Capuan political corruption, Carthaginian moral corruption, and Carthaginian defeat. In other words, we have here a causal sequence that makes sense only on the moral level, but ostentatiously does not on the level of physical action and chronological sequence.

Capua, moreover, is an implicit model for the defections from Rome in the next two books. At 24.2.8, in the context of the revolt of Croton, Livy comments that 'one (so to speak) disease had invaded all of the Italian states: the populace was at odds with the optimates, the Senate supporting the Romans, the populace taking the state to the Carthaginians' (*unus velut morbus invaserat omnes Italiae civitates, ut plebes ab optimatibus dissentirent, senatus Romanis faveret, plebs ad Poenos rem traheret*). In fact, as various scholars have observed,[98] Livy's own narrative does not bear out this generalization, since a good proportion of the states which defect do so as a result of elite rather than popular impetus—Tarentum is an especially clear example (25.8.3–4). But Livy provides enough examples of popular disaffection against Rome, especially in the immediate wake of the Capuan revolt, to provide a superficial justification for his claim,[99] especially given that Capua itself is his first detailed account of a defection, and the political dynamic there thus looms largest in the reader's mind. More importantly for us here, the opacity of the mechanism which connects popular politics and pro-Carthaginian moves at Capua is mirrored later: the language of disease at 24.2.8 suggests anti-Roman attitudes spreading from state to state without

[98] See e.g. Reid (1915: esp 98, 112), Ungern-Sternberg (1975: 63–76).
[99] See 23.14.7, 23.39.7, and 24.13.8 (Nola); 24.1.7 (Locri—but note the contradictory account at 23.30.8, and cf. above, 54–5); 24.23.10 (Syracuse).

any visible causal connection.[100] Capua acts as the archetype, and it is followed by a series of moral and political collapses in other cities which likewise transcend any attempt to provide a rational explanation for them.

The moral problems surrounding Capua recur with its recapture by Rome in Book 26, and in some respects they have not changed. In particular, the Capuans are still marked by wealth and luxury, most obviously when Vibius Virrius and his colleagues decide to commit suicide rather than surrender, and do so at a dinner party (26.13.17–18), where they use the alcohol in order to distract themselves from their imminent deaths (26.14.3)—though with the ironic consequence that the food and drink make it harder for them to die swiftly (26.14.5). Moreover, the political topsy-turviness at Capua has continued and indeed been accentuated. The Senate has abandoned its responsibilities, refusing even to hold a meeting (26.12.7–9) until they are bullied and threatened into doing so by the people (26.13.1). The leader of the state, Seppius Loesius, is not an aristocrat, but 'born to an obscure position and slender means' (26.6.13 *loco obscuro tenuique fortuna ortus*), whose mother, on hearing it prophesied that her son would become the leader, joked—with ironic accuracy—that it would be under a condition where 'the Campanian polity was ruined' (26.6.15 *perditas res Campanorum*). Loesius achieves power through accusing the aristocracy of abandoning the state (26.6.17), something which they certainly have done, but he himself proves no better: his inadequacy for the post removes its authority (26.12.8), and he appears to share the Senate's feckless disregard for their responsibilities (26.13.1). In Pacuvius Calavius Capua had a leader of high birth and personal authority, whatever his moral failings; Loesius appears to represent the very fate from which Pacuvius thought he had saved the city when he persuaded the people that none of them could be fit substitutes for the senators (23.3).

But in other respects the situation diverges strikingly from what went before. One difference is the self-sacrifice of the Capuan rebels. In Book 23 heroic action was confined to pro-Roman activists like Decius Magius, who defies Hannibal even though it could potentially cost him his life. Here heroism is found primarily among those who defy the Romans to the end: above all Vibius Virrius, who warns his countrymen of the likelihood of Roman revenge and who leads a group of them to suicide instead (26.13.2–14.5), and Vibellius Taurea, who voluntarily chooses to join his countrymen in their punishment, seeking execution and then committing suicide when

---

[100] Compare above, 352–3 for the significance of disease metaphors in the context of the overturning of an existing social order.

execution is denied to him (26.15.11–15).[101] Both of these complicate the association of Campanian luxury with moral decline that is implicit in much of the treatment.

But a more far-reaching difference is the involvement of the Romans. In Book 23 Carthage is corrupted through association with Capuan luxury; that is no longer foregrounded,[102] though the Carthaginians' failure to support their allies in Capua remains a focus of attention.[103] But the primary focus—and the primary complication—is on the Romans' treatment of the Capuans, and in particular on the question of what punishment they will or should receive if they surrender. At 26.12.5 the Roman proconsuls[104] promised in the name of the Senate that any Capuans who defected 'before a set deadline would be unharmed' (*ante certam diem . . . sine fraude esset*). Livy does not say what the deadline was. His narrative sequence implies that the Capuans missed it, when he immediately continues by noting that 'no defection occurred' (26.12.6 *nec ulla facta est transitio*). But he does not state that explicitly, and it is not inevitable, especially given that the reason the Capuans failed to act was that they did not believe that the Romans would in fact pardon them, in light of their earlier crimes: if they are right then the precise deadline is irrelevant. So from the very start Roman mercy is present in principle, but that goes hand in hand with scepticism about the likelihood of its being exercised in practice.

---

[101] However, Livy does slightly undercut Vibellius' heroism by presenting an alternative version of his death (one of a long sequence of queries that he raises at 26.16.1–4—see further below, 369–70). In this second version Vibellius is due to be executed in any case, and his defiance consists merely in insulting Fulvius by insisting on his own superior courage (26.16.2–3).

[102] Note however 27.3.2, where Fulvius, after the capture and punishment of the city, removes his soldiers from it 'fearing that the excessive pleasantness of the city would weaken his army too, like Hannibal's' (*metuens ne suum quoque exercitum sicut Hannibalis nimia urbis amoenitas emolliret*). Even in defeat Capua retains its potential to destroy those associated with it.

[103] The Carthaginian garrison is explicitly said to be more concerned for themselves than for the Capuans (26.12.10); Hannibal, having induced the Capuans to remain loyal by promising that his march to Rome will raise the siege (26.7.6–8), does not return after the plan fails and so abandons to their fate not only the Capuans but his own troops (26.12.1–4, 26.12.11–14).

[104] The usual reading of the text is *proconsulum*. The fifth-century Puteaneus MS, however, has the abbreviation *procos*. It is possible that this reflects only the spelling of a copyist in later antiquity, but it is a standard abbreviation on inscriptions, and it is at least possible that it stood that way in Livy's original text also. If so, it is worth noting that the abbreviation does not distinguish between the singular *proconsulis* and the plural *proconsulum*, and so leaves it ambiguous whether the edict was issued in the name of one proconsul or both. Other things being equal we would naturally assume the latter, since both proconsuls are present, but the ambiguity is significant in the light of the later narrative, where it emerges that Fulvius, unlike Appius, is inclined to treat the Capuans harshly and to circumvent senatorial decrees to the contrary. The split in Roman attitudes towards the Capuans is thus present as a possibility from the start, and gives colour to the Capuans' immediate suspicions about their sincerity.

The same double set of possibilities appears in the ensuing episode. The Capuans change their minds on seeing the brutal punishment the Romans mete out against the Numidians who attempt to circumvent the blockade (26.12.15–19): they demand the senatorial action that was previously lacking (26.13.1; cf. 26.12.7) and propose sending a delegation to surrender to the Romans (26.13.2–3); they do so in confidence that the Romans will treat them mercifully (26.14.2). Against this, however, is Vibius Virrius' opposition (which leads him and his fellows to commit suicide instead), based on the argument that the Romans are certainly going to punish atrociously any Capuans who surrender to them. He graphically describes what he imagines surrendering Capuans will undergo, culminating in a destruction of the city comparable to the destruction visited on Alba Longa in the opening years of Rome's (and Livy's) history (26.13.14–16). He points out the implacability of the Romans' prosecution of the siege (26.13.7–13), and the offences that the Capuans themselves committed (26.13.5–6). Indeed, he misrepresents both of the last of these. As far as the implacability of the Romans goes, Livy at the beginning of the book comments that the Romans' determination to take Capua was less the result of their anger against Capua (justified though that was), but was because of the propaganda value that would result from its recapture (26.1.2-4; cf. 26.5.2, 26.16.13). As for the offences, the Capuans did not send Hannibal to attack Rome, contrary to what Vibius says at 26.13.6: it was Hannibal's spontaneous choice, and done without their prior knowledge (26.7).

So Livy sets up the Capuan surrender in such a way as to leave both possible outcomes available and indeed plausible: the Romans may show mercy (as is eventually predicted by the Capuans, and as was guaranteed by a promise which may or may not have expired) or they may punish the Capuans relentlessly (as was originally feared by the Capuans in spite of the Romans' promise, and as was graphically foretold by Vibius Virrius). And that question remains open even after the surrender, because there is immediately a dispute between the two proconsuls, Appius Claudius and Fulvius Flaccus, the former of whom wants to pardon the Capuans, while the latter is harsher (26.15.1). Claudius proposes to refer the matter to the Senate, presumably on the assumption that they will share his view that mercy is preferable, though the specific—and apparently disingenuous[105]—reason he gives is to allow the Senate to question the Capuans about the other allies' support for their revolt

---

[105] Fulvius is no less disingenuous in his response, however: he claims that he does not want to place the allies at risk of unjust accusations (26.15.4), when his real aim is manifestly to be able to execute the Capuans without senatorial interference.

(26.15.2–3). That dispute between the commanders draws on but also extends the contrasts between other pairs of commanders in the work, some of which I discussed in Chapter 3. The issue of the proper treatment of defeated enemies has already been emphasized with Marcellus at Syracuse in Book 25, and will continue to be explored through the contrast between him and Fabius in Book 27, and through the magnanimity of Scipio, especially at the end of Book 26 and with the defeat of Carthage in Book 30. But here the description of Claudius and Fulvius aligns that question with the old issue of 'rash commanders' versus 'cautious commanders'. There is obviously no reason why rashness in battle should correlate to harsh treatment of the defeated or *vice versa*, but Livy hints at such a correlation. Fulvius, like Flaminius or Varro, 'speaks defiantly' (26.15.5 *ferociter loquentem*) and seeks to circumvent the instructions he receives from the Senate: Appius, on the other hand, appears simply to assume that Fulvius will wait, and so does nothing active to oppose him—if indeed he has the opportunity, a matter which, as we shall shortly see, Livy leaves surprisingly open.

For Livy first sets up a clear story and then carefully muddles it. His initial account is that Fulvius, though receiving orders from the Senate in support of Appius' plan to defer the punishment, deliberately evades those orders (26.15.6). First he dashes to Teanum so as to be able to execute the twenty-eight Capuan senators held there before even hearing from the Senate (26.15.7–8). Then he rides to Cales, where he receives the Senate's instructions; but he does not open the message until after he has completed the executions (26.15.8–10), on the (correct) assumption that it was ordering him to spare the prisoners. But Livy then confuses the issue by immediately citing a series of alternative versions. First, he questions the dispute between Claudius and Fulvius, suggesting that Claudius might have died before the Capuans surrendered (26.16.1): in this version his advocacy of mercy—if it existed at all—never had a chance of being put into practice. Another alternative is that Fulvius actually did read the Senate's letter—but that the letter, rather than ordering him to remit the prisoners to the Senate, gave him the right to make the final decision for himself (26.16.4). The fact that this is cited only as an alternative to the main story would tend to lead the reader to place less weight on it—except that the subsequent narrative makes sense only on the second version. Fulvius' next act is to move from Capua to Atella and Calatia and execute the Capuan senators held there (26.16.5), which indicates that even after reading the Senate's letter he was still willing to continue the policy of executions. Indeed, it emerges from 26.17.1 that the Capuans' punishment described in detail in 26.16.6–13, which appeared to be Fulvius' initiative, was in fact the punishment that the

Senate had decreed.[106] In other words, Livy does here precisely the same thing as I showed that he did with the chronological discrepancy at 21.15 (above, 59–60): he uses his discussion of alternative versions in order to make a transition between a narrative sequence dependent on one version and a sequence dependent on a second, incompatible one. In the first version the Senate, like Appius, is merciful and Fulvius deliberately sabotages their policy; in the second Appius has disappeared from the scene and the Senate has given Fulvius permission to carry out his harsh policy. The ambiguous picture of Roman harshness and mercy that has been running through the story of Capua remains thus far unresolved.

Nor are the terms of the Capuans' punishment easy to make sense of. They consist not only of executing the Capuan senators, but also of imprisoning several hundred noblemen and selling the great mass of the Campanians into slavery (26.16.6). The city is left intact, populated by foreigners, freedmen, and workers, but it is deprived of all independent political structures, and ownership of all the land is handed over to the Romans (26.16.7–10). Livy in his own voice praises this solution as the ideal combination of harshness towards the guilty and mildness towards the physical town (26.16.11–13), and it partly—but only partly—gives the lie to Vibius Virrius, since he had wrongly foretold that the Romans would destroy the city, though he was right to anticipate the ill treatment of the populace (26.13.14-16). This thus appears to resolve the ambiguities by showing how the Romans synthesize their instincts towards harshness and mercy into a single effective policy.

However, the issue of the punishment of the Capuans recurs the following year, which introduces a new set of complications. Here, in response to the Capuans' appeal, the senators reach a decision which is similar but not identical to their earlier one. Two Capuan women who had helped Rome have their property and freedom restored (26.34.1); other Capuans have their property confiscated and they and their families are sold into slavery (26.34.3); others are imprisoned to await later judgement, while still others are allowed to keep their property intact (26.34.4). All movable property, including animals and female and child slaves, is restored to its owners (26.34.5); all Campanians, save those who actively served with Hannibal, are allowed to be free but not to possess Roman citizenship or Latin status (26.34.6–7). Finally the entire population is expelled from the city and surrounding region, though sent to different places and with different restrictions placed on them depending on the degree of their guilt in the defection

---

[106] Cf. Ungern-Sternberg (1975: 81–2); as he observes, the terms in which the punishment is described make more sense as an account of a senatorial decision than as something decided by the proconsul in the field.

(26.34.7–10). This decree is in some respects less sweeping than the previous one—in particular, more account seems to be taken of individual guilt or innocence, and the bulk of the population is expelled rather than being enslaved *en masse*. On the other hand, the earlier decree explicitly ensures that a rump population remains in order to work the city and its lands, whereas the later decree appears to strip Capua of almost all of its inhabitants.[107] But either way the Capuans are presented as deserving their punishment: just as before Livy praised the Senate's wisdom, so here he ends the scene with the Capuans ceasing to blame the Romans and attributing their fate to the gods and their bad fortune—though not, perhaps revealingly, their own moral missteps (26.34.13).

The usual understanding of this is that it is a doublet: there was only one senatorial decree, but Livy has read it in two separate places in his sources (albeit in slightly different versions) and has therefore recorded it twice. As a matter of historical reality that may well be correct: it seems unlikely that the Senate would pass two decrees in successive years with such similar terms.[108] But even if that is true, Livy's account is not the result of inadvertent doubling (cf. above, 54–5), but rather recreates the earlier episode in a new way: the Senate is offering a new version of their earlier decision. The Capuans appeal directly to the Senate for protection, and this time make an argument which they had not used previously: that they themselves were closely tied to Rome by blood and marriage, and indeed hold Roman citizenship (26.33.3).[109] This point is then addressed by M. Atilius Regulus, who, though hostile to the Capuans, accepts that any decree affecting citizen rights has to be ratified by the people (26.33.10–11): a plebiscite authorizing senatorial action is then passed (26.33.12–14). The implication is that the previous senatorial decree was invalid in as much as it failed to take Roman citizenship into account. But that point is never made explicitly—it would, after all, mean stating directly that the Senate had violated citizen rights. Instead one gets two separate versions of the punishment of Capua, both of which are apparently justifiable, but which respond to different conditions.

But this second version has moral complexities of its own. As before, the Capuans have to contend not only with the Senate, but with the harsher

---

[107] We may contrast here Zonaras 9.6, who is explicit that the second decree was harsher than the first, and interprets this as punishment for the Capuans' accusations against Fulvius, which were delivered too boldly as a result of their 'ignorance' (ἀπαιδευσίας).

[108] So e.g. de Sanctis (1968: 330–1), Ungern-Sternberg (1975: 81–9), Frederiksen (1984: 244–6), Urso (1995), Pobjoy (1996: 6). However some historians (e.g. Briscoe 1989: 77; Pina Polo 2006: 181–2) accept Livy's account of two separate senatorial decrees.

[109] Compare the similar point that Livy had made in his initial account of the Capuan defection (esp. 23.4.7); cf. also above, 222–7.

instincts of Fulvius. The Capuans' complaint to Laevinus concerns Fulvius' cruelty, rather than the senatorial decision (26.27.10, 26.27.15–16).[110] He insists to Laevinus on the justifiability of their punishment, given the unparalleled hatred of Capua for Rome, and warns against even allowing them to enter the city (26.27.11–14). And while Fulvius does not attend the Senate, his legates do, and their spokesman, Atilius Regulus, endorses his harsh actions (26.33.7–9). And on the face of things, Fulvius' treatment of the Capuans is ultimately endorsed by the Senate, exactly as it was first time round. But Livy's detailed account leads to another conclusion. Fulvius' explanation for his harshness towards Capua is that the Capuans are universally and irredeemably hostile to Rome. Likewise Regulus claims that no one except the two women he names showed any support for Rome, and that the guilt in the defection was universally shared in the population—those executed were singled out because of their greater *dignitas*, not their greater *culpa* (26.33.9). And this interpretation of the Capuans' actions appears to be supported by the episode directly prior to their appeal to Laevinus, where a group of Capuans commit arson in Rome (26.27.1–9)[111]—something that Fulvius immediately cites as proof of the danger that Capua poses (26.27.13–14).

Yet this picture of Capua as the site of universal and undifferentiated anti-Roman feeling is repeatedly undermined. The arsonists are said to have been motivated by the fact that their fathers had been the victims of Fulvius' executions (26.27.7)—in other words, they are acting on a private grudge, not demonstrating the universal unreliability of the nation, and Fulvius' harsh treatment of them appears to have been self-defeating. Fulvius' description of the Capuans as 'wild beasts' (26.27.12 *feras bestias*) appears exaggerated, not least because it recalls precisely the same phrase that Vibius Virrius had used of the Romans in arguing that the Capuans should not surrender (26.13.12). And the Senate's decree this time—unlike the version in 26.16—rejects rather than endorses Fulvius' approach.[112] Whereas Fulvius and his supporter Regulus premised their case on the undifferentiated guilt of the Capuans, the bulk of the Senate's decision is precisely founded on differentiations between levels

---

[110] Cf. Ungern-Sternberg (1975: 84–5), who uses this as the key evidence to show that the inconsistency is simply the result of Livy drawing on a different version of the story. This overlooks the greater rhetorical effectiveness of an appeal against an individual; it is also relevant that Livy is carefully constructing the episode as a parallel to the Syracusans' complaint against the alleged cruelty of Marcellus.

[111] See Briquel (2002) for an exhaustive analysis of the historical background to this episode.

[112] Appius is no longer in the picture here, since he is said to have died 'after the capture' (26.33.4 *post captam*). This implies that we are now assuming the version in which he had opposed Fulvius' treatment of the Capuans on the city's surrender, and consequently that Livy has retreated from the version at 26.16.1 (above, 369) in which Appius died before Capua fell.

of Capuan guilt. People who served with Hannibal are treated more harshly than those who did not. Those who remained in Capua during the siege are treated more harshly than those who did not. Those who were in Capua during the defection are treated more harshly than those who were not. Those who went over to Rome before Hannibal's arrival in Capua are treated more leniently still, being kept close to the city. It is true that most Capuans suffer to some degree, but Fulvius' universal attack on them is not endorsed. In other words, whereas in the first account of the Capuans' punishment Livy started by indicating a division between the harshness of Fulvius and the leniency of the Senate, only to alter the version into one where the Senate endorses Fulvius' harshness, here he returns to the earlier division, and shows the Senate rejecting Fulvius' assessment in devising the punishment. The punishment is, as I said, similar (though not identical) in both cases. The primary change is the way Livy sets it in dialogue with more brutal alternatives.

This second account of the Capuans' punishment is not only set against Fulvius' approach, however; it also is influenced by the wider narrative. The Capuans' appeal to Rome does not come in isolation, but is closely linked with a similar appeal by the Syracusans. The plan for the Syracusans to address the Senate had admittedly been arranged slightly earlier (26.26.5–9), but it is postponed until the arrival of Laevinus, who accordingly reaches Rome with both Sicilians and Capuans in his train and appears to be supporting both (26.27.16–17). There are moreover obvious parallels between the Syracusans' case and the Capuans'. Both have abandoned their alliance with Rome in favour of Carthage, both have now been recaptured by the Romans, and are primarily complaining about their harsh treatment by the commander who captured their city (Marcellus in the case of the Syracusans, Fulvius for the Capuans), and Marcellus in his defence associates himself with Fulvius as the object of (implicitly unjust) criticism (26.30.12). The moral issue in the case of Syracuse is no less complex than that of Capua, as I discussed in Chapter 3, although it is also quite different in its details. Marcellus' treatment of the Syracusans was less straightforwardly brutal than Fulvius' of the Capuans, but also exhibited a greater degree of evasiveness and moral complacency, as he failed to follow through his apparently merciful instincts. Moreover, the focus on the plunder of the city—something that does not appear to be a central concern with Capua, despite its proverbial wealth—is extremely uncomfortable (see above, 208–13). The Syracusans' arguments for their own innocence are largely disingenuous,[113] but their plight arouses sympathy in the Senate, especially because of the physical

---

[113] See Pelling (1989: 204–5).

despoliation of the city (26.32.4). The question of Syracusan guilt or innocence is also complex and nuanced, since their defection was bound up with
the actions of their autocratic rulers: even if that does not exculpate them as
completely as they hope, it is an excuse which, as Livy immediately observes
(26.33.2), the Capuans cannot use. The final decision (26.32.6) is that the
Senate ratifies Marcellus' past actions, but also takes direct oversight for the
future to ensure that the city is treated better subsequently: the Syracusans
have already (with Marcellus' agreement) achieved their aim of having him
removed from their province (26.29).

But even if the debate over the Syracusans is necessarily conducted in quite
different terms and reaches a different resolution from that over Capua, it is
still highly relevant to Livy's handling of the Capuan debate. For while the
Capuans are—justifiably—treated much more harshly by the Senate than
the Syracusans were, one essential feature remains the same: that the Senate,
while notionally ratifying the commander's approach, undermines it by
treating the captured city in quite different terms, ones which implicitly
undercut the claims of the commander to have acted appropriately. If we
ask why Livy not only returns to the Capuan episode after having apparently
resolved it in 26.16, but constructs the relationship between the commander's
approach and the Senate's differently from the way he had in 26.16, one likely
reason is that the way it is framed here is influenced by the parallel episode of
Marcellus and the Syracusans, an episode with which it is explicitly united and
compared.

Hence the recapture of Capua, like its defection, illustrates many of the
ways in which Livy sets up a narrative that does not work in terms of our ideas
of normal causal connection and sequence. In the capture of the city Livy
moves between two incompatible versions of events. The first gradually
establishes a division between the two commanders Appius and Fulvius, the
latter of whom undermines the Senate's attempt to block his brutal policies.
A moral resolution is reached, but only because the narrative switches to an
alternative version in which Appius has disappeared from the scene, with the
Senate and Fulvius working together. The episode is however repeated—again
partially inconsistently—in the following year, where a similar decision is
ultimately reached, but based partly on new considerations which were never
previously mentioned, and where the Senate's approach and Fulvius' once
again diverge. And in this second episode both the framing of the question
and the decision that is reached on it appear to be governed partly by what has
happened in the parallel case of Marcellus with which it is entwined.

All of this makes little sense if one is looking for a narrative where cause and
effect operate at a purely material level, since it depends on moving between
avowedly inconsistent accounts. It does, however, make sense in terms of

morality: the Romans twice debate the appropriate punishment of the Capuans, each time in a narrative in which different moral considerations are to the fore, and twice reach a resolution in which a balance is struck between mercy and harshness appropriate to those considerations. It moreover makes sense in terms of the overall movement of Livy's narrative, as the Capuan and Syracusan stories are wound up together in similar terms: this is then followed by Livy's famous accounting of the balance between the Romans and Carthaginians in the war at 26.37, which in turn is followed by the new departure as Scipio achieves his first victories in Spain. Those, it seems, are the primary ways in which causation in Livy is to be understood.

5.5. THE INTELLECTUAL CLIMATE

The example of Capua shows how completely the anomalous features of Livy's version of causation are interwoven with one another. Chronological dislocations, character discontinuities, apparently unexplained events, and connections governed by narrative junctures all sit side by side within a single sequence. The picture of the world that emerges is thus a very strange one. Yet in one respect it is reassuringly comprehensible as well. The single aspect of causation which controls our understanding of events when everything else appears to have broken down is also the one which is the most readily familiar, namely the moral one. The most straightforward way of understanding what Livy is doing with his causal sequences is to see the moral question as primary, and everything else as ancillary to that. Things in Livy happen above all because that is the right way for them to happen. Moral behaviour comes out on top, immoral behaviour meets with disaster. And if in practice the consequences of action in Livy are generally more complex and double-edged than that, this is a fair reflection of the fact that although Livy is clear that morality and immorality meet with appropriate consequences, the possiblility of clear moral judgement in any individual episode is tempered by his preference for the morally complex, and his tendency to shape his account in order to highlight the moral problems inherent in human action rather than to produce a clear and unambiguous answer to those problems.

Yet that is not a fully satisfactory answer to the problem of anomalous causation in Livy. Granted that he shows us a world which makes sense in moral terms; this does not do nearly enough to explain why he is prepared to organize it so strangely in other terms. It may be that, as I suggested in the case of Capua, he is using these causal anomalies precisely in order to invite the reader to interpret events less in the light of material events and more in terms of the moral sphere. As I discussed in Chapters 2 and 4, Livy challenges the rationalist picture of the world propagated by Polybius, under which there is (or should be) a clear connection between plans and outcomes, and accordingly, rational commanders typically meet with success. Livy describes a world where things can and do happen for no material reason, where attempts by commanders to plan rationally fail as often as they succeed, but where victory may follow nevertheless. His treatment of causation is of a piece with that non-rationalist and non-mechanical image of the world: he repeatedly shows us that it is a vain exercise to seek to interpret the world in purely material terms. But even so, it remains extremely uncomfortable that Livy's picture of events is so remote from one that we can recognize. As an historian, Livy purports to represent reality; yet a universe full of causal anomalies is one which is hard for us to see as a representation of reality. My aim in this section, therefore, is to argue that Livy's picture of causation is one that, if not precisely identical to that found in other ancient thinkers, at any rate appears less bizarre when seen in the light of those thinkers.[114]

Perhaps the most obvious—and useful—starting point is Stoicism. Admittedly, Livy's picture of causation is impossible to see as merely a Stoic one. For one thing, the Stoic picture of the universe was strongly materialist, and their notion of 'cause' was not only something corporeal, but something that actively produced an effect.[115] In consequence they required a material connection for causation to operate: the broader connections that are typical of Livy are hard to analyse closely in Stoic terms. For the same reason, the temporal dislocations that are among Livy's most rebarbative features are alien to Stoicism. It is true that Stoics distinguished different temporal fields in which causation could take place, separating those causes which were concomitant with their effects from those which were antecedent to them.[116] But there is no place in Stoic thought for causation which appears to be independent of any temporal sequence, let alone the wilder aspects of Livy's picture of the world, such as a causal sequence which depends on running together two avowedly incompatible time-frames.

---

[114] Compare Hunter (1982: 117–296) on the way in which for Herodotus and Thucydides the process of history implies an explanatory framework that is independent of any precisely calibrated chronological sequence. Her conclusions cannot be applied directly to Livy, since his chronological dislocations are more overt and he does not appear to have his Greek predecessors' interest in using their narratives to illustrate the working out of general theses about human behaviour and the world, which for Hunter is the key explanation for the apparent anomaly. But the comparison at all events demonstrates that Livy's oddities would not have appeared as unfamiliar to an ancient reader as they do to us.

[115] For the corporeality of Stoic causes, see e.g. Sextus Empiricus, *Adv. Math.* 9.211 = *SVF* II 341; for the Stoics' (influential) limitation of causes to active causes see Frede (1980).

[116] For this distinction see Bobzien (1999: 203–4).

But even if these features of Livy's picture of the world are not Stoic, there are parts of Stoicism that can help us make sense of some of them. Most important is the Stoic picture of a causal nexus: the idea that all events in the universe are bound together causally. One consequence of this is that all things are fated; but a no less important consequence for our purposes is that apparently unrelated events will turn out to be causally related, albeit indirectly, because there is a chain of causation that links all events, even if in practice we are unable to discern the individual links in that chain.

This, for a Stoic, had serious practical consequences, the most relevant of which here is the notion of sign-inference. In a variety of fields, ranging from divination to medicine, Stoics were prepared to deduce outcomes from signs that were apparently unrelated to those outcomes, arguing that although there was no discernible causal connection, the universal causal nexus meant that a connection necessarily existed beneath the surface, and it then simply became an empirical question to demonstrate that certain signs did indeed correlate with certain outcomes. This forms Cicero's explicit justification (in the mouth of Quintus) in *De Divinatione* for the validity of divination. He emphasizes (*Div.* 1.29) that he is not claiming that signs directly cause the outcomes, but that both the signs and the outcomes are connected through a general causal system established in such a way that the one always precedes the other (*Div.* 1.125–7):

fieri igitur omnia fato ratio cogit fateri. fatum autem id appello, quod Graeci εἱμαρμένην, id est ordinem seriemque causarum, cum causae causa nexa rem ex se gignat. ea est ex omni aeternitate fluens veritas sempiterna. quod cum ita sit, nihil est factum, quod non futurum fuerit, eodemque modo nihil est futurum, cuius non causas id ipsum efficientes natura contineat . . . ita fit, ut et observatione notari possit, quae res quamque causam plerumque consequatur, etiamsi non semper (nam id quidem adfirmare difficile est), easdemque causas veri simile est rerum futurarum cerni ab iis, qui aut per furorem eas aut in quiete videant.

    praeterea cum fato omnia fiant . . . si quis mortalis possit esse, qui conligationem causarum omnium perspiciat animo, nihil eum profecto fallat. qui enim teneat causas rerum futurarum, idem necesse est omnia teneat, quae futura sint. quod cum nemo facere nisi deus possit, relinquendum est homini, ut signis quibusdam consequentia declarantibus futura praesentiat. non enim illa, quae futura sunt, subito exsistunt, sed est quasi rudentis explicatio sic traductio temporis nihil novi efficientis et primum quidque replicantis. quod et ii vident, quibus naturalis divinatio data est, et ii, quibus cursus rerum observando notatus est. qui etsi causas ipsas non cernunt, signa tamen causarum et notas cernunt.

Therefore reason compels us to admit that everything happens by fate. I am calling 'fate' what the Greeks call *heimarmene*, namely the order and sequence of causes, since cause bound to cause produces something out of itself. That is an everlasting truth flowing from all eternity. Since this is so, nothing happens that was not going to be, and similarly nothing is going to be where Nature does not contain the causes bringing that very thing about...So it happens that it can be known even by observation what thing generally—even if not invariably (for that is certainly difficult to assert)—follows what cause, and it is likely that the same causes of future events are seen by those who see them either in a state of madness or in sleep.

Besides, since all things happen by fate...if there can be any mortal who mentally perceives all of the chain of causes, certainly nothing would deceive him. For the person who apprehends the causes of future events necessarily apprehends all things that will happen. But since no one except a god can do this, it must be left to man to foresee the future by means of certain signs which declare what will follow. For those things that will be do not suddenly come into existence, but, like the unfurling of a rope, the passage of time produces nothing new but unfolds each thing one after the other. Those who have been granted natural divination see this, as do those who know it through observing the course of events. The latter admittedly do not see the causes themselves, but they recognize the signs and marks of causes.

It is reasonably likely that Cicero here is reproducing the argument of Posidonius, who is quoted at both the beginning and end of the section (*Div.* 1.125, 1.130);[117] but if so, Posidonius here is reflecting a broader Stoic position.[118] Both the universal causal nexus and the understanding of divination as a sign-system where the signs are not the direct causes of events but certain concomitants within that nexus are significant parts of the overall Stoic deterministic system.

Nothing of this intricate philosophical system, naturally, is present in Livy. But there are parts of its general conceptual framework that make it much easier to understand some of the oddities of causation within his narrative. In particular, the idea that the signs from which diviners work may in some sense be causally related to the outcomes without being direct causes of the outcomes is relevant not only to Livy's handling of prodigies and divination, but more broadly to his picture of atemporal causation. For if things may be related to other things even though appearing remote from them, with the connection formed by some unseen chain within the overall nexus of causes, there is no reason why those connections need to follow strict temporality. In practice in divination the sign that signals an effect precedes that effect, but there is no particular reason from the point of view of the Stoic causal system why it needs to (save, of course, for the important point that it would not be useful to the diviner if it did not).[119]

---

[117] So Long (1976: 75), Schäublin (1985: 163–7).

[118] Kidd (1988: 428); cf. Wardle (2006: 407). The exception was Panaetius, who appears to have rejected divination (Diogenes Laertius 7.149).

[119] This is not a negligible consideration, since another aspect of the Stoic theory of divination is that the system of signs and inferences is providentially established by the divine in order that humans may be able to profit from the knowledge that they offer. Indeed, the classic proof of divination offered by the Stoics depended on the idea that a providential universe would not leave humans bereft of such knowledge: see Cicero, *Div.* 1.82–4.

A sign of something can occur after the thing of which it was a sign, or before it, or simultaneously with it, but it is no less a sign of it, and no less connected to it indirectly through the causal chain. So too the idea that things remote from one another may be causally connected through that indirect chain is a familiar concept within the Stoic system. And above all, the central role that Livy gives to morality is likewise fundamental to the whole of the Stoic model. The nexus of causes is not merely a mechanical consequence of actions and interactions, but is controlled by a divine mind which is itself a moral force organizing the world according to a moral system.

One might in this context speculate whether Livy's presentation of causation might owe anything to the way in which Posidonius handled the topic in his own history, but unfortunately not nearly enough of the latter survives to allow much more than speculation.[120] In one respect, however, Livy appears highly un-Posidonian, and thus unlikely to derive from Posidonius' own historical practice. As I have explained, Livy signals the failure of mechanical causation by having outcomes determined by events which are themselves not fully explained. Posidonius, however, regarded it as important to explore the entire chain of causes—he appears to have placed particular emphasis on searching them out and explaining them.[121] Livy in this aligns himself more closely with orthodox Stoic positions: Chrysippus in particular believed that not all causes were capable of being apprehended, and that some would inevitably remain opaque.[122] Livy's history illustrates the point graphically.

I should emphasize, however, that Livy's position overall is far from being a Stoic one. The most obvious difference is that the Stoics did not see divinatory signs as causes: they may be indirectly connected with certain other events through the broader nexus, but are not themselves causes of those events.[123] Hence while signs may be remote or indeed atemporal for Stoics, causation certainly is not, as I have already observed. For Livy the distinction

---

[120] See, however, Malitz (1983: 415–22), who suggests that in general Posidonius' history was designed to show that historical events were all connected within an ethically governed universe. Note also the arguments of Kidd (1989) and Hahm (1989: 1357–61) that Posidonius saw history as ancillary to ethics, being a way of illustrating ethical causation which does not involve the rigorous analysis of philosophy but supplies practical if less systematic examples.

[121] See in particular Posidonius T85 (Edelstein–Kidd) = Strabo 2.3.8 and F165.75–102 (Edelstein–Kidd); cf. Kidd (1971: 210–11). Admittedly Strabo reports this in the context of Posidonius' scientific rather than his historical writing, but it seems a plausible inference that Posidonius applied similar methods to history (compare Kidd 1988: 72–4). See Malitz (1983: 410–11), who suggests that it was precisely this interest in determining causes that led Posidonius to write history in the first place; cf. Kidd (1989: 49).

[122] *SVF* II 351, 973; Strabo 2.3.8 suggests that by contrast Posidonius' practice owed more to Aristotle than to Stoicism.

[123] Compare Long (1982: 170–1).

between the two does not appear to be significant: it is virtually impossible to understand (for example) the connection between Hannibal's arrival in Gaul and the revolt of the Boii (above, 335) in terms of 'signs' rather than actual causes. But the fact that the Stoic system allowed for connections which are both atemporal and have a causal dimension (even while not actually being causes) makes it easy to see how a writer with a conceptual framework in which causes and signs were not sharply distinguished could regard the atemporality of causes or lack of proximity to their effects as an acceptable understanding of the way the world works—especially given that he shared with the Stoics an understanding of the central role of morality within the causal system.

This takes us some way down the road to explaining how Livy's version of causation might have appeared less bizarre within contemporary intellectual culture than one might initially have suspected. Moreover, there is another aspect of Stoic metaphysics which is perhaps even more relevant, not least because it represents a strand of ancient thought that extended well beyond Stoics: the concept of cosmic sympathy. This too is referred to by Cicero in *De Divinatione*, albeit in the sceptical response rather than in Quintus' original presentation of the arguments in favour of divination (2.34):

quid de fretis aut de marinis aestibus plura dicam, quorum accessus et recessus lunae motu gubernantur? sescenta licet eiusdem modi proferri, ut distantium rerum cognatio naturalis appareat. demus hoc; nihil enim huic disputationi adversatur; num etiam, si fissum cuiusdam modi fuerit in iecore, lucrum ostenditur? qua ex coniunctione naturae et quasi concentu atque consensu, quam συμπάθειαν Graeci appellant, convenire potest aut fissum iecoris cum lucello meo aut meus quaesticulus cum caelo, terra rerumque natura?

Why should I say more about the straits or the tides of the sea, whose ebb and flow are governed by the movement of the moon? Let us bring forward thousands of examples of that sort, so that the natural affinity of distant things appears. Let us grant that; for it provides no objection to the current argument; surely, if there is some sort of fissure in a liver, no gain is indicated by it? What conjunction of nature and (so to speak) harmony and concord, which the Greeks call *sympatheia*, can match either a fissure of a liver with my petty profits or my wretched income with the heavens, the earth, the nature of the universe?

It is important first to recognize that the argument here concerns something different from what I was discussing earlier, although it looks superficially similar.[124] The previous discussion concerned the possibility that apparently unrelated things were nevertheless *indirectly* connected through the long chains of causation which govern the world. Cicero's argument here is against

---

[124] For the distinction cf. Hankinson (1988: 149–53).

a different claim: that certain aspects of nature that are apparently unrelated may affect one another *directly,* because they are in natural harmony with one another—something he is prepared to grant in principle, at least for the sake of argument, but where he denies that the specific connections postulated by the diviners can fall into those categories. Belief in such natural harmonies was a Stoic position,[125] but more generally it was a view held widely in many intellectual movements: that certain things were able to affect other things through natural sympathy with or antipathy to them.[126] So, for example, Pliny in the final book of his *Natural History* claims that his entire work has been devoted to explicating the principles of sympathy and antipathy under-lying the universe;[127] theories of both astrology[128] and alchemy[129] were founded in notions of natural sympathies, and the former at least was widely practised and believed. Above all it was a fundamental principle of much ancient medicine,[130] which prescribed therapy on the basis of these presumed sympathies and antipathies between parts of the human body and various external agents.[131] And related to all of these, though partly distinct from them, was the even more widespread acceptance of magic, the practice which frequently assumed causation over distances of both time and space based merely on affinities between the devices used by the magician and the effect that the magician intended to produce.[132]

---

[125] See e.g. Sextus Empiricus, *Adv. Math.* 9.78–9 = *SVF* II 1013. Reinhardt (1926) argues that the doctrine was not part of earlier Stoicism, but was incorporated into it by Posidonius; see however *contra* Kidd (1988: 423–5).

[126] See e.g. Stemplinger (1919: esp. 5–32), Préaux (1973: esp. 9–57).

[127] Pliny, *NH* 37.59: *totis voluminibus his docere conati sumus de discordia rerum concordia-que, quam antipathian Graeci vocavere ac sympathian*; cf. *NH* 20.1-2, 24.1, 29.61. On the significance of these concepts in Pliny's thought see Gaillard-Seux (2003), Gaide (2003: 129–44).

[128] Sextus Empiricus reports that astrologers 'say that the seven stars offer a foundation of efficient causes for making each of the things that happen in life occur' (*Adv. Math.* 5.5 δραστικῶν μὲν αἰτιῶν λόγον ἐπέχειν φασὶν εἰς τὸ ἕκαστον τῶν κατὰ τὸν βίον συμβαινόντων ἐκβαίνειν τοὺς ἑπτὰ ἀστέρας). Cf. Préaux (1973: 14–18).

[129] On alchemy see Keyser (1990: esp. 360–1).

[130] Pliny, *NH* 29.61 offers it as a widely-held generalization that 'medicines are produced from that sympathy or antipathy of the universe' (*illa concordia rerum aut repugnantia medi-cinae gignuntur*); cf. *NH* 24.1–4.

[131] On sympathy in ancient medicine see e.g. Stemplinger (1919); Keyser (1997); Gaide (2003). Galen, *On the Natural Faculties* 1.14–15 (44–60) (cf. also 2.3 (80–8), 2.7 (106–7), 3.15 (206–7)) offers a lengthy and polemical demonstration that certain substances intrinsically possess attractive and repulsive forces towards other substances, and that this both controls the natural functions of the body and should govern therapeutic treatments: Galen contrasts this with the mechanistic explanations of such attractions and repulsions posited by thinkers like Epicurus.

[132] On ancient ideas of magical causation see Collins (2003: 17–49). He argues (2003: 37–44) that it is a mistake to see concepts of natural sympathy at work in ancient magic, but fails to observe how closely analogous magical practices were to other ancient disciplines in which such 'sympathy' was explicitly adduced as an explanation, which at least suggests that by the Roman

Here too nothing in Livy directly suggests that he was working within such a theoretical framework—although it would not in fact be especially surprising if he was tacitly subscribing to aspects of it, given that notions of natural sympathy were widespread and not confined to a particular philosophical dogma. But the fact that he was writing in an intellectual climate in which it was widely accepted that even without a direct mechanical connection, things could and did influence one another simply through some form of natural affinity, goes some way towards explaining why his picture of causation depends so heavily on what appear to a modern reader very loose connections between cause and effect, and indeed connections which seem at time to consist of little more than seeing one event as a reaction to another proximate event. While it would once again be hard to trace the specifics of such a theory through the particular examples of causation in Livy's history[133]—and there is no reason to think that Livy himself either did trace it or expected the reader to do so—it unquestionably helps us to understand his approach if we appreciate that he was writing in a world in which the remoteness of a connection was not in principle a sign of a lack of connection.

Livy's notions of historical causality, in short, may look bizarre, but they also are in many respects comprehensible when set against broader ancient concepts of causation and connection, even if they extend rather than precisely replicated those concepts. But this still leaves a serious difficulty, one which the discussion so far has skirted around rather than confronted directly. Part of Livy's anomalous presentation of causation, as I set it out in this and earlier chapters, concerns not merely connections that would appear loose or indeed counterintuitive to the modern reader, but things which he himself indicates do not represent reality. A prime example is his account of the chronology of the first year of the war (above, 56–61), where he indicates the incompatibility of the two possible versions, but uses that discussion to move between them, so conflating them into a single sequence of events which his own account has already demonstrated could not have occurred in that form. And there are many other cases where it seems unlikely that the causal sequence is one that Livy or his readers could genuinely have expected to have happened in the way he presents it. Examples include the arguments of the Cannae veterans to Marcellus (above, 337–9), which Livy constructs as if they were addressed

---

period magic would have been interpreted in those terms (as it certainly was by Plotinus, *Enneads* 4.4.40–4, admittedly in a philosophical context). See Gordon (1999: 184–5, 232–9); on the blurred line between medical and magical notions of 'sympathy' see Keyser (1997).

[133] Compare Clarke (1999a: 185–92) for a (slightly strained) attempt to argue that Posidonius' historical work reflected Stoic notions of cosmic sympathy.

to the Senate—although they were not—and which assume circumstances which are not in fact the circumstances under which the speech was ostensibly delivered. Then there is the circular reasoning which leaves the Sicilians' visit to Marcellus and to Syracuse each as the cause and the effect of the other (above, 331–4), or Livy's account of the battle of Silpia (above, 296–8), which seems to depend on simultaneously accepting two incompatible accounts of the relative size of the armies.

This is an area where examination of the philosophical and broader intellectual background is unlikely to be helpful. The problem is a contradiction between the nature of Livy's text, which is self-consciously moving away from a direct representation of reality, and what appear to be the assumptions of the genre of historiography, that what is represented should be an accurate—or at any rate a plausible—reflection of reality. Livy's technique, as I briefly noted in Chapter 1 (above, 61) may be paralleled in verse, but that is a genre which does not usually purport to—and is not assumed by readers to—represent literal truth. Historiography is another matter.[134] The only way that such a contradiction can be resolved is to consider the nature of the genre itself. And this brings me to the final conclusions of this book.

Scholarly dispute over the nature of ancient historiography has subsided in recent years after a great deal of activity in the late 1980s and early 1990s,[135] but the argument has still not reached a firm resolution.[136] The problem is

---

[134] Thus O'Hara (2007: 43–4) argues that the chronological inconsistencies in Catullus 64 (above, 61) are there precisely to accentuate the readers' awareness of the poem's fictionality. Whether or not that is true of Catullus, Livy is unlikely to be readily interpreted in those terms, as I shall explain.

[135] The key work in this debate is Woodman (1988), itself a more radical and systematic development of ideas put forward by Wiseman (1979, 1981) and Woodman (1983). Other important contributions include Wheeldon (1989), Pelling (1990c), Feichtinger (1992), Moles (1993a), Rhodes (1994), Bosworth (2003). The debate has been influenced by the wider debate over the relationship between history, truth, and fiction initiated by the work of Hayden White, although the issues are distinct, since the generic boundaries of ancient historiography are universally accepted to be to some degree different from its modern counterpart. I shall be discussing some of these questions further below.

[136] The most recent (and rather overwritten) salvo, by Lendon (2009), scores one good point in noting that literary scholars have often failed to pay sufficient attention to Roman historians' own claims of veridicity and to evaluate the genre accordingly, but unfortunately most of the essay descends into an exercise in throwing out a large number of babies along with a small draining of bathwater. I shall here simply mention two of the points where Lendon's eager polemic has drawn him into conceptual problems that undermine his entire position. One is his heavy and repeated reliance on Livy's demonstrably faithful dependence on Polybius in the Fourth and Fifth Decades, from which Lendon extrapolates that Roman historians in general were equally respectful of their sources (Bosworth 2003: 172–5 makes a similar point). As I proved at length in Chapter 2 (above, 126–63), this argument is circular on more than one level, and a fuller accounting of Livy's use of Polybius shows how extensively he is prepared to transform his predecessor's entire narrative when it suits his wider narrative aims. A second

straightforward to state. On the one hand historians like Livy purport to be describing real events, and are usually—if not invariably—taken by other writers who draw material from them to be describing real events.[137] Moreover, on many—though certainly not even close to all—of the occasions when we can test them they demonstrably *are* describing real events, even if they apply some literary colour which may change the tenor of the narrative. On the other hand, those same historians at other times no less demonstrably invent and distort in ways that go well beyond the application of literary colour: it appears to involve outright fiction. This is uncomfortable. The sheer extent of invention precludes reading historians merely as factual accounts. Yet it is no less unsatisfactory to read historiography as a brand of fiction, without taking into account that historians both claim to be, are regularly assumed by others to be, and in fact often are, representing the truth. Few if any scholars are prepared in practice to eschew employing historians as evidence for the events they describe, given their central importance for providing our entire narrative framework for the ancient world, and, more significantly, given the reasonable inductive argument that if the testable portion of their material is very often accurate, we should be able to assume that the non-testable parts are also.

I do not intend here to rehash this entire debate, which necessarily draws on a wide range of evidence from a wide variety of historians and other ancient sources. The relevant point here is to see that the aspects of Livy under discussion in this chapter must significantly affect the terms in which the debate is constructed. For even the most radical scholars rarely deny that ancient historians generally purported to represent reality (save only for those times when the historians themselves note their distance from the time they describe or lack of reliable sources for it and accordingly present their

---

problem is that in extending his attack to those scholars whose approaches are informed by varieties of modern literary or political theory, Lendon is led (largely, it seems, by dislike of their writing styles) into the absurd claim that no account of an ancient historian can be considered acceptable unless couched in terms that the historian himself would have found familiar—as if a writer can only be doing things which he can articulate as a conscious intention. Even those who, like myself, regard writers' intentions as not merely legitimate but important objects of study, rarely do (and never should) regard them as the sole legitimate object of study. For a lucid explanation of this, see Heath (2002).

[137] This point is stressed by, in particular, Wheeldon (1989) and Lendon (2009), who between them supply a number of examples. As is noted by Wiseman (1993: 122–5), there is an alternative view, represented by Seneca, *NQ* 7.16.1–2 and *Historia Augusta* 2.1–2, that historians as a class falsify the truth (one can of course add many more examples of individual historians who are accused by others of misrepresentation on particular occasions, as Wiseman extensively discusses). However, Bosworth (2003: 169–70) observes that Seneca at least is inconsistent in this, since elsewhere in *Natural Questions* he is perfectly prepared to use data from historians when it suits his purposes.

accounts with appropriate caveats).[138] So Woodman, who presents the most rigorously thought out and far-reaching explanations for the capacity and willingness of ancient historians for outright invention, arguing that historiography was seen as a branch of rhetoric and that its truth-claims were accordingly evaluated in a manner comparable to those of rhetoric,[139] nevertheless accepts that historians expected their works to be at least plausible to their readers, just as orators did.[140] Yet in Livy we have an historian who presents narrative sequences which are avowedly impossible in the terms in which he sets them up, and not because he regards the period as one that is inaccessible, but simply because that allows him to create a narrative that makes sense of his wider moral and political themes. Since the impossibility of the narrative sequence in Book 21 emerges from Livy's own explicit argument, it follows that he expects his readers to recognize its impossibility. So it cannot be a sufficient explanation to suggest that he is simply creating a plausible and persuasive account as an orator might do. An orator might covertly produce an impossible narrative, but it is unlikely that he would actively draw attention to its impossibility, or expect it to be persuasive in the event that he were to do so. It is true that one can find analogies to these moments in Livy in more widely recognized and accepted practices of ancient historians, such as the habit of reporting stories which one then claims not to believe, so achieving the colour and innuendo supplied by those stories while simultaneously critically undermining them.[141] But the resulting narrative in such cases is rarely impossible: it will make sense even if the crucial episode is detached. In Livy's account of the first year of the war the story cannot be read independently of either version, since each supplies a crucial segment of the account which is not present in the other. Yet reading them together creates a story which demonstrably cannot have occurred.

Some more fruitful analogies emerge from Pelling's account of Plutarch's practice. He extends Wiseman and Woodman in one crucial direction: whereas they suggested that the historians' justification for their superstructure of invention was that it 'must have happened that way',[142] Pelling argues that the occasions where Plutarch presents things that 'must have happened like that' shade into occasions where Plutarch must have known that it in fact

---

[138] Plutarch, *Theseus* 1 is a clear example of such caveats: for an interesting discussion of Plutarch's handling of the truthfulness of his *Theseus–Romulus* pair, see Pelling (2002: 171–95).

[139] See esp. Woodman (1988: 70–116, 197–215).

[140] E.g. Woodman (1988: 91–3).

[141] Lateiner (1989: 76–84) is thought-provoking on this: 'The historian finds cultural meaning and historical significance even in fictions . . . false or inadequate histories can contain valuable truths' (77).

[142] Wiseman (1981: 389), Woodman (1988: 93).

did not happen like that.[143] It is true that Pelling never mentions any place where Plutarch presents an account that *could not be true* in the abstract; but he certainly demonstrates numerous points where Plutarch presents an account which not only was not true but which *he knew was not true*, but which he was nevertheless prepared to include in pursuit of his wider aims—the phrase Pelling uses here is 'true enough'. Indeed, one of Pelling's examples is of Plutarch chronologically rearranging what he knew to be the correct order of events in Caesar's early career in order to provide a neater sequence.[144] It is not a great step from that to Livy's willingness not only to manipulate chronology to present an account that is 'true enough', but to do so in a way that draws the readers' attention to the fact that it is no more than 'true enough'.

Even so, that willingness remains startling, because it seems to challenge so directly the usual expectations of the genre. Historians do not generally actively present their own account as impossible, even though they may hedge it with all sorts of caveats about the limitations of their sources or possible alternative versions.[145] Yet that is what Livy appears to do on the occasions I have considered here. In my earlier book on Livy I discussed what appears superficially to be a similar case:[146] where Livy narrates supernatural events while signalling two alternative and incompatible interpretations of those events, one in which they are genuine and expressions of the gods' will, one in which they are either imaginary or at least unconnected with the divine. I argued there that this was part of a strategy of involving the reader in the process of historical discovery, since in order to make sense of the narrative he is forced to take an active role, weighing up the evidence for each interpretation.[147] However, the passages we are now discussing are consider-

---

[143] Pelling (1990c: 35–52, revised in Pelling 2002: 152–61); cf. also along similar lines Moles (1988: 36–46), Feichtinger (1992), Moles (1993a: 115, 118–21). Compare Feichtinger (1992: 33) on Livy: 'Auch wenn Livius nicht *absolute Wahrheit* erzählt, offenbart er uns doch viel *Wahres* über Rom und seine Vergangenheit, was eine rein faktenorientierte Historiographie kaum vermöchte' [emphasis in original].

[144] Pelling (1990: 39 = Pelling 2002: 154–5); he originally discussed this and other similar examples in Pelling (1980: 128–9, revised in Pelling 2002: 92–3).

[145] Cf. Moles (1993a: 120–1) on what he sees as the rhetorical necessity in historiography 'to maintain the illusion of strict historicity'; in the context of Thucydides Gribble (1998) discusses the way in which authorial interventions are calibrated precisely so as to reinforce the sense of the text's historicity and its distance from fiction.

[146] Levene (1993: esp. 29–30). My reading of the double picture of religion in Livy has been challenged by Davies (2004: 21–142); but see *contra* Levene (2006b).

[147] On Livy's 'openness' cf. also more broadly Kraus (1994a: 13–15). The practice is, however, not unique to Livy, or indeed to historiography: see now the fundamental article by Starr (2001), who demonstrates through the practices and expectations of literary commentators in antiquity that readers were expected to be actively involved in creating the meaning of the work by selecting between possible interpretations.

ably more problematic. In the case of Livy's double-edged handling of the supernatural, either interpretation available to the reader would appear to work on its own terms even were the other one removed. But we have seen here several cases where Livy, for example, forms a single narrative by stringing together two avowedly incompatible accounts. Neither of those accounts can exist if the other is removed, because each only tells half the story; but the story that results from their combination is an impossible one, and it is hard to see how this leaves any opening for even an active reader to interpret it as something possible.

An alternative explanation might be to see Livy as a radical anti-realist, undermining his own account of the Hannibalic War in the interests of challenging the entire claim of historiography to tell the truth at all.[148] That is a type of reading towards which many modern scholars are instinctively sympathetic; but the problem is that it seems to create a distorted picture of the work. For one thing, as I have already observed, much of Livy's picture of the Hannibalic War is not affected by these anomalous features, even if they are more widespread than we find comfortable; nor are they generalized into wider comments about the problems of arriving at the truth. On the other hand, he does frequently make points which appear to be premised precisely on his general account of the past reflecting reality—not least in his discussion of and criticisms of other historians who may have failed to reflect reality as accurately as he has.[149]

But if this is an unacceptable conclusion, then we are inevitably led in the opposite direction: that in some sense, even when Livy presents impossible sequences of events, he is doing so on the understanding that he is not acting outside the generic limits of historiography—in other words, that he is actually offering the reader some form of the truth. And this returns me to an issue that I have already discussed in Chapter 1, as well as earlier in this chapter.

The oddity of causation in Livy's account of the Hannibalic War, as I have set it out here, is not simply that he presents impossible sequences of events, but that with some sequences of events, even when they are possible, he implies that they

---

[148] Compare the account of Livy's self-presentation by Miles (1995: 8–74). The bulk of Miles's account, however, centres on the period before the Gallic Sack, a period for which Livy expressly states that reliable historical material did not exist (6.1.2–3: cf. Plutarch, *Numa* 1.1, but see Cornell (1995: 24–6) and Oakley (1997: 381–2) for reasons to doubt that the Gallic Sack genuinely represented a watershed in the survival of authentic documentation). Miles (1995: 57–62) does argue that Livy's citations of variants and expressions of doubt later in his work show that his historiographic *aporia* extends to all history, not merely ancient history; but he has little evidence that Livy intends the reader to see any aspect of his narrative in those later books as doubtful, apart from the limited places where his sources are expressly said to be at variance.

[149] Cf. Wiehemeyer (1938).

are connected simply by virtue of being adjacent in his text. Moreover, some aspects of his chronology are likewise best explained in terms of the dominance of the text over literal chronological possibilities, such as his non-transitive concept of simultaneity, under which the forward movement of the narrative is assumed to take us forward in time even when literal chronological statements indicate that no such movement has taken place (above, 45–8). Likewise his handling of character, as I described it in Chapter 3, privileges the moral dynamic set out in his text over the ancients' more usual ideas of psychological consistency. Livy regularly writes, in other words, as if his text actually was a form of reality: that things are true simply in consequence of his having written them in a particular way. Livy literally has recreated the world of the past, one which may not—indeed, on his own account, sometimes manifestly does not—mirror consistently the past as it originally occurred, but which partially supersedes that with a reality of its own. Rome's past literally is what Livy has made of it.

That idea, I imagine, sounds bizarre to many of my readers—but not perhaps to as many as it should. That is because it bears a certain superficial resemblance to what is known as the 'linguistic turn', a scholarly approach to historiography which has become increasingly prominent in the last thirty-five years.[150] According to this body of scholarship, history cannot simply be reduced to a discipline in which evidence is rationally weighed and conclusions are reached accordingly. Historians construct their pictures of the past by selective forms of plotting which are in many respects identical with the techniques employed by the writers of fictional narrative.[151] Those plots (on this view) do not exist in history independent of the historian's writing about them, and there are many equally valid ways of plotting the same historical events. The historian creates the plot: he does not discover it.

Both opponents and supporters of this approach to historiography have sometimes sought to relate it to the claim (which did not originate in historiographical contexts) that it is not merely the 'plots', but the events themselves which do not exist independent of the texts describing them.[152] This has the

---

[150] It is associated above all with Hayden White (esp. 1973, 1978, 1987). The subsequent bibliography has been vast (see e.g. Ankersmit 1983, 1989a, 1989b, 2001; Cohen 1986; Hutcheon 1988: esp. 87–177; Jenkins 1991, 1999, 2003; Southgate 2003, 2005; Munslow 2006; cf. Koselleck 2004).

[151] So, for example, White (1978: 23, cf. also 46–7) accepts that 'knowledge of history' is possible—only then to undercut that by arguing that the sort of 'knowledge' at issue is no different from the 'knowledge' of the world that we may obtain from fictional texts or indeed other works of art.

[152] The claim is especially associated with thinkers like Richard Rorty (e.g. Rorty 1979; cf. also Brandom 2000) and Roland Barthes (1989: 127–40; cf. Ankersmit 1989a for a reading of historiography in Barthean terms). Rorty popularized the phrase 'linguistic turn' before it was specifically applied to historiography (see Rorty 1967). For an ancient historian who explicitly adopts a relativist standpoint see Fox (1996: 31–43). Opponents who interpret the 'linguistic

inevitable corollary that historical 'truth' is a chimera: for if there is no history outside texts, then there can be no reason to think that any text represents history more accurately than any other does. This extreme relativism, however, is (I venture to suggest) demonstrably absurd.[153] Our own lived experience of the world depends on our recognition that certain events happened and others did not. We may misremember or *mis*represent those events, but the very notion of misremembering or *mis*representing assumes that there are determinate events which can be relayed more or less accurately. Even if someone were to narrate an account of my family in which my parents were childless and where David Levene consequently does not exist, this would not mean that I cease to exist (or perhaps exist in an indeterminate state depending on whose narrative happened to be followed at any particular point). My own experience tells me that I exist, no matter what other people may narrate (or fail to narrate) about me. If this is true of our own experience, then it is no less true of the experiences of others, whether those others are in the present or past, alive or dead.

The example most often used, because of its sharp contemporary political implications for the relativist, is Holocaust denial, though countless other examples could be given as well. There are, as is well known, people who narrate a history of the twentieth century according to which the Holocaust never took place. The relativist either has to claim that this history is just as accurate as the standard one—and confront the survivors with that claim—or else has to acknowledge that some representations of the past are more accurate than others. Few professed relativists are prepared in practice to take the former step (though some seek to avoid the argument rather than addressing its implications directly). In practice the best-known proponents of the 'linguistic turn' are not (on their own showing) relativists in this sense: they see historians constructing history only within certain limits, they accept that there is a substratum of things that genuinely happened independent of any historical (or other) text, and they thus acknowledge that narratives may represent those things more or less accurately.[154]

---

turn' in historiography as entailing relativism include Mandelbaum (1980: 49–53), Evans (2000: 93–128, 238–43, 309–13).

[153] The refutation of relativism that I offer here is necessarily brief and sketchy. For a fuller and more systematic set of arguments see Boghossian (2006, esp. 25–57), though he does not mention the neo-Cartesian argument that I employ here. The radical claim that 'nothing exists outside texts' is given a superficial plausibility because it is sometimes confused with the less controversial claim that our knowledge of the past is acquired solely through texts. The latter claim may well be true, if we have a sufficiently expansive definition of a 'text' and a sufficiently restricted definition of 'knowledge of the past'; but it does not entail the broader metaphysical point that some would wish it to.

[154] E.g. White (1978: 81–100, 121; 1987: 40–9), Ankersmit (2001: 29–74, 249–61, see esp. 36: 'From whatever angle we choose to look at the linguistic turn it can never be construed as an attack on truth or a license for relativism'; also 53: 'My own interest in narrativism...has nothing whatsoever to do with a belittling of historical research, that is, with the process of gaining factual information about the past (to be expressed in true descriptions)'); Jenkins (1991: 32–6); cf. Carroll

Livy, however, did not have to confront the politics of Holocaust deniers, nor does he offer a systematic account of the relationship between historical events and historical texts that might meet the objections I have outlined above. Hence he can take the step that few today would, and indicate that his account of the Hannibalic War—although literally impossible—has actually constructed the war the way it happened. But he does not in fact seem to be an historical relativist—he does, as I observed above, repeatedly suggest that his own account of history is closer to the truth than that provided by some of his predecessors—although were he to take his practice to its logical conclusion it is hard to see how he could avoid relativism. His position seems rather to be that his account creates the history: he does not make any comparable claims for other historians. And since his account creates the history, it also creates—and thus represents—the truth.

In case it is still not obvious, I do not believe Livy's position to be intellectually coherent, any more than I believe atemporal causation or causation through cosmic sympathies to be intellectually coherent, even though Livy has created a picture of the Hannibalic War which draws on both. It is nevertheless not a completely alien idea. That Livy in some way sees his text as representing Roman history has been a significant theme of recent Livian scholarship, taking its cue not least from Livy's programmatic description of his own work as a 'conspicuous monument' (*Praef.* 10 *inlustri . . . monumento*), and the way in which the language of the Preface (and elsewhere) slips ambiguously between language describing his work and language describing the subject-matter of his work, as if the two were identical (e.g. the use of *res* at *Praef.* 4).[155] Especially important in this context is Andrew Feldherr's argument that this is related to Livy's use of techniques of *enargeia* ('vivid description'), and that it is a way of acquiring authority of a sort which his social status did not entitle him to: he creates a monument that is not only analogous

---

(1990), Jenkins (1999: 118–20, 134–9), Koselleck (2004: 148–51), Munslow (2006: 159–61). Even Rorty towards the end of his life retreated to a certain extent from his earlier positions, and accepted that texts can be properly judged against things in an external world which they 'get right' to a greater or lesser degree (see Rorty 2000). There is an interesting analogy here with Woodman's argument that ancient historians had a set of 'hard-core facts' which were unalterable, although they would invent and construct a narrative around those facts which needed to be no more than plausible (Woodman 1988: 88–94), although the analogy is not an exact one. On Woodman's account the ancients' 'hard-core facts' are far more narrowly circumscribed than is historical fact as conceived by White or Ankersmit, for Greek and Roman historians were prepared to invent events which did not take place. Conversely, the ancients do not appear to make the metaphysical distinction between genuinely existing 'fact' and historian-constructed 'emplotment' which is central to the proponents of the 'linguistic turn'.

[155] See Kraus (1994b); on the *Preface* see Moles (1993b: esp. 142–4). On the idea of Livy's work as a monument see also Jaeger (1997: 15–29).

to, but that substitutes for and supersedes, the physical monuments created by Roman aristocrats.[156]

Most importantly, Feldherr draws an analogy with the practice of augury.[157] Under Roman augural law, magistrates did not merely interpret signs sent by the gods: they effectively created those signs by a decision to recognize them and to accept their significance, something they could do whether or not there was actually a sign there of the appropriate sort. That is why Marcellus could, according to an anecdote relayed by Cicero (*Div.* 2.77), avoid unfavourable signs by riding in a closed litter and so not seeing them; or why Appius Claudius, according to another anecdote in Cicero (*Div.* 1.29-30), blamed the tribune C. Ateius for causing Crassus' defeat at Carrhae by falsely announcing a bad omen before the expedition—the point being that the announcement of a bad omen, even if false, created a bad omen in reality.[158] Hence the idea that a person of appropriate authority could, simply by stating something, construct reality around that statement, was a normal position within the Roman conceptual universe.

Admittedly, as we have seen elsewhere, Livy's position, while recognizably part of a Roman thought-world, extends it in surprising directions. Even when it came to augury alone the interpretation that the augur constructs reality was not uncontested: in the case of Ateius and Appius Claudius, Cicero—an augur himself—goes on to reject as absurd the claim that Ateius by falsifying the auspices caused the defeat.[159] It is startling and bold to extend the idea of the creation of reality out of the narrow confines of augury to apply to an entire history. One might baulk at its implications, and prefer to see Livy's claims to be producing the history itself as a mere metaphor: but that would not fit the evidence that I have set out here. For Livy, his text actually does constitute the thing it is describing. Strange though it sounds, it makes better sense of Livy than any alternative reading does.

Livy thus stands on one end of a continuum within ancient historiography, a continuum which is hard for the modern reader to appreciate because neither end of it is quite familiar to us. Even with the most apparently 'modern' historians, Thucydides or Polybius, the relationship between

---

[156] Feldherr (1998: 1–50). For Livy's construction of history via the creation of authority see also Sailor (2006: esp. 366–83).

[157] Feldherr (1998: 53–5; cf. 64).

[158] See Schäublin (1986); also Linderski (1986: 2206–7, 2214–15, 1993: 60–1). We might also draw an analogy with the central role in magic played by the magician's volition (see Collins 2003: 34–7).

[159] Cicero's critique is, however, in the mouth of Quintus, not in his own voice, and moreover in a philosophical context. What appeared as illogicality to a philosopher may not have appeared so in other contexts: thus Cicero himself a few months later would accuse Antony of potentially bringing disaster on Rome by falsifying auspices (*Phil.* 2.83; cf. 2.88).

ancient historiography and truth is not a stable one.[160] Different ancient historians (and indeed different parts of the same ancient historian) vary in their commitment to literal factual truth, but also in what they offer as alternatives to literal factual truth. Some historians do indeed highlight their critical handling of evidence, but for others their role as providers of emotional pleasure is more important, while for still others it is their moral role that takes precedence. These are not of course mutually exclusive, and all historians to some degree may be argued to participate in them all. But there is little doubt that for Livy it is morality that matters above all. His self-presentation centres on showing himself as a provider of ethical lessons,[161] and, as I demonstrated in this chapter, he highlights his presentation of causation in ethical terms, and the reader is forced to interpret it in those terms not least because it is so hard to make sense of it in any other terms. Livy's world is an ethical world: it is also a real world. But the real world is one where causal sequence, chronology, human behaviour and everything else are subordinated to the moral structure that Livy offers, and which he implies is also the moral structure of the universe. Ethics effectively controls everything else. The ultimate understanding of how Livy can present his text, with its self-acknowledged contradictions, as if it were reality, may be that he regards the moral picture that his text presents as a valid account in its own right, but also an accurate demonstration of the way the world works. By reading through Livy's text one learns its moral lessons—complex and contested though they are—and one is obliged to focus on morality precisely because there is no other way of making sense of that text. And it is in those lessons, for him, that the truth of the Hannibalic War resides.

---

[160] Pelling (1990c: 45–51), revised in Pelling (2002: 158–61), Moles (1993a: 118).
[161] Cf. Levene (2006a).

Bibliography

Achard, G. (2002). 'Tite-Live et les grecs', in Defosse 2002: 3–11.

Adam, B. (1990). *Time and Social Theory*. Philadelphia, PA: Temple University Press.

Adams, J. N. (2003). *Bilingualism and the Latin Language*. Cambridge: Cambridge University Press.

Allen, G. (2000). *Intertextuality*. London: Routledge.

Aly, W. (1936). *Livius und Ennius*. Leipzig: B. G. Teubner.

Ankersmit, F. R. (1983). *Narrative Logic: Semantic Analysis of the Historian's Language*. The Hague: Martinus Nijhoff Publishers.

—— (1989a). *The Reality Effect in the Writing of History: The Dynamics of Historiographical Topology*. Amsterdam: Koninklijke Nederlandse Akademie van Wetenschappen.

—— (1989b). 'Historiography and Postmodernism'. *History and Theory* 28: 137–53.

—— (2001). *Historical Representation*. Stanford, CA: Stanford University Press.

Aranita, A. (2009). 'A Plague of Madness: The Contagion of Mutiny in Livy 28.24–32'. in P. R. Bosman (ed.), *Mania: Madness in the Greco-Roman World. Acta Classica Supplement III*. Pretoria, 36–51.

Asheri, D. (1991–92). 'The Art of Synchronization in Greek Historiography: The Case of Timaeus of Tauromenium'. *SCI* 11: 52–89.

Aymard, A. (1954). 'Polybe, Scipion l'Africain et le titre de "roi"'. *Revue du Nord* 36: 121–8.

Badian, E. (1958). 'Aetolica'. *Latomus* 17: 197–211.

Barber, G. L. (1935). *The Historian Ephorus*. Cambridge: Cambridge University Press.

Barthes, R. (1989). *The Rustle of Language*, tr. R. Howard. Berkeley, CA: University of California Press.

Bayet, J. (1969). *Histoire politique et psychologique de religion romaine*. 2nd edn. Paris: Payot.

Bearzot, C. (2002). 'Filisto di Siracusa', in R. Vattuone (ed.), *Storici greci d'occidente*. Bologna: Società editrice di Mulino, 91–136.

Beauregard, O. C. de (1977). 'Time Symmetry and the Einstein Paradox'. *Il Nuovo Cimento* 42B.1: 41–64.

Beck, H. (2002). 'Interne *Synkrisis* bei Plutarch'. *Hermes* 130: 467–89.

Bernard, J.-E. (2000). *Le portrait chez Tite-Live: Essai sur l'écriture de l'histoire romaine*. Brussels: Collection Latomus.

—— (2002). '*Historia magistra mortis*: Tite-Live, Plutarque et la fin de Marcellus', in Defosse 2002: 30–9.

Berry, D. H. (1996). *Cicero: Pro P. Sulla Oratio*. Cambridge: Cambridge University Press.

Beyerchen, A. (1992–93). 'Clausewitz, Non-Linearity, and the Unpredictability of War'. *International Security* 17.3: 59–90.

Birley, E. (1950). 'The Governors of Numidia, A.D. 193–268'. *JRS* 40: 60–8 = Birley 1988: 115–23.

—— (1954). 'Senators in the Emperor's Service'. *Proceedings of the British Academy* 39: 197–214 = Birley 1988: 75–92.

—— (1988). *The Roman Army. Papers 1929–1986.* Amsterdam: J. C. Gieben.

Black, M. (1955–56). 'Why Cannot an Effect Precede its Cause?' *Analysis* 16: 49–58.

Bleckmann, B. (2006). *Fiktion als Geschichte: Neue Studien zum Autor der Hellenika Oxyrhynchia und zur Historiographie des vierten vorchristlichen Jahrhunderts.* Göttingen: Vandenhoeck & Ruprecht.

Bloch, R. (1976). 'Interpretatio', in R. Bloch (ed.), *Recherches sur les religions de l'Italie antique.* Geneva: Librairie Droz, 1–42.

Bobzien, S. (1999). 'Chrysippus' Theory of Causes', in K. Ierodiakonou (ed.), *Topics in Stoic Philosophy.* Oxford: Clarendon Press, 196–242.

Bocci, S. (1995). 'Il ritratto "paradossale" di M. Claudio Marcello nella biografia plutarchea', in *Miscellanea greca e romana XIX.* Rome: Istituto Italiano per la Storia Antica, 161–88.

Boghossian, P. A. (2006). *Fear of Knowledge: Against Relativism and Constructivism.* Oxford: Clarendon Press.

Boissevain, U. P. (1895). *Cassii Dionis Cocceiani Historiarum Romanorum quae supersunt*, vol. 1. Berlin: Weidmann.

Bonjour, M. (1975). *Terre natale: études sur une composante affective de patriotisme romaine.* Paris: Societé d'édition "Les Belles Lettres".

Bonnefond, M. (1982). 'Le sénat republicain et les conflits de générations'. *MEFR* 94: 175–225.

Borca, F. (2003). *Luoghi, corpi, costumi: determinismo ambientale ed etnografia antica.* Rome: Edizioni di Storia e Letteratura.

Bornecque, H. (1933). *Tite-Live.* Paris: Boivin & Compagnie.

Borzsák, I. (2003). 'Eine kleine Historiographie'. *AAntHung* 43: 323–9.

Bosworth, A. B. (1980). *A Historical Commentary on Arrian's History of Alexander*, Vol. 1. Oxford: Clarendon Press.

—— (2003). 'Plus ça change . . . Ancient Historians and their Sources'. *CA* 22: 167–98.

Bouvier, D. (2000). 'Temps chronologique et temps météorologique chez les premiers historiens grecs', in C. Darbo-Peschanski (ed.), *Constructions du temps dans le monde grec ancien.* Paris: CNRS Éditions, 115–41.

Boyer, P. (1994). *The Naturalness of Religious Ideas: A Cognitive Theory of Religion.* Berkeley, CA: University of California Press.

Brandom, R. B. (ed.) (2000). *Rorty and his Critics.* Malden, MA: Blackwell Publishers.

Breebaart, A. B. (1980). Review of Tränkle 1977. *Mnemosyne* 33: 425–8.

Brennan, T. C. (2000). *The Praetorship in the Roman Republic.* Oxford: Oxford University Press.

Briquel, D. (2002). *Le forum brûle. 18–19 mars 210 av. J.-C.: un épisode méconnu de la deuxième guerre punique.* Paris: L'Harmattan.

Briscoe, J. (1973). *A Commentary on Livy: Books XXXI–XXXIII.* Oxford: Clarendon Press.

—— (1978). Review of Tränkle 1977. *CR* 28: 267–9.

—— (1981). *A Commentary on Livy: Books XXXIV–XXXVII.* Oxford: Clarendon Press.

—— (1989). 'The Second Punic War'. *CAH* 8: 44–80.

—— (1993). 'Livy and Polybius', in Schuller 1993: 39–52.

Brizzi, G. (1984). *Studi di storia Annibalica*. Faena: Fratelli Lega Editore.

—— (2005). 'Cartagine e Roma: dall' intesa al confronto', in C. Bearzot, F. Landucci, G. Zecchini (eds.), *L'equilibrio internazionale dagli antichi ai moderni*. Milan: Vita e Pensiero, 29–43.

Brock, R. (1995). 'Versions, "Inversions" and Evasions: Classical Historiography and the "Published" Speech'. *PLLS* 8: 209–24.

Brodersen, K. (2003). *Terra Cognita: Studien zur römischen Raumerfassung*. 2nd edn. Hildesheim: Georg Olms Verlag.

Brown, C. W. jr. (1989). 'Thucydides, Hobbes and the Linear Causal Perspective'. *HPTh* 10: 215–56.

Bruckmann, H. (1936). *Die römischen Niederlagen im Geschichtswerk des T. Livius*. Diss., Münster.

Bruns, I. (1898). *Die Persönlichkeit in der Geschichtsschreibung der Alten*. Berlin: Verlag von Wilhelm Hertz.

Brunt, P. A. (1975). 'Stoicism and the Principate'. *PBSR* 43: 7–35.

Burck, E. (1943). 'Das Bild der Karthager in der römischen Literatur', in J. Vogt (ed.), *Rom und Karthago*. Leipzig: Koehler & Amelung, 297–345.

—— (1962). *Einführung in die dritte Dekade des Livius*. 2nd edn. Heidelberg: F. H. Kerle Verlag.

—— (1964). *Die Erzählungskunst des T. Livius*. 2nd edn. Berlin: Weidmannsche Verlagsbuchhandlung.

—— (1969). 'Pleminius und Scipio bei Livius (Livius 29,6–9 und 29,16,4 – 22,12)', in P. Steinmetz (ed.), *Politeia und res publica: Beiträge zum Verständnis von Politik, Recht und Staat in der Antike*. Wiesbaden: Palingenesia, 301–14 = Burck 1981: 238–50.

—— (1971). 'The Third Decade', in T. A. Dorey (ed.), *Livy*. London: Routledge & Kegan Paul, 21–46.

—— (1981). *Vom Menschenbild in der römischen Literatur*, Vol. 2. Heidelberg: Carl Winter Universitätsverlag.

—— (1982). 'Die römische Expansion im Urteil des Livius'. *ANRW* II 30.2: 1149–89.

—— (1992). *Das Geschichtswerk des Titus Livius*. Heidelberg: Carl Winter Verlag.

Caltabiano, M. (1975). 'La morte del console Marcello nella tradizione storiografica'. *CISA* 3: 65–81.

Campbell, B. (1975). 'Who were the *viri militares*?'. *JRS* 65: 11–31.

—— (1984). *The Emperor and the Roman Army: 31 BC–AD 235*. Oxford: Clarendon Press.

—— (1987). 'Teach Yourself How to be a General'. *JRS* 77: 13–29.

—— (2002). *War and Society in Imperial Rome: 31 BC–AD 284*. London: Routledge.

Carawan, E. M. (1984–85). 'The Tragic History of Marcellus and Livy's Characterization'. *CJ* 80: 131–41.

Carroll, N. (1990). 'Interpretation, History, and Narrative'. *The Monist* 73: 134–66.

Catin, L. (1944). *En lisant Tite-Live*. Paris: Société d'édition "Les Belles Lettres".

Ceausescu, P. (1976). 'Altera Roma: histoire d'une folie politique'. *Historia* 25: 79–108.

Chaplin, J. D. (2000). *Livy's Exemplary History.* Oxford: Oxford University Press.

Chaplin, J. D., and Kraus, C. S. (eds.) (2009). *Oxford Readings in Classical Studies. Livy.* Oxford: Oxford University Press.

Charles, M. B., and Rhodan, P. (2007). '*Magister elephantorum*: A Reappraisal of Hannibal's Use of Elephants'. *CW* 100: 363–89.

Chase, K. (1984). *Eros and Psyche: The Representation of Personality in Charlotte Brontë, Charles Dickens, and George Eliot.* New York, NY: Methven.

Chassignet, M. (2004). *L'Annalistique romaine III: annalistique récente, l'autobiographie politique.* Paris: Les Belles Lettres.

Chlup, J. T. (2004). 'Beyond the Foreigner: Representations of Non-Roman Individuals and Communities in Latin Historiography'. PhD thesis: Durham.

Cipriani, G. (1984). *L'epifania di Annibale: saggio introduttivo a Livio*, Annales *XXI.* Bari: Adriatica Editrice.

Cizek, E. (1995). *Histoire et historiens à Rome dans l'antiquité.* Lyons: Presses universitaires de Lyon.

Clarke, K. (1999a). *Between Geography and History: Hellenistic Constructions of the Roman World.* Oxford: Clarendon Press.

—— (1999b). 'Universal Perspectives in Historiography', in Kraus 1999b: 249–79.

—— (2008). *Making Time for the Past: Local History and the Polis.* Oxford: Oxford University Press.

Clauss, J. J. (1997). '"*Domestici hostes*": The Nausicaa in Medea, the Catiline in Hannibal'. *MD* 39: 165–85.

Cohen, S. (1986). *Historical Culture: On the Recoding of an Academic Discipline.* Berkeley, CA: University of California Press.

Collins, A. (1984). 'Action, Causality, and Teleological Explanation'. *Midwest Studies in Philosophy* 9: 345–69.

Collins, D. (2003). 'Nature, Cause and Agency in Greek Magic'. *TAPhA* 133: 17–49.

Collins, J. H. (1972). 'Caesar as Political Propagandist'. *ANRW* I 1: 922–66.

Connolly, J. (2007). *The State of Speech: Rhetoric and Political Thought in Ancient Rome.* Princeton, NJ: Princeton University Press.

Consolo Langher, S. N. (1991). 'Il problema delle fonti di Diodoro per la storia di Agatocle: Diodoro e Duride', in Galvagno and Molè Ventura 1991: 152–86.

—— (1998). *Storiografia e potere: Duride, Timeo, Callia e il dibatto su Agatocle.* Pisa: Edizione ETS.

—— (2005). 'Polibio e gli storici contemporanei di Agatocle', in G. Schepens and J. Bollansée (eds.), *The Shadow of Polybius: Intertextuality as a Research Tool in Greek Historiography.* Leuven: Peeters, 165–81.

Conte, G. B. (1986). *The Rhetoric of Imitation: Genre and Poetic Memory in Virgil and Other Latin Poets*, tr. C. Segal. Ithaca, NY: Cornell University Press.

—— (1992). 'Proems in the Middle'. *YCS* 29: 47–59.

Cornell, T. J. (1995). *The Beginnings of Rome: Italy and Rome from the Bronze Age to the Punic Wars (c.1000–264 BC).* London: Routledge.

Cornell, T., Rankov, B., and Sabin, P. (eds.) (1996). *The Second Punic War: A Reappraisal.* London: Institute of Classical Studies.

Crouzet, S. (2003). 'Les statuts civiques dans l'Afrique punique: de l'historiographie moderne à l'historiographie antique'. *MEFRA* 115: 655–703.

Culham, P. (1989). 'Chance, Command, and Chaos in Ancient Military Engagements'. *World Futures* 27: 191–205.

Cuppy, W. (1951). *The Decline and Fall of Practically Everybody.* London: Dennis Dobson.

D'Huys, V. (1987). 'How to Describe Violence in Historical Narratives'. *AncSoc* 18: 209–50.

—— (1990). 'χρήσιμον καὶ τέρπνον in Polybios' Schlachtschilderungen: Einige literarische Topoi in seiner Darstellung der Schlacht bei Zama (XV 9–16)', in H. Verdin, G. Schepens, and E. de Keyser (eds.), *Purposes of History: Studies in Greek Historians from the 4th to the 2nd Centuries B.C.* Leuven: Peeters, 267–88.

Daly, G. (2002). *Cannae: The Experience of Battle in the Second Punic War.* London: Routledge.

Dauge, Y. A. (1981). *Le barbare. Recherches sur la conception romaine de la barbarie et de la civilisation.* Brussels: Latomus.

Davidson, D. (1963). 'Actions, Reasons, and Causes'. *Journal of Philosophy* 60: 685–700.

Davidson, J. (1991). 'The Gaze in Polybius' *Histories*'. *JRS* 81: 10–24.

Davies, J. P. (2004). *Rome's Religious History: Livy, Tacitus and Ammianus on their Gods.* Cambridge: Cambridge University Press.

Dawe, R. D. (1963). 'Inconsistency of Plot and Character in Aeschylus'. *PCPhS* 9: 21–62.

De Lacy, P. H. (1977). 'The Four Stoic *Personae*'. *ICS* 2: 163–72.

Defosse, P. (ed.) (2002). *Hommages à Carl Deroux: II – Prose et linguistique, médecine.* Brussels: Éditions Latomus.

Deininger, J. (1983). 'Gelon und die Karthager 216 v. Chr. (Liv. 23, 30, 10–12)', in Lefèvre and Olshausen 1983: 125–32.

Dench, E. (1995). *From Barbarians to New Men: Greek, Roman, and Modern Perceptions of Peoples of the Central Apennines.* Oxford: Clarendon Press.

—— (2005). *Romulus' Asylum: Roman Identities from the Age of Alexander to the Age of Hadrian.* Oxford: Oxford University Press.

Derow, P. (1976). 'The Roman Calendar, 218–191 B.C.'. *Phoenix* 30: 265–81.

—— (1994). 'Historical Explanation: Polybius and his Predecessors', in Hornblower 1994: 73–90.

Doblhofer, E. (1983). 'Livius und andere "Imperialisten"', in Lefèvre and Olshausen 1983: 133–62.

Dowe, P. (1996). 'Backward Causation and the Direction of Causal Processes'. *Mind* 105: 227–48.

Dray, W. (1957). *Laws and Explanation in History.* Oxford: Oxford University Press.

Ducos, M. (1987). 'Les passions, les hommes et l'histoire dans l'oeuvre de Tite-Live'. *REL* 65: 132–47.

Duff, T. E. (1999). *Plutarch's Lives: Exploring Virtue and Vice.* Oxford: Oxford University Press.

Dummett, A. E. (M.) (1954). 'Can an Effect Precede its Cause?'. *Proceedings of the Aristotelian Society: Supplementary Volumes* 28: 27–44.

Dummett, A. E. (M.) (1964). 'Bringing About the Past'. *Philosophical Review* 73: 338–59.

Dutoit, E. (1946). 'Les petites causes dans l'histoire romaine de Tite-Live'. *Lettres d'humanité* 5: 186–205.

Dyck, A. R. (2004). *A Commentary on Cicero*, De Legibus. Ann Arbor, MI: University of Michigan Press.

Easterling, P. E. (1973). 'Presentation of Character in Aeschylus'. *G&R* 20: 3–19.

—— (1990). 'Constructing Character in Greek Tragedy', in Pelling 1990b: 83–99.

Eckstein, A. M. (1985). 'Polybius, Syracuse, and the Politics of Accommodation'. *GRBS* 26: 265–82.

—— (1987). *Senate and General: Individual Decision-Making and Roman Foreign Relations, 264–194 B.C.* Berkeley, CA: University of California Press.

—— (1989). 'Hannibal at New Carthage: Polybius 3.15 and the Power of Irrationality'. *CPh* 84: 1–15.

—— (1995). *Moral Vision in* The Histories *of Polybius*. Berkeley, CA: University of California Press.

—— (2002). 'Greek Mediation in the First Macedonian War, 209–205 B.C.'. *Historia* 51: 268–97.

Edgeworth, R. J. (1989). 'Saguntum: A Livian Overture'. *Eranos* 87: 39–45.

Edmunds, L. (2001). *Intertextuality and the Reading of Roman Poetry*. Baltimore, MD: Johns Hopkins University Press.

Eigler, U. (2003). 'Aemilius Paullus: ein Feldherr auf Bildungsreise', in Eigler *et al.* 2003: 250–67.

Eigler, U., Gotter, U., Luraghi, N., Walter, U. (eds.) (2003). *Formen römischer Geschichtsschreibung von den Anfängen bis Livius*. Darmstadt: Wissenschaftliche Buchgesellschaft.

Erdkamp, P. (1992). 'Polybius, Livy, and the Fabian Strategy'. *AncSoc* 23: 127–47.

Erkell, H. (1952). *Augustus, Felicitas, Fortuna: lateinische Wortstudien*. Göteborg: Elanders Boktryckeri Aktiebolag.

Erskine, A. (1991). 'Hellenistic Monarchy and Roman Political Invective'. *CQ* 41: 106–20.

—— (2001). *Troy between Greece and Rome: Local Tradition and Imperial Power*. Oxford: Oxford University Press.

Evans, R. J. (2000). *In Defence of History*. 2nd edn. London: Granta Books.

Farney, G. D. (2007). *Ethnic Identity and Aristocratic Competition in Republican Rome*. Cambridge: Cambridge University Press.

Farrell, J. (1991). *Vergil's* Georgics *and the Traditions of Ancient Epic*. New York, NY: Oxford University Press.

—— (2005). 'Intention and Intertext'. *Phoenix* 59: 98–111.

Feeney, D. (1998). *Literature and Religion at Rome: Cultures, Contexts, and Beliefs*. Cambridge: Cambridge University Press.

—— (2007). *Caesar's Calendar: Ancient Time and the Beginning of History*. Berkeley, CA: University of California Press.

Feichtinger, B. (1992). '*Ad maiorem gloriam Romae*: Ideologie und Fiktion in der Historiographie des Livius'. *Latomus* 51: 3–33.

Feldherr, A. (1998). *Spectacle and Society in Livy's* History. Berkeley, CA: University of California Press.

—— (2009). 'Delusions of Grandeur: Lucretian "Passages" in Livy', in P. Hardie (ed.), *Paradox and the Marvellous in Augustan Literature and Culture.* Oxford: Oxford University Press, 310–29.

Fish, S. (1967). *Surprised by Sin: The Reader in Paradise Lost.* Cambridge, MA: Harvard University Press.

Flew, A. (1954). 'Can an Effect Precede its Cause?'. *Proceedings of the Aristotelian Society: Supplementary Volumes* 28: 45–62.

Flower, H. (2003). '"Memories" of Marcellus: History and Memory in Roman Republican Culture', in Eigler *et al.* 2003: 39–52.

Fornara, C. W. (1983). *The Nature of History in Ancient Greece and Rome.* Berkeley, CA: University of California Press.

Forni, G. (1974). 'Estrazione etnica e sociale dei soldati delle legioni'. *ANRW* II 1: 339–91.

Foucher, A. (2000). *Historia proxima poetis. L'influence de la poésie épique sur le style des historiens latins de Salluste à Ammien Marcellin.* Brussels: Latomus.

Foulon, E. (1989). 'Polybe, X, 2–20: la prise de Carthagène par Scipion'. *RPh* 63: 241–6.

—— (1992). 'βασιλεύς Σκιπίων'. *BAGB* 9–30.

—— (1998). 'Un miracle de Poséidon: Polybe X, 8–15'. *REG* 111: 503–17.

—— (2000). 'Polybe et les Celtes (I)'. *LEC* 68: 319–54.

—— (2001). 'Polybe et les Celtes (II)'. *LEC* 69: 35–64.

Fowler, D. P. (1989). 'First Thoughts on Closure: Problems and Prospects'. *MD* 22: 75–122 = Fowler 2000: 239–83.

—— (1997a). 'Second Thoughts on Closure', in Roberts, Dunn, and Fowler 1997: 3–22 = Fowler 2000: 284–307.

—— (1997b). 'On the Shoulders of Giants: Intertextuality and Classical Studies'. *MD* 39: 13–34 = Fowler 2000: 115–35.

—— (2000). *Roman Constructions: Readings in Postmodern Latin.* Oxford: Oxford University Press.

Fox. M. (1996). *Roman Historical Myths: The Regal Period in Augustan Literature.* Oxford: Clarendon Press.

Frede, M. (1980). 'The Original Notion of Cause', in M. Schofield, M. Burnyeat, J. Barnes (eds.), *Doubt and Dogmatism: Studies in Hellenistic Epistemology.* Oxford: Clarendon Press, 217–49 = Frede 1987: 125–50.

—— (1987). *Essays in Ancient Philosophy.* Minneapolis, MN: University of Minnesota Press.

Frederiksen, M. (1984). *Campania.* Rome: British School at Rome.

Frier, B. W. (1979). *Libri Annales Pontificum Maximorum: The Origins of the Annalistic Tradition.* Rome: American Academy in Rome.

Fronda, M. P. (2007). 'Hegemony and Rivalry: The Revolt of Capua Revisited'. *Phoenix* 61: 83–108.

Fuhrmann, M. (1983). 'Narrative Techniken im Dienste der Geschichtsschreibung (Livius, Buch 21–22): eine Skizze', in Lefèvre and Olshausen 1983: 19–29.

Gärtner, H. A. (1975). *Beobachtungen zu Bauelementen in der antiken Historiographie, besonders bei Livius und Caesar.* Wiesbaden: Franz Steiner Verlag.

Gaide, F. (2003). 'Aspects divers des principes de sympathie et d'antipathie dans les textes thérapeutiques latins', in Palmieri 2003: 129–44.

Gaillard-Seux, P. (2003). 'Sympathie et antipathie dans l'*Histoire Naturelle* de Pline l'Ancien', in Palmieri 2003: 113–28.

Galvagno, E., and Molè Ventura, C. (1991). *Mito, storia, tradizione: Diodoro Siculo e la storiografia classica.* Catania: Edizioni del Prisma.

Gardiner, P. (1952). *The Nature of Historical Explanation.* Oxford: Oxford University Press.

Gauthier, P. (1968). 'L'Èbre et Sagonte: défense de Polybe'. *RPh* 42: 91–100.

Gell, A. (1992). *The Anthropology of Time: Cultural Constructions of Temporal Maps and Images.* Oxford: Berg Publishers.

Gelzer, M. (1931). 'Nasicas Widerspruch gegen die Zerstörung Karthagos'. *Philologus* 86: 261–99 = Gelzer 1963: 39–72.

—— (1933). 'Römische Politik bei Fabius Pictor'. *Hermes* 68: 129–66 = Gelzer 1964: 51–92.

—— (1963). *Kleine Schriften*, Vol. 2. Wiesbaden: Franz Steiner.

—— (1964). *Kleine Schriften*, Vol. 3. Wiesbaden: Franz Steiner.

Gerhold, M. (2002). *Rom und Karthago zwischen Krieg und Frieden: Rechtshistorische Untersuchung zu den römisch-karthagischen Beziehungen zwischen 241 v.Chr. und 149 v.Chr.* Frankfurt am Main: Peter Lang.

Gignoux, A. C. (2005). *Initiation à l'intertextualité.* Paris: Ellipses.

Gill, C. (1983). 'The Question of Character-Development: Plutarch and Tacitus'. *CQ* 33: 469–87.

—— (1984). 'The *Ethos/Pathos* Distinction in Rhetorical and Literary Criticism'. *CQ* 34: 149–66.

—— (1986). 'The Question of Character and Personality in Greek Tragedy'. *Poetics Today* 7: 251–73.

—— (1988). 'Personhood and Personality: The Four-*Personae* Theory in Cicero, *De Officiis* I'. *OSAP* 6: 169–99.

—— (1990). 'The Character-Personality Distinction', in Pelling 1990b: 1–31.

—— (1996). *Personality in Greek Epic, Tragedy, and Philosophy: The Self in Dialogue.* Oxford: Clarendon Press.

—— (2006). *The Structured Self in Hellenistic and Roman Thought.* Oxford: Oxford University Press.

Gill, C., and Wiseman, T. P. (eds.) (1993). *Lies and Fiction in the Ancient World.* Exeter: University of Exeter Press.

Gilliver, C. M. (1996). 'The Roman Army and Morality in War', in Lloyd 1996: 219–38.

Ginsberg, W. (1983). *The Cast of Character: The Representation of Personality in Ancient and Medieval Literature.* Toronto: University of Toronto Press.

Ginsburg, J. (1981). *Tradition and Theme in the* Annals *of Tacitus.* New York, NY: Arno Press.

Girod, M. R. (1982). 'La géographie de Tite-Live'. *ANRW* II 30.2: 1190–229.

Glew, D. G. (forthcoming). '*Claudi curiam iubet*: Recent Roman History and Livy's Account of the Secession of Capua (23, 2–10)'.

Goldsworthy, A. K. (1996). *The Roman Army at War: 100 BC–AD 200*. Oxford: Clarendon Press.

Gordon, R. (1999). 'Imagining Greek and Roman Magic', in B. Ankarloo and S. Clark, *Witchcraft and Magic in Europe: Volume 2, Greece and Rome*. London: The Athlone Press, 159–275.

Gorovitz, S. (1964). 'Leaving the Past Alone'. *Philosophical Review* 73: 360–71.

Gray, C. S. (2002). *Strategy for Chaos: Revolutions in Military Affairs and the Evidence of History*. London: Frank Cass.

Gray, V. (1987). '*Mimesis* in Greek Historical Theory'. *AJPh* 108: 467–86.

Gribble, D. (1998). 'Narrator Interventions in Thucydides'. *JHS* 118: 41–67.

Gries, K. (1951). 'Subconscious Repetition in Livy'. *CPh* 46: 36–7.

Griffin, M., and Barnes, J. (eds.) (1989). *Philosophia Togata: Essays on Philosophy and Roman Society*. Oxford: Clarendon Press.

Gruen, E. S. (1979). 'The Consular Elections for 216 B.C. and the Veracity of Livy'. *CSCA* 11: 61–74.

Guittard, C. (2004–5). 'La réforme des Saturnales de 218/17 av. J. C.: un problème de chronologie livienne (Tite-Live XXII, 1, 19–20)'. *ACD* 40–41: 77–94.

Habel, E. (1931). 'Ludi publici'. *RE* Suppl. V: 608–30.

Habinek, T. N. (1998). *The Politics of Latin Literature: Writing, Identity, and Empire in Ancient Rome*. Princeton, NJ: Princeton University Press.

Händl-Sagawe, U. (1995). *Der Beginn des 2. punischen Krieges: ein historisch-kritischer Kommentar zu Livius Buch 21*. Munich: Editio Maris.

Hahm, D. E. (1989). 'Posidonius' Theory of Historical Causation'. *ANRW* II 36.3: 1325–63.

Haley, S. P. (1989). 'Livy's Sophoniba'. *C&M* 40: 171–81.

—— (1990). 'Livy, Passion, and Cultural Stereotypes'. *Historia* 39: 375–81.

Hall, E. (1989). *Inventing the Barbarian: Greek Self-Definition through Tragedy*. Oxford: Clarendon Press.

Halliwell, S. (1990). 'Traditional Conceptions of Character', in Pelling 1990b: 32–59.

Hammond, N. G. L. (1983). *Three Historians of Alexander the Great*. Cambridge: Cambridge University Press.

Hankinson, R. J. (1988). 'Stoicism, Science and Divination', in R. J. Hankinson (ed.), *Method, Medicine and Metaphysics: Studies in the Philosophy of Ancient Science*. Edmonton: Academic Printing and Publishing, 123–60.

—— (1998). *Cause and Explanation in Ancient Greek Thought*. Oxford: Clarendon Press.

Hanson, V. D. (1989). *The Western Way of War: Infantry Battle in Classical Greece*. New York, NY: Alfred A. Knopf.

Hardie, P. (1994). *Virgil: Aeneid Book IX*. Cambridge: Cambridge University Press.

Harris, W. V. (1979). *War and Imperialism in Republican Rome 327–70 B.C.* Oxford: Clarendon Press.

Harris, W. V. (2005). 'Can Enemies too be Brave? A Question about Roman Representation of the Other', in M. G. Angeli Bertanelli and A. Donati (eds.), *Il cittadino, lo straniero, il barbaro, fra integrazione ed emarginazione nell'antichità. Atti del I Incontro Internazionale di Storia antica, Genova, 22–24 maggio 2003.* Rome: Giorgio Bretschneider Editore, 465–72.

Harrison, S. J. (1991). *Vergil: Aeneid 10.* Oxford: Clarendon Press.

Harrison, T. (2003). ' "Prophecy in Reverse"? Herodotus and the Origins of History', in P. Derow and R. Parker (eds.), *Herodotus and his World: Essays from a Conference in Memory of George Forrest.* Oxford: Oxford University Press, 237–54.

Hasse, P. (1996). 'A Remarkable Pattern in Livy 21–45'. *AClass* 39: 5–16.

Haynes, I. (1999). 'Military Service and Cultural Identity in the *Auxilia*', in A. Goldsworthy and I. Haynes (eds.), *The Roman Army as a Community.* Portsmouth, RI: JRA Supplementary Series No. 34, 165–74.

Heath, M. (1987). *The Poetics of Greek Tragedy.* London: Duckworth.

—— (1989). *Unity in Greek Poetics.* Oxford: Clarendon Press.

—— (2002). *Interpreting Classical Texts.* London: Duckworth.

—— (forthcoming). 'What's wrong with formalism, and why is it so useful?'.

Heinze, R. (1915). *Virgils epische Technik.* 3rd edn. Leipzig: B. G. Teubner.

Herrmann, W. (1979). *Die Historien des Coelius Antipater: Fragmente und Kommentar.* Meisenheim am Glan: Verlag Anton Hain.

Heusch, C. (2005). 'Die Ethopoiie in der griechischen und lateinischen Antike: von der rhetorischen Progymnasma-Theorie zur literarischen Form', in E. Amato and J. Schamp (eds.), *Ethopoiia: la représentation de caractères entre fiction scolaire et réalité vivante à l'époque impériale et tardive.* Salerno: Helios Editrice, 11–33.

Heuss, A. (1983). 'Zur inneren Zeitform bei Livius', in Lefèvre and Olshausen 1983: 175–215.

Hinds, S. (1982). 'An Allusion to the Literary Tradition of the Proserpina Myth'. *CQ* 32: 476–8.

—— (1998). *Allusion and Intertext: Dynamics of Appropriation in Roman Poetry.* Cambridge: Cambridge University Press.

Hoch, H. (1951). *Die Darstellung der politischen Sendung Roms bei Livius.* Frankfurt am Main: Vittorio Klostermann.

Hocutt, M. (1974). 'Aristotle's Four Becauses'. *Philosophy* 49: 385–99.

Hoffman, U. (2002). '"Der Anfang reicht bis zum Ende": drei Bemerkungen zu Polybios' teleologischer Denkweise'. *Saeculum* 53: 193–225.

Hoffmann, W. (1942). *Livius und der zweite Punische Krieg.* Berlin: Weidmannsche Verlagsbuchhandlung.

—— (1960). 'Die römische Politik des 2. Jahrhunderts und das Ende Karthagos'. *Historia* 9: 39–72.

Hornblower, S. (ed.) (1994). *Greek Historiography.* Oxford: Clarendon Press.

Horsfall, N. (1985). 'Illusion and Reality in Latin Topographical Writing'. *G&R* 32: 197–208.

—— (2000). *Virgil, Aeneid 7: A Commentary.* Leiden: Brill.

Hoyos, B. D. (1992). 'Sluice-Gates or Neptune at New Carthage, 209 B.C.?'. *Historia* 41: 124–8.

—— (1998). *Unplanned Wars: The Origins of the First and Second Punic Wars.* Berlin: Walter de Gruyter.

—— (2001). 'Generals and Annalists: Geographic and Chronological Obscurities in the Scipios' Campaigns in Spain, 218–211 BC'. *Klio* 83: 68–92.

—— (2003). *Hannibal's Dynasty: Power and Politics in the Western Mediterranean, 247–183 BC.* London: Routledge.

—— (2006). 'Crossing the Durance with Hannibal and Livy: The Route to the Pass'. *Klio* 88: 408–65.

Humbert, M. (1978). *Municipium et civitas sine suffragio: l'organisation de la conquête jusqu'à la guerre sociale.* Rome: École Française de Rome.

Hunt, P. (2006). 'Warfare', in A. Rengakos and A. Tsakmakis (eds.), *Brill's Companion to Thucydides.* Leiden: Brill, 385–413.

Hunter, V. (1982). *Past and Process in Herodotus and Thucydides.* Princeton, NJ: Princeton University Press.

Hus, A. (1979). Review of Tränkle 1977. *RPh* 53: 362–3.

Huss, W. (1989). 'Der "Panafrikanische" Gedanke im zweiten punischen Krieg', in H. Devijver and E. Lipiński (eds.), *Studia Phoenicia X: Punic Wars.* Leuven: Uitgeverij Peeters, 185–91.

Hutcheon, L. (1988). *A Poetics of Postmodernism: History, Theory, Fiction.* London: Routledge.

Isaac, B. (2004). *The Invention of Racism in Classical Antiquity.* Princeton, NJ: Princeton University Press.

Jaeger, M. (1997). *Livy's Written Rome.* Ann Arbor, MI: University of Michigan Press.

—— (1999). 'Guiding Metaphor and Narrative Point of View in Livy's *Ab Urbe Condita*', in Kraus 1999b: 169–95.

—— (2003). 'Livy and the Fall of Syracuse', in Eigler *et al.* 2003: 213–34.

—— (2006). 'Livy, Hannibal's Monument, and the Temple of Juno at Croton'. *TAPhA* 136: 389–414.

Jahn, J. (1970). *Interregnum und Wahldiktatur.* Frankfurt: Michael Lassleben Kallmünz Opf.

Jal, P. (1997). 'Historiographie annalistique et historiographie thématique dans l'antiquité classique: quelques remarques'. *REL* 75: 27–37.

—— (2001). 'Lire Tite-Live aujourd'hui', in J. Leclant and F. Chamoux (eds.), *Histoire et historiographie dans l'antiquité.* Paris: Diffusion de Boccard, 113–21.

Janni, P. (2003). 'La cartografia di Polibio', in Santos Yanguas and Torregaray Pagola 2003: 89–102.

Jehne, M. (2006). 'Römer, Latiner und Bundgenossen im Krieg. Zu Formen und Ausmass der Integration in der Republikanischen Armee', in Jehne and Pfeilschichter 2006: 243–67.

Jehne, M., and Pfeilschichter, R. (eds.) (2006). *Herrschaft ohne Integration? Rom und Italien in republikanischer Zeit.* Frankfurt am Main: Verlag Antike.

Jenkins, K. (1991). *Re-Thinking History.* London: Routledge.

—— (1999). *Why History? Ethics and Postmodernity.* London: Routledge.

—— (2003). *Refiguring History: New Thoughts on an Old Discipline.* London: Routledge.

Jocelyn, H. D. (1973). 'Greek Poetry in Cicero's Prose Writing'. *YCS* 23: 61–111.

Johner, A. (1996). *La violence chez Tite-Live: mythographie et historiographie*. Strasbourg: AECR.

de Jong, I. (2001). 'The Anachronical Structure of Herodotus' *Histories*', in S. J. Harrison (ed.), *Texts, Ideas, and the Classics*. Oxford: Oxford University Press, 93–116.

Jumeau, R. (1964). 'Un aspect significatif de l'exposé livien dans les livres XXI et XXII', in M. Renard and R. Schilling (eds.), *Hommages à Jean Bayet*. Brussels: Latomus, 309–33.

Kagan, K. (2006). *The Eye of Command*. Ann Arbor, MI: University of Michigan Press.

Kajanto, I. (1957). *God and Fate in Livy*. Turku: Turun Yliopiston Kustantama.

Kaster, R. A. (2005a). *Emotion, Restraint, and Community in Ancient Rome*. Oxford: Oxford University Press.

—— (2005b). 'The Passions', in S. Harrison (ed.), *A Companion to Latin Literature*. Malden, MA: Blackwell Publishing, 319–30.

Keay, S., and Terrenato, N. (eds.) (2001). *Italy and the West: Comparative Issues in Romanization*. Oxford: Oxbow Books.

Keegan, J. (1976). *The Face of Battle*. London: Penguin Books.

—— (1987). *The Mask of Command*. New York, NY: Viking.

Kelly, G. (2008). *Ammianus Marcellinus: The Allusive Historian*. Cambridge: Cambridge University Press.

Keppie, L. (1997). 'The Changing Face of the Roman Legions (49 BC–AD 69)'. *PBSR* 65: 89–102.

Keyser, P. T. (1990). 'Alchemy in the Ancient World: From Science to Magic'. *ICS* 15: 353–78.

—— (1997). 'Science and Magic in Galen's Recipes (Sympathy and Efficacy)', in A. Debru (ed.), *Galen on Pharmacology: Philosophy, History and Medicine*. Leiden: Brill, 175–98.

Kidd, I. G. (1971). 'Posidonius on Emotions', in A. A. Long (ed.), *Problems in Stoicism*. London: The Athlone Press, 200–15.

—— (1988). *Posidonius: II. The Commentary*. Cambridge: Cambridge University Press.

—— (1989). 'Posidonius as Philosopher-Historian', in Griffin and Barnes 1989: 38–50.

Kienast, D. (1969). 'Augustus und Alexander'. *Gymnasium* 76: 430–56.

Kincaid, J. R. (1995). *Annoying the Victorians*. New York, NY: Routledge.

Klaffenbach, B. (1954). *Der Römische-Ätolisch Bündnisvertrag vom Jahre 212 v. Chr.* Berlin: Akademie-Verlag.

Klingbeil, P.-E. (2000). 'La marche d'Hannibal: ravitaillement et stratégie'. *AntAfr* 36: 15–37.

Klotz, A. (1936). 'Über die Stellung des Cassius Dio unter den Quellen zur Geschichte des zweiten punischen Krieg'. *RhM* 85: 68–116.

—— (1940–41). *Livius und seine Vorgänger*. Leipzig: B.G. Teubner.

Knauer, G. N. (1964). *Die Aeneis und Homer: Studien zur poetischen Technik Vergils, mit Listen der Homerzitate in der Aeneis*. Göttingen: Vandenhoeck & Ruprecht.

Koestermann, E. (1971). *C. Sallustius Crispus: Bellum Iugurthinum*. Heidelberg: Carl Winter Universitätsverlag.

Koselleck, R. (2004). *Futures Past: On the Semantics of Historical Time*, tr. K. Tribe. New York, NY: Columbia University Press.

Kostial, M. (1995). *Kriegerisches Rom? Zur Frage von Unvermeidbarkeit und Normalität militärische Konflikte in der römischen Politik*. Stuttgart: Franz Steiner Verlag.

Kowalewski, B. (2002). *Frauengestalten im Geschichtswerk des T. Livius.* Munich: K. G. Saur.

Kraus, C. S. (1994a). *Livy: Ab Urbe Condita Book VI.* Cambridge: Cambridge University Press.

—— (1994b). 'No Second Troy: Topoi and Refoundation in Livy, Book V'. *TAPhA* 124: 267–89.

—— (1998). 'Repetition and Empire in the *Ab Urbe Condita*', in P. Knox and C. Foss (eds.), *Style and Tradition: Studies in Honor of Wendell Clausen.* Stuttgart: B. G. Teubner, 264–83.

—— (1999a). 'Jugurthine Disorder', in Kraus 1999b: 217–47.

—— (ed.) (1999b). *The Limits of Historiography: Genre and Narrative in Ancient Historical Texts.* Leiden: Brill.

Kremer, B. (1994). *Das Bild des Kelten bis in augusteische Zeit.* Stuttgart: Franz Steiner Verlag.

Kühner, R., and Stegmann, C. (1955). *Ausführliche Grammatik der lateinischen Sprache: Satzlehre*, Vol. 1. 3rd edn. Leverkusen: Gottschalksche Buchhandlung.

Kukofka, D. A. (1990). *Süditalien im zweiten punischen Krieg.* Frankfurt am Main: Peter Lang.

Laird, A. (1999). *Powers of Expression: Expressions of Power.* Oxford: Oxford University Press.

—— (2000). 'Design and Designation in Virgil's *Aeneid*, Tacitus' *Annals*, and Michelangelo's *Conversion of Saint Paul*', in Sharrock and Morales 2000: 143–70.

Lateiner, D. (1989). *The Historical Method of Herodotus.* Toronto: University of Toronto Press.

Lazenby, J. (1978). *Hannibal's War: A Military History of the Second Punic War.* Warminster: Aris & Phillips.

Le Roux, P. (2002). 'L'amor patriae dans les cités sous l'empire romain', in H. Inglebert (ed.), *Idéologies et valeurs civiques dans le Monde Romain: Hommage à Claude Lepelley.* Nanterre: Picard, 143–61.

Lee, A. D. (1996). 'Morale and the Roman Experience of Battle', in Lloyd 1996: 199–217.

Leeman, A. D. (1963). *Orationis Ratio The Stylistic Theories and Practice of the Roman Orators, Historians and Philosophers.* Amsterdam: Adolf M. Hakkert.

Lefèvre, E., and Olshausen, E. (eds.) (1983). *Livius: Werk und Rezeption: Festschrift für Erich Burck zum 80. Geburtstag.* Munich: Verlag C. H. Beck.

Leidig, T. (1994). *Valerius Antias und ein annalistischer Bearbeiter des Polybios als Quellen des Livius, vornehmlich für Buch 30 und 31.* Frankfurt am Main: Peter Lang.

Leigh, M. (2004). *Comedy and the Rise of Rome.* Oxford: Oxford University Press.

Lendon, J. E. (1999). The Rhetoric of Combat: Greek Theory and Roman Culture in Julius Caesar's Battle Descriptions'. *CA* 18: 273–329.

—— (2005). *Soldiers and Ghosts: A History of Battle in Classical Antiquity.* New Haven, CT: Yale University Press.

—— (2009). 'Historians without History: Against Roman Historiography', in A. Feldherr (ed.), *The Cambridge Companion to the Roman Historians.* Cambridge: Cambridge University Press, 41–61.

Lengrand, D. (1993). 'M. Valerius Muttines'. *CT* 165: 31–45.

Levene, D. S. (1992). 'Sallust's *Jugurtha*: An "Historical Fragment"'. *JRS* 82: 53–70.

Levene, D. S. (1993). *Religion in Livy.* Leiden: E. J. Brill.

—— (1997). 'Pity, Fear and the Historical Audience: Tacitus on the Fall of Vitellius', in S. M. Braund and C. Gill (eds.), *The Passions in Roman Thought and Literature.* Cambridge: Cambridge University Press, 128–49.

—— (2006a). 'History, Metahistory, and Audience Response in Livy 45'. *CA* 25: 73–108.

—— (2006b). Review of Davies 2004. *CPh* 101: 419–24.

Levene, D. S., and Nelis, D. P. (eds.). (2002). *Clio and the Poets: Augustan Poetry and the Traditions of Ancient Historiography.* Leiden: Brill.

Lewis, D. (1986). 'Causal Explanation', in *Philosophical Papers* II. Oxford: Oxford University Press, 214–40 = Rubin 1993: 182–206.

Liebeschuetz, W. (1967). 'The Religious Position of Livy's History'. *JRS* 57: 45–55.

Linderski, J. (1986). 'The Augural Law'. *ANRW* II 16.3: 2146–312.

—— (1993). 'Roman Religion in Livy', in Schuller 1993: 53–70.

Lipovsky, J. P. (1981). *A Historiographical Study of Livy Books VI–X.* New York, NY: Arno Press.

Lloyd, A. B. (ed.) (1996). *Battle in Antiquity.* Swansea: Classical Press of Wales.

Lomas, K. (1997). 'Constructing "the Greek": Ethnic Identity in Magna Graecia', in T. Cornell and K. Lomas (eds.), *Gender and Ethnicity in Ancient Italy.* London: Accordia Research Institute, 31–41.

Long, A. A. (1976). Review of L. Edelstein and I. G. Kidd, *Posidonius. Volume I: The Fragments* (Cambridge: Cambridge University Press, 1972). *CR* 26: 72–5.

—— (1982). 'Astrology: Arguments Pro and Contra', in J. Barnes, J. Brunschwig, M. Burnyeat, and M. Schofield (eds.), *Science and Speculation: Studies in Hellenistic Theory and Practice.* Cambridge: Cambridge University Press, 165–92.

—— (1983). 'Greek Ethics after MacIntyre and the Stoic Community of Reason'. *Ancient Philosophy* 3: 184–97 = Long 1996: 156–77.

—— (1996). *Stoic Studies.* Berkeley, CA: University of California Press.

Lorsch, R. S. (1997). 'Augustus' Conception and the Heroic Tradition'. *Latomus* 56: 790–9.

Luce, T. J. (1965). 'The Dating of Livy's First Decade'. *TAPhA* 96: 209–40 = Chaplin and Kraus 2009: 17–47.

—— (1977). *Livy: The Composition of his History.* Princeton, NJ: Princeton University Press.

Macaulay, G. C. (1885). *Livy: Books XXIII and XXIV.* London: Macmillan and Co.

McCulloch jr., H. Y. (1984). *Narrative Cause in the Annals of Tacitus.* Königstein: Verlag Anton Hain.

McDonald, A. H. (1956). Review of Klaffenbach 1954. *JRS* 46: 153–7.

—— (1957). 'The Style of Livy'. *JRS* 47: 155–72 = Chaplin and Kraus 2009: 222–58.

McKeown, J. C. (1987). *Ovid: Amores: Text, Prolegomena and Commentary,* Vol. 1. Liverpool: Francis Cairns.

Mackie, H. (1996). *Talking Trojan: Speech and Community in the* Iliad. Lanham, MD: Rowan & Littlefield.

Mackie, J. L. (1974). *The Cement of the Universe: A Study of Causation.* Oxford: Clarendon Press.

Mader, G. (1993). ʼ*Ἀννίβας ὑβριστής*: Traces of a "Tragic" Pattern in Livy's Hannibal Portrait in Book XXI?ʼ. *AncSoc* 24: 205–24.

Mahé-Simon, M. (2003). ʼLʼItalie chez Tite-Live: lʼambiguïté dʼun conceptʼ. *RPh* 77: 235–58.

Malitz, J. (1983). *Die Historien des Poseidonios.* Munich: C. H. Beckʼsche Verlagsbuch-handlung.

Maltby, R. (1996). ʼSense and Structure in Tibullus (2.2.21–2, 1.1.78, 2.1.83–90, 1.5.1–8, 1.6.5–8)ʼ. *PLLS* 9: 93–102.

Mandelbaum, M. (1980). ʼThe Presuppositions of *Metahistory*ʼ. *History and Theory* 19.4 Beiheft 19: 39–54.

Mantel, N. (1991). *Poeni foedifragi: Untersuchungen zur Darstellung römisch-karthagischer Verträge zwischen 241 und 201 v. Chr. durch die römische Historiographie.* Munich: Editio Maris.

Marchetti, P. (1972). ʼLa deuxième guerre punique en Sicile: les années 215–214 et le récit de Tite-Liveʼ. *BIBR* 42: 5–26.

Marincola, J. (1997). *Authority and Tradition in Ancient Historiography.* Cambridge: Cambridge University Press.

—— (1999). ʼGenre, Convention and Innovation in Greco-Roman Historiographyʼ, in Kraus 1999b: 281–324.

—— (2003). ʼBeyond Pity and Fear: The Emotions of Historyʼ. *AncSoc* 33: 285–315.

—— (2005). ʼConcluding Narratives: Looking to the End in Classical Historiographyʼ. *PLLS* 12: 285–320.

Martin, J. M. K. (1941–42). ʼLivy and Romanceʼ. *G&R* 11: 124–9.

Mattern, S. (1999). *Rome and the Enemy: Imperial Strategy in the Principate.* Berkeley, CA: University of California Press.

Mauersberger, A. (ed.) (1956). *Polybios-Lexicon* I.1. Berlin: Akademie-Verlag.

Maurach, G. (1988). *Der Poenulus des Plautus.* Heidelberg: Carl Winter Universitäts-verlag.

Meister, K. (1967). *Die sizilische Geschichte bei Diodor von den Anfängen bis zum Tod des Agathokles.* Diss, Munich.

—— (1979). Review of Tränkle 1977. *AAHG* 32: 175–82.

—— (1991). ʼAgatocle in Diodoro: interpretazione e valutazione nella storiografia modernaʼ, in Galvagno and Molè Ventura 1991: 187–99.

Mensching, E. (1996). ʼÜber Livius, den alten und den jungen Marcellusʼ, in C. Klodt (ed.), *Satura Lanx: Festschrift für Werner A. Krenkel zum 70. Geburtstag.* Hildes-heim: Georg Olms Verlag, 257–77.

Meritt, B. D. (1962). ʼThe Seasons in Thucydidesʼ. *Historia* 11: 436–46.

—— (1964). ʼThe End of Winter in Thucydidesʼ. *Hesperia* 33: 228–30.

Meyer, E. (1958). ʼHannibals Alpenübergangʼ. *MH* 15: 227–34.

Miles, G. B. (1995). *Livy: Reconstructing Early Rome.* Ithaca, NY: Cornell University Press.

Miltner, F. (1943). 'Zwischen Trebia und Trasimen (218/17 v. Chr.)'. *Hermes* 78: 1–21.

Mineo, B. (2006). *Tite-Live et l'histoire de Rome*. Paris: Klincksieck.

Moles, J. L. (1988). *Plutarch: The Life of Cicero*. Warminster: Aris & Phillips.

—— (1993a). 'Truth and Untruth in Herodotus and Thucydides', in Gill and Wiseman 1993: 88–121.

—— (1993b). 'Livy's Preface'. *PCPhS* 39: 141–68.

Molin, M. (2003). 'Les *Histoires* de Polybe entre essai d'objectivité et déformation historique: l'exemple du livre III', in G. Lachenaud and D. Longrée (eds.), *Grecs et Romains aux prises avec l'histoire*. Rennes: Presses Universitaires de Rennes, 279–95.

Möller, A., and Luraghi, N. (1995). 'Time in the Writing of History: Perceptions and Structures'. *SStor* 28: 3–15.

Momigliano, A. D. (1966). 'Some Observations on Causes of War in Ancient Historiography', in *Studies in Historiography*. London: Weidenfeld & Nicolson, 112–26.

Mommsen, T. (1879). *Römische Forschungen*, Vol. 2. Berlin: Weidmannsche Buchhandlung.

Moore, T. J. (1989). *Artistry and Ideology: Livy's Vocabulary of Virtue*. Frankfurt am Main: Athenäum Verlag.

Moreschini, C. (1984), 'Livio e il mondo greco'. *SCO* 34: 27–57.

Moret, P. (1997). 'Les Ilergètes et leurs voisins dans la troisième décade de Tite-Live'. *Pallas* 46: 147–65.

Mueller, H.-F. (1999). 'Imperial Rome and the Habitations of Cruelty', in S. N. Byrne and E. P. Cueva (eds.), *Veritatis Amicitiaeque Causa: Essays in Honor of Anna Lydia Motto and John R. Clark*. Wauconda, IL: Bolchazy-Carducci Publishers, 165–96.

Münzer, F. (1897). *Beiträge zur Quellenkritik der Naturgeschichte des Plinius*. Berlin: Weidmannsche Buchhandlung.

Munn, N. D. (1992). 'The Cultural Anthropology of Time: A Critical Essay'. *Annual Review of Anthropology* 21: 93–123.

Munslow, A. (2006). *Deconstructing History*. 2nd edn. London: Routledge.

Needham, R. (1976). 'Skulls and Causality'. *Man*, NS 11: 71–88.

Nelis, D. (2001). *Vergil's Aeneid and the Argonautica of Apollonius Rhodius*. Leeds: Francis Cairns.

Nissen, H. (1863). *Kritische Untersuchungen über die Quellen der vierten und fünften Dekade des Livius*. Berlin: Weidmannsche Buchhandlung.

O'Gorman, E. (1993). 'No Place Like Rome: Identity and Difference in the Germania of Tacitus'. *Ramus* 22: 135–54.

O'Hara, J. J. (2007). *Inconsistency in Roman Epic: Studies in Catullus, Lucretius, Vergil, Ovid and Lucan*. Cambridge: Cambridge University Press.

Oakley, S. P. (1992). 'Livy and Clodius Licinus'. *CQ* 42: 547–51.

—— (1997). *A Commentary on Livy Books VI–X*, Vol. 1. Oxford: Clarendon Press.

—— (1998). *A Commentary on Livy Books VI–X*, Vol. 2. Oxford: Clarendon Press.

—— (2005a). *A Commentary on Livy Books VI–X*, Vol. 3. Oxford: Clarendon Press.

—— (2005b). *A Commentary on Livy Books VI–X*, Vol. 4. Oxford: Clarendon Press.

Ogilvie, R. M. (1965). *A Commentary on Livy Books 1–5*. Oxford: Clarendon Press.

Otto, A. (1890). *Die Sprichwörter und sprichwörtlichen Redensarten der Römer*. Leipzig: B. G. Teubner.

Palmieri, N. (ed.) (2003). *Rationnel et irrationel dans la médecine ancienne et médiévale*. Saint-Étienne: Publications de l'Université de Saint-Étienne.

Parry, A. (1981). *Logos and Ergon in Thucydides*. New York, NY: Arno Press.

Paschoud, F. (1993). 'Refléxions sur quelques aspects de l'idéologie patriotique romaine de Tite-Live', in Schuller 1993: 125–49.

Paul, G. M. (1982). '*Urbs Capta*: Sketch of an Ancient Literary Motif'. *Phoenix* 36: 144–55.

Pearson, L. (1960). *The Lost Histories of Alexander the Great*. New York, NY: American Philological Association.

—— (1987). *The Greek Historians of the West: Timaeus and his Predecessors*. Atlanta, GA: Scholars Press.

Pédech, P. (1964). *La méthode historique de Polybe*. Paris: Société d'édition "Les belles lettres".

Pelling, C. B. R. (1980). 'Plutarch's Adaptation of his Source-Material'. *JHS* 100: 127–40 (revised version in Pelling 2002: 91–115).

—— (1988). 'Aspects of Plutarch's Characterization'. *ICS* 13: 257–74 (revised version in Pelling 2002: 283–300).

—— (1989). 'Plutarch: Roman Heroes and Greek Culture', in Griffin and Barnes 1989: 199–232.

—— (1990a). 'Childhood and Personality in Greek Biography', in Pelling 1990b: 213–44 (revised version in Pelling 2002: 301–38).

—— (ed.) (1990b). *Characterization and Individuality in Greek Literature*. Oxford: Clarendon Press.

—— (1990c). 'Truth and Fiction in Plutarch's *Lives*', in D.A. Russell (ed.), *Antonine Literature*. Oxford: Clarendon Press, 19–52 (revised version in Pelling 2002: 143–70).

—— (1992). 'Plutarch and Thucydides', in P. A. Stadter (ed.), *Plutarch and the Historical Tradition*. London: Routledge, 10–40 (revised version in Pelling 2002: 117–41).

—— (1997a). 'Is Death the End? Closure in Plutarch's *Lives*', in Roberts, Dunn, and Fowler 1997: 228–50 (revised version in Pelling 2002: 365–86).

—— (1997b). 'Tragical Dreamer: Some Dreams in the Roman Historians'. *G&R* 44: 197–213.

—— (2002). *Plutarch and History*. Swansea: Classical Press of Wales.

—— (2007). '*De Malignitate Plutarchi*: Plutarch, Herodotus, and the Persian Wars', in E. Bridges, E. Hall, P. J. Rhodes (eds.), *Cultural Responses to the Persian Wars: Antiquity to the Third Millennium*. Oxford: Oxford University Press, 145–64.

Petersen, H. (1961). 'Livy and Augustus'. *TAPhA* 92: 440–52.

Pfeilschifter, R. (2000). 'Andere Länder, andere Sitten? *Mores* als Argument in der republikanischen Außenpolitik', in B. Link and M. Stemmler (eds.), *Mos Maiorum: Untersuchungen zu den Formen der Identitätstiftung und Stabilisierung in der römischen Republik*. Stuttgart: Franz Steiner Verlag, 99–140.

Pianezzola, E. (1969). *Traduzione e ideologia: Livio interprete di Polibio*. Bologna: Casa Editrice Pàtron.

Piégay-Gros, N. (1996). *Introduction à l'intertextualité*. Paris: Dunod.

Pina Polo, F. (2006). 'Deportation, Kolonisation, Migration: Bevölkerungsverschiebungen im republikanischen Italien und Formen der Identitätsbildung', in Jehne and Pfeilschichter 2006: 171–206.

Plathner, H.-G. (1934). *Die Schlachtschilderungen bei Livius.* Diss., Breslau.

Plöger, H. (1975). *Studien zum literarischen Feldherrnporträt römischer Autoren des 1. Jahrhunderts v. Chr.* Diss., Kiel.

Pobjoy, M. (1996). 'Rome and Capua from Republic to Empire'. DPhil thesis: Oxford.

Podes, S. (1990). 'Handlungserklärung bei Polybios: intellectualisme historique?'. *AncSoc* 21: 215–40.

Polverini, L. (1998). 'Le regioni nell' Italia romana'. *GeogrAnt* 7: 23–33.

Pomeroy, A. J. (1989). 'Hannibal at Nuceria'. *Historia* 38: 162–76.

Poznanski, L. (1994). 'La polémologie pragmatique de Polybe'. *JS* 1994: 19–74.

Prandi, L. (1979). 'La "fides punica" e il pregiudizio anticartaginese'. *CISA* 6: 90–7.

Préaux, C. (1973). *La lune dans la pensée grecque.* Brussels: Palais des Académies.

Pritchett, W. K. (1964). 'Thucydides V 20'. *Historia* 13: 21–36.

Prontera, F. (2003). 'La geografia di Polybio: tradizione e innovazione', in Santos Yanguas and Torregaray Pagola 2003: 103–11.

Pucci, J. (1998). *The Full-Knowing Reader: Allusion and the Power of the Reader in the Western Literary Tradition.* New Haven, CT: Yale University Press.

Rambaud, M. (1980). 'Exemples de déformation historique chez Tite-Live: le Tessin, la Trébie, Trasimène'. *Caesarodunum* 15 bis: 109–26.

Ramosino, L. C. (2004). *Plinio il vecchio e la tradizione storica di Roma nella* Naturalis Historia. Alessandria: Edizioni dell'Orso.

Ravinel, R. de (1962). 'La bataille du Métaure et l'hostilité entre M. Livius et Cl. Néron (à propos d'un *sed*)'. *LEC* 30: 3–19.

Rawson, E. (1975). 'Caesar's Heritage: Hellenistic Kings and their Roman Equals'. *JRS* 65: 148–59 = Rawson 1991: 169–88.

—— (1991). *Roman Culture and Society: Collected Papers.* Oxford: Clarendon Press.

Reeve, M. (1987). 'The Future in the Past', in M. Whitby, P. Hardie, and M. Whitby (eds.), *Homo Viator: Classical Essays for John Bramble.* Bristol: Bristol Classical Press, 319–22.

Reid, J. S. (1915). 'Problems of the Second Punic War: III. Rome and Her Italian Allies'. *JRS* 5: 87–124.

Reinhardt, K. (1926). *Kosmos und Sympathie: Neue Untersuchungen über Poseidonios.* Munich: C. H. Beck'sche Verlagsbuchhandlung.

Reinhold, M. (1985). 'Human Nature as Cause in Ancient Historiography', in J. W. Eadie and J. Ober (eds.), *The Craft of the Ancient Historian: Essays in Honor of Chester G. Starr.* Lanham, MD: University Press of America, 21–40.

Reinmuth, O. W. (1933). 'Vergil's Use of *interea*, A Study of the Treatment of Contemporaneous Events in Roman Epic'. *AJPh* 54: 323–39.

Rhodes, P. J. (1994). 'In Defence of the Greek Historians'. *G&R* 41: 156–71.

Rich, J. W. (1976). *Declaring War in the Roman Republic in the Period of Transmarine Expansion.* Brussels: Collection Latomus.

—— (1978). Review of Tränkle 1977. *JRS* 68: 226–7.

—— (1984). 'Roman Aims in the First Macedonian War'. *PCPhS* 30: 126–80.

—— (1996). 'The Origins of the Second Punic War', in Cornell, Rankov, and Sabin 1996: 1–37.

—— (1997). 'Structuring Roman History: The Consular Year and the Roman Historical Tradition'. *Histos* 1 http://www.dur.ac.uk/Classics/histos/1997/rich1.html (revised version in Chaplin and Kraus 2009: 118–47).

Riggsby, A. M. (2004). 'The Rhetoric of Character in the Roman Courts', in J. Powell and J. Paterson (eds.), *Cicero the Advocate*. Oxford: Oxford University Press, 165–85.

—— (2006). *Caesar in Gaul and Rome: War in Words*. Austin, TX: University of Texas Press.

Rizzo, F. P. (1983–84). 'Baton di Sinope: storico di Geronimo'. *RSA* 13–14: 127–41.

Robert, C. (1914). 'Zu Pindars VIII Paean'. *Hermes* 49: 315–19.

Roberts, D. H., Dunn, F. M., and Fowler, D. (eds.) (1997). *Classical Closure*. Princeton, NJ: Princeton University Press.

Rodgers, B. S. (1986). 'Great Expeditions: Livy on Thucydides'. *TAPhA* 116: 335–52.

Rood, T. (1998). *Thucydides: Narrative and Explanation*. Oxford: Oxford University Press.

Rorty, R. (ed.) (1967). *The Linguistic Turn: Essays in Philosophical Method*. Chicago, IL: University of Chicago Press.

—— (1979). *Philosophy and the Mirror of Nature*. Princeton, NJ: Princeton University Press.

—— (2000). 'Response to Bjørn Ramberg', in Brandom 2000: 370–7.

Rosenberg, B. (1996). *Little Dorrit's Shadows: Character and Contradiction in Dickens*. Columbia, MO: University of Missouri Press.

Rosenstein, N. (1990a). *Imperatores Victi: Military Defeats and Aristocratic Competition in the Middle and Late Republic*. Berkeley, CA: University of California Press.

—— (1990b). 'War, Failure, and Aristocratic Competition'. *CPh* 85: 255–65.

—— (1993). 'Competition and Crisis in Mid-Republican Rome'. *Phoenix* 47: 313–38.

Ross, S. A. (2005). '*Barbarophonos*. Language and Panhellenism in the *Iliad*'. *CPh* 100: 299–316.

Rossi, A. (2002). 'The Fall of Troy: Between Tradition and Genre', in Levene and Nelis 2002: 231–51.

—— (2004). 'Parallel Lives: Hannibal and Scipio in Livy's Third Decade'. *TAPhA* 134: 359–81.

Roth, J. P. (2006). 'Siege Narrative in Livy: Representation and Reality', in S. Dillon and K. Welch (eds.), *Representations of War in Ancient Rome*. Cambridge: Cambridge University Press, 49–67.

Rubin, D.-H. (ed.) (1993). *Explanation*. Oxford: Oxford University Press.

Rudd, N. (1976). *Lines of Enquiry: Studies in Latin Poetry*. Cambridge: Cambridge University Press.

Rüger, J. (1965). *Barbarus: Wort und Begriff bei Cicero, Livius, Caesar*. Diss., Göttingen.

Russell, D. A. (1979). '*De Imitatione*', in West and Woodman 1979b: 1–16.

Rutherford, I. (2001). *Pindar's Paeans*. Oxford: Oxford University Press.

Sabin, P. (1996). 'The Mechanics of Battle in the Second Punic War', in Cornell, Rankov, and Sabin 1996: 59–77.

—— (2000). 'The Face of Roman Battle'. *JRS* 90: 1–17.

Sacks, K. S. (1981). *Polybius on the Writing of History.* Berkeley, CA: University of California Press.

—— (1990). *Diodorus Siculus and the First Century.* Princeton, NJ: Princeton University Press.

—— (1994). 'Diodorus and his Sources: Conformity and Creativity', in Hornblower 1994: 213–32.

Sailor, D. (2006). 'Dirty Linen, Fabrication, and the Authorities of Livy and Augustus. *TAPhA* 136: 329–88.

Saller, R. P. (1982). *Personal Patronage under the Early Empire.* Cambridge: Cambridge University Press.

Salmon, E. T. (1984). 'Scipio in Spain and the Sucro Incident'. *StudClas* 24: 77–84.

Samoyault, T. (2001). *L'intertextualité.* Paris: Éditions Nathan.

Sanctis, G. de (1968). *Storia dei Romani,* Vol. 3.2. 2nd edn., Florence: La Nuova Italia.

Santoro L'Hoir, F. (1990). 'Heroic Epithets and Recurrent Themes in *Ab Urbe Condita'. TAPhA* 120: 221–41.

Santos Yanguas, J., and Torregaray Pagola, E. (eds). (2003). *Polybio y la península Ibérica.* Zarautz: Vitoria-Gasteiz.

Schäublin, C. (1985). 'Cicero, "De Divinatione" und Poseidonius'. *MH* 42: 157–67.

—— (1986). 'Ementita Auspicia'. *WS* 20: 165–81.

Schmitt, T. (1991). *Hannibals Siegeszug: Historiographische und historische Studien vom allem zu Polybius und Livius.* Munich: Tuduv.

Schuller, W. (ed.) (1993). *Livius: Aspekte seines Werkes.* Konstanz: Universitätsverlag Konstanz.

Schwarte, K.-H. (1983). *Der Ausbruch des zweiten punischen Krieg—Rechtsfrage und Überlieferung.* Wiesbaden: Franz Steiner Verlag.

Schwartz, E. (1905). 'Diodoros'. *RE* V: 663–704.

Scott, P. (1986). 'Qualities of Leadership in Livy's History'. D.Phil. thesis: Oxford.

Scullard, H. H. (1930). *Scipio Africanus in the Second Punic War.* Cambridge: Cambridge University Press.

—— (1981). *Festivals and Ceremonies of the Roman Republic.* London: Thames and Hudson.

Seeck, G. A. (1983). 'Livius: Schriftsteller oder Historiker? Zum Problem der literarischen Darstellung historische Vorgänge (Livius, Buch 21)', in Lefèvre and Olshausen 1983: 81–95.

Seemüller, J. (1908). *Die Dubletten in der dritten Dekade des Livius.* Neuburg: Griessmayersche Buchdruckerei.

Seibert, J. (1988). 'Der Alpenübergang Hannibals: ein gelöstes Problem'. *Gymnasium* 95: 21–73.

—— (1993a). *Hannibal.* Darmstadt: Wissenschaftliche Buchgesellschaft.

—— (1993b). *Forschungen zu Hannibal.* Darmstadt: Wissenschaftliche Buchgesellschaft.

Sélincourt, A. de (tr.) (1965). *Livy: The War with Hannibal.* London: Penguin Books.

Sharrock, A. (2000). 'Texts, Parts, and (W)holes in Theory', in Sharrock and Morales 2000: 1–39.

Sharrock, A., and Morales, H. (eds.) (2000). *Intratextuality: Greek and Roman Textual Relations.* Oxford: Oxford University Press.

Shaw, P.-J. (2003). *Discrepancies in Olympiad Dating and Chronological Problems of Archaic Peloponnesian History.* Stuttgart: Franz Steiner Verlag.

Sherwin-White, A. N. (1973). *The Roman Citizenship.* 2nd edn. Oxford: Clarendon Press.

Skutsch, O. (1985). *The Annals of Quintus Ennius.* Oxford: Clarendon Press.

Small, J. P. (1997). *Wax Tablets of the Mind: Cognitive Studies of Memory and Literacy in Classical Antiquity.* London: Routledge.

Smith, B. H. (1968). *Poetic Closure: A Study of How Poems End.* Chicago, IL: University of Chicago Press.

Soltau, W. (1894a). 'Die griechischen Quellen in Livius' 23–30. Buch'. *Philologus* 53: 588–628.

—— (1894b). *Livius' Quellen in der III. Dekade.* Berlin: Mayer & Müller.

—— (1897). *Livius' Geschichtswerk: seine Komposition und seine Quellen.* Leipzig: Dieterich'sche Verlags-Buchhandlung.

Sontheimer, W. (1934). 'Der Feldzug Hannibals in Oberitalien bis zur Schlacht an der Trebia bei Livius und Polybius (Livius XXI 39–56; Polybius III 56–74)'. *Klio* 9: 84–121.

Sorabji, R. (1980). *Necessity, Cause and Blame: Perspectives on Aristotle's Theory.* Ithaca, NY: Cornell University Press.

Southgate, B. (2003). *Postmodernism in History: Fear or Freedom?* London: Routledge.

—— (2005). *What is History For?* London: Routledge.

Spencer, D. (2002). *The Roman Alexander: Reading a Cultural Myth.* Exeter: University of Exeter Press.

Stadter, P. A. (1972). 'The Structure of Livy's History'. *Historia* 21: 287–307 = Chaplin and Kraus 2009: 91–116.

Stahl, H.-P. (2003). *Thucydides: Man's Place in History.* Swansea: The Classical Press of Wales.

Stanton, G. R. (1971). '*Cunctando Restituit Rem*: The Tradition about Fabius'. *Antichthon* 5: 49–56.

Starr, R. J. (1981). 'Cross-References in Roman Prose'. *AJPh* 102: 431–7.

—— (2001). 'The Flexibility of Literary Meaning and the Role of the Reader in Antiquity'. *Latomus* 60: 433–45.

Stemplinger, E. (1919). *Sympathieglaube und Sympathiekuren in Altertum und Neuzeit.* Munich: Verlag der Ärtzlichen Rundschau Otto Gmelin.

Stern, S. (2003). *Time and Process in Ancient Judaism.* Oxford: The Littman Library of Jewish Civilization.

Stok, F. (1993). 'Paradigmi dell' etnografia antica'. *Il piccolo Hans* 78: 74–96.

Strevens, M. (2004). 'The Causal and Unification Approaches to Explanation Unified—Causally'. *Noûs* 38.1: 154–76

—— (2008). *Depth: An Account of Scientific Explanation.* Cambridge, MA: Harvard University Press.

Stübler, G. (1941). *Die Religiosität des Livius.* Stuttgart: W. Kohlhammer Verlag.

Stylianou, P. J. (1998). *A Historical Commentary on Diodorus Siculus Book 15.* Oxford: Clarendon Press.

Sumner, G. V. (1975). 'Elections at Rome in 217 B.C.' *Phoenix* 29: 250–9.

Swain, S. C. R. (1989). 'Character Change in Plutarch'. *Phoenix* 43: 62–8.

—— (1990). 'Hellenic Culture and the Roman Heroes of Plutarch'. *JHS* 110: 126–45.

Syme, R. (1938). 'Caesar, the Senate, and Italy'. *PBSR* 14: 1–31 = Syme 1979: 88–119.

—— (1939). *The Roman Revolution*. Oxford: Clarendon Press.

—— (1957). 'The Friend of Tacitus'. *JRS* 47: 131–5.

—— (1958a). *Tacitus*. Oxford: Clarendon Press.

—— (1958b). 'Consulates in Absence'. *JRS* 48: 1–9 = Syme 1979: 378–92.

—— (1959). 'Livy and Augustus'. *HSCPh* 64: 27–87 = Syme 1979: 400–54.

—— (1979). *Roman Papers*, Vol. 1, E. Badian (ed.) Oxford: Clarendon Press.

Talbert, R. J. A. (1984). *The Senate of Imperial Rome*. Princeton, NJ: Princeton University Press.

Texier, I. G. (1979). 'Quomodo apud Livium Afri depingantur', in *Africa et Roma: acta omnium gentium ac nationum conventus Latinis litteris linguaeque fovendis*. Rome: "L'Erma" di Bretschneider, 174–84.

Thiel, J. H. (1946). *Studies on the History of Roman Sea-Power in Republican Times*. Amsterdam: North Holland Publishing Company.

Thomas, R. F. (1986). 'Virgil's *Georgics* and the Art of Reference'. *HSCPh* 90: 171–98.

Thompson, L. A. (1981). 'Carthage and the Massylian *coup d'état* of 206 B.C.'. *Historia* 30: 120–6.

Toppani, I. (1977–78). 'Una regina da ritrovare: Sofoniba e il suo tragico destino'. *AIV* 136: 561–78.

Tränkle, H. (1968). 'Beobachtungen und Erwägungen zum Wandel der livianischen Sprache'. *WS* 2: 103–52.

—— (1977). *Livius und Polybios*. Basel: Schwabe.

Twyman, B. L. (1984). 'The Consular Elections for 216 BC and the *Lex Maenia de patrum auctoritate*'. *CPh* 79: 285–94.

Ungern-Sternberg, J. von (1975). *Capua im zweiten punischen Krieg: Untersuchungen zur römischen Annalistik*. Munich: C. H. Beck'sche Buchhandlung.

Urban, R. (1991). 'Die Kelten in Italien und in Gallien bei Polybios', in J. Seibert (ed.), *Hellenistische Studien. Gedenkschrift für Hermann Bengston*. Munich: Editio Maris, 135–57.

Urso, G. (1995). 'La deportazione dei Capuani nel 211 a.c.', in M. Sordi (ed.), *Coercizione e mobilità umana nel mondo antico*. Milan: Vita e Pensiero, 161–76.

—— (2003). '*Pro Italia vobis est pugnandum*: Annibale al Ticino'. *RSA* 33: 67–90.

Vallet, G. (1961). 'Un exemple de partialité chez Tite-Live: les premiers combats autour de Gereonium (Liv. XXII, 24)'. *REL* 39: 182–95.

—— (1964). 'Caius Terentius Varron ou l'expression d'une antipathie chez Tite-Live', in M. Renard and R. Schilling (eds.), *Hommages à Jean Bayet*. Brussels: Latomus, 707–17.

—— (1966). *T. Livi Ab Urbe Condita Liber XXII*. Paris: Press Universitaires de France.

Vasaly, A. (2002). 'The Structure of Livy's First Pentad and the Augustan Poetry Book', in Levene and Nelis 2002: 275–90.

Veen, J. E. van der (1996). *The Significant and the Insignificant: Five Studies in Herodotus' View of History*. Amsterdam: J. C. Gieben.

Verbrugghe, G. P. (1989). 'On the Meaning of *Annales*, On the Meaning of Annalist'. *Philologus* 133: 192–230.

Villard, F. (1994). 'Les sièges de Syracuse et leurs pestilences', in R. Ginouvès, A. M. Guimer-Sorbets, J. Jouanna, L. Villard (eds.), *L'eau, la santé et la maladie dans le monde grec*. Paris: Bulletin de correspondence hellénique 28, 337–44.

Vretska, K. (1955). *Studien zu Sallusts Bellum Iugurthinum*. Vienna: SAWW 229.4.

Vrettos, A. (2000). 'Defining Habits: Dickens and the Psychology of Repetition'. *Victorian Studies* 42.3: 399–426.

Walbank, F. W. (1947). 'The Geography of Polybius'. *C&M* 9: 155–82.

—— (1957). *A Historical Commentary on Polybius*, Vol. 1. Oxford: Clarendon Press.

—— (1967). *A Historical Commentary on Polybius*, Vol. 2. Oxford: Clarendon Press.

—— (1972). *Polybius*. Berkeley, CA: University of California Press.

—— (1975). '*Symploke*: Its Role in Polybius' *Histories*'. *YCS* 24: 197–212 = Walbank 1985: 313–24.

—— (1979). *A Historical Commentary on Polybius*, Vol. 3. Oxford: Clarendon Press.

—— (1985). *Selected Papers*. Cambridge: Cambridge University Press.

Walcutt, C. C. (1966). *Man's Changing Mask: Modes and Methods of Characterization in Fiction*. Minneapolis, MN: University of Minnesota Press.

Waldherr, G. H. (2000). '"Punica Fides" – das Bild der Karthager in Rom'. *Gymnasium* 107: 193–222.

Walsh, P. G. (1958). 'Livy and Stoicism'. *AJPh* 79 (1958), 355–75.

—— (1961). *Livy: His Historical Aims and Methods*. Cambridge: Cambridge University Press.

—— (1965). 'Massinissa'. *JRS* 55: 149–60.

—— (1973). *Livy: Book XXI*. London: University Tutorial Press.

Walter, U. (2003). 'Opfer ihrer Ungleichzeitigkeit: Die Gesamtgeschichten im ersten Jahrhundert v. Chr. und die fortdauernde Attraktivität des "Annalistischen Schemas"', in Eigler *et al.* 2003: 135–56.

—— (2004). '"Ein Ebenbild des Vaters": Familiale Wiederholungen in der historiographische Traditionsbildung der römische Republik'. *Hermes* 132: 406–25.

Wardle, D. (1998). *Valerius Maximus: Memorable Deeds and Sayings Book 1*. Oxford: Clarendon Press.

—— (2006). *Cicero: On Divination Book 1*. Oxford: Clarendon Press.

Weber, C. (1983). "Two Chronological Contradictions in Catullus 64'. *TAPhA* 113: 263–71.

Webster, J. (2001). 'Creolizing the Roman Provinces'. *AJA* 105: 209–25.

Webster, J., and Cooper, N. (eds.) (1996). *Roman Imperialism: Post-Colonial Perspectives*. Leicester: School of Archaeological Studies, University of Leicester.

Weçowski, M. (2004). 'The Hedgehog and the Fox: Form and Meaning in the Prologue of Herodotus'. *JHS* 124: 143–64.

Weippert, O. (1972). *Alexander-Imitatio und römische Politik in republikanischer Zeit.* Diss., Würzburg.

Weissenborn, W. (1872). *Titi Livi Ab Urbe Condita Libri*, Vol. 4. 3rd edn. Berlin: Weidmannsche Buchhandlung.

West, D., and Woodman, T. (1979a). 'Epilogue', in West and Woodman 1979b: 195–200.

West, D., and Woodman, T. (eds.). (1979b). *Creative Imitation and Latin Literature.* Cambridge: Cambridge University Press.

Wheeldon, M. J. (1989). '"True Stories": The Reception of Historiography in Antiquity', in A. Cameron (ed.), *History as Text.* London: Duckworth, 36–63.

Wheeler, E. L. (1988). *Stratagem and the Vocabulary of Military Trickery.* Leiden: E. J. Brill.

Wheeler, S. M. (1999). *A Discourse of Wonders: Audience and Performance in Ovid's* Metamorphoses. Philadelphia, PA: University of Pennsylvania Press.

White, H. (1973). *Metahistory: The Historical Imagination in Nineteenth-Century Europe.* Baltimore, MD: Johns Hopkins University Press.

—— (1978). *Tropics of Discourse: Essays in Cultural Criticism.* Baltimore, MD: Johns Hopkins University Press.

—— (1987). *The Content of the Form: Narrative Discourse and Historical Representation.* Baltimore, MD: Johns Hopkins University Press.

Wiehemeyer. W. (1938). *Proben historischer Kritik aus Livius XXI–XLV.* Diss., Münster.

Wilcox, D. J. (1987). *The Measure of Times Past: Pre-Newtonian Chronologies and the Rhetoric of Relative Time.* Chicago, IL: University of Chicago Press.

Will, W. (1983). 'Imperatores victi: zum Bild besiegter römischer Consuln bei Livius'. *Historia* 32: 173–82.

Wille, G. (1973). *Die Aufbau des Livianischen Geschichtswerk.* Amsterdam: Verlag B. R. Grüner.

Williams, J. H. C. (2001). *Beyond the Rubicon: Romans and Gauls in Republican Italy.* Oxford: Oxford University Press.

Wills, J. (1996). *Repetition in Latin Poetry: Figures of Allusion.* Oxford: Clarendon Press.

Wiseman, T. P. (1971). *New Men in the Roman Senate: 139 B.C.–A.D. 14.* Oxford: Oxford University Press.

—— (1979). *Clio's Cosmetics: Three Studies in Greco-Roman Literature.* Leicester: Leicester University Press.

—— (1981). 'Practice and Theory in Roman Historiography'. *History* 66: 375–93.

—— (1993). 'Lying Historians: Seven Types of Mendacity', in Gill and Wiseman 1993: 122–46.

Wisse, J. (1989). *Ethos and Pathos from Aristotle to Cicero.* Amsterdam: Adolf M. Hakkert.

Wissowa, G. (1912). *Religion und Kultus der Römer*, 2nd edn. Munich: C. H. Beck'sche Verlagsbuchhandlung.

Witte, K. (1910). 'Über die Form der Darstellung in Livius Geschichtswerk'. *RhM* 65: 270–305, 359–419.

Woodman, A. J. (1979). 'Self-Imitation and the Substance of History: *Annals* 1.61–5 and *Histories* 2.70, 5.14–15', in West and Woodman 1979b: 143–55 = Woodman 1998: 70–85.

—— (1983). 'From Hannibal to Hitler: The Literature of War'. *University of Leeds Review* 26 (1983), 107–24 = Woodman 1998: 1–20.

—— (1988). *Rhetoric in Classical Historiography: Four Studies.* London: Croom Helm.

—— (1989). 'Tacitus' Obituary of Tiberius'. *CQ* 39: 197–205 = Woodman 1998: 155–67.

—— (1998). *Tacitus Reviewed.* Oxford: Clarendon Press.

—— (2006). 'Mutiny and Madness: Tacitus *Annals* 1.16–49'. *Arethusa* 39 (2006), 303–29.

—— (forthcoming). 'Community Health: Metaphor in Latin Historiography'. *PLLS* 14.

Woodman, A. J. and Martin, R. H. (1996). *The Annals of Tacitus: Book 3.* Cambridge: Cambridge University Press.

Woolf, G. (1998). *Becoming Roman: The Origins of Provincial Civilization in Gaul.* Cambridge: Cambridge University Press.

Yardley, J. C. (tr.) (2006). *Livy: Hannibal's War.* Oxford: Oxford University Press.

Zadorojnyi, A. V. (2005). 'Plutarch and the Forbidden City: *Demosthenes* 1–2', in A. Pérez Jiménez and F. Titchener (eds.), *Historical and Biographical Values of Plutarch's Works.* Malaga: International Plutarch Society, 493–512.

Zetzel, J. E. G. (1980). 'Horace's *Liber Sermonum*: The Structure of Ambiguity'. *Arethusa* 13: 59–77.

Zimmerer, M. (1937). *Der Annalist Qu. Claudius Quadrigarius.* Diss., Munich.

Ziolkowski, A. (1993). '*Urbs direpta*, or How the Romans Sacked Cities', in J. Rich and G. Shipley (eds.), *War and Society in the Roman World.* London: Routledge, 69–91.

Zoepffel, R. (2002). *Untersuchungen zum Geschichtswerk des Philistos von Syrakus.* Diss., Freiburg im Breisgau.

Zorzetti, N. (1978). *Interpretazioni Latine.* Padua: Liviana Editrice.

Index Locorum

General Index

Except in the case of well-known Roman authors like Sallust, Cicero, and Tacitus, and emperors and other members of the imperial family, the index gives the full names of Roman citizens, as far as these are known. Standard Roman abbreviations are used for the following personal names: Appius (abbreviated as Ap.), Aulus (A.), Decimus (D.), Gaius (C.), Gnaeus (Cn.), Lucius (L.), Manius (M.'), Marcus (M.), Publius (P.), Quintus (Q.), Spurius (Sp.), Tiberius (Ti.), Titus (T.). These names are ignored in alphabetization.